Classical and Contemporary Social Theory
Investigation and Application

Tim Delaney

State University of New York at Oswego

PEARSON

Boston   Columbus   Indianapolis   New York   San Francisco   Upper Saddle River
Amsterdam   Cape Town   Dubai   London   Madrid   Milan   Munich   Paris   Montréal   Toronto
Delhi   Mexico City   São Paulo   Sydney   Hong Kong   Seoul   Singapore   Taipei   Tokyo

Editor in Chief: Ashley Dodge
Publisher: Nancy Roberts
Editorial Assistant: Molly White
Director of Marketing: Brandy Dawson
Executive Marketing Manager: Kelly May
Marketing Coordinator: Theresa Rotondo
Managing Editor: Denise Forlow
Program Manager: Maggie Brobeck
Senior Operations Supervisor: Mary Fischer
Operations Specialist: Diane Peirano

Manager, Central Design: Jayne Conte
Cover Designer: Suzanne Behnke
Cover Image: Design Pics Inc. / Alamy
Director of Digital Media: Brian Hyland
Digital Media Project Manager: Tina Gagliostro
Full-Service Project Management and Composition: Integra Software Services, Pvt. Ltd.
Printer/Binder: Courier
Cover Printer: Courier
Text Font: Minion Pro, 10/12

Credits and acknowledgments borrowed from other sources and reproduced, with permission, in this textbook appear on the appropriate page within text.

Many of the designations by manufacturers and sellers to distinguish their products are claimed as trademarks. Where those designations appear in this book, and the publisher was aware of a trademark claim, the designations have been printed in initial caps or all caps.

Library of Congress Cataloging-in-Publication Data
Delaney, Tim.
  Classical and contemporary social theory : investigation and application / Tim Delaney, Ph.D., State University of New York at Oswego.
    pages cm
  ISBN-13: 978-0-205-25416-3 (alk. paper)
  ISBN-10: 0-205-25416-0 (alk. paper)
  1. Sociology—History. 2. Sociology—Philosophy. 3. Social sciences—Philosophy. I. Title.
  HM435.D45 2014
  301—dc23

                                                                        2013017919

10 9 8 7 6 5 4 3 2 1

ISBN 10: 0-205-25416-0
ISBN 13: 978-0-205-25416-3

Dedication

This book is dedicated in fond memory of Professor Herman Loether, Professor of Sociology at California State University at Dominquez Hills (CSUDH). Herm served the California State University system for forty years, ten at Cal State Los Angeles,and thirty at CSUDH. During those years he was awarded the Distinguished Professor award three times: once at CSULA and twice at CSUDH. Herm wrote several books and was known primarily for his social statistics textbook. But Dr. Loether was also an outstanding social theory professor. I met Dr. Loether while contemplating my own path in life after a near-fatal car crash on the 91 Highway near the 605 intersection in Los Angeles in 1988. Living in Redondo Beach, I decided to visit the nearby campus of CSUDH. Herm was the graduate coordinator of sociology at that time. He strongly encouraged me to attend graduate school and begin my studies by taking his social theory course. I loved it! In fact, I developed a passion for social theory that continues today. To Herm, thanks for the much-needed encouragement, and may you rest in peace. I will always remember you and our talks about social theory and life in general.

BRIEF CONTENTS

CONTENTS

PREFACE

The study of sociological theory is a requirement of nearly all sociology majors across North America and around the world. Social theory tells the story of sociology. Social theory courses are designed to impart sociological knowledge and stimulate a student's ability to think critically and abstractly. *Classical and Contemporary Social Theory: Investigation and Application* provides extensive coverage of the major classical social theorists and the major sociological schools of thought in the contemporary era. The primary purpose of tackling such an enormous project in one text is an effort to address the growing number of social theory courses that cover both classical social theory and contemporary social theory.

Classical and Contemporary Social Theory: Investigation and Application is divided into three parts. Part I, "The Classical Period of Sociological Theory," consists of seven chapters that describe the early giants of sociological thought. Chapter 1 provides highlights and insights to the earliest roots of sociological thought, including the influence of the Enlightenment, social and political revolutions, and such early social thinkers as Niccolo Machiavelli, Thomas Hobbes, John Locke, Jean-Jacques Rousseau, Claude-Henri Saint-Simon, Auguste Comte, and Herbert Spencer. Chapters 2–5 and 7 are centered on specific sociological social thinkers who have distinguished themselves in the field. In each of these chapters, discussion begins with a biographical review of the theorist. The biography of a person provides the reader with valuable insights into that theorist; such insights often foreshadow and predict the future ideology of that individual. As students read about the biography of famous social thinkers, they cannot help but wonder how their current life choices and decisions will influence who they become in the future. The biographies of social theorists also reveal that they are, after all, just human, and that they are/were just as capable of failings and misdeeds just like any one of us. In the world of reality TV and social networking, where the biographies of people draw the curiosity of millions, it should be clear then just how relevant the discussion of the biographies of social theorists is. A clever professor might teach this material as if it were current-day tabloid fodder: Now that would make a social theory course exciting. The major academic influences on each theorist will also be examined. This examination will help to reveal the social chain of knowledge that exists. In addition, it should be obvious that students need to be exposed to the key concepts and contributions of each theorist. Each chapter provides ample examples of specific concepts and ideas of the social theorist. The material is presented in a clear but academic manner. It is the discussion and analysis of each theorist's ideas and concepts that address the "Investigation" aspect of the title of this text. We will investigate the concepts and their sociological meanings. In Chapter 6, "Contributions from Women to Classical Social Theory," a number of significant social thinkers and their ideas are presented. Chapter 6 also explains how women have had to fight for equality in all spheres of life for centuries, and these struggles include the academic realm. It is worth noting that this is one of the very few texts on social theory that provides coverage of women's contributions to classical social theory.

Perhaps the most important goal to teaching social theory, or any class for that matter, is demonstrating the relevance of the materials taught in course to the students' daily lives. The word "Application" in the book title addresses the ideal of demonstrating the relevancy of sociological concepts. When students learn how to apply the ideas of classical social theorists to their own worlds, the concepts become more real to them. Before long, they will learn to apply any and all sociological concepts to their daily lives. The application of concepts and social thought is a primary goal of this text, and ample examples of the relevancy of these theoretical constructs appear in all 16 chapters.

Upon successful completion of Part I, students should be able to describe and explain who the founders of and early thinkers of sociology were, as well as their contributions to the discipline and to social thought in general; demonstrate an understanding of classical sociological theories; demonstrate an ability to utilize these theories to analyze social phenomena; and think about past and contemporary social problems and social issues critically and analytically.

In Part II, "The Contemporary Period of Sociological Theory," the major schools of sociological thought are discussed. The contemporary period of sociological theory is notably different from the classical era. The classical period, which includes, more or less, the first 400+ years of social theory, was characterized by significant individual theorists, or grand theorists. The contemporary era of social theory, which begins roughly in the mid-twentieth century, is highlighted by the ideas of a collection of like-minded social thinkers whose combined efforts led to the formation of a "school of thought." In most cases, these schools of thought were influenced by social thinkers from the classical period, but old concepts were modified or replaced and a vast array of new concepts introduced. There are, in fact, so many new sociological concepts and social theories that it would be literally impossible to chronicle them all. As lofty of a goal put forth in this text (a text supported by approximately 900 bibliographic references), it was certainly not the intent of this author to attempt to chronicle every single social theory or sociological concept in existence today. Instead, the focus is on the "major," or the most popular, contemporary schools of thought.

This "schools of thought" approach to sociological social theory is easily understood when one realizes that in the social sciences, and sociology in particular, the disciplines have become very broad, while areas of specialty among individuals have become very narrow. Consequently, contemporary sociological theory has become dominated by "schools of thought" rather than by single theorists. In *Classical and Contemporary Social Theory: Investigation and Application*, coverage of the major schools includes a review of the intellectual roots of each theory and the early theorists who contributed to the theory (e.g., Marx's influence on the development of conflict theory and George Herbert Mead's influence on symbolic interactionism). This is provided to show the continuity from the classical period and to highlight the reality that nearly all contemporary ideas are influenced, at least in part, by past ideas. Next, discussion centers on the leading proponents of each of the major social theories. In fulfillment of the "Investigation" theme of the text, each school's major concepts are examined and the significant contributions of each theory to sociological thought are also discussed. Once again, the application of each theory to contemporary society is presented in an effort to demonstrate its relevancy. A brief review of the criticisms of each school of thought and a summary are provided at the conclusion of each chapter.

Upon successful completion of Part II, students should be able to demonstrate an understanding of the sociological perspective, demonstrate an understanding of current sociological theories and schools of thought, think about problems critically and analytically, and apply sociological understanding to real-world social issues.

Part III, "Consistent and Significant Themes in Sociological Theory," is applicable to the study of both classical and contemporary social theory. Chapter 16 provides a synopsis of several social themes of sociological significance that have revealed themselves as we study classical, contemporary, or both classical and contemporary social theory. These themes include a general belief in progress and cultural evolution; technological growth; scarce resources; threats associated with overpopulation; capitalism and globalization; the development of a universal language; the dominant role of religion in society; and social injustice and the imbalance of power. Not only have past and present sociological social thinkers concerned themselves with these eight themes, but it is likely that future social thinkers will also have to contend with them. After all, any theme that has existed for 500 years is likely to extend itself into the future.

This text is available in a variety of formats—digital and print. To learn more about our programs, pricing options, and customization, visit www.pearsonhighered.com.

ACKNOWLEDGMENTS

I would like to acknowledge the folks at Pearson who helped with this project in production and editing, in particular, Mayda Bosco, Karen Hanson, and Nancy Roberts. I appreciate the assistance of the copy editors at Pearson and the helpful comments provided by reviewers: Lilli Downes, Polk State College; William Lugo, Eastern Connecticut State University; Allen Richardson, Cedar Crest College; Sharon Sarles, Austin Community College; and Catherine Solomon, Quinnipiac University.

As always, a very special thanks to my continued inspiration, Christina.

ABOUT THE AUTHOR

Tim Delaney has taught both classical and contemporary social theory courses along with combined classical and contemporary social theory courses for the past two decades. Regularly teaching social theory courses has kept Delaney focused on the presentation of the key concepts and ideas of classical theorists and contemporary "schools of thought." In addition, Delaney also realizes that social theory is often abstract, and as a result, the application of theory to every-day life presents many opportunities for new and inventive ways of interpretation of theoretical perspectives. Teaching social theory courses on a regular basis has allowed Delaney to maintain a close connection with students and the material they find interesting and relevant. With these important points in mind, *Classical and Contemporary Social Theory: Investigation and Application* provides a thorough review of important theorists and their concepts while doing so in a student-friendly manner.

Delaney holds a Ph.D. in sociology from the University of Nevada Las Vegas (1994) and an M.A. in sociology from California State University Dominguez Hills (1991). He is currently teaching at the State University of New York at Oswego, where he serves as an Associate Professor and Department Chair of Sociology. Delaney has published numerous books, chapters in books, encyclopedia articles, journal articles, and book reviews. Among his published books are *Classical Social Theory: Investigation and Application* (2004), *Contemporary Social Theory: Investigation and Application* (2005), *American Street Gangs* (2006), *Shameful Behaviors* (2008), *The Sociology of Sports: An Introduction* (2009) (co-authored), *Environmental Sustainability* (2011) (co-authored), *Connecting Sociology to Our Lives: An Introduction to Sociology* (2012), and *American Street Gangs, 2nd edition* (2013).

Delaney regularly presents papers at regional, national, and international conferences. His commitment to scholarly activity allows him to travel the world and learn first-hand the great diversity, and similarity, found among people from different cultures. Delaney maintains membership in more than a dozen academic associations and has twice served as President of the New York State Sociological Association.

PART I

The Classical Period of Sociological Theory

Part I, "The Classical Period of Sociological Theory," consists of seven chapters that describe the early giants of sociological thought and those who have, arguably, made the greatest and most lasting contributions to the field. Chapter 1 provides highlights and insights to the earliest roots of sociological thought, including the influence of the Enlightenment, social and political revolutions, and such early social thinkers as Niccolo Machiavelli, Thomas Hobbes, John Locke, Jean-Jacques Rousseau, Claude-Henri Saint-Simon, Auguste Comte, and Herbert Spencer. Chapters 2–5 (Karl Marx, Emile Durkheim, Georg Simmel, and Max Weber) and Chapter 7 (George Herbert Mead) center on specific sociological social thinkers who have distinguished themselves in the field of sociology. In Chapter 6, "Contributions from Women to Classical Social Theory," a number of significant female social thinkers and their ideas are presented. Chapter 6 also explains how women have had to fight for equality in all spheres of life for centuries, and these struggles include the academic realm. It is worth noting that this is one of the very few texts on social theory that provides coverage of women's contributions to classical social theory.

1 The Early Roots of Sociological Theory

 Listen to the **Chapter Audio** on **MySearchLab**

Chapter Outline

- Hobbes, Locke, and Rousseau
- The Age of Enlightenment
- Social and Political Revolutions
- Claude-Henri Saint-Simon (1760–1825)
- Auguste Comte (1798–1857)
- Herbert Spencer (1820–1903)
- Summary
- Discussion Questions

Declaring a particular year as the starting point of the classical period of sociological social theory is difficult and open to one's interpretation of what constitutes the distinction between philosophical thought and social theory. In some ways, the two approaches that attempt to explain human behavior overlap. Nonetheless, there is a difference between the two distinct disciplines. In this chapter, we will attempt to establish a starting point for the classical social theory era, identify some of the early philosophers that would influence sociological thought, describe the influence of the Enlightenment and political and social revolutions on social thought, and introduce the earliest key sociologists who helped to establish the initial direction(s) of social theory.

There has been philosophical speculation on the nature of society and social life at least as far back as the ancient Greeks. In fact, the term *philosophy* derives from the Greek words for "love of wisdom." In practice, however, philosophy is much more than just a "love"; it involves serious thought on some of the most basic questions confronting humanity, such as

1. What is the meaning of life?
2. What is nature, and what is our role with nature?
3. What constitutes ethical and moral behavior?"

Generally, though, the Greek philosophers' search for a universal understanding of values and reality was primarily driven by speculative thought rather than empirical evidence to support their beliefs. To this day, philosophy remains mostly a discipline entrenched in the application of deep thought in its analysis of human life.

As an academic discipline, philosophy predates sociology. Furthermore, until the early 19th century, many of today's academic disciplines, including physics, chemistry, biology, astronomy, psychology, mathematics, logic, ethics, music, and sociology, were under the philosophical umbrella. This explains why most doctorate degrees are designated as Ph.D.—doctorate of philosophy. Thus, if your sociology professors have a Ph.D., they have a doctorate in philosophy, and not something else like an So.D., a doctorate in sociology. (This holds true for other college professors outside philosophy with a Ph.D.)

As with such other academic disciplines as physics, chemistry, and psychology, sociology would emerge with its own parameters of specific interest and make its break from philosophy. To distinguish itself from its predecessor, sociology developed as a field that attempts to support its social theories with empirical research (systematic data collection). To this day, sociological theory overwhelmingly maintains a commitment to the scientific approach to the study of human behavior. Sociological theory also brings with it a *critical* aspect to its examination of social reality. That is to say, sociological theory examines societies, social institutions, and social systems as they exist in reality, rather than in the abstract. Such an approach is not about creating an ideal type of society and calling upon other societies to conform to that ideal (as was often the case with ancient philosophy).

So when did sociology make this break from philosophy? Scholars disagree on the precise answer to this question, but sociologist Roberta Garner (2000) suggests that the story of sociology begins with Niccolo Machiavelli (1469–1527) and *The Prince*, a book he wrote in 1513 (but was not published until 1532), at the height of the Italian Renaissance. During the period of 1450–1525, Europe was experiencing dramatic social change. For example, in 1453, the Turks captured Constantinople (now Istanbul) from the Greeks and demonstrated the proficient use of cannons and gunpowder. The eastern Mediterranean became part of the Islamic world, and European rulers, merchants, and adventurers felt pressure to expand westward and southward beyond the Straits of Gibraltar. In 1458, Johann Gutenberg printed the Bible on his movable-type printing press and spearheaded the movement of mass dissemination of the printed word. In 1492, Columbus "discovered" the "New" World, triggering the burst of expansion by European nations onto the rest of the world. In that same year, the sovereigns of Christian Spain completed their reconquest of the peninsula from Islamic rule and expelled the remaining Moors and Jews (Garner, 2000).

The Prince, it can be argued, sparked sociological theory because in contrast with Plato and Aristotle, who would likely insist on an imaginary ideal society to serve as the model for princely behavior, it instead concerned itself with ruthless and tyrannical princes from the real world. *The Prince* was a controversial book for its time, because it provided a realistic view of human actions and challenged the long-held belief that kings had a "divine right" to rule. Until the Renaissance, most books upheld general notions of normative behavior, were non-empirical, and did not observe, describe, or analyze actual human behavior. Machiavelli (2006) included into his book all the violent, fierce, savage, coercive, and sometimes even compassionate acts that the ruler must implement in order to stay in power. *The Prince* was based on reality, observations of real people, and not just moral ideals. It is for this very reason that it shocked its readers and was widely censored and banned. This is the very type of publication that illustrates modern social science—to write about society as it really is, not only as the power elite says that it is, or should be; and to be critical of social institutions that do not operate in the best interest of the people.

Garner puts forth a relatively strong argument about the importance of *The Prince* as a focal point to mark the distinction between philosophical thought and a starting point for sociological theory. However, because of its initial limited readership, one might argue that a contemporary of Machiavelli, Martin Luther (1483–1546), might actually serve as a better representation. Luther, a German priest and professor of theology, was one of the first advocates of mass education. He also challenged the powerful social institution of the Catholic Church and its assertion that the only true interpretation of the Bible should come from religious leaders. Luther, in contrast, believed that it was the right, even the duty, of all Christians to interpret the Bible for themselves (Stayer, 2000). For this to happen, the masses would have to learn to read, which required mass education. In 1517, Luther challenged the Catholic Church by nailing his 95 theses to the door of the cathedral in Wittenberg, Germany, lighting the fires of the Reformation and Protestantism.

It was his time spent in the monastery at Wittenberg that allowed Luther the opportunity to learn about the Catholic Church. And while he appreciated the Church's general values and beliefs, he was displeased with its position on how to spread the word of the Bible to the people. Luther's proposals on how the Bible should be taught became so popular it encouraged others to share their doubts with the Church and protest its medieval ways (bear in mind, Luther lived during part of the medieval period). Among Luther's complaints of the ancient Catholic Church was the Communion of the Saints, Penance, Purgatory, infused justification, the Papacy, the priesthood, and sacramental marriage (Armstrong, 2012). One of the practices of the Church that Luther was most critical of involved the Church's offer to provide forgiveness, at a price, to those who committed sins (known then as indulging in sinful behavior). Luther felt that one should be truly sorry for their sins and be granted absolution through penance rather than paying for absolution. The Castle Church in Wittenberg, Germany, was known as one of the most infamous churches for the collection of holy relics or religious artifacts as offerings for forgiveness. The Church would display the offerings and the viewer was granted forgiveness for "indulging" in sin (Brecht, 1985). The sociological relevance of Luther's beliefs are plentiful but center on his criticism of an existing social institution, and a powerful one at that, while other alternative courses of action (he would create Lutheranism and spearhead the Protestant Reformation). Like sociologists today, Luther was critical of a social system that disadvantaged certain citizens, primarily the poor, while it empowered the ruling class. The poor could not afford to pay for absolution for their sins while the rich could, thus enabling the rich a religious dispensation to commit sin and get away with it.

Although the sixteenth-century ideas of both Machiavelli and Luther provide us with good examples of what could be considered sociological thought, rather than philosophical thinking, we are still centuries away from the official birth of sociology. As a result, a number of other significant antecedents to sociology are worthy of discussion. We begin with a brief look at the ideas of sixteenth- and seventeenth-century philosophers, Thomas Hobbes, John Locke, and Jean-Jacques Rousseau. Our attention will then shift to the "Age of Enlightenment" and a number of social and political revolutions that spirited the eighteenth century. We conclude with a look at the contributions of Claude-Henri Saint-Simon; an examination of the "founder" of sociology, Auguste Comte; and an analysis of the sociology of Herbert Spencer, an early giant of sociological thought.

HOBBES, LOCKE, AND ROUSSEAU

Thomas Hobbes, John Locke, and Jean-Jacques Rousseau each provided an examination of human-made social order. As we shall see in the following pages, many of their ideas are still relevant today.

Thomas Hobbes (1588–1679)

Hobbes was born in Wiltshire, England, on April 5, 1588. His lifetime was part of an era where the medieval ways were being questioned but the replacement system was yet to be formed (Harrison, 2003). Among Hobbes's primary contributions to social thought is his belief that the social order was made by human beings and therefore humans could change it (Adams and Sydie, 2001). Even under authoritarian rule, Hobbes believed that authority is given by the subjects themselves; that, by their consent, the rulers maintain sovereign power. As a political and social theorist, Hobbes wondered what life and human relations would be like in the absence of government. In 1651, Hobbes published his greatest work, *Leviathan*. In this book he provides a disturbing account of society without government. From his viewpoint, society would be filled with fear, danger of violent death, and the life of man would be solitary, poor, nasty, brutish, and short.

In his brief introduction to the *Leviathan*, Hobbes describes the state as an organism analogous to a large person. He shows how each part of the state parallels the function of the parts of the human body. The idea of society as an organism with each part serving a function would serve as a forerunner to the ideas of Auguste Comte, Herbert Spencer, and the school of thought known as Structural Functionalism—all of which will be discussed later in this text. Hobbes notes that the first part of his project is to describe human nature, insofar as humans are the creators of the state. To this end, he advises that we look into ourselves to see the nature of humanity in general. Hobbes argues that, in the absence of social condition, every action we perform, no matter how charitable or benevolent, is done for selfish reasons. Even giving to charity is a way of showing one's power to do so. Today, this concept is often referred to as psychological egoism. Hobbes believes that any description of human action, including morality, must reflect the reality that man is self-serving by nature. Hobbes also noted that there are three natural causes of conflict among people: competition for limited supplies of material possessions, distrust of one another, and glory insofar as people remain hostile to preserve their powerful reputation. Given the natural causes of conflict, Hobbes concludes that the natural condition of humans is a state of perpetual war of all against all, where no morality exists, and everyone lives in constant fear.

It is interesting to note that Hobbes certainly had his own fears, and perhaps this was to be expected in an era of transition from one type of repressive social system to a yet-developed one. But Hobbes, one might argue, was a bit of a coward. Reflecting back on the state of the country at his birth, Hobbes commented that his mother "brought twins to birth, myself and fear at the same time" (Rogow, 1986:17). In November 1640, when the Long Parliament began to show signs of activity threatening civil war, Hobbes was one of the first to flee to France, and he even described himself as a "man of feminine courage" (Hobbes, 1994). Additionally, when *Leviathan* was one of two books mentioned as blasphemous literature, Hobbes was seriously frightened, and it is said that he attempted to mend his estrangement with the Anglican Church (Rogow, 1986).

Thomas Hobbes developed a theory of human nature wherein it was "natural" for people to believe that they have a right to all things (Ewin, 1991). Because of this nature of humanity, it was difficult for individuals to coexist in a society. Furthermore, Hobbes argued that humans are shaped by religious and political beliefs, beliefs that can vary quite differently from person to person. Because individuals do not share the exact same beliefs as one another, they develop different self-interests. Self-interests are shaped by selective perception, and consequently, reality is a projection created by individuals based on their beliefs and their nature. Hobbes felt it important, then, that society should instill a system of morals that would be the same for everyone; in this manner, conflict could be minimized. Hobbes's view of morality as based on self-interest was one that would be shared by many Enlightenment thinkers (Gray, 2003).

Hobbes presented a variety of evidence to support his contention that the state of nature is brutal. For example, in the absence of a system of morality to guide people, individuals are in constant competition with one another because of their desire to acquire things (Johnson, 1993). Hobbes argued that an individual's sense of pride was a contributing factor that led to conflict (Rogow, 1986). In addition, we can see signs of mistrust among people in our daily lives. At the macro level, we see in countries that have yet to be civilized, people treating others in barbaric forms. In the absence of international law, strong countries will prey on the weakness of weak countries. Hobbes argued that mistrust and preying on the weak were prime factors that led to war. In fact, it is the nature of humanity to be in constant competition with one another because of their desire to gain (Johnson, 1993). Hobbes wrote *Behemoth*, a history of the English Civil Wars (1640–1660) wherein he analyzed the causes of these wars. He concluded that it was the very nature of men to be in conflict with another. Hobbes finished *Behemoth* in 1668 and submitted it to the English king for publication, but he was denied. The book was published posthumously in 1682. Hobbes did counter his belief in war as a natural state of humans by arguing that there were three motivations for ending this state of war: the fear of death, the desire to have an adequate living, and the hope to attain this through one's labor. Nonetheless, during war, it was the nature of man that led each person to believe that he has a right to everything, including another person's life.

For Hobbes, the state of nature is not a specific period in history, but rather a way of rationalizing how people would act in their most basic state. Advancing on the individualism put forth by René Descartes ("I think, therefore I am"), Hobbes uses the individual as the building block from which all of his theories spring. He formulated his theories by way of empirical observation. Hobbes believed that everything in the universe was simply made of atoms in motion, and that geometry and mathematics could be used to explain human behavior.

According to his theories, there were two types of motion in the universe: vital (involuntary motion, such as heart rate) and voluntary (things that we choose to do). Voluntary motion was further broken down into two subcategories that Hobbes believed were reducible to mathematical equations—desires and aversions. Desires were things one was moved to or that were valued by the individual, while aversions were fears or things to be avoided by the individual. Further, individuals' appetites constantly keep them in motion, and in order to remain in motion, everyone needs a certain degree of power. Thus, the pursuit of power is the natural state of humans. Humans are in a constant struggle for power, and above all else, they want to avoid a violent death.

Consequently, humans must find a way to maintain peace. Hobbes draws on the language of the natural law tradition of morality which emphasized the principles of reason. Hobbes reasoned that people would be willing to give up "individual rights" for the security offered by a peaceful cooperative society. He believed that a "social contract," an agreement among individuals, would accomplish this. But, because human nature would never allow this to happen (because of greed, jealousy, etc.), and with no way to enforce the contract, people would eventually break it in an attempt to control a greater share of power over others.

Realizing this, Hobbes proposed that an authoritarian government would come to power in order to enforce the social contract by whatever means necessary. He gave this government the name Leviathan (from the Bible), meaning monster. Individuals would give up all of their rights to the leviathan except for the right to self-preservation. People might give up their rights to the leviathan, but by their very nature, they would not be able to abandon their passion and quest for power. This drive would need to be channeled into what Hobbes called "commodious living" (a condition in which human passions are no longer a source of destructive conflict), so that individuals could pursue more constructive goals such as trade, industry, and other business ventures. The government would insure that all individuals were free to maximize their self-interests while protecting them from each other.

Hobbes was certainly considered a "liberal" in his day. He emphasized the importance of the individual and made them the center of politics. Government should derive from human beings, and not some divine sense of purpose or a birthright. If Hobbes can be thought of as the first liberal thinker, then it is only fitting that attention is now turned to John Locke, whom some consider to be the father of liberal democratic thought.

John Locke (1632–1704)

John Locke was born in a village in Somerset, England, on August 29, 1632. Locke was the son of a country attorney and small landowner (John Locke Sr.) who served as a captain in the parliamentary army when civil war broke out, and Agnes Keene Locke (Cope, 1999). Not much is known about Locke's mother except the fact that she was nearly ten years older than Locke's father (Cope, 1999). Both sides of the family came from the Puritan social class, but Locke Sr. rose a step up on the social ladder by becoming an attorney. Locke had two siblings, but only his brother Thomas survived past infancy. His father had hoped that John would follow in his footsteps and become a lawyer, but Locke decided on medicine instead.

John Locke grew up amid the civil disturbances which were plaguing seventeenth-century England. He was educated at home until the age of 14, when he went to Westminster School (Thomson, 1993). In 1652, Locke attended Christ Church, Oxford, where he studied Aristotelianism and remained a student for many years. He would come to revolt against the medieval scholasticism of the Oxford curriculum and became more interested in the "new science" or "natural philosophy" introduced by Sir Robert Boyle, who ultimately founded the Royal Society (Thomson, 1993).

Locke was interested in the great philosophical and scientific questions of his time. He was a secretary and confidante of Lord Ashley and held a number of government posts while Ashley was in office. He gave economic advice to the government, and held the important position of secretary to the Board of Trade and Colonies from 1696 to 1970 (Ayers, 1999).

As an educated man, Locke had a number of ideas on the education of children. In his 1693 publication, *Some Thoughts Concerning Education*, Locke proposed the concept of *tabula rasa* (Baggerman and Dekker, 2004; Palmer, 2001). *Tabula rasa* was the idea that children are born with minds that were akin to a "blank slate" unmarked until experience imprints it. In this regard, children are not born with innate ideas and marked with "original sin." Because children are free of preconceived notions of norms and values, they are easily persuaded to act based on their experiences and social environments. It was the role of education, then, to turn the self-centered infant into a well-rounded citizen of society. Locke emphasized the role of parents as the primary teachers and guides on the thoughts and experiences that children will undergo throughout their lifetimes. This notion of *tabula rasa* was not only unique in Locke's era, it preceded George Herbert Mead's same notion of a child being born with a "blank slate" (see Chapter 7).

Locke embraced many of the ideas presented by Hobbes in his theories on the state of nature and the rise of government and society. Hobbes, as we have learned, believed that the government should exist to insure that all individuals were free to seek their self-interests while protecting them from each other. Locke, too, realized that there are times when the government needs to enact *salus populi suprema lex esto* (supreme law that allows the government to take extreme measures during times of drastic circumstances) (Cope, 1999). Locke believed that such a policy should only be utilized when available laws are inadequate to handle emergency situations. As a proponent of a government with limited powers, Locke proposed that individuals engage in a "social contract" with other members of society as a means of maintaining some sort of civility in society. Locke and Hobbes shared a common view of the importance and autonomy of the individual in society. The extent to which they agreed varies, but one important belief was constant between the two social thinkers—people existed as individuals before societies and governments came into being. They each possessed certain rights and all had the freedom to do as they pleased, unrestricted according to Hobbes, and with some restrictions placed on them by God, according to Locke. This freedom of the individual was important for it represents the foundation for modern liberal democracy.

The value of individual self-preservation and freedom from tyrannical rule of the government led Locke to provide instances (in his *Second Treatise of Government*) wherein government should be shut down and/or overthrown by the people. As detailed by Cope (1999), Locke describes three instances (the first of which has four subparts) in which revolution could be justified:

1. Alteration in legislation:
   a. A governmental leader sets up his or her own arbitrary will in the place of laws.
   b. The governmental leader hinders the right of individuals to assemble.
   c. The governmental leader alters or tampers with the election of the people's representatives to the legislature.
   d. The governmental leader delivers his or her people to the subjection to a foreign power.
2. When existing laws can no longer be put to execution.
3. The existing government acts contrary to the people's trust.

Under any of these conditions, argued Locke, the people have the right to protest and overthrow the government, if necessary. Locke also made it clear in his *Second Treatise of Government* that the government exists for the benefit of the people, and not vice versa.

Besides a general right to self-preservation (relatively) free from government interference, Locke believed that all individuals had a natural right to appropriate private property. This natural right carried with it two preconditions of natural law. First, since the earth was given by God to all individuals, people must be sure to leave enough property for all to have, and second, nothing may be allowed to spoil. These conditions met, an individual was granted exclusive rights to any object that he mixed with his labor.

Locke agrees with Hobbes that, human nature being the way it was, people eventually would find a way around the natural law restrictions on property accumulation through the creation of money. People were granted the ability to accumulate unlimited money based upon their industriousness. This meant that some people acted more rationally than others and thus were more deserving of property. Locke so despised the use of money that he argued it led to the disproportionate and unequal possession of the Earth.

However, Locke recognized that money "turns the wheels of trade." He argues that riches consist of gold and silver and countries filled with mines have an interest in maintaining the gold standard. Such countries grow richer either through conquest or commerce. In his *Some Considerations of the Consequences of the Lowering of Interest and Raising the Value of Money* (1691), he states the importance of a uniform code and a steady measure of values. A few years later, in *Further Considerations* (1695), he argues against devaluing the standard that he had proposed earlier. He reestablishes his commitment to maintaining standards in money *An Essay for the Amendment of the Silver Coins* (1695).

For Locke, the state of nature was still a horrible place, but God's law created moral imperatives preventing humans from partaking in the total free-for-all that Hobbes described. People left the state of nature, according to Locke, not out of fear of violent death, but as a matter of convenience and in order to protect their property. They would not have to give up all their rights to an absolute authoritarian government; instead, they formed two distinctively separate agreements: the contract of society and the contract of the majority of society and government, or "trustee relationship" as it is often referred to. The contract with society takes place when people give up the total freedom that they enjoyed in the state of nature. This society was made up of two types of people: property and non-property owners. Property owners, being rational individuals, were given the right to suffrage, while non-property owners, viewed as not being industrious, were not. In order to fulfill the contract of the majority of society and government, the society as a whole contracts an impartial third party to act as the government. This agreement is often referred to as a trustee relationship because the government has no rights, only responsibilities to the people, and therefore acts only in the best interest of the members of the society. The government is given its power to act by the property-owning portion of the population, not by society as a whole.

Locke's *Two Treatises of Government* (1967/1690) has been viewed as the classic expression of liberal political ideas. It is read as a defense of individualism and of the natural right of individuals to appropriate private property. It served as an intellectual justification for the British Whig Revolution of 1689 and stated the fundamental principles of the Whigs (Ashcraft, 1987). It would also serve as a primary source to the American Declaration of Independence. The key elements in Locke's political theory are natural rights, social contract, government by consent, and the issue of private property. Labor becomes the source and justification of property. Contract or consent is the ground of government and repairs its boundaries. Locke also believed that society had the right to overthrow the government. Since a majority created it, they have the power to remove it. This introduces the idea that government should be accountable to the people. Clearly, Locke was in favor of a limited government, not an authoritarian one like Hobbes described.

The constitutional and cultural life of the United States was deeply influenced by Locke's *A Letter Concerning Toleration* (1991/1689), which argued for the rights of man and the necessity of separating Church and State. Locke wrote that the commonwealth seems to be a society of men constituted only for the procuring of, preserving, and advancing their own civil interests. Locke referred to civil interests as liberty, health, and indolency of body; and the possession of outward things, such as money, lands, houses, furniture, and the like. It is the duty of the civil magistrate, by the impartial execution of equal laws, to secure unto all the people in general and to every one of his subjects in particular the just possession of these civil interests.

In *A Letter Concerning Toleration*, Locke detailed in great length the need for the separation of church and state. Locke states that whatsoever is lawful in the Commonwealth cannot be prohibited by the magistrate in the Church. Any law created for the public good overrides the church and any conflict with interpretations of God's will shall be judged by God alone, not by religious zealots. Further, the magistrate ought not to forbid the preaching or professing of any speculative opinions in any Church because they have no manner of relation to the civil rights of the subjects. Locke argued that the Roman Catholic Church was dangerous to public peace because it professed allegiance to a foreign prince. Locke generally goes out of his way in many of his theological writings not to take issue with the Christian faith and adherence to the Bible. He treated religion like any other subject; he uses an intellectual approach, something quite admirable and ahead of its time.

Together with Newton's *Principia*, Locke's *Essay Concerning Human Understanding* (1975/1690) effectively decided the issue in the battle between "gods" and "giants." Locke details in *Essay* the need for analysis and study in regard to issues of morality and religion. The *Essay* represents Locke's greatest philosophical contribution and centers on traditional philosophical topics: the nature of the self, the social world, God, and the ways in which we attain our knowledge of them. His initial purpose of thought was to halt the traditional analyses of the Cartesians (or the medievalists) and to derive a method of dealing with the important difficulties in normative conduct and theological discussion. In Book IV of the *Essay*, Locke reveals that he is at one with the rationalist theologians of his century in their antagonism toward those who would ignore reason. Locke (1975/1690) proclaims that reason must be our last judge and guide us in everything.

Whether or not Locke can be labeled a "rationalist" is debatable. Some social thinkers come to view a person as a rationalist if they ground their thoughts with reason as a means to interrupt the social world. Philosophers label Locke an empiricist. Thomson (1993), for one, argues that Locke was an empiricist, and describes empiricism as beginning "with sense experience and claims that all knowledge must be derived from it.... Empiricist principles reject the possibility of a priori knowledge of the world" (p. 210). Modern-day empiricists, including sociologists, would agree with the notion of rejecting a priori knowledge. However, grounding their thoughts with "reason" is not enough to be considered an empiricist. Systematic data collection and statistical interpretation are requirements of modern empiricism, and therefore in order to be labeled an empiricist, one must collect data and employ statistical analysis of such data. Thomson (1993) provides no evidence that Locke conducted empirical research; in fact, Locke's pursuit of a medical degree was hampered by this critical limitation. Philosophers may label Locke as an empiricist during his era, but as the criteria of empiricism have evolved, there are few modern social scientists that would label him an empiricist based on a contemporary perspective.

The debate over whether or not Locke is a true empiricist is relatively unimportant especially compared to his many other concepts and contributions that still have relevancy today. For Americans, perhaps the most important contribution from Locke is his liberal notions regarding the role of government. After all, he laid the foundation for much of the groundwork of the U.S. Constitution and the U.S. federal government.

As we have seen, many of Locke's beliefs and ideas had great social significance. His contemporaries, especially among those in England, felt the impact of Locke's theories on morality, government, and religion. However, his lasting impact rests with the fact that he laid the foundation for much of the groundwork of the U.S. Constitution and the U.S. Declaration of Independence and, thus, the federal government. For example, Locke's ideas of government (detailed in his *Second Treatise*) are clearly reflected in the opening segment of the Declaration of Independence, which states,

> Whenever any Form of Government becomes destructive of these ends [the unalienable Rights], it is the Right of the People to alter or abolish it, and to institute new Government, laying its foundation on such principles and organizing its powers in such form, as to them shall seem most likely to effect their Safety and Happiness." (The Declaration of Independence, 1776)

The passage of the Declaration that declares "unalienable rights" of life, liberty, and the pursuit of happiness are also from Locke's writings and especially evident by one's right to own private property. In addition, one of the most heated debates in contemporary society—the separation of church and state—was a concept articulated by Locke and embraced by the "founding fathers" of the United States.

Jean-Jacques Rousseau (1712–1778)

Rousseau was a fascinating individual whose unorthodox ideas and passionate prose caused a flurry of interest in eighteenth-century France, and his republican sentiments for liberty, equality, and brotherhood led eventually to the French Revolution. He was born to artisan Isaac Rousseau and his wife, an academic elite, Suzanne Bernard, on June 28, 1712, in Geneva, Switzerland. He was baptized into the Calvinist faith. Rousseau left home at age sixteen. He studied music and devised a new system of musical notation, which was rejected by the Academy of Sciences. Nonetheless, throughout his life, Rousseau often earned his living by copying music. In Paris in the 1740s (he arrived for the first time in 1742), he entered literary society and wrote both words and music for an opera *Les Muses galantes.*

Rousseau has a number of significant published works. As Broome (1963) states, Rousseau's first discourse was published in 1750, entitled *Discourse on the Arts and Sciences.* This publication was a prize-winning essay written for the Academy of Dijon. He argued that the more science, industry, technology, and culture became developed and sophisticated, the more they carried human societies from decent simplicity toward moral corruption (Cranston, 1983. In his second publication, *Discourse on the Origin of Inequality*, Rousseau elaborated on the process of how social institutions had developed extreme inequalities of aristocratic France, where the nobility and the church lived in luxury, while the poor peasants had to pay most of the taxes. The theme of *Inequality* is that society alienates man from his natural self, thus creating a situation of inner dissension and of conflict with other men (Crocker, 1968). In his *Discourse on Political Economy*, he suggested remedies for these injustices. He suggests that the individual should choose to regard himself as part of the whole society. He argues that civil freedom must accompanied by moral freedom. Through the practice of moral freedom, the citizen reaffirms his original integration in the civil unity. Rousseau states,

> ... [M]en are trained early enough never to consider their persons except as related to the body of the State, and not to perceive their existence, so to speak, except as part of the State's, they will eventually come to identify themselves with this larger whole; to feel themselves to be members of the homeland; to love it with that delicate sentiment that any isolated man feels only for himself (Cullen, 1993:87).

In 1756, he retreated to a simple country life and wrote a romantic novel, *La Nouvelle Heloise*, which won the hearts of many. Some historians consider Rousseau the initiator of the romantic rebellion in art and literature.

In 1762, Rousseau published his famous *The Social Contract.* According to Rousseau, society could only be accounted for, and justified as, a means for enabling men to advance to a higher level of achievement than could be arrived at in its absence. Society had to be regarded as a necessary means to the development of the moral potentialities of man's original nature. Man's development from primitive to organized societies would provide the foundation for his conception of the necessary elements of social obligations—man is born free and everything is in chains.

Rousseau believed that nature ordained all men equal and that the State's conformity to natural law involved the maintenance of public order and the provision of opportunities for the happiness of individuals. Rousseau's idea of a "perfect" society would include the following:

- A society which grew only to the extent that it could be well governed.
- A society in which every person is equal to his occupation; no one is committed to another's function.
- That society and individuals have the same goals.
- That all members of society have an equal voice.
- That no single member is above the law, and further, that no such individual is able to dictate to the state to be obliged to recognize individual superiority of power.
- That society should be aware of a dramatic increase of new members, and take measures to make sure that these new members do not restructure the state so that they enjoy unequal power.
- Society should be free from threat of conquest by other societies and should not attempt to gain control of others.
- As society grows, it becomes necessary for magistrates to "run" it, but their power must be limited.

It is clear that Rousseau wanted a democratic society, but he was also aware of the potential of individuals acting in self-interest. He believed that the only primitive instinct of man is the desire for self-preservation. He will love what tends to conserve it and abhor what tends to harm it. Man's attempt at societal social order would be the source of all evil, for man in his earliest or natural condition was an isolated being; there were no institutions, political or social; no government, no family, no property, none of the usages of society. Man survived in nature by self-sufficiency. The first moment that man becomes aware of self-consciousness signals the beginning of the decline of man. For now, reflection led him to the fatal knowledge of his superiority to the other animals. Thus, with human pride comes the divorce of nature. Man, now apart from nature, sets out to subdue the world, to advance himself in knowledge and power, and to perfect his place in the environment by this awakening reason. Man now must agree to created laws, equally binding all, and assuring the peace and well-being of everyone. But the very vices that had rendered government necessary rendered the abuse of power inevitable. Rousseau, therefore (like Hobbes and Locke), believed that the State is to have a limited role in societal matters, with its primary function to protect the members from outside threat as well as internal self-concerning individuals.

Rousseau's view on private property was quite different from John Locke's. Rousseau believed that God provided nature and that humans should not own nature; for if they did, it would lead to their corruption. This corruption would occur because of the jealousies among people in a given society that inevitably would arise because of the different amounts of property that individuals own. Rousseau believed that those without property ownership would eventual revolt against those who did (Gildin, 1983). Property, then, according to Rousseau, should belong to all people as a collectivity. In this manner, Rousseau was a forerunner to Karl Marx and his view of private property (see Chapter 2).

The work of social thinkers like Hobbes, Locke, and Rousseau emphasized the grand, general, and very abstract systems of ideas that made rational sense. Their work, along with many other thinkers, such as Voltaire (the pen name of François Marie Arouet), Charles de Montesquieu, and René Descartes, would spearhead a new movement of social reasoning known collectively as the "Age of Enlightenment."

THE AGE OF ENLIGHTENMENT

The "Age of Enlightenment" (also known as the "Age of Reason"), the collective term used to describe the trends and writings in Europe and the American colonies during the eighteenth century, appeared prior to the French Revolution. The phrase was frequently employed by writers of the period itself, convinced that they were emerging from centuries of darkness and ignorance into a new age enlightened by reason, science, and a respect for humanity. The Enlightenment was a period of dramatic intellectual development and change in philosophical thought. It was a time when humans began to use reason to discover the world and cast off the superstitions and traditions of the medieval world. The desire to discover natural laws that govern the universe led to scientific, political, and social advances.

The Enlightenment thinkers kept a watchful eye on the social arrangements of society. They emphasized the pursuit of happiness and fulfillment in the here and now rather than in some heavenly future. They stressed rational education and scientific understanding as the means to attain social progress (Adams and Sydie, 2001). Progress could be attained because humans hold the capacity for reason. Further, reason should not be constrained by tradition, religion, or sovereign power.

The roots of modern sociology can be found in the work of the philosophers and scientists of the "Great Enlightenment," which had its origins in the scientific discoveries of the seventeenth century. That pivotal century began with Galileo's "heretical" proof that the Earth was not the center of the universe, as the Church had taught, and ended with the publication of Sir Isaac Newton's *Principia Mathematica* (Kornblum, 1994).

The work of Enlightenment thinkers was not dispassionate inquiry, for they were deeply disturbed by the power of the Church and its secular allies in the monarchy. Freedom of inquiry and diversity of thought were not tolerated, and free-thinkers were often tortured and executed (Garner, 2000).

The Enlightenment is most readily characterized as "liberal individualism." It was a movement that emphasized the individual's possession of critical reason, and it was opposed to traditional authority in society and the primacy of religion in questions of knowledge (Hadden, 1997). According to Seidman (1983), liberalism arose as a reaction against a static hierarchical and absolutist order, which suppressed individual freedom.

Of the basic assumptions and beliefs to philosophers and intellectuals of this period, perhaps the most important was an abiding faith in the power of human reason. The insistence on the ability of people to act rationally was anathema to Church and State (Hadden, 1997). Social thinkers were impressed by Newton's discovery of universal gravitation. If humanity could so unlock the laws of the universe, God's own laws, why could it not also discover the laws underlying all of nature and society? Scientists came to assume that through a rigorous use of reason, an unending progress would be possible—progress in knowledge, in technical achievement, and even in moral values. Following the philosophy of Locke, the eighteenth-century social thinkers believed that knowledge is not innate, but comes only from experience and observation guided by reason.

Through education, humanity itself could be altered, its nature changed for the better. A great premium was placed on the discovery of truth through the observation of nature, rather than through the study of authoritative sources, such as Aristotle and the Bible. Although they saw the church, especially the Catholic Church, as the principal force that had enslaved the human mind in the past, most Enlightenment thinkers did not renounce religion completely. They saw God as a Prime Mover, a motivator of sorts (Garner, 2000). But they still believed that human aspirations should be centered on improving life on earth and not centered on the promises of an afterlife. Worldly happiness was placed before religious promises of "salvation." No social institution was attacked with more intensity and ferocity than the church, with all its wealth, political power, and suppression of the free exercise of reason.

The Enlightenment was more than a set of ideas; it implied an attitude, a method of thought. There was a clear desire to explore new ideas and allow for changing values. It is important to note that not all of the social writers that comprised the collectivity of enlightened reason were intellectuals. There were many popularizers engaged in a self-conscious effort to win converts. They were journalists and propagandists as much as true philosophers, and historians often refer to them by the French word *philosophes*.

For the most part, the homeland of the philosophes was France. Political philosopher Charles de Montesquieu, one of the earliest representatives of the movement, had begun publishing various satirical works against existing social institutions. Voltaire was another famous French writer of political satire, poems, and essays and aided tremendously in popularizing the works of the philosophes. Voltaire and other philosophes relished the concept of a philosopher-king enlightening the people.

The philosophes valued both education and practical knowledge. They believed that educated persons would exercise their critical reason for their own happiness and, consequently, their acts and deeds would benefit society overall. The philosophes also placed a great deal of importance on practical knowledge—how to farm, how to construct bridges and dams, how to relate to follow citizens (Adams and Sydie, 2001). Hard work and education were believed to be the foundation to human and social progress. As quoted in Gay (1969:170), Denis Diderot (co-author of the *Encyclopedie*, volumes from 1751–1765) believes that "nature has not made us evil; it is bad education, bad models, bad legislation that corrupt us." Thus, reason is learned; it is not innate.

The Enlightenment was also a profoundly cosmopolitan and antinationalistic movement with representatives in many other countries: Immanuel Kant in Prussia, David Hume in England, Cesare Beccaria in Italy, and Benjamin Franklin and Thomas Jefferson in the American colonies all maintained close contacts with the French philosophes but were important contributors to the movement in their own right.

The Conservative Reaction

History will show that whenever a new and radical movement begins to challenge and change the very core beliefs and values of society a corresponding, usually a reactionary, conservative backlash will result. The Enlightenment and the French Revolution created a powerful backlash. The Enlightenment thinkers are generally considered to be the intellectual forbearers of the French Revolution (1789–1794). Intellectuals who represented the interests of the absolute monarchy and the aristocracy (the Conservatives) wrote against the new ideas of freedom of thought, reason, civil liberties, religious tolerance, and human rights (Garner, 2000). They argued for a return to rigid hierarchies, with fixed status groups, established religion, and misery for the masses. Many of the Conservatives questioned the legitimacy of individual freedom and rights, including the right to happiness. They argued that society is not a collection of individuals, but is instead a social unit in its own right, and must be protected from free thought.

The extreme irrationality of the Conservatives included suggestions from some that society should go back to the medieval-era style of rule. Louis de Bonald (1754–1840), for example, was so disturbed by the revolutionary changes in France that he yearned for a return to the peace and harmony of the Middle Ages. In his view, God was the source of society and therefore, reason, which was so important for the Enlightenment thinkers, was seen as inferior to traditional religious beliefs. Furthermore, de Bonald opposed anything that undermined such traditional institutions as patriarchy, the monogamous family, the monarchy, and the Catholic Church (Blum, 2006).

The Conservatives had idealized the medieval order, conveniently forgetting, or not caring about, the misery that the vast majority of people were subjected to throughout their short, labor-filled lives. As a challenge to the principles of the *philosophes* and a critique of the post–Revolutionary "disorder," the conservatives advanced a number of propositions about society. Zeitlin (1981) outlines ten major propositions of this conservative reaction about society, which are shown in abbreviated form as follows:

1. Society is an organic unity with internal laws and development and deep roots in the past. Society is greater than the individuals who comprise it.
2. Society is superior to individual man, for man has no existence outside a social group or context, and he becomes human only by participating in society.
3. The individual is an abstraction and not the basic element of a society. Society is composed of relationships and institutions.
4. The parts of a society are interdependent and interrelated. Therefore, changing one part undermines the stability of the whole society.
5. Institutions are positive entities because they provide for the needs of individuals.
6. All the various customs and institutions of a society are positively functional; nothing is dysfunctional, not even prejudice (which can serve the function of unifying groups).
7. The existence and maintenance of small groups are essential to society. The family, neighborhood, religious groups, etc., are the basic units of society (not individuals).
8. The Conservatives wanted to preserve the older religious forms, Catholicism not Protestantism, and sought to restore the religious unity of medieval Europe.
9. The Conservatives insisted on the essential importance and positive value of nonrational aspects of human existence. Man needs ritual, ceremony, and worship. The philosophes were merciless in their criticism of those activities, labeling them irrational vestiges of the past.
10. Status and hierarchy were also deemed as essential to society. A hierarchy was necessary to assure that the Church remained on top of the social order.

The propositions brought forth by the Conservatives would greatly influence such thinkers as Saint-Simon, Comte, and Durkheim. But what is most important is that both the Conservatives and the Enlightenment thinkers contributed substantially to the foundation of sociological thought. The Enlightenment thinkers stressed liberal individualism, with its emphasis on reason, individual freedom, contractual relations, and a reverence for science as the way to examine and explain all spheres of experience, including the social. The Conservatives stressed collectivism, which emphasized the importance of maintaining social order for the good of society itself. Tradition and church authority are sacred and must be maintained.

SOCIAL AND POLITICAL REVOLUTIONS

Reactionary beliefs and hopes of the Conservatives that society should turn back to a way of life that existed in the Middle Ages were, of course, never to be realized. Progress, it seems, can never be stopped, and the rise of reason and science had already transformed the social order. The vehicle of social change was not science itself, since relatively few individuals of any society were practicing scientists. Instead, social change was a product of the many new social ideas that captured people's imagination during the Enlightenment. A series of revolutions took place in Europe and America that were, at least in some part, a result of the social movements unleashed by the triumphs of science and reason. The ideas of human rights for all, not just the elites, of democracy versus rule by an absolute monarch, of self-government for colonial peoples, and of applying reason and science to human issues in general are all streams of thought that arose during the Enlightenment (Kornblum, 1994).

Political Revolutions

The age of reason allowed for the questioning of the traditional order of society. Faith and tradition were slowly being challenged by secular thinking. Knowledge was replacing sacred tradition and ritual. The concept of individual, natural rights for all people influenced the study of law and law-making, and debates about justice in society began to replace the idea that kings had a "divine right" to rule. From the Renaissance on, especially in Western societies, social thinkers and political revolutionists would extol the virtues of reason and scientific discovery.

From the standpoint of Europeans, the American Revolution and the Declaration of Independence indicated that, for the first time, some individuals were going beyond the mere discussion of enlightened ideas and were actually putting them into practice. The American Revolution would encourage further attacks and criticisms against existing European regimes. "Thomas Jefferson's preamble to the Declaration of Independence, a prime example of Enlightenment thinking, assumed that all 'rational' individuals would agree with the 'self-evident truths' that 'all men are created equal' and endowed with 'inalienable rights' of 'life, liberty, and the pursuit of happiness'" (Adams and Sydie, 2001:12). By praising the value of democracy and citizen's rights, Jefferson was striking a blow against tyrannical authority.

The British Empire directly felt the impact of the American Revolution, as they learned that the convictions and desires of the oppressed would not be tolerated by free-thinking citizens armed with the tools to fight back. Indirectly, it was the French who were perhaps influenced the most by the revolution in America. The citizens of France were no longer willing to be subjected to traditional forms of authority. The ideas of democracy had a great impact on the French people and provided a spark to ignite the French Revolution of 1789. The French revolutionary mob chanted, "Liberty . . . We shall not yield" during its June 1789 riots (Rude, 1988:57). The revolution was "won" on July 14, 1789, with the well-known storming of the Bastille, a medieval fortress and prison in Paris. The Bastille represented the royal authority center of the monarchy. As the monarchy fell, the feudal system in France collapsed along with it (Goodwin, 1970; Hampson, 1963).

The Age of Enlightenment is usually said to have ended with the French Revolution of 1789. As mentioned earlier, some see the social and political ferment of this period as being responsible for the Revolution. The French Revolution brought the French people the opportunity to build a new social order based on the principles of reason and justice. The changes were indeed revolutionary, as many nobles were killed, and their dominant role in French society was ended forever (Cockerham, 1995). A series of laws enacted between 1789 and 1795 produced a number of other fundamental social changes. Churches were now subordinated to the state and forbidden to interfere in politics and the conduct of civil government. Each social class was given equal rights under the law, and each son in a family was entitled to equal amounts of inherited property (opposed to just the eldest son). The total impact of the French Revolution was far more intense than the American Revolution. The Americans were fighting for freedom from the imperial British government, while the French were fighting for the near-complete restructuring of society.

While embodying many of the ideals of the philosophes, the French Revolution in its more violent stages (1792–1794) served to discredit these ideals temporarily in the eyes of many European contemporaries. France was forced to fight several wars against Britain, Russia, and virtually all its neighbors in order to preserve its new social and political order. The French society was at total war and would reach its zenith of power under one of its generals, Napoleon Bonaparte, who became a dictator in 1799. For the next fifteen years, Napoleon was the dominant figure in European politics. In a series of brilliant battles, Napoleon would conquer most of Europe. He met his political demise at Waterloo in 1815.

As France returned to a period of stability under an imposed peace settlement, intense debate erupted among French intellectuals about the many social changes that had occurred. As Giddens (1987) states, the French Revolution marked the first time in history that an entire social order was dissolved by a movement guided by purely secular ideas of universal liberty and equality.

The long series of political revolutions ushered in by the French Revolution and continuing into the nineteenth century was a dramatic factor in the rise of sociological theorizing. The impact of these revolutions on many societies was enormous and resulted in many positive changes. It also attracted the attention of many early theorists who concentrated on the negative effects of such changes. These writers were particularly disturbed by the resulting chaos and disorder that revolution and war bring with them, especially in France. An interest in the issue of social order was one of the major concerns of classical sociological theorists, especially Comte and Durkheim.

The Industrial Revolution

The Industrial Revolution was at least as important as the political revolutions were in shaping sociological theory. It began in the late eighteenth century in England and quickly spread through many Western societies, including the United States. The Industrial Revolution was not a single event but, instead, a number of interrelated developments that culminated in the transformation of the Western world from a largely agricultural society to an overwhelmingly industrial system.

The Industrial Revolution involved the substitution of machines for the muscles of animals and humans, which resulted in a dramatic increase in productivity. This increase in productivity led to an increased demand for more machines, more raw materials, improved means of transportation, better communication, better-educated workers, and a more specialized division of labor.

Large numbers of people left their farms and rural ways of life in hopes of finding employment in the rapidly developing urban cities. Industrialized factories created a high demand for labor. More and more people left their agrarian lifestyle behind them, not sure of what to expect in the city. Large sections of many medieval cities were transformed into sprawling, chaotic slums characterized by poor sanitation. Laborers worked long hours for little pay.

The Industrial Revolution changed the face of Western society. No longer did the majority of people live in small, rural villages with an extended kinship system and produce for themselves most of what they needed in order to survive. The rise of trade had dissolved the subsistence economy of medieval society and created a system of political power based on financial wealth rather than ownership of land. A wide range of social problems that had never existed before industrialization became the new topic of concern among intellectuals and social thinkers. Issues of social change and social order were joined by questions of why modernization was not occurring elsewhere in the world. Why weren't Africa, China, India, and other nations experiencing the same social changes as the West? These concerns would soon come under the domain of sociological thinking.

CLAUDE-HENRI SAINT-SIMON (1760–1825)

Born in 1760 into a noble family, Saint-Simon lived in comfort as a member of the aristocracy. He was the eldest of nine children and was educated by private tutors. Saint-Simon met Rousseau and was taught the leading ideas of the Enlightenment philosophers of France. Brilliant in many ways and certainly egotistical, Saint-Simon instructed his servant to wake every morning with a greeting, "Remember you have great things to do." In 1776, Saint-Simon joined the military. Three years later he became a captain, as the common practice of the aristocracy's enjoying rapid promotion. Under the orders of the absolute monarch, King Louis XVI, Saint-Simon served in the American Revolution as a volunteer on the side of the colonists. The monarch supported the colonists because of his disdain for the British. Saint-Simon fought under the command of George Washington at Yorktown. Fighting with the French in colonial war in the West Indies, he was captured (1782) by the English and served a prison term of several months. In 1783, Saint-Simon went to Mexico and designed the concept of building a canal across Panama. The following year Saint-Simon returned to France. He took no part in the French Revolution, believing that the old regime was weak enough, so why bother with war? He did, however, use the opportunity to make a fortune, by purchasing, at a fraction of the price, land that was confiscated from the Church and other aristocrats that fled France following the Revolution.

Saint-Simon spent the first forty years of his life as a soldier and speculator. It is said that Charlemagne, the first and greatest Holy Roman Emperor, appeared in a dream and told him to become a "great philosopher." This vision persuaded him to pursue a career in "saving humanity." Saint-Simon's desire for social improvement led him into the purchase of an aristocratic and church property from the government, and a financial partnership he formed to this end met with great success. He lavished his wealth on a salon for scientists but spent his later years in poverty, sustained by the faith that he had a message for humanity. With the support of a former servant, Saint-Simon found time for full-time study and would soon begin his scientific studies.

Saint-Simon maintained that Newton had uncovered the structure of the universe (structure is viewed here as recurrent patterns that could be observed and studied in astronomy) via his "Three Laws of Motion." He thought it was possible to study the structure of society and uncover its laws. In his work, Saint-Simon wrote about the necessity of creating a science of social organization. The very term *organization* meant "organic structure" to him. He maintained that society, like an organism, was born and grew. The major challenge was to understand such growth (social change) and the forces behind social stability (social order). He believed that laws exist to explain these issues of organization and social stability.

In his *Introduction to the Scientific Studies of the 19th Century* (1807), Saint-Simon stated that the observation of patterns over a long period of time was essential. Those observations must then be brought together in a general theory of history capable of explaining the fundamental causes of historical change, not only in the past and at the present time, but also in the future; for the causes of future events must already be in existence. The implication was that if one could forecast the future, then one might be able to shape the future as well. This line of thought was influenced by Nicolas de Condorcet's belief that he could document the operation of progress in the past and project the course of history for the future. For Condorcet, the idea of infinite perfectibility was a foregone conclusion (Coser, 1977). Ironically, Condorcet was a victim of the terror of the French Revolution.

In his 1813 *Essays on the Science of Man*, Saint-Simon suggests that the methodology of a social science should be

1. Study the "course of civilization" and look for regularities, patterns, and processes of change.
2. Observations will disclose patterns or "laws of social organization." The broad historical trends will outline the history of social evolution.
3. Once the laws are discovered, they can be used to reconstruct society on the basis of a plan.

Consequently, the study of society should be based on science, including the use of history and observation, in the search of regularities.

Foreseeing the triumph of the industrial order, Saint-Simon called for the reorganization of society by scientists and industrialists on the basis of a scientific division of labor. He had an essentially authoritarian and hierarchical view of society, believing that it was inherently divided into rigid social strata. Social classes would be determined by the new social order being ushered in by positivism. Positivism (the reliance of scientific study, laws, regulations, and reason) was to be directed by the most "competent" members of society. Saint-Simon referred to the competent class as people like bankers, lawyers, industrialists, and intellectuals. Saint-Simonian thought dictated that action taken by this class was to be evaluated and analyzed from a positivistic perspective. The social strata were further divided into categories based on the different capacities of people. For example, emotional persons would become the artists and poets, and those with strength and motor skills would become the workers and organizers (Collins and Makowsky, 2010).

The control over the social order created by this science would come in the form of a religious force. Saint-Simon was associated with a religious revival outlined in his most significant publication, the *New Christianity* (1825). He called for a newer, more humanistic, approach to Western religion. Saint-Simon believed that science and religious ideas would eventually combine to form a positivistic religion, or a *terrestrial morality* as he called it. Saint-Simonian groups (followers of the ideas of Saint-Simon) sprung up all across Europe preaching the message of Saint-Simon's philosophy. They were bourgeoisie intellectuals and officeholders (both public and private) who were, not surprisingly, mainly bankers, industrialists, and intellectuals considering themselves to be the "competent" class. They emphasized the need for order, discipline, efficiency, public control of the means of production, and the gradual emancipation of women. Being in their predominant social position, Saint-Simonians were mainly interested in material productivity and control of society by qualified experts (the competents, like themselves). Partly because of their eccentricities, the Saint-Simonians achieved brief fame. Although the movement developed into a moral-religious cult and had split and was disintegrated by 1833, it exerted much influence, especially on later socialist thought.

Saint-Simonians embraced the label "socialist" although its meaning was much vaguer back then compared to today's sociopolitical understanding of the term. The Saint-Simonians paid little attention to the importance of private property rights; instead, they were more concerned with coordinating the activities of society through large social projects—building canals, railroads, and steamship lines (Collins and Makowsky, 2010).

Ideologically, Saint-Simon envisioned a planned society, an international community, and as such, he was in favor of technological growth and industrialization. He believed that all societies would unite, forming a worldwide community. In this regard, we could look upon Saint-Simon as an early proponent of globalization. However, Saint-Simon recognized that many of the "common" people would be unable to grasp such a concept as a worldwide community based on science coupled with the need for the cultural "elites" to oversee such a huge endeavor. Thus, Saint-Simon felt that the ideas of science should be introduced to the masses through artists and their art, therefore reducing complicated issues above the intellectual limitations of the common people to a level they could understand. Today, many relatively complicated issues dealing with science (e.g., climate control) and technology (e.g., computer programming) remain above the understanding of those too ignorant to comprehend its meaning. Is it any wonder there are so many "how-to" books within the genre of "... for Dummies." A quick Goggle search will reveal such books as *Sex for Dummies, How to Fix Everything for Dummies, Stock investing for Dummies, Facebook Advertising for Dummies,* and *Small Business Kit for Dummies.* Saint-Simon might wonder whether humanity has evolved at all since his era. In reality, however, we have evolved, as a people, as our general level of intelligence has increased; it's just that society has become increasingly complicated, and most of us are specialized in our skills.

Saint-Simon employed an adaptation of the survival-of-the-fittest attitude, believing that everyone must work and be productive members of society, and if you do not, you do not eat. He was against welfare (care for the elderly, homeless, etc.) because he believed that it leads to a dependency on the state, which would eventually drain productive societies. Such an attitude would seem to be the opposite of socialism from today's perspective.

The most lasting and important influence of Saint-Simon on sociological theory lies with one of his former pupils and one-time personal secretary—Auguste Comte. For it was Comte who would more successfully transform many of Saint-Simon's ideas and formulate them into a specific and challenging discipline called sociology.

AUGUSTE COMTE (1798–1857)

Auguste Comte (1798–1857), French philosopher who coined the term *sociology* for his positive philosophy.   (SZ Photo/Alamy)

Isidore Auguste Marie François Xavier Comte was born on January 19, 1798, in the southern French city of Montpellier during the era of chaos and instability that followed the Revolution. To add to the instability in his own immediate setting, his parents were devout Catholics and ardent royalists, affiliations not conducive to one's personal safety (Hadden, 1998). His father, Louis-Auguste Comte, was a petty government official who was employed at a tax office, and a serious man who was opposed to the French revolution (Standley, 1981). Auguste Comte (he had shortened his name early on in life) and his father disagreed about most of their beliefs except for the idea that social order was of the utmost importance (Thompson, 1975).

There are two outstanding events in Comte's early life, which help to explain and shaped his more mature thought. The first was his attendance at the École Polytechnique in Paris. Founded in 1794 at the height of the radical phase of the French Revolution, the École Polytechnique trained military engineers and was quickly transformed into a school for the advanced sciences. Under Napoleon, it grew to become the foremost French scientific institution.

For Comte, however, the École Polytechnique became a model for a future society ordered and sustained by a new elite consisting of scientists and engineers.

The second great event in Comte's life took place in the summer of 1817 when he was introduced to the French utopian socialist Claude-Henri Saint-Simon, then the director of the periodical *Industri*. Comte became Saint-Simon's secretary, or more accurately his protégé, and the two were very close despite the vast differences in their ages. Saint-Simon was nearly sixty years old when the two met, but he was attracted to Comte's brilliant mind and came to view him as his "adopted son." As Saint-Simon's apprentice, Comte was paid quite handsomely, but when Saint-Simon experienced financial troubles, Comte continued to work without pay.

It is difficult to determine who benefited more from this collaboration, and scholars have debated this for some time. In acknowledging his debt to Saint-Simon, Comte states, "I certainly owe a great deal intellectually to Saint-Simon...he contributed powerfully to launching me in the philosophic direction that I clearly created for myself today and which I will follow without hesitation all my life" (Durkheim, 1928:144). Saint-Simon stated that changes in social organization take place (and are necessary) because of the development of human intelligence. He suggested that any scientific study has to look at the moral ideas of a period because at any particular time in history, the form of organization of a society is a direct reflection of the prevailing social code. Saint-Simon claimed that there were three different moral ideas in Western Europe and each was separated from the others by a transition—during that period, one moral system declines and another replaces it. The process of replacement–transition results from accumulated scientific knowledge, which changes the philosophical outlook of the society. For Saint-Simon, the three moral systems were

1. Supernatural-polytheistic morals: Greece and Rome
2. Christian theism: Socratic science, feudalism, and Middle Ages
3. Positivism: industrial society.

Saint-Simon's three moral systems would have a direct influence on Comte's "Law of Three Stages." Many other ideas of Comte's are derived from Saint-Simon's writings: the emphasis on the key role of industrialists in ordering the temporal affairs of society; stressing the need to reconstitute spiritual power in the hands of elite scientists; the realization that society must be rebuilt after the chaos of the Enlightenment and the Revolution; and the emphasis on the need for a hierarchy and on the creative powers of the elites. These are but a few of the influences of Saint-Simon on Comtean notions (Coser, 1977).

Eventually, Comte came to dislike Saint-Simon's method of developing theories, and he "...became critical of Saint-Simon's lack of scientific knowledge and his unsystematic approach" (Standley, 1981:20). Comte and Saint-Simon split over publishing rights for the *Plan des Trauvaux Scientifiques*, which Saint-Simon later published in 1824, failing to acknowledge his secretary. This falling out caused Comte to reassess his opinion of Saint-Simon, and in his later years, he described his relationship with Saint-Simon as "catastrophic," adding, "I owe nothing to this personage" (Pickering, 1993:240). Suffice it to say that his mentor influenced Comte in a major way, but the ideas of Comte's were most likely already in formation.

Concepts and Contributions of Auguste Comte

While working with Saint-Simon, Comte came to embrace the concept of "positivism." Comte would create a discipline from this concept that remains popular today, sociology. Comte also set the tone for sociology by insisting that scientific research methods be utilized while studying matters of social interest. He also introduced two enduring sociological terms of importance—*social statics* and *social dynamics*.

SOCIOLOGY   It was in his multivolume the *Course of Positive Philosophy* that Comte proposed the word *sociology* for his new positivist science. As Pickering (2000) notes, it was specifically in 1839 that the term first appeared. (Note: That Auguste Comte coined the term *sociology* forever secured his place as the official founder of the discipline and his importance to the field.) The word *sociology* is a hybrid term compounded of Latin and Greek parts. Comte preferred "social physics" to describe his new social science but later found out that Belgian social statistician Adolphe Quetelet had "stolen" the term from him (Coser, 1977). The use of the term *social physics* made it clear that Comte wanted to model sociology after the "hard sciences."

Comte acknowledged that physics was the first field of knowledge to free itself from the grip of theology and metaphysics; the decisive moment was Galileo's struggle with the Catholic Church, which tried to suppress his findings and teachings in astronomy, especially the Copernican model of the solar system and the discovery of the moons of Jupiter (Garner, 2000). Though Galileo was silenced and confined to virtual house arrest for the last ten years of his life, his findings soon were accepted by all educated people in Europe. Chemistry was the next discipline to liberate itself from theology and metaphysics. The struggle was still underway in biology and sociology, the fields closest to human affairs and therefore most likely to challenge religious doctrine.

Since the French Revolution had failed to establish a stable order based on Enlightenment principles, Comte attempted to organize those principles which, he thought, could do the job. Above all, the reorganization of society required intellectual reform. It would also involve replacing Catholicism with his positive philosophy (Hadden, 1997). Comte's idea of positive philosophy, or positivism, is one of many major contributions to sociology.

POSITIVE PHILOSOPHY   Although many individual sciences, such as physics, chemistry, and biology, had been developing at a steady pace, none had yet synthesized the basic principles of these sciences into a coherent system of ideas (Hadden, 1997). Comte envisioned a system that was led by an intellectual and moral basis and that allowed for science to intervene on behalf of the betterment of society.

There are social thinkers who believe that the social world can be studied in the same manner as the natural sciences and their belief in the existence of natural laws. This approach is generally referred to as *positivism*. Social positivists seek to discover social laws that will enable them to predict social behavior. Through observation of behavior, certain social relationships and arrangements should become identifiable; these observations could be explained as "facts" and in casual terms without interference of the researcher's value judgments. Therefore, positivism claims to be the most scientific, objective research tradition in sociology (Adams and Sydie, 2001).

Comte is remembered to this day in sociology for his championing of *positivism* (Scharff, 1995; Turner, 1990). Comte's idea of positivism is based on the idea that everything in society is observable and subject to patterns or laws. These laws could help explain human behavior (Simpson, 1969). Comte did not mean than human behavior would always be subjected to these "laws"; rather, he saw positivism as a way of explaining phenomena apart from supernatural or speculative causes (Simpson, 1969). Laws of human behavior could only be based on empirical data. Thus, positivism was based on research guided by theory, a premise that remains the cornerstone of sociology today. The very purpose of sociology as a discipline is to define and create social patterns of development in society (Thompson, 1975). Comte believed positivism would create sound theories based on sufficient factual evidence and historical comparisons to predict future events. The discovery of the basic laws of human behavior will allow for deliberate courses of action on the part of both individuals and society. Decision-making guided by science would, indeed, be positive.

Positivism, or the use of science, is revered today as a logical way to explain nearly all facets of life. However, whereas scientists in the era of Comte were happy to use science to discover and explain phenomenon, today we recognize that the most important aspect of science is to *predict* future events. After all, what good is it to simply discover and explain something if that knowledge cannot help us foresee future behavior? The application of foretelling behavior can help individuals, groups, organizations, and societies plan accordingly. For example, we have discovered and explained how and why earthquakes occur, but ultimately, we need to be able to predict them in order to save lives.

THE LAW OF THREE STAGES   Comte's first major publication was *A Prospectus of the Scientific Operations Required for the Reorganization of Society*, which he referred to as the "great discovery of the year 1822" (Hadden, 1997). It is here that he describes the plan for an empirical science of society by introducing his evolutionary theory of "The Law of Three Stages." It involves the notion that the history of societies can be divided rather neatly into three distinct periods and that each kind of society is produced and supported by a different form of thought or philosophy (Hadden, 1997). Since society of his day was experiencing a period of crisis and great disorganization, he set out to discover the causes or reasons for this phenomenon. He concluded that European societies were in the midst of a difficult transition from one stage to the next.

For Comte, evolution or progress was a matter of the growth of the human mind. The human mind evolved through a series of stages, and so too must society, he proposed. The transition is always difficult, filled with periods of great disorganization and reorganization based on the newly emerging form of thought. Comte argued that an empirical study of historical processes, particularly of the progress of the various interrelated sciences, reveals a law of three stages that govern human development. He analyzed these stages in his major work, the six-volume *Course of Positive Philosophy* (1830–1842). The three different stages are

1. **Theological:** This stage relies on supernatural or religious explanations to explain what man otherwise could not. Intellectual efforts were hampered by the assumption that all phenomena are produced by "supernatural beings." The theological stage has three sub-stages: (a) animism—ordinary objects are turned into items of tremendous purpose and are worshipped; (b) polytheism—belief and worship of many gods; and (c) monotheism—the highest point of development in the theological stage wherein the idea of a single God replaces the former belief in a proliferation of gods. To illustrate this stage, ask yourself, why do heavy objects fall? The theological response would be, "Because God, or some spirit, willed them to fall."

2. **Metaphysical:** This stage is a mere modification of the first stage and centers on the belief that abstract, even mysterious, forces control behavior. To illustrate this stage, ask yourself the same question as above—why do heavy objects fall? The metaphysical response would be, "It is the nature of heavy objects to fall."

3. **Positive:** In this final stage of societal development, there comes the realization that laws exist. Through the use of reason and observation to study the social world, human behavior can be explained rationally. This stage is highlighted by a reliance on science, rational

thought, empirical laws, and observation. Once again, ask yourself—why do heavy objects fall? The positivistic response would be, "The law of gravity dictates that heavy objects fall down, and certainly they do not fall upward."

Beyond the evolution of the human mind, each of the three stages, Comte believed, is correlated with certain political developments as well. The theological stage is reflected in such notions as the divine right of kings. The metaphysical stage involves such concepts as the social contract, the equality of persons, and popular sovereignty. The positivist stage entails a scientific or "sociological" approach to political organization. Quite critical of democratic procedures (primarily because it would allow the uneducated masses too much say in how future society would operate), Comte envisioned a stable society governed by a scientific elite who would use the methods of science to solve human problems and improve social conditions. Although Comte recognized an inevitable succession through these three stages, he acknowledged that at any given point in time all three might exist. It was Comte's hope, and belief, that in the future, humanity would be dominated by the ideals of positivism and that theological and metaphysical thinking would no longer exist.

RESEARCH METHODS   In line with his doctrine of positivism, Comte insisted that sociology utilize the methods of the natural sciences (observation, experimentation, comparison) and historic analysis of social events as a means of supporting theory and obtaining new knowledge. When using observation, the scientist looks for specific social facts in order to validate laws or theories involving the phenomena of social behavior. Comte claimed that no social fact can have any scientific meaning until it is connected with some other social fact (Simpson, 1969). Comte thought an individual trained with the scientific method will be able to convert almost all impressions from the events of life into sociological data when experience is combined with a talent to interrelate them.

The second research method promoted by Comte is experimentation. Experimentation is generally better suited for natural scientists because it is easier for them to set up controlled environments. Conducting experiments in the active social world is far more difficult for social scientists because there are a near infinite number of variables to control. Regardless, a number of sociologists do conduct experiments, and it is common to use breaching experiments in conjunction with ethnomethodology (see Chapter 12).

The third research method of investigation is comparison, which Comte divided into three subtypes. First, we can compare humans to lower forms of animals. Second, we can compare a variety of societies from different parts of the world. Third, we can compare societies to others in the same stage of development (Ritzer, 2000). In the first type of comparison, Comte felt that there was great value in comparing whatever rudiments of social life are found among the lower animals with that found among humans. Comte thought that the first germs of social relations could be discovered among the lower animals; according to Simpson (1969), this method has since proven of some advantage in such subsidiary fields of sociological study as the family, the division of labor, and socialization. By Comte's comparing humans to lower animals, he undermined ruling classes that considered mankind a special species above all other species.

According to Comte, the primary use of the method of comparison is the discovery of social structures, social classes, social functions, and patterns of social behavior, which are universal. This discovery is made through the study of coexisting states of society in different parts of the world. Comparing coexisting societies is an important tool for positive sociology, but Comte believed that the comparison of consecutive stages through which society passes over time was also needed.

This is where the fourth, and "chief scientific device" of sociology, comes into play. The fourth method is the historical investigation of human evolutionary growth. Comte states, "Our existing state cannot be understood simply through study of as it is, but only by seeing it as part of the series of social states from which it has emerged and which have left their imprint upon our minds" (Simpson, 1969:21). By attributing human reason to history, history provides more than "counsel" and "instruction"; it provides a "general direction" for humans to proceed.

Although Comte spent a considerably greater amount of time engaged in theorizing in an attempt to establish laws of the social world than he did in conducting research, his emphasis on utilizing the scientific method in support of theory established the foundation of sociology. That is, sociologists must conduct scientific research in order to claim any form of legitimacy with regard to theory formulation. The legitimacy of sociology, not only as a science, but as a discipline, is predicated on Comte's idea that theory and methods go hand in hand.

SOCIAL STATICS AND SOCIAL DYNAMICS   Through his notions of social statics and social dynamics, Comte established a direction for social research. He believed that just as biology found it useful to separate anatomy from physiology, it was just as desirable to make a distinction in sociology between statics and dynamics (Coser, 1977). *Social statics* is a term used to describe the social processes that hold society together, while *social dynamics* refers to mechanisms of change. Thus, Comte gave sociology not only its name, but also its initial orientation, which distinguished it from other disciplines (Cockerham, 1995).

In his description of social statics (sociologists today would refer to this as *social structure*), Comte was anticipating many of the ideas of later structural functionalists (see Chapter 8). As a product of post–Revolution in France, Comte possessed a lifetime fascination with the social processes designed to keep society intact. He preferred an orderly society where individuals and social institutions worked in harmony with one another in order to maintain societal stability. Subordination to government authority would be necessary but not to the degree where individualism was hindered. In fact, Comte promoted the idea of individualism because the creative and forward-thinking individuals of society stimulate further evolutionary thought. This evolutionary way of thinking is articulated by his concept of "social dynamics."

Because he was a proponent of social evolution, Comte devoted a great deal of attention to social dynamics (today's term would be *social change*). He found social dynamics to be more interesting and of greater importance than social statics. Social dynamics were more important because social evolution would make society better overall. Social dynamics deals with the laws of social movement, or progress. Utilizing two of the research methods he promoted—the historic and comparative—Comte was able to explain social change in a variety of societies by examining their histories and comparing them to others. He could also examine a society in terms of its stage of development (from the Law of Three Stages).

HERBERT SPENCER (1820–1903)

Herbert Spencer was born in Derby, England, on April 27, 1820. Derby was a bleak and dismal British industrial town. He was the oldest of nine children and the only one to survive infancy. One can only speculate how this would affect his personality and subsequent development. This comment will become clearer when we learn about Spencer's concept of the "survival of the fittest."

Concepts and Contributions of Herbert Spencer

Throughout most of Spencer's life, he enjoyed critical acclaim for his works and theories, and during the early years of American sociology, his ideas were much more influential than those of Comte, Marx, Durkheim, and Weber. A sampling of his most significant contributions—social evolution, the processes of evolution and dissolution, his influence on the development of functionalism, and the survival-of-the-fittest concept—are discussed in the following pages.

SOCIAL EVOLUTION Human beings are distributed widely throughout the planet and face an array of climates and environments. Why is it, then, that humans did not evolve into separate species, as occurred among other animals (as Spencer's contemporary, Charles Darwin, had observed during his extensive exploration voyage abroad the *HMS Beagle* in the early 1830s)? According to Spencer, the fact that humans, unlike other species, have remained similar even on different continents must be explained by the fact that we adapt to changes in our environment through the use of culture rather than biological adaptation. Geertz (1973) terms this process *cultural evolution*, in that the most successful adaptations are handed down to the next generation. Spencer simply called this process the *survival of the fittest*, meaning that those who are most successful at adapting to the changing environment are most likely to survive and to have children who will also be successful: "These successful individuals pass on their adaptive advantage to their offspring, the cumulative effect of this process over many generations is the adaptation of the entire population to its environment" (Andreski, 1971:221).

Spencer believed that this process of social evolution could not be stopped, and therefore, the government should not intervene with social policies other than to police and protect the public (from both internal and external threat). Spencer used the industrial revolution to explain the idea of social evolution and why some people prospered while others barely scraped by. The people who were leaving their farms behind and moving to the slums of the city to work in factories were less well equipped culturally to succeed in an urban environment than those who could innovate and invent. Ideas such as these made Spencer very popular in the Western world during the mid-1800s for it justified the prevailing economic sentiment of competition and capitalism by those who controlled industry and growth.

EVOLUTION AND DISSOLUTION In Spencer's early writings, one might come to the conclusion that he believed that the evolutionary process was inevitable and that human societies were destined toward continued progress. The mature Spencer recognized that although the evolution of mankind as a whole was certain, particular societies may retrogress as well as progress. He did not believe that societies develop irreversibly through predetermined stages, as Comte had stated, but rather, they developed in response to their social and natural environment.

Many people fail to recognize that Spencer viewed the universe as in a constant and cyclical process of "structuring" and "destructuring," or, in his terms, "evolution" and "dissolution." Too often Spencer is viewed by his detractors as a strict evolutionist when, in fact, he was interested in the transformations of structures, whether these transformations involved the development or dissolution of phenomena. He felt that evolution is the change of the matter from a homogeneous and incoherent form to a heterogeneous and coherent form by means of the dissipation of movement and the integration of matter. In *First Principles*, Spencer uses the example of gas to explain evolution. He elaborates that the evolution of gas is an absorption of motion and a disintegration of matter.

Spencer recognized that evolution and dissolution are related processes. Dissolution occurs when a society ceases to proceed. If there is no advancement of society, Spencer believed it would fall. Further, if surrounding societies are evolving while one society remains stagnant, it will be unable to compete and risks being conquered or overwhelmed by more dominant and advanced societies. He believed that the history of mankind had generally been one of evolution, but some populations and societies have evolved and then completely dissolved.

Like Comte, Spencer created "laws" to explain social phenomena. Utilizing his laws might make Spencer's definition of evolution a little more understandable. Some *force* (e.g., economic capital, a new technology, a deed to gather resources, new values and beliefs) sets into *motion* system growth. This *motion*, as it acts differently on various units, sends them in different directions and "segregates" them such that their differences are "multiplied." Conversely, to the extent that integration is incomplete and/or the force that drives the system is spent and cannot be replaced, then dissolution of the system is likely. Thus, social systems grow, differentiate, integrate, and achieve some level of adaptation to the environment, but at some point the system may fall into a phase of dissolution.

FUNCTIONALISM   Most functionalist theories share the assumption that as societies develop they become ever more complex and interdependent. Within sociology, this assumption can be traced to Spencer (1860), who argued that societies change from "incoherent homogeneity to coherent heterogeneity." Much of Spencer's discussion of social institutions and their changes are expressed in functional terms. He analyzed social institutions in relation to the general matrix in which they were variously embedded. Spencer makes great efforts to show that social institutions are not the result of deliberate intentions and motivations of actors, but arise from structural requirements.

In his *First Principles*, Spencer links the role of industry with that of an evolving government. The growth of regulative structure is important in both government and industry. An industry evolves within itself a structure, regulated by the parts, which also have to be directed. Now comes the operative part of each industry. The division of labor is grouped into producers and distributors, each with various grades and kinds. Thus, each industry affects other industries, and these effects advance each other. This is similar to governments (societies) affecting other governments in various ways (the multiplication of effects).

SURVIVAL OF THE FITTEST   In 1864, in his *Principles of Biology*, Spencer first uses the phrase "survival of the fittest." This would be, arguably, Spencer's greatest contribution to social thought, and ironically, this concept is often credited to Darwin. It should be pointed out that Darwin used the term *natural selection*. Darwin later suggested that he actually preferred Spencer's phrase (Hadden, 1997). Carneiro (1967) further explains Darwin's potential preference for "survival of the fittest" over his own concept because his term, natural selection, suggests an intelligent agent—nature—doing the selecting for humanity's benefit. In contrast, Spencer's term reveals the fact that nature does not select so much as it eliminates the "unfavorable" variations of species. Spencer's survival of the fittest has an even greater implication than Darwin's natural selection, in that Darwin focused on the process of transformation for each species, while Spencer focused on both the biological and the social processes, and on the end result—the survival of the fittest (Peel, 1971).

The evolution of species or societies, for Spencer, is ultimately a matter of the survival of the fittest. According to this notion, evolutionary processes filter out the "unfit" species, with the eventual outcome of a more perfect society. Since he viewed this outcome as a result of a natural process, he was adamant about his laissez-faire or nonintervention policy. Adaptation is the key to this process; if individuals are to survive in society, they must change with the changing society (and environment). At a level far more basic than an individual surviving in a society, each of us must find a way to survive physically. That is, individuals must find support with their families or find a way to take care of themselves. Each of us must take personal responsibility for survival or face the consequences. (Now you can ask yourself, "How might Spencer react to his being the only child of nine siblings to survive?")

The application of the relevancy of the survival-of-the-fittest concept to contemporary society is evident in nearly all spheres of life and reflects the notion of social evolution as well. For example, advancements in the field of communications occur so quickly (e.g., from email to cell phones, to BlackBerry, to Twitter, and so on) that people who wish to stay current need to keep up with the pace of social change. Private entrepreneurs recognize that that it is imperative to keep up with current trends, both social and technological. People who invest money need to keep abreast of numerous current events that may impact their investments. Cultural norms and values change as well. Customs and language that were once acceptable (e.g., using derogatory terms) may be deemed insensitive under different social ideals, and those who fail to keep up with the times may be viewed as bigots, or simply "out of touch." The survival-of-the-fittest doctrine is applicable to nearly all of the professions; for example, medical doctors must be aware of the latest advancements and techniques; lawyers must keep informed with new court rulings; police officers must enforce new laws; and so on. College students see the validity of the survival-of-the-fittest concept with grades; they need to earn average grades to graduate, much higher grades to enter graduate school, and very high grades to be considered at the most selective graduate schools. And students, how about the dating world? Who dates whom is a product of who makes the best "fit" for another. Athletes and sports fans alike see the validity of the survival-of-the-fittest concept on a regular basis. The Spencerian-based cliché it's a "dog eat dog world" is certainly relevant today.

Summary

As we have learned in this chapter, the roots of sociological theory predate the actual creation of the academic discipline of sociology. Theorizing about the social world, the meaning of life, and the nature of humanity has long been a concern among philosophers. Philosophers like to ponder things and create "what-if" scenarios. Sociological theory is more interested in posing questions that can be answered or, at the very least, provide the opportunity to collect data that may lead to possible explanations. In other words, sociology attempts to ground its theories with empirical data through such means as observation, experimentation, comparison, historical analysis, and in later sociology, survey research. It is debatable and perhaps impossible to pinpoint a precise time and situation when sociological thought became distinguishable from philosophical thought, but academics have presented their ideas. Part of the reason it is difficult to differentiate between philosophical thought and sociological thought is the overlap between the two even in the contemporary era.

A number of significant early influences on sociological thought were discussed in this chapter, including the noteworthy ideas of Thomas Hobbes, John Locke, Jean-Jacques Rousseau; the Age of Enlightenment; the Industrial Revolution and political revolutions; and Claude-Henri Saint-Simon. The most lasting and important influence of Saint-Simon lies with one of his former pupils and one-time personal secretary—Auguste Comte. For it was Comte who would more successfully transform many of Saint-Simon's ideas and formulate them into a highly challenging discipline called sociology.

Auguste Comte coined the term *sociology*. And thus, in the strictest sense, nothing can be truly labeled as a sociological theory until after Comte's founding of the discipline. It will always remain true, however, that many social thinkers prior to Comte did theorizing that could be considered sociological. Comte did much more than create a new academic field; he set the tone for future sociologists. He believed that there are invariant laws of the social world and it was the task of sociologists to discover those laws. The contemporary and future relevance of Comte begins with his systematic and theoretical presentation of society as a scientific discipline, emphasizing empirical analysis. In line with his doctrine of positivism, Comte insisted that sociology utilize the methods of the natural sciences (observation, experimentation, comparison) and the historic analysis of social events. These methods (and others, including survey research) are still used by sociologists today and will surely be used throughout the next millennium.

In the early years of American sociology, Spencer's ideas were much more influential than those of Comte, Durkheim, Marx, and Weber. There are several explanations for this. First, Spencer wrote in English, while the others did not. Additionally, Spencer did not write very technically, thereby making his work broadly accessible. Spencer offered a scientific orientation that was attractive to an audience becoming consumed with science. He offered a comprehensive theory that seemed to deal with the entire sweep of human history. The large volume of work produced by Spencer offered many things to many people. Finally, and perhaps most important, his theory was soothing and reassuring to a society undergoing the wrenching process of industrialization. Society was, according to Spencer, steadily moving in the direction of greater and greater progress. Spencer's most famous American disciple was William Sumner, who accepted and expanded many of Spencer's evolutionary ideas. Sumner argued that a failure to accept the *survival-of-the-fittest* concept left just one alternative, accepting a *survival-of-the-unfittest* doctrine (Curtis, 1981). Spencer teaches us that one should never be satisfied with simply surviving; one must learn to succeed. In society, only those who adapt to changes in the social system will succeed.

 Study and **Review** on **MySearchLab**

Discussion Questions

1. Thomas Hobbes argued that it was natural for humans to act on the basis of self-interest, to mistrust others, and to prey and take advantage of the "weak." He felt that civil law and a sense of communal morality would help to eliminate conflict and war. That bullying, domestic violence, acts of terrorism, and war exist today would seem to suggest that Hobbes's contention on the nature of man was correct. Do you agree, or disagree? Explain.

2. John Locke proposed a separation of church and state when it comes to governmental matters. The United States often claims to embrace such a policy, and yet there are many exceptions to this; for example, our currency states, "In God We Trust." Do we have a true separation of church and state in society? Give examples where this is true and examples where this is not true.

3. If Auguste Comte had his way, sociology would be called "social physics" and that would mean that sociology majors today would, instead, be called social physicists. Would you prefer being labeled a social physicist major or a sociology major? Explain.

4. Both Comte and Spencer argued that society is evolving culturally and technologically and that these evolutionary changes assist the betterment of society. Do you agree or disagree? Explain your answer by providing examples.

5. Do you believe that the concept of the "survival of the fittest" is still applicable today? Why or why not?

MySearchLab® Connections

MysearchLab is designed just for you. Each chapter features a customized study plan to help you learn and review key concepts and terms. Dynamic visual activities, videos, and readings found in the multimedia library will enhance your learning experience.

 Watch on **MySearchLab**

▶ George Ritzer: Importance of Sociological Theory
▶ Michael Kimmel: How Sociology Looks at the World

 Read on **MySearchLab**

▶ Berger, Peter L. Invitation to Sociology.

CHAPTER

2   Karl Marx 1818–1883

 Listen to the **Chapter Audio** on **MySearchLab**

Chapter Outline

- Biography
- Intellectual Influences
- Investigation and Application of Marx's Concepts and Contributions
- Summary
- Discussion Questions

Karl Marx (1818–1883) is among the more controversial and well-discussed social thinkers of any era. At some colleges and universities, entire courses are offered to discuss Marxist thought. Political systems around the world are, or have been, created and established because of his ideas. Marx was not a sociologist per se; rather, sociology "claims" him because of his varied societal insights (e.g., on social conflict and class theory). In fact, many academic disciplines, including philosophy, economics, political science, and history, discuss the concepts and contributions of this controversial social theorist. Indeed, Karl Marx may be one of the most influential and well-known people not in a position of political power since Jesus Christ or the Prophet Mohammad. That Marx's influence is only surpassed by prominent religious leaders is equally profound in light of his disdain for religion.

In 1999, the British Broadcasting Corporation (BBC) conducted an online poll asking respondents, "Who was the greatest thinker of the second millennium?" Although the poll is not considered a representative survey, the results are noteworthy nonetheless. In order, the top ten vote getters were Karl Marx, Albert Einstein, Sir Isaac Newton, Charles Darwin, St. Thomas Aquinas, Stephen Hawking, Immanuel Kant, René Descartes, James Clerk Maxwell, and Friedrich Nietzsche (BBC News, 1999). The BBC concluded that Karl Marx was the most influential socialist thinker to emerge in the nineteenth century; although dictatorships throughout the twentieth century have distorted his original ideas, his work as a philosopher, social scientist, historian, and revolutionary is still respected in academics today.

Karl Marx (1818–1883), German philosopher, historian, political activist, economic determinist, and humanist. (Library of Congress Prints and Photographs Division(LC-USZ62-16530))

In this chapter, we will learn a great deal about the social thinker considered among the most brilliant of all time. In particular, we will learn about his ideas on communism—perhaps the primary reason so many people have heard of Marx—alienation, human potential, class theory (including a discussion on the proletariat and the bourgeoisie), capital, private property, and religion. We begin with a look at the personal life of Karl Marx.

BIOGRAPHY

Carl Heinrich Marx was born on May 5, 1818, in Trier, Prussia, a city in the far western province of the Rhineland. Its proximity to France, and its temporary rule under Napoleon, allowed the rationalism of French culture to function as an alternative to the conservatism of Prussian-dominated Germany (Seidman, 1983). Trier benefited from the progressive philosophy of the Enlightenment in ways such as its public works projects. As such, the young Marx could directly observe the positive impact of enlightened reason.

Carl was one of nine children, and the only male among four who lived to be over 40. In the mid-1820s, Carl—later called Karl—and his sisters, and eventually his mother, were baptized as Christians (Adams and Sydie, 2001). Karl's parents, Heinrich (born Hirschl Halevi) and Henrietta Marx, were both descended from a long line of rabbis, Heinrich's in the Rhineland and Henrietta's in Holland (Carr, 1934). Heinrich Marx was a successful lawyer, who would rise to become head of the bar, and was able to provide for his family a fairly typical bourgeois existence. Heinrich broke away from his religious heritage by becoming the first to obtain a secular education. This was a very significant event, for it not only signaled a departure from Jewish teaching, but it highlighted the fact that the doors of trades and professions were now open to Jews. It was the Napoleonic regime that created equality for the Jews, and since they owed their emancipation to Napoleon, they supported his regime with great zeal. The doors of trades and professions, which had hitherto remained rigidly barred, were open to Jews under Napoleon. With the fall of Napoleon and the assignment of the Rhineland by the Congress of Vienna to Prussia, the Jews were once again deprived of their civil rights (Coser, 1977; Strathern, 2001). Threatened by the potential loss of his law practice, Heinrich Marx decided in 1817 to convert to the mildly liberal Lutheran Church of Prussia. Having no real contacts with the synagogue, Heinrich did not regard the conversion as an act of moral significance; rather, it was simply the practical thing to do.

As a youth, Karl Marx was influenced less by religion than by the critical, sometimes radical, social policies of the Enlightenment. His Jewish background exposed him to prejudice and discrimination that may have led him to question the role of religion in society and contributed to his desire for social change. His father's conversion to Lutheranism most likely influenced Marx's deep concern that all people should have the opportunity to reach their full human potential and certainly led to his questioning of the validity of religion.

Karl's father had an excellent education, unlike his mother, who was so poorly educated that she had difficulty writing correct sentences. As a result, his mother had little academic significance upon his life. His father, on the other hand, taught him the importance of a proper education. Early on in his life, Karl formed and developed an intellectual bond with his father, who introduced him to the value of knowledge while exposing him to the works of the great Enlightenment thinkers and both the German and Greek classics. His father had become aware early on that while his other children were in no way remarkable, in Karl he had an unusual and difficult son, with a sharp and lucid intelligence combined with an obdurate and domineering temper (Berlin, 1971).

Another significant figure in the young Marx's life was Baron Ludwig von Westphalen, a next-door neighbor. Westphalen was a very intelligent man who would encourage Karl by lending him books and conversing with him on frequent walks about classical works by Shakespeare and Cervantes. Often on these walks they would discuss political as well as social doctrines. The bond between the two was close, with Westphalen, a distinguished upper-class Prussian government official, becoming the spiritual mentor of the greatest general thinker in the history of socialism.

Education

Karl Marx attended high school in Trier and participated in customary student activities. The school was under police surveillance because it was suspected of harboring liberal teachers and pupils. In fact, the principal was a disciple of Kantian liberalism (Seidman, 1983). During this time, Marx wrote about Christian idealism and a longing for self-sacrifice on behalf of humanity. Marx's high school papers revealed his absorption of the Enlightenment legacy of liberal humanism.

Marx went off to college at the age of seventeen, based upon his father's advice, to the University of Bonn, where he enrolled in the faculty of law. Marx spent a great deal of time reading and writing romantic poetry. His poems reflect the primary themes and ideas of the romantics: idealism, expressionism, and the search for spiritual renewal and unity (Seidman, 1983). Marx would eventually abandon writing poetry, but his romantic concern for individual and collective fulfillment would continue throughout his life's work. While at Bonn, Marx also reveled in his rebellious nature as he fought duels and spent a day in jail for being drunk and disorderly. Marx presided at the Tavern Club, which was at odds with the more aristocratic student associations, and joined a poets' club that included some political activists.

In 1836, Marx abandoned Bonn and the study of law for the University of Berlin and the study of philosophy. The move to this more exciting and lively capital city would prove to be the decisive turning point in the young man's life (Coser, 1977). Hegel was already dead when Marx enrolled at Berlin, but his spirit still dominated. It was here that Karl was first introduced to the radical band of heretic philosophers known as the Young Hegelians, and he was soon initiated into their spirit. The informal *Doktorklub* (Doctor Club) was comprised of young marginal academics. They were a radical, somewhat antireligious and bohemian group of thinkers. Most outstanding among them were the brothers Bruno and Edgar Bauer, both radical and freethinking Hegelians of the Left, and Max Stirner, the later proponent of ultra-individualistic anarchism (Coser, 1977). Under the influence of these men, Marx resolved to devote himself to philosophy. He also became a "social" drinker who frequently was found in saloons around Berlin, where the Young Hegelians debated for hours on the fine points of the Hegelian doctrine.

This group had many interests concerning German society. They debated everything along the lines of religion to politics. Specifically, the Young Hegelians criticized traditional Christianity, the Prussian monarchy, and the lack of democratic freedom (Schmitt, 1987; Pampel, 2000). The Young Hegelians are even considered to be Germany's first known political party: "They began in other fields, and only slowly concentrated on politics as the process of secularization advanced" (McLellan, 1969:28). Marx was important to the Young Hegelians because he and other young radicals, who included Friedrich Engels, Moses Hess, Lorenz von Stein, and Michael Bakunin, represented the second generation of Hegelians (Brazill, 1970). Marx did not stay with the Young Hegelians for long, due primarily to an opposition to the teleological spiritual idealism of Hegelian philosophy. The heart of the Hegelian philosophy Marx declared to be nothing but "the speculative expression of the Christian-Germanic dogma of the opposition between spirit and matter, God and the world" (Hook, 1962:268).

During the University of Berlin days, Marx had envisioned himself as a future professor of philosophy. Bruno Bauer had found a teaching appointment at Bonn and promised Marx that he would find him a position there as well. Unfortunately, Bauer's position was short-lived as he was fired for his antireligious, liberal views. Marx abandoned forever his hope of an academic position (Coser, 1977). Marx's student life would end in 1841 with the submission of his dissertation *On the Differences Between the Natural Philosophy of Democritus and Epicurus*. Marx's doctorate was a dry philosophical treatise, except for a burning antireligious preface, which, upon the advice of his friends, was not submitted to the academic authorities.

Marx Learns About Communism

In 1841, after spending five years in the "metropolis of intellectuals," Marx returned to Bonn. At that time, the first "New Era" was in vogue in Prussia. Frederick William IV had declared his love of a loyal opposition, and attempts were being made in various quarters to organize one (Engels, 1869). Later, Moses Hess, an admirer and socialist friend of Marx, asked him to become a regular writer for the new liberal–radical and bourgeois paper *Rheinische Zeitung* in Cologne. Hess, Germany's first communist, viewed private property as a source of evil and had recently converted a young Friedrich Engels to his philosophy (Pampel, 2000).

At this time, Marx knew little about communism, but he impressed Hess with his own opinions about philosophy. Marx jumped at the opportunity to write for this paper, and he exhibited an unprecedented daring to criticize the deliberations of the Rhine Province Assembly in articles that attracted great attention. Marx wrote a series of articles on social conditions, among them the misery of the Moselle vine-growing peasantry and the horrible treatment the poor received for the theft of timber in forests to which they thought they had a communal right (Coser, 1977). The government had passed laws forbidding the winegrowers from using firewood available in the nearby forests during the winter (Pampel, 2000). Ten months later, Marx took over the editorship himself and was such a thorn in the side of the censors that they did him the "honor" of sending a censor from Berlin. Battles with the censors would continue until Marx wrote an article condemning the Russian government. Russian emperor Nicholas I, who had read the article, complained to the Prussian ambassador, and shortly after, the *Rheinische Zeitung* ceased publication. As editor, Marx had increased circulation from 400 to 3,400 (Pampel, 2000).

At seventeen, Marx had become secretly engaged to Jenny von Westphalen, a charming, beautiful, auburn-haired daughter of one of Trier's leading citizens, the aforementioned Baron von Westphalen. Because of social differences, most of her family did not approve of the relationship (Yuille, 1991). They revealed religious and class bigotry in their concerns over Marx's Jewish origins and lower social position. Jenny's family was wealthy and informed her that she would be cut off financially if she married Karl. Only her father, a follower of the French socialist Saint-Simon, was fond of Karl. Karl and Jenny's daughter, Eleanor (Tussy) Marx, recounts the love relationship between her father and mother in her 1897 paper "Biographical Comments on

Karl Marx." Karl was a young man when he became engaged to Jenny, but for them the path of true love was not a smooth one. Karl's parents did not want him to get married at such an early age, so he waited seven years, which seemed so much longer "because he loved her so much." Having played together as children, the couple went hand in hand through the battle of life. And it was a battle, as Eleanor would explain, years of bitter pressing need and, still worse, years of brutal suspicion, infamous calumny, and icy indifference. But through it all, in happiness and unhappiness, the two lifelong friends and lovers never faltered, never doubted, and they were faithful unto death. Karl kept with him in his breast pocket a poem he had written to Jenny and pictures of his wife, daughter, and father. Engels laid them to rest in Marx's coffin (Marx, 1897).

Four months after their marriage, the young couple moved to Paris, which was then the center of socialist thought and of the more extreme sects that fell under the name of "communism." This is where Marx first became a revolutionary and a communist and began to associate with communist groups of French and German working men. Influenced by communist thought, Marx published his *Critique of Hegel's Philosophy of Right* and *On the Jewish Question* in 1843. One year later, Marx wrote a series of articles that were posthumously published as the *Economic and Philosophical Manuscripts of 1844*. It was in a Paris café in 1844 that Marx had his first conversation with a German traveler, Friedrich Engels, who was on his way home from England. The two had met briefly earlier (1842 in Cologne), but they now realized the commitment and strength of their common beliefs and agreement on philosophical and political matters (Yuille, 1991). In 1845, Marx published his *Theses on Feuerbach*.

By the beginning of 1845, Marx was expelled from France by the Guizot government, acting under Prussian instigation. The Prussian government viewed his writings as acts of treason (Marx and Engels, 1978). Marx, now with family and unemployed once again (as he would be most of his life), moved to Brussels, where he pursued established contacts with German refugees. In particular, he sought out the remaining members of the dissolved radical "League of the Just," an international revolutionary organization formed in 1836 by German radical workers. In 1847, it would change its name to the "Communist League" and commissioned Marx and Engels to draw up a manifesto on its behalf (Marx and Engels, 1978).

Meanwhile, in Manchester in 1845, Friedrich Engels had made the acquaintance of Mary Burns, a factory worker who was involved in organizing the English workers' movement (Adams and Sydie, 2001). The two became and remained friends until her death in 1863. From Burns, Engels learned of worker solidarity and social movements. When Engels returned to Germany later in the year, he learned of the German working-class movement and continued to explore communist ideas. By the end of 1845, Engels had joined Marx in Brussels, where they enjoyed trips to the country and late evenings in cafés. Ever focused, Marx devoted most of his time to developing his materialistic theory of history. Together, Marx and Engels collaborated on *The German Ideology*, in which they sought to disparage the views of other contemporary philosophers (Yuille, 1991).

Marx and Engels formed the Communist Corespondence Committee, which served as the model for the future International Association. The primary purpose of the committee was to establish links among the communists in France, Germany, and England. Close ties were made with the London Communist League, at the time the largest and most organized group, composed mainly of German refugees. At the end of 1847, Marx and Engels attended the Second Congress of the Communist League, where they presented a detailed program of how the league should be organized. This became *The Communist Manifesto*. Viewing himself as an international revolutionist, Marx attempted to organize German and Belgian dissidents. He critiqued the current version of socialism in an 1847 paper titled *The Poverty of Philosophy*. In that work can be found the many essential points of theory that would be presented at the Second Congress conference. Additionally, in December 1847, Marx gave a series of lectures in Brussels, later published as *Wage, Labour and Capital* (1849).

The year *The Communist Manifesto* was published was a year of general unrest in Europe, involving uprisings in eight European countries or city states (Yuille, 1991). In March of 1848, Marx was suspected of taking part in preparations for a revolt in Brussels and was expelled from Belgium, together with his wife and three children. Marx returned to Paris at the invitation of the French provisional government that had just exiled King Louis Philippe. The tidal wave of the revolution throughout European cities had pushed all scientific pursuits into the background; what mattered now was to become involved in the movement.

Shortly after his arrival in Paris, news came of an uprising in Berlin. Marx and his communist followers traveled immediately to Germany. Marx and Engels took active parts in the revolution of 1848–1849 in Germany, co-editing *Neue Rheinische Zeitung* in Cologne. Marx and Engels took freedom of the press to the extreme in their attacks on the Prussian government. Twice Marx was put before authorities for inciting people to refuse to pay their taxes; he was acquitted on both occasions. Marx called for German unity, a German constitution, and a revolutionary war against Russia.

Frederick William IV, king of Prussia, rejected the proposed constitution, and a violent uprising occurred in Dresden. Eventually, martial law was declared and the rebellion was silenced. Marx wrote an article expressing his sympathy with revolutionaries and his condemnation of the king. Because he was no longer viewed as a Prussian subject, the government expelled Marx from Germany, and he returned to Paris. Shortly after, Marx was expelled from Paris again, triggering his move to London, a city in which he would reside until his death.

In London at that time were refugees from all the nations of the European continent. Revolutionary committees of every kind were formed. For a while Marx continued to produce his *Neue Rheinische Zeitung* in the form of a monthly review, but later he withdrew into the British Museum and worked through the immense, and as yet for the most part unexamined, library for all that it contained on political economy (Engels, 1869). Marx had now become known as a social historian of distinction. He was a regular contributor to the *New York Tribune*, for an eleven-year period until the outbreak of the American Civil War, as the editor on European politics. Some of Marx's most brilliant historical pamphlets were published during this time: *The Class Struggles in France* (1850) and *The Eighteenth Brumaire of Louis Bonaparte* (1852).

As the London years passed by, Marx and Engels continued to wait in anticipation of the communist revolt. Along the way Karl and his wife Jenny had been arrested for selling arms to revolutionaries and were continually involved with planning revolutions in hopes of spearheading the new ideology. Such a revolution never occurred in his lifetime. His brilliant works would continue to be published, chief among them *Capital*, Volume One in 1867 and Volumes Two and Three by 1880. *Capital* was published in Russia in 1872.

Economic deprivation and family tragedy played a significant role in the Marx family life, and Engels would often have to assist Karl financially. Toward the end, Engels had become quite prosperous and gave Marx an annuity, enabling him to spend his last few years in relative comfort. Earlier in their lives, Karl and Jenny lost two children in infancy, and their son Edgar in 1855, at age eight, died of tuberculosis. Karl would have to borrow money from Engels for his son's burial. For the most part, Marx was devoted to his wife and daughters. He read his children stories, encouraged educational pursuits, and would often go on day-long picnics with them. Marx was fully conscious of the burden to his family his devotion to the communist cause had cost. Jenny accepted her husband's priorities and willingly spent hours copying Karl's illegible manuscripts. In 1881, Jenny passed away, and on March 14, 1883, Karl Marx died. Only Engels and eleven others attended his funeral. Mourners throughout the world sent letters expressing their sympathies. The following year a demonstration was held on March 16 to commemorate both Marx and the Paris Commune. Between five and six thousand people marched with bands and banners along Tottenham Court Road to Highgate Cemetery. They were greeted by five hundred policemen, who had locked the gates to the cemetery and refused them entry. Even Eleanor and a few close family friends with flowers were refused admittance.

Today, ironically, people pay money at the Highgate Cemetery entrance to (among other things) visit the grave of Karl Marx, the person who led a crusade against capitalism.

INTELLECTUAL INFLUENCES

There were many influences on Karl Marx. As Marx was born in Trier, a city in the far western province of the Rhineland with its proximity to France and temporary rule under Napoleon, the French culture, dominated by thoughts of rationalism, influenced the young Marx. Later it was the conservatism of German idealism that would affect Marxist thought. The decisive turning point in Marx's intellectual development occurred when he met Friedrich Engels in Cologne, in November of 1842, with the two developing a lifelong friendship. The primary influences of Marx are discussed in the following pages.

The Enlightenment and Romanticism

During the formative years of Marx's intellectual development, he was consumed with the liberal spirit of the Enlightenment. Karl's father and Ludwig von Westphalen had a deep love for the Enlightenment and for the philosophy of Spinoza. Marx's early college years were dominated by the composition of poetry, with chief concerns including idealism, expressionism, and the search for spiritual renewal and unity. By 1839, Marx no longer composed poetry, but the romantic concern for individuals, collective struggles, and personal and societal integration remained central components of Marxian thought.

There were many divergent doctrines of Enlightenment thought. The French *philosophes* were rationalists; the British, including Locke, sensationalists; others like La Mettrie were materialists. But they all shared the common belief in the possibility of altering the human environment in such a way as to allow a fuller and more wholesome development of human capacities. Most believed that man does not have a divine soul, that he is an object in nature, but that he has the capacity for self-improvement through education and environmental changes (Coser, 1977). Man must learn to release himself from superstitions and the irrational beliefs of religion in order to come into his own true sense of being. People are creatures of circumstances and socialization; consequently, changes in such social conditions can lead to self-fulfillment. Marx sought revolutionary change as a precondition for the realization of liberal ideals of secularism, universalism, and rationalization. Marx's ideas of self-realization, human potential, guidelines for society, and the search for "laws" and regularities of the evolutionary form were all influenced by the Enlightenment and romanticism.

German Idealism

The doctrines of the Enlightenment, which stressed the gradual and amicable progress of mankind, were countered toward the end of the century by the harsher philosophy of Kant. Kant took a more pessimistic view of human progress, believing that the antagonism between men was the ultimate driving force in history. He believed that men were given to an "unsociable sociability" (Coser, 1977). Progress came about through antagonistic cooperation. Thus, as Marx would come to believe, conflict is inevitable.

In his *Second Discourse*, Rousseau provides a vivid description of the natural goodness of man being corrupted by society. He believed that individuals were deprived of their natural desires and needs by oppressive and unjust societal laws. In his *Social Contract*, he would demonstrate how people could form a new community, by associating together voluntarily, by forging new bonds. Many German thinkers were influenced by Rousseau's insights. Others, like Friedrich Schiller, were unimpressed by his idyllic description of the "nobility of savages." Schiller (1967) called it "the tranquil nausea of his paradise." Despite the debate among German thinkers as to the validity of his theories, Kant's *Second Discourse* was an early source for Marx's notion of alienation.

Marx's philosophical studies took place in an intellectual climate dominated by the thought of Hegel and his followers. In many ways, Hegelian thought follows the ideas found in the Enlightenment, in the conservative reaction, and in Comte. The Enlightenment's emphasis on reason, the Conservatives' on tradition and culture, and even Comte's focus on the primacy of forms of thought can be seen in the development of German Idealism from Kant to Hegel (Hadden, 1997). Kant believed that Newton's science had provided adequate evidence that permanent "laws" existed in nature. He questioned how such insights of nature were possible since nature does not provide any privileged access to its operation. Kant believed that man was capable of sorting data into categories of knowledge. The foremost of these categories were "space," "time," and "causality" (Hadden, 1997).

As German Idealism developed from Kant through to Hegel, the focus of attention shifted outside the human subject. Hegel (1770–1831) viewed human development as a historical process. Whereas Comte had seen historic progress in terms of the development of mind, Hegel did not. Hegel did not believe that any amount of hard, positivist thinking or analysis could make any ultimate claims of "truths." The world and its contents simply do not form a rational whole, Hegel believed, because reason (mind, spirit) had not, as of yet, developed adequately. In Hegel's German, the word "spirit" (*Geist*) does not have the supernatural meaning it does in English; rather, it refers to culture or "spirit of the times" (Hadden, 1997). (In contemporary society, the word "zeitgeist," which is derived from Hegel's philosophy, refers to the common cultural, intellectual, ethical, spiritual, and/or political climate within a given society.) Hegel thought that every process of change—and above all, the unfolding of human history—moves forward through the simultaneous negation and transformation of what existed before (Garner, 2000).

Hegel taught that objectivity is a product of the mind's activity, and that we fall into "bondage" of the laws and events that we create. Hegel emphasized that we must be aware of the fact that we are the producers of such categories of thinking, and through participation in society we help maintain (reaffirm) it. Marx's concept of reification came from these ideas of Hegel.

Hegelian philosophy was the most dominant during Marx's early years. What attracted Marx to Hegel, after the romanticism of his year at Bonn and his brief enthusiasm for the idealism of Kant and Fichte, was the bridge he conceived Hegel to have built between what is and what ought to be. In a letter written to his father in 1837, Marx wrote:

> A curtain had fallen, my holy of holies had been shattered, new gods had to be found. Setting out from idealism—which, let me say in passing, I had compared to and nourished with that of Kant and Fichte—I hit upon seeking the Idea in the real itself. If formerly the gods had dwelt above the world, they now become its center (Marx and Engels, 1980:8).

Marx's general aim was to evaluate Hegel's political philosophy, which gave him scope to criticize existing political institutions and, more broadly, to discuss the question of the relationship of politics to economics. He treated Hegel's philosophy dialectically; he negated or discarded Hegel's spiritual mystification and Hegel's enthusiasm for the state as an institution. Marx retained the concept of the logic of historical change but eliminated spiritual notions and emphasized instead the material and political dimensions of human history. He believed that during the course of history, human beings grow in their understanding of nature and society, and in the sophistication of their modes of production; as this understanding expands, they develop a consciousness of, and an ability to create, society as a collective undertaking. Society, then, is no longer viewed as a taken-for-granted God-given "natural" force, but as a social construct that can be shaped and reshaped. Therefore, it is possible to construct a society in which all human beings can realize their unique and full potential, be creative, develop both their individual talents and their sense of community, and experience freedom as well as solidarity.

During the Berlin days, Marx was exposed to the thoughts of Hegel through a group of his disciples collectively referred to as the "Young Hegelians." The Young (or left) Hegelians debated the current issues of the day, and religion was one institution that they believed must be eliminated. For the Old (or right) Hegelians, religion was seen as the true moral bond of human beings in society. Authority and tradition guided by religion were seen in a positive light by the Old Hegelians. German culture was still dominated by an unenlightened and oppressive religiosity during this period. Hence, for the Young Hegelians, the critique of religion was the major philosophical task of importance. In 1835, David Strauss, a Young Hegelian, published the critical *Life of Jesus*, in which he used the Hegelian historical method to show that certain portions of the Gospels were pure creative inventions, whereas others were only reflections of semi-mythological beliefs common in primitive Christian cultures. Bruno Bauer, a more radical Young Hegelian, went even further in his critique by denying the very existence of Jesus and treating the Gospels as works of pure imagination—as simple reflections of the ideology of the time. According to the Young Hegelians, if you rid the world of religious illusions, you remove the misery from people's real condition. On the other hand, the Old Hegelians believed that if you maintain religious authority and tradition, you provide the final ingredient that binds people together in a proper and reasonable human society (Hadden, 1997).

During the early 1840s, Marx was infatuated with the Young Hegelian position, especially in their battle against religion. But Marx would soon become quite critical of the Hegelian perspective, whether it was the Young or Old Hegelians. From his point of view, they both granted religion more influence than was justified. In a series of articles published as the *Critique of Hegel's Philosophy of Right* (1843), Marx describes his philosophical differences with Hegelian thought. There are four primary areas of criticism (McLellan, 1990; Marx and Engels, 1978):

1. A general criticism of Hegel for starting with abstract ideas instead of with concrete reality.
2. A criticism of Hegel's defense of the monarchy.
3. Disagreement with Hegel on the role of bureaucracy. Hegel believed that bureaucracy represents the "spirit" of society, whereas Marx's analysis of bureaucracy revealed its tendency to form a state within a state.
4. Disagreement on the issue of the sovereignty of the state. Hegel treats the state as an independent entity that is objectified. Marx saw the state and people as one and the same.

Despite these criticisms, the influences of Hegel and the Young Hegelians would have an impact on Marxian thought. Marx learned of the *holistic* approach through Hegel's ideas of totality. The totality approach states that everything should be considered, that the truth is a whole, not just a part. To find the truth, then, one must look at the totality of incidents that leads to a particular point in time or behavior. The German ideology would influence Marx's idea of the division of labor, which was a product of a historic process that begins with the family and is maintained by the ownership of private property. Marx's version of communism was to free humankind from the division of labor. In fact, as Marx learned through the ideas of Kant, the entire history of mankind was marked by class struggle.

Ludwig Feuerbach

Although Feuerbach can be categorized as a Young Hegelian, special attention is given to him here. Ludwig Feuerbach (1804–1872) was an important link between Hegel and Marx. Feuerbach was critical of Hegel for, among other things, his excessive emphasis on consciousness and the spirit of society (Ritzer, 2000). Because of Feuerbach's adoption of a materialistic philosophy, he stressed the importance of the material reality of real human beings, rather than the subjective idealism of Hegel. Feuerbach is said to have commented on the importance of materialism over spiritualism: "To think, you must eat." Feuerbach was also highly critical of Hegel's emphasis on the value of religion. To Feuerbach, God is merely a projection created by humans. People set God above themselves, believing that He is perfect, almighty, all loving, and holy, while believing themselves as flawed humans. Feuerbach argued that, through reification, religion serves as an alienating force that must be eliminated. Real people, not abstract ideas like religion, were the cornerstone of Feuerbach's materialist philosophy.

Karl Marx had read and was influenced by Feuerbach's *Essence of Christianity* (1841), where he described religion as the self-alienation of man. Marx believed that Feuerbach had successfully criticized Hegel's concept of the spirit of man and agreed that the "Absolute Spirit" was a mere projection. Marx was also struck by the *humanistic* aspects of Feuerbach's work. Marx read *Essence* just before submitting his dissertation. Most people attribute Feuerbach's writings as of permanent importance and a major influence on Marx (McLellan, 1969). Breckman (1999) suggests that Feuerbach had an influence upon Marx far earlier than has been recognized. Marx's philosophical efforts can be seen as a combination of Hegel's dialectic and Feuerbach's materialism.

However, Marx certainly did not agree with Feuerbach on everything. In the spring of 1845, as he and Engels were starting their collaborative work on *The German Ideology*, Marx wrote the *Theses on Feuerbach*. Engels found them in one of the notebooks that had come into his possession after his friend had died. He published them as an appendix to his essay of 1888 on *Ludwig Feuerbach and the End of Classical German Philosophy*, and described them in the foreword to this publication as "the brilliant germ of the new world outlook" (Marx and Engels, 1978). The following eleven points summarize Marx's disagreements with Feuerbach:

1. Feuerbach does not conceive human activity itself as objective reality; hence, he does not grasp the significance of "revolutionary," practical activity.
2. The question whether objective truth can be attributed to human thinking is not a question of theory, but is a practical one. The dispute over the reality or nonreality of such thinking is purely a scholastic question.
3. The coincidence of the changing of circumstances and of human activity, or self-changing, can be conceived and rationally understood only as a revolutionary practice.
4. Feuerbach starts from the fact of religious self-alienation and believes the world should be secular. Marx believes that this is just the starting point. The secular world must detach itself from itself and establish itself as an independent realm.

5. Feuerbach, not satisfied with abstract thinking, wants contemplation, but he does not conceive sensuousness as practical, human-sensuous activity.
6. Feuerbach resolves the religious essence into the human essence. But the human essence is no abstraction inherent in each individual. In its reality, it is the ensemble of the social relations.
7. Feuerbach, consequently, does not see that the "religious sentiment" is itself a social product and that the abstract individual whom he analyzes belongs to a particular form of society.
8. All social life is essentially practical. All mysteries that mislead theory into mysticism find their rational solution in human practice and in the comprehension of this practice.
9. The highest point reached by contemplative materialism, that is, materialism that does not comprehend sensuousness as practical activity, is the contemplation of single persons in civil society.
10. The standpoint of the old materialism is *civil* society; the standpoint of the new is *human* society, or social humanity.
11. In one of Marx's most famous quotes, he criticizes philosophers by stating, "The philosophers have only *interpreted* the world, in various ways; the point, however, is to *change* it" (p. 145).

Although Marx did not agree with Feuerbach on all aspects of human social life, he was most definitely influenced significantly by him. From Feuerbach's ideas, Marx was able to use religion as a good example of reification; he agreed that God and Heaven are mere projections based upon human activities; he viewed human history as manmade, not a creation by God, and therefore held that we should realize our happiness in this world, for there is no guarantee of an afterlife. Utilizing Feuerbach's materialistic approach, Marx conceived of the world as an often distorted view. He believed that religion was the root cause of this distortion. From this line of thinking, Marx would develop the concept of *false consciousness*.

Friedrich Engels

The most important and influential person in Karl Marx's life was, by far, Friedrich Engels (1820–1895). Engels was born on November 28, 1820, in Barmen, in the Rhine Province of the kingdom of Prussia. His father was a successful manufacturer. In 1838, Engels, without having completed his high school studies, was sent to Bremen for business training. Engels worked as an unsalaried clerk in an export business. Commercial affairs did not prevent him from pursuing his scientific and political education. He had come to hate autocracy and the tyranny of bureaucrats while still at high school. The study of philosophy, especially that of Hegel, led him to further despise the autocracy. Although Hegel himself was an admirer of the autocratic Prussian state, his teachings were revolutionary, and Engels, like Marx, would initially find himself an admirer of Hegelian philosophy.

During 1841–1842, Engels served in the Household Artillery of the Prussian Army, attended lectures at the University of Berlin, and joined the circle of Young Hegelian radicals, "The Free." He wrote articles for *Rheinische Zeitung*. In November of 1842, Engels and Marx met for the first time in the office of *Rheinische Zeitung* in Cologne (Marx and Engels, 1978). Engels had stopped there while on his way to join his father's business in Manchester, England. Engels would stay in Manchester, to complete his business training in the firm of Ermen and Engels, until 1844. While in Manchester, Engels studied English life and literature, read political economists, joined the Chartist movement, published in the Owenite paper *The New Moral*

World, and wrote *Outlines of a Critique of Political Economy*. Engels was gathering materials for a social history of England and on the condition of the English working class. Residing in the center of English industry, Engels made himself familiar with the proletariat by wandering about the slums in which the workers were cooped up, and saw their poverty and misery with his own eyes.

Even though Engels was not the first to describe the sufferings of the proletariat and of the necessity of helping it, he *was* the first to say that the proletariat would rise in revolution to help save itself. He believed that the working class would inevitably realize that its only salvation lies in socialism. Additionally, socialism would only become a force when it becomes the aim of the political struggle of the working class. These are some of the main ideas of Engels' book *Condition of the Working Class in England* (1845). This book was written in an absorbing style and filled with the most authentic and shocking pictures of the misery of the English proletariat. The book was a terrible indictment of capitalism and the bourgeoisie and created a profound impression; never before or since had there appeared so striking and truthful a picture of the misery of the working class (Lenin, 1896).

During this same time, Engels was sending Marx articles for publication in *Deutsch-Französische Jahrbücher*. A double issue of *Jahrbücher* was published (1844) in Paris under the editorship of Marx and Arnold Ruge. Ruge was a radical left-Hegelian writer. Returning from Manchester to Germany, in August of 1844, Engels visited Paris for a second meeting with Marx. This would mark the commencement of their many future collaborations. Their first collaborated work, *The Holy Family*, was published in 1845. The "Holy Family" is a facetious nickname for the Bauer brothers, the philosophers, and their followers. The Bauers looked down on the proletariat as an uncritical mass. Marx and Engels vigorously opposed this absurd and harmful tendency. In the name of the worker, who was trampled down by the ruling classes and the state, Marx and Engels demanded a better order of society. They, of course, regarded the proletariat as the force that is capable of waging this struggle. Even before *The Holy Family*, Engels had published in the *Deutsch-Französische Jahrbücher* his "Critical Essays on Political Economy," in which he examined the principal phenomena of the contemporary economic order from a socialist standpoint, regarding them as necessary consequences of the rule of private property. Contact with Engels was undoubtedly a factor in Marx's decision to study political economy (Lenin, 1896).

In April 1845, Engels joined Marx in Brussels. During the summer of that year, Marx visited Manchester with Engels, returning to Brussels in late August. Here Marx and Engels established contact with the secret German Communist League, which commissioned them to expound the main principles of the socialism they had worked out. Thus arose the famous *Manifesto of the Communist Party*, published in 1848.

The revolution of 1848, which broke out first in France and then spread to other West European countries, brought Marx and Engels back to their native country. The two friends were the heart and soul of revolutionary-democratic aspiration in Rhenish Prussia. They fought for the freedom and in the interests of the people. Marx was exiled and lost his Prussian citizenship. Engels took part in the uprising in South Germany as an aide-de-camp in Willich's volunteer corps in the unsuccessful Baden rising (Marx and Engels, 1978). After three battles, the rebels were defeated, and Engels fled, via Switzerland, to England. Marx had settled in London.

Engels soon became a clerk again, and then a shareholder, in the Manchester commercial firm in which he had worked in the 1840s. He lived in Manchester until 1870, while Marx lived in London, but this did not prevent their maintaining a most lively interchange of ideas, as they corresponded almost daily. In 1870, Engels moved to London, and their strenuous intellectual life continued until 1883, when Marx died. On August 5, 1895, Engels died in London.

Linked in ideology and friendship, the names Marx and Engels seem synonymous. However, as Richard Schmitt (1987) indicates, there were a number of personal differences between the two social thinkers:

- Marx was mercurial; Engels was even-tempered.
- Marx was careless with money and his appearance; Engels was an astute businessman and a person of fine taste who cared for his appearance.
- Marx was a family man; Engels, though capable of deep lasting attachments—he lived with Mary Burns for twenty years and was deeply saddened when she died—never married or had children.
- Marx was a deeper thinker; Engels had the greater facility as a writer.

Individual differences aside, it was through Engels that Marx was introduced to the concrete conditions and the misery of the working class. Marx and Engels were the first to show that the working class and their struggles were a result of the ruling class's attempts to oppress the proletariat. They believed that all recorded history hitherto had been a history of class struggle, of the succession of the rule and victory of certain social classes over others. This would continue until the foundations of class struggle and of class domination—private property and anarchic social production—disappear. The interests of the proletariat demand the destruction of these foundations, and therefore the conscious class struggle of the organized workers must be directed against them. Further, every class struggle is a political struggle. Marx and Engels attempted to organize the working class in revolution, for their own good, so that they could attain economic and political freedom, thus allowing for each individual an opportunity to reach his or her full human potential.

INVESTIGATION AND APPLICATION OF MARX'S CONCEPTS AND CONTRIBUTIONS

As one of the most influential social thinkers of all time, Marx's contributions are immense. Entire books written on Marx's concepts and contributions often fall short of grasping the true impact of Marxist thought. Consequently, a modest effort to touch upon some of the major concepts and thoughts of Marx are presented here. We begin with the concept of Marx as a humanist. Although the concept of "humanism" has varied meanings for different folks, we will view Marx as a humanist because his life mission was centered on the idea that all people should have a chance to reach their full human potential. Thus, the notion of humanism, as it is being used here, means a system or mode or thought that emphasizes human dignity and human fulfillment in the natural world rather than in the afterlife. As we shall see, nearly all of Marx's concepts and contributions to sociological theory revolve around the idea of Marx as a humanist who wished to help the proletariat reach their full human potential. Ultimately, Marx proposed, communism represents the best method to reach one's full potential.

Human Potential

Marx was a humanist who was deeply hurt by the suffering and exploitation that he witnessed among the working class under capitalism. In his later life, Marx would come to view capitalism was a necessary "evil" stage toward communism. Capitalism was necessary because it increased the capacity for surplus food and shelter; and the technological advancements helped to free many humans from hard labor. The nature of societies prior to capitalism had been too repressive to allow the masses to realize their potential. Still, Marx saw capitalism as too oppressive an environment to allow most people to develop their human potential. It was Marx's belief that communism would provide the type of environment wherein people could begin to express that potential fully. Marx believed that the communists would lead the proletariat (the people) to victory over the bourgeoisie (the capitalists) and to the formation of a society free from class antagonisms, in which the free development of each is the condition for the free development of all (Acton, 1967).

Marx was concerned with the powers and needs of people. Powers refer to the faculties, abilities, and capacities of humans, not just as they are now, or as they were in the past, but what they could be in the future under different circumstances (Ollman, 1976). Needs are the desires people have for things that are not immediately available to them in their social setting (Heller, 1976). Marx often used the Hegelian notion of "species-being" (or *Gattungswesen*), which argued in favor of the absolute uniqueness of humans. The use of the concept "species-being" allowed Marx to distinguish between animals and humans. Marx believed that *natural* needs and powers are those that people share with other animals, whereas *species* needs and powers are those that are uniquely human. The primary distinction between animals and humans is the fact that people possess a sense of consciousness. The sense of consciousness transcended an awareness of self, like animals also have, and extended to conscious awareness of one's place within the species as well as within nature itself. For example, while animals just "do" things, people can set themselves off mentally from whatever they are doing. Humans can choose to act or not to act; they control their own course of action. Though Marx thought that human beings take meaningful action, he also recognized that external, societal forces shape the way in which we act. Thus, as Marx indicated in *The Eighteenth Brumaire of Louis Bonaparte* (1852), human beings make their own history, but not in circumstances of their own choosing.

The concept of seeking one's full human potential is certainly applicable today. For example, many people attend college in hopes of attaining a degree that should translate into finding a high-paying job. Historically, people went to college to expand their knowledge level as a means of reaching their full potential. In addition, there is an entire industry related to assisting individuals reach self-fulfillment goals. There are a number of service and self-help organizations designed to help people feel good about themselves, and thus strive for maximizing their full potential. Parents are told of the importance of enhancing their children's self-esteem. Psychologists have created a number of labels designed to lessen the burden and responsibilities of individuals so that they can feel good about themselves—a kind of "don't blame me; it was someone else's fault" mentality.

On the other hand, some people attempt to reach their full human potential by feeling good about themselves through voluntarism and helping others. At many colleges and universities, professors (including this author) implement service learning in their classes. Service learning techniques generally include a number of options for students to volunteer as little as one hour a week at various community centers and agencies (e.g., Habitat for Humanity, the Boys and Girls Clubs, etc.). Service learning is designed to help eliminate social problems and social injustice through activism. Marx would support the efforts of people helping others, especially if it involves the "haves" assisting the "have-nots." Community involvement should benefit the volunteer, those receiving the help, and the community. It could potentially decrease the level of violence and tension found in many communities.

Class Theory

The previous discussion of human potential introduced two key Marxist terms—the proletariat and the bourgeoisie. The term *proletariat* refers to the workers, the masses, and/or the people in general. The term *bourgeoisie* refers to the capitalists and/or the (business) owners of the means of production. These two terms represent class distinctions during Marx's era. Marx frequently uses the term *class* in his writings, but he does not have a systematic treatment on its usage (So, 1990). Ollman (1976) interprets Marx's usage of social classes as reified social relations or relations between men that have taken on an independent existence. Dahrendorf (1959) describes Marx's social classes as interest groupings, emerging from certain structural conditions, which affect structural changes. Marx regarded the theory of class as so important that he postponed its systematic exposition time and time again in favor of refinements by empirical analysis. When reading Marx's works on social class, it becomes clear that in his mind, people are categorized into a social class based on their relation to the control of the means of production. Those who control the means of production, the bourgeoisie, are the ruling class; while those who do not control the means of production, the workers, are in the bottom social class.

The relations to production are the result of the distribution of property. The possession of property becomes the critical issue of industrial production, which, in turn, constitutes the ultimate determination of the formation of classes and the inevitable development of class conflicts. Marx's thesis that political conditions are determined by industrial conditions seems to stem from the generalized assertion of an absolute and universal primacy of production over all other structures of economy and society. Inherent in capitalistic society is a tendency for the classes to polarize. As the classes polarize, their class situations become increasingly extreme. At the same time, the two classes become more and more homogeneous internally. Once history has carried these tendencies of development to their extremes, the point is reached at which the fabric of the existing social structure breaks and a revolution terminates it (in this case, capitalist society). Marx's image of capitalist society, then, is the image of a society undergoing a process of radical change.

The existence of classes is bound only to the particular, historical phase of development of that society. Social classes, understood as conflicting groups arising out of the authority structure of imperatively coordinated associations, are in conflict with one another. The class struggle necessitates the dictatorship or control of the proletariat. Because conflict is variable, the intensity of authority and control over the workers, by the ruling class, is also variable. Marx believed that this dictatorship, or control, itself only constitutes the transition and eventual abolition of all classes through communism.

In the United States, societies of the West, and most other nations, social class distinction remains as a hallmark of society. Many nations, including the U.S., have three distinguishable social classes with a number of subsets: the upper class, which also includes the rich and very rich; the middle social class, which includes an upper-middle, middle-middle, and lower-middle; and, the lower social class, which includes the working class, the working poor, and the poor. Most people still do not control the means of production and the workers remain subject to the whims and economic decision-making practices of those who own the means of production. Thus, at any time, massive numbers of workers may lose their jobs, through no fault of their own, simply because a capitalist decides to close operations in one nation (e.g., the United States) and move them to another (e.g., Vietnam) where labor and raw materials are cheaper. In this regard, the capitalists are as greedy today, if not more so, than during Marx's era. Furthermore, the importance the discipline of sociology places on social class is reflected in the many diverse courses offered by sociology departments along with specialized courses on the topic.

Historical Materialism and the Historic Process

The general conception of historical materialism is established in Marx and Engels' *The German Ideology* (1845–1846). *The German Ideology* was written to settle accounts with Marx and Engels' former philosophic views (Marx and Engels, 1978; McLellan, 1990). In addition, Marx wanted to achieve a reconciliation of materialism and idealism, to combine the critical and scientific aspects of materialism with the dynamic and historical components of idealism. In opposition to monistic and dualistic theories, Marx sought a dialectical theory, which he first called "Naturalism" or "Humanism" and later specified as "Historical Materialism" (Giddens, 1971). In Marx's dialectical approach, mind and matter, spirit and nature, constitute the unified structure of reality. Thus, Marx was attempting to combine material and ideal factors or structural and cultural factors, and to illustrate a reciprocal relationship. Marx's dialectical position regarding the unity between thought and being, structural and cultural factors was connected to a normative model of the individual and society, and the developing harmony between members of society. These contradictions are what Hegel referred to as "the dialectic." As Ritzer explains,

> Hegel used the idea of contradiction to understand historical change. According to Hegel, historical change has been driven by the contradictory understandings that are the essence of reality, by our attempts to resolve these contradictions, and by the new contradictions that develop (Ritzer, 2011:45).

While Marx accepted the basic idea of Hegel that history is filled with contradictions, he rejected Hegel's notion that such matters could be solved philosophically. Marx emphasized action; specifically, from the proletariat. In essence, Marx accepted, to a point, Hegel's dynamic and dialectical process but embraced the materialistic view of Feuerbach. The result of this process is *historical materialism*: the process of change in the real world of material, physical reality. Marx explained that freedom and slavery are not just ideas: They exist in the real world; they are material. In contrast, religion is spiritual, not material, and not of this world.

Marx maintained that bourgeois society was but one phase of historical development, but it was a critical stage, for it creates the universal conditions for the realization of the harmonious development with the individual among other individuals, nature, and the community. It was in the *1844 Manuscripts* where Marx wrote about his desire for the unity of material and ideal factors.

The importance that Marx places on using a historic perspective reflects his evolutionary ideas of human society. Whereas Comte and Hegel based their evolutionary theories on *ideas*, Marx's evolutionary theory was based on man's need for *material* satisfaction. Marx's focus on social change lies with his insistence that men make their own history. Human history is the process through which mankind changes itself, even to the point where they pit themselves against nature and attempt to dominate it. During the course of history, mankind has increasingly transformed nature to make it better serve its own purposes. By changing nature, humans change themselves. Whereas animals can only passively adjust to nature, humans have created, among other things, tools that allow them to become actively involved with nature. Mankind distinguishes itself from animals as soon as it consciously realizes that it can *produce* its own means of subsistence, rather than being dependent on what nature provides.

Marx explained that ancient society resulted from the union of several tribes into small towns and cities. They were able to produce little more than what they needed to survive; consequently, there was little class distinction. Through the period leading to the Middle Ages, the process of feudalism allowed an elite few to enjoy the benefits of the labor of peasants. By the early period of the sixteenth century, there existed in England the beginnings of a new economic order highlighted by the rapid and vast expansion of overseas commerce. This allowed a slightly larger number of people to enjoy a high level of economic success, while most people struggled to get by. Marx believed that this led to two broad stages of productive organization that would signal the beginning of the capitalist period. The first stage was dominated by manufacture, and the second stage was the ushering in of the Industrial Revolution.

The Industrial Revolution gave way to capitalism with its class distinctions between the proletariat and the bourgeois. The bourgeois society that sprouted from the ruins of feudal society heightened class distinctions, caused greater class antagonisms, and simplified class antagonisms (Farganis, 2011).

Although contemporary society is not characterized by a simple two-class system, there have been signs that the middle class is shrinking in the United States and that the divide between the haves and have-nots is widening. The wealthiest capitalists continue to make great profits even while the national unemployment rate hovers around nine percent. In April 2011, a *USA Today* report of the salaries of the nation's top companies revealed that the median CEO pay increased 27% in 2010. In contrast, workers' pay nearly stalled and increased just 2.1% in 2010 (Krantz and Hansen, 2011). Based on Standard & Poor's 500 Index, the median CEO salary in 2010 was $9 million (Krantz and Hansen, 2011). This wide salary increase differential prompted even conservative commentators such as national syndicated columnist Cal Thomas (2011) to comment that the United States is characterized by a new "gilded age" as the top capitalists continue to profit despite a sustained economic down spiral.

Capital

During the discussion on historical materialism, the term *dialectic* was used to describe historic contradictions. The contradictions within the capitalistic socioeconomic system are what drove Marx's fury against the capitalists. In brief, the capitalists, who own the means of production, must keep the workers subjected to their authority in order to make a profit from the labor of the workers. In contradiction, the capitalists are also dependent upon the labor of the workers. Generally, the workers seek to keep, and expand, a proportion of the profits that result from their labor, while the capitalists attempt to limit wages. Furthermore, the workers are generally content with a certain level of labor and a respectable corresponding wage. (The implication here should be clear: that workers realize they never get paid the full value of their labor and freely turn over the profit of their labor to the capitalist.) The capitalists, however, never seem content, and they seek to continually increase production—through the labor of the workers—in order to invest their profits into further expansion. This augmented expansion occurs via the amplified exploitation of the workers. As summarized by Schmitt (1987), there are three important points that Marx uses to characterize capitalism:

1. Once the capitalists are oriented toward growth, they will attempt to increase profits.
2. The economic system would not exist (as is) if people were not willing to compete for larger profits.
3. Capitalism is frequently identified with industry and industrial development.

The capitalists control the means of production and therefore exert great influence over the socioeconomic political system. As far as Marx was concerned, the social system, or social structure, is the result of the mode of production (the economic base). The prevailing ideology of a society is directly tied to its form, or structure, of economic production. The state represses the plurality of ideologies in order to maintain its own economic structure. This helps to explain why Marx is often referred to as an economic determinist.

The most general economic structural element in Marx's work is *capital*. Capital involves the social relationship between buyers and sellers of labor power. Marx believed that the workers were exploited by a system that they had forgotten they produced through their labor and, therefore, have the capacity to change. Actors tend to reify capital by treating it as a natural phenomenon. In *The Economic and Philosophic Manuscripts of 1844*, Marx states, "Capital itself does not merely amount to theft or fraud, it requires still the cooperation of legislation to sanctify inheritance" (Marx, 1964:136). Capital becomes a governing power over labor and its products. The capitalist possesses this power, not on account of his personal or human qualities, but inasmuch as he is an owner of capital (Marx, 1964).

Capital, Volume One, published in 1867, is the book generally referred to simply as *Capital* and consists of two distinct parts. The first nine chapters contain very abstract discussions of such central concepts as value, labor, and surplus value. It is not only this abstraction that makes them difficult to understand; it is also the Hegelian mode of expression and the fact that, while the concepts used by Marx were familiar to mid-eighteenth-century economists, they were abandoned by later scholars. Modern economists have tended to discuss the functioning of the capitalist system as given and concentrate particularly on prices, whereas Marx wished to examine the mode of production that gave rise to the capitalist system and that would, he believed, bring about its own destruction.

Following the first nine chapters, there is a masterly account of the genesis of capitalism which makes pioneering use of the statistical material just then becoming increasingly available. It is one of the best illustrations of applied historical materialism (McLellan, 1990). *Capital, Volume Two* is rather technical and discusses the circulation of capital and the genesis of economic crises. *Volume Three* begins with a discussion of value and prices and the tendency of profits to fall, but it trails off toward the end with the dramatically incomplete section on classes.

In short, Marx believed that the sum total of the relations of production (raw materials, labor, and the technology used for production) and those who control the means of production (the capitalist) constitute the whole cultural *superstructure* of society. Consequently, those who control the means of production and private property are in the position to impose their will onto those who do not.

It is the nature of capitalists to continually seek additional profits. As we have witnessed in the contemporary era, the expansion of capitalism comes at the cost of not only the workers, but also smaller capitalists, who are squeezed out by the huge conglomerates. The technological advancements of early industrialization freed many workers from manual labor, but such developments were spirited by greedy capitalists who sought to simply increase profits (rather than ease the physical burden of workers). Advancements in technology today have made many workers obsolete. These former workers are pushed aside and become the unemployed. Capitalism encourages unemployment because it creates a steady reserve army of potential laborers who are willing to work for a lower wage. Marx had envisioned such a development. He had hoped, however, that such a revelation of the true nature of capitalism would lead to a proletariat revolution. Although there are various proletariat revolutions from time to time across the globe, there remains no clear sign of mass proletariat revolution.

Marx may have envisioned the capitalists' further exploitation of the workers, but he failed to foresee capitalistic-driven globalization. It is globalization that has kept the powerful capitalistic nations secure. As Collins and Makowsky explain,

> The more advanced countries, like Britain, France, Germany, and the United States, have been able to avoid domestic economic ills by exploiting the rest of the world. If capitalist countries overproduce, they can dump their excess goods in the markets of India or South America. Extra capital to invest can go to the same places; even labor can be exploited internationally, by using low-cost native labor to produce raw materials cheaply (Collins and Makowsky, 2010:37).

Thus, by exploiting the rest of the world, the capitalists of the wealthy nations can continue to increase profits off cheaper foreign labor. Once again, there are a number of worldwide protests against global capitalism, but none of them has been powerful enough to bring down capitalism. However, with the economic downturn that began in the late 2000s, the globalized economic system may bring about its own downfall.

Private Property

In order for the capitalists to control the means of production, they must control private property. Marx used the historic process to analyze how the concept of private property came to be. Starting with the basic premise that people need to sufficiently secure the basic needs of food, clothing, and shelter, Marx acknowledged that once primary needs have been satisfied, humans seek new *needs*, or secondary needs. This is also the first sign of a division of labor, because some people reach the secondary level before others. Class struggle becomes the next inevitable stage in the historic process. Class distinctions are influenced heavily by the possession of personal property, which is determined simply by family lineage. These property relations give rise to different social classes. Different locations in the class system lead to different class interests. The poor pursue primary needs' satisfaction, while the wealthy pursue secondary needs (e.g., self-esteem, self-actualization, the arts, leisure).

Private property is derived from the labor of workers and is reified under capitalism. Marx generally meant by private property the private ownership of the means of production by the capitalist. Thus, it is a product and is external to the worker. It is the product of alienated labor. In order for people to realize their human potential, they must overthrow the validity of private property. The overcoming of alienation, Marx declared, hinges upon the suppression of private property, and what is demanded is a reorganization of society, based upon the eradication of the contemporary relationship between private property and wage labor (Giddens, 1971). Marx believed that the means of production should be shared equally through public ownership.

In the contemporary era, most of us think of private property as the land on which our homes are built. Americans in particular praise the notion of the right to own property as a means of reaching our full potential. Marx was not against the idea of individuals having the right to own private property; rather, he was against the idea of the means of production in the possession of the few (the capitalists). Lenin misinterpreted Marx's dismissal of private property as justification for the state to own all property and forbade individuals from owning land. This is not what Marx had in mind. In fact, it was the exact opposite. Marx wanted all property to be owned collectively by the people. Communal ownership of the means of production is a hallmark of communism. It was not until (former) Russian President Vladimir V. Putin signed a land code into law in 2001 allowing Russians to own small tracts of land—known as a *dacha*—did ownership of private property come to fruition in Russia. As a frequent visitor to Russia, this author has witnessed firsthand the pride that Russians take in their newly found right to own private property. In a few cases, private Russian citizens own small tracts of land for agriculture as well as the land where their buildings and factories are situated. Nonetheless, the vast bulk of land in Russia remains in the hands of the government, which leases it to farmers, businesses, or other individuals.

Class Consciousness and False Consciousness

As demonstrated in the discussion on private property, Marx stated that some people manage to satisfy their primary needs before others and then move on to the pursuit of satisfying secondary needs. Other people are left to quench primary needs. The difference between these two categories of people leads to the early formation of social classes. As Marx has argued, capitalism further expands the differences between people. Through capitalism, the existence of a surplus was created. Those who controlled the means of production also controlled the surplus. The existence of a surplus made it possible for classes to develop. Heilbroner (1970) explains that with the appearance of surplus comes as well the appearance of a class division within society. The material surplus is accompanied by an unequal appropriation of this surplus among the members of the community, which, in turn, creates a struggle between the bourgeois and the proletariat. Social classes were directly linked to this division of labor. Through communism, Marx believed that structural barriers such as the division of labor would be eliminated. Not that Marx ever believed that under communism all people could become, for example, doctors, artists, or lawyers, but rather the artificial barriers preventing people from developing to their fullest would be eliminated.

Marx also believed that people are consciously aware of their position within the class system. The possession of consciousness as well as our ability to link this consciousness to our activities is what separates people from animals. In his extensive look at the history of humanity, Marx came to the conclusion that all of human history is one of class struggles. Antagonism exists between the exploiter and the exploited, the buyers and sellers, and so on. Class consciousness is illustrated by one's relative position to the means of production and access to scarce resources. Class consciousness is the sense of a common identification among members of a given class.

The concept of *false consciousness* is a derivative from Marxist theory of social class. False consciousness refers to the inability to clearly see where one's own best interests lie. In other words, it is often the case that people fail to see the instruments of one's own oppression or exploitation even when it is right in front of him or her and, worse, of his or her own creation. In this manner, members of the oppressed become unwitting participants of their own demise via such methods as adopting the views of the oppressor class. It was Marx's belief that once the exploited (workers/proletariat) become conscious of their plight and misery, they would unite in revolution.

When discussing the related terms of class consciousness and false consciousness, Marx was not talking about individual levels of consciousness, but rather the consciousness of the class as a whole. Additionally, the concepts of class and false consciousness are not static; instead, they are dynamic idea systems that make sense only in terms of social change and development.

Marx was surprised that his vision of a worldwide, proletariat-led revolution never occurred in his lifetime. Many critics argue that Marx overestimated the ability of the workers to act collectively in their own best interest. In addition to suffering from false consciousness, many people, according to Karl Mannheim, fail to reach the basic level of class consciousness. In any society, oppressed and dominated groups will form. The oppressed group, wanting equality, envisions a better life, but rarely knows how to go about attaining it rationally. Mannheim (1936) describes such oppressed groups as possessing a "collective unconscious," that is, behavior guided by wishful representation and the will to action. The collective want change, but they are disorganized, and therefore go about trying to change things irrationally—they rely too much on unconscious action. Not that the action itself is unconscious, but the collectiveness of rational action toward specific goals is missing. That people fail to attain class consciousness is a clear leading explanation as to why people suffer from false consciousness too.

Marx would apply the concept of false consciousness to any nonwealthy person who would support the efforts of powerful businesspeople and government officials who attempt to dismantle labor unions. Unions have fought hard to secure higher wages from the profiteers of capitalism. Collective bargaining, one of the few weapons workers possess (in their attempt to secure a greater slice of the profit pie), is being taken away by representatives of the greedy capitalists in many social institutions. Marx would warn workers of today to remain strong in solidarity. He would be proud of the workers who formed unions, as unions, ideally, represent the needs of the workers. From a Marxist perspective, unions may be viewed as representatives of the people, the working class and the "have-nots." The business owners, conversely, represent the "haves," the people who control the means of production, and the capitalists who attempt to make the maximum profit through the labor of others. Marx stated in *Capital, Volume One* that individuals have isolated labor power, but collectively, the workers have much more. The capitalists, Marx warned, will attempt to end collective action as it represents the only true power the workers possess (Tucker, 1978). Today, there are many government officials and business owners attempting to disband unions and limit the ability of workers to bargain collectively.

In the state of Maine in 2011, Governor Paul LePage removed a 36-foot-wide mural from the state's Department of Labor Building in Augusta. The mural depicted historically accurate scenes of Maine workers, including colonial-era shoemaking apprentices, lumberjacks, a "Rosie the Riveter" in a shipyard, and a 1986 paper mill strike. A spokesperson for the governor ordered the removal of the mural after several business officials complained about the pro-union message of the mural (Greenhouse, 2011). There are so many attempts to break the power of the worker today that it would seem that instead of the proletariat organizing a revolution against the capitalists, the opposite is occurring in the United States. Marx would suggest that any worker supporting the anti-union, anti-collective bargaining movement was suffering from false consciousness.

Fetishism of Commodities

Marx's conception of *commodity* is rooted in his materialist orientation, with its focus on the productive activities of actors. People produce objects they need to survive. A commodity is an object that satisfies some want or need. If we have a particular need, we attempt to acquire an object that is capable of satisfying that need. For example, if one is hungry, one must find food. Objects that are produced for use by oneself have *use* value. Objects are products of human labor and cannot achieve independent existence, because they are controlled by the actors. However, under capitalism, actors produce objects for someone else (the capitalist). These products take on an *exchange* value.

Marx distinguishes between *use value* and *exchange value* when describing the role of production found under capitalism. Products produced by the capitalist, such as yarn or boots, have a use value in that they are useful commodities for people. In *Capital, Volume One*, Marx acknowledges that the capitalist is a "progressit," and yet he does not manufacture boots for their own sake (the need for boots) but rather because boots possess an exchange value. (Clearly, the contemporary era is filled with examples of exchange-value commodities production.) Marx states,

> Our capitalist has two objects in view: in the first place, he wants to produce a use-value that has a value in exchange, that is to say, an article destined to be sold, a commodity; and secondly, he desires to produce a commodity whose value shall be greater than the sum of the values of the commodities used in its production, that is, of the means of production and the labour-power, that he purchased with his good money in the open market (Tucker, 1978:351).

In short, Marx is against someone making a profit based on the labor of others. He begrudges the cunning mind of the capitalist the opportunity to profit because of his organizational skills.

Marx's concept of the *fetishism of commodities* reflects the notion of *false consciousness*. The *fetishism of commodities* involves the process by which actors fail to recognize that it is their labor that gives commodities their value (Dant, 1996). Actors tend to believe that value arises from natural properties of things; the exchange value of one commodity is expressed in terms of its use value. Thus, the "market" takes on a function in the eyes of actors that only actors should perform. It appears natural, and this is due to the historic development of capitalism. Marx explicitly cautions against the pursuit of purchasing exchange values commodities as it helps to maintain the material order of capitalists (Mukerji, 2010). Marx borrowed the term *fetishism* from the early French anthropologist Charles de Brosses. De Brosses used "fetishism" to describe certain features of animistic religions, where some cultures created attributions of demons or spirits and then found themselves controlled by their very own mental products.

Religion

Religion represents another example of false consciousness. Influenced by such social thinkers as Ludwig Feuerbach, Marx developed strong negative feelings toward religion. Marx believed, as Feuerbach, that religion does not make man, rather, man makes religion. Marx viewed religion as another abstract creation that had become reified throughout time. Aside from economic issues, Marx believed that religion was one of the biggest factors hindering actors attempt to reach their full human potential. Marx believed that earthly misery was not lessened through prayer or hopes of a possible "eternal salvation" after death. He challenged people to consider a possible reality that there is no life after death, and therefore one should strive for one's full potential while alive on earth. Marx believed that the power elites encouraged the weak-minded masses to embrace afterlife consideration because the support of the status quo on earth kept them in power. In fact, Marx went so far as to suggest that "religion is the opiate of the masses" (McLellan, 1987; Hadden, 1997). An opiate is a drug used to dull the senses; if one is not thinking clearly, one is likely to believe most anything. Religion exists only because individuals will its existence (Carlebach, 1978). That people turned to religion, Marx believed, is a sure sign of their suffering on earth as a result of being alienated from their true essences (human potential) (Rubel and Manale, 1975).

Marx was against religion for three reasons. First, he believed that religion was a distraction for man from his essence. Second, he felt that while man was in this distracted state, he allowed himself to become shamefully exploited and controlled. Third, because man is being distracted, exploited, and controlled, he loses sight of his human essence. In other words, a religious person is no longer in control of his own destiny (Carlebach, 1978). Marx referred to religion as a form of slavery; it was not healthy, it was explicitly evil or, at least, harmful to society. Further, Marx felt religion was responsible for secular deficiencies, and that religions contain forms of prejudice (McLellan, 1987). Marx believed that religion is based upon the imagination of man. Over time, man's imagination has elaborated to form stories which have become historic events passed on from one generation to the next. He believed that there is no higher form than man.

Marx's family, it will be remembered, had converted to Christianity for practical reasons. The Jews, and even those who had converted, were victimized by discrimination and prejudice. Many of Marx's Jewish contemporaries, including those who had attained intellectual eminence, were still considered socially inferior. Marx was among those who employed an expression of Jewish self-hatred. Marx's lifelong attempt to dissociate himself from his Jewish heritage led him to be highly critical of Jews. In his *On the Jewish Question* (1843), Marx wrote of the Jew as the usurer and the moneychanger; the Children of Israel forever danced before the Golden Calf. In his later career, Marx was subjected to anti-Semitic abuse and it is evident that even before that time he suffered tremendously from his marginal status as a Jew and never came to terms with it (Coser, 1977). Marx was close to his father, but he was always embarrassed by the way his father constantly exhibited attributes that he associated with a specifically Jewish defect: weakness and submissiveness (Coser, 1977).

In 1843, Bruno Bauer wrote *The Jewish Question*. He criticized the Jews for requesting civic and political emancipation, saying that no German was emancipated, so why should the Jew be? Bauer would continue his tirade throughout the essay. He also addressed the issue of why Jews and Christians could not get along with each other. Bauer concluded that religious opposition is impossible to overcome. Therefore, the only solution was to abolish religion. When religion was no longer a barrier between people, human harmony and cooperation would occur. In Marx's response *On the Jewish Question*, he agreed with Bauer, that peace was impossible between major religious groups. Marx believed that Christians, Jews, and all others must abandon religion in order to become free.

Religion remains as a regular fixture among social institutions in nearly all societies. In some nations, their ideology is based around religious tenets. Other countries attempt to embrace religious diversity but with a separation of church and state philosophy. The functions and dysfunctions of religion have been well discussed in a vast majority of publications and are certainly beyond the scope of this text. Many people find solace, spirituality, and inner peace through religion. Suffice it to say, Marx would not be pleased by the continued proletariat embracement of religion. He would argue that people who embrace religion are alienated from their true essence and/or suffering from false consciousness. A religious person may counter, "But religion helps me to reach my full potential." There is little wonder why the topic of religion and Marx's views on it remain controversial today. Clearly, many people disagree with Marx's assessment of religion.

Marx tried to convince people that there was no God and that they should seek happiness on earth rather than accept the idea of eternal happiness in the afterlife (e.g., Heaven). Marx did recognize that people often feel the need to turn to a higher power, especially in times of strife and life-threatening situations. Perhaps the deadliest of all settings is the front line of battle. There is an expression in the military that "there aren't any atheists in foxholes." The primary meaning of this profound statement is the idea that when bullets are flying all around you and you fear imminent death, there is comfort to be found by praying to God or some higher power. If you live, it was because God saved you. If you died, it was part of God's mysterious plan. Either way, praying at least provided a last comfort to soldiers in dire situations. Are there atheists in foxholes? And if so, how do they find comfort in dire situations? In 2011, the U.S.

Army reported that there exists a group of military service persons at Fort Bragg, one of the biggest military bases in the country, who count themselves as atheists, agnostics, humanists, and other assorted skeptics (Breen, 2011). The group hopes to receive official recognition from the Army so that they can meet on the base. Sgt. Justin Griffith, chief organizer of Military Atheists and Secular Humanists, or MASH, states, "We're in foxholes." Lt. Samantha Nicoll, a West Point graduate, admits, "People look at you differently if you say you're an atheist in the Army" (Breen, 2011). The group takes comfort in military training and fighting skills and acknowledges that death is a possible outcome in combat. Marx, undoubtedly, would look favorably upon this MASH unit.

Interestingly, two key ideas from Christianity influenced Marx's concepts. The idea of a perfect life in Heaven where everyone lives in communal harmony influenced his ideas of communism and a utopian society. We will discuss communism shortly. The concept of "original sin" influenced Marx's ideas of alienation, conflict, and obstacles to reaching one's full human potential. The concept of "original sin" refers to the doctrine that holds that human nature has been morally and ethically corrupted because Adam and Eve disobeyed God and were consequently thrown out of the Garden of Eden (*Theopedia Encyclopedia of Biblical Christianity*, 2012). As a result of this transgression, all of humanity is ethically debilitated and powerless to rehabilitate themselves unless they turn to God and seek His forgiveness. Not all religions believe in original sin, and there are different interpretations of what exactly constitutes "original sin"; nonetheless, the primary point of the concept centers on the idea that humans are, by their nature, flawed. John Calvin, an influential French theologian and pastor during the Protestant Reformation during the 1500s and architect of Calvinism, who was trained as a humanist lawyer, believed that humans are corrupt and depraved by their very nature as a result of original sin (Gordon, 2007). Despite his doubts on several religious aspects of the Church, Hegel believed in the theological dogma of original sin and concluded that man is evil by nature. Influenced by Hegel, Marx argued that once individuals learn that they are born flawed, they develop feelings of alienation and self-doubt; they become alienated from their very essence. In his 1908 publication *Orthodoxy*, G. K. Chesterton—a Christian apologetic writer—stated that the doctrine of original sin is the only part of Christian theology that can be proved (Chapter 2, *Orthodoxy*). Chesterton argued that the history of humanity is sufficient proof to demonstrate the evil nature of humans. In 2012, David Buss, an evolutionary psychologist at the University of Texas, in an effort to ascertain the validity of humans as naturally evil, asked his students if they had ever thought about seriously killing someone, and if so, to write out their homicidal fantasies in an essay. The results of this study appeared throughout most of the world in a variety of publications including *The New York Times*. *Times* syndicated columnist David Brooks reported that Buss found that 91% of the men and 84% of the women had detailed, vivid homicidal fantasies and that many of the students had taken steps toward carrying them out (Brooks, 2012).

Alienation

As described above, Marx argued that original sin leads to feelings of alienation. It would be interesting to apply a Marxist study similar to Professor Buss's and test whether or not homicidal thoughts directly lead to feelings of alienation. Neither Marx nor anyone else has published such a study. Marx did, however, write about alienation; based on his historical analysis, Marx concluded that humans are becoming increasingly alienated. *Alienation*, according to Marx, was a condition in which humans become dominated by the forces of their own creation, which confront them as alien powers (Coser, 1977; Cooper, 1991). They are distortions of human nature that cause one to feel alien and mechanical in the process of labor. The capitalist society, by the very nature of its structure, was responsible for four general types of alienation on the worker, all of which can be found in the domain of work.

First, workers are alienated from the object(s) they produce. The product of their labor does not belong to them; it belongs to the capitalists to do with as they please. This implies that capitalists sell the workers' labor for a profit—an alienating realization to learn that someone else benefits more than you do from your own labor. Furthermore, the workers often lack detailed knowledge of aspects of the production process in which they are personally involved. The object produced by labor becomes alien to the worker. The worker does not receive the product, but instead a wage. All the while, the capitalists, who did not work on production, receive all of the end products and sell them, at a profit, as exchange commodities.

Second, workers in the capitalist system are alienated from the process of production. They are not actively involved in the productive activity; that is, they are not working for themselves in order to satisfy their own needs. Instead, they are working for the capitalist. This becomes an alienating force because it is not satisfying for the worker, and he often becomes bored from the monotonous, tedious activity.

Because the worker feels alienated from the productive activity and the object being produced, it is no surprise that he also becomes alienated from himself. Through the process of specialization, the worker is not allowed to fully develop his skills. This underscores one of Marx's primary concerns; namely, that the worker cannot reach his full human potential if he is alienated from self. The result is a mass of alienated workers, because individuals are not allowed to express themselves fully. Consequently, the worker feels more like himself only during times of leisure, when he is allowed the opportunity to express himself as he pleases.

Finally, the worker is alienated from his fellow workers, the human community, i.e., from his species-being. Marx's assumption was that man basically wants and needs to work with others cooperatively in order to appropriate from nature what they require to survive. In capitalism this cooperation is disrupted, and in fact, the worker may find himself isolated, or worse, in a position where he must compete with fellow workers. This isolation and competition tend to make workers in capitalism feel alienated from their fellow workers.

In short, Marx believed that capitalism alienated man from reaching his full human potential and the community of his fellows. Communism would be a system that reestablishes the interconnectedness that had been destroyed by capitalism. One of Marx's most brilliant examples of the perversion of humanity by capitalism is found in his discussion of money. From his *Early Writings*, Marx describes money as the alienated essence of man's work and existence; the essence dominates him and he worships it. In the *Economic and Philosophic Manuscripts of 1844*, Marx states that money is the pimp for man's needs. Money becomes the object of desire and alienates man from his true essence. Marx, in his *Essay on Money*, states that money leads to the distortion of society and that money equals power.

Many people still suffer from all forms of alienation. Although most of us are not working on production assembly lines, many of us are restricted to our specific jobs—and this division of labor role creates distance between us and the final product. The student reading this text may feel alienated from friends and family because she is doing homework. When we are away from home, we may feel alienated. Many people feel lost in society and wonder about their place in the world; they too feel alienated. Interestingly, many people have turned to technology to keep in touch with friends and family. Facebook, for example, has over 500 million members worldwide. Most people join Facebook to communicate with others. Ironically, actors are often so consumed with communication via cellular phones and the Internet that they have become alienated from the people in their immediate proximity. Technology may create the means to alleviate alienation, but it also seems to be a source of it.

How would Marx feel about the Internet and social networking? One the one hand, the Net allows people the opportunity to connect with friends whenever *they* want—power to the people! And yet, all the electronic devices that the proletariat purchase to stay connected fills the pockets of the capitalists. It is not a coincidence that "new" and "improved," "must-have" products are produced in increasingly rapid fashion. The consumer has been duped by the capitalist to spend. Marx would not be pleased by this. Marx would also be interested in a 2012 United Kingdom survey that suggested 66% of respondents showed symptoms of nomophobia—the fear of losing or being unable to use a cell phone (Wrenn, 2012). Although the study was released by a cell phone security company, it was conducted by outside researchers. In brief, the study reveals what many people, especially college professors, have witnessed in the classroom, namely that some people, among them students, seem to be addicted to their cell phones and have a constant need to check for messages. When separated from their cell phones for any length of time, even the short classroom time of one hour (plus or minus a few minutes), students become alienated from their sense of selves and their very essence. One possible explanation for this separation anxiety, or alienation, is the release of dopamine in the individual's system when they receive a message. Dopamine is a chemical that the brain produces in anticipation of a reward. How do you know if you suffer from nomophobia? Among the warning sings, the compulsive checking for messages, fearing that the cell phone has been lost, and waking up at night to check the phone.

Communism

Marx is perhaps best known for his ideas on *communism*. Throughout this chapter, references to communism have been commonplace. For example, we learned that Marx was influenced by the Christian ideal of Heaven as a perfect utopian society in the afterlife. Marx wanted to create an earthly life similar to this perfect communal spiritual sphere because he wanted all humans to reach their full human potential. He hoped to eliminate alienation, the class society, religion, private property, and other obstacles that he believed hindered this goal. Marx believed that capitalism was a major barrier, and therefore, he hoped to overthrow it. Marx devoted a great deal of his life to understanding capitalism through scientific study and to ending capitalism through revolution (Pampel, 2000).

Philosophically, Marx's primary ideas of communism were described in *The Communist Manifesto*, a book cowritten with Engels. In the introduction of *Manifesto*, Marx and Engels (1978) state that all of Europe is aware of the growing spectre of the Communist party and proclaim that "it is high time that Communists should openly, in the face of the whole world, publish their views, their aims, their tendencies, and meet this nursery tale of the Spectre of Communism with a Manifesto of the party itself" (p. 473). Interestingly enough, people are still intimidated by the spectre of communism today.

The Communist Manifesto, then, was a type of official "coming out" statement by the radicals who called themselves communists. The *Manifesto* has four sections. The first section ("Bourgeois and Proletariats") begins with the famous line, "The history of all hitherto existing society is the history of class struggles." Section 1 provides a history of society, indicating that throughout time all societies suffered from class conflict, which in the long run had always ended either with the destruction of the society, or with the emergence of the subordinate class as victors. With a new dominant class comes a new mode of production and a new social order. "In ancient Rome we have patricians, knights, plebeians, and slaves;

in the Middle Ages, feudal lords, vassals, guild-masters, journeymen, apprentices, serfs; in almost all of these classes again, subordinate gradations" (Marx and Engels, 1978:474). The bourgeoisie emerged from feudal society in Western Europe and with it came a growth in colonization, manufacturing, new technologies of production and transportation, and the growth of global markets. Marx and Engels (1978) successfully envisioned the future role of the bourgeoisie by proclaiming, "The bourgeoisie cannot exist without constantly revolutionizing the instruments of production, and thereby the relations of production, and with them the whole relations of society" (p. 476). The constant revolutionizing of the instruments of production takes away the "charm" of the workman, reducing him to merely a machine operator. This results in lower production costs, higher profits, lower worker wages, and the beginning of alienating labor.

The second section describes the position of communists within the proletariat class; rejects bourgeois objections to communism; characterizes the communist revolution and the measures to be taken by the victorious proletariat; and outlines the nature of the future communist society. The role of the communists with the proletariat is to seek the best interests of the labor class as a whole and not splinter working-class parties. The bourgeois fear the communists because the communists represent the needs of the people, not the capitalists. This sentiment continues in contemporary society. The communists would lead the proletariat in revolution and establish a society that best befits the workers. Marx and Engels established ten specific aspects of the future Communist party. Among the tenets of future communist society: abolition of private property; a heavy progressive or graduated income tax; abolition of all right to inheritance; establishment of a State bank; and free education for all children in public schools.

The third section contains an extended criticism of other types of socialism—reactionary, bourgeois, and utopian. As "representatives" of the entire working class, Marx and Engels viewed other socialist parties and splinter groups that interfered with their goal of uniting all of the proletariats. The final section of the *Manifesto* provides a short description of communist tactics toward other opposition parties and finishes with an appeal for proletarian unity.

Marx and Engels believed that the capitalist class would be overthrown and that it would be eliminated by a worldwide working-class revolution and replaced by a classless society. The *Manifesto* influenced all subsequent communist literature and revolutionary thought in general. Marx and Engels truly believed that the world would be a better place with communism. They believed that class inequality would end with the collective control of property and with the size and growth in power of the working class. Under Marxist communism, government was deemed unnecessary. Consequently, the governmental abuse of workers would end with the dismantling of government (Pampel, 2000).

Criticisms

Marx was a highly influential person during his lifetime; as demonstrated throughout this chapter, much of his work is still relevant today. However, there are legitimate criticisms of Marxist ideas, beginning with one of his most important contributions, his theory of communism. It has become commonplace to refute his ideas of communism, especially as an inevitable outcome following the proletariat's awareness of inequality and, therefore, attaining class consciousness. Perhaps even more problematic for Marxists is the realization that the proletariat often fail to act in their own best interests; consequently, any expectation of mass organization among the proletariats that leads to enlightenment and collective revolution was naïve, at best. In addition, many nations that were once inspired by the communistic doctrine have converted to capitalism, or a mixed economy that includes aspects of capitalism or a market system. Furthermore, the concept of communism serving as a guiding force toward some sort of perfect society is utopian and unrealistic.

Karl Marx believed that communism would create an environment wherein the proletariat would be given an opportunity to reach their full human potential. Capitalism, he argued, prevented people from attaining this goal. However, how does anyone really know what his full potential is? And, how does one know when he or she has attained his or her full potential? Each of us can ask this question to ourselves, "What is my full potential?" The concept is vague and therefore open to criticism. Marx also argued that the proletariat were exploited and alienated because of the capitalistic system. He failed to realize, or acknowledge, that people in all sorts of socioeconomic political systems experience forms of discontent. As evidenced by the start of the year 2011, people throughout North Africa (i.e., Tunisia, Egypt, Libya, Bahrain, Jordan, Saudi Arabia, Yemen, and Algeria) rebelled against the monarchies that ruled them. These proletariat revolutions were not inspired by a distaste of capitalism and a desire for communism, but instead by a desire to be treated equally within a traditional totalitarian society.

In addition, Marx failed to envision the many changes that would occur in the capitalist system. As he and Engels observed the misery of the working poor throughout Western Europe, they failed to realize that they were merely seeing the initial stages of capitalism, where it is common that societies first introduced to industrialization witness many forms of exploitation against the workers. As the capitalistic process continues in any given society, changes introduced to the system bring about many potential benefits. For example, governments can create laws to protect the workers from exploitation. Political pressure targeting the government will be far more effective than aiming it toward the capitalist. Workers can form unions and make demands for higher wages, more sick days, maternity and paternity leave, and so on. The creation of joint-stock ownership helps to eliminate feelings of alienation. Along with the decomposition of both capital and labor, a new stratum emerged within, as well as outside, the industry of modern capitalist societies. This development was, of course, the middle class. All of these changes led to another unforeseen phenomenon, that of social mobility. Although it is true that Marx failed in some of his analyses of capitalism, he can hardly be blamed for not properly predicting the future. After all, few are capable of such vision.

Summary

Karl Marx was many things: He was a poet, philosopher, socialist theoretician, economist, historian, and a major contributor to sociological thought. He was a brilliant thinker, whose ideas have been subjected to many diverse interpretations and, in some cases, outright misinterpretations. Add to this, his theories are opposed by many who have not read much, if any, of his works. Marxist thought is without question the most fraught with controversy and opposing interpretations (Hadden, 1997).

Marx was not optimistic about future society, as he believed that conflict was inevitable. It exists at multiple levels. At the class level, because of the growth and complexity of modern societies, conflict has become institutionalized. Conflict exists among social classes, sexes, races, ethnicities, and competing religions. Marx has been proven correct that religion continues to serve as a barrier against peace and accord. The world continues to be ravaged by religious conflicts and war. For example, there most certainly will never be peace in the Middle East unless Jews and Muslims abandon religion. Marx would argue that this idea on ending organized religion needs to be extended to all other forms of religion if mankind has any hope for a lasting existence.

On March 17, 1883, Marx was buried at Highgate Cemetery in London. Perhaps the best summary of Marx's immense and profound works and contributions can be found in Engels' speech at his friend's funeral:

> An immeasurable loss has been sustained both by the militant proletariat of Europe and America, and by historical science, in the death of this man. The gap that has been left by the departure of this mighty spirit will soon make itself felt. Just as Darwin discovered the law of development of organic nature, so Marx discovered the law of development of human history: the simple fact, hitherto concealed by an overgrowth of ideology, that mankind must first of all eat, drink, have shelter and clothing, before it can pursue politics, science, art, religion, etc.; that therefore the production of the immediate material means of subsistence and consequently the degree of economic development attained by a given people or during a given epoch from the foundation upon which the state institutions, the legal conceptions, art, and even its ideas on religion, of the people concerned have evolved, and in the light of which they must, therefore, instead of *vice versa*, as had hitherto been the case (Engels, 1883).

Engels described Marx as a revolutionist who wanted to overthrow capitalist society and the state institutions which it had brought into being, and to contribute to the liberation of the modern proletariat. Marx fought with a passion and tenacity for the rights of workers. Although it is true that only a few people attended Marx's funeral, telegrams from throughout the world, including such groups as the French Workers' Party, the Russian Socialists, and the Spanish Workers' Party, were received expressing their condolences. Also, as previously mentioned, people still visit his grave today. Furthermore, the ideas of Marx are taught at nearly all college campuses around the world. The overall relevancy of Karl Marx to social thought in general, and to sociological thought in particular, is well secured.

 Study and **Review** on **MySearchLab**

Discussion Questions

1. Marx spent most of his life promoting communism and criticizing capitalism. He was also economically poor most of his own life. And yet, today, people pay money at the entrance to Highgate Cemetery to visit the grave of Karl Marx. How do you suppose Marx would react to the idea of people paying money to a capitalistic entity in order to view his gravestone?

2. Ludwig Feuerbach is said to have commented, "To think, you must eat." Explain what this statement means to you. What did Feuerbach mean by the idea that God is merely a projection created by humans? Do you believe him? Why or why not?

3. Although Marx used the term *class consciousness* to refer to a class of people, the concept can be applied to the individual level. That is, most of us, at one point or another in our lives, came to realize our individual class standing. (Colleges use the term "class standing" to identify the categories of freshman, sophomore, junior, and senior students.) In other words, we know whether or not we are wealthy, middle-class, or poor. Explain the circumstances that first led you to recognize your social class standing. Where do you see yourself, from a social class perspective, in the future?

4. It is understandable why wealthy capitalists would be against collective bargaining, but why would the average person be against this? Marx would say that this is a clear example of false consciousness. What do you think?

5. What does Marx's notion of "religion as an opiate of the masses" mean to you? Do you agree or disagree with Marx's views on religion? How are you similar and how are you different from his perspective?

MySearchLab® **Connections**

MysearchLab is designed just for you. Each chapter features a customized study plan to help you learn and review key concepts and terms. Dynamic visual activities, videos, and readings found in the multimedia library will enhance your learning experience.

 View on **MySearchLab**

- ▶ Karl Marx's Model of Society
- ▶ Marx's Model of the Social Classes
- ▶ Marx's Model of Historical Change

 Read on **MySearchLab**

- ▶ Marx, Karl. Manifesto of the Communist Party.

3 Émile Durkheim

 Listen to the **Chapter Audio** on **MySearchLab**

Chapter Outline

- Biography
- Intellectual Influences
- Investigation and Application of Durkheim's Concepts and Contributions
- Summary
- Discussion Questions

Émile David Durkheim is one of the most influential figures in French sociology and is acknowledged as the founder of modern sociology (Garner, 2000). Durkheim did more than anyone else to establish sociology as an academic discipline (Hadden, 1997). Compared to Karl Marx, he had little influence on world politics and social movements. But Durkheim, more than any other theorist, defined sociology as a separate discipline with its own goals, methods, and objects of study (Pampel, 2000). "No one, not even Weber, has so eloquently set forth for us the essentials of the scientific method as it bears upon social phenomena. No one else has seen so clearly the legitimate boundaries of sociology among the sciences" (Nisbet, 1974:vii). Durkheim would become the first full professor of sociology. He is described as "a master to whom all students of human nature and of the nature of society owe a great debt; he set an example of the great humanist or, rather, of the genuine sociologist, and left behind him a promise and vision of great achievements to be undertaken by future generations of social scientists" (Roche de Coppens, 1976:46). Among the topics for which Durkheim is most renowned are his ideas on morality, collective conscience, solidarity, anomie, and suicide. His work on suicide helped to establish sociology as a legitimate field in the eyes of other academics, and it is also a topic that students can relate to, because by the time they have completed their college education, many students will know someone, or know of someone, who attempts or actually commits suicide.

Émile Durkheim (1858–1917), French sociologist generally acknowledged as the "founder of modern sociology." (Library of Congress Prints and Photographs Division (LC-USZ62-16530))

BIOGRAPHY

Émile Durkheim was born on the evening of April 15, 1858, at Épinal, the capital town of Vosges in the eastern French province of Lorraine, France. His mother, Melanie, came from a family that was involved in "trade-beer and horses" (merchants) (Mazlish, 1993:196). His father, Moise, was the Rabbi of Épinal since the 1830s and was also Chief Rabbi of the Vosges and Haute-Marne. Raised in a very strict Jewish home, Émile spent part of his early school years in a rabbinical school, studied Hebrew and the Talmud, and seemed destined to follow in the footsteps of his patriarchal lineage of Jewish rabbis (Mazlish, 1993). Émile's grandfather, Israel David Durkheim, had been a rabbi in Mutzig (Alsace), as had his great-grandfather Simon, appointed in 1784 (Lukes, 1972). His desire to become a rabbi was short-lived, and by the time he reached his teens, he had largely disavowed his heritage (Strenski, 1997). At the age of thirteen, he was influenced by a Catholic schoolteacher, which eventually led Durkheim to become agnostic. From that point on, Durkheim's lifelong interest in religion was more academic than theological (Mestrovic, 1988).

Durkheim was the youngest of four children. His siblings were Felix, Rosine, and Celine. All the children were raised in the Ashkenazi Jewish faith and tradition characterized by such traits as scorn for the inclination to conceal effort, disdain for success unachieved by effort, and horror for everything that is not positively grounded (Lukes, 1972). The Jews of eastern France had been emancipated for more than two generations at the time of Durkheim's youth, but they still maintained a cultural identity. Matters that concerned the Jewish community were generally overseen by appointed elders (parnassim) or rabbis. Rabbis and their families were, consequently, assured a certain level of prestige within the community. Economically speaking, the Durkheim household would be considered a middle-class family by today's standards. Durkheim's eventual break from his father and the Jewish tradition must have been quite a traumatic event in his life.

When Durkheim was twelve years old, France was defeated in the Franco-Prussian War. During the time that the Germans occupied France, Durkheim was exposed to a great deal of anti-Semitism. He wrote later in life about those experiences: "Anti-Semitism had already been in the regions of the East at the time of the war of 1870; being myself of Jewish origin, I was then able to observe it at close hand. The Jews were blamed for the defeats" (Lukes, 1972:41).

The level of anti-Semitism experienced by Durkheim led him to abandon his Jewish faith and drove him to higher levels of secular patriotism toward France and a desire to help reshape its society. The intervening century had been politically uncertain, but after the defeat, those who favored a rational, industrial society (in order to compete with Germany) began to carry the day (Hadden, 1997). In his *Professional Ethics and Civil Morals*, Durkheim (1957) wrote, "As long as there are states, so there will be national pride, and nothing can be more warranted. But societies can have their pride, not in being the greatest or the wealthiest, but in being the most just, the best organized and in possessing the best moral constitution" (pp. 154–155).

Education

Durkheim was a brilliant student who possessed a razor-sharp intellect and excelled at the Collège d'Épinal, earning a variety of awards and honors. With his driving ambition to continue his education, Durkheim transferred to one of the great French high schools, the Lycée Louis-le-Grand in Paris. Here he prepared himself for the rigors of the prestigious École Normale Supérieure, home to many of the intellectual elite of France. The École accepted only the brightest and most intelligent students, and those young men who were accepted into this elite institution were expected to go on and become great, influential people. Candidates went through a rigorous selection process. The governing board did not accept Durkheim in his first two attempts. Unfortunately, his father had become very ill, and the emotional distress experienced by Durkheim had negatively affected his studies.

Finally, in 1879, he passed the entrance examinations. Academic life at the École was nothing like the college experience that students enjoy today. The school monitored the students' comings and goings; they were under strict curfews that allowed off-campus activities, of any kind, only on Sundays and Thursday afternoons (and only once a month) (Lukes, 1972). The strict instruction generally encouraged bonding and a sense of camaraderie among students. The intense training that existed at the École was something the students remembered for a lifetime. Students rose at 6:30 A.M. (6:00 in the summer), ate a quick breakfast, and proceeded to attend classes and study for the next 11 hours (Pampel, 2000). It was almost like an educational "boot camp." It is unlikely students in the contemporary era would find school to be as much fun as it can be today if they had schedules such Durkheim's.

Durkheim had two close friends while at the École: Henri Bergson and Jean Jaures. It is thought that these two friends influenced Durkheim in his final break from Judaism (Lukes, 1972). Bergson, who was to become the philosopher of vitalism, and Jaures, the future socialist leader, had entered the École the year before Durkheim. Maurice Blondel (a Catholic philosopher who generally demoted/deemphasized, at least in his earlier thinking, the role of rational demonstration as a basis for action) was admitted two years after Durkheim. Pierre Janet, the psychologist, and Goblot, the philosopher, were classmates of Durkheim. The École, which had been created by the First Republic, was now enjoying a renaissance with leading intellectual and political figures of the Third Republic (Coser, 1977).

Once admitted to the prestigious École Normale, a major achievement for anyone, Durkheim became uneasy with the course curriculum. He longed for training in scientific methods and moral principles opposed to the more general academic approach at the École. Durkheim would earn the nickname "the metaphysician" by his peers (Coser, 1977). He rebelled against a course of studies in which the reading of Greek verse and Latin prose were deemed more important than actually learning philosophical doctrines or recent scientific findings. Durkheim viewed his professors as showy and shallow, knowing a little about a lot of subjects, but not knowing a lot about a few specialized subjects. When he pressed them for further details, they demonstrated a lack of true in-depth knowledge (Pampel, 2000). His professors were not happy being challenged by a student and generally punished him with low grades. Durkheim did, however, admire a few professors. He became friends with Charles Renouvier and Émile Boutoux, both philosophers. He also became a friend with Numas-Denis Fustel de Coulanges, who was a historian who taught him the use of critical and rigorous method in historical research. Durkheim dedicated his Latin thesis to the memory of Coulanges, and his French thesis, *The Division of Labor*, to Boutroux.

Post-Student Years

After graduating from the École in 1882, Durkheim decided that he would concentrate on the sociological scientific study of society. However, because sociology as an academic discipline was still relatively new, Durkheim taught philosophy in a number of provincial schools in the Paris area between 1882 and 1887 (Nisbet, 1974). His thirst for science was satisfied during a visit to German universities (1885–1886), where he was exposed to the scientific psychology being pioneered by Wilhelm Wundt (Durkheim, 1887). In the years immediately following his visit to Germany, Durkheim began to publish extensively. At age 29, he had been recognized in Germany as a promising figure in the social sciences and in social philosophy. This recognition, along with his recent publications, helped him to gain a position in the department of philosophy at the University of Bordeaux in 1887. Not everyone was pleased by his appointment because he was a social scientist and the Faculty of Letters at Bordeaux was predominately humanist.

At Bordeaux, Durkheim offered the first course in social science in a French university. This was an astounding point in French sociology, for only a decade earlier, a furor had erupted in a French university by the mere mention of Auguste Comte in a student dissertation (Ritzer, 2000b). That student, Alfred Espinas, would become a colleague of Durkheim's at Bordeaux. Espinas refused to delete the name of Comte from the introduction of his thesis. Throughout the Bordeaux period, Durkheim emphasized the value of sociology and moral education. Durkheim enjoyed teaching courses in education to schoolteachers. He was trying to encourage educators to emphasize morality in an effort to help reverse the moral degeneration he saw around him in French society (Ritzer, 2000b). He felt education was important because it was an area where sociology could make the greatest impact on society (Giddens, 1978).

Around the time of his academic appointment to Bordeaux, Durkheim married Louise Dreyfus. They had two children, Marie and André, but little is known of his family life. Louise seems to have followed the traditional Jewish family pattern of taking care of the family as well as devoting herself to Émile's work by performing secretarial duties including proof-reading. Durkheim's marriage and family life are described as a "happy family existence" (Mazlish, 1993).

In 1893, Durkheim published his French doctoral thesis, *The Division of Labor in Society*, as well as his Latin thesis on Montesquieu. In *The Division of Labor*, Durkheim demonstrates his abiding concern with unity and solidarity, and he defends modern society as capable, in principle, of rational integration while fostering individual autonomy (Hadden, 1997). Two years later, his major methodical statement, *The Rules of Sociological Method*, was published, and within another two years *Le Suicide* appeared. *Rules* represents the formal presentation of frameworks and procedures already initiated in *The Division of Labor*.

In *Suicide*, Durkheim becomes the first social scientist to actually apply the scientific method to the study of social phenomena. He demonstrates that suicide, which is generally an individual and antisocial act, can be understood sociologically. For whatever the "reasons" individuals may have for this act, sociology alone is capable of understanding factors contributing to varying *rates* of such behaviors, factors having to do with faulty regulation of individual tendencies (Hadden, 1997). In addition, Durkheim notes in the preface of *Suicide* that sociology was now "in fashion." These works were major accomplishments that pushed Durkheim to the forefront of the academic world. In 1898, Durkheim became a full professor at Bordeaux. In the same year, Durkheim put aside his work on the history of socialism and put all of his efforts into establishing a single scholarly journal devoted entirely to sociology.

Within two years, he had established *L'Année sociologique*, the first social science journal in France. *Année* was successful from the beginning, and the continued collaboration between Durkheim and its key contributors helped to form a cohesive "school" of thought eager to defend the Durkheimian approach to sociology. Also in 1898, Durkheim published his famous paper *Individual and Collective Representations*, which served as a kind of manifesto for the Durkheimian School. Durkheim would add a number of other publications to his résumé, including the famous *The Elementary Forms of Religious Life* in 1912. In this book, despite his agnostic and scientific mentality, Durkheim held that society could not exist independently of religious forms of sentiment and action (Cuzzort, 1969). He argues that the basis of religiously conceived moral authority and suasion lie, in fact, in an impersonal, anonymous, collective, social, and moral authority. Whereas the religious believer sees this force as divine in origin, Durkheim argues that it represents the complex assertion of collective group forces (Hadden, 1997). These group forces are developed through the socialization process inherent in human society, and modified throughout history.

Émile Durkheim returned to Paris, summoned to the famous French university the Sorbonne in 1902, with a reputation as a powerful force in sociology and education. Durkheim was the first to be promoted to full professorship in the social sciences in France. He occupied the chair for six years and in 1906 was named Professor of the Science of Education. In 1913, the title was changed to Science of Education and Sociology. After more than seventy-five years, Comte's brainchild had finally gained entry at the University of Paris (Coser, 1977).

André Durkheim, Émile's son, who himself was a brilliant linguist, was killed in April 1916, at the Bulgarian front in the war between Germany and Belgium (World War I). This was a terrible blow to Durkheim from which he never fully recovered. He suffered a stroke and died a year later on November 15, 1917. He is considered to be one of the most influential people in the development of sociology and was a celebrated figure in French intellectual circles. It was twenty years later, with the publication of Talcott Parson's *The Structure of Social Action* (1937), that Durkheim's work became a significant influence on American sociology.

The Alfred Dreyfus Case (1894–1906)

By today's standards, Durkheim's academic works are considered relatively conservative. But in his time, he was considered a liberal. His liberal tendencies were revealed, in part, by the fact that he was a founding and active member of the Dreyfusard Ligue pour la Defense des Droits de l'Homme (the Dreyfus Defense) (Fournier, 2007; Gartner, 2001). The "Dreyfusard Defense" referred to a group of generally liberal, anticlerical, humanitarian thinkers of the left (Nisbet, 1974). The Dreyfusard were formed to fight the perceived anti-Semitism that existed in France in general, but specifically to overturn the conviction of Captain Alfred Dreyfus. Dreyfus was a French army captain of Jewish background who was court-martialed in 1894 for treason (allegedly selling military secrets to the Germans) (Goldberg, 2008). The Dreyfusard considered the decision to court-martial Dreyfus as a result of anti-Semitism in France. (Note: This court case would lead Durkheim to publish his brief but suggestive article, "Anti-Semitism and Social Crisis.")

Despite proclaiming his innocence, Dreyfus was sentenced to Devil's Island for life. Devil's Island was the collective name given to three small islands in the Atlantic Ocean, 20 miles off the coast of French Guiana, which once contained leper colonies (Farrington, 2000). Devil's Island served as part of France's penal colonies; for months Dreyfus was the only prisoner held at this facility. The conviction of Dreyfus led to public demands to bar Jews from political life and state service, a repeal of the emancipation that the French state had given to Jews in 1791, and even cries to expel Jews from France altogether (Goldberg 2008; Vital, 1999). Anti-Jewish riots swept through France in early 1898; some of the riots involved as many as a thousand people and lasted for days (Goldberg, 2008).

Meanwhile, evidence pointed to a conspiracy against Dreyfus by army officials and the right-wing government. Luminaries and a few newspapers were proclaiming his innocence, and Durkheim was among the first to sign a public appeal on Dreyfus's behalf. In 1899, the French government issued a pardon, permitting Dreyfus's return from Devil's Island. He was exonerated following a further inquiry in 1906.

The Dreyfus case revealed the lingering anti-Semitism that existed among the masses in France and it also divided the educated elite of France. Chad Alan Goldberg (2011) argues that Durkheim's sociology is often tied to French anti-Semitism in France, sometimes explicit as in the case of the Dreyfus case and more implicit in other cases, such as issues tied to morality. Durkheim did not attribute this anti-Semitism to racism among the French people; instead, he saw it as a symptom of moral sickness confronting French society as a whole (Birnbaum and Todd, 1995). Durkheim's interest in the Dreyfus affair stemmed from his deep and lifelong interest in a common morality.

INTELLECTUAL INFLUENCES

Durkheim was an ardent reader and a highly cultivated man open to a variety of intellectual ideas. Consequently, it is difficult to describe all the major influences on his thoughts. It is well established that Durkheim has roots in the French tradition, especially with the works of Montesquieu, Saint-Simon, Comte, and Rousseau, and both German and British social thought. The significant influence over Durkheim's mature intellectual position came from distinctly French intellectual traditions. The overlapping interpretations, which Saint-Simon and Comte offered of the decline of feudalism and the emergence of the modern form of society, constitute the principal foundation for the whole of Durkheim's writings (Giddens, 1971).

The French Tradition

Many French thinkers influenced Durkheim. Rousseau and his concept of a *volonté generale* (general will) influenced Durkheim's idea of "solidarity" (let the people unify). French democracy is characterized by its defense of the intrinsic connection between liberty and equality (Seidman, 1983). Rousseau had insisted that genuine freedom and social progress presuppose social equality and participatory democracy. Of Rousseau's idea of freedom, Durkheim (1965) wrote, "Man is only free when a superior force compels his recognition, provided, however, that he accepts this superiority and that his submission is not won by lies and artifice. He is free if he is held in check" (p. 88). Freedom, then, presupposes a social and moral framework of rules and regulations that must be self-imposed or based on consensus. Rousseau saw this moral framework as the general will.

Durkheim (1965) acknowledged that he learned of the distinction between social and psychological phenomena from Rousseau when he wrote, "Rousseau was keenly aware of the specificity of the social order. He conceived it clearly as an order of facts generically different from purely individual facts. It is a new world superimposed on the purely psychological world" (p. 83). For Durkheim, a society of solidarity has a *body* (an organic effect), but also an *attitude/ sentiment* (feeling of belonging). Thus, Durkheim reveals thoughts of functionalism, but also a social–psychological effect.

Durkheim believes, "Man is himself only in and through society. If man were not a part of society, he would be an animal like the rest" (Aron, 1979:105). Thus, Durkheim believes that human investment into the creation and maintenance of society is what separates humans from the other animals; society is what makes a human "human." Durkheim states, "Rousseau demonstrated a long time ago, if we take away from man everything he derives from society, all that remains is a creature reduced to sensation and more or less indistinguishable from the animal" (Aron, 1970:106). Clearly, Rousseau influenced Durkheim in this regard.

Rousseau and Durkheim differed on at least one primary issue—politics. For Rousseau, politics were "the essence," while Durkheim, "although keenly interested in the political state, saw it as but one of the associative influences on man" (Nisbet, 1974:25).

In his Latin doctoral thesis, Durkheim expressed an indebtedness to Montesquieu for pointing to the interrelatedness of social phenomena and the idea of the connectedness of all social and cultural phenomena. Montesquieu held that all the elements of society form a whole and that if taken separately, without reference to the others, they cannot be understood. All elements of society are related to one another: law and morality, trade, social structure and culture, religion, and so on. Durkheim's holistic, or functional, view of society owes much to Montesquieu.

Studying with his teacher Boutroux, Durkheim came to view sociology as having a distinct method and field. Durkheim found philosophy a very important subject, but only within certain criteria. He believed that in order for philosophy to be valid, it must be applied to either politics or society. Perhaps of greater influence was the philosopher Charles Renouvier, whose brand of rationalism recommended a scientific approach to social cohesion and morality while upholding the notion of the autonomy of the individual (Hadden, 1997). Renouvier's long life, from 1815 to 1903, enabled him to live during the same time as Saint-Simon, Comte, and Durkheim. Renouvier was once a student of Comte and was greatly influenced by Saint-Simon. During the Revolution of 1848, he was involved in distributing socialist propaganda to the people of France. Later, Renouvier served as editor of *La Critique philosophique*, which enabled him to have tremendous influence over the people of France. Although Durkheim disagreed with Renouvier's rejection of historical laws and their relationship with society, he did agree with Renouvier's beliefs that ethical and moral considerations occupy a central role in philosophical thought; that there is a need for a science of ethics; that philosophy should serve as a guide to social action; that the reconstruction of the Third Republic must include a moral unity; and that the fundamental moral concept of modern society is the dignity of the human process.

French sociologist and social philosopher Gabriel Tarde, considered to be Durkheim's major rival, was another person to influence Durkheim. They had many debates and confrontations that most likely helped to sharpen both their intellect and earn the respect of each other. Tarde was a provincial magistrate, not an academian, but his successful legal career provided adequate financial income and free time to allow him to devote much of his energy to developing a system of social theory (Coser, 1977). Tarde was primarily concerned with criminology and social theory. Tarde published a number of works, with *The Laws of Imitation* (1890) as the most noteworthy. He was interested in how ideas and new innovations spread throughout a society. He believed that new ideas became diffused when members communicated with another. Tarde referred to this process as "imitation." He believed that society was an aggregate of individuals in interaction, and human behavior was imitated by the masses from the actions of social elites/leaders. Durkheim's contrary notion was that society is a reality, and therefore explanations of human behavior must be grounded in structural, rather than in social–psychological, terms.

The French theorist Saint-Simon was another influence on Durkheim, especially Saint-Simon's ideas on socialism. "Unquestionably it was from reading Saint-Simon that Durkheim got his full measure of the effects on French thought generally of the politically conservatives who flourished immediately after the French Revolution" (Nisbet, 1974:25). Durkheim states, "For all of us, all that is essential in socialist doctrine is found in the philosophy of Saint-Simon" (LaCapra, 1972:189). Moreover, Saint-Simon's theories on class conflict in the post–Revolutionary society of France were of the utmost importance in influencing Durkheim's theories on the same subject. Saint-Simon believed that "the new conditions could lead to a hierarchical but *nonetheless organic* order of social peace and stability. Integration was to be achieved primarily by instituting the appropriate moral ideas" (Zeitlin, 1968:236). This theory helped Durkheim formulate his system with regard to the division of labor. It appears evident that it was Saint-Simon, and not Comte, whom Durkheim regarded as his intellectual master (Zeitlin, 1968:236).

Durkheim accepted Comte and Saint-Simon's concept of positivism. Durkheim credits Saint-Simon with being a more consistent formulator of positivism than Comte. Saint-Simon had not only emphasized the growth of mind as the precursor of science, but also the growth of forms of social organization (Hadden, 1997). Comte's position on sociology lies with his insistence on empirical research. Science, unlike theology and Hegelian philosophy, does not recognize a priori that a pattern or an inner logic of things defined by ideal concepts exists. Scientists have to find patterns by studying phenomena (Garner, 2000). Durkheim was the sociological pioneer in the use of positivism, or the scientific method: data collection, the use of statistics, and quantitative data analysis. Statistics based on large numbers of individuals provide the proper insights into human behavior and social patterns. It is the ability to hypothesize, collect data, and test the hypothesis against the data collected that made sociology a legitimate science. Durkheim utilized the scientific method extensively when writing his dissertation and his work on suicide. Commenting on the use of the scientific method when analyzing society, Durkheim states, "No further progress could be made until it was established that the laws of societies are no different from those governing the rest of nature and that the method by which they are discovered are identical with that of the other sciences. This was Auguste Comte's contribution" (Lukes, 1972:68).

It is clear that Comte did have a major impact on Durkheim and his work. In some regards, Durkheim can be viewed as a successor to Comte (though others say he is a successor to Saint-Simon). *The Division of Labor* contains seventeen references, most of them favorable, to Comte. Durkheim points out that Comte recognized the division of labor as a source of solidarity, while Durkheim viewed the division of labor as a way of binding one to another within a society because each member is dependent on the others. Further, Durkheim believed that the members of society are consciously aware of this important interdependent relationship. Comte's idea of *consensus* directly influenced Durkheim's notion of a *collective conscience* (common morality).

Durkheim did not agree with all of Comte's ideas. He was not at all impressed by Comte's later "theological" writings or by his metaphysics, and he disagreed with many other Comtean approaches. Durkheim was especially critical of Comte's view of social order, with its obvious ties to conservative values. By professing a cosmological worldview as a necessary basis of social order, Comte failed to grasp the differing modes of solidarity characterized by modern society (Seidman, 1983). Durkheim argued that modern society was characterized by a decline of a worldview cosmic order and was replaced by an increase in secular order and appearance. Durkheim believed that the most recent religions were not cosmologies, but are disciplined morals. In distinguishing secular from cosmic worldviews, Durkheim was able to incorporate the idea of a moral order founded upon collective beliefs (Seidman, 1983).

The English Liberal Tradition

Historians have pointed out that the philosophes drew their inspiration and ideology from the English liberal tradition (Lichtheim, 1970; Sabine, 1965; Smith, 1962). The primary figures for the French Enlightenment were Newton and Locke. The French philosophes looked to the English constitution and its pluralistic social order as a model of a sound society. English liberal themes included the doctrine of the constitutional balance of powers, parliamentary government, economic individualism, the ideal of a market economy, and the minimal role of the government (Seidman, 1983). In the English tradition, freedom implied the separation of the individual from the artificially created social constraints of society. A polarized relationship was inherent between the individual and society.

Durkheim's sociology was a response to the underlying problem of the Third French Republic: the crisis of liberalism. Durkheim attempted to account for the recurring failure of French liberalism by pointing to such factors as class polarization, the tradition of agrarian France, and moral disorder (Seidman, 1983). He believed that the social and political failure of liberalism was due to the conceptual shortcomings of its doctrine.

Among the non-French influences on Durkheim, Spencer had perhaps the most profound effect on his thoughts. In fact, there are forty references to Spencer in the *Division of Labor*, far more than to any other social thinker. Spencer never abandoned or substantially modified the chief tenets of English liberalism. Spencer compared society to an organism, believing that all the parts make up the whole. Durkheim viewed Spencer's social theory to be of immense historical significance. Durkheim consistently praised Spencer for his analytical accomplishments: grounding society more rigorously as a "natural" entity; specifying social types and the diversity of social development; and orienting sociology to particular problems of an empirical nature. Durkheim appreciated how Spencer was able to examine institutions and classify societies into categories. Most of Durkheim's evolutionary views are derived from Spencer, as evidenced by Durkheim's conception of evolution as moving from systems of mechanical to systems of organic solidarity. This concept is very similar to Spencer's observation regarding evolution that societies evolve from incoherent homogeneity to coherent heterogeneity. In *Division of Labor*, Durkheim used a "reliance on Spencer's ideas of evolution as a movement from homogeneity to differentiation" (LaCapra, 1972:119–120).

Despite his admiration of Spencer, Durkheim did not view him as a sociologist. Instead, he viewed Spencer as he did Comte—as a philosopher. Durkheim remained unimpressed both by Spencer's overall hypothesis and by his particular social theories (Lukes, 1972). Specifically, Durkheim disagreed with Spencer's individualistic premises (because self-interest cannot account for or help maintain social order), with the aspects of Spencer's organicism, and with his simplistic extension of the biological paradigm to sociology. Durkheim especially criticized Spencer's sustained attachment to the ideology of English liberalism. Durkheim criticized the English liberal idea of private property attained through inheritance. Durkheim believed that inheritance creates inequalities among persons at birth that are unrelated to merit or service. Durkheim recommended a recasting of the morals of property so that property ownership by individuals should be equivalent to the services they have rendered in the society. In opposition to English liberalism, Durkheim formulated a doctrine that was responsive to the needs and critical disposition of the working classes, yet in accord with the tradition of moral idealism among the democratic middle class (Seidman, 1983).

German Idealism

In regard to German social thinkers, the philosopher closest to Durkheim was Immanuel Kant (the one-time bearer and destroyer of Western rationalism). In his positive view of the role of a priori reason and his methodical pursuit of knowledge, Kant expanded the Western rationalist tradition. However, once Kant rejected the concept of a complete system of knowledge because he believed the world to be unknowable in itself, he turned away from the dogmatic claims of rationalism (Seidman, 1983). Regardless, by stressing the active role of mind in the origins of knowledge and moral law, Kant created a uniquely German form of rationalism.

What attracted Durkheim to Kant was not his epistemology nor his general philosophy, but rather his commitment to the examination of moral duty. Durkheim acknowledged that his version of sociology, which emphasized the desirability of moral acts, was just an extension of Kant's notion of duty and moral obligation. In regards to morality, Durkheim (1938) wrote,

> Everything which is the source of solidarity is moral, everything which forces man to take account of other men is moral, everything which forces him to regulate his conduct through something other than the surviving of his ego is moral, and morality is as solid as these ties are numerous and strong (p. 398).

Durkheim had published a number of lengthy critical reviews of the works of many German thinkers, including Simmel, Schäffle, Gumplowicz, and Toennies. The influence of Ferdinand Toennies, author of *Gemeinschaft und Gesellschaft*, can easily be traced to Durkheim's similar distinction between organic and mechanical societies.

Another German thinker to influence Durkheim was his personal friend Wilhelm Wundt. Wundt has been called the father of experimental psychology, but he worked in other academic areas as well. Durkheim was very impressed by the amount of work that Wundt produced—he wrote or revised 53,735 pages (Coser, 1977). Durkheim appreciated Wundt's commitment to scientific methodology and the scientific research conducted at his famous psychological laboratory at Leipzig. Specifically, Durkheim agreed with Wundt's notion of the *Volksseele* (the group soul), which he substituted for the more common Hegelian term *Volksgeist*. This notion is again similar to Durkheim's concept of the collective conscience.

In addition, Durkheim enjoyed Wundt's contention that moral phenomena had to be treated as "facts of social existence, *sui generis*"—meaning, as facts irreducible in "origin and operation to individual acts" (Thompson, 1982:36). Durkheim would come to see social facts as "things"—objective and measurable things.

INVESTIGATION AND APPLICATION OF DURKHEIM'S CONCEPTS AND CONTRIBUTIONS

With such credits as the "father of functionalism," the "father of French sociology," "founder of modern sociology," and the first full professor of sociology, it is clear that Durkheim contributed greatly to sociological social thought. He offered a more coherent theory than any other classical sociological thinker. He articulated a clear theoretical orientation and utilized a variety of specific concepts in his works. A brief review of his key contributions to social thought and their relevancy to contemporary society begins with his doctoral dissertation, *The Division of Labor*.

The Division of Labor

Durkheim is considered one of the founders of "empirical" sociology. His *The Division of Labor* was an attempt to treat the facts of moral life according to the method of the positive sciences. As Warren Schmaus (1995) states,

> Educated as a philosopher, Durkheim held that the very idea of a scientific explanation requires that there be real essences in nature and patterned his concept of a sociological explanation after what he took to be the model of explanation followed by the natural sciences (p. 57).

Durkheim would come to believe that the simpler societies were founded on moral consensus or a collective conscience (terms to be discussed later) while modern societies were maintained through mutual dependence among the members.

Durkheim believed that the object of sociology as a whole is to determine the conditions for the conservation of societies. He argued that social solidarity, which is the bond that unites persons, is the key to maintaining society. In his conception there are two ideal types of society. The more primitive type, characterized by *mechanical solidarity*, has a relatively undifferentiated social structure, with little or no division of labor. "Mechanical solidarity is a solidarity of resemblance" (Aron, 1976:11). This solidarity of resemblance, or common conscience, is enforced by coercive or repressive sanctions (Bellah, 1973). The modern society is characterized by *organic solidarity*, which develops out of differences in the economic and social structure, and has a much greater and refined division of labor highlighted by specialization. "Organic solidarity is one in which consensus, or the coherent unity of collectivity, results from, or is expressed by, differentiation" (Aron, 1967:11).

It is important to note that the dramatic increase in the number of people *and* an increase in the interaction among them—which Durkheim referred to as *dynamic density*—lead to the change from mechanical to organic solidarity. Durkheim argued that neither population increase nor an increase in interaction, when taken separately, is a significant factor in societal change.

Durkheim was bothered by the question: If preindustrial societies were held together by common ideas and sentiments, by shared norms and values, and enforced by coercive or repressive sanctions, what holds an industrial/modern society together? Durkheim believed that changes in the division of labor have enormous implications for the structure of society. Whereas primitive societies are held together by their similarities and generalism, modern societies are held together by the specialization of people and their need for the services of many others. Further, Durkheim indicated that large-scale societies can only exist when there is specialization within it (Lukes, 1985). Modern legal systems of law and order and judicial decision-making help to keep an organic-based solidarity society bound together via the shared values and norms of the greater society.

The role of the division of labor is critical in Durkheim's analysis of society.

> Social harmony comes essentially from the division of labor. It is characterized by a cooperation that is automatically produced through the pursuit by each individual of his own interests. It suffices that each individual consecrate himself to a special function in order, by the force of events, to make himself solidarity with others (Durkheim, 1993:200).

The division of labor is simply the separation and specialization of work among people. As industry and technology advances, and population increases, society must become more specialized if it is to survive. In modern society, this is especially evident, as labor has never before been so concentrated, and the current trend is toward an even further increased specialization.

However, as Comte had pointed out, it is the same specialization that holds a society together that pulls it apart. Durkheim too was concerned with the social implication of increased specialization. As specialization increases, people are increasingly separated, values and interests become different, norms are varied, and subcultures are formed. Because people perform different tasks, they come to value different things than others. "A society made up an extremely large mass of unorganized individuals, which an overgrown state attempts to limit and restrain, constitutes a veritable sociological monstrosity" (Durkheim, 1984:liv). Since the era of industrialization, many social thinkers have expressed concerned over the changing social structure. "The man of today is no longer able to understand his neighbor because his profession is his whole life, and the technical specialization of this fate has forced him to live in a closed universe" (Ellul, 1964:133).

Durkheim did not see the division of labor as the downfall of the social order, but he did recognize that it gave rise to a new social order, or solidarity: *organic solidarity*. He believed that even as mankind and society continue to evolve, the whole common conscience does not cease to exist. There will always remain a cult of personality, of individual dignity, and of individual consciences. The primary characteristic of modern society—specialization—forces individuals to remain in contact with one another, which, in turn, strengthens the bonds between persons. These bonds help to create a group morality within the division of labor. The individual becomes cognizant of his dependence upon society and the forces that keep him in check and restrain him. As Durkheim (1933) summarizes, "Since the division of labor becomes the chief source of social solidarity, it becomes, at the same time, the foundation of the moral order" (p. 401).

In the contemporary era, we see that Western societies are highly specialized. The implication for individuals is the need for each of us to develop particular qualifications that are suited for the modern division of labor. Attending a trade school or college is an avenue that many people utilize in their search for a finding a niche in society. Others will gain experience in a variety of jobs and make their way through life. The advancement of social networking, such as Facebook, Twitter, LinkedIn, and email, helps to keep people together who are no longer in the same physical proximity with one another. In May 2012, there were over 900 million people in the world who had a Facebook account. Facebook is available in more than 70 languages, and with one click people who speak different languages can communicate with one another. It would seem that social network sites like Facebook serve as a mechanism for maintaining organic solidarity.

Solidarity

Durkheim's *The Division of Labor in Society* is, in part, an attempt to discover the grounds of solidarity and unity in modern, industrialized society (Hadden, 1997). To that end, Durkheim carried out a systematic, scientific study of solidarity. His research was guided by a quest to address to specific concerns. First, Durkheim wanted to quite the detractors of modern society and its increased division of labor. Durkheim proposed that the organic solidarity, or unity based on the interdependence of people in modern societies, was the functional response to the passing of traditional forms of societies to more modern ones. He went so far as to propose the idea that the modern division of labor created a form of solidarity that could reduce conflict and war. As Farganis (2011) explains,

> In contrast to mechanical solidarity, where different groups performed the same functions,
> could exist independently of one another, and thus were liable to fight among themselves

for scarce resources, the increasing interdependence of social groups under organic solidarity would, according to Durkheim, make it harder for any group to be done away with or oppressed (p. 53).

But Durkheim also wished to show that sociology could be an academic discipline that could reveal and explain social currents and trends and more importantly, apply them to specific circumstances such as an aid in the restoration of France.

For Durkheim, solidarity was defined as the bond between all individuals within a society. He was particularly interested in social cohesion. In *The Division of Labor*, Durkheim traces examples of social cohesion throughout human history; he uses demographic and economic factors—namely, increasing social density and an increasingly complex division of labor—for an explanation of the changes he observes. He found that in societies characterized by *mechanical solidarity*, social cohesion was based upon the likeness and similarities among individuals in a society, and largely dependent on common rituals and routines.

> The major characteristic of a society in which mechanical solidarity prevails is that the individuals differ from one another as little as possible. The individuals, the members of the same collectivity, resemble each other because they feel the same emotions, cherish the same values, and hold the same things sacred (Aron, 1970:11).

It follows that in a society of mechanical solidarity, a consensus should not be difficult to attain, as the bond is strengthened by similar beliefs, opinions, and values. Furthermore, it follows that there would not be as much of a division of labor, as people would be performing similar duties. "The society is coherent because the individuals are not yet differentiated" (Aron, 1970:11). Durkheim believes that primitive societies are characterized by mechanical solidarity because of the lack of technological advancements. Technology mandates specialization, which results in the formation of a division of labor.

In modern societies, highlighted by *organic solidarity*, social cohesion is based upon the dependence that individuals have to one another. A society characterized by *organic solidarity* is "one in which the consensus, or the coherent unity of the collectivity, results from, or is expressed by differentiation" (Aron, 1970:11). Even though differences in values and priorities exist among the people, the very survival of society depends on their reliance on each other to perform their specific task. "The individuals are no longer similar, but different; and in a sense…it is precisely because the individuals are different that consensus is achieved" (Aron, 1970:12). As a result of the fact that there is a distinct division of labor in a society with organic solidarity, consensus occurs as a result of the fact that members must rely (social bond) upon each other for services.

The division of labor provides a basis for solidarity, a concept that would seem to be always relevant. Immigrants to foreign countries nearly always bond together in ethnic communities, especially before becoming assimilated. Persons who share a characteristic that leads to discriminatory actions against them often unite in a form of solidarity. Environmental groups rally together in attempt to pass laws aimed at saving the planet from potential destruction. Examples of the application of solidarity are nearly endless.

As previously described, the values and norms found in a mechanical solidarity are enforced via coercive and repressive sanctions. Organic solidarity is characterized by a legal system that relies on restitutive justice—people pay, one way or another, for their social transgressions. In the contemporary era, modern societies are still characterized by restitutive sanctions when we use civil, commercial, or administrative law. Restitutive sanctions may come in the form of penal laws with designated forms of incarceration. That repressive sanctions are deemed necessary in mechanical societies and restitutive sanctions are deemed necessary in modern societies reveals that full societal solidarity is rarely achieved. In reality, we are often provided with glimpses of how fragile the social fabric of society really is.

Collective Conscience and Collective Representations

Durkheim became increasingly uneasy with his original typology of mechanical solidarity and organic solidarity and after the publication of *The Division*, seldom referred to it again (Nemedi, 1995). However, a number of central concepts, such as the *collective conscience* and *collective representations*, remained as themes of his overall work. Durkheim described the *collective conscience* as

> The totality of beliefs and sentiments common to average citizens of the same society forms a determinate system which has its own life; one may call the *collective* or *common conscience*. . . . It is, thus, an entirely different thing from particular consciences, although it can be realized only through them (Durkheim, 1938:79–80).

The *collective conscience* is an example of Durkheim's nonmaterial *social fact*. It occurs at the societal level as a sum of all individual conceptions of conscience and is a determinate of cultural expectations on individual behavior. The *collective conscience* can be differentiated on four dimensions:

1. **Volume:** the number of people involved;
2. **Intensity:** how deeply individuals feel about it;
3. **Rigidity:** how clearly defined it is;
4. **Content:** how it is formed.

As one may deduce, the greater the number of people involved and the more intensely they feel about a social situation, the greater the collective conscience. The collective conscience will be more intense if people have a clear idea of the parameters of the social situation. For example, the expression "family values" is not rigid, and although most people would say they favor "family values," there is not a fixed understanding of the meaning of the concept. Historical realities often dictate the content of the collective conscience and how strongly people feel about a given social situation.

In *The Division of Labor in Society*, Durkheim shows that societies have moved from harsh, punitive, and universally shared collective conscience to a more attenuated and individualized form. In "primitive" societies, the collective conscience is harsh, intense, rigid, and universally shared. Law associated with this level of conscience is usually repressive; the deviant is severely punished for violating rules. In "modern" societies, the collective conscience is less harsh, less punitive, less intensely felt, and less shared than in primitive societies. For example, white-collar criminals (embezzlers, tax cheats, insider traders) almost never experience the level of public loathing they deserve. Law shifts from largely repressive normative regulation to restitution, such as payment for fines.

Durkheim also spoke of *collective representatives*, which may be seen as specific states or substrata of the collective conscience. As Nemedi (1995) explains, the word "representation" occurs frequently in Durkheim's writings, especially as a scientific concept (e.g., when describing items as sacred and profane in his studies on religion). According to Durkheim, collective representations comprise a realm of moral facts. These representations not only have authoritative power in the form of obligations but are also desirable. Moral phenomena, in Durkheim's view, have this dual character of obligation and desirability.

It was Durkheim's belief that the essential problems of modern society were moral in nature and that the only real solution to modern society's problems rests with reinforcing the strength of the collective morality. He labeled the modern form of the collective conscience as the *cult of the individual* (Chriss, 1993; Tole, 1993). The basic idea conveyed by Durkheim here is that individualism is becoming the moral system of modern society.

Durkheim came to believe that the role of individuals would continue to grow in the future. Individualism was inevitable in modern society, and there was no way of returning to the *collective conscience* style of society that dominated the past. The modern version of the collective conscience would be dominated by the *cult of the individual* (Chriss, 1993). These "cults of man" or the "cult of personality" would replace the role of religion in society.

> In so regulating human behavior, these "cults of man" would be performing the same function as religion in the traditional societies. The difference would lie in the focus of this regulation: the defense of the individual rights and liberties would be of paramount impor-tance to the new cults (Westly, 1983:7).

The cult of the individual is very evident today. In fact, some people are famous just for being famous (e.g., people like Paris Hilton, who come from prominent families and allow them-selves to be pursued by the paparazzi).

The relevancy of the concepts of collective conscience and collective representations is rather self-evident. There are many moral ideals that make up a society's collective conscience that most people agree with (e.g., the dignity of persons; freedom from oppression, prejudice, and discrimination; protecting children from predators; and so on). Collective representations are not only illustrated within social institutions (e.g., all religions utilize symbols); they *are* social institutions in the form of the contemporary usage of the term *agents of socialization*—the family, marriage, religion, occupation, military, sports, and so forth. Collective representatives help to alter our behavior and thus reinforce a certain sense of morality.

Methodology

In his classic *The Rules of Sociological Method* (1895), Durkheim explicates the methodological suppositions already applied in *The Division of Labor*. In *Rules*, Durkheim states that it is not enough to look abstractly at a phenomenon; rather, it should be studied empirically. Since sociol-ogy grew from philosophy, it must separate itself (empirically) to become a science. Researchers cannot study by a priori reasoning or by introspective examination; they must study social facts, which are external and, therefore, physically observable. He argues for the existence of a collec-tive realm of facts, which are accessible by the scientific method.

Durkheim's analytical commitment to methodological holism and social idealism and his concern with social solidarity fall squarely within the theorizing of the French tradition. He believed that the sociological, empirical approach to research allowed for generalization, which was critical in order to discuss such concepts as solidarity, collective conscience, and social facts. His methodological critique was aimed at the liberal tradition and rooted in a basically a priori, deductive, and subjective methodology (Seidman, 1983).

In the preface to the second edition of the *Rules*, Durkheim addresses the objections made to his most basic premises: treating things as social facts. According to Durkheim, being able to treat things as social facts allows the researcher to be objective and detached, which is critical to empirical science. In *Rules*, Durkheim (1938) states, "To treat phenomena as things is to treat them as data, and these constitute the point of departure of science" (p. 101). He defines *social facts* as "ways of acting, thinking and feeling, external to the individual, and endowed with a power of coercion, by reason of which they control him" (p. 3). Individuals act, think, and feel, but the *ways* in which they do this are not of their creation. Social forces, or *social facts*, are imposed on individuals; hence, they are external to them; they are powerful and regulate their behavior.

Durkheim's *The Rules of Sociological Method* represents his "methodological manifesto" (Platt, 1995). It also represents the notion of how to conceive of the vast array of social things that exist in society and their interrelatedness (Turner, 1995). Although *Rules* did not always clearly articulate the relationship between social things, Durkheim's work paved the way for future sociologists in their attempt to apply the scientific method to the study of human behavior. Like Comte before him, Durkheim made it clear that sociologists should utilize the scientific method.

Social Facts

In order to distinguish itself from philosophy and psychology, Durkheim argued in *Rules* that the distinctive subject matter of sociology should be the study of *social facts.* Porter (1995) states that *Rules* does not provide a clear definition of the term *social facts*, but in French, the term *fait social* can "just as well be social action as a hard nugget of sociological truth" (p. 15). It is helpful to think of social facts as things; and because they are "things," they can only be studied empirically, not philosophically. Durkheim (1895) believed that ideas can be known introspectively (philosophically), but *things* "cannot be conceived by purely mental activity"; they require for their conception "data from outside the mind" (p. xliii).

Social facts are the social structures and cultural norms and values that are external to, and coercive of, actors. They are independent of individuals and they cannot be ignored or wished away. They are rooted in group sentiments and values. They are coercive in the sense that if you ignore them, you may be subject to punishments, public ridicule, and/or sanctions. *Social facts* are manifested in external indicators of sentiments such as religious doctrines, laws, moral codes, and aphorisms. Social facts comprise a distinct subject matter for sociologists because, as collective representations, they are independent of psychological and biological phenomena. Even though persons have individual actions, thoughts, and feelings, they tend to live their lives through social institutions: family, work, school, sporting events.

Durkheim (1895) made distinctions between two types of social facts: *material social facts* and *nonmaterial social facts*. Material social facts are the clearer of the two types, because they are real, material entities that are external to the individual. Examples of material social facts include any given society, structural components of society (social institutions), and morphological components of society (housing arrangements, income distribution, access to technology). Nonmaterial social facts are more complex because they deal with mental phenomena: morality; collective conscience; collective representations; and social currents (trends, great movements, which do not arise in any one individual consciousness).

Durkheim was very concerned with what he perceived as the lack of morality in French society. It is safe to say that all societies today and in the future will wrestle with issues of morality. In *Suicide* (1897), Durkheim demonstrated that social facts, and particularly *social currents*, are external to, and coercive of, the individual. Besides religion, the political institution of a given society will often dictate *social currents*. If the government is a repressive one, the citizens will have little say in the manner in which institutions and organizations are operated. In extreme cases, revolutions may result. Even in democratic societies, *social currents* can be influenced by the governing political party and office holders. When a political party that has definite ideas on reshaping society comes into power and is not kept in check by the other representatives of society, a new agenda can be forced unto the citizenry. Where *law* once provided a woman's right to control her own body and have a legal abortion, a new election may put into place representatives who can make such a behavior illegal. Other examples of political influence on social issues centered on moral implication are nearly endless, including proposed cuts to Planned Parenthood, National Public Radio (NPR), the Environmental Protection Agency (EPA), Social Security and Medicare; the debate over legalizing gay marriage; alternative energy solutions, including decisions on whether or not to use hydro-fracking to find natural gas; and so on. The *law*, along with the *division of labor*, and *dynamic density* are examples of Durkheim's *material social facts*.

Suicide

In *Suicide*, Durkheim firmly established the method and discipline outlined in *Rules* (Hadden, 1997). *Suicide* provides an example of a sociological study that emphasizes social facts rather than individual experiences (Phillips, 1993). Durkheim chose to study suicide because it is a relatively concrete and specific phenomenon. He applies empirical methods to a behavior that seems to be exclusively an individual act. Individuals can be seen as having many "reasons" for committing the act of suicide, but Durkheim wanted to establish sociological "causes" that influence suicide. As Farganis (2011) explains,

> Durkheim shifts our attention away from psychological questions about the motivations of particular individuals who commit suicide, a focus he viewed as reductionist, to sociological questions concerning larger social conditions associated with suicide rates (p. 52).

In his attempt to explain differences in suicide *rates*, Durkheim examined data on suicide in Austria, France, England, Switzerland, Denmark, Prussia, Greece, and Italy, among others, and found that there appeared to be a different "predisposition to suicide" in different societies. Durkheim attempted to find out what caused this predisposition (Hadden, 1997).

Le Suicide is among the very first modern examples of consistent and organized use of the statistical method in social investigation. *Suicide* is an outstanding work in the study of causation and the application of his concepts of *collective representations* and the *collective conscience*. Durkheim believed that there were a number of social factors that explained why some people are more likely to commit suicide than others. He also felt that groups differ in the degree of their integration, and that suicide varies inversely with the degree of integration. When society is strongly integrated, it holds individuals under its influence and control. Integration refers to the degree to which collective sentiments are shared.

Durkheim outlined four types of suicide: *egoistic*, *altruistic*, *anomic*, and *fatalistic*. He linked each of the categories of suicide to the degree of integration into, or regulation by, society. *Egoistic suicide* is associated with a low degree of integration, whereas *altruistic suicide* occurs when there is a high degree of integration. *Fatalistic suicide* is associated with high regulation, and *anomic suicide* with low regulation. Durkheim defined regulation as the degree of external constraints on the members of society. The following is a brief description of Durkheim's four types of suicide.

High rates of *egoistic suicide* are more likely to be found in those societies, collectivities, or groups in which the individual is not well integrated into the larger social unit. These societies are characterized by excessive individualism. Durkheim defined integration as a product of social interaction and the strength of shared beliefs among group members (Pampel, 2000). In the case where society has a stranglehold on a person with egoistic tendencies and a person considers himself at society's service, that person considers killing himself (Durkheim, 1951). *Egoistic suicide* is usually committed by people of the higher social class because they have more things to have an ego over. Egoistic suicide occurs because society allows for the separation of society and the individual, being insufficiently amassed in some parts or even the whole. *Egoistic suicide* is deeply rooted in the refined ethics, which places personality on an extremely high pedestal. Generally, a person who commits egoistic suicide is highly depressed, such as the case with Kurt Cobain, the former lead singer of Nirvana.

The second type of suicide described by Durkheim is *altruistic suicide*, which occurs when social integration is too strong, and the individual is literally forced into committing suicide. Durkheim believed that if extreme individuation can lead a person to his or her death, then so too can the lack of individuation. In general, those who commit *altruistic suicide* do so because they feel it is their duty (e.g., the followers of Jim Jones in Jonestown, Guyana, who committed mass suicide; Japanese kamikaze pilots). Durkheim (1951) divided *altruistic suicide* into three categories. The first is the suicide committed by persons on the threshold of old age or stricken with illness. If a person feels that he is no longer useful in a community, then he may realize that it is time to let go. In many primitive cultures, to die of old age was considered taboo. The second subcategory of *altruistic suicide* involves a wife killing herself because of her husband's death; the third category is that of followers/servants on the death of their chiefs.

When people decide to kill themselves in this manner, it is because they feel they are obligated to do so. The relationship between the social levels of each person plays an important role in *altruistic suicide*. In these societies, the individual plays a small role, and most people live similar lives. There is social prestige that is attached to suicide. Durkheim (1951) labeled the most altruistic type of suicide when a person kills himself for the joy of sacrifice because renunciation is considered praiseworthy. Many of today's terrorists are willing to kill themselves because they feel so strongly about their cause and believe that they will be rewarded in the "afterlife." These people are extremely dangerous to civil societies because they are not concerned with the lives of innocents or the laws that pertain to the "here and now."

Anomic suicide occurs when periods of disruption unleash currents of *anomie*. Durkheim (1951) noted that during an 1873 financial crisis in Vienna, the number of suicides immediately rose for the next couple of years. (Stock market crashes are almost always accompanied by suicides.) The rate of suicides increased as life became increasingly difficult. In cases of economic disaster, a declassification of persons is likely to occur, meaning that persons who were once in a high social class may be forced to become a part of a lower social class. All the advantages of their previous class standing become obsolete, and they cannot adjust (Nisbet, 1965). The same can happen if the opposite occurs. If someone who never knew wealth and power suddenly obtains it, he may have difficulty handling his newfound prosperity. Many of today's big-dollar lottery winners have reported that their lives were ruined by their new economic fortune.

Durkheim made little mention of the fourth category of suicide, *fatalistic*, as it was only a footnote in *Suicide*. It is most likely to occur when regulation is excessive and is characterized by high degrees of external constraints. When these constraints are forced upon a society, the people may feel suffocated and get restless. People believe that their lives are not going to get any better, or things will continue to get worse, which leads them to commit suicide. An example would be a slave who takes his own life because of the hopelessness associated with the oppressive regulation in his every action and behavior.

Through the use of *empirical methodology*, Durkheim's study of *suicide* was evidence that sociology has a legitimate place in the social sciences. Not only did he establish that external social factors influence an individual's decision to commit suicide, but he demonstrated that rates and patterns could also be ascertained. For example, the New York State Parks Police in Niagara Falls have established a "suicide season" at the Falls. According to a pattern that emerges from statistics going back to 1856, the suicide season begins in the spring and then drops off drastically in October (Michelmore, 2000). In addition, statistics at Niagara Falls show that Monday is the most common day suicide is committed, and the most popular time is 4 P.M. Niagara Falls is second only to San Francisco's Golden Gate Bridge as the nation's most popular place to commit suicide (Michelmore, 2000).

The topic of suicide is certainly still relevant today. According to the Centers for Disease Control (CDC), suicide, with 12.0 deaths per 100,000 people, was the 10th leading cause of death in the United States in 2009 (CDC 2012a). Nearly 37,000 (36,909) suicides occurred in the U.S. in 2009, with slightly more than half the result of the use of a firearm, followed by suffocation and poisoning (CDC, 2012a). In the U.S., there is one suicide every 15 minutes (CDC, 2010). For every two homicides committed in the U.S., there are three suicides (CDC, 2011). It is even more commonplace for people to think about committing suicide. According to the CDC (2010), among young adults ages 15–24, there are approximately 100–200 attempts for every completed suicide. Suicide statistics also reveal that women are more likely than men to attempt suicide, but men are almost four times as likely to succeed (CDC, 2010). Data collected by the CDC during the years 2005–2009 reveal that the highest suicide rates were among American Indian/Alaskan Native males, with 27.61 suicides per 100,000, and non-Hispanic white males, with 25.96 suicides per 100,000. Of all female race/ethnicity categories, the American Indian/Alaskan Natives and non-Hispanic whites had the highest rates with 7.87 and 6.71 suicides per 100,000, respectively (CDC, 2012b). Most experts in the study of suicide conclude that women attempt suicide as a "cry for help," while men attempt suicide to actually succeed at it. This point is further illustrated by the passive methods used by women (e.g., taking pills) and aggressive methods used by men (e.g., use of a firearm). The CDC (2010) reports that firearms are the most commonly used method of suicide among males (55.7%).

There are a number of social factors involved with suicide, such as "suicide pacts," or predetermined plans on how and why to end their lives, that are sometimes made between couples (dating or married partners) or among groups of people (e.g., cult members). A large number of people who attempt and/or succeed in suicide tell someone of their plans to commit suicide, but that information was not acted upon. The CDC (2010) also reports that anywhere from 33–66% of suicide victims leave a note behind to explain their actions—thus revealing the social aspect of their suicide. An alarming social fact about suicide involves the high percentage of veterans who commit suicide, about one in five (CDC, 2011). Coupled with the reality of multiple wars in the Middle East throughout the 2000s, it is highly conceivable (and predictable) that an increasing number of veterans will commit suicide in the decade beginning with 2011.

There is a debate in the United States, and other nations, as to whether or not a person should have the legal right to commit suicide. Among the social issues related to the legal right to kill oneself are euthanasia, "do not resuscitate" (DNR) orders, and withdrawal of treatment decisions. People who support these concepts as legal rights claim that they would rather die with "dignity" than be kept alive by machines. As of 2011, in the United States, only Oregon, Washington, and Montana permit physician-assisted suicide. Oregon and Washington passed laws, and Montana's Supreme Court determined that assisted suicide is a medical treatment. The Oregon law allows that an adult who has been determined by doctors to be suffering from a terminal disease, and who has voluntarily expressed a wish to die, may make a written request for medication for the purpose of ending his or her life in a humane and dignified manner (*The Citizen*, 6/4/11). The Washington law is modeled after Oregon's but requires the attending physician to identify the terminal disease as the cause of death on the patient's death certificate (rather than identifying suicide as the cause of death—a practice that will hamper methodological studies on suicide). Worldwide, only the Netherlands, Belgium, and Luxembourg permit euthanasia and assisted suicide. If a third party performs the last act that causes a patient's death (e.g., lethal injection), euthanasia has occurred. If the person who dies performs the last act, the death is considered an assisted suicide (*The Citizen*, 6/4/11).

Opponents argue that euthanasia would be difficult to regulate and worry about a "slippery slope" of decision-making that could lead to doctors and medical insurance companies making decisions to euphemize persons against their will. Some opponents also believe that it is unethical to engage in practices that support death under any conditions. And a number of religious persons believe that it is morally wrong to kill oneself. As most of us understand, religious beliefs influence a great deal of decision-making among people. Durkheim certainly understood that religion plays a role in society and argued that role was too influential.

Religion

It was revealed earlier in this chapter that Durkheim's family had deep roots in Judaism; however, when he was a young boy, he came to view religion negatively as a result of the anti-Semitism that took place in France following its defeat in the Franco-Prussian War. His loss of faith was replaced by a deepened sense of patriotism. Durkheim believed that people should worship society rather than any religion. Durkheim's innovative perspective on religion and God is clearly outlined in his last major book, *The Elementary Forms of Religious Life* (1912). In this book, Durkheim argues that religious feeling, the spiritual, the sacred, and God are nothing more than collective representations of the human experience. *Religion* is the ultimate *nonmaterial social fact* that is associated with the *collective conscience*. In primitive societies, religion is all-encompassing.

Religion arises from the need to explain and understand, and from sociability. Durkheim stated that religion was, at each moment of history, the totality of beliefs and sentiments of all sorts relative to the relations of man with a being or beings, whose nature he regarded as superior to his own. Durkheim believed that as societies modernized people would become progressively emancipated from traditional sources of influence (e.g., faith and tradition) and would evolve toward greater individualism, or the "cult of the individual" (Tole, 1993). Cults of individualism served many of the same functions of religion, but would focus mainly on the rights and liberties of people.

Where *Suicide* focused on a large amount of statistics from varying sources, *Elementary Forms* used one in-depth case study of the aboriginal Arunta tribe in Australia. Durkheim chose this group because he felt they represented the most basic, *elementary* forms of religion within a society. Durkheim wanted to show two things: the fact that religion was not divinely or supernaturally inspired and was, in fact, a product of society; and he set out to identify the common things that religion placed an emphasis upon, as well as what effects those religious beliefs had on the lives of the members of society.

The Arunta, a hunting and gathering tribe, participated in totemism. Totemism is a primitive form of a religious system in which certain things, particularly animals and plants, come to be regarded as *sacred* emblems (totems) of the clan. With totemism, an image or representation is placed on a totem pole. The images at the highest points of the totem were the most sacred. In addition to the physical aspects of totemism is the moral character. There are occasions when the members of the tribe come together at the totem and share a number of emotions, sentiments, and rituals.

Using the descriptions of ethnographic studies, Durkheim concludes that the Arunta religion is nothing more than the collective representations of the overwhelming power of society. In so doing, he is also saying the same thing about Judaism and Christianity (Garner, 2000). The general conclusion of *Elementary Forms* is that religion is eminently social and serves as a source of solidarity and identification for the individuals within a society. Religion provides for a meaning of life, for authority figures, and, most importantly for Durkheim, it reinforces the morals and social norms held collectively by all within a society. He did not dismiss religion as mere fantasy, for Durkheim recognized that it provides social control, cohesion, and purpose for people, as well as another means of communication and gathering for individuals to interact and reaffirm social norms.

In a comparison of religions from different cultures, Durkheim also concluded that a belief in a supernatural realm is not necessary or common among religions, but the separation of different aspects of life, physical things, and certain behaviors into two categories—the *sacred* and the *profane*—is common. Objects and behaviors deemed *sacred* were considered part of the spiritual or religious realm and were set apart from the *profane* or mundane, commonplace items. Durkheim (1973a) described "*sacred* things as simply collective ideals that have fixed themselves on material objects" (p. 159).

In contemporary society, we see many examples of profane items taking on sacred meaning. The Jonas Brothers, for example, a teen-pop boy band that first gained popularity on the Disney Network, promote a wholesome lifestyle by wearing "purity rings" on their left ring finger. The purity ring represents a commitment to abstinence from sex (before marriage), drugs, alcohol, and tobacco. For the Jonas Brothers and their fans, the rings represent a type of sacred behavior. In reality, the rings are made of profane minerals (silver and gold) with no inherent meaning. The collective representation of a purity ring is what makes them sacred. In fact, nearly any profane item can gain sacred status when it serves as a representation of religious or moral meaning. In 2011, a piece of World Trade Center steel was molded into an angel in the memory of a girl who was born on September 11, 2001, and died in a barrage of gunfire in the Tucson, Arizona, shooting rampage that injured Rep. Gabrielle Giffords (January 2011) (*The Post-Standard*, 3/24/11). The memorial angel was set to be installed outside a Little League field outside Tucson. The artist, Lei Hennessey-Owen, has created other steel "angels" and placed them at various locations, including (but not limited to) the site of the fallen Twin Towers in New York City and in a Pennsylvania field where the hijacked Flight 93 crashed. In some cases, the angels were removed because the artist never went through the proper bureaucratic channels (Ruelas, 2011).

The religious realm often claims to be the voice of morality and ethical behavior, but Durkheim would challenge that notion as well.

Morality

Some believe that we are born with the need for morality; others argue that it evolved over history. According to Wundt (Giddens, 1972), the true object of morality is to make man feel he is not a whole, but part of a whole—and how insignificant he is by reference to the plurality of contexts that surround him. Morality appears to us to be a collection of precepts, of rules of conduct. Violation of these rules sets forth consequences. Morality constitutes a category of rules where the idea of authority plays an absolutely preponderant role.

In *Moral Education*, a book first published in 1925 and likely taken from his lecture notes first developed at the Sorbonne, Durkheim articulates his view as to the role of sociology in investigating and reforming society and thought (Hadden, 1997). Morality, as with all social phenomena, can best be examined sociologically. Sociology, as a true science, must examine the criteria that make up morality. Durkheim states that art, by definition, moves in the domain of the unreal, of the imaginary. Morality, on the contrary, is the domain of action and can only be grasped in relation to real phenomena; otherwise, it is lost in the void. To act morally is to do good to beings of flesh and blood. In order to feel the need to change, transform, and improve reality, we cannot abstract ourselves from it. On the contrary, we have to embrace it and love it, in spite of its ugliness, its pettiness, and its meanness (Giddens, 1972).

Essentially, Durkheim considered himself a moral scientist (Kenny, 2010). Moral ideas and sentiments are to be retained, according to Durkheim (1973), but the historical bond with religion must be broken. Indeed, Durkheim believed that notions of morality must evolve as humanity has evolved (Kenny, 2010). He believed that educational institutions and the wider society should forge, and create, a new sense of morality, especially a morality that emphasizes the fact that inherent with freedom are rights, privileges, and duties. All of this was necessary if people are to worship society as Durkheim promoted. After all, why should people worship society if it was immoral? A moral society based on secular notions of individual rights, privileges, and duties would help to reaffirm a sense of social solidarity. Society can only be prosperous and evolve if it develops a clear sense of morality. Durkheim argued that because societies evolve based on their own needs and form a social structure designed to meet their needs, each society develops its own sense of morality. As explained by Iddo Tavory (2011), "The Durkheimian position is realist in that there is a true morality for each kind of society; it is structural in that the structure of the society defines the shape of the moral" (pp. 274–275).

The relevancy of morality, or the lack thereof, in contemporary society abounds. Today, as with every era in humanity, there are people who act immorally. However, with the idea of promoting individual rights, many forms of immoral behavior (e.g., slavery, prejudice and discrimination, and oppression) are outlawed in civil societies. There is a growing acceptance among younger generations to embrace diversity and the rights of individuals to pursue their version of moral, individual happiness. Furthermore, it has become increasingly clear to many that people can act morally and ethically without claiming to be religious. In fact, the opposite, that people who claim to be religious can act immorally and unethically, is also clear to open-minded people. And although the majority of people around the world believe in some form of organized religion, there is a growing secular movement that emphasizes morality and a common good without the fear of retribution from an angry God whenever misdeeds are committed. Secular people emphasize that people will follow societal laws because, among other things, they do not want to risk their life on earth as an incarcerated prisoner. In brief, one does not have to embrace an organized religion to be moral. Durkheim would be pleased by such a development.

Anomie

Although Durkheim promoted a new morality separate from the realm of religion, he recognized that modern industrial societies separate people and weaken their social bonds as a result of increased complexity and the division of labor. As a result, Durkheim believed that members of Western society are exposed to the risk of *anomie*. The word "anomie" comes from the Greek *anomia*, meaning "without law." Individuals are especially vulnerable to anomie when they are not faced with sufficient moral constraint or do not have a clear concept of what is and what is not acceptable behavior. For example, Durkheim (1973) states in *Moral Education*,

> If the rules of the conjugal morality lose their authority, and the mutual obligations of husband and wife become less respected, the emotions and appetites ruled by this sector of morality will become unrestricted and uncontained, and accentuated by this very release; powerless to fulfill themselves because they have been freed from all limitations, these emotions will produce a disillusionment which manifests itself visibly (p. 173).

Durkheim viewed anomie as a type of pathology of modern society (Harcourt, 2001). By thinking of *anomie* as pathology, Durkheim was saying that the problems of the world could be "cured" (via moral education). Thus, the proper level of regulation, both in terms of issues of morality and civility, would guarantee a cohesive and smoothly operating society.

Durkheim defined the term *anomie* as a condition where social and/or moral norms are confused, unclear, or simply not present. Thus, people experience a sense of normlessness—a condition that arises when the established norms of society have broken down or disappeared. That is, when people are unclear of their role in society, they may experience anomie. Marx spoke of alienation as an economic force that creates conditions favorable for alienation. Durkheim, on the other hand, offered a multidimensional context from which to understand social regulation in modern societies (Acevedo, 2005). That is, modern societies, Durkheim reasoned, are characterized by a number of social institutions, including economics that create conditions favorable for anomie.

The relevancy of Durkheim's concept of anomie to contemporary society is evident in a variety of ways. During the late 2000s, and extending to the early 2010s, many people have been faced with the financial consequences of banks collapsing, retirement pensions and funds that have disappeared, homes repossessed, attacks on labor unions, and jobs that have disappeared. As Steven Lukes (2008) states, "No wonder the world is in despair" (p. 10).

Before the worldwide financial crisis took hold, starting in 2008, individuals in modern society have always been, and continue to be, confronted with feelings of *anomie* when they find themselves in a dramatically new environment. The first-year, or transfer, student who is attending college hundreds of miles from home, has yet to meet new friends, and is having a hard time navigating the campus that seems so imposing may feel *anomie*. Any individual who starts a new job, feels overwhelmed by the demands, and has no one to turn to in order to ask for advice may feel *anomie*. People who start new romantic relationships or end existing ones may also experience anomie. In short, any number of people may experience anomie without proper social bonds to significant others.

Functionalism

"Durkheim identifies functionalism as the method for achieving objective knowledge of phenomena; to be objective, we must study facts or phenomena in functional relationships" (Jones, 1995:34). Durkheim believed society and social structures are realities at a level above the individual human organism. He shares Comte's functionalist, evolutionary, and positive premises (Garner, 2000). The functionalist perspective views society as a sum total (the whole) of a large number (the parts) of persons, groups, organizations, and social institutions. Sociologists who utilize this perspective examine the role of society as it attempts to execute the necessary functions needed in order to maintain such needs as national defense, internal social order, consumer production and distribution, food, clothing, and shelter demands from its citizens, and so on. It should be made clear, however, that Durkheim's use of the term *function* does not indicate static relations between social institutions, but changing and variable relations (Jones, 1995).

Consequently, the social structure is a complex system whose parts are said to be well integrated and in a state of equilibrium when functioning properly. During periods of rapid social change, or with the introduction of a new and dramatic force (whether social or natural), the social structure may be thrown out of equilibrium. When this happens, the various structures of society can become poorly integrated, and what were formerly useful functions can become "dysfunctional."

Functionalism, for Durkheim, is the idea that society is a system, and its parts (institutions) contribute to its stability and continued existence. His functionalist outlook did not include a value judgment, nor did he imply that some societies were "better" than others; rather, that the parts of the system are interconnected and attempt to meet the demands of each particular society. When this occurs over a period of time and stability is met, the system is said to be functioning properly. His functionalist perspective was evolutionary in that he was interested in how societies change over time. He recognized that societies, as social systems, are not static and are therefore subject to change at any time.

Durkheim's (1914) view on *functionalism* can be summarized with this quote from *The Dualism of Human Nature and its Social Conditions*:

> A great number of our mental states, including some of the most important ones, are of social origin. In this case then, it is the whole that, in a large measure, produces the part; consequently, it is impossible to attempt to explain the whole without explaining the part—without explaining, at least, the part as a result of the whole (p. 149).

Durkheim's ideas on functionalism were so significant they would influence the eventual formation of structural functionalism—the first major sociological theoretical schools of thought. We will explore the relevancy of functionalism in Chapter 8.

Crime

Durkheim proposed that crime and deviance serve a *functional* role in society because they help to unite its members. From *The Division in Labor in Society*, Durkheim states, "Crime brings together honest men and concentrates them" (Giddens, 1972:127). All groups, organizations, institutions, and societies create laws and norms of expected behavior. When a law or major social norm is violated, it is met with a moral public outrage. The members of the community cling together in opposition to the violation, thus reaffirming that society's bond and its adherence to certain standards of expected behavior. Recognition and punishment of crimes are, in effect, the very reaffirmation of the laws and moral boundaries of a society. The existence of laws and norms are representations of a shared sense of morality within society. "We must not say that an action shocks the *conscience collective* because it is criminal, but rather that it is criminal because it shocks the *conscience collective*. We do not condemn it because it is a crime, but it is a crime because we condemn it" (Durkheim, 1984:40).

Punishing violators for their crimes reminds the nonviolators (society as a whole) not to risk deviating from the law, or they too risk sanctions. Punishment, then, helps to reaffirm the sense of morality within a community because it serves as a reminder to those who question authority and dare to deviate from the norm.

Durkheim believed that crime could also help to promote social change. Occasionally, a violation may not be greeted with public opposition and instead may stimulate a reevaluation of such a behavior on the part of the members of that society. Therefore, an activity that was once considered deviant may be reconsidered and become part of the norm simply because it gained support by a large portion of the society. In short, deviance can help a society to rethink its boundaries and can ignite social change.

Durkheim also examined the relationship between crime and law. He found that a society with mechanical solidarity is characterized by *repressive law*. In this close-knit type of society, members are very similar in their beliefs and share a strong sense of common morality. Consequently, a criminal is likely to be severely punished for violations of the law. On the other hand, a society with *organic solidarity* is characterized by *restitutive law*. In this more modern type of society, there is a greater concern with restitution (or making good) than severe punishment. There are few crimes committed that cause an outrage among societal members due to the lack of a strong common morality.

In *The Division of Labor in Society*, Durkheim said that *crime* served a *functional* role in society because it helped to promote social change when a violation of a *law* caused such a public outrage that demands for change occurred. This happened when Rosa Parks refused to give up her seat to a white person, as law dictated at the time. Demands for the end of police brutality and laws to protect citizens during arrest often follow well-documented cases of abuse. Public outrage was so intense during the Rodney King arrest that a *social current* of mistrust was fueled among African Americans in Los Angeles, in 1992. The acquittal of the four LAPD officers accused of beating King led to rioting in Los Angeles and other cities across the United States and Canada.

Durkheim's ideas of anomie combined with his thoughts on crime and the law are the roots of the "broken windows" philosophy in policing that is so popular in the United States at the end of the twentieth century and the beginning of the twenty-first century. This theory can be traced to James Q. Wilson and George L. Kelling's 1982 article, "Broken Windows." The basic premise of the broken windows approach states that if minor forms of disorder, such as graffiti, littering, panhandling, and prostitution, are left unattended, it will result in neighborhood decline and encourage increased serious criminal activity. Contemporary examples of this policy in action include former New York City mayor Giuliani's implementing of an order-maintenance policing strategy emphasizing proactive and aggressive enforcement of misdemeanor laws against quality-of-life offenses such as graffiti, loitering, public urination, public drinking, aggressive panhandling, turnstile jumping (at subways), and prostitution (Harcourt, 2001). The city of Chicago enacted an anti-gang loitering ordinance prohibiting citizens from standing together in any public place "with no apparent purpose" (Harcourt, 2001). There is a very similar parallel between Durkheim's emphasis on legal regulation and the broken windows emphasis on order. Durkheim explains in *The Division of Labor* that social cohesion of modern society is at its optimal level when there is proper and sufficient legal regulation. Regardless of whether or not the "broken windows" philosophy continues as a popular form of policing, Durkheim's impact on the study of crime and the law and social order will remain a constant study for future sociologists.

Public Involvement

Durkheim's scholarly work is very impressive, but that was not the extent of his contributions to society. Always the crusader for a common morality, he possessed a strong commitment to society, was an active defender of Dreyfus, and was a key figure in the reorganization of the French university system. He managed to combine scientific detachment with an intense commitment to morality. He abandoned his religious roots and preferred to be known as a Frenchman first and foremost. His nationalistic pride did not deter him from his goal of a liberal cosmopolitan civilization in which the pursuit of science was meant to serve the enlightenment and guidance of the whole humanity (Coser, 1977).

Durkheim would encourage sociologists and sociology students alike to fight for causes that assist the common good. He would be in favor of people taking a stand to fight for the rights of individuals and individualism. Durkheim would be in favor of those who fought for the rights of the oppressed and victims of prejudice and discrimination. He would also be in favor of promoting secularism and national pride over religion. In particular, he would take the side of Americans who wish to return the "Pledge of Allegiance" to its original form as written shortly after the Civil War—"I pledge allegiance to the flag of the United States of America and to the republic for which it stands: one nation, indivisible, with liberty and justice for all." (Note: The original version did not include a pledge to God, just a pledge to a united nation, just as Durkheim would have promoted in France. Nonetheless, the majority of Americans believe that "God" should be inserted into the pledge of allegiance to American society and view this notion as a reflection of their collective conscience and sense of morality.)

Criticisms of Durkheim

In his *Division of Labor*, Durkheim describes society as advancing from *mechanical* to *organic solidarity*, which develops out of differences in the economic and social structure. It is too simplistic to characterize societies into just two categories. To be fair to Durkheim, he mostly ignored this overly simplified view of the evolution of societies. Nonetheless, societies today are often categorized in terms of their development (e.g., developing, developed, and postdevelopment nations). This reality provides us with a perspective of the worldwide division of labor.

Durkheim was incorrect in his belief (or perhaps, hope) that modern (organic) solidarity would eliminate war and conflict; instead, it has created larger wars as now blocs of "like-minded" nations team together in their quest for scarce resources and in a defense of their socioeconomic political ways of life.

Durkheim's notion of *social fact* is sometimes criticized as being objectively vague. And when the parameters of a subject matter are themselves vague, any research on that subject is potentially compromised.

Durkheim was consumed with instilling a common sense of morality among people of a given nation. His belief that sociology could best address this goal is flattering for the discipline but could cause sociologists to impose their own sense of morality as that which is best for society. Modern sociologists wrestle with this problem today, as their sense of moral reform often reflects their own personal biases of how things should be rather than describing things as they are.

Summary

Durkheim enjoyed a social background that provided an opportunity for potential greatness. He came from a family that could provide relative economic security and received the best education. "He was rigorously educated in lower schools in France, at a lyceum in Paris, and then at the École Normale Supérieure in Paris" (Simpson, 1963:1). It was, however, Durkheim's taking proper advantage of his educational opportunities that prepared him to contribute so substantially to sociology and his beloved society of France.

Durkheim presented a coherent sociological theory and applied his orientation in a wide variety of specific ways. He was a man of character who attempted to mold events in order to put his cherished principles into practice (Coser, 1977). He founded and edited *L'Année sociologique*, a professional sociological periodical. He provided the basic schematic for structural and functional analysis in sociology, and he insisted on the usage of empirical methodology, so that sociology could accurately claim itself as a science. Durkheim hoped that a scientific sociology would help to create a moral reeducation in the Third Republic and, at the same time, would help to replace religion, as the source of morality, with a secular morality.

With the advent of World War I, Durkheim felt obliged to help France in some way. He became the secretary of the Committee for the Publication of Studies and Documents on the War, publishing several pamphlets attacking pan-Germanism. Durkheim lost his son André, who died from war wounds, just before Christmas 1915. André had followed his father to the École Normale and had begun a most promising career as a sociological linguist (Coser, 1977). Émile took the death of his son very badly. He was able to write very little after this dramatic event and eventually died on November 15, 1917, at the age of fifty-nine.

Durkheim's public involvement extended far beyond his academic achievements and includes serving on innumerable university committees, advising the Ministry of Education, helping to introduce sociology into school curriculum, and influencing Europe as well as many other parts of the world. Durkheim's ideas were taught in American universities by Talcott Parsons and Robert Merton. As Coser (1977) states, "He is, if not the father, then the grandfather of us all" (p. 174).

Émile Durkheim was, and remains, one of the greatest social thinkers of all time. His works will remain relevant well into the third millennium.

 Study and **Review** on **MySearchLab**

Discussion Questions

1. Explain the connection between Durkheim's active role in defending Alfred Dreyfus and his call for "public involvement" as a means to enhance common morality.

2. Can you think of examples of the collective conscience, common morality, and collective representations that exist in society? Are there any examples of behaviors that most, or nearly all, citizens would agree are socially acceptable, or socially unacceptable?

3. Do you think people should have the right to commit suicide? How do you feel about euthanasia? If a patient signs a "do not resuscitate" or a "withdrawal of treatment" form, should medical personnel and family members go along with the decision? What role, if any, should the government play in such decisions?

4. Is it possible for people to act morally and ethically without being religious? Conversely, is it possible for people who claim to be religious to act immorally and unethically? Explain.

5. Have you ever experienced anomie? What about any of your close family members or friends? How are they coping, or how did they cope, with anomie?

MySearchLab® Connections

MysearchLab is designed just for you. Each chapter features a customized study plan to help you learn and review key concepts and terms. Dynamic visual activities, videos, and readings found in the multimedia library will enhance your learning experience.

 Watch on **MySearchLab**

  ▶ John Macionis: Who Are the Great Pioneers of Sociology?

 Read on **MySearchLab**

  ▶ Durkheim, Emile. The Division of Labor in Society.

4 Georg Simmel

 Listen to the **Chapter Audio** on **MySearchLab**

Chapter Outline

- Biography
- Intellectual Influences
- Concepts and Contributions
- Investigation and Application of Simmel's Concepts and Contributions
- Summary
- Discussion Questions

Georg Simmel was a "modern" man in a culturally active and vibrant environment, though he often felt as alienated as the "stranger" he would later describe in one of his most brilliant works. Born a metropolitan, he would live and die a world citizen (Spykman, 1966). Simmel's focus was not on large-scale social institutions and their affect on individuals; instead, he placed an emphasis on the importance of social interaction, including friendship, love, and city life. With an emphasis on the form of social interaction rather than the content, Simmel observed everyday aspects of life including the bonds that keep people together, group dynamics, the intrigue of secrets, and fashion. And because of this, urban folks, in particular, find his concepts and ideas to be fascinating and relevant today. Among the topics discussed in this chapter are social forms (of interaction), social types (of people), social geometry (the significance of numbers and social distance during human interaction), secrecy, secret societies, the philosophy of money, fashion, and mass culture.

BIOGRAPHY

Georg Simmel, the youngest of seven children, was born on March 1, 1858, in the heart of Berlin. The house he was raised in stood on the corner of Leipzigerstrasse and Friedrichstrasse, an area that Coser (1977) compares to Times Square in New York City. Facing anti-Semitism, Georg's

Georg Simmel (1858–1918), German micro-sociologist and founder of the "formal school" of sociology. (Interfoto/Alamy)

paternal grandfather, born Isaac Israel, had changed his last name to Simmel in 1812 in order to become a German citizen. Simmel's father later converted to Catholicism and married a Jewish woman whose family converted to Lutheranism. Georg Simmel was baptized as a Protestant (Pampel, 2000). He never identified with any of the religions of his family's background and never attended church services of any kind.

His father was a prosperous businessman and partner in a well-known chocolate factory that still manufactures candy bars in Germany today (Helle 2009). (Note: The chocolate factory was called Felix & Sarotti and later changed its name to simply Sarotti and is known for its high-quality chocolate and ingredients.) While Georg was quite young, his father passed away. A friend of the family, and founder of an international music publishing house, was appointed Simmel's guardian. Upon the guardian's death, Georg inherited a huge fortune, enabling him to live as an independent scholar.

Simmel's mother was said to be very temperamental and domineering (Wolff, 1950). Georg's relationship with his mother was apparently very distant, and he did not seem to have a sense of roots in any secure family environment. Feelings of marginality and insecurity plagued Simmel from an early age (Coser, 1977).

At the age of twelve, Georg entered the Gymnasium (an academic high school) and after six years was admitted to the University of Berlin (Spykman, 1965). At the University of Berlin, he followed a regular course of study, concentrating mostly on philosophy, psychology, and history. Simmel was able to study with some of the most important academic figures of the day. These scholars included historians Theodor Mommsen, Johann Droysen, Heinrich von Sybel; the philosopher Eduard Zeller; the ethnologist Adolf Bastian; and the art historian Herman Grimm (Coser, 1977).

Simmel's first efforts at a dissertation were rejected, and one of his professors commented, "We would do him a great service if we do not encourage him further in this direction" (Frisby, 1984:23). Despite this setback, Simmel received his doctorate in philosophy in 1881 with a dissertation (entitled "The Nature of Matter According to Kant's Physical Monadology") on Kant's concept of matter. Simmel so loved Berlin that he refused to follow the example of most German academic men who moved from one university to another both during and after their studies. Instead, he stayed at Berlin, where in 1855 he became a private lecturer (*Privatdozent*) in philosophy. As a private lecturer, he was dependent on student fees, in place of a regular salary. He lectured on a wide variety of subjects and theorists, including logic, principles of philosophy, history of philosophy, modern philosophy, pessimism, ethics, psychology, Kant, Lotze, Schopenhauer, Darwin, and Nietzsche, among others. In spite of his marginality as a *Privatdozent*, Simmel was an extremely popular lecturer, not only among students, but also with the cultural elite of Berlin. His lectures were described as clear, logical, artistic, and inspirational (Spykman, 1965).

During his fifteen years as a lecturer, Simmel developed quite a reputation in German academic circles as well as internationally. He was especially popular in the United States, where his work was of great importance in the birth of sociology (Ritzer, 2011). Simmel's academic activities were not limited to teaching. His prolific writing included more than a hundred essays and a number of volumes of considerable size. Among the more critically acclaimed during this period were "Moral Deficiencies as Determining Intellectual Functions" (1893), "The Fundamental Problems of Sociology" (1895), "Superiority and Subordination as Subject-Matter of Sociology" (1896), "The Persistence of Social Groups" (1898); and "A Chapter in the Philosophy of Value" (1900).

In 1900, Simmel received the title of *Ausserordentlicher Professor* ("professor extraordinary") at the University of Berlin. It was official recognition long overdue, but it was an honorary, rather than a remunerative, title. His new position did not give him full academic status, and it kept him apart from the academic community. Furthermore, it failed to remove the stigma of an academic outsider (Ritzer, 2011). In spite of the support of such scholars as Max Weber, Simmel was unsuccessful for years in obtaining full academic recognition. It wasn't until 1914 at Strasbourg that Simmel finally received a position as professor (*Ordinarius*) of philosophy. He hated the idea of leaving Berlin, but financial reasons forced him to leave the place where he had worked and taught for nearly thirty years.

There were two primary reasons why Simmel's slow advancement in academic rank stood in contrast to his wonderful reputation as a speaker and thinker. First, being of Jewish descent, Simmel was victimized by anti-Semitism. Being a Jew in Germany has seldom been advantageous, and nineteenth-century Germany was not an exception. Berlin University was Prussian in its atmosphere, and the Prussian perspective of things was not likely to lead to a speedy promotion and official encouragement of Jewish teachers (Spykman, 1965). In a report written to the minister of education, Simmel was described as "an Israelite through and through, in his external appearance, in his bearing, and in his mode of thought" (Frisby, 1981:25).

The second reason Simmel had difficulty being promoted rests on the very nature of his works. Although his lectures attracted enthusiastic audiences of students and the cultural elite, his ideas were not welcomed by senior scholars in Germany, who favored heavy topics and many footnotes. They believed he gave too much attention to superficial and frivolous topics like fashion, sociability, and everyday life; and they particularly disliked his writing style, which was witty, ironic, aphoristic, and free of citations (Garner, 2000). He acquired a reputation as an "academic showman" (Giddens, 1979). Additionally, academic criticism centered around the fact that many of Simmel's articles appeared in newspapers and magazines and were written for the general audience rather than academic sociologists (Rammstedt, 1991). His academic colleagues saw him as having a "destructive" rather than a "constructive" intellect. Consequently, while he was quite popular with the students and other members of the social community, his academic associates seemed to be a little "put-off" or even jealous of him.

When a failed attempt on the part of Weber to obtain a professorship for Simmel at Heidelberg in 1908 was realized, Simmel wrote to Weber stating that he believed that some of his contemporaries viewed his (Simmel's) serious work as too critical, possessing even a destructive spirit, and that his lectures led one only to negation (Wolff, 1950). Simmel believed that his works were misunderstood. He believed that his work tended exclusively toward the positive, toward the demonstration of a deeper insight into world and spirit. Simmel even believed that it was part of his fate to be misunderstood, and he was convinced that the minister's (of education) "unfavorable mood" went back to some such miscommunication (Wolff, 1950).

However, it would be a mistake to conclude that Simmel failed to have a support system that included his contemporaries. Simmel was very active in cultural events throughout Berlin. He attended meetings of philosophers and sociologists and was the co-founder, with Weber and Toennies, of the "German Society for Sociology." He was friends with two leading poets of Germany, Rainer Maria Rilke and Stefan George. Though he was discriminated against by a number of academic persons, Simmel enjoyed the friendship and support of such eminent academic persons as Max Weber, Heinrich Rickert, Edmund Husserl, and Adolf von Harnack (Coser, 1977).

Simmel was comfortable in many cultural circles. This sense of ease was enhanced by the financial security he enjoyed most of his life. Simmel and his wife, Gertrud, whom he had married in 1890, lived a comfortable bourgeois life. Gertrud was a philosopher in her own right who published work on religion and sexuality under the pseudonym Marie-Luise Enckendorf. Their home was a stage for cultivated gatherings where the sociability about which Simmel wrote so perceptively found a perfect setting (Coser, 1977).

After enjoying many years of success as a lecturer, Simmel moved to Strasbourg, where he could fulfill a lifelong dream of becoming a full professor. Unfortunately, Strasbourg would become a source of many disappointments. First, he was deprived of practically every opportunity to lecture to students. Second, Simmel wrote of his displeasure at the lack of a true academic life in Strasbourg in a letter to Weber's wife: "We live…a cloistered, closed-off, indifferent, desolate external existence. Academic activity is = 0, the people…alien and inwardly hostile" (Frisby, 1981:32). The third disappointment was the biggest problem of all. A short time after he arrived in Strasbourg, the war broke out, and with it came the complete demoralization of academic life. Strasbourg was a university at the borderline between Germany and France. The lecture halls were converted into military hospitals. The youth of Germany were sent to the front, and the faculty, with no students, contributed to the gruesome care of the dead and wounded. Simmel's effort to secure a chair position at Heidelberg failed. He would stay at Strasbourg and lecture to what few students were available until shortly before his death, on September 28, 1918.

Simmel felt the pain of war indirectly. He feared that the war threatened the very foundation of European culture, and he despised the ethnocentric behaviors of the nation-states. He was equally displeased by the frenzied patriotism displayed by scientists and philosophers. He felt that many scientists and philosophers had given up their eternal calling and had become political propagandists (Spykman, 1965). Simmel's faith in European culture was shaken, and because he saw himself more as a European than a German, he was pushed even further toward the edge of acceptability by his own countrymen.

Simmel never enjoyed a normal academic career, and he died as a marginal figure in German academia. Although he had many students during his thirty years of teaching, he never established a "school of thought" in the traditional sense of the term. However, Simmel successfully left his lasting mark through a great number of publications. After his dissertation, his first publication, entitled *On Social Differentiation* (1890), centered primarily on sociological issues. *The Problems of the Philosophy of History* and the two volumes of the *Introduction to the Science of Ethics* were published in 1892–1893. During this period, Simmel sought to isolate the general forms or recurrent regularities of social interaction from the specific content of definite kinds of activity, such as political, economic, and aesthetic. Special attention was given to the problem of authority and obedience. In 1900, one of Simmel's most critically acclaimed works was published, *The Philosophy of Money*, a book as much about sociology as philosophy. Here he applied his general principles to a particular subject, economics; he stressed the role of a money economy in specializing social activity and depersonalizing individual and social relationships.

In 1908, Simmel produced his major sociological work, *Sociology: Investigations on the Forms of Sociation*. Much of this work had been published previously in various journal articles. Many of these articles were published in the United States, especially in *The American Journal of Sociology*. Simmel's sociology first became influential in the United States through the translations and commentaries of Albion Small (1854–1926), one of the first important American sociologists. Park and Burgess gave Simmel a prominent position in their classic *Introduction to the Science of Sociology* (1921). Spykman's (1925) *The Social Theory of Georg Simmel* provided further evidence of the enthusiastic reception for Simmel's work. *The Sociology of Georg Simmel*, translated by Kurt Wolff (1950), comprises Simmel's *Soziologie* (1908) and other works.

INTELLECTUAL INFLUENCES

There exists a wide variety of influences on Simmel's thoughts. Apart from his immediate teachers, the other formative influences included such divergent thinkers as Husserl, Marx, Weber, Hegel, Cohen, Goethe, Heraclitus, and Schopenhauer. Simmel addressed many of the same themes as the philosopher Friedrich Nietzsche and openly shared Nietzsche's pleasure in contradictions, his aphoristic and unconventional style, and his combining of lightheartedness and despair about the human condition (Garner, 2000). Heraclitus, for whom he had the most profound admiration, had a great influence on the formulation of his relativism, and there is too much similarity in Simmel's and Hegel's dialectic to attribute it to a mere coincidence (Spykman, 1965).

Simmel was well versed in history, philosophy, and psychology. Unfortunately, he had an annoying habit of ignoring footnotes (or any other form of reference documentation). Consequently, it is difficult to distinguish his original ideas from those whom he read. Early in his career, Simmel was influenced by French and English positivistic thought and Darwinian and Spencerian evolutionary thought (Coser, 1977). He then turned to Kant and the neo-Kantians, a period when he produced some of his most substantial sociological work.

During his lifetime, Simmel published an estimated 200 articles and 22 books. These works covered a wide range of topics, including morality, history, society, money, religion, art, philosophy, and the artists, writers, and philosophers themselves (Weingartner, 1962).

Spencer and Darwin

Simmel was clearly influenced by Spencer's evolutionary conceptions, especially his idea of differentiation. Evidence of this can be found in Simmel's works of the 1890s, specifically in *On Social Differentiation* and in the *Introduction to the Science of Ethics*. Frisby (2002) claims that the basic ideas (e.g., the persistence of force and the doctrine of relativity) of Simmel's differentiation theory of society came from Spencer. According to Simmel, differentiation has the evolutionary advantage of saving energy in the relation between the organism and the environment (Coser, 1977). Charles Darwin was a focus of many of Simmel's lectures. He held seminars on Darwinism and its consequences on society. Simmel's ideas on self-preservation of social groups were influenced by Darwin's theory of species preservation. Darwin's ideas on evolution, especially from the *Descent of Man*, had an impact on Simmel's work on "truth." Simmel believed that individual conduct is based on knowledge of others. We preserve and acquire not only truth, but ignorance and error, in our judgment of others. People sometimes lie to others as a means of self-preservation (an evolutionary coping device). In modern society, a lie has more dire consequences in social relations because information spreads so quickly via technological advancements in communication. The "lie" becomes a power move similar to holding secrets. (Secrets will be discussed later in this chapter.)

He did not accept all interpretations of cultural evolution. In fact, Simmel was disturbed by current political attempts to implement Darwinian doctrines to support notions of superiority. Simmel was against the idea that all individuals and species were engaged in constant battles for dominance. However, Simmel did employ some modes of Spencerian and Darwinian reasoning to address the issues of the day. For example, in *Philosophie des Geldes*, Simmel argued that marriages engaged in for the sake of money (the tradition of the royals) lead to genetic mixtures, which biology has recognized as the cause of direct and deleterious racial degeneration. In another one of his 1890s' articles, *Einfuehrung in die Moralwisscenschaft* (1892), Simmel maintained that criminal dispositions were hereditary, and he even protested against the preservation of the weak, who will transmit their inferiority to future generations.

Simmel came close to Spencer's idea that societies evolve through stages, from primitive immersion in the group to autonomous individual growth in modern society. These beliefs were reinforced by many of the German thinkers during this era, including Adolf Bastian, a former teacher of Simmel's. In Germany, this type of evolutionary thought was referred to as "parallelism." Simmel was partly convinced of the optimistic and comforting belief in future perfectibility.

Kant and Neo-Kantian Thought

A discipline known as the Kant *Philologie*, concerned with the history, development, and works of Kant, has preempted a considerable portion of philosophical historiography since 1860. These studies began with immense commentary on the *Critique of Pure Reason*, produced in 1881–1892 by Hans Vaihinger, known for his philosophy of the "As If" (which emphasizes man's reliance on pragmatic fictions), and with the founding of the new journal *Kantstudien* (1896) and the Kant-Gesellschaft ("Kantian Society," 1904).

The fundamental question of Kant's philosophy, "How is nature possible?" was answered (by Kant) by saying that nature was nothing but the representation of nature. Thus, the notion of the realm of nature, the sensible world, is organized by human understanding in accordance with certain a priori principles of knowledge. Kant argued that man could never attain "true" knowledge of things in himself, but only a knowledge that was mediated through certain fundamental mental categories, or "givens."

Like Kant, Simmel's philosophy is relativistic. Simmel distinguishes sharply between subject and object, between knowing mind and known world, between the organizing functions of the mind and the data of experience, between form and matter. But Simmel's relativism is much less severe than Kantian formalism. Simmel's relativism was something dynamic and functional. It was not primarily a formal structure, a doctrine; it was a mode of thinking, a thought form, a method of approach.

For Simmel, the truth is relative, not absolute. A single idea is true, is valid, only in relation to another idea, and a whole body of knowledge is available through experience in relation to the external world. The peculiar tendency of the human mind to accept notions of a truth from "significant others" (e.g. religious beliefs, rumors regarding other people) is proof of man's potential for infinite regression. Circular reasoning and dogmatic approaches to life hinder the discovery of the truth.

When Simmel asked himself in his famous essay, "How is society possible?" he used Kant's reasoning in explaining how nature was possible. Simmel viewed society as a result of the unity of reciprocal parts. He resolved that the fixed, the permanent, the substantial elements of society worked with social forces, movements, and the historical process of growth. With his emphasis on process and function rather than on product and content, he approaches Nietzsche and Bergson in their conception of life itself as the ultimate value (Spykman, 1965).

Simmel's approach to sociology primarily centers around the idea that society consists of a web, or a network, of patterned interactions, and it is the role of sociology to study the forms of these interactions as they occur and reoccur in different historical times and settings. In *Fundamental Problems of Sociology* (1895), Simmel describes society as "the sum of all those modes and forces of association which unite its elements" (p. 422). Thus, society, according to Simmel, is merely the name for a number of individuals, connected by interaction.

Karl Marx

Simmel's idea of the dualism of life and objects of the mind, and the objectivation of the human mind, come from Marx's idea of self-alienation. Simmel states,

> This dialectic is not a historical phenomenon of capitalism, but the general destiny of mature civilizations. The works of men lose the human coefficient and are established in autonous contexts of their own. These intermediate layers of civilzation threaten the genuine and natural unity of man and his values (Simmel, 1965:135).

The issue of dualism appears later in this chapter with Simmel's discussion on the mass culture. His use of the term *coefficient* is important within the framework of his concept of "social geometry."

CONCEPTS AND CONTRIBUTIONS

Simmel's approach to sociology can best be described as a conscious attempt to reject the organic (analogy) theories of Comte and Spencer and the German historical description of events. He did not see society as a thing or an organism (organicist), nor merely as a convenient label for something that was an abstract creation (idealist). Society was the sum of all individual patterned interactions. Simmel did not believe that sociology was the science of everything human; its legitimate subject matter lies in the description and analysis of particular forms of human interaction. He believed that all human behavior is individual behavior, but much of it can be explained in terms of the individual's group affiliation and in terms of the constraints imposed upon him or her by particular forms of interaction (Coser, 1965). Simmel is especially discussed as a "formal" sociologist (De La Fuente, 2008).

Formal Sociology

Simmel—sometimes called the founder of the "formal school" of sociology—viewed society as a process that is real and not merely an abstraction, and built on this idea that the focus of sociology should consist of a systematic analysis of social forms. That is to say, social interactions between people take certain forms, and it was Simmel's belief that sociology should study the forms of social interaction. His insistence on the forms of social interaction as the dominant focus of sociology was a decisive response to those historians and other representatives of the humanities who denied that a science of society could ever explain the novelty and the uniqueness of historical phenomena. Simmel never denied that particular historical events are unique because, when utilizing the sociological perspective, one need not concern oneself with the uniqueness of events but, rather, with their underlying uniformities. (Note: In 1959, C. Wright Mills used his term the *sociological imagination* in place of Simmel's concept of the *sociological perspective*.) Simmel justified this belief by pointing out that similar forms of socialization occur with quite dissimilar content, and similar social interests are found in quite dissimilar forms of socialization.

It cannot be denied that this is the case. There are similar forms of relationships between individuals in groups that are completely dissimilar in purpose and goal. Superiority and subordination, competition, imitation, division of labor, personal bias, and countless other forms of relationships are found in all types of groups. A sociologist can always predict that the larger the group size, the greater the probability of differences in opinions and power that will exist.

From Simmel's standpoint, the real world is composed of innumerable events, actions, interactions, and so forth. To cope with this maze of reality, people attempt to order it by imposing patterns, or forms, onto it. In fact, one of Simmel's dominant concerns was the *form* rather than the *content* of social interaction. Therefore, instead of a bewildering array of specific events, the individual is confronted with a limited number of forms. The sociologist's task is to do precisely what the layperson does, that is, impose a limited number of forms on social reality, on interaction in particular, so that it may be better analyzed.

For Simmel, *contents* represent the total array of everything that individuals bring with them in social interactions with others. Contents are seen as drives, interests, and purposes—phenomena residing in the individual (or the raw material of form). *Social forms* reflect common patterns and routines of behavior from which individuals select during social interactions (Pampel, 2000). Forms are supra-individuals, or interactional entities within which individuals are engaged and realize their interests. Simmel believes that forms cannot live independently of content (Larwrence, 1976). Forms indicate the way some infinite potentialities of life can be organized in such a manner that it attains structural stability.

Simmel's approach to formal sociology can be defended on a number of fronts. First, he did reflect a number of real-life categories in his methodology. Second, he did not impose arbitrary and rigid categories on social reality but tries instead to allow the forms to emerge from social reality. Third, Simmel did not possess a strict theoretical orientation in which he tried to force all aspects of social life.

As described by Simmel, social life is filled with a nearly endless number of examples of social forms. Thus, the relevancy of this concept is evident in a vast array of situations. For example, at the beginning of a semester, a college professor can almost always predict what percent of the class will earn what letter grade. Who specifically will earn an "A" or "B" and so on will be determined during the semester, but the form remains relatively constant for any professor who teaches consistently over a period of time. Upper-class students (juniors and seniors) generally have a good idea what grade they are likely to earn in a particular course based on their own past experiences. Students also realize that the courses they take toward graduation are not chosen randomly. Instead, students must take courses that fit a certain form such as core and elective courses in their major, general education courses (including the many subcategories, or forms, of general education courses), and free electives.

On a daily basis, most individuals interact with an assortment of people in a variety of settings. Behavioral patterns are adjusted according to social environment. The college student may wake in the morning to the sounds of her roommate's stereo; join fellow dormmates at the dining hall for breakfast; attend classes with a number of other students and professors; go to work and interact with customers and co-workers; and finally get home in time to shower and dress for her date. These are just a few of the real-life categories and patterned interactions that will occur.

Preferences in choices of television shows (e.g., comedy or reality shows), films (e.g., action or romance), and music genres (e.g., metal, rap, or country) are also established by individuals.

As an illustration, people who know you well will have a good idea whether or not you will enjoy a new film release based on your past preferences. If you liked the first *Hangover* movie, there is a good chance you will like *Hangover Part II* and any subsequent films to follow. Social form is relevant with regard to proper dining etiquette. When you go to a fancy restaurant for fine dining, it is expected that you will have knowledge of proper etiquette and proceed accordingly (e.g., never start eating until everyone is served and use the utensils farthest from your plate first). You will be careful not to make a mess and use the napkin that you already placed on your lap. However, if you are at a bar watching a ballgame and eating chicken wings, you will pick them up and, most likely, make a mess. Napkins, or even paper towels, will be used as necessary. But this is okay in this form of dining out. Entire books have been written to describe proper form when dining.

Social Types

Simmel constructed a number of *social types* (categories of persons) to complement his inventory of social forms. Among them were "the stranger," "the spendthrift," "the mediator," "the adventurer," "the renegade," "the impartial," and "the poor."

The stranger, in Simmel's terminology, is not just a wanderer, a person who is here today and gone tomorrow; rather, *the stranger* is a person with a fixed position within a particular spatial group. As Lawrence (1976) explains, the stranger represents a person "who comes today and stays tomorrow." Wolff (1950) adds, "If wandering is the liberation from every given point in space, and thus the conceptional opposite to fixation at such a point, the sociological form of the 'stranger' presents the unity, as it were, of these two characteristics" (p. 402). This phenomenon reveals that social distance within the group is based on spatial relations on one hand, but can be symbolic on the other. The stranger unites nearness of the group and remoteness concurrently.

In Simmel's description of *the stranger*, distance plays a central role. If the individual is too close with the other group members, then he is not a stranger. On the other hand, if the individual is too far from the group, then she has no contact with the group. Being both near and far, the stranger is often called on as a confidant. Confidences entrusted to strangers run little risk of negative consequences and yet allow for some relative feedback. Often, the stranger is more objective with group members because he is not tied to either of the conflicting parties. The stranger is bound by no commitments that could prejudice her perception, understanding, and evaluation. The stranger is not bound in action by habit, piety, or precedent.

Fontana and Frey (1983) apply the concept of *the stranger* in their brilliant article "The Place-kicker in Professional Football: Simmel's Stranger Revisited." The placekicker in professional football often feels the effect of cultural marginality. He is both near and far from the group, as shown by his predominant ethnic and cultural differences, his soccer (or other sports) background, along with the different methods of entry and socialization to football. Sometimes he may even go barefooted, a clear violation of the norm. His teammates usually shun him and seldom associate with him, even on the playing field. With the rule changes that have occurred in the National Football League (NFL) over the past decades, it is the placekicker who has ironically come to dominate the game. The leading scorer on most NFL teams is the kicker (field goals and extra points after touchdowns). Thus, his kicking ability thrusts the kicker in a *superordinate* position within the team. His teammates, who do most of the work, become the *subordinates.*

Many people may experience the characteristic of being a "stranger." The student who has moved hundreds of miles away from home to start her college studies, the young man who has crossed the country to start a new job, or the young child who finds herself residing at a new army base for the third time in five years all share one common attribute—they are *the stranger.*

Simmel's description of *the stranger* is not bound by physical distance; it includes the individual who is having a hard time blending in with the cultural environment. Add to this Simmel's lucid insights regarding urban life, it is easy to see why so many people experience a level of social distance even when surrounded by thousands of people and a near-endless bombardment of stimuli.

The poor as a social type is defined in terms of social relationships. The poor emerge only when a society recognizes poverty as a special status and then assigns others to assist them. Once the poor accept assistance, they are removed from their private status and become a public issue. Society assigns them a negative status, a burden. Aid to the poor is often viewed as a requirement of society, more than a moral requirement to help the less fortunate. As Simmel explains,

> The obligations we have toward the poor may appear as a simple correlate of the rights of the poor. Especially in countries where begging is a normal occupation, the beggar believes more or less naively that he has a right to alms and frequently considers that their denial means the withholding of a tribute to which he is entitled. Another and completely different characteristic—in the same category—implies the idea that the right to assistance is based on the group affiliation of the needy (Levine, 1971:151).

Clearly, the poor are defined in terms of social relationships. The poor may feel that society owes them, and the non-poor may feel obligated to help or they may not. From a functional standpoint, Simmel felt that society must aid and support the poor so that they do not become active and dangerous enemies of society. Thus, aid to the poor is for the sake of society. Simmel recognized the poor in terms of *relative deprivation;* that is, people at all socioeconomic levels may feel poor compared to others in their group. Regardless of one's income, most people live on what they earn and always seem to want more money.

The social type of the "poor" is as relevant today as at any point in history. In 2011, there were 46.2 million people living in poverty in the United States, with the official poverty rate at 15.0% (U.S. Census Bureau, 2012). The poverty rate for children under 18 was 21.9% and for people aged 65 and older was 8.7% in 2011 (U.S. Census Bureau, 2012). Using the calculation of living on $1.25 or less per day, the World Bank (2012) reports that there are nearly 1.4 billion poor people in the world. People who live in poverty are generally malnourished; they are refugees, are homeless, or have inadequate shelter; they have no health care; their homes and neighborhoods have little or no sanitation or clean water supplies; they are usually illiterate and have no access to education or educational opportunities; they have no energy supplies; they are often unemployed or underemployed; and because they are generally powerless, they are generally the social class with the least amount of human rights. Applying Simmel's perspective to the poor, people who have nothing have nothing to lose and thus become a threat to humanity. Thus, not only should we help the less fortunate because we are civil people, but we should help the less fortunate before they rise and take what they need.

Dialectical Thinking

Simmel's sociological approach was guided by dialectical thinking. A dialectical approach is multicausal and multidirectional, integrates fact and value, rejects the idea that there are concrete dividing lines between social phenomena, focuses on social relations, and is deeply concerned with conflicts and contradictions. Simmel believed that "the world can best be understood in terms of conflicts and contrasts between opposed categories" (Levine, 1971:xxxv).

The forms of social life are constantly influencing individual decision and behavior:

> The forms of social life impress themselves upon each individual and allow him to become specifically human. At the same time, they imprison and stultify the human personality by regressing the free play of spontaneity. Only in and through institutional forms can man attain freedom, yet his freedom is forever endangered by these very institutional forms (Coser, 1977:184).

Simmel's (1904) fascinating and dualistic essay on *Fashion* illustrates a form of social relationship that allows those who wish to conform to the demands of society to do so. By imitating the latest fashion styles, individuals satisfy their need for social adaptation. For some people, this is a critical component of who they are. The fashionable person may be regarded as "cool" and "current" and become the desire of envy. On the other hand, fashion allows those who choose to ignore current trends an opportunity to deviate and remain individualistic. As a result, those who ignore the current fashion trends may look negatively upon those who are preoccupied with the latest styles. The study of *fashion* is dialectical in the sense that the success and spread of any given fashion lead to its eventual downfall. That is, the distinctiveness of fashion is lost once large numbers of people come to accept it, from Paris and New York fashion runways to the Wal-Mart, Kohl's, and Old Navy racks. Dialectically speaking, once "everyone" is doing that which is fashionable, it is no longer fashionable.

One of Simmel's primary interests was interaction (*sociation*) among conscious individuals, and his intent was to look at a wide variety of interactions. For Simmel, *sociation* always involved potential opposite extremes: Harmony involves conflict; attraction, repulsion; and love with hate. He believed that human relations are characterized by imperfect modes of *sociation* resulting in the potential of both positive and negative outcomes during interaction. Even couples involved in a "loving" relationship with one another need to "blow off steam" (a safety valve) in order for loving relations to endure. Friends, too, need to blow off steam from time to time. It is a good test of friendship when a person learns to keep their cool while the other is losing his or her cool.

Social Geometry

Simmel's formal sociology is a clear effort to develop a *geometry* of social relations. *Social Geometry,* or "Quantitative Aspects of the Group," is among Simmel's best-known works. The analogy of sociology to geometry represents an attempt on Simmel's part to identify complex social interactions and reduce them to simple patterns wherein constructs of an entire range of possible formations can be reduced to a relatively few postulates (Simmel 2009). Simmel's admiration of geometry's ability to consider forms of empirical bodies that can be reduced to uncomplicated molds of explanation compliments his formal sociology. Two of the geometric coefficients that interested him the most are social distance (e.g., *the stranger*) and numbers (e.g., *dyad* and *triad*). The role of distance in social relations can be summed as, "The properties of forms and the meanings of things are a function of the relative distances between individuals and other individuals or things" (Levine, 1971:xxxiv). The value of something is determined by its *distance* from the individual. According to Simmel, an item will not be valuable if it is either too close and too easy, or too distant and too difficult, to obtain. Objects attainable only through great effort are the most valuable.

The basic principles of group structure and quantitative size (*numbers*) are best illustrated with Simmel's concepts and usage of the *dyad* and the *triad*. The numerically simplest structures that can still be designated as social interactions occur between two elements. The isolated individual (one number) is someone who does not interact with others and is thus eliminated from group structure analysis. The dyadic group has a typical sociological form based on the fact that the most divergent individuals uniting for the most varied motives will show combinations of the same formation. Further, the dyadic characteristic holds true in the case of an association between pairs of groups (e.g., families) and other combination forms (e.g., organizations) (Spykman, 1965).

The strongest bonds are formed between two people, be they best friends, lovers, or married couples. Each member retains a high level of individuality, but they are aware of the fact that their social structure is immediately dependent upon one another. There is no independent structure within the *dyad*. Each member is directly responsible for any collective action; neither individual can deny responsibility by shifting the blame to the group; there is maximum involvement by both persons with a degree of intimacy; and if either person departs, the group ceases to exist.

The *dyad* possesses unique characteristics that distinguish it from other forms of *sociation*. The dyadic group, in contrast with all other groups of more numerous elements, is characterized by the fact that it does not attain a higher, superindividual life, so that the individual might feel independent of himself. In a dyad, when one member leaves the group (e.g., a person breaks up with his or her partner), the group ceases to exist.

The simple addition of a third person to the dyad causes radical and fundamental changes to the group structure (form). This three-person group Simmel called a *triad*. It is worth noting that Simmel believed that the form of dyads and triads may exist between groups as well as individuals. The *dyad* has a closeness between the two members; the third modifies it entirely, but it is also further complicated by the fact that a further extension is not followed by a modification of a corresponding degree (Spykman, 1965). The addition of a third element provides the opportunity for the development of an external superindividual and the internal development of divisions. The direct and immediate reciprocity found in the *dyad* is replaced by an indirect relationship that both reinforces and interferes with the immediate reciprocity. The new group is less dependent on the immediate participation of the elements; it absorbs less of the total personality; and it can continue its existence if one element leaves.

The dyadic group shows synthesis and antithesis. The entrance of a third element means transition, conciliation, and renunciation both of the immediate reciprocity and of the direct opposition (Spykman, 1965). The third becomes an intruder, but with whom will she join? The original *dyad* has an intimacy, which is the tendency of relations between two persons. Is the reason why the third person joined the group to weaken this intimacy, or to intensify it?

The third person may become the nonpartisan arbitrator or mediator. In this case, the third element serves the group as a whole. The conciliator or arbitrator aims to prevent a disruption of the existing unity between the original two elements. The nonpartisan can, however, also use his advantageous position for his own selfish interests. In such a case, his position becomes that of the *tertius gaudens*, Latin for "the third who enjoys." This previously unconnected nonpartisan may spontaneously seize upon the opportunity that conflict between the other two offers. He may do this because the other two conflicting elements will compete for the third person's favor and therefore gain power of the group. Finally, the third person may implement a strategy known as *divide et impera*, Latin for "divide and rule" or "divide and conquer." According to Simmel, this occurs when the third element intentionally produces conflict in order to gain a dominating position. The third person may do this in order to maintain power over the group, or if she has plans to ally herself with one of the original two members and then remove the other member.

There are numerous examples of the application of the relevancy of social geometry. Students, in particular, may have shared some of these experiences. For example, if we examine social distance and its relation to grade distribution, we will find that earning a high grade in a course where it is well known that the professor is a "hard" grader will bring a greater sense of accomplishment to the student than earning a high grade with a professor who is an "easy" grader. (Although it should be noted that my students tell me they appreciate *all* their high grades!) In addition, if a student had to work really hard to achieve a high grade (overcoming social distance), that grade will be cherished compared to earning a high grade in a class that required little effort. Getting a date with someone you are highly attracted to after a significant effort in pursuit will have greater value than getting a date with someone who says "yes" easily.

The significance of numbers is also relevant to all of us. In 2004, Jack White, one half of the Grammy award–winning group The White Stripes, an alternative rock band that has sold millions of records, was asked to reflect on his band's success. The band has only two members: Jack, who plays guitar and sings, and Meg White, who plays drums. Jack White indicated that having only two people in the band has its advantages—there isn't a third person to take sides and cause discord (*The Post-Standard*, 6/17/04). In the interview, White went on to proclaim the advantage of a dyad. Fast forward to 2011 and we learn that The White Stripes "officially ended" their partnership (*Entertainment Weekly*, 2011). Perhaps a third person, either a counselor or another musician with creative input, could have prolonged this group's continued success.

There are times when business partners, co-workers, friends, and loving couples may be impacted by the introduction of a third person. Couples and friends have "split up" because of the third person's role. There are times in your life where you may fall victim of the third person, and there may be occasions where you find yourself in the role of the third person. The third person can, however, serve a positive role, such as a mediator or counselor. Anyone interested in the field of counseling as a career will need to learn about the dynamics of the dyad and triad. People seeking power or advancement within the corporate ranks may utilize the *divide et impera* principle. In the business world, it is a "dog-eat-dog" world of the survival of the fittest. Learning how to play the "numbers" game can serve as a valuable tool for success.

There are times when a couple may be involved in a relationship and one person is "cheating" on the other. When this cheating is unbeknown to the other, it is usually the result of a secret being held. In the contemporary world of social networking, when one indicates on their Facebook profile page that "It's complicated" for his or her relationship status, one reason might be because they are involved in a "secret" relationship—as in SBF (secret boyfriend) or SGF (secret girlfriend). Secrets can play a very important role in all types of social relationships. Simmel's work on secrets is the next topic we will discuss.

Secrecy

The *secret* is the hiding of realities by one or more persons from another person or persons. This can be done by either negative or positive means. According to Simmel, *secrecy* is one of man's greatest achievements. It represents an advancement from one's childish stage in which every conception is expressed at once, and every undertaking is accessible to the eyes of all. The secret offers a possibility of a second world alongside the manifest world; and the latter is decisively influenced by the former (Wolff, 1950).

In order for interaction to occur among persons, there exists the reality that these people must know at least some bit of information about each other. This is true whether we are talking about interactions with friends, family, colleagues, or less impersonal contacts. Over time we tend to know certain people very well, but we can never know them absolutely. We do, however, form some sort of unitary conception of other people through the bits of information we do have. Simmel (1906) sees a dialectical relationship between interaction (being) and the mental picture we create of others (conceiving) based upon the reciprocal relationship already established. In all aspects of life, we acquire not only truths concerning others, but half-truths, false-truths, and flat-out errors of judgments.

The fact is, even if someone wanted to reveal *all* aspects of their personal life, it would be impossible to communicate such a huge amount of information. The contemporary phrase "TMI" ("too much information") comes to mind here. There are times when people want to keep certain portions of their lives secret from others and intentionally hide information. In extreme cases, they may even resort to lying. The intentional hiding of information takes on greater intensity when it clashes with the intention of revealing.

There comes a time when someone may confide previously hidden information with trusted others. In this case, he or she shares information that is unknown to others. "Whether there is secrecy between two individuals or groups, and if so how much, is a question that characterizes every relation between them" (Wolff, 1950:330). Even in the case where one of the two does not notice the existence of a secret, the behavior of the concealer, and hence the whole relationship, is modified by it. The secret contains a tension that is dissolved in the moment of its revelation. The secret is surrounded by the possibility and temptation of betrayal; an external danger of being discovered is interwoven with internal danger of giving oneself away.

It is easy to apply Simmel's concept of *social geometry* to the issue of *secrecy*. As for the element of *distance*, we tend to expect relative strangers to hold back information, but we are hurt and/or offended when it involves someone close to us. Thus, we can better accept lies from those who are distant from us. The lie of a lover is far more devastating than a lie from a movie celebrity or politician. *Secrecy* is also linked to the size (*numbers*) of society. In small groups, it is difficult to develop secrets because of the closeness of circumstances. People who grew up and/or live in small towns often comment how they "could not get away with anything" because everyone knows each other and their business. In larger groups, secrets can more easily develop and are much more needed because of the many different characteristics of group members. Thus, people who live in large metropolitan areas can participate in secretive behavior in public, often with little or no consequences. As a result, if a person is cheating on their significant other in an area where "everyone" knows who they are, there is a greater risk of the secret coming out.

If we examine the issue of power, those who possess knowledge of other's secrets have at their disposal a valuable tool. As the old adage states, "Knowledge is power." Knowing the right moment to reveal a secret is a demonstration of power. On the other, more honorable hand, being able to keep secrets and knowing with whom one can confide in is also a sign of power. Politicians, management, military personnel, family members, and friends all need, at times, to be able to hold onto a secret when an important guarded social action is being undertaken. As an example of a military and political secret, on May 1, 2011, President Obama ordered a clandestine mission to kill Osama bin Laden, the mastermind behind the worst terrorist attack on U.S. soil. Guarded intelligence reports gathered by the CIA and a variety of informants led to the strong belief that bin Laden was hiding in Abbottabad, Pakistan. For months President Obama was aware of bin Laden's hiding spot. Obama had to wait for the right opportunity to send in the Joint Special Operations Command forces (Navy SEALs), and he felt it best not to inform the American media or citizens or officials in Pakistan—a secret that, understandably, upset Pakistan officials. If the information on bin Laden had turned out to be false, Obama's secretive mission would have cost him his political career. The success of the mission may have prolonged it.

Interestingly, Simmel also pointed out the importance of *faithfulness*. Simmel describe faithfulness as a significant sociological form because such a trait is necessary for social relationships to continue to exist. This is true with micro friendships and macro-societal cooperation. Faithfulness is followed by psychological bonds, affective interests, and social autonomy. At the personal level, a person secretly dating the "cheating" person will always have to consider the reality that he or she may fall victim to the other's cheating in the future. At the macro level, when one nation violates a faithful agreement with another, relations will, naturally, be strained.

In an article published with the *Journalism and Mass Communication Journal*, this author has applied Simmel's ideas of flirting and secrecy to the Facebook relationship status of "It's complicated." After conducting interviews with people who reported that they claimed the "It's complicated" relationship status (ICR) on Facebook, Delaney (2012b) found that the most common reason cited involved one person who was already in a committed relationship but wished to hide the secret relationship with the third-party person. This person would not change his or her relationship status, but the third-party person would claim the ICR status on Facebook. Thus, the ICR is a variation of a secret dating, or having an affair. Unlike other relationship status options on Facebook, when one is involved in a secret relationship, they cannot mention their partner's name for risk of being discovered.

The Secret Society

The first internal relation typical of the *secret society* is the reciprocal confidence among members. It is required because the purpose of secrecy is protection. Of all the protective measures, the most radical is to make oneself invisible. *Secret societies* offer a very impressive schooling in the moral solidarity among members. Above all, is the oath of silence. The gradual initiation of a member into the *secret society* creates a hierarchy. With increased growth come increased rituals. Features of the *secret society* include separateness, formality, consciousness, seclusion, degrees of initiation, group egoism, centralization, and de-individualism.

There are many secret societies; some, not so ironically, are unknown because they *are* secretive. Other secret societies, such as fraternities and sororities, government spy agencies (e.g., the Central Intelligence Agency), and military covert operations are known to the general public, but their daily activities and interworkings are not. The secretive nature of the Greek system (frats and sororities) on college campuses is relatively limited to such things as secret handshakes, rituals, and symbolism, but still relatively known to college university administrators. Someone working as a CIA agent, on the other hand, is far more enigmatic. As a rule, CIA agents do not reveal their true identity to anyone outside the organization. They may admit to working for the government (e.g., the State Department), but the average citizen has no clue about their true motives. A CIA agent, for example, could be disguised as graduate student who travels the world presenting research papers at conferences as a guise to conduct covert government activities.

Superordination and Subordination

According to Simmel, the most important form of relationship in the whole social world is the one between the leader and his followers, between the superior and his *subordinates*. It is a form of socialization critical for social life and the main factor in sustaining the unity of groups. Superiority and *subordination* constitute the sociological expression of psychological differences in human beings (Spykman, 1965). Simmel claimed that superordination may be exerted by individuals, groups, or an objective force (social or ideal).

The subordination of a group under an individual can help unite the group members into a cohesive unit. As a result, the *superordinate* and the *subordinate* have a reciprocal relationship. The *superordinate* (e.g., boss and leader) expects the *subordinate* (e.g., employee and follower) to follow the rules. Domination does not lie in the unilateral imposition of the *superordinate's* will upon the *subordinate,* because of the reciprocal nature between the two. Even in the most extreme forms of domination, the subordinate has some degree of personal freedom and choice of action. The choices may be limited between submission and punishment; however little consolation the existence of this alternative may bring to the individual in question, it shows, nonetheless, that the superior–inferior relationship cannot be established without some active participation on the part of the *subordinate.* Thus, submission is not purely passive but has an active aspect as well, and the resulting relationship is a form of *sociation.*

The sociological situation between the superordinate and the subordinate is completely changed as soon as a third element is added (Wolff, 1950). One might assume that an alliance between the *subordinates* would emerge because of their common form and thus jeopardize the power of the *superordinate.* But Simmel viewed this transformation of a numerical into a qualitative difference as no less fundamental if viewed from the master's standpoint. It is easier to keep two rather than one at a desired distance; in their jealousy and competition, the master has a tool for keeping them down and making them obedient, while there is no equivalent tool in the case of *one* servant. Simmel summarized the structure found in the triad is completely different from the dyad but not, on the other hand, specifically distinguished from groups of four or more members (Wolff, 1950).

Today, more than ever, most people work for someone else. Simmel's ideas of the *superordinate* (employer/boss) and *subordinate* (employee/worker) are easily understood in the context that one finds himself possessing one role or the other. In some work settings, the employees enjoy relative autonomy. They may belong to a strong union or they are lucky enough to have an employer who truly values their contributions. In other work environments, the employees are not treated so graciously and they may actually dislike their boss and dread going to work. Many people also willingly abide by the parameters of social (e.g., the constructs of democracy) or religious (e.g., the Ten Commandments) ideals of proper behavior.

Sociability

We have already learned that the term *sociation,* for Simmel, means social interaction between at least two conscious persons. Simmel defined *sociability* as the "play form of *sociation*" (Martindale, 1988). *Sociability* is the association of people for its own sake and for the delight of interacting with others. The character of the gathering is determined by personal qualities and personalities of the participants. Interaction always arises on the basis of certain drives or for the sake of certain purposes. Interaction can be based on necessities, one's intelligence, wants and desires, will, creativity, and other elements that are a part of life. The limits of sociability rest purely with the participating interactants. For example, many people flirt. Flirting can take many forms, ranging from the pure fun of flirting (e.g., smiling at a stranger just to make him happy) with others to flirting for some specific end goal (e.g., romance). People may flirt for a free drink at a bar, and people have been said to be "flirting with disaster" when they attempt an endeavor that may backfire. Academics intellectually flirt with the challenge of conquest over some unexplained phenomenon—although this type of flirting might be considered boring work by those not familiar with the "rush" of seeking and obtaining new knowledge (Delaney, 2012b). In the cyber world, flirting is often accomplished via texting or sexting (sending photos of a sexual content) with the person with whom one is enamored. According to the Crisis Intervention Center (2011), sexting is most common between people in relationships; but sexting someone you have a crush on is the second most common form.

Sociability emerges as a very peculiar sociological form. As such, Simmel (1895, 1908) categorized many characteristics of *sociability*:

1. *Tact and impersonality.* In the group setting, there is seldom an external guide overseeing interpretations of proper behavior. Tact fulfills this regulatory function. Its most essential role is to draw limits, which result from the claims of others, of the individual's impulses, ego stresses, and intellectual and material desires. Impersonality occurs when people are not acting socially. It is considered tactless because it interferes with sociability (social interaction).

2. *Sociability thresholds.* Humans are a totality of dynamic complex ideas, wants, desires, and possibilities. According to motivations and relations of life and its changes, man makes himself a differentiated and clearly defined social phenomenon. Each person develops her own tolerance toward socializing with others, thus creating different sociability thresholds.

3. *The "sociability drive" and the democratic nature of sociability.* As a foundation of law, Kant posited the axiom that each individual should possess freedom to the extent which is compatible with freedom of every other individual. Kant's law is thoroughly democratic. These democratic ideas are to carry over to society and assumingly social drives. One must note that the form of social drives varies from individual to individual.

4. *The artificial world of sociability.* The world of sociability is an artificial one, maintained only through voluntary interaction. Because of the often harsh reality of one's real life, it is easy to understand why persons often prefer the deceptive social world they have created and work so hard at maintaining.

5. *Social games.* Many members of society will take part in interactions that attempt to outdo others, and resort to participating in social games. The seriousness of life often requires an emotional and physical outlet. Games are created and people actually "play society."

6. *Coquetry.* "In the sociology of sex, we find a play-form: the play-form of eroticism is coquetry" (Wolff, 1950:50). In general, the erotic question between the sexes is that of offer and refusal. Simmel believed that the nature of feminine coquetry (flirting) is to play up, alternately, allusive promises and allusive withdrawals—to attract the male but always stop short of a decision, and to reject him but never to deprive him of all hope. Her behavior swings back and forth between "yes" and "no" without stopping at either. Despite these and many other potentially sexist remarks Simmel makes in this section, few would disagree that the very nature of coquetry makes it an element of sociability, played by both sexes.

7. *Conversation.* In brief, conversation is the most general vehicle for socializing. It is language that separates man from the other animals. Humans are capable of serious and frivolous conversation. Knowing how to master both is a huge asset in sociability.

8. *Sociability as the play-form of ethical problems and of their solution.* Individuals must function as a part of a collective in the world in which they live. They have their own personal set of ethics and values that often come in conflict with those of society. Sociability allows for the temporary shelter of these conflicts through participation in groups who share the same beliefs.

9. *Historical illustrations.* A general conception of sociability is well illustrated throughout time. For example, Simmel shows that in the early German Middle Ages, there existed the brotherhoods of knights.

> **10.** ***The "superficial" character of sociability.*** A simple fact remains: Persons choose to form groups and societies for a wide variety of reasons, but at any time they are free to remove themselves. Thus, sociability has a very superficial character.

It could be argued that sociability is what makes life enjoyable and durable. We cannot work or study all the time. It is necessary for everyone to take some time off and enjoy life. Sociability provides that avenue.

Philosophy of Money

Simmel's magnum opus, *The Philosophy of Money* (1907), demonstrates that his theoretical scope rivals that of Marx, Weber, and Durkheim. *The Philosophy of Money* demonstrates conclusively that Simmel deserves at least as much recognition for his general theory as for his essays on microsociology. It is a difficult book that has daunted many would-be readers. Nevertheless, Simmel's insights about money are as valid today as they were more than a hundred years ago.

According to Simmel, economic exchange is best understood as a form of social interaction. His focus is exchange. Exchange is a universal form of interaction. In economics, not all exchange involves money, but money becomes a social tool. A society that uses money has replaced the barter system and, consequently, it reflects social evolution because of its acceptance of growth and rationalization. "The phenomena of the money economy are born primarily of that type of mental energy which is called intellect as distinguished from sentiment and feeling" (Spykman, 1965:232).

The use of money changes a society. The value of money is based on the faith (rationalization) that the currency can be used to purchase products. With the barter system, the items offered for exchange are tangible, they exist, and they are readily available. History has shown that people are reluctant to make such drastic changes in their economic culture. "The impulsive and emotional character of primitive people is undoubtedly due in part to the shortness of their teleological series" (Spykman, 1965:232).

In the economic realm, money serves both to create distance from objects and to provide the means to overcome it. Once we obtain enough money, we are able to overcome the distance between ourselves and the objects. The value of an object relates to the level of desirability and the degree of unattainability. In the process of creating value, money also provides the basis for the development of the market, the modern economy, and, ultimately, the capitalistic society.

Like Marx, Simmel was concerned with capitalism and the problems created by a money economy. But Simmel saw the economic problems of his time as simply a specific manifestation of a more general cultural problem. Marx, as an economic determinist, viewed capitalism as the primary problem of society and therefore subject to eventual change (for the better) through communism. Simmel viewed the economic structure as a part of the greater objective nature of society, which alienated man's subjective nature. The objective nature of society, including economics, was something inherent with human life and not subject to change. Simmel, then, attempted to show that the economic system was integrally connected with the other major social institutions of modern society (Raison, 1969).

As Simmel described, social relationships are influenced by money. In some relationships, money is more important than personal relations; it becomes a social means to an end. Many people today have their social relationships influenced in great part by money, whether that involves the ability to pay bills, buy gifts, or take someone on a romantic trip. We may not like to admit it, but money can be a means toward happiness, or at the very least, the means by which we afford our daily consumption of goods and services.

Exchange

Simmel views exchange as the purest and most concentrated form of human interaction. Generally, all interactions can be viewed as exchanges. An interesting characteristic of exchange is that the sum of values is greater than it was before the exchange took place. Economic exchange, regardless of whether it involves material objects or labor, entails the sacrifice of some good or service that has potential value for others (Levine, 1971). Thus, to some extent, value attached to a particular object comes about through the process of exchange.

Value and exchange, according to Simmel, are inseparable. Value is put on the objects that are exchanged. Value is not always contained with the specific object, but is a product of comparison. The individual determines the value of something through comparison with something else.

Simmel conceives economic activity as sacrifice in return for a gain. The value of the gain is determined from the value of the sacrifice involved in order to obtain an object. Value is always situationally determined. The exchange is always "worth it" to the parties involved, at least at the actual instant that the exchange takes place. If a sacrifice is too high, then the value is too low and exchange does not take place.

As we shall learn in Chapter 11, Simmel's ideas of social exchange will have an influence on George Homans, the creator of social exchange theory. Homans proposed basically the same idea as Simmel that in all relationships there is some sort of cost–benefit analysis that takes place in the minds of actors. If the exchange is rewarding, the interaction will continue; conversely, if the individual(s) is incurring greater costs and rewards, the behavior will cease. As Simmel proposes, our daily activities are exchange propositions. What do you think?

Mass Culture

The term *mass culture* was not coined by Simmel, but his works reflect the concept. He believed central themes reflect social and cultural life in all epochs of history. Scholars must understand these *themes* to understand current culture.

Whenever life progresses beyond the animal level to that of the spirit, and spirit progresses to the level of culture, an internal contradiction appears. The whole history of culture is the working out of this contradiction. We speak of culture whenever life produces certain forms in which it expresses and realizes itself: works of art, religions, sciences, technologies, laws, and innumerable others (Etzkorn, 1968). Culture, having spirit, ceaselessly creates such forms, which become self-enclosed and demand permanence. These forms are inseparable from life; they are fixed identities.

Like Marx, Simmel is concerned with the ineradicable dualism inherent in the relation between individuals and objective cultural values. An individual can attain cultivation only by assimilating to the cultural values that surround him. But these values threaten to engulf and enslave the individual. Beyond the fetishistic character that Marx attributed to the economic realm of commodity production, Simmel indicates that these cultural contents have been created by people and they were intended for people, but they attain an objective form and follow an immanent logic of development, becoming alienated from their origin as well as from their purpose (Coser, 1977). Thus, people come to reify social reality; and Simmel viewed social reality as "objective culture."

In the last years of his life, Simmel reflected on the drastic changes of the times—the phenomenon of *mass culture*. Simmel saw a tension between the way individuals experience and create culture ("subjective culture") and culture embodied in material objects and institutions ("objective culture"). He believed that the latter was growing rapidly, overwhelming the former so that individuals were crushed by the weight and force of culture that existed outside their control (Garner, 2000).

"The Metropolis and Mental Life"

One of the most well-known and influential works on the urban mentality was written by Simmel in an essay called "The Metropolis and Mental Life" (1903). Simmel described mental life as a combination of three basic traits: emotional reserve; an attachment to personal freedom; and a willingness to seek out and reward extreme individuality.

Emotional reserve, or indifference, is a self-protective device designed to shield the individual from the fast-paced tempo of urban life. Urban dwellers are bombarded by so many images that they must maintain a certain emotional distance from this sensory onslaught. Learning to react with one's mind rather than heart is a protective mechanism necessary in metropolitan life.

Maintaining *an attachment to personal freedom* is described by Simmel as the emotional indifference that metropolitan persons exhibit toward one another. Caring for one's neighbor, which is such a critical element in some rural villages and towns, is viewed as pettiness in the urban setting. Unfortunately for the urban dweller, this individual freedom can create loneliness and despair.

The third trait of metropolitan life, *extreme individuality,* stems from the metropolitan need to do something drastic in order to attract social attention. Urban dwellers seem to almost be relieved when such individuals display their radical forms of behavior.

Simmel's ideas of life in a metropolis were first articulated as a lecture at the Dresden exhibition on city life wherein he described the differences between rural and urban life. Rural life, according to Simmel, was characterized by a slow, regular pattern of ongoing sociation conducted at the same place(s) over and over but allowing for emotional connections to form between interactants. The regularity of behavior tends to form a "like-minded" cultural mindset among rural people that was both comforting and disconcerting (due to its lack of diversity). With urban life, contrastingly, people are surrounded by strangers with diverse opinions and habits and yet no affective bonds to unite them.

With Simmel's study on the metropolitan life, we can find yet another example of the relevancy of "numbers." For example, during the 1960s, two social psychologists, Bibb Latane and John Darley, noted how people in urban areas often ignore serious crimes that occurred around them. They concluded that the greater the number of persons in the group, the less personal responsibility any one person assumes (*diffusion of responsibility*). Thus, when 38 residents of an apartment complex in New York City (1964) did nothing in response to the screams of a young woman (Kitty Genovese) being repeatedly stabbed in an attack by a stranger, they all shifted intervention responsibility to the others (Baron and Byrne, 1997).

The diffusion of responsibility theory hypothesizes that when one person sees someone in need of help, the bystander's responsibility is clear; but with multiple witnesses to an emergency, the duty of assistance is spread equally among all the bystanders. For example, if a motorist has broken down in an isolated area, the first passerby is likely to offer assistance because he or she realizes it could be some time before another motorist might drive by. Conversely, if a motorist breaks down on a busy interstate, numerous passersby will ignore the disabled driver and justify their behavior because they do not bear the brunt of solo responsibility.

The differences between rural and urban life are as pronounced today as during Simmel's era, if not more so. More people live in urban environments today than 100 years ago, and people who live in one environment can easily point out the differences in the other. And, just as in the past, each environment has advantages and disadvantages. Inevitably, it comes down to a life choice when deciding which environment meets an individual needs.

Criticisms

The term *form* may not have been the best choice for Simmel, as he received a great deal of resistance in acceptance of its usage by other sociologists, who viewed it dubiously at best. Modern sociologists are more comfortable using terms such as *social structure*, *role*, or *status* in place of *form*. Simmel has also been criticized of imposing a sense of order where there may be none.

Simmel was, primarily, a micro theorist, and as a result, his analysis of the macro structure is relatively weak. Any micro theorist will be questioned for his or her lack of in-depth coverage of the macro structure, and that may not be exactly fair, but Simmel's definition of society as simply interaction among large numbers of people is weak.

Simmel wrote a large number of papers on a wide variety of topics. Although he could be commended for such an endeavor, he is often criticized for his lack of a coherent, systematic study.

Summary

Simmel can best be described as a microsociologist who played a significant role in the development of small-group research, symbolic interactionism, and exchange theory. Simmel's grounding of sociology in some psychological categories is one reason why his sociology has proven attractive not only to symbolic interactionists, but to social psychologists as well.

Simmel's main micro-sociological concern was with social process and the forms of interaction patterns in which individuals structure and restructure the social world. Simmel operated with a dialectical orientation that was demonstrated in a variety of ways. He was concerned with the conflicts that develop between individual culture and objective culture. His formal sociology and social geometry provided a schematic of an individual's social location, which would allow later investigators to locate and often predict the moves of social persons involved in webs of group relations.

At the macro level, Simmel paid little attention to social structures, often reducing them to little more than interaction patterns. His real interest at the macro level resides with his work on objective culture. This concern was best illustrated in his essays of the metropolitan life. In *The Philosophy of Money*, Simmel discussed problems inherent with the capitalistic system, to problems of life in general.

The revival of interest in Simmel's thoughts, which has emerged in the English-speaking world since the 1970s, has brought to the forefront the attention of his contributions to cultural theory, in particular, his works on the concept of *spiritual life* (a thinker must push beyond the confines of his era and anticipate the problems of the future), his works on "the crisis of culture," and "the conflict of modern culture." Although Simmel does not use the concept of "modernism," he identifies a number of contemporary cultural phenomena that would later be grounded under that term (Turner, 1990).

As the founder of the "formal school," Simmel successfully showed that society, as a process, is a real entity, and not merely an abstraction. Forms of interaction do exist and are subject to systematic analysis. His insistence that the focus of study for sociologists should be on these *forms* of behavior provides a guideline for microsociology. It also provides a legitimacy for the discipline.

Although most of Simmel's works are essays, his works are nonetheless substantial. It should be clear that students of social theory, and social thinkers in general, will continue to read the many important contributions that Simmel has provided to sociology.

Study and **Review** on **MySearchLab**

Discussion Questions

1. Identify at least five social forms from your daily life as a student. How are these social forms different from your family life?
2. What do you think about fashion? Is it necessary for you to keep up with the latest forms of fashion? Why or why not? What do you think about people who always have to be involved with the latest social trends or fashion styles?
3. Have you ever been asked to keep a secret for someone? Or have you ever discovered someone else's secret? How did it make you feel to have secret knowledge of someone? Have you ever had a secret of your own found out by someone? How did you react to that revelation?
4. Explain the term *sociation*. Provide examples from your own life that illustrate this concept.
5. Describe the characteristics of your home environment, urban or rural. What are positives and negatives of such a life? Do you see yourself living in the opposite environment some day? Why or why not?

MySearchLab® Connections

MysearchLab is designed just for you. Each chapter features a customized study plan to help you learn and review key concepts and terms. Dynamic visual activities, videos, and readings found in the multimedia library will enhance your learning experience.

 Watch on **MySearchLab**

▶ Michael Kimmel: Sociology Looks at Both Social Order and Social Conflict

Read on **MySearchLab**

▶ Simmel, Georg. Dyads, Triads, and Larger Groups.

CHAPTER

5 Max Weber

 Listen to the **Chapter Audio** on **MySearchLab**

Chapter Outline

- ▪ Biography
- ▪ Intellectual Influences
- ▪ Investigation and Application of Weber's Concepts and Contributions
- ▪ Summary
- ▪ Discussion Questions

Max Weber was a German social thinker who excelled in many different fields, including sociology, economics, history, law, jurisprudence, and linguistics. He was a person of encyclopedic knowledge who displayed scholarly brilliance at an early age; he quickly learned other languages as these provided access to materials helpful in his worldwide investigations. His areas of research ranged from studies of Polish farm workers to ancient religions and medieval entrepreneurs (Hadden, 1997). Weber, like Marx, spent a great deal of time analyzing the effects of industrialization on society. Unlike Marx, Weber lived long enough to see many of the benefits of industrialization (e.g., a rising standard of living for a greater number of people), but he also paid close attention to a number of new problems (e.g., increased rationalization, depersonalization in the decision-making process, the negative role of bureaucracy) that were not so apparent during Marx's era. Weber hoped to explain why industrialization rose as a socio-economic system in some parts of the world but not in others. He tied the work ethic of the Protestant religion to the spirit of capitalism as his answer. Weber is also well known for his studies on types of authority and social class and inequality. Clearly, a number of Weber's concepts and contributions are still relevant today.

Max Weber (1864–1920), German social thinker considered among the true masters of sociology.   (Keystone Pictures USA/Alamy)

BIOGRAPHY

Max Weber, son of Helene and Max Weber, was born on April 21, 1864, in Erfurt, Germany. He was the eldest of eight children, all of whom lived into adulthood except for two—Anna, who died in infancy, and Helene, who died at the age of four of diphtheria (Weber, 1988). Max himself was a sickly child and continued to suffer from physical and mental torment throughout his life. As a child in 1866, he became ill with unilateral meningitis (Weber, 1988). The many medical problems that confronted the Weber children led Helene to be an extremely devoted mother.

The Webers were a prominent family of industrialists and civil servants with a considerable amount of political and social connections (Miller, 1963). Both of Max's parents descended from a line of Protestants, who had been refugees from Catholic persecution in the past. Weber's mother's family was originally a part of the Huguenot line, with her ancestors tracing back to Wilhelm von Wallenstein (Kassler, 1988). Weber's paternal grandfather had been a prosperous linen dealer in Bielefeld, where the family had moved after being driven from Catholic Salzburg because of their Protestant beliefs (Coser, 1977). While one of the sons took over to expand the business, another, Weber's father, went into politics.

Max's mother, Helene Fallenstein Weber, was born in 1844 to Georg Friedrich and Emilie Fallenstein. Her father, who descended from a long line of schoolteachers and had been a teacher himself, fought in the war of liberation against Napoleon and then settled down to a life of a Prussian civil servant. Helene was the youngest of four girls. She was a very religious woman, a Calvinist, who desired to become closer to God and placed all of her confidence in Him (Weber, 1988). In her mind, the physical aspect of marriage was a heavy sacrifice and a sin that was justified only by having children. This belief led Helene to desire becoming old so that she would be relieved of this "duty." Her husband, however, did not share Helene's intellectual and religious interests (Weber, 1988). The senior Weber, a politician, was most attentive to his political and social life, which caused a great deal of tension in his marriage.

The senior Max Weber was born in 1836 to Karl August and Lucie Wilmans Weber. He married Helene in 1863 and in 1869 began an active career in politics. He was a lawyer, a Berlin municipal councilor, at times a member of the German parliament, later a member of the Prussian House of Deputies, a member of the National Liberal Party, and well connected to eminent intellectual, industrial, and political figures in Berlin (Weber, 1988; Hadden, 1997). As a person very much a part of the political "establishment," the senior Weber enjoyed indulging himself and leading a life of leisure. His self-satisfied, pleasure-loving, and shallow life was fairly typical of German bourgeois politicians.

The Webers moved to Berlin in 1869 and settled in an upscale suburb (Charlottenburg) favored by academics and politicians. The Weber household entertained a number of notables from Berlin society. Among the houseguests whom Weber met at a young age were the historians Heinrich Treitschke, Heinrich von Sybel, Wilhelm Dilthey, and Theodor Mommsen.

The intellectual and political people who came to visit the Weber home served as an influence on Max. Weber learned to believe that three great recent developments had occurred in Germany: that Germany had become a national state rather than a series of principalities, duchies, and kingdoms; that rapid industrialization was good; and that German imperialism had become a part of state policy (Miller, 1963). Unfortunately, his parents' marriage was showing obvious signs of trouble and increasing tension, which did not go unnoticed by the children. Weber's mother, with her strict religious commitments and Calvinist sense of duty, was in direct opposition with his father's hedonistic ethic.

Initially, the Bohemian lifestyle of his father was more attractive to the junior Weber. Father and son enjoyed each other's company and would often be found drinking and socializing with others. They also enjoyed duels. Later on, however, Max became closer to his mother's approach to life. Having parents with such diversity in temperament will eventually cause a great deal of strain on Max's mental well-being.

Weber's Education

As a student, Max received an orthodox, mainly classical education (Macrae, 1974). He was a good student, but his teachers complained about his lack of respect for their authority and his lack of discipline. On the plus side, Weber was an avid reader, who by the age of fourteen was writing essays with references to Homer, Virgil, Cicero, and Livy. He had mastered an extensive knowledge of Goethe, Spinoza, Kant, and Schopenhauer before he entered college (Coser, 1977).

In 1882, at age eighteen, Weber entered the University of Heidelberg. Although intellectually prepared, Max was thin and socially shy. His shyness quickly disappeared when he joined his father's dueling fraternity. He became very active in dueling and drinking with his mates and can best be described as "one of the boys." Drinking large quantities of beer with his fraternity brothers and proudly displaying dueling scars on his ever-expanding body had transformed Weber into a heavy-set Germanic boozer eager to take up an intellectual conversation or dueling challenge.

Identifying with his father's lifestyle was not limited to the realm of leisure. Weber had also chosen law as his academic pursuit. Despite his heavy partying, Max managed to maintain high grades and expanded his studies to economics, medieval history, and philosophy. After three terms at Heidelberg, Weber left for military service in Strasbourg.

During his time in Strasbourg, Weber came under the influence of his uncle, the historian Hermann Baumgarten, and his uncle's wife Ida, Helene Weber's sister. The Baumgartens became a second set of parents for Max, and their influence on his development would be instrumental in shaping the course of his future. Hermann treated Weber more as an intellectual peer compared to his father, who patronized him. Weber's own letters testified to the fact that Baumgarten was his main mentor and confidant in matters of politics and academics. His aunt Ida was a spiritually devoted Calvinist, who, contrary to Max's mother, was able to spark Weber's interest in religious readings. He began to appreciate the values and beliefs of his mother through the actions of his aunt. Weber even began to view his father as an amoral hedonist.

Weber's own moral behavior could be questioned when it becomes known that his first love was his cousin, Emmy, the Baumgartens' daughter. His engagement to her lasted six tumultuous years. Emmy suffered from frail health both physically and mentally and was often confined to a sanitarium. Emmy was a lovely young woman, but she had inherited the nervous problems of her mother and grandmother which caused exhaustion and melancholia (Weber, 1988). After years of agonizing guilt, Weber ended the engagement.

With the completion of his military service, Weber returned to his parents' Berlin home, in the fall of 1884. His father wished to separate Max from the influence of the Baumgartens. The senior Weber provided financial support for Max while he attended graduate school at the University of Berlin. Except for one term at the University of Goettingen and short periods of further military service, Weber stayed at his parents' home for the next eight years. He developed a greater understanding of his mother and came to resent his father's intimidating behavior toward her.

Weber's doctoral thesis, *History of Commercial Societies in the Middle Ages*, an analysis of the impact of legal regulations on economic activities, was successfully defended in 1889. His tireless work habits allowed for the completion of his postdoctoral thesis (a requirement for a university appointment), *The Agricultural History of Rome in Its Relation to Public and Private Law* (Macrae, 1974). Weber became a lawyer and started teaching at the University of Berlin. In 1893, he became professor of economics at the University of Freiburg, moving from there to the chair of economics at Heidelberg, where he succeeded the renowned economist Karl Knies (Martindale, 1981).

Max and Marianne (Schnitger) Weber

Max Weber suffered continuous mental torment throughout his adolescence and into his twenties. He had become closer to his mother and learned to detest his father. Weber's inner turmoils and struggles all seemed to dissipate by 1893 when he married Marianne Schnitger, the twenty-two-year-old daughter of a physician (a cousin on his father's side). Marianne was born in Oerlinghausen on August 2, 1870. She was a very intellectual young woman who wanted to develop her own path in life, something that was not encouraged in rural areas. Here, the women were usually trained in domestic skills (i.e., cooking, sewing).

Marianne was most supportive of Weber's career and hosted many prominent intellectuals of the day in Heidelberg, just as Max's parents had in the Berlin of his youth. Max and Marianne enjoyed an intense intellectual and friendly relationship—but it appears that the marriage was never consummated. The prominent psychologist Sigmund Freud treated Max for impotency. Sexual fulfillment came to Weber only in his late forties, in an extramarital affair (Coser, 1977). Max and Marianne did, however, adopt his youngest sister Lily's four young children after she committed suicide (Weber, 1988).

From 1893 to 1897, Weber was a young teacher and politician. He was nervously irritable at times and overloaded himself with teaching assignments and lectures and other tasks that left little free time for leisure (Weber, 1988). He reported for the Evangelical-Social Congress, joined the Pan-German Union, was a professor of economics (1894) and a professor of political science (1896), and declined to run for election to the Reichstag (1897) because he was interested in pursuing other things (Weber, 1988).

In July 1897, a major fight broke out between Max's parents. His mother wished to go on vacation alone to see her children, but his father wanted to join her and supervise the trip. He was jealous of all the close relationships that his wife had with others. When the family was all together, Max lashed out at his father and sided with his mother. Max accused his father of treating his mother unjustly and cruelly, and kicked his father out of his home. The two never reconciled, and his father died the next month (Weber, 1988).

As one can imagine, this dramatic event led to more psychological problems for Max, who then suffered a series of nervous breakdowns. He resigned from the Pan-German Union and from teaching. Weber also suffered from insomnia, a sleeping disorder. He was institutionalized for a brief time in a sanitarium and was treated by a number of specialists, but to no avail.

It took over five years for him to recover. During this period, Weber lived as a private scholar in semi-seclusion in Heidelberg. Weber's colleagues encouraged him to write about the university's restoration, which sparked his interest in writing again. Unexpectedly, in 1903, Weber became co-editor of the *Archiv fuer Sozialwissenschaft*, which became the leading social science journal in Germany. His editorial duties allowed him to reestablish contacts with academic colleagues and German socialites that he had lost during the years of his illness. He resumed his teaching duties during World War I.

In 1904, Weber delivered his first lecture in six and a half years while on a visit to the United States, a trip that aided his recovery and left him with an enduring fascination with America. In the States, Weber witnessed a clear example of secular capitalism that was so profound it would influence his writings on economics and religion. His former colleague from Goettingen, Hugo Muensterberg, then at Harvard, invited him to read a paper before the Congress of Arts and Sciences in St. Louis. The lecture Weber delivered was on the social structure of Germany.

Between the years 1892 and 1905, Weber composed a series of essays and speeches that, according to Seidman (1983), addressed the failure of German idealism. These works dealt with the social and economic conditions in eastern Germany and revealed Weber's material-ist orientation. Seidman provides as evidence the strong influence of Marxist writings, Weber's examination of the changing economic foundations of Prussian political and cultural hegemony, and the political tone of the essays aimed to discredit the Prussian Junker class by means of a materialist critique. By utilizing a materialist analysis, Weber argued that recent historical devel-opments pointed to the inevitable triumph of industrial capitalism and the bourgeoisie as the future of Germany. The Junkers are viewed as a historically obsolete, economically declining, and politically dangerous class with no value to Germany's future. In 1904 and 1905, Weber would actively attempt to politicize the German bourgeoisie.

As a note of historic relevance, in the 1870s Germany was unified under the controlling authority of Prussia, which implied the political and cultural dominance of the Prussian Junker class. The Junkers were originally a landed aristocracy. They had appropriated the peasants' land and were actively engaged in the economic affairs of the state. Eastern Germany was charac-terized by extremely large land estates organized along the lines of a feudal-manor economy. Since the Junkers' economic livelihood was directly tied to the productive side of the estate, the development of industrial and commercial capitalism was a major threat to their existence. The survival of the Junkers was dependent upon control of the economic sector.

Weber maintained that the spirit and practice of German liberalism never disengaged itself from the ideological hegemony of Prussian conservatism. Consequently, industrial capitalism in Germany was not founded upon the independent rationality of individualism operating in a competitive open market system, but rather through the controlling power of the state, with its policy of state enterprises, protectionism, and cartelization, which functioned as the guiding mechanism of economic progress (Seidman, 1983).

His many writings and speeches on social and economic organizations, religion, science, and politics rarely appeared as books during his lifetime. Some of them were inspired by the social currents of the time, while many others were historical in character. Weber's works gradu-ally found their way into English translation. A complete listing of his works in English would take up a great deal of space; thus, a brief mention of his most significant publications is provided below.

The Webers' trip to America seemed to inspire Max, as his intellectual output was aston-ishing. In 1905, his classic *The Protestant Ethic and the Spirit of Capitalism* was published. In this work, Weber used religion, on an academic level, to explain why capitalism took place in some parts of the world and yet failed to take hold in other parts. Weber published his studies of the world's religions in a global-historical perspective. These include *The Religion of China: Confucianism and Taoism* (1916), *The Religion of India: The Sociology of Hinduism and Buddhism* (1916–17), and *The Sociology of Religion* (1921). At the time of his death, Weber was working on his most important work, *Economy and Society*.

Before World War I, the Webers' home in Heidelberg had regained its status as a center of bourgeoisie and intellectual gatherings. When the war broke out, Weber, in accord with his nationalist convictions, volunteered for service. As a reserve officer, he was commissioned to run the nine military hospitals in the Heidelberg area. Initially, Weber felt the war was good for Germany, because it would help to unite it. He then became the first German (of any sociopolitical position) to oppose it. He criticized the ineptness of German leadership and was particularly enraged by the increasing reliance on submarine warfare, which, he prophesied, would bring America into the war and lead to the eventual defeat of Germany.

In the last few years of his life, Weber became increasingly political. He wrote a number of major newspaper articles on politics, was a founding member of and active campaigner for the newly organized Deutsche Demokratische Partei, and served as an adviser to the German delegation to the Versailles peace conference. Proposals to make him a candidate for the presidency of the Republic failed. In October of 1919, his mother Helene passed away. The following year, on June 14, 1920, Max Weber died of pneumonia.

INTELLECTUAL INFLUENCES

Max Weber had a thirst for knowledge and learning. He read the works of, and was influenced by, many that came before him. As an adolescent, he read Greek and Latin classics: Homer, Virgil, Cicero, and Livy. Homer was a favorite of Max's because of the great naturalness with which all the actions were related. Weber enjoyed Homer because he wrote stories in which he did not present a chain of successive actions but describes the origin and the calm sequence of actions (Weber, 1988). Weber's concept of *social action* would be influenced by Homer. Significant influences on Weber's works were supplied by the ideas of Marx, Nietzsche, and especially Kant and the neo-Kantians.

Friedrich Nietzsche and Karl Marx

The influence of both Nietzsche and Marx on Weber is especially evident in his sociology of ideas and interests. Weber believed that material and ideal interests directly govern individual conduct. Even world images are a product of created ideas one has. Social action is governed by the dynamic of individual interests. Weber placed greater significance on ideas than either Nietzsche or Marx, but he was affected by Marx's notion that ideas were expressions of public interests and served as weapons in the struggle of classes and parties (Coser, 1977).

Weber's historic materialistic orientation reveals a strong Marxist influence, and his theories of stratification and economic behavior have their roots in Marxian theory. They both agreed that modern methods of organization increased the effectiveness and efficiency of production and that this new rationalized efficiency threatens to dehumanize its creators. However, Weber believed that alienation, the negative side of rationalization, was not limited to capitalistic social systems and instead would be found in all social systems, including socialism. Weber did not agree with Marx that the economic order was solely determined by the class struggle and the owners of the means of production. Instead, Weber emphasized that the character of political power and the effect of the military were also important factors in determining power relationships. Weber states that the charismatic leader as well as the economic producer were the engines of history (Miller, 1963). Additionally, *The Protestant Ethic and the Spirit of Capitalism* is, in part, a reaction to the Marxist metaphysical assumption that all the events of civilizations are reducible to a single cause, namely, the economic order (Kasler, 1988). Weber, like many of the intellectuals of his time, believed that Marx's economic theory was superficial and misleading because of his its failure to include such social aspects as religion, politics, and law (Poggi, 2006). Marx's historical method had an impact on Weber as well, though he used it as a *heuristic* principle.

Weber was aware of Nietzsche's analysis of the psychological mechanisms by which ideas become rationalizations utilized in the service of private aspirations or power and mastery. Notions of *disenchantment* and *charisma*, though not directly tied to Nietzsche, were elaborated by Weber with the assistance of powerful stimulation from the author of *Beyond Good and Evil*. Weber's personal ethic of heroic stoicism was also inspired by Nietzsche. As Coser (1977) states, "There was much of *Zarathustra* in Wax Weber" (p. 250). Weber shared with Nietzsche a view that objective reality was something that could not be grasped by the human mind because of individual experiences, histories, and values (Weber, 1978b). As we shall see with the discussion of *values and value relevance*, Weber argued that each person brings his own interpretation to the particular experience or observation that is based on the lens of perception that is unique to each person up to that particular point in time (Weber, 1978b). Nietzsche and Weber were both worried about the future of humanity and warned that the twentieth century would be filled with horror and tyranny.

As alluded to earlier in this chapter, Weber's historic materialistic orientation reveals a strong Marxist influence. His theories of stratification and of economic behavior have their roots in Marxian economics and sociology. Weber shared Marx's contempt for the abstract mystifications of the German idealistic philosophical tradition. Despite the fact that Weber came to regard Marx's economic interpretation of history as overly simplified, he remained respectful of Marx's intellectual prowess. Weber saw in Marxian revolutionary ideology the articulation of democratic ideals. Weber instructed his Munich students that all contemporary scholars owed a debt to the brilliance of Nietzsche and Marx. A large amount of Weber's work was influenced by these two brilliant thinkers.

Kant and the Neo-Kantians

Because of his feelings about the bourgeois, Weber became fascinated with the neo-Kantian movement. During the last half of the nineteenth century (the "Back to Kant" movement began in the 1860s), neo-Kantianism was considered to be the secularized modern scientific methodology, or new process of casual investigation in Germany (Eliaeson, 2002). Neo-Kantianism was a broad cultural movement focused on an intellectual critique of the currents of positivism, naturalism, and materialism which followed the aftermath of the decline of German idealism. In opposition to the viewpoint that deterministic currents of materialism and collectivist idealism dictated human behavior, the neo-Kantians affirmed the autonomy of individuals. In the tradition of Kant, the neo-Kantians assumed a critical posture toward all institutions, cultural forms, and traditions that suppressed autonomy (Seidman, 1983). The neo-Kantians, then, became critical of social domination, which in the eyes of many democrats provided the ethical and idealist underpinnings of a repressive government. "Weber tried to synthesize the Kantian and neo-Kantian, and idealistic and neo-idealistic tradition in Germany" (Martindale, 1981:377).

Weber strongly identified with the neo-Kantian movement. His Germany had a highly developed industrial economy, with a political structure dominated by the semifeudal values of Prussian conservatism, patriarchal authoritarianism, and a highly developed formal legalism.

The middle classes prospered economically while maintaining political indifference. The working class was completely excluded from the decision-making process. Weber was not happy maintaining the status quo and resented the continued political dominance of the Junkers. To Weber, the Junkers were the caretakers of the feudalistic traditions that hampered the emergence of a truly modern bourgeois class. Weber proposed a unified Germany where all people, including the working class, worked together toward the German national mission. He demonstrated in great detail the advantages of the rational, methodical ethic of work, which is the very foundation of the spirit of capitalism. Rational capitalism, to Weber, was an economic miracle.

He maintained a commitment to a critical and formal rationalism, moral individualism, and liberal-democratic values, ideas that are consistent with neo-Kantian beliefs. From the ideas of Friedrich Naumann—who stressed that the renovation of German liberalism can only occur if the bourgeois-liberal elements recognize that the workers must form the basis of future liberal organization—Weber conceived of the Protestant social reform movement.

The antipositivistic, neo-Kantian influence of thinkers like Rickert is seen in Weber's belief that reality is not reducible to a system of laws. He believed that no body of laws can exhaust a science of culture, nor can one ever expect to achieve complete predictability, since prediction is successful only within limited or closed systems. Society and culture are a result of an ongoing *process*, and consequently, history is never predetermined; it moves toward unknown ends. Weber felt that there could be no objective ordering of the historical process (Mommsen, 1989). He regarded "historicism" as a "narrow-minded patriotism of the field" (Kasler, 1988:9). In response, Weber came to utilize the "ideal type" methodology to study society.

INVESTIGATION AND APPLICATIONS OF WEBER'S CONCEPTS AND CONTRIBUTIONS

Max Weber is considered one of the "founding fathers" of sociology:

> Weber was a man of enormous scholarly ambition, sporadic and volcanic energy, and wide learning. As a result, a great deal that he intended to complete, fill out, or refine was left in a kind of chaos of articles, treatises, schema, lecture notes transcribed by students, and so on.... No man should be condemned merely for attempting in the intellectual sphere more than he could actually accomplish (Macrae, 1974:4–5).

His works are complex, varied, and subject to many interpretations.

Verstehen

Weber recognized that sociologists had an advantage over natural scientists in that they possessed the ability to *understand* the phenomena under study. Natural scientists cannot gain a similar insight of the behavior of an atom or a chemical compound. The German word for understanding is *verstehen*. Weber's sociology is primarily interpretative based on *verstehen*. He believed that sociologists must look at the actions of individuals and examine the meanings attached to these behaviors. For example, understanding *why* an individual says something—what meanings did they attach to the situation? Weber was interested in action and meaning; he thought it was important to understand how people give meaning to their actions. Today, this goal is similar to techniques such as interviewing, focus groups, or ethnographic observation (Garner, 2000).

In its easiest translation, according to Weber, *verstehen* is a rational way to understand and study the world. His theoretical use of the term *verstehen* underscores some of the basic problems with his methodological approach. As Burger (1976) indicates, Weber was neither very sophisticated nor very consistent in his methodological pronouncements. Weber employed a series of definitions of *verstehen*:

1. *deuten*, generally translated as "interpret";
2. *sinn*, generally translated as "meaning";
3. *handeln*, concrete phenomenon of human behavior, or "action";
4. *verhalten*, a broad term referring to any mode of "behavior."

Weber's use of the term *verstehen* was common among German historians of his day and was derived from a field of study known as *hermeneutics* (Pressler and Dasilva, 1996). The German tradition of *hermeneutics* was a special approach to the understanding and interpretation of published writings. The goal was not limited to merely understanding the basic structure of the text, but the thinking of the author as well.

Utilizing this approach, for example, in his studies on the relationship between religion and capitalism allowed Weber to learn what Hebrew prophets thought about God, or how Calvinists wrestled with the implications of predestination, by reading the words of Isaiah and Calvin (Garner, 2000).

Critics of the *verstehen* method claim that it is little more than "intuition" and that it represents a "soft," irrational, subjective research methodology. Weber vehemently denied this criticism and countered that *verstehen* was a rational procedure of study involving systematic and rigorous research. In fact, Weber's very definition of sociology includes the *verstehen* approach. He describes sociology as a science concerning itself with the interpretive understanding of social action and thereby providing a causal explanation of both the course and consequence of such behavior (Swedberg, 1998).

Weber's concept of *verstehen* is still utilized today by both academics and laypersons. Certainly, each of us tries to understand why people act the way they do. This is especially important with loved ones. A simple comment on your part may lead to a surprising reaction on the part of another. The person you have recently started to date suddenly stops texting or calling you. Why? Your mind wanders to any number of possible explanations—did I do something wrong; did something happen to her; did she lose her phone; is she breaking up with me; or is her phone dead and she forgot her charger? The interpretative approach is popular with social scientists, who are interested in understanding "why" certain behaviors occur. Potentially, it allows for a great deal of insightful academic information into the character of human behavior.

The hermeneutic approach to verstehen becomes even more complicated, and perhaps more fruitful. For example, did the author of this text actually have specific people in mind when he used the example of dating someone new and wondering about the meaning of a sudden end of texts from the loved one? Or was it just a simple example that seems applicable to the lives of students? There are definitely occasions when authors incorporate "hidden" messages in their texts. These messages have little or no meaning to most readers, but others may put "the pieces together." A number of people have long speculated that there are hidden meanings in *The Da Vinci Code*. For example, what is the "Holy Grail"? Does it represent the bloodline of Jesus? Even the 2006 court case that surrounded *The Da Vinci Code* involved hermeneutic intrigue. Peter Smith, the High Court judge who presided over the copyright infringement suit brought by authors (Baigent, Leigh, and Lincoln) of the nonfiction book *The Holy Blood and the Holy Grail* against the publisher of Dan Brown's best-selling *The Da Vinci Code*, encoded a message in his 71-page judicial decision. The message read, "Jackie Fisher who are you Dreadnought"—a reference to Admiral Jackie Fisher, who developed the battleship *HMS Dreadnought*. Judge Smith has a fondness for Admiral Fisher and wanted to honor him. A sequence of italicized letters was sprinkled throughout the text, with the first ten spelling out "Smithy code." Justice Smith added a typographical error deliberately to "create further confusion" (*BBC News*, 2006). London lawyer Dan Tench cracked Smith's code and reported it to *The London Times*. When asked about it, Smith said he inserted the code "for my own pleasure" (*BBC News*, 2006).

The lesson to be learned from the hermeneutic approach to verstehen is that sometimes there are hidden messages to be found "in between the lines." Will someone write about you without using your name directly? What do you think?

Social Action

The techniques of *verstehen* and hermeneutics help sociologists to explain social action. Weber believed that human action cannot be regarded as mere reactions to stimuli. To understand social action, we need to comprehend the images that the actors are bearing in their minds (Lachmann, 1971). Weber was concerned with understanding the reasons behind the actions of actors. "When social actors go about their affairs they are typically pursuing certain ends, and they pursue those ends through the deployment and means which, they conceive, will be effective in delivering the ends they seek" (Hughes et al., 1995:137). Weber put forth that people have goals and certain expectations before they take actions toward these goals. This affects choices of action. Weber argued that this explains why actors' values are important when trying to understand courses of social action.

Weber conceived of sociology as a comprehensive science of *social action*. His initial theoretical focus was on the subjective meaning that humans attach to their actions in their interactions with one another within specific historical contexts. By *action*, Weber meant meaningful, purposive behavior. Weber envisioned the study of society as the study of *social action* among humans. This perspective is in complete contrast to Durkheim's view of society as external structures that function apart from human purpose and will.

Weber treated the individual action as the basic unit, as an atom. He believed that sociology should reduce concepts to the understanding of action. Social acts are created by the actor. If the behavior is oriented toward others, it is a *social act*. *Social action* can be active or nonactive (failure to react). For example, if a construction worker whistles (active action) at a woman who walks by the construction site, but the woman ignores his behavior, she has demonstrated nonactive action. *Social action* can be past, present, or future behavior. Action can be nonsocial if it is oriented solely to the behavior of inanimate objects (e.g., an individual picking up trash at the beach). Active social action causes a reaction, whereas nonactive social action does not involve a reaction.

Social action does have its complications. Actors have subjective meanings that may be unique or different to others. In addition, meanings can change over time (for example, the term "gay" used to refer to feelings of happiness or giddiness; today the term is applied to homosexual behavior). Therefore, Weber believed that in order to fully understand the meaning of action, the researcher must incorporate the sociological method of *verstehen*.

Weber distinguishes among four major types of *social action*: zweckrational, wertrational, affective action, and traditional action. *Zweckrational* can be roughly translated as "technocratic thinking" (Edwards, 1997). It is defined as action in which the means to attain a particular goal are rationally chosen. It is often exemplified in the blueprints of an engineer who builds a bridge in the most efficient manner that allows passage over a body of water. Individuals who pursue a college degree in hopes of attaining a job that provides financial security are exhibiting Weber's zweckrational behavior.

Wertrational, or value-oriented rationality, is characterized by striving for a goal that in itself may not be rational, but that is pursued through rational means. The values come from within an ethical, religious, philosophical, or even holistic context—they are rationally "chosen" (Edwards, 1997). An example would be an individual seeking salvation through following the teachings of a prophet, or living a certain way of life in hopes of reaching "eternal salvation."

Affective action centers on the emotional state of the person, rather than in the rational weighing of means and ends. Sentiments are powerful forces in motivating behavior. Choosing a college strictly because one's girlfriend is enrolled at the same school is an example of *affective action*.

Finally, *traditional action* is guided by customary habits of thought, by reliance on what Weber called "the eternal yesterday" (Edwards, 1997). Many students attend college simply because it is traditional for their social class and/or family to attend—the expectation was always there; it was never questioned.

The central importance of Weber's work on *social action* is his idea that human behavior has become increasingly formally rational over the course of history. "Formal rationality" means careful, planned, and deliberate matching of means to ends; in formally rational action, human beings identify and use means that they believe are most likely to bring about a desired end. "All human beings engage in action, in meaningful behavior, but such behavior is not always formally rational. Only in modern societies does the mode of formal rationality pervade all spheres of action" (Garner, 2000:88). Weber used the term *disenchantment* to illustrate the point that in modern, rational society, certain modes of action once considered magical or miraculous were now easily explained scientifically.

From Weber's viewpoint, purposive rationality is viewed as fundamental for social action (Habermas, 1987). "Weber believed that if individuals are informed about the effects of different kinds of action, they will have a greater capacity to make decisions that are value-oriented but implemented rationally" (Ashley and Orenstein, 1985:210).

Weber's insights into *social action* reveal his initial theoretical focus on the subjective meaning that humans attach to their interactions with one another. People behave (nearly all the time) in a manner that is calculated to meet some sort of desired outcome. *Social action* is behavior directed toward another; all social relationships are mutual to each other. The *values* that people hold play an important role in their relationships. Consequently, understanding *(verstehen)* the values of others comes into play during social interaction. The more one knows about the other (including their values), the more likely their behavior can be predicted. Every individual lives with this reality on a daily basis and is very unlikely to ever change.

Ideal Types

The interpretative approach of *verstehen* and hermeneutics guided Weber's theoretical approach to scientific study of social action. His use of ideal types represents Weber's favorite methodological approach (Symonds and Pudsey, 2006). At its most basic level, an *ideal type* is a concept constructed by a social scientist, based on his or her interest and theoretical orientation to capture the principal features of some social phenomenon. An *ideal type* is essentially a "measuring rod" whose function is to compare empirical reality with preconceived notions of phenomena. *Ideal types* are *heuristic* devices used in the study of slices of historical reality. According to Weber (1958/1915), ideal types allow social researchers to see if particular traits (or the totality) of specific phenomena approximate our construction of that phenomena.

An *ideal type* provides the basic methodology for historical-comparative study. It is not meant to refer to the "best" or to some moral ideal. The problem for comparative method is to get cases that can actually be compared. Weber's solution was the *ideal type*. As he conceived them, *ideal types* are hypothetically concrete creations (personalities, social situations, changes, revolutions, social institutions, classes, and so on), constructed out of their relevant components by the researcher for the purpose of instituting precise comparisons (Martindale, 1981). An *ideal type* is an analytical construct that serves as a measuring rod for social observers to determine the extent to which concrete social institutions are similar and how they differ from some defined measure.

The *ideal type* involves determining the "logically consistent" features of a social phenomenon. The *ideal type* never corresponds to concrete reality but is a description to which researchers can compare reality. An *ideal type* of bureaucracy would be based on the immersion of historical data in order to compare it to some existing bureaucracy. "Ideal capitalism" is composed of four basic features: private ownership, pursuit of profit, competition, and laissez-faire.

To some extent, *ideal types* are like stereotypes. But stereotypes are evaluative concepts, designed to close rather than to open analysis. Finally, *ideal types* are not averages based on some sort of arithmetic computations appropriate only to the investigation of quantitative variations along a single dimension (Weber, 1903). Average Protestants in a given area at a given time may be quite different from "ideal Protestants."

The use of ideal types remains in vogue in a variety of settings today. An ideal type can be applied to specific persons, institutions, or social systems. We can examine the performance of athletes, actors, singers, musicians, and so on in terms of an ideal-type construction. Some of us have constructed an ideal type of a perfect mate. When a nation promotes its socioeconomic political systems, such as democracy, as an ideal type, it is comparing other social systems to its own.

Rationalization

The idea of *rationalization* lies at the heart of Weber's substantive sociology. Weber did not explicitly articulate the idea that the world is becoming increasingly dominated by norms and values of *rationalization*; rather, it was a theme that one must extract from his specific studies. Weber's use of rationality is complex and multifaceted and was used most powerfully and meaningfully in his image of the modern Western world.

Weber believed that Western capitalistic civilization is unique; that it has properties not replicated by any other civilization. A general theme throughout Weber's works was the problem of the nature, causes, and effects of *rationality* on modern society. Only in the West, for example, has science, the most rational mode of thought, become the norm of thought and the guide of behavior. Weber noted that precise knowledge and refined observation appeared in India, China, Babylonia, and Egypt; but Babylonian astronomy lacks a mathematical foundation, Indian geometry lacks the rational proof, medicine was developed in India but without a biochemical foundation, and a rational chemistry was absent everywhere except in the West. China lacked the historic method, Indian political thought had no systematic method or rational concepts, and only in the West had a rational jurisprudence developed (Martindale, 1981).

In his *Protestant Ethic and the Spirit of Capitalism* (1904–05), Weber's description of the contrast between the West and non-West extends to the arts and architecture. In music, for example, polyphonic sounds are widely diffused over the earth, but the rational tone intervals do not appear outside the West. In architecture, only in the West had the pointed arch and cross-arched vault been rationally employed for distributing pressure and creating many kinds of spaces. Further, while printing appears in China, only in the West does a literature designed only for print appear.

From Weber's perspective, the spirit of capitalism involves the rational and calculating pursuit of maximum profit. He argued that only in modern capitalism does the desire for unlimited profit combine with the efficient use of reason (Pampel, 2000). The popular writings of the American Benjamin Franklin revealed his own spirit of capitalism, in that he hated wasted time and wasted money. This belief is easily illustrated in Franklin's belief that since time is money, those who spent time in leisure or relaxation were throwing away money (Pampel, 2000). Weber especially believed that Protestant beliefs encouraged the use of rational decision-making in the pursuit of unlimited profit.

Stephen Kalberg (1980) has identified four basic types of rationality in Weber's work. These types of rationality provided Weber with the basic heuristic tools needed to scrutinize the historical realities of Western and non-Western societies.

The first type is *practical rationality*, which is defined as every way of life that an individual evaluates worldly activity and its effects on that person. It reflects a purely pragmatic and egoistic viewpoint when engaging in daily events. People who exercise *practical rationality* accept given realities and constraints in society and merely calculate the most expedient ways of dealing with the difficulties that they present. This type of rationality is in opposition to anything that threatens to alter the everyday routine.

Theoretical rationality involves a cognitive effort to master reality through such abstract means as logical deduction, induction, and attribution of causality rather than through action. This type of rationality allows individuals to transcend daily realities in a quest to gain enlightenment on such things as the "meaning of life."

Substantive rationality dictates courses of action based on a value system in which individuals' behaviors are limited. This type of rationality is not limited to the West and exists transculturally and transhistorically, wherever consistent value postulates exist.

The final category is *formal rationality*. Courses of action are dictated by universally applied rules, laws, and regulation. This type of rationality is critical for capitalism, for formalistic law, for bureaucratic administration, and so forth; it must be in operation for a rational enterprise to flourish. Universal laws and regulations characterize *formal rationality*.

According to Weber, *rationalization* is the product of scientific specialization and technical differentiation, in other words, a striving for perfection and refinement of the conduct of life (Freund, 1968). Similar to Marx's notion of alienation, *rationalization* as well as *bureaucratization* seemed, for Weber, an inescapable fate for future society. This inescapable notion is captured in Weber's description of future society as an "Iron Cage." Instead of being able to roam and do what one pleases, bureaucracies consist of rational and established rules, and limited activity. These rules reflect the norms and values of society. Weber also noted, however, that rationalization also paradoxically affords individuals a limited degree of autonomy in their social lives (Lowith, 1982). That is to say, if we work within the parameters of the established society, we are free to choose many courses of actions in our pursuit of fulfillment and happiness.

Weber believed society, as a whole, benefited from rational principles. The idea that future society would be closer to an "Iron Cage" than a "Garden of Eden" rests primarily with the growing presence of bureaucratization. Bureaucracy, the engine that runs rational society, would become so omnipresent, Weber predicted, that it would cause great depersonalization for humanity.

Bureaucracy

According to Weber, *bureaucracies* are goal-oriented organizations designed according to rational principles in order to efficiently attain the stated goals. Offices are ranked in a hierarchical order, with information flowing up the chain of command, directives flowing down. Operations of the organizations are characterized by impersonal rules that explicitly state duties, responsibilities, standardized procedures, and conduct of office holders. Offices are highly specialized. Appointments to these offices are rationally made based on specialized qualifications. All of the ideal characteristics of the *bureaucracy* are centered around the efficient attainment of the organization's goals.

In his *Economy and Society,* Weber (1968/1921; 1978) defined the bureaucracy ideal type by these characteristics:

1. Official business is conducted on a continuous basis.
2. Business is conducted in accordance with stipulated rules.
3. Every official's responsibility and authority are a part of a hierarchy of authority.
4. Officials do not own the resources necessary for them to perform their assigned functions, but they are accountable for the use of those resources.
5. Offices cannot be appropriated by their incumbents in the sense of property that can be inherited or sold.
6. Official business is conducted on the basis of written documents.

Weber described *bureaucracy* as an *ideal type* in order to more accurately describe their growth in power and scope in the modern world. He notes that as the complexity of society increases, *bureaucracies* grow. The *bureaucratic* coordination of the action of large numbers of people has become the dominant structural feature of modern societies. It is only through this organizational device that large-scale planning and coordination, both for the modern state and for the modern economy, become possible. The consequences of the growth in the power and scope of these organizations is critical in order to more clearly understand our world.

In his historic examination of the origins of *bureaucracy*, Weber (1978) explains that the modern rational organization could not have been possible without two important developments: the separation of the household from the place of work, and the development of rational bookkeeping. The growth of *bureaucracy* is dependent on the social and economic preconditions that a money economy exists in order to provide payment of officials who work in the bureaucratic administration.

As Perrow (1986) summarizes, Weber's model of bureaucracy contains three groups of characteristics: those that relate to the structure and function of organization; those that deal with means of rewarding effort; and those that deal with protections for the individuals. In regard to the structure and functioning of the organization, Weber states that the business of the organization is conducted on a continuous basis, that there is a hierarchy of offices, and that this hierarchy entails a systematic division of labor. The second group of characteristics, dealing with rewards, addresses the issue of salaries, which are based on rank and what is deemed appropriate by the position one holds. Finally, Weber insisted that the rights of individuals should be protected to prevent the arbitrary use of power.

Weber's (1947) core idea that bureaucracies found within organizations are designed to do something ("purposive activities") has been retained by most organizational analysts. His analysis and definitions of bureaucracy and organization have served as the basis for many other researchers (Hall, 1987).

It would be inaccurate to assume that Weber was a fan of *bureaucracy* just because he viewed it as a necessity in a rational society. Weber noted the dysfunctions of *bureaucracy*: It excludes emotion and personal involvement in favor of rational decision-making, and it has led the modern world into a world that is often depersonalized. Organizations dominated by a bureaucratic framework are also characterized by a hierarchical ranking order of personnel where information flows up the chain of command and directives flow down the chain of command. Operations of the organization are characterized by impersonal rules that explicitly state duties, responsibilities, standardized procedures, and conduct of office holders. Because we all deal with organizations characterized by a bureaucracy and because most of us will work in such an environment, the applicability of Weber's notions of rationalization and bureaucracy are quite relevant.

Perhaps the best illustration of the relevancy of Weber's concepts of rationalization and bureaucracy comes from George Ritzer and his description of the McDonald's fast-food restaurant chain as presented in his critically acclaimed book entitled *The McDonaldization of Society* (1993, first edition). According to a 2011 *Wall Street Journal* report, there were 33,749 McDonald's restaurants worldwide at the end of 2010 (*UPI*, 2011). The success of McDonald's, Ritzer (2000c) argues, is attributed to the simple formula it offers consumers, workers, and managers: efficiency, calculability, predictability, and control (through the increased use of nonhuman technology).

1. **Efficiency:** Customers walk up to the counter, place an order, receive their food, gather their own utensils, condiments, and napkins, and proceed to a table to dine. Workers are trained to follow steps in a predesigned process, and they are supervised by equally trained managers. The orderly fashion of the entire operation ensures efficiency.
2. **Calculability:** An emphasis on the quantitative aspects of products sold (portion size, cost) and services offered (the time it takes to get the product). For McDonald's, quantity has become equivalent to quality; that is, "a lot of something, or the quick delivery of it, means it must be good" (Ritzer, 2000c:12).
3. **Predictability:** McDonald's prides itself on the idea that its products and services will be the same in all locales at all times. Customers find a certain comfort in knowing that an Egg McMuffin tastes the same in New York, Alabama, or California. Workers and managers behave in predictable ways as well. They follow the corporate rules.
4. **Control through nonhuman technology:** One of the best ways to eliminate human error is to eliminate human decision-making. In an increasing number of ways, machines have replaced humans, for example, the soft drink dispenser that shuts itself off when the cup is full, the French fry machine that rings and lifts the basket out of the oil when the fries are crisp, the preprogrammed cash register that eliminates the need for the cashier to calculate prices, and so on.

According to Ritzer (2000c), the McDonaldization process reveals a fifth idea/principle, the "irrationality of rationality." That is, McDonaldized systems tend to have a negative effect on the environment and dehumanize the world. Ritzer points out that in a McDonald's type of systems, the pursuit of rationality often leads to irrational consequences. For example, the need for the "perfect" potato for its French fries has led to the creation of huge farms in the Pacific Northwest that produce potatoes that rely on the extensive use of chemicals. Furthermore, the need to produce the perfect fry means that much of the potato is wasted, with the remnants either fed to cattle or used for fertilizer. The underground water supply in the area of these farms now contain high levels of nitrates, which may be traceable to the fertilizer and animal wastes (Ritzer, 2000c).

Ritzer's concept of the *McDonaldization of Society* has inspired economists to establish the "Big Mac Index." The "Big Mac Index," also known as "Burgernomics," is based on the theory of purchasing-power parity (PPP), the notion that a dollar should buy the same amount in all countries (*The Economist*, 2011). The concept goes as follows:

> The exchange rate between two countries should move towards the rate that equals the prices of an identical basket of goods and services in each country [in this case] the basket is a McDonald's Big Mac, which is produced in about 120 countries. The Big Mac PPP is the exchange rate that would mean hamburgers cost the same in America as abroad (*The Economist*, 2011).

The PPP would compare prices of the meal (bread, vegetables, meat, etc.), labor, rent and advertising, and monetary exchange rates. Utilizing the "Big Mac Index," *The Economist* (2009) provides us with this analysis: If the cost of a Big Mac is $3.54 in the United States, it would be $5.75 in Switzerland, $5.74 in Norway, $3.39 in Brazil, $2.36 in Mexico, and $1.44 in South Africa. Interestingly, *The Economist* introduced a companion to the Big Mac Index via the "Tall Latté Index." The idea is the same, except that the Big Mac is replaced by a cup of Starbucks coffee, acknowledging the global spread of the overly rationalized coffee chain.

The concepts of rationalization and bureaucracy described by Weber and expanded upon by Ritzer seem to be applicable to a growing number of businesses and organizations. The term "Megachurches," or "McChurches," has been used to described the open auditorium-style churches where thousands of people attend service each weekend. McChurches are characterized by McPastors, who preach sermons that reassure McParishioners and utilize techniques that emphasize the "experience" of going to church rather than promoting a solid doctrine. Mood lighting, candles, scents, comfortable furniture, emotionally affirming music, and positive sermonettes are characteristics of the McChurch (Gospel-driven Disciples, 2011).

When the new de Young Museum opened in San Francisco in 2005, it was described as "modern" or "postmodern" by some critics and patrons of art, but it has also been described as an example of McArchitecture by others (della Cava, 2005).

Willis, Mastrofski, and Weisburd (2004) describe the policing technique of COMPSTAT (short for Computer Statistics or Comparative Statistics) as an example of the McDonaldization of policing. COMPSTAT reinforces certain traditional features of police bureaucracy but emphasizes its accountability mechanism, persistence of bureaucratic features-functional specialization, formalization, routine, and uniformity. There seems to be a movement to "McDonaldize" all organizations. Ritzer (2000c) concludes,

> Fast-food restaurants...have been heavily McDonaldized, universities moderately McDonaldized, and mom-and-pop grocers only slightly McDonaldized. It is difficult to think of social phenomena that have escaped McDonaldization totally, but some local enterprise in Fiji may yet be untouched by this process (p.19).

Predictably, McDonald's Corp. is not pleased with the popularity of Ritzer's portrayal of its chain of restaurants; they are especially upset that the word "McJob" appears in the dictionary—defined by *Merriam-Webster* as "a low-paying job that requires little skill and provides little opportunity for advancement." In response to the negative image of its restaurant practices, McDonald's Corp announced on April 19, 2011, "National Hiring Day" as it sought to recruit 50,000 full- and part-time employees. McDonald's announced in a press release that about 40% of the company's staff started out in the lower-level positions before being promoted to management positions. Undoubtedly, McDonald's is not happy with headlines like that of the *Southern Business Journal*, which read, "Need a McJob? McDonald's Hosting National Hiring Day April 19" (*The Southern Business Journal*, 2011).

Causality

Weber firmly believed in the *multicausality* of social phenomena. He expressed *causality* in terms of the probability that an event will be followed or accompanied by another event. Weber believed that it was not enough to simply record events as historians do; rather, sociologists should report the reasons for and the meanings behind the action taken by the participants. Thus, Weber believed in both historical and sociological *causality*.

The notion of predicting human behavior is generally viewed as a difficult task, especially considering the many social influences and near limitless potential courses of action open to individuals. But Weber (1958/1904) argued, for example, that human action is generally very predictable, except in the case of the "insane." Humans enjoy routines and regular courses of action. They like the "feeling" of freedom, but even their leisure time arises precisely when it has been rationally calculated to fit their schedule.

Most researchers would agree that attaining *causal* certainty in social research is impossible. Weber believed that the best that can be done is to focus sociological theories on the most important relationships between social forces, and to forecast from that theory in terms of probabilities. For example, Weber disagreed with Marx's assertion of the absolute primacy of material conditions in determining human behavior. Weber's system invokes both ideas and material factors as interactive components in the sociocultural evolutionary process. He argued that Marx had presented an overly simplified theory that had emphasized just one *causal* chain, the one leading from the economic infrastructure to the cultural superstructure. This, according to Weber, could not adequately take into account the complex web of *causation* linking social structures and ideas.

Weber (1958/1904) attempted to show that the relations between ideas and social structures were multiple and varied, and that *causal* connections went in both directions. While Weber basically agreed with Marx that economic factors play a key role in understanding the social system, he gave much greater emphasis to the influence and interaction of ideas and values on sociocultural evolution.

Weber (1978) maintained that there were three primary topics of *causality*:

1. Human actions cannot be explained in terms of absolute "laws," such as cause and effect.
2. To grasp the meaning of human actions would require a different method from any known to, or required by, practitioners of social science (something beyond positivism).
3. The social scientist's own moral, political, or aesthetic values will enter into her conclusions in a way that those of the natural scientists do not.

Weber's methodological approach is enhanced by his firm belief in the *multicausality* of social phenomena. That multiple social forces affect persons all the time is impossible to argue with; the more variables the researcher can control, or "allow" for, the more likely she is to accurately predict human behavior. Weber firmly believed, however, that "laws" of human behavior are impossible to create. Many sociologists (e.g., critical and postmodern theorists) disagree with Weber's conclusion and strive to create such "laws." This is a debate that will surely continue throughout the third millennium.

Values and Value Relevance

Weber believed that social scientists have a more difficult time than natural scientists in creating "laws" because inevitably the investigator's own values and interests interfere with judgment (Bendix, 1960). Further, he believed that there is no absolutely "objective" scientific analysis of culture or social phenomenon. To illustrate this point, Weber insisted that a *value* element inevitably enters into the very selection of the problem an investigator chooses to study. This phenomenon is referred to as *value relevance*, meaning the very selection reflects the investigator's *values*, because he will most likely study events in which he is already interested. *Value relevance* is extended to the macro level as well, in that the *values* of a society which the researcher is from influences/clouds decision-making and scientific study. In sum, *values*, according to Weber, play a crucial role before, during, and after the social research study.

One might think that Weber felt social scientists should *not* let their personal values influence their scientific research in any way. This is not completely true. While Weber was most adamant that teachers must control their personal values in the classroom, he believed scholars have a perfect right to express their personal values freely in speeches, in the press, and in their research. Students should be presented with the facts; attendees at a conference, scholars interviewed by the mass media or at some other public gathering should expect to hear opinionated comments supported by facts.

It is important to remind the reader that Weber felt social scientists have at least one major advantage over natural scientists, that is, their ability to understand the social phenomenon under study. In regard to human action, researchers can do more than simply record protocols of recurrent sequences of events; they can attempt to understand the motives by interpreting human's actions and words. Unlike the positivists, who insist on scientific, quantitative data to support their theories of human behavior, Weber believed that human behavior could best be understood through *verstehen*. Social researchers have access to the subjective (meaning, motivation, etc.) aspects of action, whereas the natural scientists do not. This schema is consistent with Weber's (1964) definition of sociology as the "science which aims at the interpretative understanding (*verstehen*) of social behavior in order to gain an explanation of its causes, its course, and its effects" (p. 29).

The social scientist is certainly capable of deriving facts from empirical study, but according to Weber (1964), this research cannot tell people what they "ought" to do. An empirical science cannot tell anyone what he "should" do—but rather, what he "can" do—under certain circumstances. Weber (1903–17) believed that the role of the social sciences was to help people make choices among various ultimate value positions. In his view, there is no way of scientifically choosing among alternative value positions; thus, social scientists cannot presume to make such choices for people. "The social sciences, which are strictly empirical sciences, are the least fitted to presume to save the individual the difficulty of making a choice" (Weber, 1903–17/1949:52). That is why Weber is fundamentally at odds with those who argue for a morality based on science. Conversely, one might wonder, if not science, then what other criteria?

Although most contemporary social thinkers would agree with Max Weber that complete objectivity is nearly impossible, if not completely impossible, many have not heeded his advice to keep personal opinion out of the classroom. Weber would most likely encourage professors to offer an opinion if a student asks for it, but most students do not want the personal agendas and biases of professors forced upon them. They want to be educated so that they can form their own educated opinion of matters of social relevance. There are a number of social science professors, including sociologists, however, that feel certain topics (e.g., racism, sexism, ageism, prejudice and discrimination) need to be presented in such a way as to enlighten students on the importance of specific social issues.

Types of Authority

Weber's discussion of authority relations provides another insight into the changing structure of the modern world. He wondered on what basis do men and women claim authority over others? Why do men and women give obedience to authority figures? Weber traced a parallel historical process in forms of authority and organization. He defined *power* as the ability to impose one's will onto another, even when the other objects and offers resistance. *Authority* is legitimate power, power that is exercised with the consent of the ruled. Weber argued that people voluntarily comply with authoritative expectations and directions of those with authority because it becomes embedded within each of us to do so (Garcelon, 2010). Weber's sociological interest in the structures of authority was influenced, at least in part, by his own political aspirations. And although Weber was nearly as critical as Marx of the modern capitalistic system, he was nowhere near as radical. Instead of promoting a proletariat revolution, Weber expressed the need for a gradual change in society rather.

According to Weber, distribution of power and authority is the basis of social conflict. He stated that power is the probability that one actor within a social relationship will be in a position to carry out his own will despite resistance, regardless of the basis on which this probability exists. Whereas power is essentially tied to the personality of individuals, authority is always associated with social positions. Weber also stated that while power is merely a factual relation, authority is a legitimate relation of domination and subjection. In this sense, authority can be described as legitimate power. Authority is a universal element of social structure: it both realizes and symbolizes the functional integration of social systems. If individuals in a given society are ranked according to the sum total of their authority positions in all associations, the resulting pattern will not be a dichotomy, but rather like scales of stratification according to income and prestige (Dahrendorf, 1959).

In every association, the interests of the ruling group (maintenance of the status quo) are the values that constitute the ideology of the legitimacy of its rule, whereas the interests of the subjected group constitute a threat to this ideology and the social relations it covers. Employees obey superiors by custom and for material compensation, but a belief in legitimacy is also necessary. "According to the kind of legitimacy which is claimed, the type of obedience, the kind of administrative staff developed to guarantee it, all the mode of exercising authority, will all differ fundamentally" (Weber, 1978:213). One's relation to power and authority reflects the desire to maintain the social system. Consequently, the dominant seeks status quo, and the subordinate seeks change.

Social class signifies conflict groups that are generated by the differential distribution of authority in imperatively coordinated associations. The elites will always be smaller in number, but more organized. The masses, as implied, will be larger in number, and far less organized. Classes, understood as conflict groups arising out of the authority structure, are in conflict primarily over the issue of power.

Weber uses an *ideal type* as an analytical tool in his discussion of authority relations. Weber proposed that there are three *types of authority* (legitimate forms of domination): rational-legal, traditional, and charismatic. All *types of authority* require an administrative staff characterized by efficiency and continuity (Dronberger, 1971).

Rational-legal authority is based on rational grounds and anchored in impersonal rules that have been legally enacted or contractually established. This *type of authority* has come to characterize social relations in modern societies. This is the *type of authority* found in the United States, characterized by *bureaucracies*. The authority exists in the position that one holds, not in the individual. The professor–student relationship illustrates this point. The professor has complete authority over the student in the classroom (class assignments, tests, term paper requirements, etc.), but no authority in social worlds such as nightclubs, ballgames, and so forth, because his authority is limited to the workplace. As another example, elected officials have the authority to make decisions for the district that they represent. The authority is in the "office," not the individual.

Traditional authority is a dominant type of authority in pre-modern societies. It is based in the sanctity of tradition, of "the eternal yesterday." Here,

> Loyalty is attached to the person of a leader because he serves and is guided by tradition: attendant powers of control are handed down from the past...persons exercising authority are designated according to traditionally transmitted rules...the object of obedience is the personal authority of the individual which is enjoyed by virtue of traditional statues...the group is primarily based on relations of personal loyalty (Dronberger, 1971:305).

Traditional authority is attained through inheritance or it may be invested by a higher author-ity (e.g., religious authority). An example of an inherited *traditional authority* would be monarchies (often referred to as "royalty"). Because of the shift in human motivations, it is often difficult for modern students to conceive of the hold that tradition held in pre-modern societies. There are still some societies ruled by monarchies even as humankind has entered the third millennium.

Charismatic authority rests on the appeal of leaders who claim that they possess extraor-dinary virtuosity. This type of authority is naturally unstable because it only holds up as long as the leader is alive, the leader maintains his or her charisma, and the people believe in the leader's virtuosity. Unlike the *rational-legal authority, charismatic authority* has no roots in anything legitimate or stable. The power *is* with the individual, not the political system. Weber believed that charisma was a revolutionary force. Charisma is by its nature unstable; it exists in its pure form only as long as the charismatic leader lives. In the long run, charisma cannot be routinized; inevitably, the social system must be transmitted into either *traditional* or *rational-legal authority*.

Weber's typology of authority is important for many reasons, but particularly on the fol-lowing two counts. First, he was one of the earliest political theorists who conceives of authority in all its manifestations as characteristic of the relation between leaders *and* followers, rather than as an attribute of the leader alone (Coser, 1977). Second, even though Weber never clearly defined charisma, its importance lies with his sociological approach in the understanding of "why" humans behave as they do.

Weber's analysis of the *types of authority* and the role of power remains a foundation in conflict theory. Modern society is characterized by a *rational-legal authority*. And yet, in a rational-legal authority-based society like the United States, a person can become elected to political office, even the office of the president, because of charismatic charm. This was true for John F. Kennedy in 1960 and Barack Obama in 2008. A number of other politicians are elected because of their charisma as well. And in some cases, people who come from political families may continue the tradition of serving the people.

On a daily basis, each of us is subjected to the authority of others, in some cases to the power of others. In a rational society, it is impossible to escape the authority of others. In all types of societies, people are subjected to the power of others either directly or indirectly. People in democratic nations have rights and privileges, but they must also abide by the legitimate rules of society.

Social Class and Inequality

Power differential is one of the distinguishing characteristics that give rise to differentiated social classes. Weber's description of social class was similar to that of Marx, in that he defined a social class as a category of persons who have a common specific causal component of their life chances. Furthermore, this causal component is represented by economic interests (possession of goods and opportunities for income) and the conditions of the commodity or labor market (Gerth and Mills, 1946). Weber's theory of stratification differed from Marx in that he intro-duced an additional structural component to the formation of class, that of "status group" (Gerth and Mills, 1946).

A classification of this sort is based on consumption patterns rather than the process of production. Members of a status group come to identify one another based on lifestyles and by the social esteem and honor accorded to them by others:

Linked with this are expectations of restrictions on social intercourse with those not belonging to the circle and assumed social distance toward inferiors....A status group can exist only to the extent that others accord its members prestige or degrading, which removes them from the rest of social actors and establishes the necessary social distance between "them" and :us." (Coser, 1977:239)

As Weber came to recognize, those with money, over time, will eventually ascend to the top of the status position in society. Equally true is the reality that the economically poor will almost always find themselves at the bottom of the social prestige ladder. Social stratification, then, will always consist of the "haves" and the "have-nots." There are individuals who bridge the gap between low economic status and yet possess high status (e.g., a priest, a successful community activist, etc.), but this is impossible for an entire social class of low economic status. The inequality that persons experience will be the result of the lack of power due to low economic status and/or low social prestige.

Weber's ideas on social class and inequality continue to assist sociologists today. His attempts to identify and explain the variables that give rise to social class stratification have inspired many social thinkers in this area, especially with regard to the "haves" and the "have-nots" concept. Members of similar social groups (whether it is based on religion, race, ethnicity, social prestige, or economic status) generally create a "we" category in order to identify themselves as a community. Through social interaction and group participation, a sense of "we-ness" is created, where the term "we" becomes an extension of their identity. Sports fans will use the phrase "we won the game." An ethnic group, such as the Irish, might state, "We have long been oppressed by the English." Ethnic and racial groups often attempt to maintain their distinctive "we-ness" (Shibutani and Kwan, 1965). By so doing, external groups come to view the group by their "they-ness" (Rose, 1981). Consequently, by establishing a "we" group, a "they" label is also created. In reality, these "we–they" categories are often similar to the "haves–have-nots" labels. Studies in race and ethnicity relations reveal how members of the dominant, or majority, group (the "haves") utilize prejudice and institutional racism as a means of maintaining power and control over the subordinate groups (the "have-nots"). The subordinate group serves as a scapegoat to be blamed for societal problems.

The Protestant Ethic and the Spirit of Capitalism

"Weber mused, there may be a suppressed political will waiting to be tapped and ignited. Perhaps a piercing intellectual jolt would unleash the stored-up critical energies of German liberalism. The jolt, of course, was the Protestant Ethic" (Seidman, 1983:218).

The Protestant Ethic and the Spirit of Capitalism was Weber's best-known work and marked the beginning of a Weberian sociology of worldview. Weber (1904–05) traced the impact of Protestantism—primarily Calvinism—with the rise of the spirit of capitalism. He investigated a causal relation between Puritanism and the psychological and cultural presuppositions of "spirit" of modern capitalist culture. Paretskaya (2010) states that Weber's analyses of the "spirit of capitalism" is based solely in Puritan terms and assess the quality of new capitalistic systems by the presence or absence of an ethic of asceticism.

Weber came to believe that the *Protestant ethic* broke the hold of tradition when it encouraged men to apply themselves rationally to their work. Calvinism, he found, had developed a set of beliefs around the concept of predestination. Followers of Calvin believed that one could not do good works or perform acts of faith to assure a place in Heaven; either you were among the "elect" or you were not (Edwards, 1997). However, wealth was taken as a sign that you were one of God's "elect," thereby providing encouragement for people to acquire wealth. *The Protestant Ethic* fostered a religious spirit of rigorous discipline, encouraging people to apply themselves rationally to acquire wealth. Protestant asceticism used all its power against the relaxed enjoyment of possessions. It set limits to consumption, especially luxury consumption. It did, however, have the psychological effect of liberating the acquisition of goods from the restrictions of the traditionalist ethic (Weber, 1978).

Capitalism was, in part, a result of the *Protestant ethic*. Capitalism grew from Calvinism. Calvinism stimulated hard work, a determination to succeed, and making money. In Germany, at this time, the Protestants were economically richer than the Catholics. The Catholics believed that those who give away "goods and materials" (charitable contributions of money, clothing, etc.) will be rewarded in Heaven. Since the Calvinists believed that only a select few get into Heaven, they must look for signs of grace to see if they are one of the few chosen. Economic success was seen as the primary sign.

Protestantism succeeded in turning the pursuit of profit as a moral crusade. Ideas such as "time is money," "be frugal," "be punctual" were all in the *spirit of capitalism*. This spirit allowed capitalists to ruthlessly pursue economic riches; in fact, it was their duty. Workers would cling to their work as if it were a life purpose willed by God. *The Spirit of Capitalism* legitimized an unequal distribution of goods as if it were a special dispensation of Divine Providence. Hudson and Coukos (2005) argue that this moral obligation to work hard and accumulate wealth metamorphed over time from a religious to a cultural mandate.

The Protestant Ethic helped to explain the growth of capitalism in the West, but Weber also wished to explain why capitalism did not grow in other societies. He found that several of these preindustrial societies had the technological infrastructure and other necessary preconditions to begin capitalism and economic expansion. The only force missing was cultural encouragement and approval to abandon traditional ways. Weber found that irrational religious systems inhibit the growth of a rational economic system. In China, Confucianism led people to simply accept things as they were. Active engagement in a profitable enterprise was regarded as morally incorrect. Taoism was essentially traditional, with one of its basic tenets being to not introduce innovations. This approach to life did not produce enough tension, or conflict, among members to motivate them to innovative action. In India, structural barriers of the caste system hampered social mobility and tended to regulate most aspects of people's lives. The Hindu religion, with its belief of reincarnation, was completely opposite to the Calvinist belief in predestination. The Hindu merely gains merit for the next life. This idea system failed to produce the kind of people who could create a capitalist, rational economy.

Weber promoted multicausal explanations for any phenomenon, including the rise of capitalism, but it is clear that he felt that the *Protestant ethic* was the most powerful force in fostering its emergence.

Through his brilliant work found in *The Protestant Ethic* and *The Spirit of Capitalism*, Weber demonstrated that certain cultural barriers, especially those based on religion, hampered the growth of a rational economy system. Thus, while the West was experiencing mass industrial growth and enjoying economic wealth, other societies remained less developed. The relevance of this topic is exemplified by the great disparity between the economically rich countries and the developing poor nations. Without a change in socio-political and economic structures, the financially poor societies will never develop their full economic potential and risk further polarization. Many of the poorest nations in the world are found in Latin America and the Caribbean basin (Engerman and Sokoloff, 2006). The majority of the most economically dire nations, however, are found in Africa. Using Gross Domestic Product (GDP) per capita (U.S. dollars) data as the criterion, and starting with the poorest country, the World Bank identifies the ten poorest nations in the world as Democratic Republic of Congo, $300; Zimbabwe, $500; Liberia, $500; Guinea-Bissau, $600; Somalia, $600; Comoros, $600; Solomon Islands (not an African nation, but located in Oceanic), $600; Niger, $700; Ethiopia, $700; Central African Republic, $700 (source: Maps of World, 2008). 24/7 Wall St. (2012) cites data from the World Bank and uses the poverty rate to determine its ranking of the ten poorest countries in the world. Starting with the 10th poorest to the poorest, we find that still most of the poorest nations are found in Africa: Sao Tome and Principe (66.2% poverty rate); Sierra Leone (66.4%); Burundi (66.9%); Madagascar (68.7%); Eritrea (69.0%); Swaziland (69.2%); Democratic Republic of Congo (71.3%); Zimbabwe (72%); Equatorial Guinea (76.8%); and the poorest nation in the world is the Caribbean island of Haiti (77%). The World Bank notes that more than half of Haiti's population lives on less than $1 a day and 80% of the residents live on less than $2 a day. The presence of extreme poverty generally coincides with numerous other social problems, including limited resources, disease, famine, war, lack of quality health care, and low levels of education among its citizens. From a Weberian perspective, it not surprising that the economically poor nations of the world are those that failed to embrace industrialization, or did so much later than societies from the West.

Social Theory

Weber's works are so multifaceted that he influenced the ideas of many others. Not only did he contribute various terms and concepts (still relevant today) and an elaborate methodology, but he also made substantial contributions to *social theory*. Specifically, Weber helped to influence such theories as structural functionalism, conflict, and symbolic interactionism. (Note: Weber did not use these terms; his studies and insights helped to create these *social theories*.)

In the 1920s, after Weber's death, American sociologist Talcott Parsons discovered his work (Macrae, 1974). In the early 1960s, Parsons, partly through a reconsideration of Weber's work, transformed his *structural functionalism* (Schluchter, 1981). According to Parsons, "Weber's thesis was that the development of Western modernity, of the system of modern societies, is not only of universal significance for the history of humankind but has also a specific direction and is in this sense not accidental" (Schluchter, 1981:70).

Conflict theory maintains that the social order that does exist in society is a result of coercion created by the people at the top of the social structure. Conflict theorists particularly emphasize the role of power in maintaining order within society. Weber believed that conflict underlies all social relations and determines power (Dronberger, 1971). Every society at every point is subject to a process of change. The possession of power is a critical element in *conflict theory*. As noted earlier in this chapter, power plays a critical role in Weber's works on the *types of authority*.

Symbolic interactionism is essentially a theory that suggests people interact with one another using symbols, and these symbols come to have meanings. Symbolic interactionists call attention to how social life is "constructed" through the everyday acts of social communication. Communication involves the use of symbols that, when put together, form words. Through the use of symbols such as communication, members of society are able to interact with one another. Effective use of symbols and communication is dependent upon a shared understanding behind the meanings of symbolic interaction. *Symbolic interactionists* have warmly embraced Weber's use of *verstehen*. It was Weber who emphasized that social researchers must comprehend "why" behavior occurred opposed to simply identifying "what" happened. The idea of *verstehen*, or interpretive understanding, is the *interactionists*' guiding principle.

Criticisms

Weber's use of *verstehen* is generally viewed as a subjective approach to the study of human behavior. That in itself is not problematic, especially for those who prefer the interpretative approach; rather, it presents an inconsistency in Weber's otherwise promotion of scientific study. Science, because it promotes objectivity, is generally not receptive to subjective analysis of social phenomenon.

A second criticism of Weber centers on his use of ideal types to describe phenomena. Weber considered ideal types as "logically consistent," but they are often criticized as lacking objectivity and being subject to different interpretations based on who is conducting the research.

Max Weber viewed societies of the West as being dominated by the ideals of rationalization. He believed that the spirit of capitalism was influenced by the Protestant ethic and deemed other religiously based societies as lacking in rationality. Although this represents a version of critical analysis, George Ritzer (2011) argues that Weber lacks a critical theory. Ritzer is assuming, of course, that it is necessary for all social theorists to present a critical analysis of society. It is true that roots of sociology are firmly entrenched in moral reform (which can be viewed as critical analysis), but there is no existing mandate in sociology that social theorists *must* be critical.

Through his use of the *McDonaldization of Society*, Ritzer has demonstrated as clearly as anyone that a rational-based organization, or society, does not always act rationally. In fact, in the pursuit of rationality, many organizations and societies begin to act irrationally. Whereas Weber properly predicted that the forces of bureaucracy would create conditions favorable for an "Iron Cage" scenario, he failed to predict that the pursuit of rationality would come at the cost of human dignity, uniqueness, and independent, creative thinking.

Summary

Max Weber represents a true giant of classical sociological social thought. His contributions and ideas are diverse and intellectually challenging. And yet, grasping the concepts and contributions of Weber is quite insightful and rewarding. Weber studied the cultures of numerous societies; as a result, "Max Weber belongs, not to one particular university, one town, one country: he belongs today, even more than in his lifetime, to the whole scientific world" (Stammer, 1971:3). Furthermore, "In the opinion of some sociologists, Max Weber was the greatest social scientist of the first half of the twentieth century" (Martindale, 1981:389). Weber created the German Association for Sociology in 1909. He formed the starting point for the careers of many major sociologists of the mid- and late-twentieth century, among them Karl Mannheim, Hans Speier, Hans Gerth, Talcott Parsons, Robert Merton, and C. Wright Mills.

A full appreciation of the richness of Weber's work can be gained only through knowledge of his empirical studies, in which the theoretical and methodological concepts (described in this chapter) were combined with a truly extraordinary scholarship to bring historical data into a new and sharper focus. Many of the significant trends in contemporary social science are extensions of work begun by Weber. Among these are stratification theory, the study of bureaucracy and large-scale organization, the study of legitimate authority, the role of power, the sociology of law, the sociology of politics, the sociology of religion, and the sociology of music (Martindale, 1981).

Max Weber, a brilliant thinker, is one of the "Founding Fathers" of sociology. "His *detached concern* for the trials, the tragedies, and the occasional successes of social action made him an as yet unsurpassed master of the art and science of social analysis" (Coser, 1977:260).

Study and **Review** on **MySearchLab**

Discussion Questions

1. Now that you have completed reading the chapter, do you think that the ideas of Nietzsche and Marx or Kant and the Neo-Kantians had a greater impact on the works and ideas of Max Weber? Provide examples and explain why.
2. Weber argued that professors should not present their personal opinions and biases in the classroom and instead rely on presenting a factual account on issues. What do you think? That is, should professors actively try to influence the opinions of students?
3. Each of us deals with bureaucracies on a regular basis. Your college or university is dominated by a bureaucratic system. Describe at least three instances you have had when dealing with bureaucrats at your school. If any of these experiences were negative, explain why. If the experiences were positive, explain what was done properly.
4. How did Weber distinguish between the concepts of "power" and "authority"? Identify someone in your life that has power over you and someone who has authority over you.
5. Using a Weberian perspective, explain the role of religion on the economic system of at least three contemporary societies.

MySearchLab® Connections

MysearchLab is designed just for you. Each chapter features a customized study plan to help you learn and review key concepts and terms. Dynamic visual activities, videos, and readings found in the multimedia library will enhance your learning experience.

 View on **MySearchLab**

▶ Weber's Three Components of Social Class

 Read on **MySearchLab**

▶ Weber, Max. Asceticism and the Spirit of Capitalism.
▶ Weber, Max. Characteristics of Bureaucracy.

CHAPTER 6

Contributions from Women to Classical Social Theory

 Listen to the **Chapter Audio** on **MySearchLab**

Chapter Outline

- Harriet Martineau (1802–1876)
- Beatrice Potter Webb (1858–1943)
- Anna Julia Cooper (1858–1964)
- Ida Wells-Barnett (1862–1931)
- Charlotte Perkins Gilman (1860–1935)
- Jane Addams (1860–1935)
- Marianne Weber (1870–1954)
- The Ladies of Seneca Falls
- Summary
- Discussion Questions

The patriarchal reality of the social structure found in nearly all societies throughout most of human history has negatively affected women in many spheres of social life. This includes premodern academia. As a result, it should come as no surprise that contributions from women to classical social theory were limited. Nonetheless, a number of women have contributed to social theory and social activism, leading to a revised way of thinking about the role of women in society. This chapter provides a brief review of a number of women who deserve recognition for their participation in the formulating of social thought.

The story of sociology is generally a history of men (e.g., Comte, Spencer, Marx, Durkheim, Weber, and so forth) and their contributions to the formation of the field. Missing from most classical social theory books is any significant mention of women and their contributions to social theory. It was as if women were "invisible" from early sociology. Not so coincidently, some of the women to be discussed in this chapter originally received their credit in sociology because they were linked to men in sociology.

The women to be discussed in this chapter are Harriet Martineau (1802–1876), Beatrice Potter Webb (1858–1943), Anna Julia Cooper (1859–1964), Ida Wells-Barnett (1862–1931), Charlotte Perkins Gilman (1860–1935), Jane Addams (1860–1935), Marianne Weber (1870–1954), and Elizabeth Cady Stanton (1815–1902). Stanton is included here partly because of the "uniqueness" she brings to any volume on the discussion of women contributors to social theory, but mostly because it allows for the sociological examination of her wonderful insights into human behavior. Also, discussion of Stanton allows for an introduction to the "Ladies of Seneca Falls" and the first Women's Rights Convention, held in Seneca Falls, New York, in 1848. Because of this convention, Seneca Falls is considered the birthplace of the Women's Rights Movement. The efforts of these women combined with the abolitionist movement of the 1830s led to the development of the feminist movement, sometimes referred to as the "first wave" of feminism. As we shall learn in Chapter 13, there are three waves of feminism. In short, the second wave of feminism began in the 1960s and was influential in the passage of a great deal of legislation designed to assure gender equity, and the third wave of feminism and feminist thought refers to the more recent trend of feminist concern with civil rights, gay and lesbian issues, homelessness, AIDS activism, environmental concerns, and human rights in general.

The women whose recognition in the past was linked primarily to men include Martineau, as Comte's translator; Weber, as the wife of a genius (Max), Webb as Sidney's partner, Addams, as "secular saint"; and Gilman, as the eccentric authors of the publication "The Yellow Wall-Paper" (Lengermann and Niebrugge-Brantley, 1998). These women, however, made significant contributions to sociological thought in their own right.

HARRIET MARTINEAU (1802–1876)

Harriet Martineau was born in Norwich, England, on June 12, 1802. She lived during a period that witnessed the beginnings of modern sociology. Although it is true that she was Comte's translator, she herself was a prominent writer and thinker. She was born in 1802 to Thomas and Elizabeth (Rankin) Martineau and was raised in a strict, but loving, family environment. She was often ill as a child and suffered a number of ailments. She could not taste or smell, and she lost most of her hearing at an early age. Her parents were slow to recognize her hearing disability and for years did not provide her with a hearing-assistance aid that serves as a crude early version of hearing aids today. As a child she enjoyed reading and writing and was a studious person. Her parents generally encouraged her to speak her mind and stand by her sociological beliefs; this was congruent with the English Dissenting tradition (Herbert Spencer). The city of Norwich was prosperous in industry and possessed an intellectual culture that embraced the dissention tradition. Dissenters belonged to a range of Protestant sects—Baptist, Methodist, Quaker, Presbyterian, and Unitarian—that refused to accept Anglicanism, the state religion of Britain, and were thus barred from various civil rights afforded to other citizens such as voting and attending university (Lengermann and Niebrugge-Brantley, 1998). The Martineau family were Unitarians who emphasized the value of education and did not believe in worshiping a God; instead, they encouraged a commitment to meeting social needs. Harriet and her sisters, who were all home-schooled, enjoyed a higher level of education than compared to most British women, but she regretted for her whole life that she was barred from attending a university.

Thomas Martineau was a successful textile manufacturer. He was a Unitarian and a political radical and imparted these beliefs and values to his children (Pichanick, 1980). Thomas was a hard worker and understood that the success of his business was dependent on happy employees who were sharing in the profits of industry. The phenomenon of the "Industrial Revolution" transformed the entire socioeconomic makeup of England, and this was especially true in Norwich. By the 1820s, the Martineau family business and most of the prosperity of Norwich disappeared because of industrialization (Webb, 1960). Harriet took note of these events and came to believe that society was greatly influenced by two variables: politics and economics. "Political economy," the emerging science of economics, as it was known then, became a common topic of conversation in the Martineau family. These experiences would greatly influence Harriet's future writings in social science.

The 1820s were a turbulent period for Martineau: The family fortune was quickly disappearing; an engagement she had ended; all of England was suffering from an economic crisis; her father passed away in 1826; and in 1829, the family business completely collapsed (Lengermann and Niebrugge-Brantley, 1998). Oddly, Martineau became engaged to a second man, a Unitarian minister with "weak nerves." When he collapsed into insanity, Martineau was relieved, and she even refused to visit him in the hospital. He finally died a month later (Hoecker-Drysdale, 1992). The family's new economic reality dictated that Harriet would have to begin working to support herself and assist the family. She lived at home with her mother and began to write fictional tales on economic issues for the *Monthly Repository*. Interestingly, she had published an article anonymously in 1822, "Female Writers on Practical Divinity," in the *Monthly Repository* (a Unitarian journal). In 1830, Martineau produced 52 pieces for the *Repository*, plus a novel, a book-length religious history, and essays for contests sponsored by the Unitarian Association (Lengermann and Niebrugge-Brantley, 1998). She was clearly taking advantage of her Unitarian background in order to get published, but it is hard to fault her for this, as she was establishing her name for future publications.

Present-day critics of Martineau do fault her and point to this high output of mostly general journalistic articles, essays, and commentaries as evidence of her lightweight intellectual status (Adams and Sydie, 2001). Martineau's writings can be defended on at least two fronts (Adams and Sydie, 2001). First, she was writing for a wage; this was her livelihood and she was economically dependent on this income (she did not set out purposely to be an academic writer). Second, she possessed the ability to describe rather difficult subject matters in a more popular style of writing—she was attempting to appeal to an audience that did not necessarily include academia. She wanted to reach the masses. Returning from an inspirational visit to Ireland, financed by the Unitarian prize money she had won, Martineau decided to write a series of short tales illustrating the principles of political economy. After a lengthy and difficult search for a publisher, Martineau's patience and writing would be vindicated. The first volumes of her *Illustrations of Political Economy* (1832) became a runaway bestseller. In these volumes she wrote about the ideas of such people as Adam Smith, David Ricardo, Thomas Malthus, and James Mill. She produced 25 volumes in the following 24 months, each volume of about 33,000 words. By 1834, Martineau's series of short tales was selling at the unbelievable rate of 10,000 per month. She was easily outselling such notable writers of her time as Charles Dickens (Hoecker-Drysdale, 1992).

Martineau's name was now recognizable and she turned her attention toward the creation of a science of society. She visited the United States for two years (1834–1836) and wrote three books about her experience: *Society in America* (1836), *How to Observe Morals and Manners* (1838), and *Retrospect of Western Travel* (1838). Martineau (1836) describes her visit to America as a wonderful experience: She traveled to 20 of the then-24 states; she visited Congress; she had dinner with President Jackson; she liked Americans and they seemed to like her; and she met abolitionist proponents William Lloyd Garrison and Maria Westin Chapman (with whom she maintained lasting friendships). Her hosts on her journey consisted of a roll call of political, intellectual, artistic, and literary leaders of the period, including Andrew Jackson, Ralph Waldo Emerson, James Madison, and William Lloyd Garrison (Yates, 1985). Having written against slavery as early as

1830, Martineau was easily able to identify with the abolitionist cause. *How to Observe Morals and Manners* was her first text on sociological research techniques. She had started the methodological portion of the book before she left for the United States, and then applied and expanded the research strategies in her extensive American field trip. By the end of the 1830s, Martineau was acknowledged as a leading social analyst, which led to a request from her publishers that she become editor of a newly proposed sociology periodical (Hoecker-Drysdale, 1992). She turned them down and instead concentrated of her own writings in sociology and other interest areas.

During the 1840s, Martineau published many books and articles. Among them were *The Hour and the Man* (1841), a fictional account of Toussaint L'ouverture, the black liberator of Haiti; *The Playfellow* (1841), a very popular children's adventure stories; *Life in the Sick-Room* (1844), written after she had recovered from an illness due to gynecological problems; *Letters on Mesmerism* (1845), a controversial book because she promoted mesmerism (hypnotism) and proclaimed how it had helped her recovery; *Eastern Life: Past and Present* (1848), a sociological and religious account of her trip through the Middle East; and *Household Education* (1849), a sociological, pro-family examination of the early socialization process of children (Lengermann and Niebrugge-Brantley, 1998). On a personal note, in 1845, Martineau had purchased land at Ambleside, England, and designed and had built The Knoll, a family farm–type dwelling. She would live there until her death on June 27, 1876.

Martineau's quality production continued through the 1850s. In 1851, she co-authored with friend and philosopher Henry George Atkinson *Letters on the Laws of Man's Nature*, where the authors state, "The mind can be studied scientifically as material reality that forms ideas out of experience. She [Martineau] rejected the idealist thesis that the mind has immanent categories issuing directly from God" (Lengermann and Niebrugge-Brantley, 1998:28). She was promoting her atheism. In 1852, she published *Letters from Ireland*, a book written about her travels throughout Ireland and her analysis of the Irish people. In 1853, she made the contribution to sociology that most students are made aware of, her translation of Comte's six-volume *Positive Philosophy*. Martineau had come to believe that many educated middle-class English people had begun to lose their sense of moral direction during the 1840s and 1850s. Martineau (1853) wrote in the preface of her translation of *Positive Philosophy* that a large number of English people were adrift because ideals of morality were in a state of fluctuation (Vol. I: viii). As Coser explains,

> Harriet Martineau here alludes to the crisis of belief that came to be widespread in the forties. Educated men were increasingly deprived of the kind of certainties that used to be provided by traditional religion. Whereas earlier in the century those who had lost faith were sustained by the utilitarian morality of Bentham and the elder Mill, this alternative was no longer viable for the later generation (1977:121).

In 1855, Martineau became ill again, and this time, fearing her death was imminent, she began writing her autobiography. She recovered but limited her writing to mostly journalistic pieces. On her deathbed at her beloved The Knoll, Martineau (1877) wrote that she had no regrets about her life, and she saw all of humanity advancing under the law of progress.

Significant Contributions to Sociology

Martineau's name usually surfaces as a mere footnote in sociology, and even then, it is usually mentioned because she translated Comte's works into English, but she did more than simply translate Comte's ideas (she actually managed to condense and clarify much of his work); she also wrote about social issues of her time. She traveled to different countries and was able to provide cross-cultural analysis on diverse sets of beliefs (e.g., religion). Martineau was responsible for educating the public on guiding principles of sociology. If Comte is labeled the "father of sociology," it might be proper to label Martineau as the "mother of sociology." Lengermann and Niebrugge-Brantley (2000) refer to her as a "founding mother" of sociology. Martineau shared with her contemporaries a general belief in progress, that human society was constantly moving forward and becoming better. She noted, however, that progress is sometimes interrupted by various crises.

Among Martineau's contributions to sociology was her insistence on defining subject matter methodologically. The subject matter, according to Martineau, should be social life in society. This was especially true in terms of answering the question, "What constitutes a better life for people?" Examination of current living standards would allow the social scientist an opportunity to describe details that would make life better (progress). To this end, Martineau contributed to the change in the "Poor Laws" in England. The laws, which were written in the 1600s, were clearly outdated. Harriett wrote a series of articles designed to educate the parliament and encourage their support to pass the Poor Law Amendment Act of 1834. As it turned out, the new legislation created "poor houses" and did little to improve the lives of the poor (Hoecker-Drysdale, 1992).

In her attempt to create a "science of society," Martineau believed that sociology should be grounded in systematic, empirical observation. Furthermore, in order for the masses to make personal and political decisions that would help enrich their lives, this "science of society" should be made accessible to a general readership. Martineau involved herself in extensive travel, where she began to apply her systematic scientific inquiry to an understanding of society. From the time she first started traveling until she died, Martineau would conduct sociological analysis (Lengermann and Niebrugge-Brantley, 1998).

As a further example of how she attempted to study society methodologically and make it more accessible to the masses, Martineau undertook the task of dividing up its parts. "She outlined studies of the major social institutions, including religion, education, family, arts and popular culture, markets and economy, prison, government, and philanthropy" (Hill, 1991:292). She also attempted to compare studies from different societies. As Michael Hill (1991) states, "Harriett Martineau authored the first systematic methodological treatise in sociology and conducted extended international comparative studies of social institutions" (p. 291).

Martineau believed that any analysis of society must include its morals (cultural values and beliefs) and manners (social interaction). She recommended that nothing should be overlooked in the methodological pursuit of an accurate portrayal of the subject matter. She suggested that data should be sought in such places as cemeteries and prisons. Tombstone inscriptions found at cemeteries reveal the morals of the community in which the dead had resided; and because there is a prevailing moral code of *De mortuis nil nisi bonum* ("Do not speak negatively of the dead"), epitaphs everywhere indicate what were considered good qualities (Martineau, 1838). Studies of prisons are important as they reflect the morals and manners of society that are most important, because those who violate certain norms (morals) will be punished by society and find themselves in prison. In her analysis of America's democratic ideal of social equality, Martineau (1836) noticed an inconsistency in the form of the unequal status of women. She noted that the Constitution guarantees equality and democracy, but not for women. This observation would help create her feminist thinking, especially her analysis of the role of women in relation to the institution of marriage. Martineau would maintain a lifetime commitment to the betterment of women's role in society. Of sociological significance was her article "Female Industry" (1859), which analyzed women's work in Great Britain and concluded with the overall importance of female labor to the national wealth (Lengermann and Niebrugge-Brantley, 1998). Her concern over the enslavement of Blacks is another feature of her work in *Society in America.*

Martineau (1838) speaks of the importance of researchers remaining detached (impartiality) from their subjects and of remaining careful not to impose their own values (an ethnocentric view) onto their study. Martineau seemed to violate this very principle in her study of tombstone inscriptions and the corresponding idea that only good things are said about a person in epitaphs. The point is if the sociologist wants to truly understand the morals and manners of people, one must investigate the "bad" things that people do as well. She did not advocate complete value-neutrality but believed that a researcher's own biases (if any) should be acknowledged in the study. Martineau (1838) felt that the sociologist should try and develop a systematic understanding of the subject in order to better understand the meanings of an activity for the actor (Lengermann and Niebrugge-Brantley, 2000). Sympathy toward the subject is a skill that separates sociology from geology or general statistics. A researcher who fails to understand the meaning of an event that the actor participates in does not gain the full methodological picture (Martineau, 1838). Her approach is similar to Weber's *verstehen* or the Chicago School's use of sympathetic introspection.

Martineau believed that sociology should be a critical and ethical field; that is, it should work toward improving society and pointing out its ills. This is completely in tune with the prevailing theme of the early sociologists as moral reformers. Martineau was not a brilliant writer, nor was she an imaginative genius. But she put forth tremendous energy in recording numerous social behaviors in a variety of social settings. The ability to accurately capture social reality and put it to writing is praiseworthy for anyone. Martineau is truly a sociologist deserving of proper recognition for her contributions to the development of the field.

The relevancy of Martineau's works is evident today in a variety of ways. For one, sociologists still examine a number of social problems as individual entities (e.g., homelessness, poverty, crime, drug abuse, and teenage pregnancy) while finding a way to connect them to the greater social system. Her commitment to scientific methodology remains the hallmark of contemporary sociology. Martineau's belief in progress (even with occasional dips and periods of stagnation) is consistent with nearly every social thinker who embraces the scientific method. Her studies of morals and manners are looked at as values and norms by sociologists today and their significance represents a mainstay in sociological analysis. Throughout her vast number of writings, Martineau was always conscious of being female. She knew that being a woman meant that she had to do things differently from men and she must give voice to the needs of women. She was a feminist ahead of her time.

BEATRICE POTTER WEBB (1858–1943)

Martha Beatrice Potter was born on January 22, 1858, at Standish House, on the edge of the Cotswolds, near Gloucester, England (Webb, 1982). She was the eighth daughter born to Richard Potter, a businessman, and Laurencina Heyworth. Beatrice was four years old when her brother, and male heir, was born; she was seven when he died. Beatrice learned early on in her life the gendered nature of her society. Webb (1926) explains that she lived "in the shadow of my baby brother's birth and death" (p. 58). Gender issues were a major preoccupation for Webb since early on in her life:

> She seems to have experienced some basic discomfiture in gender identity, which while not the determining factor in her life, certainly left her with mixed feelings about being female. The particularity of her response is perhaps demonstrated by the fact that all of her sisters made conventionally good marriages and went on to live lives of conventional female service (Lengermann and Niebrugge-Brantley, 1998:278).

Richard Potter made his living as a railroad speculator and became a very wealthy industrialist. Laurencina was a close personal friend of Herbert Spencer, a frequent visitor to the Webb household. Richard first met Spencer when he was displaying a flying-machine (a type of airplane) that he had invented. Potter was fascinated by this and offered to finance its production; unfortunately, Spencer's flying-machine never got off the ground (Muggeridge and Adam, 1968). Spencer (1904) described Webb's parents as having an ideal marriage, "the most admirable pair I have ever met" (p. 19). Both Richard's and Laurencina's fathers had risen to industrial power early in the nineteenth century. This economically advantageous lifestyle afforded Beatrice's parents (both of liberal provincial backgrounds) an opportunity to take a passionate interest in every detail of their children's upbringing (Muggeridge and Adam, 1968). The Potter house was filled with books and intelligent friends. The girls were encouraged to read widely and to discuss candidly their impressions of what they read (Webb, 1982). The nine girls were free to roam about a very large country house farm filled with ponies, dogs, and cats. They would enjoy elaborate picnics and lavish birthdays. There were servants to take care of all their needs. The Potter home was one with many luxuries.

Beatrice, like her sisters, was home-schooled. In *My Apprenticeship* (1926), the only volume she completed of her planned autobiographical trilogy, Beatrice described her education as very broad, which included speculation of religion and philosophy, along with the study of literature and the classics, modern languages, history, mathematics, and science.

Laurencina Potter, Beatrice's mother, was described as being nearly as perfect as a human being could be. She was raised by her father to see herself as a "paragon of virtue," and her family treated her as such (Muggeridge and Adam, 1968). From the time she first met Richard Potter in Rome, where they fell immediately in love, he treated her as an "angel" as well. Richard was from a "broken" home and made every effort to assure a happy and successful marriage and family with Laurencina. In 1882, Laurencina died, and Beatrice became her father's best friend and close companion, running his households in London and in the country (Webb, 1982). She enjoyed the stimulating conversation of houseguests such as Spencer:

> Herbert Spencer never married, but—like other eminent Victorian bachelors—he loved little girls. In those days mothers were merely touched and amused if an elderly unmarried friend fell in love with their pre-pubescent daughters....He said they served as "vicarious objects of the philo-progenitive instinct." (Muggeridge and Adam, 1968:40)

Spencer enjoyed the bevy of little girls at Standish, and they looked forward to Spencer's visits.

As a teenager, Beatrice Potter traveled to America with her father as he attended to an extended business trip. When she returned to England, her anxieties resurfaced; seeking meaning in life, she began to study many religions (Radice, 1984). In her diary she wrote about such subjects as having a right to question conventional religion, but then stated that one has a duty to create a belief system of one's own. She would spend most of her life in search of her own belief system (Lengermann and Niebrugge-Brantley, 1998). As a young woman, Beatrice felt the social pressures of society's expectation that she should be looking for a husband. She was of a privileged background and taught to believe that she could accomplish whatever she put her mind to.

Unfortunately, employment opportunities for women of this era were very limited. Potter faced quite a dilemma throughout the 1880s. She was

> well-to-do, intelligent and attractive, Beatrice was apparently set for a conventionally successful marriage. But, her upbringing…left her with a profound inner conflict between emotion and intellect, between her feminine instincts and her desire to be independent and successful in a man's world….(Webb, 1982).

Beatrice was torn between her perceived duty to get married and her fond desire to make "something of herself." She pursued odd jobs in an attempt to find herself, and she pursued with obsessive passion the Radical politician Joseph Chamberlain (Webb, 1982). Nothing came of the obsession, but "she sought relief from that self-tormenting attachment in the anodyne of work in the East End of London" (Webb, 1982:xii). Potter became a "rent collector" in the Katherine Buildings, a poverty-ravaged housing slum. She was horrified and demoralized by the poor conditions in which these people were living. This was her first real witness of the differences between the wealthy class and the working class of England.

Through a family connection, Beatrice found a job working with her cousin-in-law, Charles Booth, an author and social researcher. Through Booth, Potter learned all the techniques of social research, quantitative and qualitative; personal interviewing; observation studies; content analysis; and statistical analysis. Her work with Booth convinced Potter to pursue a career as "a brain worker," a phrase she used often in an attempt to identify with other workers (Lengermann and Niebrugge-Brantley, 1998). She was also convinced that she needed to do something to help the less fortunate, and she decided that she would give her life to charity work, along with the dutiful quest of figuring out how to make the lives of the working-class better. Potter finally had her own sense of direction in life.

In 1891, living off a pension received following the death of her father, Potter published her most influential single-authored book, *The Co-operative Movement in Great Britain*. Her personal life was taking a turn for the better as well. She had met Sidney Webb, a fast-rising civil servant and Fabian ideologist, a year earlier. The Fabians were a socialist group that sought reform via a slow and bloodless process. Potter Webb first declared herself a socialist in her diary following her marriage to Sidney Webb (Nord, 1985).

Her immediate interest in Webb was strictly as a friend and intellectual partner. On July 23, 1892, Webb won over the reluctant Beatrice Potter. She insisted that the wedding be based on equality, and that it should be a working partnership (Webb, 1982). Although she had begun to come to terms with the idea that she might end up a working "spinster," she had not really turned against marriage. She was quoted to say in 1889 (the year just prior to meeting Webb), "God knows celibacy is painful to a woman" (Webb, 1982:232). Their marriage had become quite the topic of conversation, as they were both socialites and both well on their way to reshaping English society. For the rest of her life, Beatrice Potter Webb worked with her husband on a variety of social issues. Among their many collaborative publications were *The History of Trade Unionism* (1894), the companion volume, *Industrial Democracy* (1897), *The History of Liquor Licensing in England* (1903), *The Parish and the County* (1906), *The Manor and the Borough* (1908), *The Story of the King's Highway* (1913), *English Prisons under Local Government* (1922), *English Poor Law History: The Old Poor Law* (1927), *English Poor Law History: The Last Hundred Years* (1929), *Methods of Social Study* (1932), and their last work of social science, *Soviet Communism: A New Civilization* (1937). Clearly, the Webbs were proficient in their level of production. Besides their publications, the Webbs created the London School of Economics and Political Science (1895), and Beatrice founded the *New Statesman*, a periodical concerning itself with sociological issues. Potter Webb lived in Chicago for a while and conducted social research on urban poverty in an attempt to develop reform legislation. In 1928, Beatrice and Sidney Webb retired to Hampshire, where they lived until their deaths—1943 for Beatrice, and 1947 for Sidney.

Significant Contributions to Sociology

Beatrice Potter Webb helped to break the gender barrier found in professional fields, including in sociology. Webb maintained a strong commitment to the proposition that in order to claim to be a science, sociological work must be arrived at inductively, and grounded in the practice of rigorous empirical investigation. Empirical research aids sociology because it allows the social scientist to show that society is a system of emergent social structures, rather than a byproduct of individual action. She felt that the goal of sociology should be to discover how economic equity can be arrived at through a democratic decision-making process. The empirical research conducted by the Webbs "became an intellectual and political partnership which left a policy-oriented body of empirical research that laid the foundation for the twentieth-century British welfare state" (Lengermann and Niebrugge-Brantley, 2000:287).

It was Potter Webb's work with Booth that first introduced her to the importance of utilizing empirical data, but it is also where she came to the view that the capitalist system was slowly destroying the British working class and that it was the working-class people who would suffer the most. She studied the working class, empirically, in order to find ways to make their lives better. This was quite a transformation for Webb, because, as a child, she not only enjoyed the benefits of wealth, but she was raised by the Spencerian application of social evolution. Spencer, more or less, blamed poverty on individuals who were selected against, because they were not "fit" for the environment (e.g., society's economic structure). She learned of Malthus' idea that charity leads to overpopulation by allowing the unfit to survive and produce more unfit children. The very idea of governmental interference in the natural order of things went directly against the tenets of social evolution. It is quite amazing that Potter Webb became the caring, generous, crusader of the working poor.

While conducting empirical research on the working poor, Potter Webb became convinced that poverty was caused by social conditions. The problem of poverty was structural, not individual unfitness as proposed by Spencer. She felt that capitalism should be replaced by socialism. British socialism is essentially pragmatic, and not similar to Marx's radical conception of a reconstruction of society. When Potter married Webb, she became associated with the "Young Fabians" and Fabian socialism. The Fabians believed that society should be modified through slow and bloodless reform.

> They christened themselves after the Roman general Fabius: "For the right moment you must wait, as Fabius did most patiently when warring against Hannibal, though many censured his delays; but when the time comes you must strike hard as Fabius did or your waiting will be vain and fruitless" (Muggeridge and Adam, 1967:131).

The Fabians positioned themselves in government and attempted to shape policy in the socialist perspective. They believed in social progress (evolution), but they believed that it must be given directional assistance. According to Webb (1983), the workers need to be led because "judging from our knowledge of the Labour movement we can expect *no* leader from the working class. Our only hope is in permeating the young middle-class men, catching them for collectivism before they have enlisted on the other side" (p. 77).

Webb never described herself as a feminist; in fact, many contemporary feminists shun her works because of her antisuffrage stance of the 1880s and 1890s. Her simple reasoning for not identifying with the feminist movement was because she personally never experienced anything negative resulting from her gender. She had visited the Hull House on her trip to the United States, and Jane Addams read her *The Co-operative Movement in Great Britain* (Lengermann and Niebrugge-Brantley, 1998). It so happens that Webb's primary concern was the plight of the poor, not of women.

Beatrice Potter Webb was among the early female sociologists. She attempted to develop legislation that would help the working-class poor. Her desire to help the poor remains a trademark among sociologists today. She argued, as many social commentators do today, that the capitalist system is destroying the middle class. Her socialistic views, however, would be controversial in the contemporary United States. In keeping with the true sociological tradition, a tradition embraced today among the vast majority of sociologists, Webb insisted on the use of empirical data to support theory and social policy. She is a worthy contributor to the field of sociology.

ANNA JULIA COOPER (1858–1964)

"Cooper was born Anna Julia Hayward in Raleigh, North Carolina, in 1858, the daughter of Hannah Stanley Haywood, an African American woman who was a slave and 'presumably', in Cooper's words, of George Washington Hayward, her mother's white master" (Alexander, 1995:338). Her mother was a slave, but Anna described her as the finest woman she had ever known. Her mother could read the Bible and write a little bit. Anna Hayward was born during the Civil War and freed by the Emancipation Proclamation Act of 1863. She was quite a smart young girl but had to battle racism, sexism, and limited finances in her pursuit of an education. She attended St. Augustine's Normal and Collegiate Institute, an Episcopal school for African Americans. She was such a bright student that she was a tutor since the age of nine. Hayward was admitted to Oberlin College, one of the few colleges that allowed Blacks, and earned her bachelor's degree in 1884 and an honorary master's degree in 1887. Hayward would support herself as a teacher in the Washington, DC, school system for the rest of her life (Lengermann and Niebrugge-Brantley, 2000). In 1887, Anna Cooper would marry George A. C. Cooper, a native of the British West Indies. After his death two years later, she would never remarry.

Cooper valued education and the subsequent status it afforded her. She believed that she was bestowed with a Heavenly "intelligent consciousness" that pushed her in the direction of education (Alexander, 1995). Cooper felt that it was her destiny to enlighten the masses and to help reshape society. She campaigned against racism throughout her life. In 1892, she published *A Voice from the South*, her collection of essays on the issues of race, gender, education, and other topics. Throughout her teaching career, Cooper continued to work toward her Ph.D., by studying during summer recess and various academic leaves. She attended Columbia University and the Sorbonne, in Paris. Her dedication and commitment finally paid off when she successfully defended her dissertation, *Slavery and the French Revolutionists (1788–1805)*, at the age of 65. Her dissertation was written in French and made available in English in 1988. It is with these two books that Cooper demonstrated her ability as "a significant sociological theorist of race and society both in the United States and globally" (Lengermann and Niebrugge-Brantley, 2000:158).

Significant Contributions to Sociology

The post–Civil War era was not kind to African Americans. The climate of Cooper's time includes lynchings at an all-time high, overt and covert racism evident throughout the nation, an economic depression that increased tensions in 1893, a confederation of Black women being formed in Boston (1895), and many other Blacks who were speaking out against racism. In *A Voice from the South*, Cooper spoke out against the white women's movement for its racist exclusions, the emerging Black male leaders' refusal to fight for the rights of Black women, the negative portrayal of Blacks in literature, and U.S. expansionism (Alexander, 1995). Her core belief was that racism was the result of an unequal power structure found in society.

Cooper was a theorist who sought "self-consciously, to describe the patterns of social life and to stimulate herself in that work of theoretical creation" (Lengermann and Niebrugge-Brantley, 2000:314). Cooper attempted to support her theories, as would any good sociologist, with statistical data and historical documentation. She applied her theories primarily to issues of race and gender. Cooper served as an inspiration to many, and in her writings, "she forges a space for the African-American woman intellectual, working and thinking at the turn of the century" (Alexander, 1995:355).

Although at first glance it may appear that Cooper's contributions to sociological thought are limited, one must remember that as a nineteenth-century black woman, she began life under most adverse circumstances and at a time when the mental capacity of Blacks and women were questioned and disparaged (Hutchinson, 1981). When we take this knowledge of Cooper to heart, her achievements take on greater significance. And certainly she serves as an inspiration to anyone who feels the pressures of contemporary society.

IDA WELLS-BARNETT (1862–1931)

Ida Wells-Barnett (1862–1931), African American civil rights crusader, suffragist, women's rights advocate, journalist, and speaker.   (Everett Collection Inc/Alamy)

Ida Wells-Barnett was a fearless civil rights crusader, suffragist, women's rights advocate, journalist, and speaker. She was born into slavery in Holly Springs, Mississippi, in 1862 and died in Chicago in 1931, at the age of sixty-nine. Her parents were slaves who gained freedom after the Civil War. After they gained freedom, Ida's father, Jim Wells, was able to find employment as a carpenter with the man with whom he had apprenticed. Ida's mother, Elizabeth Warrenton Wells, worked as a cook for her husband's boss, and the whole family lived on his land. Elizabeth Wells enrolled at Rust College, an institution started by white Northerners for the education of freedmen, so that she could learn to read her Bible (Lengermann and Niebrugge-Brantley, 1998).

In her autobiography, *Crusade for Justice* (1970), Wells-Barnett credited her parents with instilling in her an interest for politics and a guiding principle of fighting for justice. She recalled that when her father's boss asked for her father's vote (it was a common practice in those days for a white boss to demand his black employees vote as he dictated) he refused; Jim Wells resisted, moved off his boss's land, and started his own carpentry business. Ida Wells followed in her mother's footsteps and attended school at Rust College. When Ida was just fourteen, her parents and youngest sibling fell victim to yellow fever. Symbolic of the responsibility and perseverance that characterized her life, Ida kept the family together by working as a teacher until 1883. She continued her studies at Rust during this period. In 1883, she moved to Memphis to live with her aunt. As an educated black woman, Ida quickly found that her teaching, writing, and public speaking skills were in high demand. Teaching salaries were also much higher in Memphis than compared to rural Mississippi. Ida expanded her own education by attending both Fiske and LeMoyne Institute.

It was in Memphis where Ida first began to fight for racial and gender equality. She worked as a journalist and started a one-woman campaign against lynching in 1883 by writing a series of articles detailing, with empirical data, the horrors and racial terrorism that lynching represented (Lengermann and Niebrugge-Brantley, 2000). In 1884, Ida Wells was ordered to move from her seat on a railroad car. A white man wanted to sit down, and Blacks were supposed to sit in the "smoker" cars, which were generally very dirty. Despite the 1875 Civil Rights Act banning discrimination on the basis of race in theaters, hotels, and other public accommodations, several railroad companies ignored this law. It is interesting to note that her defiant act was before *Plessy v. Ferguson* (1896), the U.S. Supreme Court decision that established the doctrine of "separate but equal," which legalized racial segregation. Wells was forcefully removed from the train, and the white passengers cheered. This incident would spark her career of protest (Thompson, 1990). When she returned to Memphis, she immediately hired an attorney to sue the Chesapeake, Ohio and Southwestern Rail Road Company. She won the decision in the lower court but lost in the Court of Appeals. She was ordered to pay court costs of $200. From this point on, Wells-Barnett was identified as a dissident. She decided to dedicate the rest of her life to fight for the rights of Blacks and women.

Her suit against the railroad company (and against Jim Crow tactics) sparked her career as a journalist. Many newspapers wanted to hear about the experience of the twenty-five-year-old school teacher who stood up against white supremacy. Her writing career progressed in papers geared toward African American and Christian audiences. In 1889, Wells became a writer and part owner of the *Free Speech and Headlight*, an anti-segregationist newspaper primarily owned by Rev. R. Nightingale. He forced his large congregation to subscribe to the paper. After writing an editorial for the *Free Speech* criticizing the school board for the inferior conditions in the segregated black schools, Ida's teaching license was revoked (Broschart, 1991). Facing unemployment, Ida Wells became a full-time journalist and eventually part owner of the *Free Speech* (Zeccola, 1996).

She often wrote about the horrors of lynching, and in her first antilynching pamphlet, *Southern Horrors*, she described a case involving one of her close friends, Thomas Moss. Moss and two of his friends, Calvin McDowell and Henry Stewart, owned a successful grocery store called the People's Grocery. Their success was cutting into the profits of white-owned grocers. A group of angry white men decided to do something about this matter and attacked the owners of People's Market. Moss and his friends fought back, and one of them shot one of the attacking white men. The black men were arrested, but a lynch-mob broke into the jail, dragged them away from town, and brutally murdered all three.

Upset by the way the white media covered the event, Wells-Barnett began a campaign against lynching and wrote about it in *The Free Speech*. "Her articles in *The Free Speech* provided ideological clarity and served as an organizing tool locally, nationally and internationally" (Boyd, 1994:9). She led a campaign of a mass exodus of Blacks from Memphis, and her open campaign against white patriarchal chivalry (even suggesting that white women might desire black male companionship) so offended Whites that they destroyed the press offices of *The Free Speech*. A white-owned newspaper in Memphis called for the lynching of Wells-Barnett, but she was attending an African

Methodist Episcopal Church convention in Philadelphia (Boyd, 1994). It became clear, however, that she could no longer live in Memphis, so she moved to Chicago and continued her journalistic attacks on southern injustices. She would live in Chicago for most of her adult life. Wells-Barnett was a friend of Jane Addams, the activist, and she admired her work at Hull House.

Chicago was host to the 1893 World's Columbian Exposition, which black Americans were not allowed to attend. In a response to this overt act of racism, Ida Wells wrote and published a pamphlet, *The Reason Why the Colored American Is Not in The World's Columbian Exposition*. The introduction was translated into German and French, and the pamphlet, which included a copy of "Lynch Law"—an essay that explains the racist psychology of American society—was distributed to patrons of the exposition (Boyd, 1994). That same year, a black women's organization founded the World's Congress of Representative Women, in order to secure representation of Blacks in the exposition. Wells-Barnett would remain a prominent figure in the women's movement. She was instrumental in the founding of the National Association of Colored Women, the National Afro-American Council, and the National Association for the Advancement of Colored People. She was now a leader of campaigns for women's suffrage. Wells-Barnett, along with Jane Addams, successfully blocked the establishment of segregated schools in Chicago.

In 1895, Ida Wells married F. L. Barnett, a Chicago lawyer and editor of a Black newspaper. In the same year she published her second major work on lynching, *A Red Record*. She used data from White newspapers as a part of her statistical analysis of lynching. Wells-Barnett would remain as social activist and writer for the rest of her life. She died on March 25, 1931, in Chicago.

Significant Contributions to Sociology

Ida Wells-Barnett, like Anna Julia Cooper, was directly influenced by her immediate environment. Born slaves, freed early on in childhood, but realizing the racist nature of society, they both possessed an intellectual and activist desire to make a positive contribution to society. They both fought for the rights of women and Blacks. Their theories were based on the premise that Blacks and women are oppressed because of the unequal distribution of power in society. Cooper and Wells-Barnett believed that oppression creates a dominate-dominated class structure. Domination by the power group is patterned by five factors: history (sets of events that lead to power discrimination); ideology (distortions and exaggerations of select events); material resources (possession of resources equals power); manners (routinization of everyday interactions between dominants and subordinates); and passion (the key to domination rests on emotion, a desire to control) (Lengermann and Niebrugge-Brantley, 1998). Cooper and Wells-Barnett both wished for a society without domination, a society that allowed for peaceful coexistence, or equilibrium.

Unfortunately, American society was not in a state of racial equilibrium, and class struggles coexisted with racial and sexual discrimination. Wells-Barnett wrote articles that demanded justice. She called upon Blacks and women to become politically active, to fight inequality. She used lynching as her exemplar of racial injustice. She spoke internationally on the topic and linked it to racial and class inequality. For Wells-Barnett, lynching involved the combination of racial and gender issues.

> She dissolves the rationale for the lynching of black men offered by white society, the myth that the victim has raped a white woman. She provides case studies of the emotional/sexual attraction between white women and black men as a normal part of social relations in the South and of the attraction of white men to black women (Lengermann and Niebrugge-Brantley, 2000:167).

Publishing ideas such as this during this particular era reflects very radical behavior. But it was this very behavior and spirited commitment to activism that provided Wells-Barnett with her huge following and support among those in the Black community.

Ida Wells-Barnett launched an international campaign against lynching and significantly influenced the ideological direction of black women's organizations. One such organization, the Ida Wells-Barnett Women's Club, would be named in her honor. The purpose of this club was for civic and social benefit of African American women. She bought and ran many different aspects of *The Conservator*, a newspaper owned previously by her husband and associates. During 1909, she went to the inaugural meeting of the National Association for the Advancement of Colored People (NAACP). At this meeting she spoke about lynchings around the country and provided data to support her contentions (Sterling, 1979). But as the years went on, Wells-Barnett often endured political and gender discrimination from within and outside the African American community. "Wells' political integrity and strong sense of social urgency was compatible with her earliest associates, but during the more conservative era of the early twentieth century, this radicalism distanced her from the new leadership of the left" (Boyd, 1994:12). She has been vindicated in the advent of Black women's studies.

Wells-Barnett contributed to sociology by means of her analysis of racial and gender issues, especially as they pertain to class inequality and injustice. "In the study of Wells' life and words, we find insight into the complex and peculiar predicament of the black female experience" (Boyd, 1994:13). Women like Ida Wells-Barnett continue to inspire contemporary generations. It is worth noting that many of the women (and men) discussed in this chapter (and book) have their legacies kept alive by present-day actors who portray them in classrooms across the United States. Tamara Johnson, for example, portrays civil rights activist Ida B. Wells. The Syracuse (NY) newspaper *The Post-Standard* conducted a wonderful interview on Johnson as she toured schools in the Syracuse area:

> Johnson is in full character, complete with a flowing black dress, a pinching corset and a riveting voice. Her crisp first-person narrative moves right along. She talks about her childhood, the death of her parents when she was 14, her struggle to raise her brothers and sisters...her banishment from a train car in 1884, and the lawsuit that follows (Herron, 2003:D-2).

Having contemporary actors portray those who contributed to sociological theory is a great way to show their relevancy to the present-day generation.

CHARLOTTE PERKINS GILMAN (1860–1935)

Charlotte Anna Perkins was born on July 3, 1860, in Hartford, Connecticut. She was the greatniece of abolitionist advocate Harriet Beecher Stowe, author of *Uncle Tom's Cabin*.

> Her childhood was characterized by loneliness, isolation, and poverty, particularly after her father, a gifted but temperamental librarian and fiction writer, abandoned the family when Charlotte was nine. Contributing to her emotional insecurity was her mother's tendency to withhold affection, which left Charlotte exceedingly wary of personal relationships (Gilman, 1998:xi).

Economic hardship caused the Perkins family to move nineteen times in just eighteen years. Transferring from school to school led Charlotte to become largely self-educated. She would visit the library on her own and read about ancient history and civilization. Charlotte's childhood developed a strong, hardworking, and independent woman.

As a teenager, Charlotte Perkins became involved in a loving relationship with her friend, Martha Luther. They were together for four years until Martha left Charlotte in 1881, to marry a man, and then moved away. Perkins was devastated, and described in *The Living of Charlotte Perkins Gilman* (1935) that the break-up was the most lasting pain she had ever known. In January 1882, Charlotte was still dealing with loss of Luther when she was introduced to Charles Walter Stetson, a handsome young man. Stetson pursued Perkins for two years until she finally agreed to marry him. Predictably, the marriage was a failure. Charlotte suffered a nervous breakdown and was institutionalized. The critical trigger of Perkins Gilman's chronic depression was her relationship with Stetson, although the origins of her depression had clearly been established early on in her life.

Charlotte Perkins had refused Stetson's marriage proposals for two reasons. The most obvious of these reasons was her uncertainty regarding her sexual orientation; she had warned him of the difficulties of pursuing an intimate relationship with her (Gilman, 1935). Second, Perkins was concerned that if she married, she would not have time to pursue a career, and she very much wanted to make her mark on society through social activism. She was totally alarmed when she found out she was pregnant. Since she had feared marriage would interfere with a career, motherhood was viewed as a curse. Katherine Beecher Stetson was born on March 23, 1885, just a little more than ten months after Charlotte and Walter were married (Gilman, 1998). Charlotte fell into a deeper depression and was sent to a Philadelphia sanitarium. Upon release, and subsequent attempts to reconcile her marriage, the depression that Charlotte Stetson felt led her to abandon her husband and move to California. She took her daughter with her, but due to economic deprivation, she decided in 1894, the year her divorce became final, to turn Katherine over to Stetson and his new wife. "Determined to have an independent lifestyle, Gilman helped effect the marriage of her best friend to her former husband and turned her daughter over to them while she pursued her public and professional career" (Lengermann and Niebrugge-Brantley, 2000:298).

During the 1890s, Perkins published numerous articles and edited a weekly magazine, the *Impress*. She joined the lecture circuit speaking on socialist issues and on women's rights throughout the United States and in England (Gilman, 1998). In 1898, Gilman gained international acclaim with the publication of *Women and Economics*, her groundbreaking work that would go through nine editions in her lifetime and was translated into seven languages. Her two other major sociological publications are *The Home* (1903) and *Man-Made World* (1911). Her literary reputation was established with her quasi-autobiographical short story depicting the mental and emotional disintegration of a young wife and mother, "The Yellow Wall-Paper" (1892). She wrote a number of popular short essays that were serialized as *Herland, With Her in Ourland*, and *The Dress of Women*. "Gilman wrote and published *The Forerunner* as an educational, sociological enterprise. The influence of works like *The Dress of Women*, presented over the course of a year in twelve monthly installments, was limited primarily to the regular readers of her magazine" (Gilman, 2002:xii). Perkins Gilman expected a large readership that would include "Gilman Circles" of small face-to-face groups who would discuss the contents of her writings. Sales were poor, and her, perhaps delusional, hope to amass a wider audience to her work never materialized. Perkins Gilman was, however, a well-known sociologist during her era. She presented papers at annual meetings of the American Sociological Association and published articles in *The American Journal of Sociology*.

As for Charlotte Perkins' personal life, she decided to give marriage one more try:

In 1900, after several passionate attachments with other women, she married a cousin, Houghton Gilman, who was considerably younger than she and who supported her need for independence and public visibility in what was to be a very satisfactory marriage for them both (Lengermann and Niebrugge-Brantley, 2000:298).

The marriage lasted for thirty-four happy years, until George Houghton Gilman died of a massive cerebral hemorrhage. "During the early years of their marriage, Katherine lived with Charlotte and Houghton much of the time and alternately with her father and stepmother, Grace" (Gilman, 1998:xiv). Charlotte Gilman, struck with inoperable breast cancer, would take her own life on August 17, 1935.

Significant Contributions to Sociology

"Gilman participated in several important intellectual movements, including: cultural feminism, reform Darwinism, feminist pragmatism, Fabian socialism, and Nationalism that shared interests in changing the economy and women's social status through social reform movements" (Gilman, 2002:xiii). Some of these movements were national or international, while others were of local concerns. Lengermann and Niebrugge-Brantley state that

Gilman was influenced by three configurations of thought popularly expressed in her era: (1) reform social Darwinism; (2) Progressivism, particularly those strands of its reform ideology that drew on non-Marxian or utopian socialism; and (3) feminism, the growing mobilization by women for rights, including the right to vote and the right to economic independence (1998:112).

Gilman admired Thorstein Veblen, a man who had an integral role in Gilman's *The Dress of Women*. She particularly enjoyed his concept of *conspicuous consumption* and his application of the term to gender issues. Gilman believed much of Veblen's works were a defense of women. In his *The Theory of the Leisure Class*, Veblen discussed the problematic nature of displaying the wealth of men and families through women's adornment and leisure. Veblen devoted an entire chapter, "Dress as an Expression of the Pecuniary Culture," that parallels Gilman's work in *The Dress of Women* (Gilman, 2002). Gilman also applied the words "savage" and "barbarian" in similar ways to Veblen's usage, as a means to refer to stages in social evolution. Furthermore, both Veblen and Gilman were described as immoral because of their sexual lives—Gilman because of her lesbianism, divorce, joint custody of a child with an ex-husband and his wife, a marriage arranged by Charlotte; and Veblen because of his public affairs and adulterous behavior.

In *The Dress of Women*, Gilman stated,

Once recognizing that human clothing in material and structure is part of our social life; that cloth is a living tissue evolved by us for social use as much as fur or feathers are evolved for individual use; then we are prepared to recognize also the action of evolutionary forces on this tissue, in all its forms and uses (2002:15).

Clothing, then, becomes a social element beyond its most obvious function to cover the body and keep it warm in cold weather. Through conspicuous consumption, clothing becomes a weapon of wealth and a public display of power. Gilman did not solely blame individuals for their display of leisure consumption; in addition, she discussed the influence of the clothing industry as a powerful economic force capable of intimidating and initiating social action. The relevance of this analysis should not be lost on any sociologist who examines the role popular culture on decision-making. Parents understand that the clothing industry has successfully penetrated the minds of young consumers to "look" a certain way. Social class differences become quite evident with the issues of clothing, fashion, and style. Gilman clearly expressed her views of the producers and consumers of fashion as

> The people contentedly, eagerly, delightedly, practicing this unspeakable foolish slavery to the whims and notions, and the economic demands, of a group less worthy to rule than any Church or Court of past—the darling leaders of the demi-monde, the poor puppets of a so-called "Society" whose major occupation is to exhibit clothes, and a group of greedy and presuming tradesmen and their employees (2002:117).

Gilman even attempted to understand the psychology behind people who consume clothing at the conspicuous level. Gilman clearly demonstrated a critical sociological theoretical approach to this and other studies.

Prior to her first real sociological writing, Gilman published the "The Yellow Wall-Paper," in *New England Magazine* (1892). This short story was written in two days, during the summer of 1890, during Gilman's "first year of freedom" that followed her permanent separation from Walter Stetson (Gilman, 1935). Loosely based on her experiences while undergoing therapy, critics claim that her writings are a reflection of progressive insanity. She insisted that the real purpose of "The Yellow Wall-Paper" was to convince Dr. S. Weir Mitchell (the doctor who treated her) of the error of his ways of treating nervous breakdowns (Knight, 1997). Today, "The Yellow Wall-Paper" remains a definitive feminist statement that continues to spark controversy (Knight, 1997). Charlotte Perkins Gilman is generally ignored in contemporary sociology, but her works make for wonderful additions to women's studies, American literature, and short fiction.

JANE ADDAMS (1860–1935)

Jane Addams was born in Cedarville, Illinois, on September 6, 1860, to Sarah and John Addams. Jane's parents had lost three babies (1850, 1855, and 1859) prior to Jane's birth and prayed that the other five children would remain healthy. Both John and Sarah Addams were descended from immigrants who arrived in the United States in the early eighteenth century (Diliberto, 1999). Jane admired her father not just because he was a good father and provider who comforted her when she awoke from horrible dreams following her mother's tragic early death (Addams was just two years old), but because he served the community in a professional manner and was admired by the community as a respectable leader and family provider (Brown, 2004).

Jane attended Rockford Female Seminary, although she did not look forward to it upon her arrival in 1877. "Jane admitted she was distraught to be starting at 'humdrum Rockford'. With its weak academic program, its emphasis on religion, and its rigid code of conduct, Rockford seemed stuck in the pre–Civil War past" (Diliberto, 1999:60). This was an era when women where first being allowed to attend college, and Rockford was one of dozens of female seminaries that had transformed itself into a real college. Upon Jane's arrival at Rockford, the college did not even offer degrees. John Addams was among the more enlightened men of the time, and he encouraged his daughters to pursue higher education. Jane had hoped to convince her father to let her transfer to Smith after one year at Rockford, but he would not allow it. Luckily for Addams, just months before she was to receive her "testimonial"—a certificate used in place of a degree—the Rockford board of trustees voted to allow degrees to those students who had completed the four-year academic program. Addams excelled in this academically weaker environment and graduated as valedictorian in 1881.

Like many college students, Jane was hoping to "find herself" at college, and she was open to new experiences:

> Jane's avidity for new experience led her, as it has college students in other eras, to experiment with drugs. One morning she and four friends swallowed crushed opium pills, hoping to induce hallucinations that would help them better understand *Confessions*, by the English essayist and opium addict De Quincey, which they planned to read once the drug took effect (Diliberto, 1999:72).

Addams discovered that she enjoyed public debate and took part in Rockford's public examination, an annual event where a panel of ministers and politicians would test the young women's knowledge of a variety of topics. In the fall of 1880, a group of men from Knox College in Galesburg, Illinois, tried to block Jane and other female debaters from participating in the state debate contest. They did not think it was proper for women and men to share a stage in public debate—etiquette books of the late 1800s agreed (Diliberto, 1999). This was a period of time, after all, where women were first entering college and were expected to be raising large families. Many of Jane's friends dropped out of college to get married. Jane was not about to marry a man. She was an ardent feminist, and feminists of this era often viewed heterosexual love as disgusting. Furthermore, "many feminists of the nineteenth-century believed that women were degraded by having sex with men" (Diliberto, 1999:75).

On August 17, 1881, John Addams died. He had a huge estate and left half to his then-wife Ann Haldeman; the other half was divided among Jane and her two sisters and brother. Jane's share included a 247-acre farm, 60 acres of timberland in Stephenson County, 80 acres in Dakota, Illinois, stocks and bonds, and $50,000—the equivalent of nearly $1 million in 1998 (Diliberto, 1999). Ann, Jane's stepmother, wanted her to get married and attempted to unite her son George with Jane. It seems that Ann was worried that her son might be gay, and she felt the marriage between Jane and George would benefit both of them. Jane was horrified by the idea. The year 1883 was especially memorable to Addams; she visited Ireland and England, but also suffered her first nervous breakdown. Throughout the 1880s, Addams seemed unsure of herself and wondered what she should do with the rest of her life. She would travel to Europe again and find inspiration in London. She was, at first, alarmed at the urban decay of London, characterized by prostitutes, drunken men, crippled children begging on the streets, streets covered with garbage and animal blood from the open slaughterhouses, and news of an unknown assailant the reporters called "Jack the Ripper" (Davis, 1973; Diliberto, 1999). But Addams also discovered in London Toynbee Hall, a "settlement" house designed to provide "relief" to the less fortunate (e.g., money, food, clothes, and other services). The idea and image of creating some sort of equivalent settlement house in America would lead to Jane Addams' greatest contribution to society and, ultimately, sociology.

In 1889, Jane Addams and Ellen Gates Starr arranged to rent the second floor of a subdivided former mansion on Halsted Street, Chicago, an area of working-class immigrants. They planned on creating a settlement house modeled on Toynbee Hall and named it "Hull House" after Chicago millionaire Charles Hull, the original owner (Elshtain, 2002). Addams and Starr had some definite ideas on what they hoped to accomplish at Hull House, but they also realized that new programs would have to be created as new needs arouse.

> Their plan, which Addams recounts in *Twenty Years at Hull-House* (1919/1990), was to try to learn and help by living simply as neighbors among the poor.... They embarked upon a range of social experiments including social clubs, garbage collection, apartments for working women, consumer cooperation, evening classes, trade unions, industrial reform legislation, investigations of working conditions, debating societies, and intervening in strikes, unemployment, and hysteria about anarchists (many of whom took part in Hull House debates) (Lengermann and Niebrugge-Brantley, 2000:303).

From the start, the settlement was a refuge for many of the children in the neighborhood "whose harsh lives were often cut short by industrial accidents and the many epidemics that raged through their squalid homes" (Diliberto, 1999:158). For the older children, Hull House provided an educational program.

Hull House was a success story in every way. It offered literary clubs, academic clubs, sewing lessons, kindergarten and daycare facilities for children of working mothers, and so much more. In fact, Hull House was so successful it "expanded from a single floor to a city-block complex of building including an art gallery, coffee shop, gymnasium, library, theater, museum of labor, dining rooms, music rooms, and housing facilities" (Lengermann and Niebrugge-Brantley, 1998:68). Hull House was now a collaborative enterprise assisting thousands of people, including recent immigrants such as the Italians, Russian and Polish Jews, Irish, Germans, and Greeks; even the Bohemians found refuge there. Many other educated women who shared Addams' activism and reform attitude joined her at Hull House, among them Florence Kelley, Dr. Alice Hamilton, Julia Lathrop, Sophonisba Breckinridge, and Grace and Edith Abbott.

Significant Contributions to Sociology

Jane Addams made a significant difference in Chicago with her Hull House settlement. Her most important contributions to sociology are directly linked to her experiences at Hull House. The communal atmosphere of Hull House led Addams to develop a sociological theory based on the idea that people must begin to work collectively and cooperatively. Sociological themes of cooperation and progressive growth are the foundation of her major publications: *Democracy and Social Ethics* (1902), *Newer Ideals of Peace* (1907), *Twenty Years at Hull House* (1910), *The Long Road of Women's Memory* (1916), *Peace and Bread in Times of War* (1922), and *The Second Twenty Years at Hull House* (1930). Her sociological outlook on society implied that diverse people must learn to accept and tolerate one another.

Addams involved modified versions of progressivism, reform social Darwinism, philosophic pragmatism, and social gospel Christianity into her general social theory (Lengermann and Niebrugge-Brantley, 1998). In an attempt to prove that the social Darwinistic, laissez-faire philosophy of government coexists with social reform, Addams proposed *reform social Darwinism*. She believed that humans had already progressed to the point where they could control evolution and therefore owed a duty to help the less fortunate. The reform social Darwinism principle stated, "Evolutionary law demanded that people find ways to work in combination with each other to secure a social environment in which all people could develop fully" (Lengermann and Niebrugge-Brantley, 1998:73). Her progressive Darwinistic approach also possessed a "social gospel" in order to provide proper moral guidance in decision-making and social action.

In the tradition of the Chicago School and the sociology that dominated that geographic area, Addams' theoretical ideology involved a "hands-on approach" to the study of human behavior. She believed that sociologists must go "native," and live with those that they study. Her micro orientation leads to the individual as the basic unit of study, and it is the individual and her interactions with the community that most dominated Addams' social theory.

Addams' theories and research reflect a feminist framework. She wrote from a gendered standpoint, employed a focus on women's lives in her research (e.g., housewives, domestics, sweatshop laborers, prostitutes), and demonstrated a commitment to changing the role of women in society. Hull House itself, despite all the other programs it offered diverse people, was as much a sanctuary for female friendship and a source for professional, practical, and material support for women.

> When Addams wrote sociology, she did not have the men of the academy as her primary audience, but the thousands of women she knew through social reform work, lecture tours, personal correspondence, and as the intended readership for her articles in popular magazines. She understood the work that she and other women activists were doing to be sociology—a sociology created primarily by women out of their life experiences (Lengermann and Niebrugge-Brantley, 1998:70).

Addams was an activist and a person who believed in social, moral change. Hull House residents, neighbors, and supporters forged a powerful reform movement. Among the projects that they launched were the Immigrants' Protective League, the Juvenile Protective Association, the first juvenile court in the nation, and a Juvenile Psychopathic Clinic. Through their efforts, the Illinois legislature enacted protective legislation for women and children (1903), the Federal Children's Bureau (1912), and passage of a federal child labor law (1916). The Hull House was located in an urban area; and with urban areas come a number of potential social problems. One problem that Addams attacked head on was city sanitation. Addams believed that the streets of Chicago (a meat-slaughterhouse city) were so dirty and repulsive that they were destructive to human health and the overall quality of life. It was common for huge garbage boxes to be left in the streets festering in filth and the corresponding rats and cockroaches that accompany street trash. As Levine explains, the piles of garbage "were the first objects that the toddling child learned to climb, their bulk afforded a barricade and their contents provided missiles in all battles of the older boys; finally they became the seats upon which absorbed lovers held enchanted converse" (1971:73). Such was the state of poor sanitation in Chicago that Addams organized protests, cited city code violations, and brought them to the attention of the city; Addams was eventually appointed the Garbage Inspector of the city (Levine, 1971). Urban, suburb, and rural residents alike can appreciate the relevancy of Addams' work to try and keep the streets clean.

The efforts and successes of the Hull House reformers would be expanded to the national level. Addams began to realize that the passing of laws would not be enough to guarantee the end of poverty, and as a result she attempted to find the root causes of poverty. She joined a number of labor groups and discussed with the working poor the reasons for poverty. Armed with specifics, Addams attempted to get lawmakers to legislate for the protection of immigrants from exploitation, limiting the working hours of women, mandating schooling for children, recognizing labor unions, and providing industrial safety. She worked in the efforts to secure women's rights to vote; she was a member of the Chicago municipal suffrage; and she became the first vice president of the National American Women Suffrage Association in 1911. Addams even became the first woman to second the nomination of a presidential candidate, Theodore Roosevelt, at the Progressive Party convention of 1912.

Addams was not without controversy. When horrible working conditions led to workers' protests and the subsequent Haymarket riot, Addams was personally attacked for her support of the workers. It resulted in a great loss of donor support for Hull House. Addams would supplement the settlement from her own resources. She was also criticized for her effort to stop the U.S. involvement in World War I. There was a great deal of patriotism at the time of the war, and her diplomatic attempts to thwart war were not popular among the masses. Many people labeled her a socialist, an anarchist, and a communist. Addams was even expelled from the Daughters of the American Revolution (1917). She made the FBI's list of "most dangerous radicals" during the "Red Scare" decade of the 1920s. However, despite these controversies, Addams had, by now, achieved international acclaim. Her participation in numerous charities and associations were highlighted by her election as the first president of the Women's International League for Peace and Freedom (a position she held until her death), her involvement with the creation of the American Civil Liberties Union, and her activism with the NAACP.

Jane Addams was many things to many people. Her Hull House settlement seemed to vindicate her beliefs that society should work more cooperatively. Much of the governmental "interference" designed toward reform social Darwinism advocated by Addams became policy under President Franklin Roosevelt. Perhaps her crowning achievement came in the form of her receiving a Nobel Peace Prize in 1931. Despite her failing health, Addams worked at Hull House until the end of her life. She died on May 21, 1935. Thousands of people came to her funeral at Hull House before she was taken to Cedarville to be buried.

MARIANNE WEBER (1870–1954)

Marianne Schnitger Weber was born on August 2, 1870, in Oerlinghausen, Germany. Marianne is mostly remembered today as Max Weber's wife and proponent of his work after his death. She also played an important role in helping organize Max's works while he lived.

> [Max] Weber's work was fragmentary and disconnected, "found in journals or left unedited." Marianne Weber's persistence and devotion played no little part in its collection and publication. *Economy and Society* was in large part written "without benefit of footnotes and other customary scholarly paraphernalia" (Mommsen and Osterhammel, 1987:383).

Marianne was the grandniece of Max Weber, Sr., father of her future husband. Her mother, Anna, who came from a wealthy family, married Eduard Schnitger, a man whom the Weber family felt was beneath her. Schnitger was a country doctor in an era when such a position was not considered prestigious. Marianne was born within the first year of this marriage but became motherless when Anna died two years later after giving birth to a second child. Shortly after the death of his wife, Eduard began to show signs of a mental illness. Marianne was sent to live with her paternal grandmother and an aunt in a small country town. At age sixteen, her wealthy grandfather Weber sent her to be educated at a fashionable finishing school in Hanover (Weber, 1975). After completing her studies in Hanover, Marianne returned to the country to live with her mother's married sister, Alwine. Marianne was bored there because she relished an intellectual environment. In 1891, she was invited to spend a few weeks with the Weber family in Berlin. It was during this visit that Marianne caught a glimpse of the world she desired. She could hardly get her fill of such a cultural and intellectual atmosphere (Weber, 1975). A year later, she went back to Berlin to live with the Weber family. Two very important elements took place during this second visit. First, she formed a solid "mother–daughter"-type relationship with Helene Weber. Helene was like the mother that Marianne never really had, and Marianne became Helene's confidant. Second, Marianne became "interested" in her cousin Max. She was extremely happy to discover he felt the same way about her, and they became engaged to marry. Determined to be an active part of her future husband's academic career, Marianne helped Max with an investigation of farmworkers he had undertaken for the Evangelical Social Congress. She wanted to familiarize herself with scholarship as soon as possible (Adams and Sydie, 2001).

The early years of their marriage found Max consumed with academic activity, intellectual production, and leftist politics. Marianne was becoming a sociologist in her own right, as she was producing sociological research on marriage and the legal position of women in that institution. Weber (1975–1926) argued for a reform of marriage, not a substitute for marriage. Marianne Weber was also among the leading women of Germany in the liberal feminist movement. "In 1918 German women obtained the vote, and in 1919 Marianne Weber became the first member of the Baden parliament" (Adams and Sydie, 2001:172). In 1897, Max Weber (see Chapter 5) had a "falling out" with his father, and, shortly thereafter, and before reconciliation, his father passed away. Max was devastated and went into a state of depression; he was in and out of mental institutions for years. During this period, Marianne took over the role of public speaker in the marriage and became actively involved in sociopolitical issues.

By 1904, Max had recovered from his nervous collapse and would manage to find a proper blend between scholarship and leisure. In this same year, the Webers visited the United States to attend a scholarly conference held during the Universal Exposition in St. Louis. Max looked forward to visiting America so that he could further examine the role of Protestantism and capitalism. He had accepted the editorship of a new journal in social science, *Archiv fur Sozialwissenschaft und Sozcialpolitik*. His article, "The Protestant Ethic and the Spirit of Capitalism," published in that journal, is now famous. Max Weber concluded that Americans were passionate only about mundane pursuits (e.g., economic wealth, consumer goods) and that their pursuits were minus any religious and ethical meaning. Marianne was far more condemning of Americans' behavior. Her religiously inspired criticism of the United States included doubts of the very core of America's ideology—freedom. She felt that freedom had brought immorality to millions "living under the scourge of gold" (Mommsen and Osterhammel, 1987:217). The Webers gathered with other German intellectuals in Tonawanda, New York, and in between visits to nearby Niagara Falls, they would compare empirical evidence of America's economic, materialistic system. During this American tour, Marianne was expanding her own sociological self. She met both Jane Addams and Florence Kelley. She published several articles on women's experience and studied the works of Charlotte Perkins Gilman. In 1907, Marianne published her famous *Ehefrau und Mutter in der Rechtsentwicklung* (*Marriage, Motherhood, and the Law*). In that same year, Marianne's grandfather Karl died, leaving her and Max free from financial worry. Max and Marianne were living a life of economic comfort, which allowed both of them to actively pursue intellectual interests. Marianne created her own "intellectual salon" where gifted speakers, including some of Max's colleagues (e.g., Robert Michels and Georg Simmel), joined with prominent feminist speakers. Unfortunately for Marianne, one of Max's interests involved a sexual relationship with their mutual friend Else Jaffe (Green, 1974). "In 1910, the Webers were in Venice with the Jaffes, friends from Heidelberg. Edgar Jaffe was Max Weber's publisher and coeditor on the *Archiv*; Else Jaffe, one of Marianne's friends, had briefly been one of Max's students" (Adams and Sydie, 2001:189). The first time Max and Else became lovers was when Marianne attended a feminist conference. Their relationship continued until Max's death, and Else was even at his bedside, along with Marianne, during his dying days (Adams and Sydie, 2001). Max claimed to have maintained his affection for Marianne during this whole period, and Marianne did stay with Max; but her writings would reveal her own emerging sense of power and critical confidence. Among her publications are "The Question of Divorce" (1909), "Authority and Autonomy in Marriage" (1912), "On the Value of Housework" (1912), "Women and Objective Culture" (1913), all of which can be found in *Frauenfragen und Frauengedanken* (*Reflections on Women and Women's Issues*) (1919).

Max and Marianne remained married and to all appearances (to the outside world) displayed allegiance to one another. Max would defend her from antifeminist attacks, and Marianne remained committed to the idea of marriage and would work hard after Max's death to make sure his intellectual legacy remained intact. It often seems odd that a couple could remain together after one of the two is known to have cheated on the other; but this is not a new development and a contemporary parallel might be drawn to Bill and Hillary Clinton. Former U.S. President Bill Clinton has been involved in extramarital affairs, and yet his feminist wife Hillary has (at least externally) remained committed to the relationship while still maintaining creditability in the feminist world with her work on female empowerment and civil rights for people around the world. After her husband's death, Marianne would remain busy in the intellectual world. She published eight books in all, and she worked on feminist issues until the Nazis came into power in Germany, in 1933. She managed to publish *Erfülltes Leben* (*The Fulfilled Life*) in an underground press. Weber survived the war, but she was devastated to learn of the true horrors created by the Nazis during World War II. Her last years of life paid witness to the construction of a prosperous and democratic West Germany. Many of the participants of her Heidelberg intellectual salon were actively involved in this reconstruction. On March 12, 1954, Marianne Weber died in Heidelberg.

Significant Contributions to Sociology

Many students of social theory first hear of Marianne Weber as the wife of Max Weber, and then they hear of her influence on the next generation of social thinkers (e.g., Talcott Parsons) through her interpretations and teachings of Max Weber's sociology. But Marianne Weber made her own significant theoretical contributions to sociology, mostly in the areas of feminism and in marriage and family. Germany had been unified in 1871 under the authoritarian and militaristic regime of the monarchy of Prussia led by Bismarck. Bismarck instilled an unquestioned male-dominated society (Lengermann and Niebrugge-Brantley, 1998). Weber proposed that patriarchy was the root cause of the superiority of men in society and that women have been subjugated and disempowered as a result of her gender (Weber, 2003). In her fight to end the subjugation of married women, Weber (2003) proposed (1) the elimination of the husband's legal decision-making authority; (2) restructure of parental rights; (3) when it comes to differences of opinion between husband and wife, the husband decides for the sons and the wife decides for the daughters; and (4) the wife should have pecuniary independence through exact definitions of the support obligations of the husband. Her feminist thoughts on the social institution of marriage have had a lasting impact on society, especially in the form of child care and spousal support.

Industrialization allowed for the creation of an emerging middle class and political activists who attempted to make many changes in government and civil society. The feminist movement began in Germany during the late 1800s and was spearheaded by an active attempt to reach economic and political equality. Around 1905, a new power group of the German feminists emerged, and their primary concern of sexual autonomy led to what is known as "the erotic movement."

Helene Stocker became the leader of the erotic movement in 1906, and under her leadership, problems of sexual politics and matrimonial law became the most important issues.

> Within the bourgeois women's movement, this shift of interest triggered off violent disagreements about the relation between sexual and economic emancipation. The Association [Association for the Protection of Mothers] attacked the conventional ossification of bourgeois marriage and propagated as an alternative a "new ethic," whereby women could claim the right to engage in sexual relations regardless of material and legal considerations (Mommsen and Osterhammel, 1987:486).

What these women were proposing, according to Max Weber, was the right to "free love" and to the illegitimate child. He viewed the erotic movement as crass hedonism and ethically immoral. (Note the relevance of this material to contemporary society, where within just the past few years it has become, more or less, acceptable for women to have a child on their own and without a paternal-figure role model.) Marianne Weber agreed with her husband's stance and wrote in her book, *Ehefrau und Mutter in der Rechtsentwicklung*, that the standpoint of the women's movement should be with the equality of women, and less concerned with moral emancipation. In 1907, Marianne Weber gave a lecture at the Evangelical-Social Congress in Strasbourg. In this talk, "She defends the ethical and legal norms of modern marriage by drawing on the theory of rationalization, introducing evolutionary motifs" (Mommsen and Osterhammel, 1987:487). Weber made it clear that she believed marriage should be a lasting, exclusive life-companionship relationship between man and woman, with mutual obligations. Thus, she made two critical points. First, women should be treated equally in the social system, especially the social institution of marriage. Second, she viewed marriage strictly as a union between a man and a woman, thus alienating many other feminists.

Weber was certainly a feminist: "She defended a woman's right to, capability of, and need for sexual pleasure in the face of late Victorian sentiments that idealized the asexual woman" (Adams and Sydie, 2001:191). She believed that women should have the right to freedom from a patriarchal marital relationship. Her feminist sociology was centered on the realization that Germany, as with most societies, was based on a patriarchal social structure and social organization model. She stressed that women should have the right to financial independence, including perhaps the idea that a housewife should be paid for her domestic chores. (Note: The idea of a housewife being paid for her work has been discussed so often in feminists' circles that it is now a part of popular culture, especially in the form of story lines on television shows.) Weber believed that under a patriarchal society, the system is designed so that males can reach fulfillment of essential needs, whereas women are expected to be subordinate to the male and help him reach his full potential. Weber concluded that this system needs to be changed so that women may also reach their full potential.

THE LADIES OF SENECA FALLS

Feminism was begun in the United States by those who advocated equal rights for women. The origins of feminism are also found in the abolitionist movement of the 1830s (Anderson, 1997). The exact birthplace of feminism is Seneca Falls, New York. As Miriam Gurko (1974) asks and answers, "Who were the ladies of Seneca Falls? Originally there were five: five ladies sitting around a tea table in 1848 in the small town of Waterloo in upstate New York" (p. 2). The leader of this group was Elizabeth Cady Stanton; the others were Quaker preacher Lucretia Mott of Philadelphia, her sister Martha Wright, Jane Hunt, and Mary Ann McClintock. They proposed to do the nearly unthinkable, to call a woman's rights convention. The five ladies committed to take action despite the fact they had no idea how to organize such a meeting. There would be many obstacles to organizing a woman's rights gathering. Many of the prevailing social institutions were designed to keep women subordinate to men. The existing sociopolitical structure worked against them. For example, "Once a woman married, she forfeited her legal existence. She couldn't sign a contract, make a will, or sue in a court of law. If she received property from her father or other source, her husband could sell it and keep the money for himself" (Gurko, 1974:8). If she didn't marry, she would be mocked as an "old maid." The church was another social institution determined to keep a woman in her place. Women were instructed to know their place—the home. The social institution of education worked against women, as college doors were not opened to them. And, the press often led the public in denouncing any woman's effort to improve her social standing. Gurko (1974) provides what she describes as a typical comment on a woman's rights convention from the now-defunct *Syracuse Daily Star*, "which labeled the proceedings as a mass of corruption, heresies, ridiculous nonsense, and reeking vulgarities which these bad women have vomited forth for the past three days" (p. 10). As Stanton and Mott would point out, the most devastating barrier to women's rights was the acceptance of these ideological beliefs by so many women.

Despite all these obstacles, the Women's Rights Convention would be held in the Wesleyan Methodist Chapel, Seneca Falls, New York, on July 19–20, 1848. More than 300 people attended this first convention of women's rights. In a replica copy of the minutes, it states that the convention was gathered to discuss the social, civil, and religious condition of woman, and called on by the Women of Seneca County, New York. The "Declaration of Sentiments" was offered for the acceptance of the convention; after a few changes were suggested, the declaration was accepted as the guiding theme of the convention. The "Declaration of Sentiments" was modeled after the "Declaration of Independence." For example, paragraph two begins, "We hold these truths to be self-evident; that all men and women are created equal" (source: Women's Rights National Historical Park Service). The "Declaration" states that women have been victims of tyranny by men: "The history of mankind is a history of repeated injuries and usurpations on the part of man toward woman, having in direct object the establishment of an absolute tyranny over her" (U.S. Constitution Online, 2011). The document set demands for equality in such areas as custody laws, property rights, educational opportunities, and the participation in the church, professions, and politics. This convention was the beginning of a seventy-twoyear battle to gain women the right to vote in the United States. The Women's Rights Convention that took place in Seneca Falls represents the "first wave" in American feminism. (Note: As previously stated, we will learn about the subsequent waves of feminism in Chapter 13.)

In 1920, the United States became the seventeenth country in the world to give women the right to vote. The first country to do so was New Zealand in 1893. Interestingly, the U.S.S.R. was the seventh nation to give women the right to vote (1917).

Elizabeth Cady Stanton (1815–1902)

Elizabeth Cady Stanton led the call for the Seneca Falls Convention and wrote the first draft of the "Declaration of Sentiments" out of a strong sense of injustice and righteous indignation at the plight of women. "Elizabeth Cady Stanton was the best known and most conspicuous advocate of women's rights in the nineteenth century. For almost fifty years she led the first women's movements in America. She set its agenda, drafted its documents, and articulated its ideology" (Griffith, 1984:xiii). For most girls in the early nineteenth century, the normal course of things included modest education, marriage, raising a family, and keeping a house. But it was quite clear from early on that young Elizabeth Cady was not about to follow the normal course of action.

Born in Johnstown, New York, in 1815, Elizabeth was the seventh of the eleven children of Daniel and Margaret Livingston Cady. Named for Sir William Johnson, an Englishman who bought the site from the Indians before the Revolution, Johnstown was an intellectual and industrial center in the early nineteenth century. The Cayadadutta River at the north end of the village supplied power for factories (Griffith, 1984). The Cady family thrived in this environment and was very wealthy, socially prominent, and politically active. Her parents encouraged Elizabeth to pursue her childhood interests in traditionally held activities such as debating, learning Greek, and horseback riding; she excelled at all of them. She did very well in school but did not attend college because no colleges were open to women. She did attend the Troy Female Seminary and received the most advanced education available to a woman in her era (Women's Rights National Historical Park, 2011).

Stanton was influenced by family members (the Livingston name tied her to the old Dutch aristocracy in New York), outstanding teachers, and the preaching of Charles Grandison Finney during the Great Troy Revival of 1831. Finney had claimed to have seen Christ on a main street in Rochester, New York, and felt he had a mission similar to St. Paul (Griffith, 1984). Stanton was raised as a Presbyterian with the gloomy Calvinistic outlook of a punitive God. Finney's strenuous style and revival enthusiasm had quite an effect on impressionable adolescents, and Elizabeth was awe-struck as well. He taught that man and woman had free will to choose between salvation and damnation. When someone confessed their sins to him, Finney granted "conversion" to a reaffirmation of faith and an acceptance of an obligation to perfect oneself and one's community (this is similar to the conversion process of being "born again"). Elizabeth Cady's conversion left her feeling bad instead of good, and her family forbade any further discussion of religion or mention of Finney. This experience would lead her to religious indecision, and eventually religious superstitions would give way to ideas based on rational, scientific facts. But some good came out of this experience as well. She had always loved to debate, and she did admire Finney's ability to command the attention of his audience.

Elizabeth Cady spent many summers at the home of her cousin Gerrit Smith, a wealthy radical reformer. She learned about and became committed to antislavery, temperance, and other reforms. In 1839, Elizabeth Cady met Henry Brewster Stanton, who was an eloquent speaker of the abolitionist movement and one of its most capable and courageous leaders. The abolitionist movement was not very popular among the masses, and he was repeatedly attacked by violent mobs. Henry Stanton was also the financial secretary of the American Anti-Slavery Society (Gurko, 1974). Elizabeth and Henry quickly fell in love with each other and announced their engagement less than one month after first meeting. Her family and friends objected to the marriage. Her father, Judge Cady, disapproved of abolitionists, especially a nonaffluent one who presumed to marry his daughter. She initially broke off the engagement but continued to see him. A year later, when Henry informed Elizabeth that he was going to London as a delegate to the World Anti-Slavery Convention, he asked her one more time to marry him; she accepted. In the wedding vows, the word "obey" was omitted, and she objected to being called "Mrs. Henry Stanton" on the basis of equality. The couple would travel to London together, further inflaming Elizabeth Cady Stanton's desire for future activism.

> The antagonism to women evident in the debate aroused Elizabeth Cady Stanton more than the antislavery questions on the agenda. She was angry at the injustice of the situation and impatient with the hypocrisy of the abolitionists. The opposition of the most liberal leaders of the most radical movement of the era to a question of women's rights stunned her (Griffith, 1984:37).

Her outrage at the London meeting ignited her interest in women's rights. But it was also at this meeting that Cady Stanton met Lucretia Mott and formed an enduring friendship.

After an extended European trip, the newlywed couple returned to Johnstown. Henry, in an attempt to mend family feeling, decided to study law with his father-in-law Judge Cady. He clerked for fifteen months. On March 2, 1842, the first of the three boys was born to Elizabeth while she and Henry were still living at the Cady family home. After Henry Stanton finished his law studies, the family settled in Boston, where they became active in reform work and in the city's intellectual and cultural life. In 1846, the Stantons moved to Seneca Falls, New York. She was experiencing the life of an average middle-class white housewife. Henry was often away working, while Cady Stanton was raising three sons and taking care of a house. She missed the intellectual stimulation she enjoyed in Boston. The true nature of her discontent surfaced at a tea party in Waterloo, New York, at the home of Jane Hunt in early July 1848. "Cady Stanton vividly described her unhappiness to four women friends: Lucretia Mott, Martha Wright, Mary Ann McClintock, and Jane Hunt. The group decided then and there to call a convention to discuss the status of women" (Women's Rights National Historical Park, 2011). A week later they met again, drafted the "Declaration of Sentiments," and the convention was on. This meeting was the formal beginning of the women's rights movement, and Cady Stanton was the leader. After the convention she continued to work for women's rights, she wrote extensively, but family responsibilities prevented her from traveling and speaking outside the local area. In 1862, the Stanton family moved to New York City. Here, she articulated that the women's rights movement should be a broad platform of change for women, including woman suffrage, dress reform, girls' sports, equal employment, property rights, equal wages, divorce and custody law reform, collective households, coeducation, birth control, and religious reform (Women's Rights National Historical Park, 2011). When her children were grown, she began to travel the country to discuss women's issues. She helped write the three-volume *History of Woman Suffrage* (1887) before publishing her controversial autobiography, *Woman's Bible* (1895). The *Woman's Bible* was a series of commentaries on biblical passages that were antiwoman. Cady Stanton took exception, for example, to the passage that states God made man, man was lonely, so God made woman. She believed this to be insulting to women. The clergy said her interpretations were the work of the devil. Even many women suffragettes disagreed with the tenets of her book. It was a "controversial" end to a women's-rights crusader.

Lucretia Coffin Mott (1793–1880)

Lucretia Coffin Mott was one of the most active and successful reformers of the nineteenth century. A devout Quaker, she attributed her strength and courage to divine inspiration. She believed that all people possess "divine" elements, and consequently, all people are equal.

Lucretia Coffin grew up on Nantucket Island, off the coast of Cape Cod. Her father, Thomas Coffin, Jr., was a sea captain, who was away from home for long stretches of time as he chased sperm whales over the deep. Her mother, Anna Folger Coffin, a successful storekeeper, was herself a model of strength and self-reliance for her daughter. The Coffin family was Quaker, and as such, women were allowed to speak freely, they had a right to an education, and they could be ministers, something quite unthinkable in nearly any other religion. Lucretia Coffin Mott would become a minister herself while still in her twenties. The very fact that she was raised in Nantucket benefited her as a woman. "The island was a great whaling and fishing center, with the men away at sea for months at a time. In the absence of their husbands, the Nantucket housewives not only managed all the family affairs, but often set up small businesses of their own" (Gurko, 1974:52). Thus, as a child, Lucretia saw women in a position of authority.

Lucretia loved the island and was heartbroken when the family moved away when she was eleven and a half. They first moved from Nantucket to Boston, and then to Philadelphia, the center of Quaker life. Lucretia started school at age four and later attended the Nine Partners boarding school in Duchess County, New York. An outstanding student, she joined the faculty after graduation and met another young teacher, James Mott. They were married in Philadelphia in 1811. In keeping with their Quaker beliefs, the marriage was quite egalitarian. Religious faith was very important to both of the both of them. With the advent of the War of 1812, Thomas Coffin took a gamble and invested all of his money in a factory for the manufacture of cut nails, a new product of the Industrial Revolution. The gamble paid off as he earned huge sums of money from his factory. On August 3, 1812, Lucretia gave birth to her first child, Anna.

As a minister in the Quaker church, Lucretia's life was consumed with social issues. Her work was becoming increasingly affected by the growing controversy within the church over the issue of slavery. Some Quakers, including Mott, spoke out against slavery and the injustice of human bondage. However, many of the conservative elders felt such discussions were inappropriate. In 1827, the more liberal "Hicksites" broke away from the authoritarian Orthodox Friends church. The Hicksites believed it was their religious duty to protest slavery, but the Orthodox church dismissed them as heretics. Mott believed that religion must be based on "inward spiritual grace," not upon rigid creeds or fixed ceremonial rituals. Mott felt that religion "must be based on justice as well as upon reason and 'inner light,' it must be express itself in 'practical godliness'" (Gurko, 1974:54).

Lucretia Mott became aware that throughout Delaware, New Jersey, and Pennsylvania, Quaker men and women were becoming increasingly troubled by the growing power and authority of the Philadelphia elders. Protest against the elders reached its peak with their treatment of the prophet-like minister Elias Hicks, a man who preached against slavery, and whom Lucretia and James Mott had entertained in their home (Bacon, 1999). The elders denounced his antislavery speeches. This was the last straw for Mott. She joined the Hicksites in 1828 and became more actively involved in the antislavery struggle. Their home became an active station in the Underground Railway. James Mott joined the Free Produce Society, refusing to sell slavemade products, including cotton and sugar, in the Mott store. In 1833, delegates came to Philadelphia to form the American Anti-Slavery Society. Lucretia Mott was one of four women invited to attend the conventions, but only as observers. They would not be permitted to join the new society. Instead, Mott met with local abolitionist women, black and white, to organize the Philadelphia Female Antislavery Society. The local white community was horrified by the idea of interracial organizations and publicly protested the women's group. Led by Mott, the organization insisted that Blacks and Whites working together was an important step in combating racism, and educated others, by their example, of interracial friendship and cooperation (Women's Rights National Historical Park, 2011).

Her battle against slavery was constantly interrupted by the "woman question." Mott was forced to fight two battles at once: one against slavery/racism, and one against sexism. Women were routinely denied access to leadership positions in the male-dominated antislavery societies and were discouraged from participating in public activities (e.g., public debates, and serving as delegates to national conventions). These issues finally came to a boil at the 1840 World Antislavery Convention in London. Mott and seven other women attended as representatives of female antislavery societies, but the male delegates were divided over whether to recognize the women as "legitimate" delegates. Seated with the Motts was Elizabeth Cady Stanton, who struck up a friendship with Lucretia. They decided to discuss women's rights issues when they returned to the United States.

It would be eight years before Stanton and Mott were able to act on this decision. Mott was traveling throughout upstate New York and was invited to a tea party at the home of Jane Hunt, a Waterloo Hicksite Quaker. As described previously in this chapter, it was this famous tea party that set into motion the women's rights convention to be held in Seneca Falls. Mott championed a wide variety of causes beyond antislavery and women's rights; she was a lifelong peace activist who opposed the Civil War (even though many follow activists tried to convince her that this was the only way to end slavery); she was in favor of Indian rights and opposed to white aggression against native tribes and the taking of their lands; and she challenged intolerance and prejudice of any form. She continued her work until her death in 1880.

Growth of the Women's Rights Movements

As concluding remarks for this section on the "Ladies of Seneca Falls," it is worth summarizing that Seneca Falls, New York, is considered the American birthplace of feminism. The events that took place at the first Women's Rights Convention in Seneca Falls on July 19 and 20, 1848, set the tone for what is labeled the "first wave" of feminism in the United States. But certainly the feminist movement had surfaced in various places across the United States, and around the world, separate from Seneca Falls. Women like Harriet Tubman, born a slave, uneducated, apprenticed as a weaver, always deeply spiritual (who claimed to have visions from God), escaped from slavery when her master died in 1849, continue to serve as an inspiration today. Naturally, she enjoyed her newfound freedom after escaping slavery, but this did not last for long, as Tubman worried about her sister and her two children and others who were still slaves. Tubman decided to try and rescue them. Her determination to help free other slaves led to the forming of the Underground Railroad. It is believed that she led over 300 slaves to freedom. She is often referred to as the "Moses of her people" (Women's Rights National Historical Park, 2011). She would go on to create a Home for Indigent and Aged Negroes on her own property in Auburn, New York.

Susan B. Anthony was a friend of Cady Stanton, and as a single woman she had the time to travel and make speeches promoting women's rights. She would visit Stanton in Seneca Falls and then take her speeches and writings with her to travel throughout the country campaigning for women's rights. Susan Anthony was active in the women's movement by her own right. She also joined the Rochester (New York) Daughters of Temperance and became its president. Anthony was a highly competent organizer and fundraiser. She served as a delegate to the many temperance conventions in upstate New York. Susan Anthony was not among the original ladies of Seneca Falls, but she became close to many of them.

Summary

In a chapter such as this, where numerous individual theorists were discussed, it would be impractical to offer a summary of each woman. Instead, we look at the collectivity of the work produced by these women who contributed to classical sociological theory and/or social activism and feminism. From Martineau, who encouraged systematic data collection in the study of many specific pieces of the social environment, to Jane Addams, whose social activism spearheaded urban renewal in a variety of fashions to help the less fortunate, as well as the greater community, to the Ladies of Seneca Falls, who spearheaded the "first wave" of feminism, all these women made unique contributions to social theory.

Undeniably, women enjoy greater equality today than during the eras of all the women discussed in this chapter. But it's been a long battle and one that is certainly not over. The women theorists of the classical period of sociological theory organized more conventions, spearheaded more social movements, and fought for legislation that granted them more rights. The unequal status of women was not completely rectified during the classical period of social thought, but much progress has been made. The feminist movement gained new momentum in the late 1960s (e.g., the formation of the National Organization for Women in 1966 by Betty Friedan and associates) and continued in the 1970s (e.g., the Equal Rights Amendment passes both houses in 1972, the *Roe v. Wade* U.S. Supreme Court decision that granted women the right to an abortion in 1973). This period is known as the "second wave" of feminism and will be discussed in Chapter 13.

 Study and **Review** on **MySearchLab**

Discussion Questions

1. Harriett Martineau is referred to as the "mother of sociology." Why did Martineau consider it important to study the morals and manners of prisoners?
2. Of all the women discussed in this chapter, which woman has the greatest relevancy to contemporary society?
3. Describe the Hull House. What inspired its creation? What was its significance to the city of Chicago? Does your hometown offer anything similar to the Hull House?
4. Of all the women discussed in this chapter, which one made the greatest contribution to sociological theory specifically? Which woman, or women, contributed the most to social activism?
5. Explain the significance of the "Ladies of Seneca Falls." What is meant by the expression "the first wave of feminism"?

MySearchLab® Connections

MysearchLab is designed just for you. Each chapter features a customized study plan to help you learn and review key concepts and terms. Dynamic visual activities, videos, and readings found in the multimedia library will enhance your learning experience.

 Read on **MySearchLab**

▶ Addams, Jane. If Men Were Seeking the Franchise.
▶ Addams, Jane. Twenty Years at Hull House.
▶ Barnett, Ida Wells. False Accusations .

7 George Herbert Mead

 Listen to the Chapter Audio on MySearchLab

Chapter Outline

- Biography
- Intellectual Influences
- Investigation and Application of Mead's Concepts and Contributions
- Summary
- Discussion Questions

The review of George Herbert Mead represents a presentation in thought quite unique from most perspectives discussed to this point. Mead was an American sociologist, philosopher, social psychologist, and pragmatist. In his Introduction to *Mind, Self, and Society: From the Standpoint of a Social Behaviorist* (1962/1934), Charles W. Morris states,

> Philosophically, Mead was a pragmatist; scientifically, he was a social psychologist. He belonged to an old tradition—the tradition of Aristotle, Descartes, Leibniz; of Russell, Whitehead, Dewey—which fails to see any sharp separation or any antagonism between the activities of science and philosophy, and whose members are themselves both scientists and philosophers (p. ix).

Echoing Morris's sentiments, Collins and Makowsky (2010) state, Mead's social thought is relational, evolutionary, and pragmatic. Upon reading Mead one is struck with a sense of what Alfred North Whitehead called

> "the interrelatedness of things." ... Mead's theoretical achievement was arrived at inductively by observation of what happens in the daily lives of human beings. For Mead the society in which we interact with one another in sundry groups constitutes an empirical reality (pp. 152–153).

Mead's works are primarily concerned with the micro aspects of human behavior; that is, instead of examining how social systems operate, he is more interested in how everyday people behave. Because of his work on issues related to one's sense of self, development of self, and social acts, students tend to find Mead's concepts and contributions to social theory relatable. Mead's discussion of the two components of self—the "I" and the "me"—may remind readers of the conversations they have with themselves when evaluating their own appearance and behavior (e.g., looking at yourself in the mirror before you leave home in the morning and reflecting upon your appearance in either a positive or negative manner—"I look pretty good in this outfit") and their evaluation of the social acts of others (e.g., as in, "What was she thinking wearing that to class?").

George Herbert Mead (1863–1931), American pragmatist, philosopher, social scientist, and primary founder of symbolic interactionism. (The Granger Collection, NYC/The Granger Collection)

BIOGRAPHY

George Herbert Mead was born on February 27, 1863, in South Hadley, Massachusetts. Mead came from a religious and educated family that encouraged his intellectual development. When Mead was seven, the family moved to Oberlin, Ohio. George's father, Hiram Mead, was a minister in the Congressional Church and taught homiletics (the art of preaching) at Oberlin Theological Seminary (Miller, 1973). Hiram Mead benefited from the progressive education for which Oberlin was known (Farganis, 2011). Oberlin was founded in 1833 by a militant Congregationalist reformer, the Reverend John Jay Shipherd (1802–1844), and was one of the first American colleges to admit Blacks. In 1841, it became the first coeducational college to grant a bachelor's degree to women (Coser, 1977). Oberlin was one of the primary stops along the route of the Underground Railroad that helped thousands of southern Black slaves to escape to the north and to Canada.

George's mother, Elizabeth Storrs Billings, came from a family background in which intellectual achievement was greatly valued (Coser, 1977). When her husband died, Elizabeth taught at Oberlin College to make ends meet and later became the president of Mount Holyoke College (Miller, 1973). Mead's only sibling, Alice, born four years before him, married Albert Temple Swing, a minister from Fremont, Nebraska (Miller, 1973).

There is little information on Mead's childhood except that the family spent a few summer vacations on a farm in New England (Miller, 1973). His mother saw to it that the young George would go through his daily regimen of prayer, study, and good works. It was her dream that George would follow in his father's footsteps in the Christian ministry (Shalin, 2000). Mead entered Oberlin College at the age of sixteen and was described as a serious, cautious, quiet, mild-mannered, and kind-hearted person (Miller, 1973). Academically, he was interested in literature and poetry, as well as English and American history.

Oberlin College was not nearly as progressive in its academic thinking as it was in displaying a sense of social conscience for the oppressed members of society. Challenging the narrow theological dogmatism of the college was strongly discouraged. Memorization of "truths" consistent with Christian theology was encouraged over intellectual debate. Mead's son recalls that while George was at Oberlin, "Questioning was discouraged, ultimate values being determined by learned men in the dogmas and passed on to the moral philosophers for dissemination" (Wallace, 1967:398). For a mind as thirsty for stimulating conversation and knowledge as Mead's, this was surely difficult, as he found throughout his lifetime that the best expression for his brilliant, encyclopedic mind came in the form of conversation.

Socially, Oberlin College did not allow dancing or drinking. Many students were active members of the Anti-Saloon League, a group founded in Oberlin that preached on the evils of alcohol. Concerned over potential interaction among men and women coeds, the college maintained separate library hours for males and females (Pampel, 2000). Mead's negative reaction to Oberlin's excessive theological agenda led him to lose his faith in the Christian ethics. "The son of many generations of Puritan theologians had lost his faith in the dogmas of the church" (Coser, 1977:342). Mead once remarked that he spent 20 years trying to unlearn what he learned the first 20 years of his life (Schellenberg, 1978). He had pushed himself in Christian ideology, for the sake of his mother, for as long as he could, and confessed to his best friend, Henry Castle, that "her happiness is bound up in me" (Shalin, 2000:303).

In 1881, Hiram Mead died, leaving very little in financial support for his family. George found a job as a waiter to pay his way through college, and his mother taught at the college. In 1883, Mead graduated from Oberlin and accepted a job to teach at a primary school. Several teachers had just resigned from the school because they were unable to cope with a large number of students who were terrorizing classmates and teachers. Mead stood up to the rowdy students and began expelling large numbers of them from school. The Board of Trustees failed to support Mead and discharged him after just four months (Miller, 1973).

For the next three years, Mead alternated between jobs as a tutor and as a surveyor for a railroad in Minnesota and Canada. He had long abandoned his one-time dream of starting a literary paper in New York, but he continued to read widely during his spare time. Mead's thirst for an intellectual outlet for his energetic mind was beginning to get the best of him. He began to write to his college friend Henry Castle. Castle came from a wealthy, well-educated family that had extensive land holdings and political influence in Hawaii (Baldwin, 1986). While at Oberlin, Mead and Castle often discussed issues related to life, God, poetry, and evolution. The two friends came to favor modern secular beliefs over religious doctrines. It is most likely Castle who had the greatest influence over Mead's reexamination and eventual break from his theological tradition (Wallace, 1967). His future interest in psychology would be shaped, at least in part, by a conscious effort to avoid direct confrontation with his past theological values (Schellenberg, 1978). Mead was also becoming acquainted with the new developments in the natural sciences, and in particular was impressed by Darwin's work on the evolution of species (Pampel, 2000).

In 1887, Castle had been admitted to the graduate program in philosophy at Harvard University and persuaded Mead to give graduate school a try. They would live as roommates and continue their philosophical discussions. Mead found his philosophy courses stimulating but too abstract and isolated from the real world (Pampel, 2000). At Harvard, Mead's philosophical interests lay in the romantic philosophers and Hegelian idealism, as taught by Josiah Royce (Baldwin, 1986). Mead also studied under William James, whom he worked for, and tutored his children (Miller, 1973). Both Royce and James left a permanent mark on Mead's life and outlook (Coser, 1977). His exposure to advanced philosophy further eroded Mead's remaining Christian beliefs (Pampel, 2000).

Unhappy with the abstract nature of philosophy, Mead decided to change his course of study to physiological psychology. Psychology was still just a branch of philosophy at that time, but Mead deemed it more practical and scientific to the obscure thought of many of the philosophers he studied. For his second year of graduate school, Mead accepted a scholarship to study in Germany, the location of the world's most renowned specialists in physiological psychology (Pampel, 2000). Mead first went to Leipzig to study with Wilhelm Wundt, whose conception of the "gesture" would greatly influence his later works (Coser, 1977). Also at Leipzig, Mead studied under Stanley Hall, the American physiological psychologist who sparked Mead's interest in that discipline (Farganis, 2000). In 1899, Mead went to Berlin to study both psychology and philosophy taught in the tradition of Simmel (Pampel, 2000). Coser (1977) speculates that Mead was taught by Simmel himself, although he was never able to confirm this.

In 1891, while Mead was in Berlin, Henry Castle brought his sister Helene with him to visit George. Over a period of just a few months, Helene and Mead became very close, fell in love, and were married on October 1, 1891. He quit graduate school (never earning a graduate degree) to accept a lecturer's teaching position at the University of Michigan, teaching philosophy and psychology (Scheffler, 1974).

At Michigan, the young and idealistic Mead hoped to combine scholarship and social action, a tradition he learned and embraced while in Germany. His colleagues included Charles Cooley, James Tufts, and the young philosopher John Dewey. Dewey served as a role model for Mead, as he was already active in social involvement and academic success. Dewey had published his first book at age 27, and his second book at age 29. This work ethic would follow Dewey throughout his life. Mead and Dewey quickly realized their similar interests and became lifelong friends. Dewey's daughter would state, some time later, that the Meads and Deweys remained friends until their death (Strauss, 1964).

In 1893, Dewey received an offer to become the chair of the department of philosophy at the University of Chicago. Although Dewey had known Mead for just one year, and George did not have a graduate degree, Dewey insisted that he be allowed to bring Mead to Chicago with him as condition of his employment. Further, despite the lack of any publications, Dewey was even able to secure the position of assistant professor for Mead at Chicago. Mead would remain at the University of Chicago for the rest of his life.

His Career

The extraordinary growth of both the city of Chicago and the University of Chicago provided Mead and Dewey with a wonderfully exciting intellectual environment. The city of Chicago was little more than a small log fort in 1833 and had become a major city just six decades later (Faris, 1967). At the time of Mead's appointment, Chicago was primarily a meat-packing center occupied by numerous slaughterhouses. Chicago boasted the first steel-framed skyscraper; reversed the flow of the Chicago River; and, as a result of massive and rapid migration along with the attendant disorganization of many slum districts, laid claim to numerous social problems. It was the perfect place for applied academic study and social reform.

The University of Chicago had just opened prior to the arrival of Mead and Dewey, through an endowment funded by such industrialists as John D. Rockefeller (Pampel, 2000). It opened its pseudo-Gothic doors in 1892 under the presidency of William Harper, a professor of Bible at Yale University, with the idea that it would compete with the older eastern universities such as Harvard, Yale, and Princeton. Harper was an aggressive president who ruthlessly raided eastern universities, offering twice the normal salary and light teaching loads, in hopes of attracting the most brilliant scholars. The original faculty included eight professors who gave up college presidencies to teach at the University of Chicago (Coser, 1977).

The city of Chicago had become a practical social laboratory for social thinkers, especially sociologists. Mead's greatest contribution to sociology and the so-called Chicago School of thought rests with his development of social psychology. Influenced strongly by Dewey and the environment of the university, Mead began to evolve a philosophy of social life that combined a number of academic interests. His philosophy aimed to combine thought with action, science and progress, and the individual and community (Pampel, 2000). Mead and Dewey were heavily involved with the philosophical school called pragmatism. "In essence, pragmatism extends the scientific methods of the natural sciences to all areas of intellectual life" (Pampel, 2000:179).

During the early years at Chicago, Mead remained in the public shadow of Dewey. When Dewey accepted a position at Columbia (leaving because he felt that the University of Chicago was not providing enough support for his educational experiments), Mead did not assume the eminent position once held by his friend. One reason was his limited publications. Mead experienced great difficulty putting his ideas in writing, but that never stopped his creative thoughts. His lectures were eagerly greeted and well attended by students. He never used notes and possessed a powerful style of presentation. Mead seldom looked directly at the students, and discouraged questions and discussion. He never entered the classroom until after the bell rang, left immediately at the end of class, and took measures to avoid contact with students interested in asking him questions. Despite this, his students loved his lectures (Pampel, 2000). Most of Mead's major works were published by graduate students from notes taken in class.

Mead expanded on Wundt's theories of the gesture by emphasizing the importance of social factors in the evolution and development of communication, role taking, mind, and self. Between 1910 and 1920, Mead worked on integrating Einstein's theory of relativity with his own thinking, attempting to bring unity to the entire scientific and pragmatic worldview. He eventually pieced together an evolutionary cosmology that integrated all the sciences and resolved philosophical problems in terms of emergence—beginning with the emergence of the solar system and planets, then dealing with the evolution of life and increasingly higher levels of animal awareness, and culminating in human mind, self, and society (Baldwin, 1986). During the last years of his life, Mead turned increasing attention toward macro-societal issues and international relationships, thus formulating his unified theoretical perspective (Baldwin, 1986).

In early 1931, after teaching at the University of Chicago for nearly forty years, Mead became embroiled in a bitter conflict between the department and the president of the university. So great was the bitterness that Mead wrote a letter of resignation from his hospital bed, indicating his desire to leave not only the university, but Chicago as well. Upon his release from the hospital the next day, April 26, he died suddenly at the age of 68. At his memorial service, James H. Tufts said, "He was the most interesting conversationalist I knew. He was informed and informing" (Miller, 1973:39). His close friend Dewey stated, "His mind was deeply original—in my contacts and my judgment the most original mind in philosophy in America, of the last generation....I dislike to think what my own thinking might have been were it not for the seminal ideas which I derived from him" (Scheffler, 1974:150).

INTELLECTUAL INFLUENCES

There were numerous influences on Mead's thoughts, as he possessed a wide variety of interests. He was knowledgeable in sociology, philosophy, psychology, history, and biology. Mead was familiar with mathematics and mathematical rationality and enjoyed music and poetry. His family's background in religion exposed him to Puritan Christianity and theological dogmatic thinking. And, as we have already learned, Henry Castle played a significant role in influencing Mead's questioning of religion and the theological restraints that existed in the United States, especially at Oberlin.

William James

The properties of Mead's social psychology and symbolic interactionism can be traced, at least in part, to William James. In his brilliant *Principles of Psychology* (1890), James called for the reexamination of the relations between individual and society (Martindale, 1981). Although James was a product of his time and accepted the instinct theory that was so prevalent, he began to believe that there were other aspects beyond biology that tended to modify behavior. His works on *habit* were of special importance as James recognized that habit reduces the need for conscious attention. If an individual is capable of forming new habits, then he is also capable of modifying his behavior. James (1890) believed that the individual acquires a new nature through habit.

A second critical aspect of James's psychology was his rethinking of the role of "consciousness." He noted that consciousness always involves some degree of awareness of the person's self. The person appears in thought in two ways:

> partly known and partly knower, partly object and partly subject....For shortness we may call one the *Me* and the other the *I*....I shall therefore treat successively of (a) the self as known, or the *Me*, the "empirical ego" as it is sometimes called; and of (b) the self as knower, or the *I*, the "pure ego" of certain authors (James, 1890:176).

The empirical self, or *me*, is the sum total of all the person can claim as one's own, their feelings, emotions, actions of self-seeking and self-preservation. People possess as many social selves as there are individuals who have images of them in mind. The self as knower, the *I*, or pure ego, is a much more complicated subject matter (James, 1890). The *I* refers to the sense of self that a particular person possesses at any given specific moment in time.

In the tradition of James, Mead (1934) argued that consciousness must be a product of the dynamic relationship between a person and her social environment. Mead stated that it is an erroneous idea that "'Mental' phenomena [are] conditioned [to] reflexes and similar physiological mechanisms—in short, to purely behavioristic terms" (p. 10). Every individual is constantly involved in a succession of interactions with others, all of which influence and shape one's mind. Consciousness is continuous, subject to the vast array of stimuli presented to it from the social environment.

Mead was clearly influenced by James in his works on the development of self. Mead even used the same terminology of the "I" and "me" in explaining the structure of the self. Mead reasoned that the self consisted of an "I" which is capable of understanding the social "me." Further discussion on Mead's usage of the "I" and "me" follows later in this chapter.

German Idealism

Learning from the ideas of Johann Gottlieb Fichte, Friedrich Wilhelm Schelling, and Georg Wilhelm Friedrich Hegel, whom Mead called "the Romantic Philosophers," Mead understood the German idealistic tradition tended to generalize, and made a philosophical doctrine of the notion of the life process (Coser, 1977). The Romantic idealists utilized the self–not-self process in experience and identified this process with the subject–object process. This subject–object process was similar to James's analysis. These German romantic idealists established a philosophy that humans see themselves through reflexive experience. As Collins and Makowsky (2010) explain, "The more we become aware of ourselves in the continuing social process, the more we increase our 'species consciousness'" (p. 153). Mead learned from this German tradition that there is no consciousness that is not conscious of something; therefore, the subject and object are inevitably interrelated. There cannot be a subject without the object being aware of it, just as there cannot be an object without it being a subject. "Mead took the idea that the development of the self requires reflexivity—that is, the ability of an individual (the subject) to be an object to himself as a result of 'taking the attitudes of others who are involved in his conduct'" (Adams and Sydie, 2001). This idea would greatly influence Mead's concept of the generalized other.

Mead came to view the German idealists as preoccupied with the relations of the self to its objects. He felt that Fichte was too concerned with moral experiences. He believed that Schelling and Hegel focused too much attention on the aesthetic experience and experience of thought, respectively (Coser, 1977). Above all, Mead found fault with Hegel for not having formulated adequate concepts of the individual and of the future. Hegel's philosophy is thus incapable of grasping individuality in its concreteness (Joas, 1985).

Having studied in Germany, Mead was most directly influenced by Wilhelm Wundt, where he became impressed by Wundt's theories of language and the gesture. Wundt was the heir apparent of the German idealistic tradition. He was able to relate German idealism to the social sciences through his psychophysical parallelism (Martindale, 1981). In the introduction to Mead's *Mind, Self, and Society*, Charles Morris clarifies the distinction between Darwin and Wundt's conception of the gesture by explaining that Wundt helped to separate the gesture from its internal emotional implication and regard it in a social context. In the tradition of Wundt, Mead viewed the gesture as the transitional link to language from human action. The gesture preceded language and mediates the development of language as the basic mechanism that allows for the "sense of self" to arise during the course of ongoing social interaction. Thus, Mead came to argue that the gesture can *only* be explained in a social context. Years later, a more mature Mead (1934) would come to describe a gesture as those phases of the act which bring about the adjustment of the response of the other.

From Hegel, Mead took the idea that consciousness and society were dialectically emergent phenomena (Adams and Sydie, 2001). Mead replaced Hegel's "Spirit" with a concept of a "unified world" that emerges through the realization of universal human potential. He believed that social development was dependent on individuals becoming aware of their "opposition to one another" and working through such oppositions (Mead, 1938).

Charles Darwin and Evolutionism

As with many of the early social thinkers, Mead was raised in a religious family. However, an analytical mind that seeks the truth and supports the validity of science is bound to question religious dogma. The primary influence on Mead's final abandonment from the theological shackles of his youth was Charles Darwin (Coser, 1977). The theory of evolution presented by Darwin was enough factual evidence for Mead to conclude that the religious doctrine that he was raised to believe was false. Darwin's influence on Mead extended to his philosophical and psychological beliefs as well.

For Mead, the key figure for a new beginning in philosophy was Charles Darwin. Darwin's model of an organism in an environment, to which it must adapt in order to survive, provides the means for the understanding and discovery of all behaviors, humans included. The knowledge of human behavior rests with the awareness of all the conditions set by nature on the organism's reproduction of itself. In addition, the organism must be able to deduce the subject's behavior within the external world that is separate from itself (Joas, 1985).

As for Darwin's influence on psychology, Mead (1934) stated,

> One of the important documents in the history of modern psychology, particularly for the psychology of language, is Darwin's *Expression of the Emotions in Man and Animals.* Here Darwin carried over his theory of evolution into the field of what we call "conscious experience" (p. 15).

Darwin showed that there are a number of acts that express emotions. The part of the organism that most vividly expresses emotions is the face. Darwin studied the muscles themselves in order to determine whether such changes in the face might actually express emotions such as anger. Darwin studied the blood flow in fear and in terror in order to determine if changes in the blood flow itself causes a change in emotions. Darwin theorized that there must be some rhythm of circulation in blood flow that corresponds to various emotions.

According to Mead (1934), Darwin discovered a greater validity in the acts or gestures of behaviors themselves. For example, dogs exhibit attitudes (gestures) of anger and intent to attack (act) with their teeth. "The attitude, or in a more generalized term, the gesture, has been preserved after the value of the act has disappeared" (Mead, 1934:16).

Mead vehemently disagreed with the psychology of Darwin that assumed emotion was a psychological state, a state of consciousness, and that this state could not itself be formulated in terms of the attitude or the behavior of the form. Mead found no evidence for the prior existence of consciousness, and concluded that consciousness is an emergent form of behavior. The social act is a precondition of the conception of consciousness.

Darwin taught Mead to think in terms of process (evolutionary process) instead of fixed forms. Mead (1936) came to realize that process will shape form. The organism has one form now, but it will have another form later, dependent on the conditions under which it is exposed. For Mead, the evolutionary process was a pragmatic, scientific approach to problem-solving. "Evolution is the process of meeting and solving problems" (Mead, 1936:143). Thus, the primary influence of evolutionary thought on Mead was the recognition that there are no fixed structures; instead, there exist changing forms through a continuing process.

Darwin's general idea of evolution was very important to Mead, but it was his idea of random variations that Mead found most intriguing. As Mead (1934) interpreted Darwin's idea that constant pressure leads to the selection of which variants are better adapted to the conditions under which selection occurs, Mead concluded that it was this randomness that allows for the unpredictability and indeterminism in the course of human evolution.

American Pragmatism

A critical influence on Mead's intellectual thinking was *pragmatism*. Although Mead would become one of the key figures in the development of pragmatism, he was initially introduced to pragmatic philosophy by John Dewey, William James, and James Baldwin. Mead (1938) viewed pragmatism as a "natural American outgrowth." It reflected the triumph of science in American society and a belief in the superiority of scientific data and analysis over philosophical dogma and other forms of inferior beliefs. Pragmatists reject the idea of absolute truths and regard all ideas as provisional and subject to change in light of future research (Ritzer, 2000). For pragmatists, truth and reality do not simply exist "out there"—they are actively created as humans act in and toward the world (Shalin, 1986). Truth is determined by humans' adaptations to their environments, therefore revealing the transitive character of both truth and consciousness.

Pragmatists believe that human beings reflect on the meaning of a stimulus before reacting. The meaning placed on various acts depends on the purpose of the act, the context in which it is performed, and the reactions of others to the act (Adams and Sydie, 2001). Mead's notion of the act as social was directly influenced by Dewey and Cooley. Dewey believed that reflexive action(s) leads to the construction of such issues as morality. Thus, Mead came to view even issues such as ethics and morality as socially constructed and not fixed entities. Different cultures are easily explained by the realization of the fact that people with different life experiences come to different interpretations of events and impose different meanings on acts.

The collaboration of ideas between Dewey and Mead was mutually beneficial. On the one hand, close examination of Mead's social psychology reveals many influences from Dewey. On the other hand, as Charles Morris (1962) states in the "Introduction" to *Mind, Self, and Society* in regard to both Dewey and Mead,

> Neither stands to the other in the exclusive relation of teacher to student; both...were of equal though different intellectual stature; both shared in a mutual give-and-take according to their own particular genius. If Dewey gives range and vision, Mead gave analytical depth and scientific precision (p. xi).

Behaviorism

Mead (1934) defined behaviorism as simply an approach to the study of the experience of the individual from the point of view of one's conduct (behavior). His version of behaviorism was not consistent with the way in which it was used by his contemporaries, especially John B. Watson. The behaviorism of Mead's time was borrowed from psychologists who studied animal behavior and applied it to humans. Watson represented the attempt to account for sociopsychological phenomena in purely behavioristic terms (Martindale, 1981). Mead criticized Watson for ignoring the inner experiences of consciousness and mental imagery.

However, Mead did believe that inner experiences could be studied by behaviorists, as long as a *social*-behavioristic approach was utilized. This social-behavioristic approach would lead to the development of *symbolic interactionism*. Instead of studying the mind introspectively, Mead focused on the act (the social act). Acts are behaviors that respond to stimuli. In a variation of the stimulus–response relationship described by behaviorists and exchange theorists, Mead described a stimulus–act relationship. The difference is that the inner consciousness responds to the stimulus before the individual responds, thus creating an *act* that takes in account the existence of the mind and free will.

INVESTIGATION AND APPLICATION OF MEAD'S CONCEPTS AND CONTRIBUTIONS

George Herbert Mead is generally described as the founder of modern symbolic interactionism. He can also be described as a social psychologist who explained the emergence of mind, consciousness, and self through human symbolic interaction. Beyond that, Mead developed a philosophical system that allowed him to construct a social theory that unifies all facets of society and social experience—subjective and objective, macro and micro (Baldwin, 1986).

As an American and influenced by the American values of liberty, equality, and individualism, Mead's experiences differed greatly from those of the Europeans who helped to create the field of sociology. American history is very different from that of Europe's history of feudal structures with a monarchy, an aristocracy, and serfdom. The American Bill of Rights was designed to limit the power of the central government so that no such past European political structures could exist in the United States. The values of freedom and individual effort contributed to the development of market capitalism relatively free from government control (Pampel, 2000). American values, concerns, issues, and ways of thinking left their marks on early American sociology as it developed a practical, can-do attitude toward the world (Garner, 2000). This attitude led to the formation of pragmatism.

As Shalin (1992) explains, for much of the twentieth century, the Europeans rejected pragmatism and dismissed it as a crude expression of Anglo-Saxon utilitarianism. Even the European thinkers sympathetic to the new American intellectual current found it inferior to the continental philosophical tradition. By the 1960s, European thinkers such as Jürgen Habermas began to acknowledge the validity of pragmatism and its counterpart, symbolic interactionism (Shalin, 1992).

Pragmatism

Mead (1964) traced the rise of American pragmatism to the scientific developments of behavioristic psychology and empirical methodology. *Pragmatism* is, in essence, the extension of the scientific method to all areas of intellectual inquiry, including psychology, sociology, and philosophy. Pragmatic analysis involves all ideas and theories being tested on their ability to solve problems and provide useful information. Thus, an idea can be evaluated in terms of its consequences. Mead's version of pragmatism, then, is like a philosophical variation of a "costs–benefits analysis." Mead (and the Chicago School social thinkers) integrated a philosophical system that is designed to advance all facets of human knowledge and improve the human condition by the rigorous application of scientific methods (Baldwin, 1986).

Pragmatism provides an intellectual justification for social action, therefore integrating consistently with the American respect for problem-solving, progress, and democracy. Mead felt that all ideas and theories should be tested in the real world for their consequences; those that make society better, help solve problems, and work in the real world are judged valid and valuable. Unlike most philosophers, Mead rejected isolated thinking, and the lack of application, as a means of relating to the real world. Rather than debates about "truths," the American pragmatic approach stressed by Mead would concentrate on testing the ideas in the real social world (Pampel, 2000). For example, in the debate over the existence of God, a question that, despite centuries of religious and philosophical debate, has failed to be answered empirically, pragmatists would concern themselves with issues of: Does the belief in God make for a better society, encourage moral action, or improve human lives?

The pragmatic philosophy sees human beings as active and purposeful creatures. Yes, humans are biological creatures, but they are also social beings capable of developing an active, coping self in society (Garner, 2000). Mead argued that humans are not fixed beings with predetermined (by biology) behavioral patterns; instead, they are products of their environment capable of learning and changing.

Societies of the West have long accepted the validity of the pragmatic approach and will certainly continue to value this scientific method in the future. Pragmatic thinking dominates business, commerce, and politics. Most of the daily decisions made by individuals are pragmatically induced as we seek the most efficient path toward a desired end. These desired ends may be simple (e.g., getting a cup of coffee before work or class), relatively more complicated (e.g., finding someone to repair your virus-ridden computer), and life-impacting (e.g., choosing the "right" major). Choosing the "right" major is an important decision for nearly all college students, and there are a number of considerations to ponder. A good place to start involves asking yourself, "What type of work can I see myself doing for the rest of my life?" If you are an accounting major but dread the idea of working behind a desk in an office the rest of your life, you may want to reconsider your major. If you want to help less fortunate people, you may want to become a social work major. However, if making lots of money after you graduate is your primary end goal, social work is not the right field for you. The highest-paying jobs, not surprisingly, are those in engineering (petroleum, aerospace, chemical, electrical, and nuclear), applied mathematics, biomedical engineering, physics, and computer engineering. As one might imagine, these fields require majoring in challenging disciplines. (All academic disciplines, of course, are challenging in their own way.) Consequently, some may find it more pragmatic to major in a discipline that matches other skills possessed by the student.

Symbolic Interactionism

Ironically, the most important thinker associated with the Chicago School and *symbolic interactionism* was not a sociologist but rather a philosopher, Mead. It must be made clear that there was no such field as symbolic interactionism per se when Mead first started teaching social psychology at Chicago. It was Herbert Blumer, following in the tradition of Mead and Cooley, who coined the term *symbolic interactionism* in 1937. It was Mead's students who put together their notes on his courses and published *Mind, Self, and Society* posthumously under his name, which had primary influence on Blumer and the development of symbolic interactionism.

Mead believed that human beings have the capacity to think and decide on their own how they should act in given situations, and that they react on the basis of their perceptions and definitions of the situations in which they find themselves (Cockerham, 1995). Mead did not ignore legitimate social forces that strongly influence or limit alternate plans, such as being born into an economically lower-class family, or losing one's job due to economic downsizing. But the symbolic interaction approach suggests that people cope with the reality of their circumstances according to their comprehension of the situation (Cockerham, 1995).

Mead placed a great importance on the symbolic meaning of the act, not just the act itself (Alexander, 1987). He insisted that "objects" exist in the social world based on the meaning social actors place upon them. As a result, some objects have a greater meaning to some people, and less meaning to others. In the National Hockey League (NHL), for example, teams compete for the Stanley Cup, a trophy awarded to the winning team following multiple (four) rounds of playoff games. For NHL players and fans, the Stanley Cup has great meaning, and any discussion about winning "the Cup" takes on symbolic meaning. However, for people who are not fans of the NHL, any discussion on "who will win the Cup this year" is lost in symbolic significance. As another example of the relevancy of symbolic meanings of mundane items (like trophies), consider the value some people place on designer handbags. For most of us, a handbag serves a pragmatic function (it carries needed items). For others, however, paying $2,695 (2011 retail price) for a Valentino studded leather bag is a "must-have" item because of its symbolic value. (Note: In 2012, the most expensive handbag, according to the Singular Investor, was the Mouawad's 1001 Nights diamond purse valued at $3.8 million.) That some people place a high value on one particular item and others value different items reflects Mead's contention that how people perceive the world is an active process as actors respond selectively to given stimuli, and these responses, social acts, are motivated symbolically.

From a sociological perspective, Mead's greatest contribution to social thought lies with his ideas on symbolic interactionism. Considered one of the "Big Three," or original three, sociological theories (along with conflict and functionalism), symbolic interactionism has maintained a steady presence within the discipline. With its brilliant insights to micro-sociological behavior, symbolic interactionism will remain a dominant theory in the future. In Chapter 10 we will learn much more about symbolic interactionism and Mead's influence on its creation. Mead also influenced the creation of other related theories (known collectively as the sociologies of *everyday life*).

Mind, Self, and Society

Mead's *Mind, Self, and Society* represents his attempt to understand individual social experiences in relation to society. He argued that there can be no self, no consciousness of self, and no communication apart from society. Mead felt that social experience is the sum of the total dynamic realities observable by the individual who is a part of the ongoing societal process (Kallen, 1956). Society must be understood as a structure that emerges through an ongoing process of communicative social acts and through interactions between persons who are mutually oriented toward each other (Coser, 1977).

Mead (1934) viewed the *mind* as a process and not a thing, as an inner conversation with one's self, which arises and develops within the social process and is an integral part of that process. The mind reflects the human capacity to conceive what the organism perceives, define situations, evaluate phenomena, convert gestures into symbols, and exhibit pragmatic and goal-directed behavior.

The mind, or mentality, resides in the ability of the organism to respond to the environment, which in turn responds, so that the individual can control responses to stimuli from the environment. The mind emerges when the organism demonstrates its capacity to point out meanings to others and to itself (Strauss, 1956). Mead feels that the human animal has the unique capacity of controlling his responses to environmental stimuli and isolating those responses during the very act itself. This ability is the product of language (Miller, 1973). Language becomes the mechanism of control during the reflection process of interaction between the organism and the environment.

The concept of *self* is a critical issue in Mead's works. The *self* involves the process whereby actors reflect on themselves as objects. Thus, the self has the rare ability to be both object and subject. The self is something which has a development; it is not initially there at birth, but arises in the process of social experience and activity. The developmental process of the self is not biological, but rather it emerges from social forces and social experiences. Even the human body is not representative of self until the mind has developed and recognizes it as such. The body can simply be there as an existent structure in the real world, but the self has the characteristic that it is an object to itself; and that characteristic can then distinguish itself from other objects and from the body (Pfuetze, 1954).

Language represents the developmental process from interpreting gestures to the capability of utilizing symbolic communication and interaction. Sharing a language allows people the ability to put themselves in the role of the other and to understand why they act the way that they do. It is this reflexivity that allows for the development of self because the persons are able to consciously adjust and modify their own behavior (Mead, 1934).

In regard to *society,* Mead states,

> Human society as we know it could not exist without minds and selves, since all its most characteristic features presuppose the possession of minds and selves by its individual members; but its individual members would not possess minds and selves if these had not arisen within or emerged out of human social process in its lower stages of development (1934:227).

Mead believed that the behavior of all humans has a basic social aspect to it. The experience and behavior of the individual is always a component of a larger social whole or process. The organization of human experience and behavior is *society*. Because humans have the ability to manipulate their environment, a wide variety of human societies may exist.

The relevancy of Mead's concepts of *mind, self*, and *society* resides with the fact that these concepts of essential elements of the sociologies of the "everyday life" (see Chapters 10 and 12). The concept of *self* is especially important as the focus of psychological and micro-sociological analysis begins here.

The "I" and the "Me"

Mead is the earliest of the social thinkers to examine the socialization process from the interactionist perspective. He believed that human behavior is almost totally a product of interaction with others. The self, which can be an object to itself, is essentially a social structure that arises from social experience. Borrowing from Locke's usage of the concept *tabula rasa* (see Chapter 1), Mead insisted that a baby is born with a "blank slate," without predispositions to develop any particular type of personality. The personality that develops is a product of that person's interactions with others.

According to Mead, the self is composed of two parts: the "I" (the unsocialized self) and the "me" (the socialized self). Both aspects of the self are part of an individual's self-concept. The self is a product of the dialogue between the "I" and "me." The "I" is the spontaneous, unsocialized, unpredictable, and impulsive aspect of the self. It is the subject of one's actions. The "me" develops gradually through interaction and internalization of the community; it monitors the "I" (Cockerham, 1995). The "me" is the part of the self that is formed as the object of others' actions and views, including one's own reflections on one's self (Garner, 2000). When an individual fails to conform to the norms and expectations of society, she is under the influence of the "I."

The "me" is the judgmental and controlling side of the self that reflects the attitudes of other members of society, while the "I" is the creative and imaginative side of the self (Pampel, 2000). The "me," then, represents the organized set of attitudes that one assumes and that one interjects on their private self, and the "I" represents the organism's response to others' acts, behaviors, and attitudes (Pfuetze, 1954). The "me" has a self-control aspect, in that it acts to stabilize the self, while the "I" is associated with change and reconstruction of the self. The combining of the "I" and the "me" leads to the creation of individual personality and the full development of self (Pfuetze, 1954).

The "me" is the aspect of self that attempts to seek conformity to the expectations of others in the community. This does not imply that the "me" represents morality or pro-social behavior, as the norms the "me" seeks to conform to may be deviant or criminal by society's standards. A gang member's "me" personality will assimilate to such behaviors as robbery, selling drugs, and acts of violence against the innocent law-abiding citizens. The emergence of the self as a product of multiple interactions with others reveals that the social environment plays the most significant role in the creation of personality.

Mead believed that we are never totally aware of the "I" aspect of ourselves, and that is why we periodically surprise even ourselves by our own behavior. We see and know the "I" only after the act has been carried out. Consequently, we know the "I" only in our memories (Ritzer, 2011). The self appearing as the "I" is the memory image of the self who acted toward himself and is the same self who acts toward other selves. Additionally, the process that goes into making up the "me," whom the "I" addresses, is the experience that is induced by the action of the "I" (Reck, 1964). The differences in our memory presentations of the "I" and the "me" are those of the memory images of the initiated social conduct and those of the sensory responses thereto. The "I" of introspection is the self that enters into social relations with other selves. It is not the "I" that is implied in the fact that one presents himself as a "me." And the "me" of introspection is the same "me" that is the object of the social conduct of others (Reck, 1964).

The concepts of *I* and *me* are as relevant today as when Mead articulated their meanings. We often have conversations with ourselves regarding our own behavior. For example, most of us have regretted saying or doing something instantly after we do it. Our conversation with self would begin, "Why did I just do that?" "That wasn't me. I don't typically say things like that." In this scenario, self-reflection questions why "I did something when that is not (the "real") "me." The "I" remains the spontaneous aspect of self that, if left unmonitored, may behave in a manner that is not typically a part of the social self, the "me."

Development of Self

The development of self is critical for the creation of consciousness and the ability of the child to take the role of the other and to visualize her own performances from the point of view of others. To understand the formation of the self, Mead studied the activities and socialization of children. Mead (1934) noted that newborn babies do not have a sense of themselves as objects; instead, they respond automatically and selfishly to hunger, discomfort, and the various stimuli around them. Very young babies do not have the ability to use significant symbols; and therefore, when they play, their behaviors are little different from those of puppies or kittens, who also learn from imitating their parents. Through play and as children grow, they begin to learn to take the role of others: "A child plays at being a mother, at being a teacher, at being a policeman; that is, it is taking different roles" (Mead, 1934:150).

In his theory of the *development of self,* Mead traced patterns of interaction that contribute to the emergence of the social self during childhood (Pampel, 2000). To learn the role of others, the child must come to understand the meanings of symbols and language. Much of this learning takes place through various forms of play. The development of self takes place through a number of stages; and although many reviewers of Mead's stages of development concentrate on just two stages (the play and game stages), it is more useful to identify all four stages in his scheme.

1. **Imitation stage:** At the most basic level of play, infants develop an emerging awareness of other people and physical objects. Babies learn to grasp, hold, and use simple objects like spoons, bottles, and blankets. As their physical skills further develop, they learn to play with objects by observing and imitating their parents. For example, the parent might pick up a ball and throw it, then coax the child to do the same thing. The infant is capable of under-standing mere gestures, and until infants learn to speak, they are capable of little more than imitating behavior. However, even imitation implies learning, as babies discover that some behaviors are positively rewarded and other behaviors bring punishments (Pampel, 2000).

2. **Play Stage:** At this stage of development, the child has learned to use language and the meanings of certain symbols. Through language, the child can adopt the role or attitude of other persons. They not only *act out* the roles of others; their imaginations allow them to pretend to be that person (Pampel, 2000). They can dress up and "play" (act) mom, a fire-fighter, a wrestler, their pet dog, or even a cartoon character. While at play, the child will act in the tone of voice and attitudes of whom he is "playing" and in doing so, "He calls or

tends to call out in himself the same response that he calls out in the other" (Mead, 1964). The child has learned to take the role of specific others. Although lower animals also play, only humans "play at being someone else" (Aboulafia, 1986:9). Mead explained that when the child learns to become both subject and object, she has conquered an important step in the development of self.

3. **Game stage:** At this stage, the child must now be capable of putting herself in the role of several others at the same time, and to understand the relationship between these roles. When the actor can take the role of others, she can respond to herself from their perspective (Deutsch and Krauss, 1965). As Mead states,

> The fundamental difference between the game and play is that in the latter the child must have the attitude of all the others involved in the game. The attitudes of the other players which the participant assumes organize into a sort of unit, and it is that organization which controls the response of the individual (1934:154–155).

Mead used the game of baseball to illustrate his point. When the ball is hit, the fielder must make the play, but he must also know the role of his teammates in order to understand such game complexities as where to throw the ball if there are already runners on base, and so forth.

Understanding the roles of others is just one critical aspect of the game stage. Knowing the rules of the game mark the transition from simple role taking to participation in roles of special, standardized order (Miller, 1973). Abiding by the rules involves the ability to exercise self-control and implies that the individual has learned to function in the organized whole to which she belongs (Mead, 1934). The game is viewed as a sort of passage in the life of a child from taking the role of others in play to the organized part that is essential to self-consciousness. Learning the diverse roles in organized games helps the child to understand the more general workings of social life (Pampel, 2000).

4. **Generalized other:** The generalized other develops from the successive and simultaneous use of many roles. The generalized other is a kind of corporate individual or a plural noun; it is the universalization of the role-taking process (Pfuetze, 1954). At this stage of development of self, individuals come to take the attitude of the whole community, or what Mead called the "generalized other." At this point, the individual identifies not only with significant others (specific people), but also with the attitudes of a society, community, or group as a whole. The generalized other is not a person; instead, it is a person's conscious awareness of the society of which he or she is a part (Cockerham, 1995).

The ability of individuals to adopt the attitude of the generalized other is what allows for diverse and unique persons to share a sense of community. The self-revealed is not "I" but the empirical self "me." The "me" develops through communication and participation as the person takes on different roles and enters the perspective of the community (Pfuetz, 1954). It is through associations with others in different places throughout the community (such as work, school, church, ballgames, etc.) that the many "selves" of an individual personality are awakened, developed, and correlated into a moral community.

The development of self is dependent on interactions with others within the community. These interactions help to shape the individual's personality. Whereas the play stage requires only pieces of the selves, the game stage requires a coherent self (Ritzer, 2000). Embracing the standards of the community is accomplished by recognizing the generalized other. The awareness of the generalized other enters a person's thinking and influences how that person will act in certain situations. In this manner, the generalized other exerts control over individual behavior. The individual may have any number of generalized others in their life, including family, friends, gang, political party, national allegiance, and so on. Some of these generalized others are more important than others but, nonetheless, are taken into account when a person decides what is relevant in choosing from courses of action.

The relevancy of Mead's concept of the development of self can be explained in a number of ways. Clearly, each child goes through stages of development, and Mead's descriptions seem as plausible as any other developmental theory; at the very least, it can serve as an ideal type. Parents can observe the development of their own children and compare their experiences to Mead's formula. Collins and Makowsky (2010) describe the relevancy of the generalized other specifically by claiming that the concept has had considerable influence on the formation of empirical social research:

> Herbert Hyman's derivative concept of the "reference group" has become one of the central analytic tools in social psychology. Robert K. Merton and Alice S. Rossi interpreted it in terms of a "social frame of reference" while analyzing the causes of varying degrees of dissatisfaction among World War II troops. Muzafer Sherif employed related concepts in experimental studies of individual conformity to group judgments (p. 158).

The Act

Mead's analysis of *the act* reveals his social-behaviorist approach to the stimulus–response process. The response to a stimulus is not automatic, because the individual has choices of behaviors in which to react. Mead (1982) states, "We conceive of the stimulus as an occasion or opportunity for the act, not as a compulsion or a mandate" (p. 28). In *The Philosophy of the Act* (1938/1972), Mead identifies four basic and interrelated stages in the act.

1. **Impulse.** The impulse involves "gut" reactions or immediate responses to certain stimuli. It refers to the "need" to do something. If the individual is thirsty, an impulse will tell him to drink. Reactions to this impulse still involve a level of contemplation and decision-making. If the immediate environment does not offer something to drink (nothing at home), then the individual must now decide whether or not to leave the environment (go to the store) to find a drink, or decide to put off the decision to drink until later (wait for roommate to come home with groceries). The environment may provide a source to secure a drink (soda machine) but still put up obstacles in attaining it (machine is out of order). As we can see, the impulse involves both the actor and the environment.
2. **Perception.** The second stage of the act is *perception*. The individual must know how to react to the impulse. People will use their senses as well as mental images in an attempt to satisfy impulses (Ritzer, 2000). Because people are bombarded with potentially limitless stimuli, they must choose among sets of stimuli that provide the characteristics most beneficial to them and ignore those which do not. Choosing to react to certain stimuli while ignoring others is the result of the meaning of things perceived by the perceiver (Mead, 1982). Some objects will stimulate an implicit reaction while others will not (Mead, 1982).
3. **Manipulation.** Once the impulse has been manifested and the object has been perceived, the individual must take some action with regard to it (Ritzer, 2000). The individual conforms himself to the environment or perhaps conforms to the environment itself in order to satisfy the impulse. Tired of waiting for his overdue roommate and feeling very thirsty, the individual decides to go to the store and purchase a beverage.

    4. Consummation. At this, the final stage, the individual has followed through on a course of action and can consummate the act by satisfying the impulse (drinking the beverage). Mead viewed the four stages of the act as interrelated. He also viewed the act as involving one person, while the *social act* involves two or more persons.

The Social Act

A social act may be defined as one in which the stimulus (or occasion) sets free an impulse (found in the very character or nature of its being) that then triggers possible reactions from those found in the environment (Reck, 1964). Mead restricted the *social act* to the class of acts that involve the cooperation of more than one individual and whose object, as defined by the act, is a social object (Reck, 1964). The basic mechanism of the social act is the *gesture*.

    According to Thayer (1968), the importance that Mead placed on gestures was influenced by Darwin's *Expression of Emotions in Man and Animals*, in which Darwin describes the physical attitudes and physiological changes as expressive of emotions (the dog baring teeth for attack). This suggested an evolutionary biological origin of the gesture of language, which Mead found appealing (Thayer, 1968). However, he objected to Darwin's subjectivistic psychological theory that emotions are inner states and gestures are the outward expressions of these ideas and meanings (Thayer, 1968).

    Mead emphasized the importance of the *vocal gesture* because the individual who sends a vocal gesture can perceive that vocal signal much the same way as the listener does. That does not guarantee that the listener will respond in the manner in which the sender anticipated (Baldwin, 1986). Verbal gestures represent signs, which, being heard by the maker as well as other parties to the social act, can serve as a common sign to all parties to the social act. The mutually understood gesture becomes a *significant symbol* (Martindale, 1981). Common gestures allow for the development of language, which consists of a number of significant symbols. Only humans developed to the point of being able to use language and develop significant symbols. Symbols allow people to communicate more easily. The development of symbolic communication leads to inner conversation with the mind, and reflective intelligence (Baldwin, 1986). The tendency for the "same" responses, of a significant symbol, leads to organized attitudes which we arouse in ourselves when we talk to others (Reck, 1964).

    Communication through vocal gestures has a special quality, in that we cannot see our own facial gestures, but we can hear our own vocal gestures. Because we can hear our own vocal gestures, they potentially carry the same meaning for both the listener and the speaker. They also provide the speaker with an opportunity to answer himself as he hopes the listener does (Pampel, 2000). Thinking about responses appropriate in social settings is what Mead called the *generalized other*.

Mental Processes of Intelligence and Consciousness

Mead (1934) defines *intelligence* broadly as the mutual adjustment of the acts of organisms. Humans exhibit a different form of intelligence from other animals in that they have the capacity to understand and use significant symbols. Through the use of symbols, humans can carry on conversations with themselves (Mead, 1934). This self-communication allows for reflective intelligence, which, in turn, allows humans the ability to inhibit action temporarily, to delay their reactions to a stimulus (Mead, 1934). Reflective intelligence is central to the development of a self-concept, self-control, role-taking, empathy, and numerous other social-psychological phenomena (Baldwin, 1986). It is also important for transmitting social customs and creates opportunities for social change.

Humans also have the ability to use reason, which allows the individual to choose among a range of actions. In short, Mead states, "Intelligence is largely a matter of selectivity" (1934:99).

Mead's analysis of the evolution (from the irrational Greek thinkers, to religious dogma, through to the Enlightenment) of knowledge regarding *consciousness* and *intelligence* provides strong support for the hypothesis that the scientific method was superior to all other means of attaining knowledge (Baldwin, 1986). Consciousness was on a continuum from low levels of feeling in simple organisms to high levels of symbolic thought in humans.

There is an ambiguity in the word "consciousness." It might be used in the sense of "awareness," or "conscious of," and to assume that it is coexistent with experience and lodged in the brain. Mead firmly believed that consciousness is explained in terms of social process and is subject to change from external stimuli found in the objective world—the environment. An environment arises for an organism through the selective power of an attention that is determined by its impulses that are seeking expression (Reck, 1964). Thus, consciousness is created through "awareness" and becomes "emergent" through social interaction (Reck, 1964).

Language

For Mead, language has its origins in gestures (Thayer, 1968). Gestures are important in the very nature of communicative behavior and they provide the basic explanation in the creation of selves (minds). Mead was influenced by Darwin and Wilhelm Wundt's work on gestures. As a student of Wundt at the University of Leipzig, Wundt introduced the basic idea of the gesture as an early phase of activity of an organism which is responded to by a second organism. Mead (1934) provided an example of a dog showing its teeth to another dog is a precursor to an attack. The second dog will then show its teeth in response to the first dog's gesture. Mead called this ongoing exchange as the "conversation of gestures." However, these gestures are nonlinguistic, and humans react differently to gestures.

For humans, the most important characteristic of the gesture is its social properties, that is, how it affects and coordinates behavior between two or more individuals (Thayer, 1968). As described earlier in this chapter, the ability to communicate through language represents the developmental process in the development of self. Members of a community who share a common language possess the ability to take the role of the other, thus providing the means for a better understanding in the other's behavior.

Mead felt that the structure of one's language has a great impact on one's train of thought. He believed that language is a social institution that is influenced by a wide variety of social groups and societies. The economically poor will speak a different language from those of the wealthy class, and the mentality of farmers is different from that of a city person. Thus, language is subject to symbolic interpretations and meanings held by certain persons, in certain places, at certain points in time.

The behavior of the individual can only be understood if one understands the behavior of the whole social group of which he is a member. An individual's actions are influenced by the larger community, their social acts go beyond themselves, and implicate the other members of the group (Strauss, 1956). According to Mead, language does not play a role in the formation of society. The formation of language is an effect of the existence of society. Society is formed through social grouping and interaction among individuals. Initial interactions were limited to gestures (facial and vocal); over time they advanced to symbolic interactions and the inevitable creation of language. In short, the social group is formed first, and then language is formed (Strauss, 1956).

The process of the development of language begins with the realization that society is made of individuals. These individuals come in contact with one another, and during these social acts individuals use gestures. Gestures become known as symbols or acts (past, present, or future). Within the community there is a shared meaning of these gestures or symbols. Each symbol signifies a certain meaning. Following facial gestures is the formation and use of vocal gestures. When vocal gestures are put together in some meaningful manner, they create language. Thus, language is the grouping together of significant vocal gestures that have understood and shared meanings between individuals. The definition of language is the significant vocal gestures that elicit the same response and meaning in the speaker as it does in the listener (Joas, 1985).

The primary contribution of symbolic interaction and language is that it provides for the means of *communication* between community members. The essential aspect of communication is that the symbol should arouse in one's self what it arouses in the other individual (Farganis, 2000). The symbol must have a degree of universality to any person who finds himself in the same situation (a contemporary example would be the universal symbol for handicapped persons). There is a possibility of communication any time individuals share the same language.

On a regular basis, each of us is presented with a nearly endless number of gestures and symbols. We filter out those with no meaning to us and react to those which do have meaning. How many examples of gestures can you think of right now?

Science and Social Progress

Mead and Dewey's pragmatic thinking reveals that they confidently accepted the unity of science and progress as much as they accepted the unity of thought and action (Pampel, 2000). They believed that science provides a clear and effective way to test ideas on how to improve future society (Pampel, 2000). Scientific analysis eliminates bias and dogmatic thinking. For Mead, the use of reason and science was clearly superior to that of the Christian evangelistic thought that he was exposed to in his youth. Science and democratic social action were far more valuable than unreasoning faith and prayer.

Darwin's theory of evolution greatly impacted Mead's thinking of science and progress. Mead believed that the evolutionary principles that Darwin attached to his studies of various species also apply to social organization and societies. Evolutionary thinking allows individuals to use their intelligence to adjust to the problems they face in everyday life (Pampel, 2000).

A proponent of science, Mead did not agree with positivist science. The fundamental mistake of the positivist theory of science is, in Mead's eyes, that it regards all events as instances of laws, and that means it conceives of all surprising facts, those which run counter to expectation, as instances of scientific laws that have not yet been ascertained (Joas, 1985). For Mead, the conceptual objects of science do not replicate an ultimate reality which causally determines the subjective phenomena of our perceptual world. Rather, they are inevitably referred to the world of our actions and immediate experiences. This is true in three ways (Joas, 1985):

1. The problem that requires a scientific solution itself makes the appearance in the world of our immediate experiences; it is linked to the observation of anomalies.
2. The testing of a hypothesis must rely on immediate experiences...
3. ...which cannot be dispensed with even by those theories that claim to effect a general reconstruction of theories themselves.

Like science, history is, for Mead, a progressive process that can never be completely planned and is essentially unpredictable, since it is the result of intentional action and of causal determination.

Two main strands of his writing indicate Mead's *worldview* perspective. First, he advocated analyzing all ideas via the scientific method. Second, he was strongly opposed to a mind–body dualism in all its forms because it split the world into two irreconcilable parts (Baldwin, 1986). Mead's scientific method included "empirical cosmology." Traditional philosophical cosmologies included nonempirical metaphysical assumptions. For Mead, science is a problem-solving system that works toward unity, without expecting to reach a final static state.

A central theme of Mead's writings is that the world of knowledge is an organic whole in which all the parts affect each other to produce a dynamically fluctuating system. His key method of approach was to organize all topics in terms of evolutionary processes, developmental processes, and other types of processes. For this reason, Mead has been described as a *process philosopher*. He believes that the temporal dimension cannot be excluded from the real; the real is not timeless, but consists of acts, happenings, and events (Baldwin, 1986).

According to Mead, both mechanism and teleology are merely postulates. They are dogma. Mead explained that internal conversation that we carry on in our heads is the "mechanism of thought"; and describing oneself objectively, as if looking at oneself from the role of others, is the "mechanism of introspection" (having an internal conversation with oneself). Mead advocated an objective, scientific approach to human conduct, placing humans in nature rather than above nature. At various points, Mead described his form of objective psychology as "behavioristic psychology" (Baldwin, 1986). It is important to note that at this time, the term "behaviorism" had just come about and there was no consensus on its meaning, just as today there is great ambiguity in the term *postmodernism*.

Ethics and Moral Responsibility

As a philosopher, Mead maintained an interest in ethics. Mead (1938) believed that ethics and moral consciousness are formed when individuals establish a bond with communities, social institutions, and customs of a society. Our behavior becomes influenced by our ethical and moral responsibility as good citizens. Mead described moral responsibility as doing that which we would want others to do. By this Mead meant that most of us do what is morally right to keep society intact. The problem is that our ability to do the right thing is limited by our own resources. In Mead's ideas on *ethical philanthropy*, an actor is always limited in his ability to do what is morally right. We want to try new things, and sometimes we push the bounds of ethical and moral responsible behavior.

Solving moral problems requires, according to Mead, creative intellectual effort and consideration of all values relevant to the given situation. For Mead, the value relation is an objectively existing relationship between subject and object, but it is not equated with a cognitive relation (Joas, 1985). Value relations and cognitive relations are distinctly different. Their differences, however, do not lie in a merely subjective character of evaluation as opposed to ascription of objectivity to cognition, but rather in their correlation to different phases in an act.

Many of Mead's scattered articles and theses can be grouped around the notion of universal morality. His analysis of the functions of "punitive justice," which in his judgment is not therapeutic but does serve to stabilize the structure of domination in a society, belongs just as much in this thematic complex as do his articles on patriotism as an ethical and psychological problem (Joas, 1985). Ethical universality is possible only through the human capacity of role-taking, aided by communication, which leads to the concept of sociality. Moral problems can be solved rationally by exploring values held by different individuals.

Mead wrote about philanthropy from the point of view of ethics. Charity implies both an attitude and a type of conduct that may not be demanded of whoever exercises it. Whatever the donor's inner obligation may be, the recipient on his side can make no claim upon it. Yet the inner obligation exists and in part limits the charity itself, for the donor cannot fail in her other commitments, because she has answered the appeals of charity too generously (Reck, 1964).

Obligation arises only with choice: not only when impulses are in conflict with each other, but when, within this conflict, they are valued in terms of their anticipated results. We act impulsively when the mere strength of the impulse decides. The kindly impulses that lead us to help those in distress may breed beggars and organized charity (which attempt to bring reason into action). That the recognition of an obligation is at the same time the assertion of a right is tantamount to the individual's identifying himself with those who make the claim upon him, for an obligation is always a demand made by another or by others (Reck, 1964).

Presumably, most of us attempt to behave ethically and morally. But some of our behaviors are justified in our own minds because we perceive them as acceptable. But if society labels some of our behaviors as unethical and immoral, how do we react to that? This is a dilemma that we wrestle with constantly. As a result, the concepts of *ethics* and *moral responsibility* will remain relevant throughout our lifetimes.

Criticisms

Mead's analysis of human behavior is centered on the concepts of *the self* and *the development of self* along with *acts* and *social acts*; yet he ignores the role of power in nearly all of his theories. How people develop and form a sense of self and how they behave are often influenced by the possession of power, or the lack thereof. As Collins and Makowsky (2010) explain, "Mead tended to ignore the ways in which humans dominate and manipulate one another in political, economic, and status hierarchies" (p. 158).

His work on *the self* includes the concepts of "I" and "me," two terms that present an operational challenge to social theorists because of their relative vagueness. His term the "generalized other" also presents operational problems. For sociologists who conduct empirical research involving data collection and analysis, the lack of clarity in these concepts serves as a barrier.

As Mead was a social psychologist and micro sociologist, it is not surprising that there is noticeably less detail and precision in macro facets of Mead's theoretical system. For example, his description of "society" as the sum activities of individuals who interact with one another is weak by any sociological standard.

A fourth criticism of Mead's work centers on his lack of attention to the unconscious and irrational acts engaged in by actors:

> Mead portrayed humans as rational beings, because they are social beings. By analyzing the philosophies of Kant and the utilitarians he arrived at a pragmatic position according to which the only rule ethics can present is that an individual should deal rationally with all the values that are found in a particular problem (Collins and Makowsky, 2010:159).

Summary

George Herbert Mead was a philosopher, sociologist, social psychologist, and a social scientist in general. He was a person of great vision, with the skill for synthesizing an enormous breadth of knowledge in an elegant, unified system. He developed a philosophy of science and beautifully integrated social theory in such a way that they are as important today as they were in his own time (Baldwin, 1986). Mead's theory combines macro- and micro-social processes, mental and physical events, academic and practical concerns.

Mead examined the development of the mind and the self, and regarded the mind as the natural emergent from the interaction of the human organism and its social environment. Within this biosocial structure, the gap between impulse and reason is bridged by the use of language. By conquering language, Mead believed humans become aware of their roles in life; this awareness allows for the emergence of the self. Intelligence, he believed, develops over time.

The potential for the development and elaboration of Mead's form of pragmatic social science is enormous. Mead's general approach could unify the many subdivisions of sociology. Mead's pragmatic social science has both theoretical elegance and practical utility. Mead's theory is also adaptive in that it allows for social change. Mead himself was dedicated to both intellectual work and social reforms; and his theory reflects his strengths in both areas. We can benefit from, and elaborate upon, both facets of his work (Baldwin, 1986).

George Herbert Mead was a gifted social theorist who was more comfortable with the accomplishments of others, especially his students, than he was interested in having the spotlight shine on his own contributions. As Coser (1977) explains, he was proud and happy to have gifted students and encouraged and guided their careers while impressing them with his classroom lectures. This is clearly evident in the fact that it was his students and colleagues who published most of Mead's works posthumously.

 Study and **Review** on **MySearchLab**

Discussion Questions

1. Describe the primary influences of William James and Henry Castle on Mead. Which of these influences was more significant? Explain.
2. Describe Mead's concepts of "mind," "self," and "society." How would your definitions of these three terms be different or be similar to Mead's?
3. Name and describe the four stages of the development of self and apply them to your own growing experiences.
4. Name and describe the four steps of Mead's "the act." Provide at least three examples of behaviors

that you have engaged in that illustrate these four interrelated stages in "the act."
5. Explain what Mead meant by ethics and moral responsibility. Describe instances from contemporary culture where a person (or persons) has displayed "proper" ethical and/or moral responsibility and where a person (or persons) has displayed "improper" ethical and/or moral responsibility. Be sure to explain the criterion used to determine proper or improper behavior.

MySearchLab® Connections

MysearchLab is designed just for you. Each chapter features a customized study plan to help you learn and review key concepts and terms. Dynamic visual activities, videos, and readings found in the multimedia library will enhance your learning experience.

 View on **MySearchLab**

> ▶ George Herbert Mead: The Self Is Born of Society
> ▶ George Herbert Mead: How We Learn to Take the Role of Others: Mead's Three Stages

Read on **MySearchLab**

> ▶ Mead, George Herbert. Self and Society.

The Contemporary Period of Sociological Theory

In Part II, "The Contemporary Period of Sociological Theory," the major schools of sociological thought are discussed. The contemporary period of sociological theory is notably different from the classical era. The classical period, which includes, more or less, the first 400+ years of social theory, was characterized by significant individual theorists, or grand theorists. The contemporary era of social theory, which begins roughly in the mid-twentieth century, is highlighted by the ideas of a collection of like-minded social thinkers whose combined efforts led to the formation of a "school of thought." In most cases, these schools of thought were influenced by social thinkers from the classical period, but old concepts were modified or replaced and a vast array of new concepts introduced. The schools of thought discussed in Part II are structural functionalism and neofunctionalism, conflict theory, symbolic interactionism, social exchange theory and network analysis, ethnomethodology and phenomenology, feminist theory, critical theory, and modern and postmodern theories.

8 Structural Functionalism and Neofunctionalism

Listen to the **Chapter Audio** on **MySearchLab**

Chapter Outline

- The Intellectual Roots of Structural Functionalism
- Defining Structural Functionalism
- Talcott Parsons
- Robert Merton
- Neofunctionalism
- Criticisms of Structural Functionalism
- Application of Structural Functionalism to Contemporary Society
- Summary
- Discussion Questions

During the 1950s and 1960s, structural functionalism, often simply referred to as "functionalism," reigned as the dominant theoretical perspective in sociology. Its primary tenets remain among the cornerstone ideas of social theory and everyday life. *Structural functionalism* has a dual focus on the structural forces that shape human behavior and the means and ways that the social system addresses societal needs. In light of shifting theoretical paradigms in sociology over the past couple of generations, structural functionalism has attempted to remain as a major school of thought via neofunctionalism and post-functionalism.

The majority of sociologists discount the validity of functional theory, claiming its concepts and central premise are out-of-date. However, in everyday scenarios, people generally evaluate relationships (e.g., "I need to get out of this dysfunctional relationship"), social situations (e.g., "I felt out of place at that gathering"), and products ("My phone is outdated"), among other things, based on functionality. Various buzzwords akin to the concept "functionalism" constantly appear in print and conversation. In January 2012, for example, State University of New York Chancellor Nancy L. Zimpher used the word "systemness" to refer to "the coordination of multiple components that when working together create a network of activity that is more powerful than any action of individual parts on their own" (SUNY, 2012). When you head a large corporation or the largest state university system in the nation, finding a way to assure the functionality of all the parts of the system is not only relevant and applicable, it's commendable. After reading this chapter, you can determine for yourself whether this theory is still relevant today.

THE INTELLECTUAL ROOTS OF STRUCTURAL FUNCTIONALISM

The most significant intellectual forerunners of functionalism were Auguste Comte, Herbert Spencer, Émile Durkheim, and Max Weber. The fields of linguistics and cultural anthropology also played a role in the foundation of structural functionalism.

Auguste Comte, the person who coined the term *sociology* and set the tone for this emerging discipline as a social science, introduced the notions of *social statics* (social processes that hold society together) and *social dynamics* (mechanisms of change). In his description of social statics (today's term is *social structure*), Comte anticipated many of the ideas of later functionalists, as the focus of structural functionalism rests with the idea that mechanisms exist in society to keep the social system intact and running smoothly. Social dynamics (today's term is *social change*) allows for the realization that society is always changing, but as structural functionalists would promote, Comte believed that change should be orderly and governed by societal laws. Comte's usage of the "organic analogy" (comparing society to a living, breathing organism) laid the groundwork for systemic and functionalist sociological approaches (Trevino, 2008).

Utilizing an "organic analogy," Herbert Spencer, like Comte, argued that society has many of the same systems' needs as any living organism. Further, if these needs are not met, the system (e.g., an organism or society) risks dissolution. It is up to the social system to find, from the environment, the necessary materials needed to survive. Spencer termed this process *requisite functionalism* (Turner, 2003). Spencer's concept of *differentiation* is of significant importance in the development of functionalism. He believed that increases in the size of both organic and social aggregates are invariably accompanied by an increase in the complexity of their structure. According to Spencer (1898), the process of growth, by definition, is a process of integration. Furthermore, integration in its turn must be accompanied by a progressive differentiation of structures and functions if the organism or the societal unit is to remain capable of survival. Social aggregates, like organic ones, grow from relatively undifferentiated states, in which the parts resemble one another, into differentiated states in which the parts have become dissimilar. As the level of complexity increases, so, too, does the level of interdependence of the parts of the organism and the social unit. Much of Spencer's discussion of social institutions and their changes is expressed in functional terms. He analyzed social institutions in relation to the general matrix in which they are variously embedded. Spencer (1860) made great efforts to show that social institutions are not the result of the deliberate intentions and motivations of the actors but arise from structural requirements.

Émile Durkheim viewed society as a social system with its parts (social institutions) contributing to the functioning stability of the whole (society). The parts of the social system, Durkheim argued, are interconnected and attempt to meet the demands of each particular society. When this occurs over a period of time and stability is met, the system is said to be functioning properly. Durkheim's functionalist approach was evolutionary in that he was interested in how societies change over time. He recognized that societies, as social systems, are not static and are therefore subject to change at any time. Durkheim's (1973/1914) view on functionalism is summarized in this quote from *The Dualism of Human Nature and Its Social Conditions*:

> A great number of our mental states, including some of the most important ones, are of social origin. In this case then, it is the whole that, in a large measure, produces the part; consequently, it is impossible to attempt to explain the whole without explaining the part—without explaining, at least, the part as a result of the whole (p. 149).

Parsons was impressed by what he saw in Durkheim's work, namely, that he formulated a number of specific concepts (e.g., collective effervescence and the sacred and profane) to explain slices of social action (Fish, 2005).

Max Weber's influence on structural functionalism is particularly evident in the works of Talcott Parsons. Parsons' dissertation, "Concept and Capitalism," was based primarily on Weber's (1958/1904–1905) *The Protestant Ethic and the Spirit of Capitalism*. Parsons was exposed to Weber's works while he studied in Europe, and he translated Weber (the first four chapters of *Wirtschaft und Gesellschaft*) into English for American sociologists. Parsons felt that Karl Marx's reductionist approach to explaining social structure and social action as being tied nearly exclusively to the economic realm was overly simplistic and not realistic. He favored Weber's unwillingness to simplify explanations of the complexity of the social system.

> Weber essentially established certain broad differentiations of patterns of value-orientations, as we would now term them....He showed how these...patterns "correspond" to the broad lines of differentiation of the social structures of the societies in which they had become institutionalized (Parsons, 1954:15).

The field of linguistics has an influence on structural functionalism because of its examination of language as a system of words, syntax, and phonics whose relationships are governed by determinate laws. Language, the mechanism that helps people communicate with one another, is structured by a system of signs which gained meanings among members over a period in interacting time. Understanding the structure and meaning of language reveals a great deal about a society and the arrangement of its parts.

A number of anthropologists, including Claude Levi-Strauss, A. R. Radcliffe-Brown, and Bronislaw Malinowski, have influenced structural functionalism. Levi-Strauss organized all forms of communication as ordered systems that are subject to structural analyses. Parsons' functionalism is closer to the anthropology of A. R. Radcliffe-Brown than it is to Malinowski's:

> Both these anthropologists were committed to a scientific methodology and were reluctant to build theory about matters for which little hard evidence exists, for example, the historical development of preliterate societies. Both chose to focus their attention on existing societies that could be observed by the ethnographer, and both chose to conceive of those societies as consisting of customs and practices that helped sustain them as ongoing, integrated wholes (Johnson, 1975:17).

Parsons learned from both Radcliffe-Brown and Malinowski to identify the various conventional patterns of behavior that contribute to the maintenance of society.

DEFINING STRUCTURAL FUNCTIONALISM

Functionalism is a macro-sociological theory that examines the characteristics of social patterns, structures, systems, and institutions. It views society as having interrelated parts which contribute to the functioning of the whole system. Functionalism has two basic assumptions. The first is the idea of interdependent parts, where all of society's social institutions (e.g., religion, politics, military, economics, education, sports, and leisure) or all of a state university's colleges are all linked together. As Levin (1991) explains, "Functionalism begins with the idea that any stable system (such as the human body) consists of a number of different, but interrelated, parts that operate together to create an overall order" (p. 76). Any change in one institution inevitably leads to changes in other institutions. In order to function properly, the system seeks equilibrium, or stability. Equilibrium allows a smoothly running system. Second, members of society must have a general consensus on values. A general agreement on issues of right and wrong, basic values, and morality issues allows the system to function properly. If people lose faith in their society (the system), they will seek change. Rapid change within the system is something that could lead to dissolution. As a result, the social system, in order to be "functional," must encourage its members to conform to the core values and norms of the prevailing culture.

It would be incorrect to assume that the functionalist approach ignores social change (what Comte called *social dynamics*). It primarily explains social change as a result of such variables as population growth (due to migration and increased childbirth rates) and increased technology (such as smart phones, social network sites, and a slew of modern devices). Functionalists are so aware of social change that they often wonder how society maintains itself at all. Society's social institutions are running most efficiently when the system is in a homeostatic mode. Consequently, the social system is designed to minimize conflict. This is true at any level (societal, institutional, and family).

TALCOTT PARSONS (1902–1979)

Talcott Parsons, the youngest of five children, was born in Colorado Springs in 1902. He came from a religious family that valued education. His father was a Congregational minister and a professor at Colorado College. His mother was a progressive and a suffragist (Camic, 1991). During his undergraduate studies at Amherst College, Parsons took courses in biology and later in the social sciences. His early exposure to biology, with its focus on the importance of the interdependence of an organism's parts, greatly influenced his outlook on social behavior. He graduated from Amherst in 1924 and a year later entered the London School of Economics. In London, he studied with Malinowski, L. T. Hobhouse, and Morris Ginsberg. Parsons accepted Malinowski's view of societies as systems of interconnected parts.

In 1926, Parsons received a scholarship from the University of Heidelberg, where he first learned of the works of Max Weber. Although Weber had died five years before Parsons' arrival, his widow Marianne Weber held meetings at her home on the works of her husband, and Parsons regularly attended. Upon the completion of his dissertation, Parsons was appointed as a nonfaculty instructor of economics at Harvard University. Parsons eventually became an inaugural

Talcott Parsons (1902–1979), structural functionalist and grand theorist. (Harvard University Archives, UAV 605, Box 10, Parsons F2170)

member of the sociology faculty at Harvard. In 1945, Parsons established the Department of Social Relations, an interdisciplinary collaboration in the behavioral sciences. He served as chair of the department for its first ten years and remained active in the department until its dissolution in 1972. A year later, Parsons retired as emeritus professor. He continued teaching as a visiting professor at such universities as Pennsylvania, Rutgers, and the University of California at Berkeley. Parsons died in May 1979.

Parsons was one of the most prominent theorists of his time. He attempted to generate a grand theory of society that explains all social behavior, everywhere and throughout history, with a single model: structural functionalism, or, more simply, functionalism. By design, his theory is often very abstract: It is nonetheless quite elaborate. His theory once dominated sociological discourse and had nearly as many detractors as supporters (Abrahamson, 1978). Parsons' analysis of social systems and social action remains relevant as a premiere sociological theory.

Structural Functionalism

The structural-functional approach of Parsons was a lifelong development and reflected the era in which he lived. The post–World War II era was highlighted by a great prosperity among many Americans. The 1950s were a decade of a relative societal calm and an increasing economic boom. "Structural-functional sociology mirrored these real-life developments. It emphasized societal stability and the match between institutions like the economy, the family, the political system, and the value system" (Garner, 2000:312). Parsons believed social systems strive for stability. "Parsons argued that the overall system and subsystems of which it is composed work together to form a balanced, stable whole and that the system naturally tends toward stability rather than toward disorder" (Levin, 1991:77). The basic premise of Parsons' functionalism of stability or equilibrium is a sound one, for it stands to reason that for any society to last a great length of time, there must be some sense of social order and interdependence among the various institutions. With its commitment to stable social institutions, the decade of the 1950s provided the perfect years for Parsons' structural-functional theory to dominate sociological thought. The conservative nature of this theoretical approach reflected American society itself.

Parsons' theoretical approach involved utilizing a number of limited but important concepts that "adequately grasp" aspects of the objective external world. These concepts thus correspond to concrete phenomena. These specific concepts would be determined after conducting empirical research on the actions of those under study. In "The Role of Ideas in Social Action," Parsons (1954) explained that his theory of action is an analytical one ("analytical realism") and that any analysis of ideas must be conducted on an empirical, scientific basis. Parsons used his analytical concepts throughout his writings, which were first presented in his brilliant book *The Structure of Social Action* (1949/1937).

Social Action Theory

In the preface to *The Structure of Social Action* (1949/1937), Parsons made clear his commitment to empirical research as the guiding force behind his theory:

> This body of theory, the "theory of social action," is not simply a group of concepts with their logical interrelations. It is a theory of empirical science the concepts of which refer to something beyond themselves.... True scientific theory is not the product of idle "speculation," or spinning out the logical implications of assumptions, but of observation, reasoning and verification, starting with the facts and continually returning to the facts (p. v).

Parsons acknowledged the subjective nature of human activity and therefore wished to make clear the distinction between the concepts of *action* (an active, creative response) and *behavior* (a perfunctory response to stimuli). Action options depend upon the actor's knowledge of her situation, which includes knowledge of the probable effects of the available choices. Parsons (1949/1937) insisted that in order to qualify as an action theory, the subjective aspect of human activity cannot be ignored.

Parsons' social action theory begins with an analysis of the process of an "act." According to Parsons (1949), there are four basic components of the *act*. First, an act involves individuals, or "actors," engaging in some sort of behavior. Second, the act has some sort of intended end goal. Third, the action engaged in by actors is predicated on given situations at the time of the behavior. And, fourth, there exists the possibility of randomness in any given social act that may lead actors to change their course of action.

Parsons (1949/1937) explained that an act is always a process in time, and that the concept of *end* always implies a future reference to a state (or situation) that does not yet exist. Actions consist of the structures and processes by which human beings form meaningful intentions and more or less successfully implement them in concrete situations (Parsons, 1966).

Parsons' theory of social action also involves four steps. First, Parsons believed that actors are *motivated* to action, especially toward a desired goal (e.g., a college degree). Parsons referred to a *goal* as the time of the termination of the actor's action in which the desired end has been reached (e.g., receiving the college diploma on graduation day). Second, the actor must find the *means* to reach the desired goal (e.g., a college fund created by the student's parents, student loans, a personal computer). Next, the actor must deal with *conditions* that hinder reaching the goal (obstacles to a student's reaching a college degree might include the lack of a proper intellect or of time to study, or a personal crisis). And finally, the actor must work within the *social system* (such as administrative rules and procedures, test taking, and all the required courses). Working within the social system is often quite challenging.

Social System

In *The Social System* (1951), Parsons attempted to further articulate his social action theory by integrating the role of structure and processes of social systems in their effect on the actor. For Parsons, a social system involves the interaction of a plurality of individual actors oriented to a situation, where the system includes commonly understood cultural symbols. Parsons believed that actors are motivated by the need to optimize their own gratification in given situations. Furthermore, actors work within their own personality constructs and the cultural norms of society.

Culture itself is a system of generalized symbols and their meanings. Through the internalization of a culture's norms and values, the individual's personality becomes integrated as a part of the social system.

> The principal mechanism by which this is accomplished appears to be through the building up of attachments to other persons—that is, by emotional communication with others so that the individual is sensitized to the *attitudes* of the others, not merely to their specific acts with their intrinsic gratification-deprivation significance (Parsons, 1965:29).

As Parsons' general theory continued to develop, the cultural element occupied a more central place.

Pattern Variables

In an attempt to make his relatively abstract theory of action more explicit, Parsons formulated *pattern variables*, which categorize expectations and the structure of relationships. These pattern variables are a set of concepts denoting some of the variable properties of social systems. Parsons had three primary thoughts in mind when developing these variables: They should be general enough to permit the comparison of relationships in different cultures; they should show relevance to action frames or reference; and they should be relevant to all social systems. These pattern variables are expressed as paired polarities that allow for the categorization of modes of orientation of social action (Buxton, 1985; Turner, 2003). Five pattern variables articulated by Parsons are

1. **Affectivity–affective neutrality:** The concern here is whether the actor can expect an emotional component in the relationship or interaction situation. A newlywed couple should expect a great deal of affection in their relationship, whereas the sales clerk–customer relationship is neutral.
2. **Diffuseness–specificity:** This pair of terms refers to a range of demands and obligations that may be expected in the relationship. If the relationship is a close one, there exists a potential for a wide range of demands and expectations (diffusion), but if the relationship is limited, there are far fewer expectations (specific needs are met).
3. **Universalism–particularism:** The issue here is how actors are evaluated. Is the actor treated on the basis of a general norm (universalism), or does someone's particular relationship with the other cause particular action? The McDonaldization process (see Chapter 5), for example, encourages a universal treatment of customers, workers, and management. By comparison, a family-run restaurant will emphasize particular ways of dealing with customers and workers.
4. **Achievement–ascription:** These pattern variables deal with the assessment of an actor. Is performance evaluated on achieved statuses (e.g., an earned college degree, setting a state record in the 100-meter dash) or on an ascribed status (such as race, gender, age)? If someone is judged simply on ascribed characteristics, the quality of the performance evaluation has been compromised.
5. **Collectivity–self-orientation:** The concern here is with the motivation of the actor. Is the behavior directed toward a particular person, or is the action directed toward the collectivity? Self-interest often overrides a commitment to the group or to specific others (Parsons, 1951).

These five dichotomies represented, for Parsons, the universal dilemmas of action.

Some of these concepts, such as self–collectivity, were later dropped from the action scheme, but others, such as universalism–particularism, assumed greater importance. The intent of the pattern variables remained the same, however: to categorize dichotomies of decisions, normative demands, and value orientations (Turner, 2003:43).

Parsons believed that these pattern variables provided a set of categories for describing the value components of action at the level of personality, the social system, and the culture (Johnson, 1975).

Adaptation, Goal Attainment, Integration, and Latency (AGIL): Functional Imperatives for All Action Systems

Soon after *The Social System* (1951) was published, Parsons developed another schema that was to prove far superior to the pattern variables. He referred to this new schema by a number of different names, including *system problems,* the *functional imperatives of any system of action,* and the *four-function paradigm* (Johnson, 1975). The term *functional imperatives* is the one that endured, and students of social theory generally call them *AGIL* (adaptation, goal attainment, integration, and latency) for short.

In 1953, Parsons collaborated with Robert Bales and Edward Shils to publish *Working Papers in the Theory of Action*. It was in this book that the conception of functional imperatives arose and came to dominate the general theory of action. Three years later, Parsons, along with Neil Smelser, published *Economy and Society* (1956) to further outline these imperatives. The experiments of Parsons and Bales (on leadership in small groups) were the source of the data used to develop their classification scheme. Wallace and Wolf (1999) indicated that the subjects used in these studies consisted of mostly white upper-middle or upper-class Protestant males and therefore suggested that the data lack generalization credibility.

The functional imperatives are a set of conditions that Parsons believed must be met if systems of action are to be stable and effective; that is, "the conditions can be thought of as processes that constitute the imperative functions of any system, from a simple two-person interaction to the most complex modern society" (Johnson, 1975:29). The functional imperatives are based on Parsons' hypothesis that processes in any social system are subject to four independent functional imperatives, or "problems," which must be met adequately if equilibrium and/or continuing existence of the system is to be maintained (Parsons, 1956a). Thus, these are tasks that must be performed if the system, or subsystem, is to survive:

1. **Adaptation:** Social systems must secure sufficient resources (e.g., raw materials, technology) from the environment and distribute them throughout the system. Thus, the system must show that it can adapt to changes in the system and/or environment. Adaptation may involve the manipulation of the environment (e.g., building dams to control flooding) in order to secure the resources which are deemed necessary to reach the goal(s) of the social system. Parsons argued that the responsibility of this function imperative rests with the economic institutions of a society. However, it is also clear that the agricultural industry needs to produce food for people to survive and there must be a distribution system set up to assure that freshly grown food reaches markets in a timely manner (Trevino, 2008).

2. **Goal attainment:** The social system must first clearly establish its goals. This need may seem obvious, but goals vary from one social system to the next. Nonprofit agencies hope to collect resources so that they may be properly distributed to the needy, whereas corporations hope to maximize profits, especially for the stockholders. In order to reach the stated goals, the social system must mobilize resources and energies, while establishing and maintaining priorities. The primary responsibility for this function in a nation-state is the political system (government).

3. **Integration:** This functional imperative involves the regulation and coordination of actors and subsystems within the greater social system in order to keep it functioning properly. The system must coordinate, adjust, and regulate relationships among the various subgroups. This is accomplished by the legal system, or the prevailing court of laws. In its attempt to reach goals, the system must often fight to maintain equilibrium and stability; consequently, it is important to keep deviance to a minimum.

4. **Latency:** Latency consists of two related problems: tension maintenance (internal tensions and strains of actors) and pattern maintenance (displaying "appropriate" behavior). The system must define and maintain a set of common values that guide and legitimate action within the system. Actors must be socialized and sufficiently motivated to play their roles (maintaining a commitment to society), and society must provide mechanisms and safety valves for actors so that they can release pent-up frustrations and other strains that they feel. This function is accomplished through such social institutions as the family, religion, education, and sports and leisure.

Table 8.1 Structure of the General Action System			
L	Cultural system	Social system	I
A	Behavioral organization	Personality system	G

Collaborating with Gerald Platt on *The American University* (1973), Parsons infused his AGIL concepts with his general action systems theory (see Table 8.1). The biological organism must learn to adapt behaviorally (*behavioral organization system*) in order to survive in the environment. The *personality system* motivates individuals toward desired goals, while society presents opportunities to achieve these goals. The *social system* is designed to integrate the diverse members of society. The *cultural system* provides the norms, values, and expectations of society that individuals must learn to incorporate into their daily lives.

In their book *Economy and Society*, Parsons and Smelser (1956) utilized their functional imperatives on a variety of subjects. One of them is presented as "The Differentiated Subsystems of Society" (p. 53). Starting with the macro-social system of society, Parsons and Smelser (1956) projected the adaptation problem onto the economy; the goal attainment problem onto the polity; the integration problem onto an integrative subsystem that includes the legal system; and the latency issue onto such subsystems as religion and education. However, in another figure, "Functional Differentiation of the Economy as a System" (p. 44), Parsons and Smelser projected the functional imperatives onto a subsystem of the society: the economy. Here, the adaptation problem was delegated to the capitalization and investment sector; the goal attainment problem to the production subsystem, including distribution and sales; the integration issue to the organization subsystem of entrepreneurism; and latency to the economic commitments found in physical, cultural, and motivational resources. The point is that functional imperatives can be used on a whole system (society) or on a subsystem (organizations and groups).

The Concept of "Society"

As Parsons (1966) stated,

> Treating societies as wholes by no means exhausts the possibilities for empirical application of the concept of social system. Many social systems such as local communities, schools, business firms, and kinship units are not societies, but rather sub-systems of a society. Also, in a sufficiently pluralistic world, many social systems, which are "partial" systems in terms of the concept of society, may be parts of more than one society (p. 1).

This is especially true of global corporations that conduct business in more than one nation. Parsons' study of societies was guided by both an evolutionary and a comparative perspective. The evolutionary framework implies that humans are integral to the organic world and the life process. Basic concepts of organic evolution such as variation, selection, adaptation, differentiation, and integration are the center of concern. "Socio-cultural evolution, like organic evolution, has proceeded by variation and differentiation from simple to progressively more complex forms" (Parsons, 1966:2).

Parsons provided a number of definitions for *society*. In *Societies* (1966), he stated, "In defining a society, we may use a criterion which goes back at least to Aristotle. A society is a type of social system, in any universe of social systems, which attains the highest level of self-sufficiency as a system in relation to its environment" (p. 9). In *The System of Modern Societies* (1971), Parsons defined a society as "the type of social system characterized by the highest level of self-sufficiency relative to its environments, including other social systems" (p. 8). All societies depend for their continuation on the inputs they receive through interchanges with the surrounding systems. The system has to be coordinated in such a way that sufficient resources may be found in the environment.

> The core of a society, as a system, is the patterned normative order through which the life of a population is collectively organized. As an order, it contains values and differentiated and particularized norms and rules, all of which require cultural references in order to be meaningful and legitimate. As a collectivity, it displays a patterned conception of membership which distinguishes between those individuals who do and do not belong (Parsons, 1969:11).

The study of societies is important not only because society represents the most critical social system, but also because of a society's tremendous impact on individuals.

ROBERT MERTON (1910–2003)

Robert King Merton was born in 1910 of Jewish immigrant parents from Eastern Europe and was raised in a South Philadelphia slum. The family lived in an apartment above his father's modest dairy store until the building burned down. His father then worked as a carpenter and truck driver. Merton's passion for learning began at an early age and was summed up in an autobiographical statement titled "A Life of Learning" (Merton, 1994/1996). Growing up in a slum did not stifle cultural opportunities for Merton. He spent a great deal of time at the nearby Carnegie library and attended concerts performed by the Philadelphia Orchestra. Interestingly, Merton was not the family name, as he was born Meyer R. Schkolnick. As an amateur magician and admirer of the magician Harry Houdini, who had changed his name from Ehrich Weiss, Meyer Schkolnick decided he wanted to change his name. Schkolnick chose the name of Robert Merlin in honor of King Arthur's famous magician. Five years later he changed his name to Robert King Merton (Calhoun, 2003).

Merton won a scholarship to attend Temple College, a school founded for the poor boys and girls of Philadelphia, and became interested in sociology while taking an introductory sociology course taught by George E. Simpson, the translator of Durkheim (Calhoun, 2003). Simpson took Merton on as a research assistant in a project on race and the media. Simpson also took Merton to the annual meeting of the American Sociological Society, where he met Pitirim Sorokin, founding chair of the Harvard sociology department. After earning his B.A. at Temple, Merton, with the help of a fellowship, attended and received his doctorate from Harvard University. Even though Sorokin took Merton on as a research assistant and starting publishing with Merton by his second year at Harvard, Merton was far more impressed by the young, then-unknown sociologist Talcott Parsons than he was by Sorokin. After earning his Ph.D. in 1936, Merton taught for two years at Tulane before joining the faculty at Columbia University in New York City. At Tulane, Merton began to read the work of Paul Lazarsfeld, a mathematically minded methodologist. The two became colleagues in 1941 at the Bureau of Applied Social Research at Columbia. They would collaborate for decades to follow.

Merton had always stressed the importance of empirical research, and his approach to functional analysis reflected this commitment. Merton's functional approach contrasted with the grand theorizing of Parsons.

> Merton's goal was to keep functional assumptions to a minimum, whereas Parsons' intent was to build a functional analytical scheme that could explain all reality.... Merton believed that grand theoretical schemes are premature because the theoretical and empirical groundwork necessary for their completion has not been performed (Turner, 2003:33).

Merton formulated empirical hypotheses and often tested them in the real world by gathering data himself and analyzing the data—true empiricism. Merton's functional theories are of the "middle-range" variety. He questioned the assumption that all systems have needs and requisites that must be met and that certain structures are indispensable in meeting these needs (Turner, 2003). Despite their differences, Parsons and Merton together would become known as the leaders of the structural-functional school of thought.

On February 23, 2003, Merton died; he had been residing in New York City. He will be remembered as one of the most influential sociologists of the twentieth century. His cumulative work contributed to his becoming the first sociologist to win a National Medal of Science in 1994 (Kaufman, 2003).

Theories of the Middle Range

One of Merton's greatest contributions to sociology was his emphasis on what he termed "theories of the middle range." He felt that grand theories were too abstract, and he deemed microanalysis pedantic inquiries. What he preferred were studies that led to further inquiry. In *Social Theory and Social Structure,* Merton (1968) described sociological theory as logically interconnected sets of propositions from which empirical uniformities can be derived. The focus of his theories is on the middle range. Merton (1968) describes *theories of the middle range* as theories that are more advanced than working hypotheses used by researchers but not as advanced as the larger, all-inclusive, more general and systematic theories designed to address a broad array of behaviors and situations.

Merton's middle-range theories are functionalist theories that consist of limited sets of assumptions, from which specific hypotheses can be derived and tested empirically. Merton viewed Durkheim's *Suicide* and Weber's *The Protestant Ethic and the Spirit of Capitalism* as examples of middle-range theories.

An important element of middle-range theory is the concept of *role sets.* Merton (1968) stated,

> The theory of role-sets begins with an image of how social status is organized in the social structure.... Despite the very diverse meanings attached to the concept of *social status,* one sociological tradition consistently uses it to refer to a position in a social system, with its distinctive array of designated rights and obligations. In this tradition, as exemplified by Ralph Linton, the related concept of *social role* refers to the behavior of others (who accord the rights and exact the obligations) (p. 41).

Role sets are multiple role expectations that are parts of the same position or status that any one person holds. For example, a student's role set might include family obligations, study obligations, work demands, significant-other demands, demands from a coach if that student is an athlete, and demands from other friends. This student must somehow find a way to meet all the demands on him or her within this role set.

Merton's theories are functionalist in perspective. For Merton, the term *function* referred to the extent to which a particular part or process of a social system contributes to the maintenance of the system or subsystem. *Function* does not mean the same thing as *purpose* or *motivation* (subjective dispositions); it refers to observable objective consequences. Merton (1968) promoted a process referred to as *codification*. Codification involves orderly, disciplined reflection; it entails the discovery of what has in fact been the strategic experience of scientific investigators, rather than the invention of new strategies of research. One of Merton's most famous middle-range theories involves his analysis of deviance.

Anomie Theory

As initially developed by Durkheim, the concept of *anomie* referred to a condition of relative normlessness in a society or group. Indicators of anomie include the perception that community leaders are indifferent to one's needs, the perception that little can be accomplished in a society which is seen as basically unpredictable and lacking social order, the perception that life goals are receding rather than being realized, a sense of futility, and the conviction that one cannot count on personal associates for social and psychological support. The success goal in American culture leads many to feelings of anomie. According to Merton (1949/1968), it is the conflict between cultural goals and the availability of using institutional means—whatever the character of the goals—which produces a strain toward anomie. This strain is especially difficult for lower-socioeconomic persons because society has created an opportunity–desire incongruence (Thio, 2010).

In brief, Merton believed that society encourages all persons to attain culturally desirable goals (such as economic success), but the opportunities to reach these goals are not equal among the members of society. Structural barriers such as economic means, racism, sexism, and ageism may hamper one's opportunity to reach culturally determined goals. Persons feeling such social pressures, without the means to attain these goals legitimately, may adapt a number of deviant behaviors in order to avoid feelings of anomie. Such terms as *cultural goals* and *institutionalized norms* are examples of explanatory factors consistent with functional analysis. Merton's primary aim "lies in discovering how some social structures *exert a definite pressure* upon certain persons in the society to engage in nonconformist rather than conformist conduct" (Merton, 1957:672). Among the several elements of social and cultural structures that exert pressure on individuals, two are of immediate importance. The first is culturally defined goals, purposes, and interests held out as legitimate objectives for all members of society. The second element is the institutionalized means that the structure defines, regulates, and controls, that is, the acceptable modes of reaching out for these goals. "Every social group invariably couples its cultural objectives with regulations, rooted in the mores or institutions, of allowable procedures for moving toward these objectives" (Merton, 1968: 187). The social system must find an effective equilibrium between these two elements. Thus, individuals must have ample opportunities to reach desired goals, but not to the extent that the social structure is threatened.

Merton (1968) described five types of individual adaptations for pursuing the coveted goals. These adaptations are schematically set out in Table 8.2, where plus (+) signifies "acceptance," minus (−) signifies "rejection," and plus/minus (+/−) signifies "rejection of prevailing values and substitution of new values."

Table 8.2 A Typology of Modes of Individual Adaptation

Modes of adaptation	Cultural goals	Institutionalized means
1. Conformity	+	+
2. Innovation	+	−
3. Ritualism	−	+
4. Retreatism	−	−
5. Rebellion	+/−	+/−

A brief description of each of these modes of adaptation reveals how the social structure operates to exert pressure upon individuals.

Merton stated that to the extent that a society is stable, adaptation Type 1—*conformity* to both cultural goals and institutionalized means—is the most common and widely diffused mode. If this were not the case, the stability and continuity of society would be compromised. This adaptation is not a deviant one, for it implies that a person has attained monetary success by socially acceptable means (by working hard and getting an education). *Innovations* such as bank robbery and racketeering will help the individual attain economic success, but they represent deviant adaptations. Merton wrote of the alarming increase in white-collar crime; he would be alarmed at the rate at which it occurs today. *Ritualistic* types of adaptation involve the "abandoning or scaling down of the lofty cultural goals of great pecuniary success and rapid social mobility to the point where one's aspirations can be satisfied" (Merton, 1968:203; Orig. 1949). This type of person rejects the cultural obligation to attempt "to get ahead in the world" but continues to abide almost compulsively by institutional norms. This type of behavior is labeled deviant. *Retreatism* (e.g., in drug addicts, social hermits, and pariahs) represents the rejection of both the cultural goals and the institutional means of attaining them, and it is therefore deviant behavior. *Rebellion* is a type of deviant adaptation that leads individuals to go outside the social structure. It involves a genuine transvaluation, where the direct or vicarious experience of frustration leads to a full denunciation of previously prized values. Rebellion represents the rejection of both societal goals and acceptable means and leads to behavior that attempts to drastically modify or overthrow the existing social structure. In extreme cases, riots or coup attempts may occur.

Manifest and Latent Functions

Merton argued that the functional approach to sociology is caught up in terminological confusion. All too often, a single term has been used to symbolize different concepts, just as the same concept has been symbolized by different terms. This confusion extends to the very word *function*. "The word 'function' has been pre-empted by popular speech with the not unexpected result that its connotation often becomes obscure in sociology proper" (Merton, 1968:74). By such a word as *function* many theorists mean one thing; specifically, if a behavior is functional, it serves some manifest trait. Merton believed that, too often, functionalists looked only at the manifest (intended) functions of behavior. Durkheim's study of elementary forms of religious life is a classic example of this, according to Merton. In his study of the Hopi Indian raindance, Merton expanded upon Durkheim's acknowledgment that the Arunta practiced totemism and that the symbols on the totem were in fact significant, in that they possessed a functional purpose. But as Merton (1968) noticed, the Hopi raindance served a manifest function as a means of attaining the needed

rain and also the latent function (unintended) of the dance behavior itself, aiding in the maintenance of group solidarity. Thus, Merton came to distinguish two primary usages for the word *function*. *Manifest functions* are those consequences that are expected, or intended; they are conscious
motivations for social behavior. *Latent functions* are consequences that are neither recognized nor
intended. The manifest function of the Hopi raindance was rain, whereas the latent function of
the dance included bringing the community together for a common cause. As another example,
education has the manifest function of providing knowledge to students, but a latent function is
providing social interaction opportunities (such as parties, and finding one's future spouse).

As Cuzzort and King (1995) explained,

> The manifest-latent distinction is a valuable one; it makes clear the nature of sociologi-
> cal investigation as perhaps few other distinctions do. Manifest functions are essentially
> "official" explanations of a given action. Latent functions are the unrecognized or "hidden"
> functions of an action. Socially patterned motives and purposes are essentially concepts for
> understanding the interaction between social structures and individual behavior (p. 251).

When a manifest function fails (if it does not rain after a raindance) but the latent function
remains important (communal gathering), there is a tendency to rationalize social action (the
lack of rain was not the result of the ceremony itself, but the fault of one, or more, of the participants). With regard to the Hopi raindance, the functionalist explains the persistence of superstitions as functional features of the social order. "Merton, aware of this disturbing feature of
structural and functional thought, has tried to get around it by introducing yet another idea—the
idea of dysfunctions" (Cuzzort and King, 1995:252).

Dysfunctions

As a functionalist, Merton examined the social structure and patterns of activity within organizations. He noticed that just setting up a system and putting it in place does not guarantee that it
will work at peak performance or that it will be *functional*. It may in fact have very negative or
dysfunctional consequences for the organization or the persons who must deal with it. "Merton
termed such system-disrupting consequences dysfunctions" (Levin, 1991:78). Furthermore,
aspects of the system may be functional for some but dysfunctional for others. For example,
a convenience store that remains open while all other grocery stores are closed during some
holiday may turn out to be quite functional for the customers who need last-minute purchases;
however, the clerk who is stuck working the holiday hours may find the store's remaining open
dysfunctional. Merton examined bureaucracy, which he described as a system set up for specific procedural strategies that foster objectivity and the smooth operation of the organization.
However, a bureaucracy, by its very design, is conservative (ritualistic) and inflexible (formalistic), and therefore unable to cope with changes or flaws within the system (Merton, 1968). For
example, if a courthouse is totally dependent on persons using computers to conduct daily business, it is rendered useless, or *dysfunctional,* during an electrical power outage. Dysfunctional
events, then, lessen the effective equilibrium of a social system.

> Dysfunctional aspects of a society imply strain or stress or tension. A society tries to con-
> strain dysfunctional elements somewhat as an organism might constrain a bacterial or
> viral infection. If the dysfunctional forces are too great, the social order is overwhelmed,
> disorganized, and possibly destroyed (Cuzzort and King, 1995:252).

Wallace and Wolf (1999) stated, "Merton's concept of dysfunctions is also central to his argument that functionalism is *not* intrinsically conservative. It appears to be only when functionalists imply that everything is generally functional in its consequences" (p. 52). A lasting issue is the concern over for whom the social structure is functional and for whom it is dysfunctional. Many institutions and subsystems possess these bipolar effects on different individuals, groups, and even entire societies.

Empirical Research

While working with Paul Lazarsfeld, Merton (with Patricia Kendall) wrote a piece on the focused interview. "Although he was never totally oriented to methods, some of Merton's most insightful pieces concerned the relation between research and theory, and the issue of problem-solving in sociology" (Adams and Sydie, 2001:363). Merton acknowledged that different research methods are necessary for different empirical problems, that research may lead to empirical generalizations, and that empirical research is useful for much more than testing hypotheses drawn from a general theory. Merton consistently drew links between theory and research. In an article written decades ago, Merton (1968) stated,

> Like all interpretative schemes, functional analysis depends upon a triple alliance between theory, method and data. Of the three allies, method is by all odds the weakest. Many of the major practitioners of functional analysis have been devoted to theoretic formulations and to the clearing up of concepts; some have steeped themselves in data directly relevant to a functional frame of reference; but few have broken the prevailing silence regarding how one goes about the business of functional analysis (p. 73).

More recently, Merton promoted the techniques employed in focus-group research that were derived from work some forty years prior (Merton, 1987). In his article "The Focused Interview and Focus Groups" (1987), Merton argued for "a set of procedures for the collection and analysis of qualitative data that may help us gain an enlarged sociological and psychological understanding in whatsoever sphere of human experience" (p. 565). Thus, for Merton, theorizing was always important, but it required methodology, research, and data analysis.

NEOFUNCTIONALISM

In the years following the primary contributions by Parsons and Merton, many other functionalists emerged, some in the tradition of the two theorists and others who rejected them. As Turner (2003) stated, "The grand architecture of the Parsonian functional scheme, as it evolved over a forty-year period at the mid-century, inspired a great amount of criticism, both inside and outside the functionalist camp" (p. 54). As a result, a new theoretical set of ideas appeared in the United States and Germany, collectively known as *neofunctionalism*. Among the most eminent neofunctionalists have been Niklas Luhmann, who wrote about social systems and maintained a commitment to producing abstract frameworks for analyzing social reality; Anthony Giddens, who rejected the Parsonian functional scheme and wrote about the process of structuration; Jeffrey C. Alexander, who is recognized as the leading proponent of neofunctionalism in the United States and published a volume titled *Neofunctionalism and After;* and Neil J. Smelser, who coauthored *Economy and Society* with Parsons. The works of these theorists are here.

Niklas Luhmann (1927–1998)

Born in 1927 in Luneburg, Germany, Niklas Luhmann would become the most prominent German, and arguably, European social theorist by the time of his death (Blute, 2002). After completing his law degree in 1949 from the University of Freiburg/Breisgau, Luhmann practiced law for a few years but became disillusioned with the repetitive nature of the legal profession and subsequently joined the civil service. During his free time he read the classic works of Descartes and Kant, as well as the functionalist theories of Malinowski and Radcliffe-Brown. In essence, Luhmann's theoretical development was the result of his own reading and of his civil service work in post–World War II Germany. Luhmann studied sociology under Talcott Parsons at Harvard from 1960–1961 and introduced German social thinkers to his works. Luhmann was highly impressed by Parsons but felt that he had failed to incorporate such critical concepts as self-reference and complexity. Having witnessed firsthand his country's defeat in a world war and German occupation by foreign troops, Luhmann was led to conclude that modern society was not a better place to live. Thus, like any social thinker, he was influenced by the climate of his times, and his pessimistic outlook on life directly contrasted with the outlook most American theorists (especially Parsons) of this era. Luhmann even argued that the modern world is too complex for such things as shared norms and values (the second core assumption of functionalism: shared values that assist in the maintenance of the social system).

Luhmann's own works were an attempt to formulate a universal or grand theory of social systems that includes his ideas described above. The resulting theory is far more complicated than the works of Max Weber.

> Niklas Luhmann not only saw the modern world as complicated—more so than during Weber's time—but mirrored it in his writing. The words are complex, the thoughts are complex, and his works are almost prohibitively so. He used a flexible and abstract set of concepts and propositions that could be combined in many different ways (Adams and Sydie, 2001:370).

The difficulty that Americans have in reading Luhmann involves the translation from German, the fact that his ideas are very abstract, and the fact that his sentences include new or little-known words. Luhmann found no reason to make theory noncomplicated, because social life itself is complicated. "The encompassing system is too large and complex to be immediately understandable. Its unity is not accessible, neither by experience nor by action" (Luhmann, 1984:59). His primary works, such as *Social Systems* (1984), have no natural starting point and lack a logical sequence of chapter ordering. Luhmann (1983) stressed the importance of grand theory: "Without universalistic theories or general frameworks, sociology will never be fully accepted" (p. 987). Luhmann (1983) described theory as not "something you invent or produce yourself; it is something already available which only needs interpretation and refinement" (p. 987). He remained steadfast in the idea that grand theory can, and should, be the primary goal of sociological theory. Luhmann (1984) stated, "Despite all skepticism and all the complaints about ideological bias which seem to be a recurrent affair…the chances for general theory are exceptionally good today. However, they require interdisciplinary orientations which are overlooked if we continue to focus on the classics" (p. 60).

Luhmann's primary contribution to social theory rests in his work on *systems theory*.

> Luhmann employs a *general systems* approach to emphasize that human action becomes organized and structured into systems. When the actions of several people become interrelated, a social system can be said to exist.… All social systems exist in multidimensional environments, posing potentially endless complexity with which a system must deal (Turner, 2003:55).

In order for any system to survive, it must learn to adapt to its environment. The complex nature of social environments makes systems integration a major concern.

The student of social theory should be able to easily recognize that the core premise of interdependent parts is a key element of Luhmann's theory. As Luhmann (1984) explained, "Social systems are self-referential systems. They are composed of elements (actions) which they produce by an arrangement of their elements" (p. 65).

This general framework distinguishes several forms of building subsystems in relation to their internal environment.

> Segmentation means that subsystems presuppose their environment in terms of a rank order of systems. Functional differentiation means that subsystems specialize themselves on specific functions and presuppose that their environment cares for the rest. These distinctions coincide roughly with the historical types of primitive societies, culturally developed societies, and modern society (Luhmann, 1984:63–64).

Interestingly, Luhmann did not view modern society as really integrated at all. As Fuchs (2001) interpreted Luhmann, society is instead

> characterized by massive parallel processing: think of all the encounters and conversations going on at the same time, with no mega-encounter coordinating or planning how this happens, or with what results. Modern society does not "go" anywhere but "drifts," without anyone at the helm (p. 130).

Luhmann described *general systems theory* as possessing two important elements. The first (as described above) is the distinction of the whole and its parts as modified by his *distinction of system and environment.* Second is the concept of *self-referential systems,* a condition necessary for the efficient functioning of systems. What this means is that the system is able to observe itself, can reflect on itself and what it is doing, and can make decisions as a result of this reflection. Luhmann (1983) stated:

> The system continually refers to itself by distinguishing itself from the environment. This is done by drawing and maintaining boundaries which can be crossed occasionally. The self-referential system is a self-reproducing or "autopoietic" unit, itself producing the elements which compose the system, and this requires the capacity to distinguish elements which belong to the system from elements which belong to the environment of the system. The distinction between system and environment is, therefore, constitutive for whatever functions as an element in a system. It is not the actor who produces the action. The meaning of the action and therefore the action itself is due to the difference between systems and environment (pp. 992–993).

Thus, Luhmann's focus remained on the system, and not on individual actors. Individuals were merely a part of the environment. Luhmann disagreed with Parsons, however, that ultimately there was an encompassing social system in society that strived for equilibrium.

According to Luhmann, social systems consist primarily of communication networks. The socialization of individuals into the social system is accomplished through communication.

Socialization is necessary to align the individual's modes of conduct with society's general shared meanings. Shared meanings are always a result of communication. Luhmann created a *communication theory* that stresses human communication as reflexive. Communication and, presumably, a shared language allow the more effective transmission of the ideas and concepts central to a society (or social system). Communicative language allows individuals to share the meaning of the key elements found in the environment. Reflexivity allows individuals to understand the meaning behind various forms of communication and therefore assists in the integration process.

Many of Luhmann's ideas are related to those of British theorist Anthony Giddens.

Anthony Giddens (1938–)

Few theorists have been as productive as Anthony Giddens. He is the author or editor of more than 40 books translated into over 40 different languages and more than 200 articles and reviews. Several of his books have become academic bestsellers (Guardian.co.uk, 2011). As a result, he is well known throughout the academic world. Giddens was born in North London (Edmonton) in 1938 and was the first member of his family to attend college, graduating from Hull University in 1959 with a B.A. in sociology. He completed his M.A. in sociology at the London School of Economics in 1970 and earned his Ph.D. in sociology from the same school in 1974 (Giddens, 2011). While working on his doctorate, he lectured in sociology at the University of Leicester, Simon Fraser University (British Columbia), and the University of California at Los Angeles (UCLA). After UCLA, Giddens went to Cambridge, where he served as a sociology lecturer and then a professor from 1970 to 1997. He is now the director of the London School of Economics and Political Science. As an active member of the Labour Party, Giddens has been among the favorite advisors to Tony Blair and, at one time, Bill Clinton.

Early in his academic career, Giddens taught the ideas of classic social theorists like Durkheim, Weber, and Marx. His functionalist perspective and interest in positivism took a turn in the 1970s and 1980s, when he started to emphasize cultural theory. Giddens believes that contemporary sociology relies too much on the theories and concepts of nineteenth-century European social theory in the application to modern social problems. He believes that the classical ideas must be radically overhauled today, and virtually all of his work is an attempt to develop a change in social theory. Evidence can be found in *Capitalism and Modern Social Theory* (1971), which Giddens (1976) described as "an exegetical preparation to an extended critique of nineteenth-century social thought" (p. 1); in *New Rules of Sociological Method* (1976); and in some sections of *Studies in Social and Political Theory* (1977), where he undertook critiques of two broad programmatic approaches to social theory: hermeneutics of the forms of "interpretative sociology" and functionalism. Although it is tempting to describe Giddens as a postmodernist because of his deconstruction of functionalism, he views postmodernism as little more than an extension of modernity due to the forces of globalization. Postmodernism, in Giddens' view, is really just the deemphasizing of traditional sociology.

Giddens' primary objective is to develop a theoretical position which attempts to draw upon the ideas of structuralism, hermeneutics, and interpretive social theory. He referred to his approach as the *theory of structuration*. Knoke (1990) described Giddens' approach as strongly influenced by Continental hermeneutics and linguistics, and as an attempt to formulate a theory of agency without lapsing into purely subjectivist phenomenology.

According to Giddens (1979), "The theory of structuration begins from an absence: the lack of a theory of action in the social sciences" (p. 2). He continued:

> The theory of structuration substitutes the central notion of the *duality of structure.* By the duality of structure, I mean the essential recursiveness of social life, as constituted in social practices: structure is both medium and outcome of the reproduction of practices. Structure enters simultaneously into the constitution of the agent and social practices, and "exists" on the generating moments of this constitution (p. 5).

Giddens (1979) went so far as to state that the theory of structuration could be read as a *nonfunctional manifesto* (p. 7). According to his theory, social systems have no purposes, reasons, or needs whatsoever; only human individuals have. It is clear that Giddens takes exception to the concept of *systems needs* because a system cannot "need" anything; it is an entity that exists because individuals within a system exist, and they are the only ones who could possibly "need" something from the environment. In functionalist theory, the guiding model of a "system" is usually that of an organism; therefore, it is viewed as a living, breathing being that has needs (as a biological organism has needs).

In contrast, Giddens (1979) views *social systems* as

> regularized relations of interdependence between individuals and groups, that typically can be best analyzed as *recurrent social practices.* Social systems are systems of social interaction; as such they involve the situated activities of human subjects, and exist syntagmatically in the flow of time. Systems, in this terminology, have structures, or more accurately, have structural properties; they are not structures in themselves (p. 66).

As Knoke (1990) observed, "In Giddens' unique terminology, social systems, as continuous flows of conduct in time and space, are distinguished from social structures, which are defined as rules and roles existing as memory traces that are revealed in actions" (p. 16). Social structures become necessary components of social systems. "Giddens believes structure can be conceptualized as *rules* and *resources* that actors use in 'interaction contexts' that extend across 'space' and over 'time'" (Turner, 2003:477). Rules are notions that actors come to understand and generally accept. "All social rules have both constitutive and regulative (sanctioning) aspects to them" (Giddens, 1979:66). A common example of a rule is "not to take the goods of another." Resources are those items that give actors power and allow those who possess resources the ability to "get things done." Giddens emphasizes the inherent "transformative" potential of rules and resources (Turner, 2003). Structural principles operate in cooperation with one another, but they also contravene each other (Giddens, 1984). In addition, structure itself is

> both enabling and constraining, and it is one of the specific tasks of social theory to study the conditions in the organization of the social system that govern the interconnections between the two. According to this conception, the same structural characteristics participate in the subject (the actor) as in the object (society). Structure forms "personality" and "society" simultaneously—but in neither case exhaustively (Giddens, 1979:69–70).

A quick summation of Giddens' theory of structuration reveals his structuralist perspective, which is revealed in Knoke's (1990) analysis of the four basic modes of structuration that occur:

1. rules for signification of meaning;
2. rules for normative legitimation of social conduct;
3. authorized resources to command persons (political power);
4. allocation of resources to command objects (economic property).

Giddens' theory of structuration (1979) links these structural modes to recurrent interactions through a duality of structure and agency. Thus, society, though consisting of social actors who interact with one another, is still a complex matrix of social systems that are interdependent.

Throughout the 1990s and 2000s, Giddens has been working in the area of globalization, especially in regard to its impact on human behavior, the global marketplace, and international finances. The global marketplace has grown so much that trillions of dollars are turned over each day on global currency markets (Giddens, 2000a:28). Among his most recent books are *The Consequences of Modernity* (1989), *Modernity and Self-Identity* (1991), *Beyond Left and Right* (1994), *In Defence of Sociology* (1996), *The Third Way and Its Critics* (2000), and *Runaway World* (2000). In *Runaway World,* Giddens described how globalization is restructuring the ways in which we live. Globalization is led from the West and bears the strong imprint of American political and economic power. Giddens pointed out that globalization affects the United States as well as the rest of the world.

Giddens views globalization as a positive influence on humanity because it is liberating women, spreading democracy, and creating new wealth. The importance that Giddens places on democracy leads him to conclude that it is worth fighting for, and that it can be achieved. It can be achieved through more government. "Our runaway world doesn't need less, but more government" (Giddens, 2000:100).

Giddens has continued to publish extensively in the 2000s. Beyond his still-popular introductory sociology texts, Giddens has published a number of books that deal with politics, specifically, introducing a new way of looking at democracy. His *The New Egalitarian* (2005) explores social inequality at a time when traditional societal values and norms have by undermined by the social current of individualism. In *Over to You, Mr. Brown* (2007), Giddens examines the leadership of the Labour Party, suggesting it stands at a decisive point in its history. In his *Politics of Climate Change* (2009), Giddens describes how climate change is a social problem that affects humanity as a collectivity and warns that if this problem continues to grow unchecked the consequences could be catastrophic for humanity. Former U.S. President Bill Clinton describes this book as a landmark study in the struggle to contain climate change.

Building upon the success of his earlier editions of *The Third Wave* books, Giddens published *The Third Wave: The Renewal of Social Democracy* in 2010. *The Third Wave* promotes a left-of-center approach to politics that emphasizes the value of democracy free from the two traditional forms (waves) of democracy—the "Old Left" and "market fundamentalism." The third way provides a political alternative to leftists and rightists.

> Third way politics, I try to show, isn't an ephemeral set of ideas. It will continue to have its dissenters and critics. But it will be at the core of political dialogues in the years to come, much as neo-liberalism was until recently and old-style social democracy was before that. Third way politics will be the point of view with which others will have to engage (Giddens, 2000b:1).

In *The Third Way and Its Critics* (2000b), Giddens expanded upon some of the ideas and themes outlined in his 1998 publication. Giddens (2000b) stated,

> The idea of finding a third way in politics has become a focus of controversy across the world. The term "third way," of course, is far from new, having been employed by groups of diverse political persuasions in the past, including some from the extreme right. Social democrats, however, have made the use of it most often (p. 1).

American Democrats describe the third way as a "new progressivism" (Giddens, 2000b:2).

> Partly borrowing from the New Democrats, and partly following its own line of political evolution, the Labour Party in Britain converged on similar ideas. Under Tony Blair's leadership, the party broke with its own "old progressivism"—Clause 4 of the Labour Party constitution. Blair started to refer to New Labour as developing a third way, eventually putting his name to a pamphlet of the same title (Giddens, 2000b:3).

Giddens described the third way as involving radical politics and

> argues that the three key areas of power—government, the economy, and the communities of civil society—all need to be constrained in the interests of social solidarity and social justice. A democratic order, as well as an effective market economy, depends upon a flourishing civil society. Civil society, in turn, needs to be limited by the other two (Giddens, 2000b:51).

It is Giddens' hope that the third way will provide a fresh approach to issues such as family life, crime, and the decay of many communities. Perhaps his faith in globalization will be realized as the third way of dealing with worldwide inequality.

Jeffrey C. Alexander (1947–)

Jeffrey C. Alexander is a Professor of Sociology at Yale University. He earned his B.A. from Harvard in 1969 and his Ph.D. from the University of California at Berkeley in 1978. He worked at UCLA from 1974 until joining Yale University in 2001. Alexander has tried to revive the functionalist theories of Parsons while addressing its deficiencies. Establishing a legitimate post-Parsonian functionalism is what Alexander calls *neofunctionalism*. His *Neofunctionalism and After* (1985) represents his first attempt to finalize the bridge between traditional functionalism and reconstructed functionalism. Alexander succeeded in establishing the legitimacy of some of Parsons' central themes and concepts while articulating newer, more contemporary issues related to functionalist theory. For example, unlike Parsons, Alexander emphasizes the micro levels of sociological analysis by including elements of symbolic interactionism. He has also attempted to incorporate a less optimistic view of modernity by utilizing aspects conflict theory.

In his 1998 publication of *Neofunctionalism and After* (1998), Alexander expands his previous ideas and describes neofunctionalism as a movement of ideas that marked a shift in the predicted slope of knowledge/power. Alexander (1998) explains:

> Faced with the emergence of a neofunctionalism in the 1980s, theorists whose formation occurred in the 1960s—when a radical sociology was supposed to have broken definitely with Parsons—spoke of a "surprisingly successful comeback" and of neofunctionalism as a refutation of the linear assumptions about scientific development that the preceding generation had continued to hold (p. 3).

Alexander acknowledged the considerable contributions of Parsons to sociological theory but stated that they are not as revered today as in the past. Alexander (1998) added:

> I have succeeded in helping to (re)establish the legitimacy of some of Parsons' central concerns, I regard this project as completed. It is this very completion that has allowed me increasingly to separate my own understanding of social theory from Parsons' own, to look beyond Parsons, to think about what comes "after Parsons," to build not only upon "Parsons," but upon strands of classical and contemporary work, to create a different kind of social theory. Still, whatever comes after neofunctionalism will be deeply indebted to it (p. 5).

Alexander views neofunctionalism as part of the evolutionary growth of postwar sociological theory. Parsons dominated the first phase (the 1940s through the mid-1960s). Theories presented in the 1970s by such social thinkers as Giddens, Habermas, and Collins that attempted to integrate different lines of thought represent the second phase of theoretical development. And finally, in a phase that Alexander (1998) described as postclassical, neofunctionalism "was an effort to relate Parsons to different forms of classical and contemporary work" (p. 8). Furthermore, "neofunctionalism has succeeded in helping to establish Parsons as a classical figure" (p. 12).

In the 2000s, Alexander has authored or coauthored a number of books expanding on his theoretical ideas, among them *The Performance of Politics—Obama's Victory and the Democratic Struggle for Power* (2010), *The New Social Theory Reader*, 2nd edition (2008), *The Civil Sphere* (2006), *Social Performance: Symbolic Action, Cultural Pragmatics and Ritual* (2006), *The Cambridge Companion to Durkheim* (2005), *Cultural Trauma and Collective Identity* (2004), and *The Meanings of Social Life: A Cultural Sociology* (2003). An underlining theme of Alexander's works is an analysis of democratic society and the challenges it faces in light of modernity and the social problems associated with it.

Neil Smelser (1930–)

Presently, Smelser serves as University Professor of Sociology Emeritus at the University of California, Berkeley. He earned both his B.A. (1952) and Ph.D. (1958) from Harvard, where he learned about functionalism first-hand from Parsons. Neil Smelser co-authored *Economy and Society* (1956) with Talcott Parsons while he was just a graduate student. Smelser is considered a top-level theorist in neofunctionalism. Smelser, more so than Alexander, incorporated the symbolic interactionist perspective in his neofunctionalist approach. Smelser (1998) believes that people seek to avoid the experience of ambivalence because it is "such a *powerful, persistent, unresolvable, volatile, generalizable,* and *anxiety-producing* feature of the human condition" (p. 6). Smelser (1998) stated that ambivalence refers to such phenomena as death and separation, retirement, and moving away from a community (traditional definitions of ambivalence—simultaneous attraction toward and repulsion from a person—might confuse the reader here with Smelser's usage of the term). When such moves are "forced" upon the individual, the negative feelings are heightened. For example, if someone loses a job and is forced to move away from a loved community, that person will experience a wide variety of negative emotions, or ambivalence. Additionally, more coercive organizations, or those closed institutions described by Erving Goffman as "total institutions," are especially conducive to ambivalence and its negative consequences. In less extreme cases, people may feel locked to a job, or a career, that they cannot escape without great cost. In such cases, co-workers must learn to cooperate and get along with one another. Unfortunately, all too often those in power abuse their authority because of a personal agenda, and the victim feels great ambivalence (among other feelings).

CRITICISMS OF STRUCTURAL FUNCTIONALISM

The functionalist perspective was spearheaded by the works of Talcott Parsons, who revolutionized a way of thinking by formulating a grand theory centered on his social action theory and his analysis of social systems. Parsons' one-time-dominant theoretical perspective came under attack on many fronts by the 1970s. One criticism of functionalism is that it fails to explain social change, that it stresses structure over process. Critics argue that structural functionalism is better suited to deal with static structures than it is dealing with processes of change. If the parts of the system are designed to maintain a functional flow, how do they allow for change? Parsons believed that he had addressed this concern about social change in his theory of evolution. However, his explanation was always in the context of strain on the system and the corresponding attempt to reach equilibrium. The emphasis of the social system is on the need for integration of the parts of society and the various actors. Consequently, a more legitimate criticism of Parsons' functionalist theory is its conservative nature.

The conservative nature of functionalism is indeed often criticized. The narrow focus of functionalism prevents it from addressing a number of important issues in the social world. Functionalism's focus on systems equilibrium leads it to support the status quo, so it is highly conservative. The assumption that the parts of the system work in cooperation with one another generally leads functionalists to ignore conflict. Functionalists have a hard time dealing effectively with conflict—another important criticism of functionalism.

Functionalism stresses the importance of shared societal values but ignores the *interests* of people. According to Wallace and Wolf (1999), although functionalism does show "the independent importance of ideas and the links between power and social consent, it neglects the coercive aspects of power and the significance of people's conflicting objectives" (p. 65). Because of the conservatism of his theories, Parsons often ignored issues of conflict and power. The social system needs to maintain equilibrium, and therefore, it must often exercise social control and seek to avoid conflict. Conflict is a cause of strain that must be stabilized so that the system can move along smoothly.

Parsons was aware of conflict but failed to address it in any significant way in his theories. The primary reason he failed to explain conflict is that he did not elaborate on the role of power and how power positions often dictate behavior. The reason most people perform their roles and act as they do is not that their behavior is functional to them, but that they find themselves on the short end of a power relationship. Parsons (1951) did acknowledge that one's participation in the social system is influenced by one's "location" in the relationship. In his article "A Sociological Approach to the Theory of Organization II" (1956b), Parsons discussed what can be achieved with power but did not articulate what constitutes power, nor did he discuss power relationships. Parsons seemed to treat conflict and power as "givens" of normal life that do not need further examination. Even toward the end of his life, when he was surely aware of the criticisms of his theoretical shortcomings, Parsons failed to examine more closely these vitally important variables of human action. In order to be a complete theory, functionalism needs to integrate the role of power and the effects and types of social conflict.

Functionalism is also attacked for its overly macro perspective on social life. It pays little attention to daily interactions among individuals. Functionalism fails to explain adequately its most important terms: *structure, function,* and *social system.* It assumes that there is a general consensus on shared values but fails to demonstrate how these values come about or how they are modified. Parsons was criticized for failing to collect empirical data, even though he admired Weber and Durkheim for using empirical data to support their theories. Parsons did not worry about such complaints, as he indicated that there must be specialists in every field: Some are specialists in research, and he considered himself a specialist in theory. His commitment to the development of sociological concepts in order to study human action reveals his dedication to social theory.

Neofunctionalism was created by those who believe in the validity of the basic core tenets of functionalism while also addressing the criticisms of it. Neofunctionalists have incorporated aspects of symbolic interactionism to address micro issues of human behavior and conflict theory to address societal conflict and power differentials. Anthony Giddens argued that systems do not have needs, people do. One could debate sociologically whether or not a system, which consists of people, has needs, or if, in fact, as Giddens suggested, only people—presumably who are outside the system—can have needs.

THE APPLICATION OF STRUCTURAL FUNCTIONALISM TO CONTEMPORARY SOCIETY

Structural functionalism, like all sociological theories, should be examined on two key criteria: its practical application (everyday use by everyday people) and its theoretical application (sociological value). From a practical perspective, functionalism is very applicable and relevant to the lives of people. The daily decision-making process utilized by nearly of all us is heavily influenced by matters of practicality and functionality. This is especially true when it comes to matters of finance. For example, we may prefer to drive a brand-new, fancy car or purchase a new consumer item (e.g., big-screen TV, new computer, or kitchen appliances), but when money is tight, we tend to make decisions based on functionality. That is, if the car runs and the computer works, we make do. Families struggle with practical decisions on a daily basis. Can we afford a family vacation to Disneyland, or do we have a "staycation"? A staycation, of course, is a vacation that is spent at one's home enjoying all that home and one's home environment has to offer. Deciding on a staycation over a vacation is generally determined out of concerns of practicality.

Many students, undoubtedly, chose to attend college based on the application of functionality. Graduating from a top-tier university (e.g., the Ivy League schools) would be nice, but for most students the state university systems and community colleges offer a more realistic and functional alternative. Furthermore, the college degree itself serves an important function of assisting graduates land a relatively high-paying job. The popularity of Facebook (over 500 million users worldwide) reflects the functional component of social networking as it allows people, especially friends and family, an opportunity to keep in touch with one another in an inexpensive and efficient manner. In other words, it is functional to those who use it. Law enforcement agencies study gang graffiti and gang tattoos because it serves a functional component in their quest to combat street gangs. Increasingly, police detectives analyze the ink worn by gangsters looking for clues about crimes committed and links to gang affiliation (Gaona, 2003). In this manner, the study of tattoos and graffiti serve a functional component for law enforcement. In short, there is nearly no end of the examples of the practicality of the functional theory in everyday life.

When examining the relevancy of structural functionalism to contemporary sociology, we should examine some of the key tenets of the theory. Let's begin by examining the most basic element of structural functionalism—the idea that society is a system of interconnected parts (social institutions). The reality is society and all modern social systems *are* comprised of interdependent parts. An examination of any social system, such as a university, large businesses, corporations, and local, state, and federal governments, reveals a structure (with varying degree) made up of a number of different departments with specialized activities conducted by people working toward the system's desired goal(s). Structural functionalists are correct when they predict that a breakdown, or strain, in one institution can cause harm to adjoining parts of the system, or the entire system itself.

If we look at the United States in 2012, we see a nation with a social system that has been deeply compromised because of a drain on financial resources. The costs of funding the social institution of the military to wage multiple wars have a profound effect on the system's ability to support other social institutions such as education, public health care, and maintaining the infrastructure. If we take a quick look at health care, for example, we will discover that the United States spent over $2 trillion dollars for health care in 2008 (National Health Care Anti-Fraud Association, 2009). The total cost of health care soars every year. The National Coalition on Health Care (NCHC) (2009) estimates that the national health spending will reach $2.5 trillion in 2009, accounting for 17.6% of the gross domestic product (GDP). The United States spends a greater percentage of its gross domestic product on health care than any other country in the world (Wallechinksy, 2007). These expenditures place a high demand on the financial resources of the U.S. And when one considers the aging population (primarily because of the aging "baby boomers") of the U.S., the demands on the healthcare system will only increase the strain on the social system. The social system needs to find a way to cope with the rising costs of health care or risk dissolution. Structural functionalists use the idea of the system needing to find equilibrium to address the issue of impending dissolution.

The second guiding principle of structural functionalism is the idea of a general consensus on values. It is this tenet that upsets so many critics of functionalism, for they feel it reflects an intolerance of differing viewpoints and is therefore conservative and supports the status quo. The truth remains, however, that in order for any social system (society, organization, family, or personal relationship with others) to remain intact and to run smoothly, there *must* be some commitment to general values, issues of morality, and goals of the relationship. To deny this reality is naive at the very least. Couples "drift" apart when they no longer share a commitment to the relationship; employees leave an organization when they realize that their attitudes and goals differ from those of the employer; and society risks dissolution when disturbances (e.g., internal conflicts, riots, protests, and civil war) cause such strain that the system itself is threatened. And although the more than 315 million people who live in the United States do not share all the same values, there are a number of key values we do share. For example, Americans share a belief that we all have basic rights and freedoms; that we should not be subject to physical attack or that people cannot take our personal possessions just because they are stronger than us; that cannibalism and pedophilia are wrong; that we should have the right to fall in love with any person we want regardless of race, ethnicity, and religion; and so on. There are numerous examples of shared values within a given society, just as there are numerous examples of values we do not share; however, as structural functionalists point out, we must have some common thread or the system risks falling apart.

Robert Merton's middle-range version of functionalism introduced many key concepts into sociological theory. The distinctions between manifest and latent functions are numerous. Many people attend sporting events to cheer for their favorite team (manifest function), but the communal gathering (especially demonstrated with "tailgating" before football games—America's number one sport) before, during, and after the game also serves a latent function.

Earning a degree is a manifest function of higher education, but finding your future mate and attending parties, sports events, and art exhibits serve as latent functions. There are many other examples of things we do for a primary purpose (manifest) that also serve secondary purposes (latent).

Merton's use of dysfunction is relevant today too. As he indicated, just because an element exists in life does not mean it is functional to all of us. Cell phones, for example, are practical and serve many manifest functions, but they are also troublesome (dysfunctional) when people use them while driving or in public places such as movie theaters or restaurants. Most people use their cell phones to text, but they become so preoccupied with texting that they forget about the people who are in their immediate proximity. And most professors would agree students using cell phones in class is very dysfunctional to the learning environment.

Many people take prescription drugs to help with various medical problems. Ritalin, Adderall, and Dexedrine are used to treat Attention Deficit Hyperactivity Disorder (ADHD). Assuming that a proper diagnosis reveals that a child needs to take a drug for ADHD (there are many professionals who remain skeptical about prescribing drugs to kids just because they are hyperactive), such medication serves a functional purpose. However, research shows that during the past few years, an increasing number of college students are using these same prescription drugs to help them study (Caplan et al., 2007). In many cases, the dysfunctional result of taking prescription drugs that were not specifically prescribed to the person can lead to substance abuse and negative chemical reactions in the body. Thus, as Merton warned us, just because certain elements exist in society does not mean they serve a functional purpose to us all.

The value of structural functionalism to contemporary sociologists has diminished since the heyday of the theory. Nonetheless, this once-popular theory should not be ignored, as many of its basic core tenets remain valuable today.

Summary

Structural functionalism dominated sociological theory in the 1950s and 1960s. In 1959, at the height of functionalism, Kingsley Davis (1959) suggested that every sociologist is a functionalist because sociology *is* functionalism. Functionalism is a theory originally designed by Talcott Parsons that now lives on through the ideas of others. Stephen Turner (1993) stated,

> Parsons underwent a much promoted posthumous "revival," and the historical and interpretive literature on Parsons, both of the hagiographic and critical sort, has expanded ever since. Parsons has been fortunate in attracting scholarly interest—of better quality, in some respects, in death and with nonstudents than in life with his students (pp. 228–229).

Robert Merton attempted to bridge the gap between the macro aspects highlighted by Parsons and the micro aspects that were neglected. He also introduced the concepts of manifest and latent functions along with the idea of dysfunctions. The contributions of neofunctionalists like Niklas Luhmann, Anthony Giddens, Jeffrey C. Alexander, and Neil Smelser demonstrate the staying power of the functionalist tradition. As Levin (1991) stated, "Functionalism is one of the major perspectives in sociology" (p. 82).

Despite the criticisms of structural functionalism, its practical application remains as relevant today as any other time in the past. The theoretical relevance of structural functionalism to sociology is less applicable to contemporary sociologists. Nonetheless, it is safe to state that the functional approach will remain in sociological discourse for as long as there is sociology. For further evidence of this, one merely needs to review any introductory sociology textbook, as the functionalist approach is regularly discussed in a variety of contexts. Lastly, functionalism, along with conflict theory and symbolic interactionism, is one of three sociological theories generally discussed in all introductory sociology courses. As a result, it remains as one of the "big three" (or "original" three) theoretical approaches in sociology.

 Study and **Review** on **MySearchLab**

Discussion Questions

1. How many items do you own or utilize because they serve a functional role in your life?
2. Using the AGIL format, describe your college's social system.
3. How does Robert Merton's functionalist theory compare and contrast to that of Parsons? Which approach seems more valid? Explain.
4. Describe the criticisms of structural functionalism. Do you think that the application of the relevancy of functionalism supercedes the criticisms or falls short?
5. Does structural functionalism deserve a designation as one of the "big three" theories of sociology? Why or why not?

MySearchLab® Connections

MysearchLab is designed just for you. Each chapter features a customized study plan to help you learn and review key concepts and terms. Dynamic visual activities, videos, and readings found in the multimedia library will enhance your learning experience.

 View on **MySearchLab**

▶ Merton's Strain Theory of Deviance.

 Read on **MySearchLab**

▶ Parsons, Talcott. The Sick Role and the Role of the Physician Reconsidered.

9 Conflict Theory

 Listen to the **Chapter Audio** on **MySearchLab**

Chapter Outline

The cornerstone of functional theory is the idea that there is a general *consensus* in values and norms of society and that the social institutions are integrated as a functioning whole. In contrast, *conflict theories* emphasize the role of *power* and the inequality found systematically throughout society. Conflict theory claims that there is no true consensus and that, instead, society's norms and values are those of the dominant group. The privileged group imposes its will on the subordinate group in order to maintain its power position. It is the existence of multiple groups, the result of stratification, and the tension and strain between them that leads to conflict with society. As Lewis Coser (1956) states, "Conflict sets boundaries between groups within a social system by strengthening group consciousness and awareness of separateness, thus establishing the identity of groups within the system" (p.34). Conflict theory rose to prominence during the 1970s because of growing disenchantment with structural functionalism, the advent of much civil unrest during the 1960s, and a renewed interest in the works of Marx, Weber, and Simmel among contemporary sociologists. With conflict, of one sort or another, evident in nearly all spheres of life, this theory would appear to be as relevant as ever.

Individuals, groups, organizations, and society are fighting over scarce resources, and yet people in power positions maintain the upper hand in the distribution of goods and services.

DEFINING CONFLICT THEORY

The conflict perspective views society as a system of social structures and relationships that are shaped mainly by economic forces. Those who are economically wealthy control the means of production and thus dominate society because of their advantageous power position. Conflict theorists assume that social life revolves around the economic interests of the wealthy and that these people use their economic power to coerce and manipulate others to accept their view of the society—and the world. Social classes are based on economics and one's relative position in regard to the means of production. Furthermore, because there is a clear power differential among individuals and social classes, resentment and hostility are constant elements of society. The obvious implication of this social reality is that conflict is inevitable.

The conflict perspective acknowledges that there are special *interest groups* that fight over the scarce resources of society. These groups have their own best interests at heart and not those of the greater society. Interest groups work to gain a power advantage over others.

> Instead of interpreting social life as normally cooperative and harmonious, conflict theorists view society as an arena in which different individuals and groups struggle with each other in order to obtain scarce and valued resources, especially property, prestige, and power (Lindsey and Beach, 2004:20).

The competition between these groups throws off the equilibrium of society until a dominant group gains control and reinstitutes stability by means of power. Conflict theorists believe that *power* is the core of all social relationships. It is the most precious of the scarce social resources. Therefore, *conflict theory* views society as composed of competing elements (interest groups) that fight over scarce resources (e.g., wealth, power, and prestige) with power differentials that ultimately determine the allocation and distribution of these scarce resources.

THE INTELLECTUAL ROOTS OF CONFLICT THEORY

Sociological conflict theory has its roots in the ideas of Karl Marx (1818–1883), Max Weber (1864–1920), and Georg Simmel (1858–1918). All three of these classical theorists contributed to the formation of contemporary social conflict theory. (For a more thorough analysis of these social thinkers, see Chapters 2, 4, and 5, respectively.)

When teaching conflict theory to students, I tell them to think of two things when they hear the term *conflict theory*: power and Marx. That conflict theory consists of two elements, "Marx" and "power," is an oversimplification of course, but it does highlight the basic roots of this sociological theory. The role of power in society is a common thread among all conflict theorists, and it is the ideas of Karl Marx that are most evident in the conflict perspective. Marx did not "create" conflict theory; rather, it was his ideas on such subjects as human potential, the historical method, class conflict, class consciousness, capitalism, exploitation, and communism that influenced future social thinkers when they created conflict theory.

Max Weber agreed with Marx that economics was an important variable in determining power differentials among individuals in society. However, he believed that social divisions were based on two other factors as well: social prestige or status and political influence. Weber acknowledged the role of power in maintaining order within society. He believed that conflict underlies all social relations and determines power (Dronberger, 1971). The possession of power is a critical element in conflict theory, and power is a central aspect in Weber's works on the *types of authority*. (Weber proposed that there are three *types of authority*: rational-legal, traditional, and charismatic.) Weber defined *power* as the ability to impose one's will on another, even when the other objects. *Authority* is legitimate power (and a legitimate form of domination); it is power that is exercised with the consent of the ruled. According to Weber, the distribution of power and authority is the basis of social conflict. He stated that whereas power is essentially tied to the personality of individuals, authority is always associated with social positions. Weber also insisted that while power is merely a factual relation, authority is a legitimate relation of domination and subjection. In this sense, authority can be described as legitimate power. Authority is a universal element of social structure; it both realizes and symbolizes the functional integration of social systems.

Georg Simmel's sociological study was guided by the *dialectical approach*. A dialectical approach is multicausal and multidirectional, integrates fact and value, rejects the idea that there are concrete dividing lines between social phenomena, focuses on social relations, and is deeply concerned with conflicts and contradictions. Simmel believed that "the world can best be understood in terms of conflicts and contrasts between opposed categories" (Levine, 1971:xxxv). The forms of social life constantly influence individual decisions and behavior. According to Simmel, the most important form of relationship in the whole social world is the one between the leader and the followers, between the superior and the subordinates. It is a form of socialization critical to social life and is the main factor in sustaining the unity of groups. Superiority and subordination constitute the sociological expression of psychological difference in human beings (Spykman, 1965). Simmel insisted that social action always involves harmony *and* conflict, love *and* hatred. If this is the case, then conflict is always present and varies only in degree.

The works of Marx, Weber, and Simmel had a tremendous impact on the development of conflict theory, and yet their influence was delayed for decades. It was not until the 1950s and the works of two German-born sociologists, Lewis Coser and Ralf Dahrendorf, that the tenets of conflict theory would resurface in the United States (Turner, 2003). The ideas of Coser and Dahrendorf, along with C. Wright Mills and Randall Collins, will be highlighted in this chapter.

LEWIS COSER (1913–2003)

Lewis Coser was born in Berlin, Germany, in 1913, to a family of Jewish bankers. His original name was Ludwig Cohen, but his father later changed the family name. He lived in Berlin through high school, where his involvement with Marxist politics and the socialist student movement was not met with tolerance during the emergence of Adolf Hitler and his Nazi regime (Coser, 1993; Perrin, 2003). Coser left Germany in 1933 and moved to Paris, explaining (1993),

> My parents were not allowed to support me financially outside Germany, and the French government did not allow foreign exiles to take regular jobs in the tough job market of the depression years. I worked as a traveling salesperson for several wholesalers, and somewhat later was privileged to work as a personal secretary to a Swiss author and journalist (p. 2).

Luckily for Coser, enrollment at the Sorbonne (University of Paris) was free, and so began his academic career. Because of his interest in social structure, Coser chose to study sociology.

With the outbreak of World War II, Coser was interned as an enemy alien. He was able to escape France with the aid of a local socialist mayor, who managed to get a visa for Coser as a political antifascist refugee (Wallace and Wolf, 1999). On the advice of an immigration official, Coser changed his first name from Ludwig to Lewis (Perrin, 2003). Coser arrived in New York via Spain and Portugal and was assigned an agent, Rose Laub, for his case with the International Relief Association. Not only did Coser remain in the United States, but he and Laub also fell in love and were soon married. Rose and Lewis remained happily married. Both Rose and Lewis earned their Ph.D. degrees in sociology from Columbia University and studied under such professors as Robert Merton and Paul Lazarsfeld.

Coser's academic writings include his first book *The Functions of Social Conflict* (1956), *Men of Ideas: A Sociologist's View* (1965b), *Continuities in the Study of Social Conflict* (1968), *Greedy Institutions: Patterns of Undivided Commitment* (1974), his brilliant review of social theory found in *Masters of Sociological Thought* (1977), and a large number of journal articles. Coser's work reflects the conflict perspective and his lifelong concern with protecting human freedoms from oppressive power groups. His work also centers on the analysis of *greedy institutions* that demand total involvement from their members. Coser was concerned with the threat of human freedom inherent in total involvement. He wrote (1974), "I consider it essential that an open society be preserved above all" (p. 17). After a long and productive life, Lewis Coser died on July 8, 2003, in Cambridge, Massachusetts.

It should be clear to the reader that Coser's life experiences played a significant role in his outlook on social life. Born and raised as a Jew in Germany, he was forced to escape from his homeland by the oppression of the Nazi regime. He learned firsthand about direct social conflict and the negative effects that a dominant group can have on a subordinate group—a lesson that, once learned, is seldom erased in future attitudes or action. Among the academic influences on Coser are Émile Durkheim, Georg Simmel, Karl Marx, Robert Merton, Talcott Parsons, and Coser's wife, Rose Laub Coser.

Conflict Theory

Coser credits Georg Simmel's work on conflict theory for turning his focus on "the conflictual rather than the harmonious aspects of social phenomenon" (Coser, 1993:7). Simmel was interested in the "web of conflict," or the cross-cutting allegiances that can both bind a society together and create antagonism and confrontations. Coser's major work on conflict theory, *The Functions of Social Conflict* (1956), is an exposition of sixteen separate propositions that attempt to develop Simmel's rather fragmented insights (Wallace and Wolf, 1999). Coser (1956) argued that although conflict always exists in society, society also consists of degrees of consensus. Combining Simmel and Marx's ideas, Coser came to view the causes of conflict as

1. The greater the deprived groups' questioning of the legitimacy of the existing distribution of scarce resources, the more likely they are to initiate conflict.
2. The more a group's deprivations are transformed from absolute to relative, the more likely the group is to initiate conflict (Turner, 1974).

By the late 1950s, many social thinkers in the United States had revitalized Marxist thought into conflict theory.

> The revolutionary and activist Marxism first developed by Marx and Engels in the late 1840s found an echo among 20th century intellectuals....Social existence determined social consciousness. The receptivity to variant Marxist doctrine was largely conditioned

by the values and attitudes of the men and women whose concrete social and historical existence was mirrored in their world view, whether as producers or as consumers of ideas (Coser, 1972a:200).

In *The Functions of Social Conflict* (1956), Coser defined and related conflict to the social world, explored the nature of hostility, discussed how conflict can lead to social change, and paid close attention to the role of people's emotions in conflict. Coser (1956) defined conflict as "a struggle over values and claims to scarce status, power and resources in which the aims of the opponents are to neutralize, injure or eliminate their rivals" (p. 8). Coser believed that conflict may take place between individuals, between collectives, or between individuals and collectives. Intergroup and intragroup conflicts are a constant feature of social life (Hilgart, 1997). Coser (1956) defined power as "the chance to influence the behavior of others in accord with one's own wishes" (p. 134). Determining the level of power that any one group holds depends on its relation to other groups.

Coser agreed with Simmel that there are aggressive or hostile impulses in people, and that in all close and intimate relationships, both love and hate are present. Love and hate are conjoined because contact is constant in close relationships; the closer the contact, the more intense the conflict. Conflict in a relationship often creates instability (Coser, 1956). Because of close proximity, people have many opportunities to develop resentment; consequently, conflict and arguments are integral parts of people's relationships and need not be signs of instability and breakup.

On the other hand, the nature of hostility and conflict varies for sociological reasons, including social structural factors that include financial stability, clearly defined societal rules, love and nurture from the family, and practical and emotional support from outside the nuclear family. Coser's work is an attempt to explain how structural factors interact with people's underlying emotions (Wallace and Wolf, 1999).

Coser came to realize that conflict serves many functions. Conflict often leads to social change, it can stimulate innovation, and during times of external (war) or internal (civil unrest) threat, it leads to an increase in the centralization of power. (Note: This idea was also articulated by Herbert Spencer.) Thus, as the title of his book implies, it was the *functions* of conflict that Coser explored. He presented a number of arguments in the form of sixteen separate propositions. A selected number of these propositions are reviewed next:

Proposition 1: Group-Binding Functions of Conflict

Conflict serves as an important agent in establishing full ego identity, autonomy, and differentiation of personality from the outside world. Conflict with other groups increases a group's consciousness and awareness of separateness and establishes boundaries between groups. A group is bound together by the individual members' similarities and the reinforcing of group awareness of such similarities. The realization of differences from other groups establishes and strengthens the group's identity. Conflict helps to create and maintain group cohesion. With a high level of conflict comes a high level of group cohesion. Each group relies on conflict for its identity and for the maintenance of the boundaries that divide it from the rest of the social world. Conflict, then, is essential to a society (Coser, 1956).

Proposition 4: Conflict and Hostile Influences

Social conflict cannot be accounted for by drives, impulses, and isolated instances of behavior; rather, it is explained by a pattern of interaction. Aggressive behavior is related to a group's structure of interactive relations. The structural variable linked to direct aggression is the degree of group cohesion. Coser (1956) defined *direct aggression* as "aggression expressed toward members of the group" (p. 57). In unorganized groups, there are many instances of aggression. Therefore, high group cohesion leads to high amounts of aggression (Coser, 1956).

Proposition 5: Hostility in Close Social Relationships

Love and hate are intricately linked. "One frequently hates the person one loves; hence it is often invalid to separate the two elements in concrete reality" (Coser, 1956:60). (Note: There is a popular song lyric that expresses this idea: "It's a thin line between love and hate.") This idea is most accurately applied to close, intimate relationships rather than all social relationships. The closer the relationship, the greater the investment, which leads to a likelihood of suppressed, rather than expressed, hostile feelings. This suppression is due to a fear of putting the relationship in danger. As hostility continues to be suppressed, these emotions accumulate and intensify. This intensity creates feelings of hatred, which may eventually be expressed in direct aggression. Therefore, the love–hate phenomenon found in intimate relationships helps to support Coser's contention that the high instances of direct aggression are found in highly cohesive groups. Studies of domestic violence could benefit from Coser's analysis of conflict in loving, close relationships.

Proposition 7: Impact of Conflict on Group Structures

As previously noted, close relationships may exhibit tendencies toward the suppression of conflict. If conflict should occur despite suppression, it tends to be disruptive to the relationship because of the intensity expressed. This intensity is attributed to the total involvement of the personality and the accumulation of hostility. Therefore, it is accurate for the participants to fear conflict because of the effects it may have on the relationship (Coser, 1956).

Proposition 10: Conflict with Another Group That Defines Group Structure

When conflict occurs between groups, the members of each group become more cohesive. They depend on each other's loyalty and dedication in order for the group to come out of the conflict victorious. Groups in conflict expect their individual members to be entirely involved. For example, bickering family members unite when a threat from the outside challenges the very survival of the family. A group engaged in continued struggle with other groups tends to be intolerant of individual deviations within the group. A member of a threatened group may be allowed only limited departures from group unity. Those who choose to deviate must either volunteer or be forced to withdraw from the group. This proposition helped Coser form his future ideas on *greedy institutions* and their demand for total involvement. Coser and his wife described in *Dissent* how the People's Temple cult and the Jonestown tragedy were an example of a greedy institution that expected such a degree of commitment from the group that the members moved away from their homes and loved ones and eventually committed group suicide (Coser and Coser, 1979).

Concluding and Connecting the Functions of Social Conflict

Social conflict creates boundaries between different groups, which, in turn, create a strong unity between the individual members of a group. Not only does social conflict promote cohesion in individual groups, but it also promotes coalitions and associations with outside groups. Several groups may be threatened by one single other group, so they may unite to fight the single threatening group. Therefore, social conflict creates an increase in cohesion inside a group and among several groups which, if not in conflict, would not normally unite.

Violence

Violence and conflict are often linked, and therefore, violence itself can lead to social change. Coser believed that violence serves three specific social functions. The first is violence as achievement. Causing violence is an achievement for some people, and the more violence they cause, the more they achieve in their own minds. As Merton articulated in his anomie theory on social deviance, society does not provide equal opportunity for all members to achieve the success goal. Consequently, some people deviate from the normal expectations of behavior and commit acts of deviance, including violence, as a means of achieving success (Coser, 1967).

The second function of violence is as a danger signal. Violence often alerts society and its members to underlying problems that need to be corrected. It acts as a warning signal (or a social barometer) that some course of action must be taken, for clearly a number of people are frustrated by the social system if they feel it necessary to turn to violence to gain attention. One might think of "road rage" as the result of people who are frustrated with the social system. Once behind the wheel of a car, the frustrated driver may think of his or her car as a weapon and other drivers as representatives of "everything that is wrong" in their lives.

The third function of violence in society is as a catalyst. This catalyst function can start the process of "correction" in solving a social problem, or it can cause an increased level of violence. "Whether given forms of conflict will lead to changes in the social system or to breakdown and to formation of a new system will depend on the rigidity and resistance to change, or inversely on the elasticity of the control mechanisms of the system" (Coser, 1967:29). Violence arouses the public and informs it that something needs to be done about specific social issues. When the society unites to solve the problem, the catalyst has completed its job. However, violence can act as a catalyst to cause more problems and attract others to join in the violence. Coser (1967) believed that violence has both positive and negative functions in society and viewed it as a necessary aspect of society.

Social Theory and Methodology

Coser's contributions to social theory were not limited to his works and ideas centered on the conflict perspective. His *Masters of Sociological Thought* (1977) was once a classic textbook in graduate and undergraduate social theory courses. In this text, Coser provides a detailed description of a number of social theorists. The chapters are divided into five sections: the work, the theorist, the intellectual context, the social context, and a summary of each theorist. Coser provided a wealth of information and offered often brilliant insights into the work of each theorist. Unfortunately, students often found the book difficult to read. It lacks a full bibliographical listing, and the order of the contents within each chapter often makes the reading even more difficult. Regardless of these minor criticisms, Coser illustrated the importance of detailing the biography of each social thinker, for one's personal life most assuredly affects one's outlook on the social world. The influences on each theorist reveal the fact that each bit of current knowledge is a mere extension or reinterpretation of past thoughts and ideas. The need to describe the contributions of each theorist is self-evident.

Coser (1976) always emphasized the need for a balanced assessment of theoretical trends. He maintained that each theoretical perspective must be given time to flourish and grow:

> Just like young trees that have only begun to bear fruit, their ultimate worth will have to be judged by a generation that is able to evaluate the quality of their products. Some of them, no doubt, will turn out to have been barren, while others will have produced an abundant harvest (p. 158).

In support of the conflict perspective, Coser (1964) warned that "sociological theory tends too frequently to focus attention exclusively on the dominant norms and patterns of behavior and to disregard the tensions and dysfunctions that full adherence to those norms might entail" (p. 884). In addition, in pursuit of the sociology of knowledge and sound social theory, Coser (1988) recommended utilizing a number of methodological techniques:

> The traditional view in the philosophy of science has assumed that there existed a close link between the logic of scientific procedure and the substantive results of empirical inquiry. This view has now been sharply challenged by post-positivist scholars who have demonstrated that the relations between methodology and substantive findings are much looser than had previously been assumed (p. 85).

Furthermore, in his 1975 presidential address delivered at the annual meeting of the American Sociological Association, Coser stated, "I am perturbed about present developments in American sociology which seem to foster the growth of both narrow, routine activities, and of sect-like, esoteric ruminations" (p. 691).

Lewis Coser made a number of significant and lasting contributions to sociological thought. His work as a conflict theorist who attempted to incorporate some of the basic constructs of functionalism is a wonderful addition to social theory. Many of his ideas will remain relevant well into the third millennium. In all societies, conflict is inevitable. Conflict serves to bind members of a group together, and it determines the boundaries of power.

C. WRIGHT MILLS (1916–1962)

C. Wright Mills was born in Waco, Texas, on August 28, 1916, into a middle-class Catholic household. His father was an insurance broker and his mother was a homemaker. By 1939 he had earned both his bachelor's and master's degrees from the University of Texas. He left Texas, for the first time in his life, to work on his doctoral studies at the University of Wisconsin (he had won a research fellowship there). At Wisconsin, Mills studied under Hans Gerth, a German émigré. "Far from the usual student-professor relationship, they soon engaged in a series of collaborative works focusing on social psychology and introducing the work of the German sociologist Max Weber to an English-speaking audience" (Kivisto, 1998:36). While working on his doctorate, Mills taught for a while at the University of Maryland. The proximity to Washington, DC, provided Mills his first taste for political life and an exposure to true power.

After earning his Ph.D., Mills moved to New York City and accepted a position at Columbia University in 1945. Mills wrote for many left-wing journals, including the *New Leader*, the *New Republic*, the *Partisan Review*, and the union journal *Labor and Nation* (Scimecca, 1977). He remained at Columbia until his untimely death in 1962 from his fourth heart attack. He was just forty-five when he died, but as we shall see, he contributed a great deal to sociological theory. Among the books that he authored are *The New Men of Power* (1948), *White Collar* (1951), *The Power Elite* (1956), *The Causes of World War Three* (1958a), *The Sociological Imagination* (1959), and *The Marxists* (1962). Mills coauthored other books and published numerous journal articles as well.

The Social Context

C. Wright Mills was a rather controversial person who enjoyed getting under the skin of people close to him as well as those not so close to him. He argued with professors while he was a graduate student and with his colleagues at Columbia. Horowitz (1983) described how Mills published a vaguely disguised critique of the ex-chair at Wisconsin and referred to the senior theorist at Wisconsin, Howard Becker, as a "real fool." Mills even turned on his friend and coauthor Hans Gerth. Gerth retaliated by calling Mills a "cowboy"—as in "a la ride and shoot" (Horowitz, 1983:72). (Note: The term *cowboy* was certainly not meant as a compliment.) According to Kivisto (1998),

> Mills had an uncanny ability to irritate people who had befriended him. His life comprised a series of fallings-out with such people, beginning with Gerth and continuing through to include Bell, Macdonald and other luminaries in the New York intellectual scene, and his sociology colleagues at Columbia (p. 37).

Although Mills had established a well-respected academic name for himself upon his arrival at Columbia, his reputation as a rebel and cowboy, combined with the conservative climate of the times, would complicate his professional and personal lives. As Garner (2000) explained,

> Of Texan origin, which contributed to his image as a maverick and radical from the heartland, he was a professor of sociology at Columbia University during the most intense period of the Cold War. The 1950s was a period of political timidity and enforced conformity when many intellectuals avoided expressing ideas and opinions for which they could have been labeled as "reds" (Communist sympathizers) or subversives. Mills courageously opposed this political timidity in his writing and teaching (p. 322).

Despite his growing marginality, Mills did not soften his positions. If anything, he became more vitriolic with the passage of time (Kivisto, 1998).

Mills was critical both of the trends of contemporary sociology and of society. He more than challenged the status quo. He questioned "grand theorizing" and the unbreakable commitment to positivism (at a time when few American sociologists had). He challenged Talcott Parsons, the dominant theorist of his day, and Paul Lazarsfeld, the dominant methodologist and Mills' colleague at Columbia. His disdain toward empirical research was the result of his belief that fragmented data collected from questionnaire responses were no substitute for a broad historical and political understanding of society (Garner, 2000). A commitment to the historical method was just one of Marx's influences on Mills. The criticism that Mills directed toward American society earned him a visit to the Soviet Union, where he was honored as a major critic of American society. However, true to his confrontational nature, Mills "took the occasion to attack the censorship in the Soviet Union with a toast to an early Soviet leader who had been purged and murdered by the Stalinists: 'To the day when the complete works of Leon Trotsky are published in the Soviet Union'" (Ritzer, 2010:88).

Conflict Theory

Like other conflict theorists, Mills was deeply influenced by the ideas of Karl Marx and Marxist thought. Mills helped to introduce American sociologists to Marxism through his edited anthology, *The Marxists* (1962). Mills did not describe himself as a Marxist, however, as he found clear differences between his ideas and those of Marx.

> Mills did not see all inequality as emerging from the mode of production; like Weber, he identified several distinct dimensions of inequality and treated power as a variable that can be independent from economic class. The concept of power elite, rather than ruling class,

signals this difference between Mills and Marxists. He did not insist on the bourgeoisie and the proletariat as the antagonistic classes of a polarized structure, nor did he share Marxist ideas about the unfolding of a historical process. In many ways, his version of conflict theory was much closer to Weber than to Marx, and his concerns about the direction of society overlapped and updated Weber's critique of bureaucracy and formal rationality. Mills also differed from many Marxists in his commitment to North American traditions of social criticism and radical democracy. His solution to the economic inequalities and power differences in corporate America was not a vanguard party and a proletarian revolution, but a reopening of political debate, public discussion, and citizen participation in politics (Garner, 2000:323).

Political power and class differences were the focus of Mills' publications. *The New Men of Power* (1948) is a study of the American labor movement. In this book, Mills wrote that the working class is not a revolutionary class capable of overthrowing capitalism. He did not believe that the rank-and-file workers were a militant force and that they were more concerned with basic daily issues than with seeking loftier goals. Furthermore, Mills concluded that labor leaders did not work in the best interests of their workers and were instead compromised by their own ambitions and government regulations. He believed that most union leaders resembled the character of their organizations and that few union leaders possessed any real power. Mills (1948) wrote,

> It is the task of the labor leaders to allow and to initiate a union of the power and the intellect. They are the only ones who can do it; that is why they are now the strategic elite in American society. Never has so much depended upon men who are so ill-prepared and so little inclined to assume the responsibility (p. 291).

Because of this lack of leadership and the unpreparedness of the working class, Mills recognized what Marx failed to, that the proletariat could never become a revolutionary force.

Power

Power is the critical element of analysis for all conflict theorists. This is especially true of C. Wright Mills.

> His work remained centered on power—the nature of power, the distribution of power, the uses and abuses of power, the person of power, the power of organizations, the myths of power, the evolution of power, the irrationality of power, and the means of observing and comprehending power in the vastness of modern society (Cuzzort and King, 1995:178–179).

Mills wrote in "The Promise" (1959) that people feel that their lives are a series of traps:

> They sense that within their everyday worlds, they cannot overcome their troubles, and in this feeling, they are often quite correct: What ordinary men are directly aware of and what they try to do are bounded by the private orbits in which they live; their visions and their powers are limited to the close-up scenes of job, family, neighborhood; in other milieu, they move vicariously and remain spectators. And the more aware they become, however

vaguely, of ambitions and of threats which transcend their immediate locales, the more trapped they seem to feel (Mills, 2002:1–2).

In "The Structure of Power in American Society" (1958b), Mills wrote that

power has to do with whatever decisions men make about the arrangements under which they live, and about the events which make up the history of their times. Events that are beyond human decision do happen; social arrangements do change without the benefit of explicit decision. But in so far as such decisions are made, the problem of who is involved in making them is the basic problem of power (p. 29).

Mills (1958) questioned whether American society was truly a society where citizens were ruled by consent and instead suggested that those in power managed to manipulate the consent.

Mills (1958b) described three types of power:

1. **Authority:** power that is justified by the beliefs of the voluntarily obedient;
2. **Manipulation:** power that is wielded unbeknownst to the powerless;
3. **Coercion:** the "final" form of power, where the powerless are forced to obey the powerful.

Mills acknowledged that in the modern era, power is more likely to be authoritarian. And yet, the reality remains that most people will always be relatively powerless and often unaware of those who truly wield power over them. Marx wrote in *The 18th Brumaire of Louis Bonaparte* (1852) that all men are free to make their own history, but they do not make it just as they please; but Mills (1958b) said that *some* men are much freer than others. Mills argued that the power elites of a society are freer to create their own paths in life because they have power and access to decision-making.

Major decisions regarding the course of history are made by political, military, and economic institutions, which, according to Mills, make up the power elite. Mills (1956) stated that this "triangle of power" is a structural fact and the key to understanding American society.

The Power Elite

Mills was convinced that the American military, industry, and politics were integrated. This connection concerned Mills because "it can lead to a disengagement of leadership from the problems of the people that leadership is supposed to represent" (Cuzzort and King, 1995:179). In *The Power Elite* (1956), Mills describes the power elite as those persons who hold positions to make decisions that have major consequences over others. The power elites are people who are at the top of major corporations and influential government persons. The power elites also control the military. Thus, there exists a triangle of power that includes business, government, and military. Mills described the triangle of power as the "tripartite elite" and warned that this triangle of power was an increasing threat to American democracy.

Mills (1958b) explained the unity of the power elite in psychological and economic terms. The members of the power elite generally share a similar origin, education, and style of life, and because of their similar social type, they easily intermingle. Additionally, since they are the "elites" of society, they share economic goals. In this regard, the power elite have a similar worldview and share a sense of class consciousness. Despite the fact that the power elite constitute a close-knit category of people, they are not part of a conspiracy that secretly manipulates events to reach some agreed upon selfish interest end goal. For the most part, the power elite peacefully operate in open view; they do not rely on terror or a secret police known for midnight arrests to assure its goals are met. Operating free from repressive techniques, the power elite maintain their advantageous positions in society through legitimate means afforded to those with great wealth and power-making decision positions within the government (politics), military, and industrial/ private sectors.

The social context of the mid-1950s was clearly an influence on Mills' writings regarding the power elite. American military technology was superior, the economy was strong but becoming increasingly dependent on foreign markets, and a repressive political climate existed because of the Cold War; all contributed to Mills' theory of the power elite.

Mills acknowledged that the power elites were not solitary rulers. They were assisted by the advisers and consultants, the spokespeople and opinion makers, and the captains of industry. Immediately below the elite were the professional politicians, as well as those of the new and old upper classes. Thus, the power elites are those who possess scarce resources. As Mills (1956) explained,

> The higher circles in and around these command posts are often thought of in terms of what their members possess: they have a greater share than other people of the things and experiences that are most highly valued. From this point of view, the elite are simply those who have the most of what there is to have, which is generally held to include money, power, and prestige—as well as all the ways of life to which these lead (p. 9).

However, simply possessing more scarce resources than others does not automatically bring wealthy people power; such people must be in a position to command situations. Mills (1956) stated,

> By powerful we mean, of course, those who are able to realize their will, even if others resist it. No one, accordingly, can be truly powerful unless he has access to the command of major institutions, for it is over these institutional means of power that the truly powerful are, in the first instance, powerful. Higher politicians and key officials of government command such institutional power; so do admirals and generals, and so do the major owners and executives of the larger corporations (p. 9).

From a Marxist perspective, Mills felt that the American people were subjected to "the will of the bourgeoisie." It is always in the best interests of the powerful to maintain the status quo. Therefore, they promote a conservative society, where challenges to authority are discouraged. History has shown that when extreme conservatism is met with a dramatically changing society, conflict is inevitable. "The challenges to the elite that burst onto the cultural and political landscape in the 1960s—the civil rights movements, the antiwar movement, and the counterculture—called into question Mills's pessimistic assessments" (Kivisto, 1998:40). Mills did not live to see these radical forces of social change, as he died in 1962.

Following in the tradition of Mills is G. William Domhoff, who has written numerous books on the power elite. Domhoff's first book, *Who Rules America?* (1967; 5th edition published in 2006), created controversy and grabbed the attention of the academic world because of his insistence that the United States has a structure favoring the upper classes because of the power of the social elites of society. The elites influence politics because of their control over large corporations, income, and wealth. Where Mills viewed American society run by the "tripartite elite," Domhoff, in his ruling class theory, viewed the power elite as those who carried out the directives of the upper class. For Domhoff (2006), the power elites were the owners and top-level managers in large income-producing properties (corporations, banks, and agribusiness) that come together as a corporate community and dominate the federal government in Washington, DC, and their real estate, construction, and land development companies that form growth coalitions and dominate most local governments. The theme of the power elites controlling American society coupled with his belief that the masses are reluctant or ignorant to acknowledge the existence of the power elite runs through all of Domhoff's subsequent book publications. Within this context, Domhoff is more of a conspiracy theorist than Mills. Like Mills, Domhoff beliefs that a substrata of elites work below the power elites to assist them in their attempt to maintain power positions and economic riches.

The Sociological Imagination

Perhaps the single concept that Mills is most known for is the *sociological imagination*. (The *sociological imagination* is taught in all introductory sociology courses.) The sociologist can gain insights into human behavior by utilizing the sociological imagination. The sociological imagination reveals how our private lives are influenced by the social environment and the existing social forces. The sociological imagination emphasizes the importance of the historical social context in which an individual is found. Combining personal biography with current behavior allows the sociologist to better understand the individual.

To highlight the importance of this point, Mills made distinctions between "the personal troubles of milieu" and "the public issues of social structure." According to Mills (1959), "This distinction is an essential tool of the sociological imagination and a feature of all classic work in social science" (p. 8). Mills (1959) described *troubles* and *issues* as follows:

1. *Troubles* occur within the character of the individual and within the range of her or his immediate relations with others. They have to do with the self and with those limited areas of social life of which the person is directly and personally aware.
2. *Issues* transcend these local environments of the individual and the range of her or his inner life. They have to do with the organization of many milieux into the institutions of a historical society as a whole and form the larger structure of social and historical life.

With this reasoning, the sociologist acknowledges that social forces, often out of the control of the individual, affect the individual's life for both the good and the bad. For example, if a company goes bankrupt and lays off all its workers, the individual employees need not view themselves negatively, because they could not control the *issues,* or causes, of their dismissal. However, if an individual loses her job when no one else does, she has personal *troubles*.

RALF DAHRENDORF (1929–2009)

Ralf Dahrendorf was born in Hamburg, Germany, in 1929. This time was a turbulent period in Germany. His father was a Social Democratic politician, a member of the Hamburg Diet at the time of Ralf's birth, and then later a member of the German Parliament (the Reichstag). The Social Democrats had political differences with both the Nazis and the Communists. The senior Dahrendorf would lose his job when the Nazis came into power in 1933. Unemployed, he moved his family to Berlin. Ralf's father was arrested twice. The second time he was sentenced to seven years in prison—and was released by the Russians at the end of the war.

Ralf Dahrendorf was also involved in opposition to the Nazi regime. In late November 1944, Dahrendorf was arrested by the Gestapo for letters that he and his friend had written to each other. Dahrendorf was sent to a concentration camp east of the Oder River, in what is now Poland. Dahrendorf escaped on January 29, 1945, while the German guards battled with the Russian army. Throughout his life, Dahrendorf actively participated in political groups that fight injustice.

In 1952, Dahrendorf earned his first doctorate in philosophy, with classics as the subsidiary subject, from the University of Hamburg. He then moved to London and to the London School of Economics, where he later earned his doctorate in sociology. Dahrendorf was a widely respected social scientist in both Europe and North America. He held academic positions in Germany, Great Britain, and the United States, including the position of director of the London School of Economics from 1974 to 1984. After a brief period in Germany, Dahrendorf returned to Britain in 1987 and served as Warden of St. Anthony's College, Oxford, a position he held until his retirement in 1997. Despite his academic commitments, Dahrendorf was very active in public life in Britain, including as a member of the British House of Lords (the upper house of Parliament). He was awarded a knighthood in 1982 and was made a life peer in 1993. Dahrendorf continued to publish in the area of conflict theory with a functionalist influence until his death in 2009.

Conflict Theory

At the beginning of this chapter, it was explained that functional theorists believe that society is held together informally by norms, values, and a general consensus on issues of morality. Additionally, functionalists believe that society is in a state of moving equilibrium—a slow, evolutionary growth that leads to orderly social change. Conflict theorists believe that social order is maintained through coercion by those at the top or, as Mills put it, the power elites. Consequently, tension is a constant in society, and radical social change is likely at any point, in any given society.

> For Dahrendorf, the social world is composed of "imperatively coordinated associations" …which represent, in terms of criteria not specified, a distinguishable organization of roles. This organization is characterized by power relationships with some clusters of roles having power over others (Turner, 1973:236).

Dahrendorf (1959) believed that sociological theories should be divided into two parts: those that concentrate on issues of consensus and those that concentrate on issues of conflict. Dahrendorf believed that conflict and consensus are both evident in any society. In fact, there cannot be conflict unless some degree of consensus has already been established. In other words, one cannot be in conflict with another until there is a lack of consensus on a matter. When a consensus has been reached, conflict disappears, temporarily. As to whether or not conflict and consensus theories can be linked, Dahrendorf (1959) believed that there was no possibility of this occurring; but he did keep an open mind that such a link could possibly exist in the future.

Dahrendorf articulates his conflict theory in *Class and Class Conflict in Industrial Society* (1959). In this publication, Dahrendorf explains that the starting point for his conflict theory resides with the notion of coercion; and this is why Dahrendorf's conflict theory is referred to as the "coercion theory of society." Dahrendorf (1959) outlined four basic tenets of his coercion theory:

1. At every point in time, all societies are subject to change, and the processes of change are ever-present.

2. Social conflict is inevitable in every society.
3. Every society sows the seeds of its own inevitable change and possible disintegration.
4. In every society, some people are coerced by others.

Dahrendorf disagreed with Marx that economic forces are the sole determinant of conflict in society. Instead, when we examine Dahrendorf's conflict theory of coercion, it is revealed that associations are structured by domination and subjection; that associations compete with one another; that each group has latent interests, which can become manifest; and that these conditions of associations and organizations can give rise to violence. The unequal distribution of political power is also a major contributor to conflict. According to Dahrendorf, (1959), the structural organization of society and groups is designed so that "some positions are entrusted with a right to exercise control over other positions in order to ensure effective coercion; it means, in other words, that there is a differential distribution of power and authority" (p. 165). Thus, coercion and conflict are impacted by power and authority.

Power and Authority

In the tradition of all conflict theorists, Dahrendorf believed that power and authority are scarce resources, and that those who have them hope to maintain the status quo, while those who lack power and authority hope to attain some portion of them. Dahrendorf (1959) assumed that the differential distribution of power and authority becomes the basis of conflict. "Identification of variously equipped authority roles is the first task of conflict analysis; conceptually and empirically all further steps of analysis follow from the investigation of distributions of power and authority" (Dahrendorf, 1959:165–166). Dahrendorf believed that power implies the coercion of some by others but recognized that in organizations and associations, the power held by certain persons is legitimate authority (Turner, 1973). In making a distinction from Marx, however, Dahrendorf suggested that authority is not bound by property rights and therefore believed that "class conflict is best seen as arising out of a dispute over the distribution of authority in a given authority structure" (Lopreato, 1967:281).

Dahrendorf (1959) used the same definitions of power and authority as Weber (discussed earlier in this chapter). Dahrendorf stated that the important difference between power and authority is that power is essentially tied to the personality of individuals, whereas authority is always associated with social positions or roles. Dahrendorf was most interested in the study of authority and came to the following conclusions:

1. The superordination–subordination relationship implies that one has authority over the other.
2. Those in superordinate positions are expected to assure that subordinates behave appropriately in social situations; in other words, they are supposed to "know their place" within social settings.
3. Expectations of individuals' behaviors are connected to their position in the superordinate–subordinate relationship.
4. The authority that one enjoys in one setting does not transcend to persons who are not a part of the superordinate–subordinate relationship.
5. When one has authority over another, they can impose sanctions to assure conforming behavior.

In his studies of authority, Dahrendorf also utilized the terms *domination* and *subjection* synonymously.

Two other issues related to authority are also noteworthy. Since authority lies in the position that one holds, it does not extend to other social arenas, and persons who lose their authority also lose their position. For example, nearly everyone has a "boss" who holds legitimate authority. But one person's boss does not have authority over someone outside that setting. Thus, someone can occupy a position of authority in one setting and a subordinate position in another. Additionally, a boss who is fired, resigns, or retires no longer has authority over his or her subordinates. With these ideas in mind, Dahrendorf argued that society is composed of *imperatively coordinated associations* (Max Weber used the term *Herrschaftsverband*). Since imperative coordination, or authority, is a type of social relation present in every conceivable social organization, it is sufficient to describe such organizations simply as associations. These associations are coordinated as organized aggregates of roles by domination and subjection because, in all associations, authority exists.

> Authority relations exist wherever there are people whose actions are subject to legitimate and sanctioned prescriptions that originate outside them but within social structure. This formulation, by leaving open who exercises what kind of authority leaves little doubt as to the omnipresence of some kind of authority somehow exercised. For it is evident that there are many forms and types of authority in historical societies (Dahrendorf, 1959:168).

More important, Dahrendorf argued that domination and subjection are a common feature of all possible types of authority.

Class Theory

Dahrendorf explained that the concept of *class* has invariably displayed a peculiar explosiveness:

> If the sociologist uses the concept of class he not only must carefully explain in which of its many meanings he wants it to be understood, but also must expect objections that are dictated less by scientific insight than by political prejudice. . . . Evaluative shifts of meaning have accompanied the concept of class throughout its history (Dahrendorf, 1959:3).

The Romans introduced the word *classis* to divide the population into tax groups, but with this economic distinction came an evaluative one as well. This is true of the American term *income bracket*, which, along with its statistical category, touches on the vulnerable point of social inequality.

Using the historical method in his analysis of class theory, Dahrendorf highlighted the significance of industrialization (as have all historically conscious sociologists). "With the industrial revolution, the history of the concept of class as a tool of social analysis began" (Dahrendorf, 1959:4). Dahrendorf (1959) examined Marx's class theory and pointed out that "Marx regarded the theory of class as so important that he postponed its systematic exposition time and again in favor of refinements by empirical analysis" (p. 8). Marx came to the conclusion that society is a two-class system, the proletariat falling far short of reaching their full human potential because of their limited access to society's scarce resources. His solution to this problem was the promotion of a classless society (under communism), where there is no private property and the people share equally in the resources.

As any student of social theory and Marxist thought is aware, it is commonplace today to point out the many flaws in Marx's general class theory because of his failure to predict the significant changes that occurred in the capitalist system (e.g., the rise of the middle class, profit sharing, and stock options). Dahrendorf commented, however, that to ignore Marx completely would be "naive and irresponsible." Marx believed that the theory of class involved a systematic analysis of the causes of the endogenous structural change in societies. At the root of all social change is social conflict. For Dahrendorf (1959), class theory can be defined as "the systematic explanation of that particular form of structure-changing conflict which is carried on by aggregates or groups growing out of the authority structure of social organizations" (p.152).

Clearly, Dahrendorf believed that the sociologist can uncover key elements of society, through empirical methods, to the point where a class theory can be applied. He was quick to note that generalizing class theory from one society to another is problematic in that each society is unique.

According to Dahrendorf (1959:153–154), to create a general theory of class, two analytically separable elements must be addressed: the *theory of class formation* and the *theory of class action*, or class conflict.

1. **The theory of class formation:** Concerned with the question of analyzing the "genesis" of social classes. The theory must establish relations which connect the specific "real phenomenon" class by way of the "theoretical phenomenon" class with patterns of social structure, and in this sense derive social classes from social structure.
2. **The theory of class action:** Based on the theory of class formation. Its subject matter consists of the general analytical elements of the interrelations between classes conceived of as structural phenomena. It is concerned in particular with patterns of class conflict and the regulation of class conflict.

Dahrendorf wrote in far greater detail about both the theory of class formation and the theory of class action in *Class and Class Conflict in Industrial Society* (1959).

As for the specific classes found in society, it is not surprising that Dahrendorf found the continual existence of two opposed classes: the "elites" and the "ruling classes" versus the "masses" and "suppressed classes." These two groups are forever in conflict, as their collective goals are in direct opposition. Social classes, then, can be understood as conflict groups arising out of the authority structure of imperatively coordinated associations that are in conflict. "In the affluent society, it remains a stubborn and remarkable fact that men are unequally placed" (Dahrendorf, 1968:151). Social stratification is a very real element of everyday life, and every person is aware of her or his "place" within the social structure.

RANDALL COLLINS (1941–)

Randall Collins was born in Knoxville, Tennessee, on July 29, 1941. His father was a professor of German literature at Maryville College, and during World War II he joined Army Intelligence, later becoming a career diplomat. Because of his father's military career, Collins traveled extensively with his parents to such places as Germany, Uruguay, Russia, and Spain. Collins received his bachelor's degree from Harvard University in 1963, his master's degree from Stanford in 1964, and his Ph.D. from the University of California at Berkeley in 1969. He has taught at several universities, including Chicago, Harvard, Virginia, Wisconsin, the University of California at Los Angeles, at San Diego, and at Riverside, and the University of Pennsylvania.

Collins has published a large number of works, including having authored a dozen books and well over one hundred articles on all aspects of sociological theory. His early work centered

Randall Collins, one of the most significant sociologists and social thinkers of the contemporary era.   (Randall Collins)

on the conflict perspective and is highlighted by the publication of *Conflict Sociology* (1974). The most recent edition of *Conflict Sociology* was published in 2009 (Paradigm Publishing). Other publications include *The Credential Society* (1979), *Weberian Sociological Theory* (1986), and *Macro-History: Essays in Sociology of the Long Run* (1999). Recently, Collins has sought to combine micro-sociological aspects within the conflict perspective. His works have been translated into Arabic, Chinese, Dutch, German, Japanese, Korean, Romanian, Russian, Spanish, and Swedish.

Conflict Theory

In his conflict theory, it is clear that Collins attempts to bridge the micro–macro division that exists within the sociological perspective. From the macro perspective, Collins incorporated the ideas of Marx and Weber and their analysis of the effect of the economic and political institutions on individuals' behaviors. Collins (1975b) described Marx as "the great originator of modern conflict theory" (p. 428). He does not agree with all Marxian thought, but he does agree with Marx's analysis of the material world and the capitalist system (e.g., that the capitalist system, by its very structure, separated people into classes, relative to the control of the means of production). Among all the theorists that Collins admired the most, Max Weber ranks number one. Collins adopted Weber's pluralistic model using an analytic framework, comparative historical approach, and nonutopian outlook of the future (Wallace and Wolf, 1999).

His focus on individuals and their inner struggles reveals a micro orientation. Collins (1975b) believed that conflict theory should incorporate the social construction of subjective realities and the dramaturgical qualities of historically conditioned material interests, and he provided a typology of the resources people bring with them to social interaction:

1. Material and technical resources, which include not only property, tools, and such skills as literacy, but also—very importantly—weapons.
2. Physical strength and attractiveness and the role they play in personal relationships.
3. The number of contacts people have will directly influence the potential for negotiating material goods and status.
4. The possession of personal resources and qualities deemed desirable by others, which will lead to opportunities for emotional bonding among people because of shared interests.

Collins' incorporation of micro principles has been consistent throughout the years as he develops his conflict theory. Collins emphasizes the idea that individuals maximize their subjective status according to the resources available to them and their rivals. That is, one's subject experience of reality is the nexus of social motivation. Furthermore, everyone constructs one's own world with oneself in it; but this reality construction is done primarily by communication, real or imaginary, with other people, and hence people hold the keys to each other's identities (Collins, 2009).

> Add to this an emphasis from conflict theories: that each individual is basically pursuing his or her own interests and that there are many situations, notably ones where power is involved, in which these interests are inherently antagonistic subjective worlds; that others pull many of the strings that control one's subjective experience; and that there are frequent conflicts over control (Collins, 2009:22).

Life, then, is a struggle for status wherein each of us is subjected to the power of others around them.

Conflict theory generally emphasizes the role of power that one group, or person, holds over another group, or person. Kemper and Collins (1990) contended

> that power and status are fundamental relational dimensions at the micro level of social interaction and perhaps at the macro level as well. Whatever else may be going on in social life, and however else one may wish to conceptualize it, human actors are deeply involved in relational issues of control and dominance (power) and of acceptance and positive association (status), and social theorists of all persuasions have necessarily dealt with these in one form or another (p. 32).

Inherent in any social system, group structure, or interpersonal relationship is an imbalance of power. Collins (1975a) assumed that there are certain "goods"—namely, wealth, power, and prestige—that people in all societies will pursue. Furthermore, all people dislike being ordered around and will therefore do what they can to avoid the subordinate role. Thus, conflict is inevitable, for everyone is in pursuit of scarce resources and the roles related to these desired resources.

His commitment to the micro–macro bridge is admirable, and as Collins (1981) stated, "A micro-translation strategy reveals the empirical realities of social structures as patterns of repetitive micro-interactions" (p. 985).

Stratification and Social Change

From a traditional conflict perspective, the basic outlines of stratification theory were set forth by Marx and Engels:

> Revolutions were class conflicts: a privileged class faced increasing pressure from a discontented rising class. The revolutionary transfer of power eventually broke through the block, setting off a new period of social change. This process was synchronized with a succession of ideological hegemonies. The ruling ideas were those of the ruling elite; as class challengers emerged, their change in consciousness acted as a barometer as well as a mobilizer for the coming revolution (Collins, 1993:117).

However, as evidenced by his commitment to micro variables, it is clear that Collins prefers Weber's notion of social stratification—that it includes aspects of political power and social prestige—to Marx's economic deterministic perspective.

In his theory of stratification, Collins (1975b) indicated that the crucial dividing lines in the social structure are dominance relations and the number of resources that one possesses. In keeping with his general program of linking structural and interactional levels of analysis, Collins attempted to cast all structural variables in terms of actual differences in the experience of face-to-face encounters. For example, in the world of employment, power relations and situations of giving and taking orders seem to be the most important variables in shaping behaviors. Collins concluded that the basic premise of the conflict perspective is that all pursue their own best line of advantage according to the resources available to them, and that social structures—whether formal organizations or informal acquaintances—are empirically nothing more than continuous negotiating power situations in any encounter.

In his 2009 publication of *Conflict Sociology*, Collins describes how stratification is generally described as "a ladder of success" with "a hierarchy of geological layers" or as a "pyramid." This notion reflects the Marxist economic view of stratification. Collins argues that society does not actually look like a pyramid or a series of ladders found at work:

> What it looks like, as all persons can verify by opening their eyes as they go about their daily business, is nothing more than people in houses, buildings, automobiles, streets—some of whom give orders, get deference, hold material property, talk about particular subjects and so on. No one has ever seen anything human that looks like a ladder or a pyramid, except perhaps in a high school variety show. What these images derive from, most likely, are the convenient ways we have for graphing statistics of occupation or wealth (15).

Collins examined stratification by education as part of his interest in the role of educational qualification (credentials) and their use as a resource in the struggle for power, wealth, and prestige (Wallace and Wolf, 1999). The educational elite use credentials to screen undesired persons from employment. (Note: It is hard to argue against the necessity of "qualified" people in most professional jobs, especially in the medical, scientific, and educational fields. What might be a better example is the law profession, which keeps raising the required LSAT score needed for admission to law school. The score is raised because too many people are already in the law profession.) Thus, the educational system serves as a "gatekeeper," which allows those who have attained a high level of education to climb in the ranks of the social hierarchy. Collins (1979) explained the reemergence of such schools as commercial trade schools and business institutes as a response to this credential requirement. (Note: It is important that professionals such as plumbers, electricians, and exterminators must also be "certified" and have licenses to perform their trades.) Collins (1979) went so far as to suggest that there is a credentials crisis, and he sought to abolish compulsory school requirements.

Beyond the field of education, Collins applied his theoretical analysis of stratification and social change to economics. He has written articles on such topics as the market system and the effects of capitalism on social structures. Collins (1997:843) noted how, historically, capitalism has gone through three key phases:

1. A small leading sector within agrarian-coercive societies set the innovative dynamic in motion.
2. The spread of capitalist market structures made agricultural production dynamic.
3. The Industrial Revolution of production by machines harnessed to inanimate energy sources set off the expansion of nonagricultural production.

Like Weber, Collins examined the role of religion as an explanation of why some world regions evolved with industrialization and others did not. In his article "Market Dynamics as the Engine of Historical Change" (1990), Collins concluded that "if past history is any precedent, the capitalism that is dominant today has plenty of upheavals in store in its future" (p. 134). Clearly, Collins has examined multiple causes of stratification including, and expanding beyond, economics.

Violence

Individual theorists differ in their specific approaches to conflict theory, but they share a commitment to understanding the role of power and its impact on people and society and they acknowledge that violence is a possible outcome of conflict. Collins examines violence from both the macro and micro perspectives. From the macro perspective, Collins examined the "state" and used Weber's definition of the state as the monopolization of legitimate force (Collins, 1999). When describing the sociopolitical state in relation to violence, Collins (2009) claims, "The state consists of those people who have the guns or the other weapons and are prepared to use them; in the version of political organization found in the modern world, they claim monopoly" (p. 170). A state may use violence in order to exercise power, gain or defend resources, or as a defense from attacking states.

Violence, of course, occurs at the micro level too. In fact, it is a very common occurrence. And just as violence by the state may serve some pragmatic purpose, so to does violence serve as a means to an end for individuals. Violence may be directed toward the other as an act of aggression, or it may be a defense mechanism. Despite his commitment to the macro–micro bridge in conflict theory, Collins does not provide an adequate description of violence at the micro level. Instead, he makes a distinction between violence that is organized as criminal or political (the state). Collins (2009) states, "Violence is never very effective except as exercised by a social coalition. Except in a very small group, one individual cannot coerce many others, even if he is bigger and holds most of the weapons. Organization is the crucial factor" (p. 183).

Interaction Ritual Chain Theory

Collins does not think very highly of functionalism, but he believes that Durkheim explained a great deal about the role of emotional bonds and how loyalties are created and maintained (Wallace and Wolf, 1999). Collins (2000) explained that in Durkheimian theory, the collective performance of rituals generates feelings of solidarity and that the recognition and use of symbols reinforce membership in the group. Collins' interaction ritual chain theory was undoubtedly influenced by Durkheim.

One of Collins' most interesting and significant contributions to sociological theory is his interaction ritual chain theory. Through the interaction ritual, Collins explained why people behave differently among different groups of people. He believes that all social encounters can be ranked by their degree of ritual intensity. Those who have a highly vested interest in the group will carry out ritualistic behavior more intensely than those who are less committed to the group (or couple). Those who have an emotional attachment to the group, share in its social identity, and participate in the group activities will experience emotional energy (Collins, 2000). Individuals carry symbols of this commitment to indicate membership and to recharge their emotional energy. There are numerous examples of this commitment to membership: Married couples wear wedding rings to show their commitment to one another; sports fans wear clothing with symbols of their favorite team; religious persons wear some token of their faith; and gang members wear tattoos to show their allegiance to the gang. In all cases, all members of the group feel accepted and welcomed because of their attachment to the group and the ritualistic behavior. As Delaney's (2001) research indicated, the same ritualistic behavior of bonding and emotional commitment is shared by members of sports booster groups. Cheering for the team and wearing team associated clothing (hats, T-shirts, and so on) contribute to the interaction ritual.

Collins expanded on his ritual theory with ideas on intellectual networks. These networks start with intellectuals, who produce decontextualized ideas and regard them with the same kind of seriousness and respect that Durkheim said believers give to the sacred items of religion (Collins, 2000). Intellectuals make their careers by entering the network of previous participants and building new arguments on past feelings. The new intellectuals try to imitate not the ideas of prior theorists, but the emotional energy (Collins, 2000). The new intellectuals hope to attract attention with their new work, but these opportunities are limited because only a limited number of positions attract proper scholarly recognition.

On certain college campuses, scholarly academic pursuits are not rewarded (compared to sports accomplishments, for example), and in some cases, those in power positions are threatened by the new intellectuals and use the resources at their disposal to hinder the careers of the aspiring intellectuals. Many of those in academia must decide whether to forge ahead in an attempt to make a lasting contribution to the field or be content with going "through the motions" so as not to challenge the existing administrative power structure.

Geopolitics

Another important concept articulated by Collins is *geopolitics*. Geopolitics represents a momentous contribution not only to sociology, but to international politics as well. Collins' work on geopolitics paid particular attention to the importance of military technology and organization (Collins was perhaps influenced by his childhood military family lifestyle). It is noteworthy that in 1980, through his geopolitical analysis, Collins predicted the collapse of the Soviet Union (eleven years before it occurred).

Other theorists have certainly presented a world-systems view of international politics and economics, but Collins' presentation of geopolitics is original enough to stand out. Collins argued that geopolitics began at the turn of the twentieth century. Powerful nations began to realize that the possession of strategic heartlands on the globe gave the state dominance over others. Since Collins did not originate the geopolitics concept, his contribution comes in the form of his geopolitical theory. Collins' (1999, 2009) geopolitical theory consists of five conditions, or principles, for the expansion and contraction of the territorial power of states. The five principles of geopolitical theory are as follows:

1. Size and resource advantage favor territorial expansion. The bigger, more populous, and more resource-rich states expand militarily at the expense of smaller, less populous, and resource-poor states.
2. Geopositional or "marchland" advantages favor territorial expansion. Those states with enemies on fewer fronts expand at the expense of states with enemies on more borders.
3. A high level of internal conflict hinders efforts to expand, whereas internal harmony, or control, allows a concentration of military efforts externally.
4. Cumulative processes bring periodic long-term simplification, with massive arms races and showdown wars between a few contenders. Bigger states swallow up smaller ones or force them into alliances. Before long there exist just a couple of "superpower" states.

5. Overextension brings resource strain and state disintegration. The costs of expansion have become overwhelming, to the point where the internal state risks dissolution.

It was the review of these five principles that first led Collins to conclude that the Soviet Union had passed its peak of power and would decline.

CRITICISMS OF CONFLICT THEORY

There are three primary criticisms of conflict theory. First, because of its focus on power differentials that are reinforced by coercion, conflict theory tends to ignore the many areas in which most people arrive at an uncoerced consensus about important values of life. The powerful and the powerless alike respect honest, hard-working people who stick by their principles and cherish family, honor, and dignity. Mundane daily behaviors, such as walking and driving on the right (in the United States, anyway), holding the door open for the person behind you, and a slew of basic manners and courtesies, are valued by people of all socioeconomic levels. Therefore, conflict might be an enduring aspect of society, but so are harmony and cooperation among diverse individuals and groups of people.

The second criticism of conflict theory is its seemingly active commitment to side with the people who lack substantial social power (Fay, 1987). The problem with this is not that the powerless are in need of being helped, but, as critics claim, activism that provides just one group violates the principle of scientific objectivity. Conflict theorists, of course, do not see this as a criticism and would charge that those who see an injustice and do nothing about it are guilty of being "moral bystanders."

A third criticism of the conflict perspective is of its focus on economic factors as the sole criteria for all conflict in society. This criticism is accurate of the Marxist approach, but not of all versions of conflict theory. Most conflict theorists today do not ignore the importance of gender, race, ethnicity, age, sexual orientation, and other factors that lead to conflict.

Conflict theory has also been criticized for being ideologically radical, underdeveloped, and unable to deal with order and stability. Thus, like structural functionalism, conflict theory has an inherent weakness of being able to explain only portions of social life.

THE APPLICATION OF CONFLICT THEORY TO CONTEMPORARY SOCIETY

As discussed throughout this chapter, the key concept of conflict theory is "power." Conflict theorists argue that an imbalance in power in society dictates nearly all relationships between people, groups, and nation-states. Among primitive and isolated societies, power is first exercised physically. The stronger person is the more powerful person: Might *does* make "right." Primitive man dominated the primitive female because of superior physical strength. The leader of the clan, as with nearly all animal species, was the physically strongest person. Eventually, empires were made because of physical strength and advanced weaponry. In many ways, physical power is still a standard of ultimate power. This is especially true in gang behavior, among inmates in prisons, on the schoolyard, in most sports, and within domestic violence. Conflict theorists view domestic violence as the result of power and control. One partner has power over the other and in an attempt to control the other uses physical violence. Conflict theorists view domestic violence as the result of a "power struggle between men and women [that] is the result of improper gender socialization" (Lawson, 2003:21). Conflict theorists argue that domestic violence between partners is likely to continue until there is gender equity in society. As Brewster (2002) explains, any inequality in the family, including dominance by a female partner, "increases the probability of violence because the dominant partner may use violence to maintain his or her position, or the subordinate partner may use violence to try to achieve a more equitable relationship" (p. 27).

In civilized societies, physical strength has been neutralized as a factor in day-to-day interactions with others. It has also been eliminated as a factor in decision-making. For example, a professor up for tenure does not physically challenge the department chair to a fistfight to determine tenure status; a physically stronger person cannot legally take a "weaker" person's home or other possessions away by means of might. Physical power has given way to "legal" and "economic" power. A person who legally owns property has claims to it. Those who control the means of production provide jobs that are necessary to the well-being of workers. Thus, being the owner of the means of production is equated with power.

In contemporary society, most societies are characterized by a legitimate means of power: authority. As Weber defined authority, it is power that is exercised with the consent of the ruled. This leads to roles such as superordinate–subordinate and domination–subjection. Since these aspects are prevalent in society, the study of these relationships will remain relevant in the future. Coser documented an interesting aspect of the domination–subjection phenomenon:

> To illustrate the sociological point that whenever rulers are greedy for power, whenever they wish to maximize their autonomy in the face of feudal, bureaucratic, or other impediments, they tend to avail themselves of the services of alien groups rootless in the country they rule. The alien, I have argued, is easily bent to the ruler's purposes and an ideal servant of power (Coser, 1972b:580).

The economically powerful often employ servants and other persons to do their housework, and they are, indeed, often "aliens."

The conflict perspective has already demonstrated, because of power differentials between groups, that conflict *is* an inevitable aspect of a number of social relations. Even though consensus and agreement can be found in many areas of society, it remains true that conflict exists in society as well. Conflict has always existed, and it always will. The study of conflict will always be important. At many colleges and universities, conflict resolution courses are taught in an effort to combat this inevitability of social life.

There are countless examples of the relevancy of power differentials in the world today. In 2011 Northern Africa, the proletariat attempted, in some cases successfully, to overthrow tyrants who rule with an iron fist and show little regard to the rights of regular citizens as human beings. The spark for this discontent began modestly in Tunisia in December 2010 when Mohammed Bouazizi, a man who sold vegetables from a cart, was repeatedly harassed by local police. Fed up with his status as a "have-not," Bouazizi poured fuel over himself and set himself afire. He did not die right away, but instead lived until January 4, 2011 (*Time.com*, 2011). There was such an outrage over his ordeal that President Zine el Abidine Ben Ali, the Tunisian dictator, visited Bouazizi in the hospital to try and comfort him. His ploy did not work, and ten days after visiting Bouazizi, following a people's revolution, Ben Ali's 23-year rule of Tunisia was over (*Time.com*, 2011).

The success of the people in Tunisia, fed by modern technology, including mobile phones, Facebook, and Twitter, led to revolutions in Egypt and demands for the ouster of Egyptian leader Hosni Mubarak. Within weeks, the people's revolution in Egypt was also a success. Revolutions sprung up in other Northern African nations as well, including Libya, Bahrain, Jordan, Saudi Arabia, Iraq, Yemen, and Algeria. In each case, the people were attempting to oust the existing power structure of political regimes and restore power to the people. In each of these later case revolutions, however, the success of the people was not realized (as of this writing). The leaders in these nations used their power position, including all available resources, to maintain the status quo.

In the United States, the "haves" were battling the "have-nots" in 2011 as well. This time the battleground was state capital buildings (e.g., the Wisconsin Capital Building) and the fight was centered on workers' rights, in particular, union workers' rights to negotiate collectively. The power elites, namely, a number of state governors, and especially Wisconsin Governor Scott Walker, stood their ground and vowed to push on with their agendas to weaken unions and the collective bargaining rights of workers. Their primary agenda was to bury labor unions by crippling their right to collectively bargain. Governor Walker used the pretense that he was trying to cut the state's budget deficit. However, instead of going after big business and the banks (e.g., by eliminating government bailouts and tax breaks and shelters for the rich) or insisting on an end to the wars in the Middle East that have cost taxpayers more than the combined deficits of all U.S. states, Walker argued that the public-sphere union workers made too much money and that their unwillingness to compromise on collective bargaining rights was somehow responsible for Wisconsin's deficit. (Note: According to the nonpartisan Center on Budget and Policy Priorities [2010], virtually the entire U.S. deficit is the result of the economic downturn, the Bush tax cuts for the rich. and the wars in Afghanistan and Iraq.) The union countered that they had made, and were willing to make more, concessions to salary, medical benefits, and retirement contributions. Union representatives also claimed that public-sphere workers do not make more money than private-sphere workers. The governor's attack on public employees was a scapegoating technique wherein he blamed the unions for the state's deficit (*On Campus*, 2011).

As it turns out, Governor Walker's proposals to eliminate the collective bargaining rights of union workers were the result of vested interests supported by the state's Republican majority. As a general rule, the Republicans support the status quo and the power elites because of their commitment to big business (e.g., tax cuts for the rich and powerful organizations). In essence, Walker admitted to working for the best interests of the power elites when he spoke to a prank caller claiming to be billionaire conservative businessman David Koch. Fully believing that he was talking with Koch, Walker explained his anti-union stand and his attempts to bust it. The phone call was recorded and released via the Buffalo Beast, a left-leaning website in New York. The audio quickly spread across the Web. Democrats, who typically support unions and working class people, used the audiotape as an indication that Walker was representing the needs of the rich and powerful (Dwyer and Khan, 2011). Koch responded by donating $300,000 in television advertising to support Gov. Walker (Dwyer and Khan, 2011).

Governor Walker, a political leader who represents the needs of the power elite, was successful in drastically reducing the collective power of union workers. Union workers vowed to fight Walker in an attempt to restore their power. Perhaps one of the most fascinating aspects of this ordeal, from a conflict perspective, is Gov. Walker's portrayal of union workers as the "haves," or the wealthy. In an attempt to rally a number of citizens of Wisconsin, Walker tried to paint a picture of unions as the elites. In reality, of course, union workers have always, and continue to be, representatives of "the people, the working class." There is an adage, within the conflict perspective, that when union workers are strong, all workers are strong. This is the case because when union workers receive their fair share of profits, all workers can point to the salaries and benefits of union workers when making demands for themselves in the private sector. That a number of non-union workers see unions in a negative light is clearly an example of what Karl Marx would describe as false consciousness. Furthermore, the telling of the story of Walker's anti-union stand from the conflict perspective also serves to alienate those who support the unions from those who do not. The telling of this divisive story was simply meant to show the nature of people, from the conflict perspective, and was not meant to reveal a personal preference on the part of the author. The reader will make up his or her own mind as to which side is "right" and that decision will be based on, according to the conflict perspective, the vested interests of each respective person.

The real power elites, or "haves," in education are the administrators, people who earn three to five times that of teachers and professors. For example, school superintendents in Syracuse, New York, earn annual salaries ranging from $176,163 to $199,000 (Moses, 2011). Teachers and professors typically make one third to one fourth that amount. So, who are the "haves" and the "have-nots"?

There are any number of individuals, groups, and organizations that exist in society and act solely in their own best interests. As Randall Collins pointed out, individuals tend to act in their own best interests. Elderly persons, for example, want to make sure that the government continues to allocate funds to Medicaid and Medicare. They do not want to hear about budget cuts or the elimination of the programs. From the perspective of an elderly person, the funds paid into the system throughout a working career should be available when it is time to retire. Every organization dependent upon government assistance wants its "piece of the pie" too. Organizations that help the mentally ill want to assure their programs are funded. So too do organizations like Planned Parenthood. Other people wonder whether or not such organizations need to be funded, especially with a multi-trillion-dollar deficit.

Powerful nations also act in their own vested interests. Noam Chomsky, linguist, political activist, and author of numerous books, is an expert on foreign policy and domestic policy analysis. During a talk to more than 1,000 people at a Syracuse, NY, high school in May 2011, Chomsky described the then-recent death of Osama bin Laden as a "planned assassination." He then described how American foreign policy is used to stabilize other countries in which it has a vested interest. For American diplomats, Chomsky explained, "stability" means we (the United States) run it (Alfonso III, 2011). As conflict theorists would point out, the United States acts like any powerful nation capable of influencing others (via their abundance of resources, including weaponry). China, Japan, Russia, France, England, and other nations do the same thing.

In an effort to maintain a power position, or in an effort to attain a power position, interest groups use political methods such as hiring lobbyists. Lobbyists are hired to work the political system in such a way as to get laws passed that are favorable to their clients. For example, the tobacco industry is among the most powerful interest groups in the world. It uses the political and economic systems to its advantage to maintain its own power position. The proof of its power is obvious: What other single product (tobacco) is responsible for the death of more than 443,000 Americans every year, costing the nation $96 billion in healthcare costs annually (CDC, 2009)? If there was a food product, automobile, child's toy, and so on that killed a fraction of this number, it would be banned from the market, and yet tobacco remains a legal product.

It is also very evident that there is a power elite in society. C. Wright Mills described the power elite as political, military, and economic institutions. These three elements are integrated and form what Mills called the *triangle of power*. The wars in the Middle East are an example of the *triangle of power* in action. Powerful companies that make money (e.g., producing war machines, private security forces) influence people in politics to convince them waging war is good, and the military receives increased funding because, well, they are at war. At the start of the 2000s, then-President George W. Bush successfully integrated these three powers by convincing Americans that such an effort was necessary to fight terrorism. As another example of the power elite, it has become common knowledge that global conglomerate General Electric receives "corporate welfare." GE, a company that has made $26 billion in profits for the five-year period between 2006 and 2010 received a $4.1 billion tax refund during that same period (Mariani, 2011). The power elite are people who transcend the ordinary environments of ordinary persons and make decisions that have major consequences. They are at the top of hierarchies of major organizations and, in short, are in charge of the "machinery" that runs society.

Among the specific contributions by the conflict theorists discussed in this chapter is Lewis Coser's functional conflict theory. Functional conflict theory illustrates the beauty of combining two major theories.

> Conflict theorists do not deny that certain types of social arrangements are functional for particular individuals or for groups, but they insist that we must always ask *for whom* they are functional. They view with great skepticism the functional assumption that many existing social arrangements can be interpreted as generally positive for an entire social system (Lindsey and Beach, 2004:20).

For example, when a president announces a "tax cut" and declares that it will benefit all of society, the conflict theorist quickly analyzes this claim and generally discovers that the tax cut is designed to help the rich. A great example of this fallacy is former president Ronald Reagan's claim that his "trickle-down" economics would benefit all of society.

C. Wright Mills is best known to college students today because of his sociological imagination concept. The sociological imagination is taught in all introductory sociology courses and is a standard of their textbooks. Mills wrote on the difference between individual troubles and public issues. This analysis is social-psychological. For example, a person who has recently been divorced or has broken up with a significant other has negative self-feelings and may think there is something wrong with him or her. The reality of this individual trouble is that it is a part of a greater public issue. There is a growing divorce rate, and people break up with each other regularly. As another example, people who lose their jobs because of corporate downsizing are not "losers"; instead, they are simply a product of the greater economic reality of a dramatically changing socioeconomic system. Consequently, the negative feelings one may have regarding oneself are simply a reflection of a greater societal occurrence. The bottom line is that, when looking at things sociologically, we see the "big picture," and not a simple snapshot view of the world. The problems that most people have (lack of economic security) are not found in individual pathologies (although there certainly are times when they are), but in mismanagement of the greater society.

Ralf Dahrendorf articulated the ideas of domination and subjection and the role of authority. Of particular interest is his insight that a person who holds a position of authority in one setting does not hold a position of authority in other social arenas. Future studies in this area should prove to be very beneficial, especially in the industrial setting.

Randall Collins has contributed a great deal to sociological theory and will continue to do so for some time. His work on geopolitics has already proved useful in the understanding of the global community. His theories on the role of persons in power positions when they mingle with subordinates in social settings and his interaction ritual chain theory are certainly relevant. First, his analysis of power persons in social settings is relevant on numerous occasions. Generally, the "boss" or the person with greater power expects to be shown a certain level of respect and deference, even in social settings. Many bosses expect that when playing a game, like golf, the subordinates will allow them to win. They expect to be allowed to "cut" into the food line rather than waiting their turn at a buffet, and they expect that their jokes will be laughed at. In short, those who hold power generally expect special treatment outside the work environment and exploit their subordinates even in social settings. Collins' interaction ritual chain theory is a revealing look at human behavior and provides an area of study that could benefit from additional research. Collins has revealed the conditions under which people continue to engage in, or disengage from, relationships with others. This theory is especially insightful on small-group behaviors.

Collins' work on the interaction ritual is both insightful and fascinating. All personal relationships can easily be examined by means of this theory. The expansion of this ritual theory to intellectual networks provided excellent insights into interpersonal relationships within a structural framework. Randall Collins is certainly a first-rate scholar in the field of sociology, in particular, and a brilliant social thinker in general. Sociological theory has certainly benefited from this gifted social thinker.

As demonstrated here, conflict theory has both a practical application (relevancy to everyday life by everyday people) and a theoretical application (sociological value). Nearly all of us are involved in multiple power-differential relationships where conflict can occur or is occurring. Sociologists regularly cite power differentials in a wide variety of areas of study, including race and ethnicity, social stratification, gender studies, conflict resolution, and so on.

Summary

Conflict theory views society as composed of competing elements, characterized by power differentials, with conflict among individuals, groups, and nation-states as the inevitable outcome. Conflict theorists believe that society is coordinated as a result of power struggles and power differentials. In brief, the conflict perspective proposes that inherent in any social system are interest groups that continually struggle for superiority and power. Those who have power want to keep it. The power elites are those who control the resources needed for the production and distribution of the goods and services deemed desirable and necessary by a society. Because they control the economic strata, the power elites have the money to help maintain their advantageous position. Those without power seek social change. Because of this reality, conflict theorists view society as a setting where groups and individuals are in constant struggle with one another in order to obtain scarce and valued resources, especially money, property, prestige, and, in short, power. Furthermore, the conflict perspective maintains that what social order does exist in society is the result of the power elites' coercion of the masses.

Karl Marx provided the foundation for modern conflict theory. He viewed power relationships as unnatural and alienating. In his era, society was basically a two-class system: the bourgeoisie (owners of the means of production) and the proletariat (workers). Marx believed that the owners of the means of production used their power position over the workers to maximize their profits. Marx argued that economics was the ingredient that had shaped human society throughout history. Contemporary conflict theorists do not limit their power analysis to the economic-class structural realm. They look at such issues as gender (feminist theory) and race, ethnicity, and sexual preference.

In short, conflict theory represents one of the "big three" traditional theories of sociology. It is taught at all levels of sociology, from introductory courses to advanced graduate courses. There is good reason. Power differentials and conflict are inevitable in human behavior and society. The impending violence that often accompanies conflict is also ever-present in contemporary society. Consequently, the sociological study of social conflict will always be relevant; and thus, conflict theory will also remain relevant for the foreseeable future.

Study and **Review** on **MySearchLab**

Discussion Questions

1. According to Lewis Coser, violence serves a number of functions. Name and describe them. Can you think of any contemporary examples of the applicability of the functions of violence?
2. C. Wright Mills described three types of power. Name and briefly describe them. Using the conflict perspective, which type(s) of authority best describes American society?
3. Name the three components of the "tripartite elite" or "triangle of power" according to Mills. Do some research and determine for yourself whether or not the "triangle of power" is applicable to the recent

wars in the Middle East (especially Iraq and Afghanistan).
4. Describe what Randall Collins means by his "interaction ritual chain theory." Apply this ritual chain to your own associations.
5. There are people who credit former President Ronald Reagan with bringing down the U.S.S.R. However, as learned in this chapter, Collins predicted the collapse of the Soviet Union a decade before it happened. Do some research and find out for yourself whether or not Reagan deserves any credit for the Soviet collapse.

MySearchLab® Connections

MysearchLab is designed just for you. Each chapter features a customized study plan to help you learn and review key concepts and terms. Dynamic visual activities, videos, and readings found in the multimedia library will enhance your learning experience.

 View on **MySearchLab**

▶ C. Wright Mills: Power in the United States: The Model Proposed by C. Wright Mills

 Read on **MySearchLab**

▶ Mills, C. Wright. The Power Elite.
▶ Mills, C. Wright. The Promise.

10 Symbolic Interactionism

 Listen to the **Chapter Audio** on **MySearchLab**

Chapter Outline

- Defining Symbolic Interactionism
- The Roots and Development of Symbolic Interactionism
- George Herbert Mead
- Herbert Blumer
- Erving Goffman
- Arlie Russell Hochschild
- Criticisms of Symbolic Interactionism
- Application of Symbolic Interactionism to Contemporary Society
- Summary
- Discussion Questions

S*ymbolic interactionism* is a term coined by Herbert Blumer and a theoretical perspective most generally associated with George Herbert Mead. Blumer had been asked by Emerson P. Schmidt to contribute an article on social psychology to his book *Man and Society* (1937). Blumer, who studied under Mead at the University of Chicago, used the term *symbolic interactionism* to describe sociological and social psychological ideas emanating from George H. Mead, but not exclusively in *Mind, Self, and Society* (1934). The primary undertone of symbolic interactionism, according to Blumer, was to study how the individual develops socially as a result of participating in groups. Norman Denzin (1969) stated, "The development of a theoretical perspective appropriate for the joint analysis of social psychological and sociological problems has long concerned the sociologist" (p. 922). As essentially a social-psychological perspective, symbolic interactionism focuses primarily on the issue of self and in small-group interactions. Joel Charon (1989) believes that "symbolic interactionism is a perspective in social psychology that is especially relevant to the concerns of sociology" (p. 22). Symbolic interactionism represents the first micro-sociological theory discussed to this point.

Symbolic interactionism is often a favorite of college students because this theory seems relatable to their everyday lives. This theoretical perspective concentrates on micro behavior, that is, the behavior of small groups and the role of the individual in groups. Symbolic interactionists study social acts (human behavior) and the use of gestures, describe how people control their presentations of self (e.g., the image you portray on social network sites such as Facebook), examine dramaturgy (e.g., the idea that life is like a drama, and in this world of reality television and social networking, drama is the cornerstone subject), and discuss the role of emotions.

DEFINING SYMBOLIC INTERACTIONISM

Symbolic interactionism is based on the idea that social reality is constructed in each human interaction through the use of symbols (Levin, 1991). Symbols include such things as words and gestures. The ability to communicate by the use of language becomes the primary method of symbolic interaction. Language allows individuals to discuss and understand ideas and events that transcend the immediate environment.

> Symbolic interactionism takes as a fundamental concern the relationship between individual conduct and forms of social organization. This perspective asks how selves emerge out of social structure and social situations.... The interactionist assumes that human beings are capable of making their own thoughts and activities objects of analysis, that is, they can routinely, and even habitually, manipulate symbols and orient their own actions towards other objects (Denzin, 1969:922–923).

Symbolic interactionism is a micro approach in sociological theory. The focus is primarily on individuals and their interactions with others. What is of utmost concern are the meanings that actors place on social acts committed by themselves and by others. Because objects found in human environments carry no intrinsic meaning, humans are capable of constructing objects' meanings. In addition, because actors are objects themselves, their sense of self is open to meaning and thus amendable.

Symbolic interactionists believe that studying social interaction is the key to understanding human behavior.

> Instead of focusing on the individual and his or her personality characteristics, or on how the social structure or social situation causes individual behavior, symbolic interactionism focuses on the *nature of interaction,* the dynamic social activities taking place between persons. In focusing on the interaction itself as the unit of study, the symbolic interactionist creates a more active image of the human being and rejects the image of the passive, determined organism (Charon, 1989:22).

The interactionist perspective maintains a belief in the ability of actors to modify their behaviors to meet the needs of the present and the immediate environment. Interactionists are steadfast in the idea that reality exists in a present. As Mead (1959) stated, "The present of course implies a past and a future, and to these both we deny existence.... Existence involves nonexistence; it does take place. The world is a world of events" (p. 1).

Additionally, during interaction, social acts and events come to be defined in some matter by participating interactants.

Because human interaction involves behavior of both the covert and overt variety, and because the meanings attached to objects often change during an encounter, and the interactionist endeavors to relate covert symbolic behavior with other patterns of interaction. This additionally demands a concern for the unfolding meaning objects assume during an interactional sequence (Denzin, 1969:925).

In short, symbolic interactionism involves people who interact with one another through the use of symbols (e.g., gestures and language) that have meaning to actors.

THE ROOTS AND DEVELOPMENT OF SYMBOLIC INTERACTIONISM

The intellectual sources that influenced the development of symbolic interactionism are both numerous and diverse. This highly American social theory includes the European precursors of evolutionism, the Scottish moralists, and German idealism, along with the American intellectual influences of pragmatism, behaviorism, and the works of William James and Charles Cooley. A brief analysis of these influences follows.

Evolution

Charles Darwin's model of an organism in an environment to which it must adapt in order to survive provides the means of understanding and discovering all behaviors, those of humans included. Mead was particularly impressed by Darwin's *Expression of the Emotions in Man and Animals*. In this book Darwin extended his theory of evolution into the field of "conscious experience" (Mead, 1934). He showed that there are a number of acts that express emotions. The part of the organism that most vividly expresses emotions is the face. Mead did not agree with Darwin's theory of consciousness. For example, Mead believed that consciousness is an emergent form of behavior, whereas Darwin viewed consciousness as a psychological state. As Reynolds (1990) explained,

> The nineteenth-century Darwinian doctrine of evolution was a major source of ideas for the American pragmatists in general and for George Herbert Mead in particular. It was, however, only to selected aspects of Darwin's theory that the founders of interactionism were to direct their attention. Mead, for example, was critical of Darwin's argument concerning emotions and their expression by animals (p. 6).

Mead's attraction to Darwin rests on his emphasis on process (evolutionary process), specifically, the idea that process gives rise to different forms (Stone and Farberman, 1970). Mead's interpretation of Darwin's ideas led him to believe that behavior is not accidental or random but formed through individuals' interactions with one another in a social environment. This adaptation to the environment is an ongoing process sustained by social interaction. "As this interaction unfolds, the person's behavior is performed in adaptation to the environment, and person and environment come mutually to influence each other" (Reynolds, 1990:7). Behavioral adaptation during social interaction often leads to emergent behavior that meets the needs of the changing environment. Thus,

> The evolutionary conceptions of the processual, emergent character of life, the adaptive function of behavior, and the mutually determinative relationship between organisms and environments were to be a part of the intellectual heritage of symbolic interactions (Reynolds, 1990:8–9).

The Scottish Moralists

Evolutionism influenced the founders of symbolic interactionism to believe that the "mind" and the "self" possessed emergence characteristics. The Scottish moralists believed that the "mind" and the "self" were social products shaped by individuals' interactions with others. Among the principal spokesmen of the Scottish moralist tradition were Adam Ferguson, Henry Homes, David Hume, Francis Hutcheson, and Adam Smith.

> The principal significance of the Scottish Moralists for the symbolic interactionists is that the former anticipated many of the key or pivotal social-psychological concepts of the latter.... The Scottish Moralists' concepts of "sympathy" and of the "impartial spectator" clearly foreshadow the interactionists' working concepts of "roletaking" and the "generalized other," and in the writings of Adam Smith are to be found views anticipating the interactionist conceptions of a spontaneous, or "I," component of self, as well as the self's "me," or internalized view of others, component (Reynolds, 1990:9).

Smith's ideas not only foreshadowed Mead's concepts of the "I" and the "me," but also Cooley's theory of the self.

German Idealism

The principal spokesmen of the variety of German idealism who influenced Mead and symbolic interactionism were Gottlieb Fichte, Friedrick Von Schelling, and G. W. F. Hegel, whom Mead called the *Romantic Philosophers*. These philosophers argued that humans construct their own worlds and their realities. "It was Fichte's concept of the 'ethical self' and Schelling's discussion of artistic creativity that led each to conclude that the world in which we live was, at least in part, created by ourselves" (Reynolds, 1990:11). The romantic idealists utilized the self–not-self process in experience and identified this process with the subject–object process. This subject–object process was similar to William James's analysis. Mead learned from the German tradition that there is no consciousness which is not conscious of something; therefore, the subject and the object are inevitably interrelated. There cannot be a subject without the object's being aware of it, just as there cannot be an object without its being a subject. Mead also believed that the development of self involves the process of reflexivity, which is the ability of an individual to be an object to himself. This idea would greatly influence Mead's concept of the generalized other.

Mead came to view the German idealists as preoccupied with the relations of the self to its objects. He felt that Fichte was too concerned with about experiences and that Schelling and Hegel focused too much attention on the aesthetic experience and on experience of thought, respectively (Coser, 1977). Above all, Mead found fault with Hegel for not having formulated adequate concepts of the individual and of the future. Hegel's philosophy is thus incapable of grasping individuality in its concreteness (Joas, 1985).

Having studied in Germany, Mead was most directly influenced by Wilhelm Wundt, especially Wundt's theories of language and the gesture. Wundt was the heir apparent of the German idealistic tradition. He was able to relate German idealism to the social sciences through his psychological parallelism (Martindale, 1988). In the introduction to Mead's *Mind, Self, and Society* (1934), Charles Morris clarified the distinction between Darwin's and Wundt's conception of the gesture by explaining that Wundt had helped to separate the gesture from its internal emotional implication and to regard it in a social context. In the tradition of Wundt, Mead viewed the gesture as the transitional link to language from human action. The gesture precedes language and mediates the development of language as the basic mechanism that allows the "sense of self" to arise during the course of ongoing social interaction. Thus, Mead came to argue that the gesture can be explained *only* in a social context. Years later, a more mature Mead (1934) would come to describe a gesture as those phases of the act which bring about the adjustment of the response of the other.

From Hegel, Mead took the idea that consciousness and society are dialectically emergent phenomena (Adams and Sydie, 2001). Mead replaced Hegel's "spirit" with a concept of a "unified world" that emerges through the realization of universal human potential. Mead (1938) believed that social development depends on individuals' becoming aware of their "opposition to one another" and working through such oppositions.

> From the larger camp of German idealism, then, symbolic interactionism was to draw upon the doctrine that dictated that what Mead termed "the World that is there" was, in fact, a self-created world. People were to be seen as responding to their own working conceptions and definitions of that self-created world and not to the world per se. And from Wundt would be taken the conception of the gesture as the initial phase of the social act (Reynolds, 1990:12–13).

Pragmatism

A brief discussion of the American influences on symbolic interactionism follows. A critical influence on symbolic interactionism in general, and on Mead specifically, was pragmatism. In fact, Reynolds (1990) stated, "If forced to single out the one philosophical school of thought that most influenced symbolic interactionism, one would be on safe ground in concluding that pragmatism provides its primary intellectual underpinnings" (p. 13). Pragmatists believe that true reality does not exist "out there" in the real world; it is actively created as we act toward the world (Shalin, 1986).

Although Mead would become one of the key figures in the development of pragmatism, he was initially introduced to pragmatic philosophy by John Dewey, William James, and James Baldwin. Mead (1938) viewed pragmatism as a natural American outgrowth (see Chapter 7). It reflected the triumph of science in U.S. society and a belief in the superiority of scientific data and analysis over philosophical dogma and other forms of inferior beliefs. Pragmatists do not believe in the concept of "absolute truths." Instead, they argue that any claim made about the "truth" of an event is subject to change in light of future research and knowledge. Truth is determined by humans' adaptations to their environments, and therefore the transitive character of both truth and consciousness is revealed. Reality, then, is always relative to individuals. Pragmatism helped to develop the idea that people base knowledge on what is most useful to them. Therefore, a construction worker is knowledgeable about tools and how to operate them properly; an auto mechanic is knowledgeable about the parts and operation of automobiles; medical doctors understand the human body and how it functions; and academics have book knowledge and know how to apply such knowledge to the relevancy of peoples' lives.

Pragmatists believe that human beings reflect on the meaning of a stimulus before reacting. The meaning placed on various acts depends on the purpose of the act, the context in which it is performed, and the reactions of others to the act (Adams and Sydie, 2001). Mead's notion of the act as social was directly influenced by Dewey and Cooley. Dewey and Mead were colleagues for a short period of time at the University of Michigan. More important, Dewey, while at the University of Chicago, was instrumental in getting Mead an appointment there. As the primary exponent of pragmatism, "Dewey stressed the process of human adjustment to the world, in which humans constantly seek to master the conditions of their environment. Thus, the unique characteristics of humans arise from the *process* of adjusting to their life conditions" (Turner, 2003:345). Dewey believed that reflexive action(s) leads to the construction of such ideas as morality. Thus, Mead came to view even ideas such as ethics and morality as socially constructed and not fixed. Different cultures are easily explained by the realization that people with different life experiences come to different interpretations of events and impose different meanings on acts.

The collaboration of Dewey and Mead was mutually beneficial. On the one hand, close examination of Mead's social psychology reveals many influences from Dewey. On the other hand, as Charles Morris stated in the introduction to *Mind, Self, and Society* (Mead, 1962/1934) in regard to both Dewey and Mead,

> Neither stands to the other in the exclusive relation of teacher to student; both...were of equal though different intellectual stature; both shared in a mutual give-and-take according to their own particular genius. If Dewey gave range and vision, Mead gave analytical depth and scientific precision (p. xi).

Behaviorism

Mead considered himself a behaviorist but not in the radical tradition of behaviorism that focuses on the simplistic formula that stimuli elicit automatic responses, or behaviors (stimulus–response mechanisms). Mead (1934) defined behaviorism as simply an approach to the study of the experience of individuals from the point of view of their conduct (behavior). His version of behaviorism was not consistent with how the term was used by his contemporaries, especially John B. Watson. The behaviorism of Mead's time was borrowed from animal psychology and was applied to humans (Ritzer, 2011). Watson represented the attempt to account for sociopsychological phenomena in purely behavioristic terms (Martindale, 1988). Because Mead recognized the importance of both observable behavior and the covert aspects of behavior, something that the radical behaviorists ignored, he criticized Watson for ignoring the inner experiences of consciousness and mental imagery. Thus, for Mead, the acts of individuals possess both covert and overt meanings.

Mead believed that the inner experiences of individuals who act can be studied by behaviorists, as long as a social-behavioristic approach is utilized. This social-behavioristic approach led to the development of symbolic interactionism. Instead of studying the mind introspectively, Mead focused on the act (the social act). Acts are behaviors that respond to stimuli. In a variation of the stimulus–response relationship described by behaviorists and exchange theorists, Mead described a stimulus–act relationship. The difference is that the inner consciousness responds to the stimulus before the individual responds, thus creating an act that takes into account the existence of the mind and freewill.

William James

The properties of Mead's social psychology and symbolic interactionism can be traced, at least in part, to William James.

> The Harvard psychologist William James (1842–1910) was perhaps the first social scientist to develop a clear concept of self. James recognized that humans have the capacity to view themselves as objects and to develop self-feelings and attitudes toward themselves (Turner, 2003:344).

In his *Principles of Psychology* (1948), James called for a reexamination of the relations between the individual and society (Martindale, 1988). Although James was a product of his time and accepted the instinct theory that was so prevalent then, he began to believe that other aspects beyond biology tended to modify behavior. His works on habit were of special importance, as James recognized that habit reduces the need for conscious attention. If individuals are capable of forming new habits, they are also capable of modifying their behavior. James (1948) believed that the individual acquires a new nature through habit.

A second critical aspect of James's psychology was his rethinking of the role of "consciousness." He noted that consciousness always involves some degree of awareness of the person's self. The person appears in thought in two ways:

> partly known and partly knower, partly object and partly subject.... For shortness we may call one the *Me* and the other the *I*....I shall therefore treat successively of (A) the self as known, or the *Me*, the "empirical ego" as it is sometimes called; and of (B) the self as knower, or the *I*, the "pure ego" of certain authors (James, 1948:176).

The empirical self, or me, is the sum total of all the person can claim as one's own: their feelings, emotions, actions of self-seeking and self-preservation. People possess as many social selves as there are individuals who have images of them in mind. The self as knower, the I, or pure ego, is a much more complicated subject (James, 1948). The I is what the person is at any given specific moment in time.

James developed a typology of selves, but this typology was never adopted by subsequent interactionists. As explained by Horace Kallen (1953), the three parts of the James's "self" were one's constituents (with three subparts: the material self, the social self, and the spiritual self), one's feelings and emotions (with numerous subcategories that allow for such things as pride or self-loathing due to our insecurities), and the self-seeking and self-preservation aspects of the self. Jonathan Turner (2003) suggests that even though James's complete typology of the self may never have caught on with symbolic interactionists, his notion of the "social self" did. Mead was clearly influenced by James in his works on the development of the self. Mead even used the same terminology of the "I" and the "me" in explaining the structure of the self.

Charles Horton Cooley

Cooley was a student of John Dewey and was well acquainted with the writings of both William James and James Mark Baldwin. Cooley and James both identified the influence of the environment on behavior. The self is viewed as a process in motion, in which individuals see themselves as objects, are aware of other objects in the environment, and modify their behaviors as the situation dictates. Individuals learn to act as society (others) wants them to act, not as they themselves might want to act (thus, individuals do not react solely on a stimulus–response mechanism). For example, two youths cannot play catch with a football during church services just because they want to; the negative reactions of others will be enough to stop the inappropriate behavior of those properly socialized. Society itself is an interweaving and interworking of mental selves. Through socialization, society is internalized in the individual psyche; it becomes a part of the individual self through the interaction of many individuals, which links and fuses them into an organic whole. Consequently, Cooley realized that the self emerges from communication and interaction with others. Through interaction and the evaluation and interpretation of acts by others, the self is developed as both an object and a subject.

Cooley argued that a person's self develops through contact and interaction with others. By identifying a sense of self, individuals are able to view themselves the same way they do any other social object. Cooley (1964) stated that there can be no isolated selves: "There is no sense of 'I'...without its correlative sense of you, or he, or they" (p. 182). Individuals gain a sense of self when they receive consistent messages from others. Actors are most interested in, and value most, the reactions of significant others, especially primary-group members. Cooley is perhaps best known for introducing sociologists to the concepts *primary groups* and the *looking-glass self* theory.

Cooley (1909) explains,

> By primary groups, I mean those characterized by intimate face-to-face association and cooperation.... The result of intimate association and cooperation.... The result of intimate association, psychologically, is a certain fusion of individualities in a common whole, so that one's very self, for many purposes at least, is the common life and purpose of the group (p. 23).

These associations are primary in several senses, but chiefly in that they are fundamental in forming *human nature*. A closer examination reveals that Cooley (1909) was trying to show that even though we are instinctively and initially bound to our natural self, in the end our true goals are aimed to help the whole.

Cooley's *looking-glass self* theory was also influenced by William James. (Note: The term *looking glass* is an old fashion way of saying "mirror.") Cooley's *looking-glass self* theory is based on the idea that individuals are interested in their own appearance because it belongs to them. We are thereby "pleased" or "displeased" by whether or not our appearance is as we would like it to be. In our imaginations we perceive in another person's mind their impression of our appearance and character; then we are affected by this perception. Cooley outlines three key principles of the *looking-glass self* theory:

1. the imagination of our appearance to the other person;
2. the imagination of their judgment of that appearance;
3. our resulting self-feeling, such as pride or mortification.

Therefore, an individual's self-image mirrors the imagined reactions of others to our appearance, demeanor, and behavior. We can think of every person we meet face to face as a mirror because we see ourselves in their reactions to us. Cooley (1902) illustrated the reflective nature of the self by comparing it to a looking glass, "Each to each a looking glass, reflected the other that doth pass" (p. 183).

GEORGE HERBERT MEAD (1863–1931)

We have discussed George H. Mead in an earlier chapter (see Chapter 7). As a result, and despite the importance of Mead to symbolic interactionism, our review here will be relatively brief. As you may recall, Mead taught at the University of Chicago. The city of Chicago itself was important in the development of symbolic interactionism as numerous social scientists first conducted ethnographic, participant–observation research in Chicago. (Recall from Chapter 6 that Jane Addams' Hull House was located in Chicago during this era of symbolic interactionism development.) During Mead's era, Chicago was flourishing and growing both industrially and commercially, immigrants were migrating to the city seeking a better life, and the city was becoming a hub of social activity. This social activity was like a laboratory for social scientists eager to mingle with people and learn about behavior first-hand for themselves and from a first-hand account of the people under study. Social scientists, like Mead, discovered that people were products of their social environments that were capable of modifying their behaviors to accommodate new environmental needs. The socialization process, symbolic interactionists surmised, was the key to understanding the human behavior.

The Social Act and Gestures

Mead's analysis of the act reveals his social-behaviorist approach to the stimulus–response process. As we learned in Chapter 7, *the act* consists of four elements: impulse, perception, manipulation, and consummation. The development of self from impulse reaction to perception reaction reflects a key change in how individuals behave, for they are no longer simply reacting to a stimulus; they are reacting based on an individual perception of the stimulus. Thus, some people may react differently to the same event because of the way they perceive things. As a contemporary example, the events surrounding the US Airways A320 jet flown by pilot Capt. Chesley "Sully" Sullenberger (Flight 1549 from New York's LaGuardia Airport) that developed mechanic trouble after flying into a flock of birds and landed on the Hudson River in 2009 is perceived quite differently by people. Some label the successful landing that resulted in no loss of life the "Miracle on the Hudson." Rational and scientific persons cite the training and skill of the pilot for the successful landing and certainly give it no significance beyond the secular realm. The plane is now in an aviation museum in Charlotte, NC, where it will be on permanent display. The plane, then, has become similar to a piece of art to be observed and perceived by onlookers.

Since humans act in accordance to their interpretations of actions (perception) and not merely the stimulus alone (impulse), the use of gestures becomes an important variant of symbolic communication (Anderson, Carter, and Lowe, 1999). A gesture, such as a smile, holds common meaning by a general consensus of a society. Gestures are a type of symbol that people utilize to interact or portray certain feelings. As Mead explains, the basic mechanism of the *social act* is the gesture. A *social act* may be defined as one in which the stimulus (or occasion) sets free an impulse (found in the very character or nature of its being) that then triggers possible reactions by those in the environment (Reck, 1964). Mead restricted the social act to the class of acts which involve the cooperation of more than one individual, and whose object, as defined by the act, is a social object (Reck, 1964).

According to Thayer (1968), the importance that Mead placed on gestures was influenced by Darwin's *Expression of Emotions in Man and Animals,* in which Darwin described physical attitudes and physiological changes as expressive of emotions (the dog baring teeth for attack). This suggested an evolutionary biological origin of the gesture of language, which Mead found appealing (Thayer, 1968). However, he objected to Darwin's subjectivistic psychological theory that emotions are inner states and gestures are the outward expressions of these ideas and meanings (Thayer, 1968). Mead emphasized the importance of the vocal gesture because the individual who sends a vocal gesture can perceive that vocal signal in much the same way as the listener. That shared perception does not guarantee that the listener will respond in the manner that the sender anticipated (Baldwin, 1986). Verbal gestures represent signs, which, being heard by the maker as well as other parties in the social act, can serve as a common sign to all parties in the social act. The mutually understood gesture becomes a significant symbol (Martindale, 1988). Common gestures allow the development of language, which consists of a number of significant symbols. Only humans have developed to the point of being able to use language and create significant symbols. Symbols allow people to communicate more easily. Consequently, a shared language greatly assists the whole society to function more efficiently. The development of symbolic communication leads to inner conversation with the mind, and to reflective intelligence (Baldwin, 1986). The "same" responses to a significant symbol lead to organized attitudes, which we arouse in ourselves when we talk to others (Reck, 1964).

Communication through vocal gestures has a special quality, in that we cannot see our own facial gestures, but we can hear our own vocal gestures, and therefore, they potentially carry the same meaning to both the listener and the speaker. The speaker can also formulate the answer he or she hopes the listener will give (Pampel, 2000).

Christian von Scheve has conducted more recent research on gestures, in particular, emotion expression. Von Scheve (2012) hypothesizes that the sociological relevance of expressive behavior becomes evident when accounting for universals in facial expressions and their function as a signal of emotional gratification as well as when emphasizing their plasticity and social calibration, that is to say, when their involuntary and embodied attunement to the practices and norms of systems of social order are encoded across the boundaries of cultural units (von Scheve 2012). Thus, while gestures and emotional expressions may vary across the world, within certain culture contexts, there exist universal patterns. The role of the sociologist is to uncover and document these patterns in order to better assure effective communication among people of the same culture and ultimately between cultures.

Symbolic Interactionism

Mead, the most important thinker associated with the Chicago School and symbolic interactionism, was not a sociologist but a philosopher. It must be made clear that there was no such field as symbolic interactionism when Mead first started teaching social psychology at Chicago. It was Herbert Blumer, following in the tradition of Mead and Cooley, who coined the term in 1937. Mead's students, who put together their notes on his courses and published *Mind, Self, and Society* (1934) posthumously under his name, had a primary influence on Blumer and the development of symbolic interactionism. Mead had published several articles by the time Blumer completed his doctoral dissertation on "Method in Social Psychology." A number of Mead's works were made available to Blumer before his assertion that he

> was compelled to develop a symbolic interaction methodology to deal '…explicitly with many crucial matters that were only implicit in the thought of Mead.' It is not clear by what criteria Blumer made his judgment that Mead's methodological perspective was 'implicit' in his written work. Our comparison of their respective epistemologies will establish that Mead's position is far more detailed and explicit than Blumer suggests. It is also quite different from the position Blumer felt compelled to develop (McPhail and Rexroat, 1979:450).

Mind, Self, and Society

Mead's *Mind, Self, and Society* (1934) represents his attempt to understand individual social experiences in relation to society. He argued that there can be no self, no consciousness of self, and no communication apart from society. Mead felt that social experience is the sum of the total dynamic realities observable by the individual, who is a part of the ongoing societal process (Kallen, 1956). Society must be understood as a structure that emerges through an ongoing process of communicative social acts and through interactions between persons who are oriented toward each other (Coser, 1977).

Mead viewed the mind as a process and not a thing, as inner conversation with oneself, which arises and develops within the social process and is an integral part of that process. The mind reflects the human capacity to conceive what the organism perceives, define situations, evaluate phenomena, convert gestures into symbols, and exhibit pragmatic and goal-directed behavior. The concept of *self* is critical in Mead's works. The self involves the process whereby actors reflect on themselves as objects. Thus, the self has the rare ability to be both object and subject. In regard to society, Mead (1934) stated,

> Human society as we know it could not exist without minds and selves, since all its most characteristic features presuppose the possession of minds and selves by its individual members; but its individual members would not possess minds and selves if these had not arisen within or emerged out of human social process in its lower stages of development (p. 227).

Mead believed that the behavior of all humans has a basic social aspect. The experience and behavior of the individual are always a component of a larger social whole or process. The organization of human experience and behavior is society. Because humans have the ability to manipulate their environment, a wide variety of human societies may exist.

The "I" and the "Me"

Mead is the earliest of the social thinkers to examine the socialization process from the interactionist perspective. He believed that human behavior is almost totally a product of interaction with others. The self, which can be an object to itself, is essentially a social structure that arises from social experience. A baby is born with a "blank slate," without a predisposition to develop any particular type of personality. The personality that develops is a product of that person's interactions with others. According to Mead, the self is composed of two parts: the "I" (the unsocialized self) and the "me" (the socialized self). Both aspects of the self make up one's self-concept. The self is a product of the dialogue between the "I" and the "me." The "I" is the spontaneous, unsocialized, unpredictable, and impulsive aspect of the self. It is the subject of one's actions. The "me" is the part of the self that is formed as the object of others' actions and views, including one's own reflections on oneself (Garner, 2000). An individual who fails to conform to the norms and expectations of society is under the influence of the "I."

Development of Self

In his theory of the development of the self, Mead traced patterns of interaction that contribute to the emergence of the social self during childhood (Pampel, 2000). To learn the role of others, the child must come to understand the meanings of symbols and language. Much of this learning takes place through various forms of play. The development of the self takes place through four stages: imitation, play, game, and generalized other. At the imitation stage, the infant is capable of understanding gestures (e.g., the parent coaxes the child to roll the ball by rolling the ball herself) and imitating behavior. This is an elementary stage of learning, but it represents learning nonetheless, as even imitation implies learning, and babies learn that some behaviors are positively rewarded and other behaviors bring punishment (Pampel, 2000). During the play stage, the child has learned language and the meaning of many symbols. By role playing, the child learns to become both subject and object, an important step in the development of the self. The game stage represents the third stage of development. As Mead (1934) stated,

> The fundamental difference between the game and play stage is that in the latter the child must have the attitude of all the others involved in the game. The attitudes of the other players which the participant assumes organize into a sort of unit, and it is that organization which controls the response of the individual (pp. 154–155).

The final stage of development is what Mead called the *generalized other*. The *generalized other* develops from successive and simultaneous use of many roles. The individual can take on the attitude of the entire community (as in, "It will be good for the community"). The generalized other is a kind of corporate individual or a plural noun; it represents the attitudes of the whole community. Thus, the development of the self depends on interactions with others within the community, and these interactions help to shape the individual's personality. Embracing the standards of the community is accomplished by recognizing the generalized other.

HERBERT BLUMER (1900–1987)

Herbert Blumer taught sociology at the University of Chicago from 1927 to 1952, having completed his doctoral dissertation in 1928 under the guidance of Ellsworth Faris, a disciple of George Herbert Mead. Although Mead was a philosopher, his courses on social psychology routinely drew a large number of sociology students. Blumer took courses from Mead, and during Mead's illness in his last quarter of instruction at Chicago, he asked Blumer to take over his major course, "Advanced Social Psychology." As Wallace and Wolf (1999) stated:

> Blumer carried on Mead's tradition for twenty-five years at the University of Chicago and for another twenty-five years at the University of California at Berkeley, where he taught until his retirement. During his Chicago era Blumer was involved in such diverse activities as playing professional football, serving as a mediator in labor disputes, and interviewing underworld figures from the Al Capone gang. Blumer's stature in the profession and the profound respect he commands are indicated by his editorship of the *American Journal of Sociology* from 1941 to 1952, his presidency of the American Sociological Association in 1956, the festschrift in his honor, and several memorial sessions at professional meetings after his death on April 15, 1987 (p. 206).

Blumer was one of sociology's most prominent and esteemed practitioners, and for an entire generation he was the leading spokesperson for the Chicago style of symbolic interactionism. His writings "attempt to capture the fluidity of social action, the reflexivity of the self, and the negotiated character of much of everyday life" (Farganis, 2000:349). Blumer believed that humans construct their own actions and are free of internal drives. Instead, actions are a consequence of reflexive and deliberate processes determined by the individual in response to the environment. Furthermore, humans act on the basis of meaning. Meanings arise during the interactive process, which itself is mediated by language. Language allows individuals to take the role and perspective of the other in order to better understand the true meaning of one's own and others' behavior.

Symbolic Interactionism

As previously stated, Herbert Blumer coined the term *symbolic interactionism* in 1937. According to Blumer (1969):

> Symbolic interactionism rests in the last analysis on three simple premises. The first premise is that human beings act toward things on the basis of the meanings that the things have for them. Such things would include everything that the human being may note in his world—physical objects, such as trees or chairs; other human beings, such as a mother or a store clerk; categories of human beings, such as friends or enemies; institutions, as a school or a government; guiding ideals, such as individual independence or honesty; activities of others, such as their commands or requests; and such situations as an individual encounters in his daily life. The second premise is that the meaning of such things is derived from, or arises out of, the social interaction that one has with one's fellows. The third premise is that these meanings are handled in, and modified through, an interpretative process used by the person in dealing with the things he encounters (p. 2).

Blumer insisted that the first premise—that "humans act toward things on the basis of meanings"—is merely common sense and cannot be argued against. And yet, many social scientists ignore or downplay the importance of this reality. Blumer (1969) stated, "Meaning is either taken for granted and thus pushed aside as unimportant or it is regarded as a mere neutral link between the factors responsible for human behavior and this behavior as the product of such factors" (p. 2).

"Blumer views symbolic interactionism as a uniquely human process in that it requires the definition and interpretation of language and gestures and the determination of the meaning of the actions of others as well" (Farganis, 2000:350). For humans to interact, they must be able to communicate; to communicate effectively, they must share a language. The simple realization that humans interpret each other's actions is the foundation of symbolic interactionism. As a result, Blumer's symbolic interactionism has three premises:

> First, the actor indicates to himself the things that have meaning. The making of such indication is an internalized social process in that the actor is interacting with himself.... Second, by virtue of this process of communicating with himself, interpretation becomes a matter of handling meanings. The actor selects, checks, suspends, regroups, and transforms the meanings in the light of the situation in which he is placed and the direction of his action. [Third] Accordingly, interpretation should not be regarded as a mere automatic application of established meanings but as a formative process in which meanings are used and revised as instruments for the guidance and formation of action. It is necessary to see that meanings play their part in action through a process of self-interaction (Blumer, 1969:5).

The importance that Blumer placed on interpretation is an elaboration of Mead's argument against Watsonian behaviorism or any mechanical stimulus–response approach. Blumer and Mead insisted that both covert (subjective meanings, the thinking process) and overt (actual, observable) behaviors be analyzed when scientific explanations of human interaction are offered (Wallace and Wolf, 1999). Furthermore, gestures are a key element in the interpretation process: They help to shape an awareness context. This awareness context is illustrated in Glaser and Strauss's (1965) study of dying patients, in which the patients learned to interpret the gestures of their nurses.

Having established his three basic premises of symbolic interactionism, Blumer (1969:50) elaborated on the methodological implications of symbolic interactionists' view of human group life and social action. These implications led to four central conceptions in symbolic interactionism:

1. People, individually and collectively, are prepared to act on the basis of the meanings of the objects that comprise their world.
2. The association of people is necessarily in the form of a process in which they indicate to one another and interpret each other's indications.
3. Social acts, whether individually or collective, are constructed by actors' noting, interpreting, and assessing the situations confronting them.
4. The complex interlinkings of acts that comprise organization, institutions, division of labor, and networks of interdependency are moving and not static.

The fact that people act on the basis of the meanings that objects have for them presents profound methodological implications. It signifies that if researchers hope to truly understand social action, they must see the objects in the same way as do the subjects of their study.

Methodology

Symbolic interactionism is sometimes criticized as a theory devoid of empirical research principles. However, this was not the case for Blumer. Instead, he spent his entire academic life articulating his methodology. Blumer was acknowledged by the American Sociological Association in 1983 when was given the Association's Award for a Career of Distinguished Scholarship. Blumer was credited with elaborating and expanding the diffusion of field studies, ethnography, and qualitative sociology. Despite his lifelong attempts to clarify the methodological needs and guidelines that are essential to the interactionist approach, McPhail and Rexroat (1979), in their article "Mead vs. Blumer: The Divergent Methodological Perspectives of Social Behaviorism and Symbolic Interactionism," drastically misinterpreted Blumer's works. In his article "Mead and Blumer: The Convergent Methodological Perspectives of Social Behaviorism and Symbolic Interactionism," Blumer (1980) blasted the assertions of McPhail and Rexroat. He referred to their article as "flawed by serious misrepresentations" (p. 409) and as "completely wrong" (p. 412).

Blumer (1980) clarified his methodology on a number of key points. First, his approach to the study of human conduct was

> naturalistic: By "naturalistic" study I mean the study of conduct and group life as these occur naturally in the everyday existence of people—in the interaction of people as they associate in their daily lives, as they engage in the variety of activities needed to meet the situations that confront them in their day-to-day existence. This natural makeup of human conduct and group life covers what is done by individuals, organizations, institutions, communities, and collectivities as they carry on their lives (p. 412).

Second, Blumer stressed the need for exploratory studies for two reasons: (1) A great deal of human group life is obscured or is hidden from immediate notice; and (2) social scientists generally do not initially have firsthand intimate familiarity with the group life that they propose to study. For these two reasons, Blumer (1969, 1980) advocated and stressed the need for exploratory study. Exploratory studies are, by definition, flexible, enabling researchers to move in new directions as their study progresses, and they allow scholars an opportunity to form a close and comprehensive acquaintance with a sphere of life that is unfamiliar and hence unknown to them.

The symbolic interactionist approach to methodology is inductive, committed to the understanding of human behavior. The researcher is to gain in-depth knowledge of a group with whom she or he becomes thoroughly familiar. This approach is the opposite of the deductive functionalist approach, which begins with a set of hypotheses. The primary modes of inquiry include exploration (as described previously); inspection, by using "sensitizing concepts," that is, clear definitions of the attributes of the persons and objects under study; and qualitative analysis, or in-depth knowledge gained by interviews and observations of the group under study. The use of concepts is critical in scientific research. Blumer warned against vagueness in defining concepts.

> The vagueness of the concept means that one cannot indicate in any clear way the features of the thing to which the concept refers; hence, the testing of the concept by empirical observation as well as the revising of the concept as a result of such observation are both made difficult (Blumer, 1940:707).

Blumer suggested that students are often repelled by the vagueness of certain concepts and theories and therefore turn their attention to the more solid character of the natural sciences. Agreeing with Blumer, this text is an attempt to explain sociological concepts while showing the relevance of abstract theory to concrete events and people in contemporary society.

Social Theory

Blumer's focus on social theory was limited to theories grounded in empirical science. Blumer (1954) stated, "The aim of theory in empirical science is to develop analytical schemes of the empirical world with which the given science is concerned. This is done by conceiving the world abstractly, that is in terms of classes of objects and of relations between such classes" (p. 3). Although Blumer's theory is generally micro in its orientation, his conception of society provides a structural framework. Blumer (1969) freely acknowledged the role of structure in human society: "There are such matters as social roles, status positions, rank orders, bureaucratic organizations, relations between institutions, differential authority arrangements, social codes, norms, values and the like" (p. 75). However, Blumer (1969) made it clear that "social interaction is obviously an interaction between *people* and not between roles, the needs of the participants are to interpret and handle what confronts them—such as a topic of conversation or a problem—and not to give expression to their roles" (p. 75). Theoretical schemes are essentially proposals as to the nature of relations between persons and their social environments. "Theory, inquiry and empirical fact are interwoven in a texture of operation with theory guiding inquiry, inquiry seeking and isolating facts, and facts affecting theory. The fruitfulness of their interplay is the means by which an empirical science develops" (Blumer, 1954:3). Blumer wrote *Industrialization as an Agent of Social Change* in the early 1960s, but because he was never happy with this book, it was not published. Maines and Morrione, however, had it published posthumously in 1990. Maines and Morrione suggest that this book reveals Blumer's macro and objectivist side. Blumer wrote this book in an attempt to explain the role of industrialization as a cause of social change.

ERVING GOFFMAN (1922–1982)

Another important figure in the field of symbolic interactionism is Erving Goffman. Goffman was born in Manville, Alberta, Canada, on June 11, 1922. He graduated from the University of Toronto in 1945 and for his graduate studies went to the University of Chicago, where he studied with Herbert Blumer. He obtained his master's degree in 1949. His master's thesis was an attempt to use statistics to understand an audience's response to a then-popular American radio soap opera called *Big Sister* (Manning, 1992). His academic focus would shift dramatically from the quantitative approach in his thesis. One of his publications before his dissertation, "On Cooling the Mark Out" (1953), foreshadowed this dramatic departure. In this article, Goffman described the exploits of a con artist. Of particular interest to Goffman was the manner in which the con artist would attempt to "cool" the anger of an angry "mark" (victim of the con) in order to defuse a potentially hostile situation that may lead to violent confrontations or criminal charges. Goffman received his Ph.D. in 1953. His dissertation, entitled "Communication Conduct in an Island Community," was based on fieldwork on a remote Shetland Island with only 300 families as permanent residents. The close proximity of the residents provided Goffman an excellent social laboratory to study their face-to-face interactions. Goffman was fascinated by the various ways that islanders spoke with one another and with strangers and visitors. Goffman's dissertation would become his classic *The Presentation of Self in Everyday Life* (1959).

In 1954, Goffman served as a visiting scientist at the National Institute of Mental Health in Bethesda, Maryland. Posing as a ward orderly at the hospital, Goffman was able to conduct participant observation research on the interactions among patients, doctors, and administrators. This work would appear later in his publication *Asylums* (1961a) and deals with issues related to performance alterations found within total institutions. In 1957, he joined the department of sociology at Berkeley, where he became a colleague of Herbert Blumer. Goffman stayed at Berkeley until 1969, when he accepted a position as professor of anthropology and sociology at the University of Pennsylvania, where he taught until his death in 1982.

Goffman's works reveal a great deal of influence of the symbolic interactionist tradition (participant observation supplemented by data from case histories, autobiographies, letters, and so on), especially the influence of Everett Hughes, who is best known for his studies of occupations, and George Herbert Mead's concept of the self. The influence of Durkheim's analysis of ritual in *The Elementary Forms of the Religious Life* (1912/1965) can be found in Goffman's discussion of ceremonial practices in a total institution *(Asylums)* and in *Interaction Ritual* (1967). Goffman was also influenced by social anthropology, especially the works of W. Lloyd Warner (Collins, 1986). But Goffman felt that calling a symbolic interactionist was too vague and narrow (Manning, 1992). He created the field of dramaturgy; he helped to shape the sociology of everyday life, ethnomethodology, and conversation analysis. The recently developed Queer Theory and its analysis of self identity parallels the works of Goffman (and Mead), especially his analysis of the presentation of self and impression management (Green, 2007; Dunn, 1997).

Presentation of Self

Perhaps Goffman's most famous work, and his first major publication, is *Presentation of Self in Everyday Life* (1959). *Presentation of Self* is very much in the tradition of symbolic interactionism because of its focus on the individual as an active and reflective self capable of making a vast number of choices in determining how the self should be presented in the varied social situations in which it must perform. In the preface, Goffman (1959) stated that the perspective used in this book

> is that of the theatrical performance; the principles derived are dramaturgical ones. I shall consider the way in which the individual in ordinary work situations presents himself and his activity to others, the ways in which he guides and controls the impression they form of him, and the kinds of things he may and may not do while sustaining his performance before them (p. xi).

The dramaturgical perspective compares all human interaction to a theatrical or dramatic performance. Society is viewed as a stage where humans are actors giving performances for audiences. While *acting,* individuals attempt to *present* themselves according to their identity constructs. The "self label" is an identity that one presents to others in an attempt to manage their impression of him or her. Individuals deliberately give off signs to provide others with information about how to "see" them. This information helps individuals to define situations and direct courses of action. Picking up on signs and clues provided by others allow the acquainted and the unacquainted alike to proceed with their interactions.

A few important points can be made from this analysis. Individuals who are with unacquainted persons can present themselves as they want others to see them, and they may be successful in this presentation because the audience has no past knowledge of them and they therefore cannot be discredited. However, audience members will attempt to fill in the pieces of missing information and may or may not be accurate in their assessment of the actor. Actors with an audience of acquainted persons can successfully present themselves if their behavior is consistent with the audience's knowledge of them. Thus, a respected professor can gain the approval of students because they already know about that professor from other students and their own previous experience. On the other hand, a professor who has already been discredited as incompetent cannot present himself or herself as a respected educator. In another example, a significant other with a history of cheating (discredited) will not be able to present herself or himself effectively by saying, "Trust me; you know I would never cheat on you." On the other hand, when one is dating someone and has little knowledge of that person's past, and he or she states, "Trust me; I would never cheat on you," he or she will be judged on the basis of past experiences that one has had in previous relationships as much as he or she is likely to be judged on his or her own merits (presentation of self). Persons who present themselves may or may not be sincere in their performance. The audience members must always guard against the likelihood that the performers are hiding their true attitudes, beliefs, emotions, and even factual accounts of events. This is especially important because most people interact with others using certain presuppositions. "A *presupposition* (or assumption, or implication, or background expectation) can be defined very broadly as a state of affairs we take for granted in pursuing a course of action" (Goffman, 1983a:1).

The person performing implicitly requests that the observers take seriously the impression that is fostered before them. They are asked to believe that the character they see actually possesses the attributes presented. Performers may sometimes believe in the sincerity of their own performance, and at other times they may doubt the effectiveness of their own performance. For example, when interviewing for a job, the applicant may believe that her presentation was effective and showed a strong candidacy for the job, or the applicant may leave the interview believing she failed in the interview. Utilizing the correct props helps the actor in a presentation.

When interviewing for a professional job, it is advisable to dress appropriately with proper business attire. Gregory Stone (1962) conducted a study of appearance and dress in this context and concluded that dress is important in telling others who we are, or in announcing our identities. Proper dress is important in many settings, and how one dresses often influences the way one is perceived. If one goes to a judicial court, one should have a dignified manner and dress properly. How one dresses when giving a student presentation to the class, attending a business function or a ballgame, and going on a date indicates the presentation of the self and reveals how one is perceived by the self and by others.

Dramaturgy

Dramaturgy in sociology was developed by Goffman as a method of examining social interaction as a series of small plays, or dramas (Levin, 1991). This is an easy concept to grasp, as many individuals already recognize that their lives are filled with drama and constant turmoil—leading to such contemporary phrases as "She acts like a drama queen." As Deegan (1989) explained, "Dramaturgy is a powerful tool for analyzing social life. Invoking the dramatic world of the theater, it allows us to analyze the profane world of everyday life and the sacred world of extraordinary life" (p. 6). Goffman's analysis of the presentation of the self is guided by the dramaturgical perspective; that is, he attempted to explain human interaction by comparing life to a staged drama. Interacting persons are viewed as *actors,* who give *performances* for *audiences* in *settings,* by using *props* and allowing their true selves to be known in the *backstage* region; but they perform for others through their *appearance* and *manner* on the *front stage.* Goffman explained the use of the dramaturgical perspective in *Presentation of Self in Everyday Life* (1959): "In developing the conceptual framework employed by this report, some language of the stage was used. I spoke of performers and audiences; of routines and parts; of performances coming off or falling flat; of cues, stage settings and backstage" (p. 254).

During social performances it is common for actors to manipulate others and engage in *impression management* in order to give and sustain a particular definition of the situation. Impression management affects the *self,* which Goffman referred to as the *product* of a particular scene that is being played out. To protect oneself in the presentation of the self, impression management is used to guard against unexpected actions, such as unintended gestures, inopportune intrusions, and other unforeseen events that may influence one's performance. Performing social actors attempt to construct a particular definition of the situation and must therefore pay close attention to details (e.g., props, the setting) if they are to have any chance of success in convincing others of their role. Many times, social actors do not perform alone; they perform with others. Goffman used the term *performance team* or simply *team* to refer to any set of individuals who cooperate in staging a single routine (1959:79). "A team is not identical to a group. In fact, members of the team may not know each other; certainly, they do not have to like or care particularly about each other" (Curra, 2003:51). For example, professionals such as hairdressers and dentists who help with one's appearance would be considered team members. Co-workers may be viewed as team members as well. In a restaurant, hostesses, waiters and waitresses, buspersons, cooks, bartenders, and management personnel are all team members who attempt to make the dining experience of customers a positive one.

Two critical distinctions in settings affect the presentation of performance: the *front stage* and the *backstage.* Front-stage behaviors are designed to give intentional performances through the use of specific props to illustrate the role that one is playing. A surgeon needs a sterile operating room, a cab driver needs a taxi, and the waitress needs a restaurant to serve patrons. Goffman (1959) described the front stage as

> that part of the individual's performance which regularly functions in a general and fixed fashion to define the situation for those who observe the performance. Front, then, is the expressive equipment of a standard kind intentionally or unwittingly employed by the individual during his performance (p. 22).

The front stage is where the individuals perform a role as they wish to be perceived, whether that is their "true" identity or not. Most people who work do not see their co-worker's entire identity (e.g., a clerk has an identity and life beyond the work label); instead, workers perform certain roles in given situations (the clerk may also be a parent who needs to take care of a child or a member of a band that must perform at a club).

In the *backstage*, actors act as they really are and let their guard down (e.g., a police officer off duty and relaxing at home may wish to watch a ballgame and have a few drinks). "Here the performer can relax; he can drop his front, forgo speaking his lines, and step out of character" (Blumer, 1959:112). The backstage is a region closed and hidden from the audience, where the techniques of impression management are relaxed and the actors can be themselves. Thus, a waitress, hoping to earn big tips, will be polite and courteous and act as if she is genuinely concerned about the well-being of her customers (front-stage behavior), but in the kitchen, she may be making fun of the patrons with the cooks and busboys (backstage behavior). Goffman's attention to one's backstage behavior highlights how difficult it can be for actors to put on a good front-stage performance. Chances are there is a student reading this text now that has a number of personal issues to deal with (backstage performance for a student). Whenever anyone is confronted with issues that may affect front-stage behavior, it is important to be skilled in impression management. This successful separation of back- and front-stage performances is found in all social arenas.

The degree to which individuals separate themselves from a given role (front-stage–backstage separation) is described in Goffman's concept of *role distance*. As Goffman wrote in *Encounters* (1961b), if the role being performed by an actor negatively impacts his self-image, he will want to quickly distance himself from that role-performance.

> It is important to note that in performing a role the individual must see to it that the impressions of him that are conveyed in the situation are compatible with the role-appropriate personal qualities effectively imputed to him: These personal qualities, effectively imputed and effectively claimed, combine with a position's title, when there is one, to provide a basis of *self-image* for the incumbent and a basis for the image of his role that others will have of him (p. 87).

Thus, a judge should deliberate with an open mind but citing judicial precedents, a pilot in the cockpit is supposed to be calm, an air traffic control operator should be awake while on the job, and an accountant should be accurate while working on a client's income tax return form.

Stigma

Stigma is a term that describes a mark of disgrace or dishonor. Persons who are stigmatized are lacking in full social acceptance, and their self-identity is negatively affected by this label. In one of his most fascinating works, *Stigma: Notes on the Management of Spoiled Identity*

(1963), Goffman presented an analysis of persons who are unable to conform to the standards which society has established as "normal." Tracing the origins of the word *stigma* and its meaning, Goffman (1963) found that the Greeks originated the term stigma to refer to bodily signs designed to negatively label slaves, criminals, and traitors. Christians also used bodily signs, but they did so to label both evil and good persons. Today, the term stigma is viewed as a sign of disgraced, as in one has been stigmatized as a "cheat."

Stigmas are not simply physical markings (such as scars, moles, the lack of a nose, or obesity); they may be seen as "blemishes of individual character" in people who are perceived as weak, those labeled as dishonest, distrustful, afraid, cowardly, traitor, and so on. A stigma can be applied at the macro level as well; there are tribal stigmas of race, nation, and religion, which can be transmitted through lineages and equally contaminate all members of a family. In the weeks following the terrorist attacks of September 11, 2001, Arabs and Muslims were stigmatized in the United States. The same can be said of Americans in many Middle East nations.

Persons considered "normal" often discriminate against those who are stigmatized. Goffman said we believe that the person with a stigma is not quite human.

> We construct a stigma-theory, an ideology to explain his inferiority and account for the danger he represents, sometimes rationalizing an animosity based on other differences, such as those of social class. We use specific stigma terms such as cripple, bastard, moron in our daily discourse as a source of metaphor and imagery, typically without giving thought to the original meaning (Goffman, 1963:5).

Cuzzort and King (1995) concluded that

> stigmata fall into three broad classes: gross physical defects, defects in character, and membership in a social class or group that is not acceptable. A stigma may be acquired at birth or at any time during the life of the individual. Although there are variations caused by the kind of stigma or the time of its acquisition, most stigmatized persons share a number of common problems and common strategies for meeting these problems (p. 337).

A stigma does not dictate all the social performances of the person having it, but it precludes social acceptability in certain settings. Goffman's sociological analysis of stigma also involves the techniques used by "different" persons in dealing with the refusal of others to accept them. The stigmatized individual uses techniques that do not fit the general categorization of that specific category of stigmas. Goffman's examples include the Jew "passing" in a predominantly Christian community and persons who lie about their past but must constantly be on guard that the audience does not learn of the deception—this is referred to as a *discreditable stigma* (Ritzer, 2000c).

Stigma, then, is viewed as a type of deviance from the normal. In an early publication, "Embarrassment and Social Organization" (1956), Goffman stated that

> it is only natural to be at ease during interaction, embarrassment being a regrettable deviation from the normal state.... He who frequently becomes embarrassed in the presence of others is regarded as suffering from a foolish unjustified sense of inferiority and in need of therapy (p. 264).

Those who face public speaking may become flustered and feel discomfort, and being unable to cope with these feelings, they become rattled.

An individual may recognize extreme embarrassment in others and even in himself by the objective signs of emotional disturbance: blushing, fumbling, stuttering, an unusually low- or high-pitched voice, quavering speech or breaking of the voice, sweating, blanching, blinking, tremor of the hand, hesitating or vacillating movement, absent-mindedness, and malapropisms (Goffman, 1956:264).

People who fail in public speaking not only feel embarrassed but are also stigmatized. Given their desire to conceal then embarrassment, they may attempt to control their performance by maintaining poise or "hiding" behind the podium. Since individuals dislike feeling or appearing embarrassed, tactful persons will avoid placing themselves in such a situation.

ARLIE RUSSELL HOCHSCHILD (1940–)

"Arlie Hochschild is one of the most imaginative and productive feminist sociologists of the last thirty years" (American Sociological Association, 2011:1). She is also considered the founder of a new subfield of symbolic interactionism: the sociology of emotions. The basic premise of this field is to demonstrate that just as humans seek to consciously control their actions to fit the expected behaviors of a situation, they may also modify their emotions to conform to the expected standards.

Hochschild received her B.A. from Swarthmore and her M.A. and Ph.D. (1962) from the University of California at Berkeley. She taught at the University of California at Santa Cruz for two years and then returned to Berkeley, where, following a distinguished career, she became a professor of emeritus in sociology. Unlike the relative advantages that women have today in entering the college job market, Hochschild (1994) faced many obstacles in attempting to combine graduate study, an academic job, and child care during the late 1960s and early 1970s. Hochschild indicates that her focus on emotions was inspired by the "collective consciousness" of the women's movement and by Goffman's work. She did not take classes from Goffman while he was at Berkeley, but she had met him and wrote to him on several occasions. His positive response to her academic writings further encouraged her to continue her sociological work on emotions (Adams and Sydie, 2001).

Hochschild's work on emotions has extended Goffman's work in two ways. First, she expanded upon his ideas of embarrassment and shame to incorporate a wider range of emotional responses of actors. Second, she not only examines the outward signs of emotional responses like Goffman did, but she also examines the inner emotional life of the self (Adams and Sydie, 2001). Hochschild (1983) was critical of Goffman for ignoring the emotive self that exists separate from "outer watchers."

Hochschild (1983) described emotion as a biologically given sense; like the other senses—like

Arlie Russell Hochschild, founder of the sociology of emotions.   (Estrada Studio, Sigrid Estrada)

hearing, touch, and smell—it is a means by which we know about our relation to the world, and it is therefore critical for the survival of human beings in group life (p. 219). She believes that emotion is a unique sense because it is related to cognition: "Broadly interpreted, cognition is involved in the process by which emotions 'signal' messages to the individual" (p. 220). Emotional states such as happiness, sadness, and jealousy are viewed as senders of signals about our way of approaching the inner and outer environment.

Emotion Work

Hochschild's theory of emotion is an expansion of symbolic interactionist ideas but is designed to expand on the limitations of the work on emotions. Her theory encompasses a wide range of emotions and focuses on how actors attempt to manage (work at) their feelings. Hochschild referred to emotion work as the act of evoking or shaping, as well as suppressing, feelings within oneself. Hochschild (1979) stated, "By 'emotion work' I refer to the act of trying to change in degree or quality an emotion or feeling. To 'work on' an emotion or feeling is, for our purposes, the same as 'to manage' an emotion or to do 'deep acting'" (p. 561).

Hochschild explained that there are two broad types of emotion work: *evocation,* in which the actor's cognitive focus is on a desired feeling that is initially absent, and *suppression,* in which the actor's cognitive focus is on an undesired feeling which is initially present. Often, emotion work is aided by creating emotion work systems. An example used by Hochschild involves a person telling friends of all the worst faults of the person one wants to "break up" with and then going to those friends for reinforcement of this view of the ex-beloved. Hochschild (1979) stated that "emotion work can be done by the self upon the self, by the self upon others, and by others upon oneself" (p. 562).

Using a content analysis study of 261 protocols given by university students, Hochschild (1979:562) identified other techniques of emotion work:

1. **Cognitive:** The attempt to change images, ideas, or thoughts in the service of changing the feelings associated with them.
2. **Bodily:** The attempt to change somatic or other physical symptoms of emotion (such as trying to breathe slower, trying not to shake).
3. **Expressive:** Trying to change expressive gestures in the service of changing inner feeling (e.g., trying to smile or to cry). This differs from simple display in that it is directed toward a change in feeling.

Emotion work becomes most necessary when the actors' feelings do not fit the situation in which they find themselves. For example, a person who has recently received some very good news (like a new job, the birth of a child) but finds himself or herself in an environment that dictates displaying emotions of sorrow (e.g., attending a funeral) needs to suspend the feelings of happiness until he or she leaves the environment demanding displays of emotional sorrow. All of this is necessary because social guidelines direct how we are to feel in given social situations. Thus, persons who display signs of sorrow overtly may actually be quite happy covertly. In other words, outward behaviors can be, and often need to be, controlled, depending on social protocols whereas feelings can be masked and kept "hidden" from the audience members. Hochschild (1979) explained, "Feeling rules differ curiously from other types of rules in that they do not apply to action but to what is often taken as a precursor to action. Therefore they tend to be latent and resistant to formal codification" (p. 566). In short, individuals try to manage what they feel in accordance with rules.

Emotion Culture

The emotion culture consists of a series of ideas about how and what people are supposed to experience in given situations. This culture is filled with emotional ideologies about the behaviors, attitudes, and feelings that members should share (these are similar to subcultural expectations placed on members within their circle of associates). Hochschild stresses that individuals are often put in situations where a great deal of emotion work must be performed; consequently, a number of Hochschild's publications deal with various work and nonwork environments that expect certain levels of conformity.

In *The Unexpected Community* (1973), Hochschild provided a descriptive account of the interactions among forty-three retired people who lived in a small apartment building near the shore in San Francisco (the Bay Merrill Court Senior Citizen Housing Project). She described the social isolation that many senior citizens experience as the norm. In preindustrial society a large proportion of old people owned or controlled the modes of production and consequently maintained a positive sense of self. Postindustrialization has led to the decline of small business owners and has caused a corresponding lowering of self-esteem among the elderly because they find themselves relatively powerless. A large number of elderly people find themselves living in retirement homes as their last years disappear. They are an example of de facto segregation, living separate from the greater society and their immediate families. Hochschild (1973) explained,

> There is a well-known theory in gerontology called the theory of disengagement. According to it, as people grow older, they reduce ties to the outside world and invest less emotion in the ties they retain. In doing so they gradually "die" socially before they die biologically. This process, according to the theory, is "natural" and is linked to the nearness to death (p. 32).

Within the retirement home it is common to form a new sense of community that develops new norms and expectations of behavior. There is a structure of "parallel leadership." The members assist in the planning of activities, purchasing flowers for those who die, helping out the disabled among them, and so on. But there are always those who refuse to join in group activities beyond having their meals together—they become deviants within the community. Ingroups and outgroups are formed, rivalries are created, and some members are judged while others do the judging.

In *The Managed Heart* (1983), Hochschild presented data that demonstrate certain consequences for many airline attendants and bill collectors. "She suggests that while laborers doing manual work may become alienated from what they produce, laborers doing emotional work may become estranged from their own emotional expressions and what they actually feel" (Reynolds, 1990:195). The growing service industry has created a large number of disenchanted workers who are required to do a great deal of emotional labor. From her studies on flight attendants, Hochschild (1983) believes there are three categories of workers:

1. Those who have their identity tied wholeheartedly with the job.
2. Those who can easily distinguish their work selves from their non-work selves (or their "truer" self.
3. Workers who perform necessary job functions but separate their work deeds from their personal selves. Thus, they perform tasks as workers that they would not perform as nonworkers.

In *The Time Bind: When Work Becomes Home and Home Becomes Work* (1997), Hochschild provided an accurate portrayal of the growing reality for many workers: working at home. Working at home creates images of "freedom" from corporate and management demands. But if the home worker has children at home, the job becomes far more complicated. The home is being invaded by the time pressures and efficiencies of work (e.g., fax machines, home computers); while for some workers the workplace is becoming a type of "surrogate home." These workers find their primary "self" identified with their work/occupation; they tend to lack an emotionally stable home environment, or they simply have no life outside the office. Hochschild spent three years at a Fortune 500 company and interviewed workers from factory hands to top executives in a variety of environments, ranging from corporate meetings to the home and at the golf course. She stated that, "As the social worlds of work and home reverse, working parents' experience of time in each sphere changes as well" (p. 45). The implication is that a trend in modern life may be that few people feel totally secure either at work or at home.

Hochschild remains active in her academic work on emotional sociology and feminism. In her edited book, *Global Woman: Nannies, Maids, and Sex Workers in the New Economy* (2003a), Hochschild and associates take a look at the globalization of women's traditional role in society. In the introduction, Hochschild (2003a) addresses the issues at hand with regard to domestic workers:

> How can we improve the lives and opportunities of migrant women engaged in legal occupations such as nannies and maids: How can we prevent trafficking and enslavement? More basically, can we find a way to counterbalance the systematic transfer of caring work from poor countries to rich, and the inevitable trauma of the children left behind? (p. 13)

The contributors to this book address these questions. In her book *The Commercialization of Intimate Life*, Hochschild (2003b) describes a number of emotional scenarios, including the capacity to feel, working on feeling, the economy of gratitude, and pathways of feeling.

CRITICISMS OF SYMBOLIC INTERACTIONISM

Despite the seeming clear merit of the symbolic interactionist approach and its contributions to sociological theory, there are critical attacks from all sides. Psychologists interested in some of the same topics as symbolic interactionists tend to regard both the ideas and the methods of symbolic interactionists as lacking in rigor and replicable procedures (Stryker, 1987). Mainstream sociology is also critical of symbolic interactionism's seeming departure from the canons of scientific methodology and the quest for objectively verifiable generalizations, which are the cornerstone of traditional sociology.

> Symbolic interactionism places great emphasis on a methodology which focuses on subjective meanings, symbols, and interpretation in the determination of how actors arrive at their courses of action. Because the processes are mental and internal, some interactionists rely on subjective and introspective insights rather than readily observable and objective data (Farganis, 2000:350).

This unscientific approach is hence "little more than tenured journalism" (Fine, 1993:65). The unscientific criticism of symbolic interactionism is extended to the vagueness of many key concepts such as mind, self, society, I, me, and generalized other. Without specific parameters established for concepts such as these, it makes it difficult to conduct comparative empirical studies.

> Ethnomethodologists are critical of the symbolic interactionism derived from Blumer

> regarding the description of social processes produced in that vein as a total gloss of human social interaction, demanding in its place the minute description of behavior, in particular language behavior, without reference to the "mind," or "self" or "society" that were the conceptual mainstays deriving from Mead that organized accounts of social life in the manner of Blumer (Stryker, 1987:84).

The strongest criticism of symbolic interactionism seems to rest on its commitment to, and overemphasis on, everyday life and the social formation of the self while virtually ignoring social structure.

> There are times when symbolic interactionists write as if the poor, the homeless, and the victims of economic dislocations were not a part of everyday life. Class relations and the constraints they place on the lines of action open to individual actors are ignored or overlooked in favor of a more optimistic view of an open society in which negotiated joint action is the relevant characteristic of human action (Farganis, 2000:350).

Fine (1993) added, "Critics might accept symbolic interactionist dominance over the study of face-to-face interaction and microrelations but reject its relevance elsewhere" (p. 65). Adding to this, the role of power in social interaction is also missing from the symbolic interactionist approach. Collins and Makowsky (2010) criticize Mead, in particular saying that he "tended to ignore the ways in which humans dominate and manipulate one another in political, economic, and status hierarchies...and his schema neglected to analyze social class and mobility" (p. 158). Of all the criticisms of symbolic interactionism, this (its lack of focus on structure) is the fairest and is of greatest concern. However, it should be noted that the symbolic interactionist perspective *is* a micro approach and the focus *is* on individual social interaction.

APPLICATION OF SYMBOLIC INTERACTIONISM TO CONTEMPORARY SOCIETY

Symbolic interactionism meets the two key criteria for its sociological relevance, as it has practical application and sociological theoretical application. Symbolic interactionism has practical relevance to all of us if for no other reason than the realization that we interact with people through the use of symbols on a daily basis. And this interaction process begins in childhood and develops through the socialization process within primary and secondary groups. We are born into a family, form childhood playgroups, attend school, join clubs, organizations, or sports, date, form new friendships, and on and on. As we meet people, it becomes rather commonplace to try and ascertain how others evaluate us. That is, we tend to employ the "looking glass self" technique. Often, when our appearance and sense of self are not perceived as we see ourselves, a negative self-feeling may emerge. Conversely, we when are perceived in the manner we see ourselves, gratification is experienced.

Erving Goffman's dramaturgy is quite relevant to most of us as well. Everyone, at some point, interacts with others in the manner described by Goffman's as the front-stage and back-stage personas. When a young man meets the parents of his new girlfriend, it is best to behave politely and respectfully (front stage), making such comments as, "I respect your daughter very much," "When would you like me to have her home?" and "You have a lovely home," rather than saying what he might be thinking (backstage): "I can't wait to make out with your daughter," or "Your home is a mess." In a different scenario, job interviewing demands that interviewees put forth their front-stage persona by highlighting their job skills and relevant experience. This behavior is opposed to what might be one's true character (backstage) and is revealed by mentioning being fired for stealing and/or embezzlement. Examples of the relevancy to the dramaturgical approach are nearly limitless.

Symbolic interactionism remains relevant in sociological discourse today. There have been studies conducted on seemingly every possible variable that affects humans. For example, Jason Jimerson, a former student of Blumer's, in his study on the use of norms in pickup basketball, has attempted to develop more realistic images of interaction. Jimerson (1999) analyzed an entire conversation between people waiting to play an informal game of basketball to illustrate how a combination of perspectives emphasizing the internalization of norms, rational use of norms, and talk about norms can influence both participants and observers. Jimerson (1999) noted that Blumer's three premises of symbolic interactionism are relevant to the meanings in pickup basketball:

> The first premise...indicates that players act toward their games and their teammates in accordance with the meanings that those games and teammates hold for them. The second premise...implies that the meaning of basketball-related activities derives from or arises out of the social interaction between players. The third premise...suggests that the meanings in pickup basketball will be handled in and modified through an interpretive process used by players to deal with the basketball-related events they experience (p. 137).

By using the three premises and explaining how they relate to pickup basketball, Jimerson (1999) was able to "go beyond 'for fun' or 'for friendship' to explain how players cocreate the meaning of fun in basketball" (p. 138). While this was the extent of Jimerson's use of symbolic interactionism in this article, his analysis provided an interesting look at everyday life from a symbolic interactionism perspective.

Patricia and Peter Adler (2000) have extended Mead and Cooley's theoretical work on *the self* with their concept of the *gloried self*. The gloried self emerges when individuals become the focus of intense interpersonal and media attention, leading to their achieving celebrity status. The gloried self reveals the creation of a sometime unintended self-identity, even in the face of considerable resistance, as a result of the actor becoming a "public person." The role of the media is an increasingly important variable that was foreign to earlier social theorists (for the obvious reason of its recent development). The media are responsible for the creation of the *medial self.* Print and video coverage of "celebrities" has led to the development of such people as "reality-TV personalities" as "human-interest" stories. The public is not only overwhelmed with information provided by the media on these individuals (e.g., the Kardashian sisters, the cast of the Jersey Shore, and Paris Hilton); they *crave* it. And as a result, people become famous for being famous. Such people may actually possess a glorified sense of self as a result of their media self.

The study of gestures has led to a great deal of research on nonverbal communication, which has shown how people in different cultures use different nonverbal signs and align themselves spatially in different ways during their interactions. Recognizing these differences in attitudes is important in interpersonal relations. Susan Goldin-Meadow, a professor of psychology at the University of Chicago and author of *Hearing Gesture: How Our Hands Help Us Think* (2003), argues that nonverbal behaviors—smiling, blushing, shrugging—reveal our emotions while gesturing exposes our thoughts. Goldin-Meadow suggests that gestures are a part of communication and yet they are not part of a codified system. As a result, gestures are free to take on forms that speech cannot assume and are therefore free to reveal meanings that speech can accommodate. Gestures become important to the listener as well. We respond to gestures because the visual input that adds to what is being said. Gestures are a key to sign language communication, as the hand movements take on a significant meaning during human exchange. Why some people are more prone to talk with their hands than others is a quasi-mystery. However, Goldin-Meadow's (2003) research reveals that children sometimes communicate different ideas with their hand gestures than with their spoken words. In addition, children whose gestures do not match their speech are particularly likely to benefit from instruction in that task. Gestures, then, according to Goldin-Meadow (2003), provide insight into the unspoken thoughts of children and reveal a child's readiness to learn.

Undoubtedly, we have all received text messages and emails that are difficult to understand sometimes because of the lack of visual signs, such as gestures, that allow the reader to understand the emotion behind the messages. As a result, the reader may assume a certain "tone" in the message received that may or may not be true (e.g., "Based on the tone of your text, I thought you were mad at me"). To avoid possible misunderstandings, it has become commonplace for people to use emoticons to express feelings. Emoticons are text gestures that take on meaning for sender and receiver. Thus, if a message, or statement, ends with a smiley face, the reader is supposed to understand the intent of the message was civil, humorous, or certainly not meant to be interpreted as threatening or hostile. Conversely, an emoticon such as this: :-@ (anger) is used to express hostility or anger. Understanding emoticons has become a challenge in its own right as some people regularly use them with others who do not understand them. Receiving a text such as this: <3 (meaning: heart or love, as in "I love you") may cause confusion for readers who do not understand its meaning but bring joy to those who do understand the meaning. A symbolic interactionist study on the use of emoticons would reveal a great deal about contemporary forms of language.

The use of emoticons represents the tip of the virtual iceberg. That is, because of the nearly complete intrusion of electronics and social networking in the lives of people, most of us now have a *virtual self*. As Karin Cetina (2009) explains,

> A substantial and increasing portion of everyday life is spent not in the physical co-presence of others but in virtual spaces. The face-to-face domain, then, simply no longer has the structural importance it once had.... [There is a] need to conceptualize, within micro-sociology and the interaction order, the presence of different electronic media and their contribution to both "situations" and the coordination of interaction (p. 64).

Electronic interaction is becoming increasingly prevalent in our technology-driven society. In a 2008 study, 65% of Americans were found to spend more time with their computers than with their significant others (Kelton Research and Support, 2008). Most people, especially students, are likely to be involved in social networking sites such as Facebook and Twitter. Facebook allows people an opportunity to keep in touch and communicate with real friends and family, who may be many miles away. Although the friends and family are real on Facebook, the interaction is not face to face. Many people are involved in "virtual worlds" such as Second Life. In this kind of virtual world, people create "avatars," which are virtual characters that people use to represent themselves. In this virtual reality. people can socialize with others, exchange virtual goods and services, and participate in virtual group life. The question has to be asked, however: "Would you rather have real friends and a real significant other, or a virtual friend and virtual significant other where the benefits from such a relationship are virtual and not real?" Think about it.

Laura Robinson (2010) uses the term *cyber self* instead of *virtual self*. She suggests that the "symbolic interactionist framework is crucial to understanding the cyberself-ing process because the cyber self is formed and negotiated in the same manner as the offline self" (Robinson, 2010: 94). Utilizing the symbolic interactionist perspective articulated by many of the theorists discussed in this chapter, Robinson (2010) describes how we develop a sense of self through the eyes of those with whom we interact. However, the cyber self is created by people online who create profiles to represent themselves. They choose what information to share with the knowledge that other people are going to be able to access that information and form judgments based on this information. When choosing what kind of information to put into a profile, a person is consciously choosing how he wishes to represent himself and his identity. The norms and values of the face-to-face world are somewhat carried over into the cyber community. In cyber space, people can control their own profiles and profile photos, but they cannot control the text and photo postings of others. Thus, their identity can still be shaped by others. Goffman's work on dramaturgy is also relevant to the development of the cyber self. The idea of the front-stage and backstage personas is comparable to the "offline" persona and the "cyber" persona. When a person makes an online profile, she is presenting her front-stage persona—an attempt to control how others view her. One's backstage persona is the offline, or real, self. Participation in online virtual worlds like Second Life is an ultimate expression of a front-stage persona. In the multi-user domains (MUD) such as Second Life, people create a virtual, or cyber, self and act in manners not possible in the real world. (This concept was illustrated in James Cameron's 2009 blockbuster film *Avatar*.)

> By role playing, MUDers may adopt characters that express parts of the self that they have found necessary to suppress or efface in the offline world, given the forces of the "generalized other's" disapproval. Online, however, these users can invest MUD characters with traits that the offline society regards with contempt or disapproval (Robinson, 2010: 98).

In sum, it is clear that the application of symbolic interactionism is as relevant today as in the past. Not only do we still participate in face-to-face associations, but we also engage in virtual reality associations. And both forms of interplay will keep symbolic interactionism relevant to sociology for the unforeseeable future.

Summary

In this chapter, the micro-oriented sociological theory of symbolic interactionism was analyzed, beginning with its roots in evolutionism, idealism, behaviorism, and pragmatism. The diverse influences from both European and American sources have led to the development of a very intriguing school of thought. The core ideas presented by George Herbert Mead, Herbert Blumer, and

Erving Goffman center on the presentation of the self and the fact that human communication and interaction often involve attempts to manage one's image and environment. Recent developments in the interactionist tradition are more diverse and have expanded its original focus. Hochschild's research on emotional sociology goes beyond that of the early symbolic interactionists. And the most recent development in symbolic interactionism involves the examination of the "virtual" self— a phenomenon that Cooley, Mead, and Blumer would never have envisioned.

Over the past few decades, symbolic interactionism has become more accepted by mainstream sociology, many of its core concepts having been accepted. The rebirth in the symbolic interactionist perspective can be attributed to many factors, including the creation of the journal *Symbolic Interaction*. Many of the leading sociological journals typically include symbolic interactionists on their editorial boards and, as a result, these journals are publishing more research articles informed by tradition (Wallace and Wolf, 1999). The symbolic interactionists have done such a good job within their domain that "the process of interaction is probably the best-understood dimension of the social universe" (Turner, 2003:364).

Symbolic interactionism applies a number of sound methodological procedures to the study of human behavior. The first is the "naturalistic" approach, where the researcher observes firsthand the conduct of group life in the natural environment of the interactants. The second is exploratory studies, where the researcher does not bring any preconceived notions regarding the subjects. The third, a qualitative inductive method, allows greater flexibility in conducting research. These techniques of study remain valuable for many forms of study of the social world.

Symbolic interactionism is of great value to sociology, and it is a tremendous complement to more traditional, macro-sociological theories. As the primary micro-sociological theoretical approach, symbolic interactionism is taught in all introductory sociology textbooks and is a mainstay in social theory courses. As a result, symbolic interactionism constitutes the third of the "big three" theories of sociology; therefore, its relevance to sociological theory will remain indefinitely.

 Study and **Review** on **MySearchLab**

Discussion Questions

1. How would you evaluate symbolic interactionism compared to structural functionalism and conflict theory? That is, what are some of the advantages and disadvantages to this symbolic interactionism compared to structural functionalism and conflict theory?

2. Why do so many people turn to the virtual world for social interaction? What is the appeal of a virtual or cyber self?

3. Explain the significance of gestures to symbolic interactionists. Give examples of gestures.

   Explain the significance of language to symbolic interactionists.

4. Explain dramaturgy. Demonstrate how this theory is relevant to your life. That is, provide a scenario that demonstrates your front-stage persona and your backstage persona.

5. Describe Arlie Hochschild's work on emotion work and emotion culture. What type of impact will her work on emotions have as a contribution to symbolic interactionism?

MySearchLab® **Connections**

MysearchLab is designed just for you. Each chapter features a customized study plan to help you learn and review key concepts and terms. Dynamic visual activities, videos, and readings found in the multimedia library will enhance your learning experience.

 Watch on **MySearchLab**

▶ Melissa Milkie: Symbolic Interactionism

 View on **MySearchLab**

▶ Blumer's Model of How an Acting Crowd Develops

 Read on **MySearchLab**

▶ Blumer, Herbert. The Nature of Symbolic Interactionism.

11 Social Exchange Theory and Network Analysis

 Listen to the **Chapter Audio** on **MySearchLab**

Chapter Outline

Social exchange theory emphasizes people's abilities to act rationally in their social interactions. For that reason, some scholars refer to exchange theory as a rational choice theory. George Homans described the first three propositions of his explanation of human behavior in terms of "rational choice." However, this categorization often leads one to fail to acknowledge the many dynamics of this truly brilliant theory and its significant contributions to social thought. The rational choice distinction also implies that exchange theory ignores the role of emotions, which is untrue. Social exchange theory is one of the most overlooked of all the major schools of thoughts. It has elements of micro analysis and has been expanded to macro concerns via network analysis. Students should find the cost–benefits aspect of daily social exchanges with others quite relevant and enlightening, as the premise put forth by this theoretical perspective seems straightforward and plausible. Examination of group behavior is also quite fascinating ranging from our obligation to one another within the group to norms and expectations of specific behaviors like gift-giving. If nothing else, this theory deserves recognition as being the only theoretical perspective to dare suggest it can explain *all* human behavior. That bold claim alone should draw the interest of even the casual intellectual.

DEFINING SOCIAL EXCHANGE THEORY

Social exchange theory illustrates an effort to fuse the principles of behaviorism and economics with other ideas and apply them to the concerns of sociologists. Exchange theory originated during the 1950s, primarily through George Homans. Most of Homans' exchange theory can be viewed as a reaction against Talcott Parsons, Émile Durkheim, and structural functionalism in general. Exchange theory is positivistic in that it assumes that human behavior can be explained by natural "laws." Because there is an exchange involved in every interaction, this theory is concerned with the interactions between people and focuses on what people seem to be getting out of their interactions and what they in turn are contributing to the relationship. Exchange theorists believe that in every interaction something is being exchanged. These exchanges are not limited to the economic realm (money or commodities), for incentives to behave socially (to take action) also come in the form of approval, esteem, love, affection, allegiance, and other nonmaterialistic or symbolic expressions.

> When two actors at least occasionally satisfy each other's interests somewhat, and do so as an exchange, we say that together they form an exchange relation. An exchange network is a set of exchange relations in which every exchange relation shares an actor with at least one other exchange relation (Whitmeyer, 2001:141).

The larger the number of the interacting members, the more complex these exchanges become. Furthermore,

> Location in a network of exchange will affect the outcomes an actor experiences when actions in one relationship affect the course of negotiations in other relationships involving that actor. Negotiations comprise a sequence of actions by which agreement is (or is not) reached (Skvoretz, Willer, and Fararo, 1993:97).

When people work together, an exchange network is established. An exchange network is a set of exchange relations in which every exchange relation shares an actor with at least one other exchange relation. One's social location in the exchange network often dictates behavioral options. Those in power positions are better able to negotiate behavior during social exchanges. Exchange theory works on a basic premise that people continue to engage in behavior they find rewarding and that they cease to engage in behaviors where the costs are too high. With this backdrop, exchange theory can be defined as a theory that envisions social behavior as an exchange or activity, tangible or intangible, and more or less rewarding or costly, between at least two persons.

THE INTELLECTUAL ROOTS OF SOCIAL EXCHANGE THEORY

The intellectual influences on exchange theory include cultural anthropology, B. F. Skinner and psychological behaviorism, utilitarian economics, and rational choice theory. The creator of social exchange theory is George Caspar Homans; direct influences on his creation of exchange theory will be discussed later in this chapter.

Cultural Anthropology

At one time, cultural anthropology was a dominant academic discipline. Cultural anthropologists, such as Clyde Kluckhohn, insisted that every culture is unique, especially in terms of social rituals. George Homans disagreed and instead insisted that human nature is generally the same the world over. He believed that, in terms of basic behavioral modes, even remote Aboriginal societies engage in typical interactional patterns. While anthropologists generally wrote about the unique beliefs of Aboriginal societies, Homans took note of their similar behavioral patterns. Consequently, he concluded that societies are not unique and that people around the world are stimulated to act by common goals and aspirations. In other words, all people have common aspirations and similar purposes for their interactions with others. The goal of social science should be to unveil these ordinary behavioral patterns.

British anthropologist Bronislaw Malinowski (1884–1942) acknowledged social exchange considerations in his studies. Malinowski believed that exchange plays an important role in social life. He spent many years among the Trobriand Islanders of the Melanesian Islands, where he concluded that exchange is the basis of social cohesion. Malinowski (1926) found that Trobriand society is guided by the principle of legal status, which involves well-balanced chains of reciprocal services. The whole division of totemic clans is characterized by a game of give-and-take, by reciprocity. The concept of reciprocity became a critical element in Homans' exchange theory. The concept of exchange itself was influenced by Malinowski's discussion of the gift. Social exchange theorists and cultural anthropologists agree that the behavioral expectations associated with gift-giving help to bind society together because of mutual obligations members have with one another.

French anthropologist Marcel Mauss, a nephew of Émile Durkheim, wrote a short book entitled *The Gift* (circa 1924). Among the premises of *The Gift* is the idea that a number of gift-giving practices are universal; chief among them is the exchange process. Among the principles of gift-giving: The obligation to give gifts, as giving gifts is a first step in building social relationships; the obligation to receive the gift, as accepting the gift implies accepting a social bond; and the obligation to reciprocate, demonstrating social integrity. The ability to provide gifts to others is a sign of power, even if the gift has little monetary value, but especially if it does. The basic exchange principles involved in gift-giving (offer a gift, accept a gift, and reciprocate) have, more or less, remained constant throughout history. A number of episodes from the TV show *Seinfeld* discussed the etiquette of gift-giving in the contemporary era, but none perhaps as cleverly as "The Label Maker" (1995) episode. In this episode, the concept of "re-gifting" as a sign of disrespect (both to the original gift-giver and the process of gift-giving itself) is introduced. The person who uses a gift he or she received as a gift to a third person is called a "re-gifter" and the gift itself is known as a recycled gift. The Seinfeld characters also introduced the concepts of "de-gifting"—when the gift giver asks for his gift back, and the "gift grace period"—a period of time where a gift giver is allowed to ask for his gift back from the person he gave it to under certain circumstances (Delaney 2006). In a more serious analysis of gift-giving in the tradition of Mauss, Gregoire Mallard applied the theory to German war reparations and Europe's sovereign debt crisis. Mallard (2011) argues that the principles of *The Gift*

> help us understand the legal (the evolving conceptions of contractual law and sanctions), political (the anti-imperialist alliance management policies), and anthropological (the ritual and temporality of gift-making practices) dynamics at work in issues of reparations and sovereign debt cancellation that still agitate the international community today (p. 245).

The application of gift-giving to the micro and macro levels of behavior also demonstrates the broad range of human activities covered by social exchange theory.

B. F. Skinner and Psychological Behaviorism

Burrhus Frederic Skinner (1904–1990), a highly esteemed Harvard professor of psychological behaviorism, was another important influence on the creation of social exchange theory. Skinner was famous for his pigeon studies and the Skinner box (an instrument used to trace changes in animal behavior). Skinner viewed social theories such as structural functionalism, conflict, symbolic interactionism, ethnomethodology, and phenomenology as "mystical enterprises." He saw these theories as constructing mystical entities that distract sociologists from the only concrete entities of study: behavior and the consequences that make behavior more or less likely to occur. Culture itself is nothing more than a collection of human behaviors. Concepts such as ideas and values are useless. What needs to be understood are things such as costs and rewards.

B. F. Skinner was a pioneer in the study of operant behavior and was fascinated by the prospects of the control of behavior of animals and human beings (Martindale, 1988). (Homans would use the word *activity* instead of *operant*.) At the core of his psychology was the notion of the stimulus–response arc: When the subject is presented with a stimulus, a response is automatically triggered (e.g., when a golfer yells, "Fore" at a golf course, nearby golfers respond by "ducking" and protecting themselves). In his studies of pigeons, Skinner proved that by reinforcing a desired behavior, he could train his birds to perform bizarre stunts. For example, he was able to get his pigeons to perform a parody of table tennis by rewarding them with corn (Martindale, 1988). Both imitation and willingness to follow instruction are the basis of reinforcement effectiveness. Skinner explained that language, the most significant human skill, arises on the basis of differential reinforcement, through the building of a basic repertoire of words and expressions. The biologically functional child is capable of learning language and does so by imitating the sounds of the parents. Through reinforcement, the child is encouraged and rewarded for furthering her or his vocabulary skills. Even creativity is explained by the principles of reinforcement, by the positive response that originality elicits from most humans.

George Caspar Homans

George Homans treated the social exchange between Skinner and his pigeons as the paradigm of all social exchange. This point helps to explain why Homans' social exchange theory is heavily influenced by the behavioral school of experimental psychology founded by Skinner. Homans' sociology is an attempt to build a theory about social life from the basic behavioristic propositions of Skinner's psychology of operant conditioning. Homans (1967) believed that all behavior can be reduced to

George Homans, founder of Social Exchange Theory. (Harvard University Archives, UAV 605.295.7, Box 2, "H")

psychological organismic behavior and that those people who dislike a theory based on pigeons simply suffer from "sentimental" problems.

Exchange theory is deterministic. There are two types of determinism: strong ontological (nature of being) and weak epistemological (nature of knowing). Homans falls into the category of strong ontological determinism, which denies conscious beings. Homans felt that consciousness is metaphysical—a leftover of religion. There is no soul; the mind replaces it. For Skinner, the mind is a "black box" and people simply react to stimuli. Consequently, the researcher does not have to understand what is going on in an individual's consciousness (as phenomenology stresses); instead, the researcher merely needs to observe actual behavior. In regard to methodology, Homans' exchange theory advocates experiments. Experiments are used within an axiomatic theoretical format in which a few highly abstract statements lead to hypotheses that can then be tested.

Utilitarian Economics

Social exchange theory incorporates a system of logic based on sound elementary economic and psychological principles. Among these principles are the following:

1. Individuals seek to maximize rewards and minimize costs in an effort to attain the greatest profit possible. The rewards individuals seek, however, are based on personal tastes and preferences.
2. The more of something a person has, the less interested he or she is in having even more of it.
3. Prices for goods and services are dictated by market demand.
4. Goods and services are generally more expensive if they are supplied by a monopolist rather than by a firm in competition with others.

The first two propositions are clearly based on the psychological interests of persons. Individuals always seek a profit in any given interaction, and their course of action is nearly always driven by specific preferences, such as one's choice of whom to date or have as friends. The second proposition may need a little clarification. It is hard to imagine that anyone who has a lot of money, property, wealth, or fame would not want even more of it. A fan of music wants as many recordings as possible but generally has little interest in having multiple copies of the same recording. The last two propositions highlight the willingness of persons to pay market prices, especially if they must give up other goods and services. There are a few commodities that most people cannot live without and therefore are willing to pay any "reasonable" price for (e.g., water, food, gasoline, heating oil, and cigarettes). However, if they have options (because of competition), many will seek the best deal in order to maximize their profits. For example, gasoline prices are generally the same from one retailer to the next, and those dependent on automobiles for transportation will pay what the market demands. On the other hand, those who smoke cigarettes and can no longer afford the increasing price of the leading brands often resort to maintaining their habit by purchasing "generic" brands of tobacco.

Homans adapted and applied these basic economic premises to human behavior. He argued that the parties involved in a social exchange approach it with a variety of interests or values, such as material rewards (certain tangible goods and products) and nonmaterial rewards (enjoyment, power, self-esteem). The tobacco industry is obviously not concerned about the health of the customers; it merely wants to increase profits. Cigarette smokers either wish to take care of the addictive need of smoking or simply wish to enjoy the "pleasurable" experience of smoking. When all of the parties involved in the exchange are happy, group equilibrium, or balance, has occurred. Homans called fair exchange *distributive justice*.

Homans' exchange theory has its roots in utilitarianism. The utilitarian approach describes people as self-interested in the sense of maximizing pleasure and avoiding pain (this approach is similar to hedonism, which emphasizes maximizing pleasure and minimizing pain). Utilitarians argue that behavior is more or less a moral activity according to the amount of utility it bestows on individuals. Utilitarianism is a theory that the greatest good for the greatest number should be the main consideration in making a choice of actions. For example, during a war, the death of soldiers (and some civilians) is justified in the name of serving the "greater good."

Rational Choice Theory

Rational choice theory, developed largely through the efforts of James S. Coleman, is derived from neoclassical economics and utilitarianism (Ritzer, 2010). As the name implies, rational choice theory explains human behavior as the result of rational decision-making toward a desired goal. Actors pursue desired goals with the anticipation that the positive experiences (rewards) will outweigh the negative ones (costs). Actors will continue with courses of action, then, as long as they are receiving an ample amount of rewards (e.g., money, praise, affection, encouragement, hope). However, as articulated in the definition of social exchange theory, power differentials can impact the courses of rational action available to actors. Furthermore, each of us can only afford to pursue rational courses of actions if we have the means (e.g., money, looks, love, affection) to do so. In other words, we have to have certain assets in order to attain certain desired goals. When people act rationally, they will come to realize whether or not a desired goal is actually attainable. Thus, if someone is pursuing the affection of another, but the other just doesn't feel the same way, or is flat out not interested, one should rationally realize that the costs outweigh the rewards. As another example, a person earning $40,000 annually should not attempt to purchase a million-dollar home.

Taking into account how rational resource-maximizing actors can remain committed to the normative structure of groups, Michael Hechter (1987) has outlined his utilitarian assumptions of rational choice theory:

1. Humans are purposive and goal-oriented.
2. Humans have sets of hierarchically ordered preferences or utilities.
3. In choosing lines of behavior, humans make rational calculations about the utility of alternative lines of conduct with reference to the preference hierarchy, the costs of each alternative in terms of utilities foregone, and the best way to maximize utility.
4. Emergent social phenomena—social structures, collective decisions, and collective behavior—are ultimately the result of rational choices made by utility-maximizing individuals.
5. Emergent social phenomena that arise from rational choices constitute a set of parameters for subsequent rational choices of individuals in the sense that they determine the distribution of resources among individuals, the distribution of opportunities for various lines of behavior, and the distribution and nature of norms and obligations in a situation (Turner, 2003; Hechter, 1987).

As presented by Hechter (1987), individuals are, at their essence, pleasure-seeking, self-fulfilling beings, but they realize they often need the help of others to reach their goals. Thus, it is in the best interests (rational) of individuals to maintaining solid group relationships.

GEORGE CASPAR HOMANS (1919–1989)

It was Homans' belief that all human behaviors could be explained by behavioral psychology. To that end, he implemented a number of propositions, all psychological in origin, to comprise a theory of rational behavior centered on the assumption that individuals act to increase their rewards and decrease their costs. Homans was so confident that his five basic propositions could explain all human behaviors he challenged everyone to prove him wrong. For all those theorists who disagree with his basic assumption, Homans argued that the burden of proof rests on their shoulders (Martindale, 1988).

A Brief Biographical Sketch

George Caspar Homans was born in Boston to a wealthy Brahmin-style family on August 11, 1910. In his autobiography, Homans (1984) described the Brahmins as gentlemen and ladies who were conscious of their class standing. The Homans lineage consisted of three consecutive generations of successful surgeons, all residing in Boston. George was the eldest of four children. He would always value academics, and he took advantage of the outstanding library in his family home—something that can only happen in a financially privileged household. "Much of what I learned from books I learned not at school but at home, from our excellent library" (Homans, 1984:46). He also benefited from the top private schools in Boston until he eventually entered Harvard, following in the footsteps of previous generations of Homanses. In September 1928, Homans entered the freshman class. As an English literature major, he learned from Bernard DeVoto (1897–1955), who was his English instructor and tutor. Homans credited DeVoto with being the biggest single influence on his intellectual life. Homans was particularly indebted to DeVoto for introducing him to Lawrence Joseph Henderson. DeVoto and Henderson were friends, and it was Henderson who had introduced DeVoto to sociology. In turn, it was DeVoto who introduced Homans to sociology.

Homans earned his bachelor's degree from Harvard in 1932, with an English literature major. Homans' sociological background came from those with whom he associated at Harvard, but his real interest in the field came as a result of reading the works of Vilfredo Pareto. His exposure to the works of Pareto would forever alter his academic and professional pursuits. In 1934, Homans co-authored (with Charles Curtis) *An Introduction to Pareto and His Sociology*. With this publication, Homans was accepted as a sociologist in the sociology community even though he had little other knowledge of the field. Pareto's sociology influenced Homans' use of basic psychology and economics as well as his desire to establish deductive theories or explanations of social behaviors. Homans would never complete his Ph.D., but he did become a major sociological giant during his era. He became a junior fellow at Harvard from 1934 to 1939, and during this time he immersed himself in the field of sociology. In 1939, Homans became an instructor of sociology, remaining so until 1941, when he left to serve in the U.S. Navy in World War II. After four and a half years in the Navy, Homans returned to Harvard and was given the position of associate professor of sociology in the Department of Social Relations founded and chaired by Talcott Parsons. Homans did respect Parsons but would come to be highly critical of his style of theorizing. In fact, a long-running public feud would develop between the two colleagues that often manifested itself in books and journals. Homans believed that social theory should be centered on empirical observation and deductive reasoning. He felt that Parsons created theoretical constructs and then found examples to fit these preconceived categories.

Homans served as the president of the American Sociological Association (ASA) and in his 1964 address followed the tradition of making controversial statements about the state of sociology. Homans verbally attacked functionalists because of their rejection of the validity of using psychological propositions, by stating that functionalism was unable to generate any adequate explanations of human behavior. Homans spent his entire academic career at Harvard, and in 1988, while serving as professor emeritus, he was awarded the ASA's Distinguished Scholarship Award.

Influences on Homans

Because of his micro orientation, the most significant influences on Homans' work came from a variety of sources that attempt to explain small-group analysis. These influences include such disciplines as biochemistry, behavioral psychology, functional anthropology, utilitarianism, and basic economics and such social theorists as Lawrence Henderson, Elton Mayo, B. F. Skinner, and Georg Simmel.

As previously mentioned, Homans worked with DeVoto and it was he who introduced George to Lawrence Henderson. Henderson (a biochemist) was conducting research on industrial work with his colleague Elton Mayo (a psychologist). Mayo was the director of the famous studies conducted at the Hawthorne Plant of the Western Electric Company in Chicago. (*Note:* Homans dedicated *Sentiments and Activities* to the memory of Elton Mayo.) Homans conducted his own follow-up studies of the Bank Wiring Room at Hawthorne years later and concluded that workers share a body of sentiments. In his 1951 article "The Western Electric Researches," Homans described how workers know better than to turn out too much work. Any worker that did so was considered a "rate-buster."

> The theory was that if an excessive amount of work was turned out, the management would lower the piecework rate so that the employees would be in the position of doing more work for approximately the same pay. On the other hand, a person should not turn out too little work. If he did he was a "chiseler"; that is, he was getting paid for work he did not do (Homans, 1951:235).

In other words, workers expected new employees to work at the same rate of production as the established norm. This "expected" pace produced enough to keep management happy but controlled an impression that other workers were not working hard enough. Newcomers to the workforce were quickly indoctrinated into these shared sentiments in the workplace culture.

Homans' *The Human Group* (1950) was partially rooted in the functionalist tradition of Durkheim and of the British anthropologists Bronislaw Malinowski and A. R. Radcliffe-Brown. His subsequent work abandoned this functional viewpoint in favor of an exchange perspective. Homans eventually broke away from these influences after he met B. F. Skinner. Homans came to view Skinner's operant conditioning research as applicable to research on humans. Homans was not implying that animals and humans are similar in behavior, however.

> We begin at what may seem a long distance from human social behavior—at the behavior of individual animals. And a long distance it is: not for one moment do we imply that the behavior of men and the behavior of animals is the same. But if they are not the same they may yet be similar, and similar in just those ways that will most interest us (Homans, 1961:17).

Homans believed that the explanations of animal behavior are more firmly established than those of human behavior; therefore, it was logical to borrow from other sciences the knowledge that they had already tested (especially because investigators can more easily experiment with animals under controlled conditions than with humans). Skinner's psychological propositions became the foundation of Homans' social exchange theory. These ideas were fused with basic economic premises to yield a cost–benefits analysis of behavior.

Georg Simmel had an impact on Homans as well. Simmel was one of the first early major social theorists who attempted to identify universal characteristics of human behavior. He was especially interested in why people are moved to make contact with others. Like modern exchange theorists, he came to believe that their motive is to satisfy needs and pursue individual goals. Simmel suggested that even though people do not always receive equal returns, their interactions are always based on some expectation of reciprocity and therefore should be viewed as kinds of exchanges (Wallace and Wolf, 1999). Simmel, then, viewed social interaction as an interactive process involving reciprocal relations, or social exchanges, between actors.

In 1958, Homans wrote an article ("Social Behavior as Exchange") for a special issue of the *American Journal of Sociology* in honor of Simmel. Homans suggested that Simmel was the ancestor of postwar small-group research, which Homans had taken to the edge of a growing scientific sociology. Homans urged small-group researchers to integrate laboratory experiments with quantified fieldwork and to limit the propositions to psychological explanations. He proudly stated in *Sentiments and Activities* (1962), "I hold myself to be an 'ultimate psychological reductionist'" (p. 279). Furthermore, Homans (1962) stated that the special virtue of exchange theory is that it brings sociology closer to economics, the oldest and most practical of the sciences of humanity.

Social Exchange Theory

Homans' basic view was that the study of sociology should concern itself with explaining individual behavior and interaction. He showed little interest in consciousness or in the various types of large-scale structures and institutions that were of primary concern to most sociologists. The most basic premise of exchange theory is that people continue to engage in behaviors they find rewarding and that they cease to engage in behaviors where costs have proven too high. Homans believed that self-interest is the motive that makes the world go around and that individuals, just like Skinner's pigeons, modify their behavior according to the positive or negative reinforcement provided by their environment (Coser, 1977). The human social world consists of interacting persons exchanging rewards and punishments, and people continue to engage in relationships that they find rewarding.

However, when people become aware that they are being exploited or treated unfairly, they leave the relationship or quit the group (Homans, 1961). In Homans' industrial observations, he concluded that if workers feel that they are not being paid enough for their work, they may form a union, bargain collectively with the employer, or even go on strike. But in taking such action, workers must weigh the potential benefits against the potential costs: losses in pay and in friendship and perhaps even their jobs. Such choices are never easy, nor are the motivations always obvious. When multiple values are involved, the rational calculation of benefits and costs becomes very difficult.

In short, Homans' exchange theory is based on both behavioral psychology and elementary economics. It is a theory that "envisages social behavior as an exchange or activity, tangible, or intangible, and more or less rewarding or costly, between at least two persons" (Homans, 1961:13). Homans outlined five clear-cut propositions that he felt explain all human behavior. Although he admitted that his "set of general propositions gets no high marks for originality" (Homans, 1961:13), they do form the foundation of his social exchange theory.

The Five Propositions of All Human Behavior

Homans made it clear that his five basic propositions used to explain all human behaviors are psychological. They are psychological in two ways. First, they are usually stated and empirically tested by persons who consider themselves psychologists. Second, they are propositions about individual behavior, rather than propositions about groups or societies. Although a particular kind of reward may be valuable to members of one group and a different kind of reward may be of value to another, and since the pursuit of different rewards may require different action, the same proposition is used. The proposition "The more valuable the reward, the more frequent or probable the action that gets the reward" holds true for both. Even if people differ genetically and biologically, they still pursue the action that is most likely to be rewarded (Homans, 1967).

Homans (1984) believed that all human behaviors can be explained by five general propositions. Of these five propositions, four of them were from Skinner, while the "frustration-aggression" proposition was stated in 1940 by John Dollard in his book *Frustration and Aggression*. The propositions are as follows (Delaney, 2004: 269–271):

1. **The success proposition:** The principle of reward. If in the past an activity was rewarded, then the individual is more likely to repeat the activity in the present. The shorter the interval of time between the behavior and the reward, the more likely the person is to repeat it. Furthermore, the more often a particular action of a person is rewarded, the more likely the person is to perform that same action. This is referred to as the *success proposition* because the individual is rewarded for certain courses of action and activity. In *The Human Group* (1950), Homans attempted to make a distinction between action and activity in stating that an activity is "an *element* of social behavior.... It might be called *action,* if *action* had not been given a more general meaning, or *work,* if *work* did not have a special meaning" (pp. 34–35).

    Homans explained that in the pursuit of *rewards,* certain *costs* are incurred. "For an activity to incur cost, an alternative and rewarding activity must be there to be foregone" (Homans, 1961:59). A *cost* is a value foregone, and it is a negative *value.* "The cost, then, of a unit of a given activity is the value of the reward obtainable through a unit of an alternative activity, foregone in emitting the given one" (Homans, 1961:60). A *profit* is measured in terms of successful rewards minus all costs. Homans (1961) stated,

    > We define psychic *profit* as reward less cost, and we argue that no exchange continues unless both parties are making a profit. Even the pigeon, when it finds its rewards and costs nicely balanced, may try to get out of the situation or indulge in emotional behavior rather than continue its exchange with the psychologist. But our argument is more familiar in the field of human buying and selling (p. 61).

For example, an individual will not continue to purchase a regular product (something consumed often, such as coffee or soda) at a high price at one store if it can be purchased cheaper at a second store. Furthermore, the seller at the first store will not be able to reduce the price if she or he does not receive a reduction in the wholesale cost. Homans regularly used economic examples to demonstrate the validity of his propositions. Homans (1961) believed that the "principles of elementary economics are perfectly reconcilable with those of elementary social behavior, once the special conditions in which each applies are taken into account. Both deal with the exchange of rewarding goods" (p. 68).

2. **The stimulus proposition:** The principle of experience. If a similar stimulus, or set of stimuli, presents itself and resembles an originally rewarded activity, the individual is likely to repeat that course of action. The more often, in a given period of time, an individual's activities reward the activity of another, the more often the other will emit the activity. This proposition reflects the concepts of *value* and *quantity*. In quantity, frequency is measured by some sort of counting over a period of time, such as the quantity of desired activities during exchange. According to Homans, (1961),

> Frequency is a measure of the quantity of activity; it is the number of units of the activity that the organism in question emits within a given period of time: the frequency of pecking is the number of pecks per minute or per hour. Frequency is measured by some kind of counting and presupposes units of activity that can be counted (p. 36).

Value may be measured in terms of the "degree of reinforcement" an individual receives per exchange. Value is a matter of degree varying from one person to another, and it is equated with rewards. The connection between the stimuli and the action is subject to both generalization and discrimination. The individual works within the bounds of how similar a stimulus must be to past rewarding stimuli in order to be considered as valuable as the original. For example, if you buy a book on Amazon.com, a list of similar books will be suggested to you as possible books to purchase. Facebook matches "likes" among its members in an attempt to generate a sense of community based on similarity. However, this generalization of similar categories inevitably runs into a snag because each of us has a unique set of "likes" which results in our preference for some items, but not all similar items (discrimination). Thus, a "sports fan" may enjoy watching football, baseball, and basketball (generalization) but not enjoy golf and soccer (discrimination).

3. **The value proposition:** Reward and punishment, the principle of value of outcome. The more valuable to an individual a unit of the activity another gives him or her is, the more often he or she will emit the activity rewarded by the activity of the other. Thus, if one person highly values the company of the other, she or he is far more likely to engage in behavior that the other finds desirable. For example, she or he tolerates watching football on television because the friend likes football. However, Homans was quick to notice that this proposition needed to be altered, for if one person highly values the company of another but the other is always accompanying the original, a feeling of satiation may occur.

   Rewards, then, vary by degree of value. The value in question is always that of a given unit of the reward, no matter how that unit is defined. The variable, value, may take either a positive or a negative form. The results of an individual's behavior that have positive values are called *rewards,* while the results that have negative ones are called *punishments.* Action that has the result of allowing an individual to avoid punishment is rewarded by that result, and that behavior is more likely to be performed in the future. Consequently, there are two classes of reward: intrinsic reward and the avoidance of punishment. In addition, there are two classes of punishment: intrinsic punishment and the withholding of a reward. Punishment, or its threat, becomes a potentially powerful motivator of action.

   Homans combined these first three propositions to form the *rationality proposition,* or *rational choice.* These first three propositions assign value to our actions as individuals seek to collect favorable outcomes (rewards). However, Homans also believed that individuals calculate which course of action has the greatest likelihood of success. Thus, an individual may prefer one reward but realize the second (and less desired) reward is easier to attain. Throughout one's life, each of us will take chances on a highly desired reward even though we realize the odds of attaining it are slim. Nonetheless, in most cases, people choose safer courses of action that are more likely to yield at least some level of satisfaction. Turner (2003) created this formula to explain the rationality proposition:

$$Action\ (A) = Value\ (V) \times Probability\ (p)$$

If Action1 is valued at "10" (on some sort of personal criteria scale), but the probability of getting the desired reward is low (0.20) and if Action2 is less valued (say, 5), but the probability of receiving it is greater (0.50), the individual is more likely to take Action course #2. Using Turner's formula, we can see why:

$$A1 = 10 \times 0.20,$$
$$A1 = 5 \times 0.50$$

We can see that Action2 results in a reward yield of 2.5 and Action1 results in a reward yield of 2.0. Although this proposition may appear relatively complicated, humans use a system similar to this on a regular basis. Decisions such as choosing what type of cell phone, television, or automobile to purchase are all determined by a rational calculation of the costs versus the rewards. One may prefer one cell phone over another, but when the costs are calculated, a less expensive cell phone is purchased.

4. **The deprivation–satiation proposition:** The principle of diminishing returns. Homans (1961) stated that "deprivation and satiation are not, of course, separate variables but low and high values, respectively, of the same variable, and we have not stated two different propositions but a single proposition" (p. 19). In Skinner's studies, deprivation was explained in terms of the pigeon's going a long period of time without food. Hunger increased the desired activity of pecking at the lever to receive a food pellet. Homans believed that this principle could also be applied to human needs beyond (and including) food. A person who goes a long period of time (deprivation) without a desired reward (e.g., contact with a loved one) becomes far more willing to engage in behavior that will lead to the desired reward. When people miss one another so much that they "ache" without the other, they will alter their behavior so that they can be with the desired one. This idea is somewhat similar to the adage that absence makes the heart grow fonder. However, an individual who is forced to go a long period of time without the desired reward will lose interest and move on, seeking other rewards from other sources. Homans referred to this as changes in kind of activity. Since human activities are not standardized exchanges incapable of change, people will change their activities to increase profits and rewards. Thus, when engaging in the dating ritual of "playing hard to get," one must be prepared for the other's simply giving up and moving on.

    When someone has more than enough of the desired reward, satiation takes place and the motivation to act a certain way is missing. In Skinner's studies, when a pigeon had had an abundance of food, its need to participate in the desired behavior (pecking at the target) disappeared. This proposition can be applied to humans in a wide variety of activities. For example, when two people spend a great deal of time together, they may grow tired of the relationship. In some cases, "familiarity breeds contempt" (as is generally the case when two bitter rivals are placed in close proximity).

Homans further elaborated that the deprivation–satiation proposition is not very precise and is subject to the value of the reward in question in relation to the time it was last presented. Food and sex satiate a person quickly, but they soon recover their value, whereas most persons are not so easily satiated by money, power, or status.

5. **The aggression–approval proposition:** The principle of distributive justice. Homans (1961) noted that "when a behavior does not receive the expected reward, or is punished unexpectedly, the response is anger or aggression. Interestingly, the aggressor will find such aggression rewarding" (p. 37). Additionally, when a person's action receives a greater reward than expected, or he or she does not receive a punishment when expected, he or she will be pleased and is more likely to perform approving behavior.

   The principle of *distributive justice* is applied here. In Skinner's pigeon's study,

   > When a pigeon pecks but gets no grain, although the stimulus-conditions resemble those under which it was previously rewarded for pecking, the pigeon displays what looks to a human observer for all the world like anger and frustration: it turns away from the target, flapping its wings and cooing hurriedly (Homans, 1961:72–73).

This principle certainly applies to humans. When individuals do not receive the same rewards as others, frustration occurs. For example, if two students both receive the same numerical grade, they expect the same letter grade. If one receives a grade lower than the other, frustration and anger will occur. As Homans (1961) explained, humans

> express anger, mild or severe, when they do not get what their past history has taught them to expect. The more often in the past an activity emitted under particular stimulus-conditions has been rewarded, the more anger they will display at present when the same activity, emitted under similar conditions, goes without its rewards: precedents are always turning into rights (p. 73).

This anger and frustration are especially directed at the person responsible for the distribution of the reward. Additionally, the more unfairly one is treated, the more frustrated and angry one becomes.

The Group System

Homans identified a number of specific elements that comprise the group system: activity, interaction, sentiment, and norms. *Activity* refers to the behavior of group members. *Interaction* involves directed behavior toward one or more members of the group. Group *sentiment* refers to the feelings of group members. The *norms* of the group are a code of behavior adopted consciously or unconsciously by the group. Homans' group system is in the tradition of Pareto, who viewed a group as external in contrast to the internal system. The group is external in that it responds to the needs of the outside environment. These environmental needs can be physical, technical, and/or social. The group is an internal system because the elements of behavior are mutually dependent.

In *The Human Group* (1950), Homans defined a group as "a number of persons who communicate with one another often over a span of time, and who are few enough so that each person is able to communicate with all the others not at secondhand, through other people, but face to face" (p. 1). Homans analyzed a series of previously conducted studies of groups found in a variety of environments, including families, school cliques, and co-workers.

Power and Authority

Homans (1961) felt that a person who influences other members has authority. An individual earns authority by acquiring esteem and acquires esteem by rewarding others. Similarly, power can be defined as the ability to provide valuable rewards. Those with power and authority are small in number, and the smallness of the number is the seed for future conflict. The leader, when directing others, inevitably causes the members to incur costs. The leader's also incurring costs will help to prevent conflict. For example, workers are less upset when the boss tells them they have to work late if the boss also stays to work late. When the rewards that are distributed seem fair (distributive justice), the individual is satisfied, especially if the reward is received within a given period of time. Humans act as if they find it valuable to realize fair exchange, and they will express emotion toward this end (the pursuit of distributive justice).

George Homans' greatest contribution to sociological theory is his development of social exchange theory. His focus was primarily on the individual and social groups, but his ideas helped to influence such exchange theorists as Peter Blau, Karen Cook, and Richard Emerson. These theorists helped to transform exchange theory from its micro-oriented roots to addressing issues at the macro level.

PETER BLAU (1918–2002)

Peter Blau was an Austrian-born, American sociologist who expanded Homans' social exchange theory of analyzing reciprocal relationships between individuals to larger structures of associations.

A Brief Biographical Sketch

Peter Blau was born in Vienna, Austria, on February 7, 1918, and died on March 12, 2002. He emigrated to the United States in 1939, and after serving in the military during World War II (earning a Bronze Star), he became an American citizen in 1943. Blau received his undergraduate sociology degree from Elmhurst College (Illinois) in 1942 and his Ph.D. from Columbia University in 1952. He taught at Wayne State University, Cornell University, the University of Chicago (from 1953 to 1970), Columbia University (becoming a professor of sociology), and then at the University of North Carolina at Chapel Hill. Blau received many honors during his career, including serving as president of the American Sociological Association in 1964 and winning the Sorokin Award from the ASA in 1968 for a book he co-authored with Otis Dudley, entitled *The American Occupational Structure* (1967). He wrote many articles and books. It was, however, his *Exchange and Power in Social Life* (1964) that propelled Blau's status as a major theorist and is of greatest relevancy to exchange theory and, consequently, this chapter.

Blau's Exchange Theory

In *The Organization of Academic Work* (1973), Blau discussed the role of theory. "A formal theory from which empirical predictions can be logically deduced plays the dominant role in research that is designed to test the predictions and thereby indirectly the theory" (p. 45). Thus, a theory needs to be presented in such a way that it allows itself to be tested empirically. Exchange theory is such a theory.

In *Exchange and Power in Social Life,* Blau acknowledged his devotion to Simmel's idea of exchange. Blau described social exchange as a central principle in social life, which is derived from primitive terms and from which complex social forces are derived. Blau stated that social exchange theory can explain behavior in groups as well as in individuals. In short, he believed that social exchange may reflect any behavior oriented to socially mediated goals. In Chapter 1 of *Exchange and Power,* Blau discussed the structure of social associations. He analyzed Durkheim's conception of suicide as a social fact by suggesting that a social fact emerges only when it has been transformed by association. Association itself is an active factor in producing social behavior. It creates social life, and it assists social integration by creating trust, encouraging differentiation, enforcing conformity to group norms, and establishing collective values. Thus, social exchange creates bonds of friendship and establishes social positions of subordination and domination.

Processes of social association can be conceptualized, if one follows Homans' lead, as an exchange of social activity, tangible or intangible, rewarding and costing, between at least two persons (Blau, 1964). Exchanges of gifts in simpler societies served latent functions of establishing bonds of friendship and establishing superiority over others. The basic foundation of any social exchange is one person's offering another person a reward at a certain cost. The relationship continues as long as both persons find the exchange beneficial or necessary. A variety of conditions affect social exchange: the stage in development and the character of the relationship between the exchange partners; the nature of the benefits in the transactions; the costs of providing them; and the social context in which the exchanges take place.

According to Blau, the social exchange process also creates opportunities for impression management. People want to be seen in a certain way to maximize their potential profits. Impressions often come at a cost to the actor, as he or she must perform the role that brings the most rewards. For example, someone who is in the early stages of dating generally behaves in a manner that ultimately brings the greatest rewards (e.g., additional dates, sex). Blau acknowledged, as Homans did, that in any relationship, one person almost always has more power than the other. Blau (1964) referred to Willard Waller's principle of least interest, whereby the partner who is less committed to the relationship has an advantage over the person who is more involved in the relationship.

Blau's conception of *reciprocity* in exchange implies the existence of balancing forces that create a strain toward equilibrium. The simultaneous operations of diverse balancing forces produce imbalances in social life, and the resulting dialectic between reciprocity and imbalance gives social structures their distinctive nature and dynamics (Blau, 1964). Humans choose between potential associates or courses of action by evaluating the experience or expected experiences with each in terms of preference ranking, and then they select the best alternative. According to Blau, social attraction is the main force that draws people together. *Attraction* is defined in terms of potential rewards for participating in the social exchange. When there are inadequate rewards, the social ties between individuals and groups is (more) likely to deteriorate. In other words, individuals continue to associate with others as long as they are getting something (rewards) out of the relationship. Irrational as well as rational behaviors are governed by these considerations. Of particular importance is the realization that not all individuals (or groups) value the same alternatives equally. Thus, one person may be willing to do just about anything to maintain the company of another, while those outside the relationship may wonder why the first person would even want to associate with the other (as in, "What does he see in her?"). Blau also makes distinctions between intrinsically rewarding exchanges (love relationships) and associations primarily concerned with extrinsic benefits (getting paid to tutor a student).

Unlike Homans, Blau never listed specific propositions designed to explain all human behaviors. Jonathan Turner (2003), however, extracted basic principles from Blau's theories and established what he called "Blau's Implicit Exchange Principles." They are listed here:

1. **Rationality principle:** People are more likely to participate in activities they find rewarding than any other activity.

2. **Reciprocity principles:** The more often people exchange rewards with one another, the stronger the reciprocal obligations are between them. The stronger the bond between reciprocal persons, the harsher the sanctions are when the norms or reciprocity are violated.

3. **Justice principles:** Solid exchange relations have an expectation of fair exchange. People who are not treated fairly are likely to seek sanctions against the violators of fair exchange.

4. **Marginal utility principle:** The more expected rewards have been forthcoming from the emission of a particular activity, the less valuable the activity is and the less likely its emission is.

5. **Imbalance principle:** The more stabilized and balanced one set of exchange relations among social units is, the more likely other exchange relations are to become imbalanced and unstable.

This impressive review by Turner (2003) provides a valuable summation of Blau's exchange theory.

Group Formation

Social exchange must be directed toward other persons; consequently, social interaction begins with social groups. Individuals choose what groups to interact with based on the rewards they can receive. Groups that offer the greatest number of rewards are the ones sought out, whereas "closed" groups, or groups that offer few rewards, will be ignored. Groups that offer rewards are attractive, and because a group is attractive, individuals want to be accepted. Of course, the individual who wishes to join an attractive group needs to provide the group members with rewards too. A good example would be pledges to a fraternity or sorority. A fraternity that has a good reputation and therefore is capable of offering many rewards (e.g., job connections, good house parties) will be sought out by many who want to be pledges, and who will attempt to impress the organization with their own ability to provide rewards (e.g., athletic ability, being from a politically powerful family).

The formation of a group involves the development of integrative bonds that unite individuals in a cohesive unit. Some of the integrative bonds discussed by Blau (1964) are the following:

1. **Impressing others:** Expectation of rewards makes association attractive. Strategies that appear impressive include taking risks, performing role distance, and being able to exhibit both strain and ease, depending on the social occasion.

2. **Social approval:** Humans are anxious to receive social approval for their decisions and actions, opinions, and suggestions. The approving agreement of others helps to confirm their judgments, to justify their conduct, and to validate their beliefs. Preoccupation with impressing others impedes both expressive involvement and instrumental endeavors. Restraints imposed by social approval are confined to circles of significant others.

3. **Attractiveness:** Opinions that are met with approval, and one's approval of another's opinion, increase one's level of attractiveness. We all like to associate with people who agree with our opinions. On the other hand, serious and persistent conflicts of opinions lead to personal rejection (unattractiveness). The role of first impressions is involved in perceived attractiveness, for impressions may be self-fulfilling as well as self-defeating. One must be cautious of first impressions, for their reflection may be distorted. Bluffing is a mechanism utilized by some people in hopes of creating a positive early impression. However, the cost of having a bluff called may be too high. For example, claiming to be economically wealthier than one really is can be embarrassing when the person of one's desire agrees to a date at an expensive restaurant where one cannot afford to dine (bluff was called).

4. **Love:** Love is the extreme case of intrinsic attraction. Love appears to make human beings unselfish, since they themselves enjoy giving pleasure to those they love, but this selfless devotion generally rests on an interest in maintaining the other's love. The exchange process is most evident in love attachments, but the dynamics are different because the specified rewards are not as clear as in social exchanges. In love relationships, there quite often is one person who is "more in love" than the other (the principle of least interest). The person less in love has the power advantage and may manipulate this advantage to gain more rewards. Although expressions of affection stimulate another's love, freely giving rewards depreciates their value, which is the dilemma of love.

Group Cohesion and Power

Group cohesion promotes the development of consensus on normative standards and the effective enforcement of these shared norms because integrative ties of fellowship enhance the significance of the informal sanctions of the group (such as disapproval and ostracism) to its individual members. Whereas social control strengthens the group as a whole, social support strengthens its members individually, particularly in relation to outsiders (Blau, 1964). Blau (1955) stated, "Common expectations and orientations arise or crystallize in the course of interaction and subsequently influence it" (p. 144).

Simmel's discussion of the dyad and the triad influenced Blau's conception of power. The simple addition of a third person to a two-person group radically changes the structure of the group. The power of an individual over another depends entirely on the social alternatives, or the lack of alternatives, of the subjected individual. Unilateral exchange generates differentiation of power. The exercise of power, as judged by norms of fairness, evokes social approval or disapproval, which may lead to legitimate organization and to social opposition, respectively. Collective approval of power legitimizes that power; collective disapproval of power engenders opposition. Furthermore, equilibrium forces on one level are disequilibrating forces on another (Blau, 1964).

Turner (2003) summarized Blau's conditions for the differentiation of power in social exchange:

1. The fewer services people must exchange for the receipt of particularly valued services, the more compliance those providing these particularly valued services can extract.
2. The fewer the alternative sources of rewards, the more compliance those providing valuable services can extract.
3. The less those receiving services from particular individuals can employ physical force and cohesion, the more compliance those providing the services can extract.
4. The less those receiving the valuable services can do without them, the more compliance those providing the services can extract.

Blau successfully demonstrated the role of power at the dyad level, the group level, and the social structural level. Power differential inevitably leads to the potential for conflict. The group system, at all levels, must find a way to successfully integrate differences in power and authority among group members if it is to succeed in maintaining its structure.

Bureaucracy and Social Organization

Blau attempted to bridge the micro–macro gap of social theory. Due to this, he realized that sociological analysis must be of bureaucracy and social organizations; it cannot rely on an examination of individual social exchanges. In his *Bureaucracy in Modern Society* (1956),

Blau described how frustrating it can be to deal with bureaucracies and red tape. Imagine how he would react today, especially in light of the growing number of automated phone processes and prerecorded menus that individuals must deal with before they can speak to a "live" person. It is as if organizations want nothing to do with their customers. Even bank tellers prefer customers to make deposits at and small withdrawals from an automatic teller machine (ATM), presumably freeing them for more important transactions.

Blau (1956) defined a *bureaucracy* as a "type of organization designed to accomplish large-scale administrative tasks by systematically coordinating the work of many individuals" (p. 14). He added,

> This concept, then, applies to organizing principles that are intended to improve administrative efficiency and that generally do so, although bureaucratization occasionally has the opposite effect of producing inefficiency. Since complex administrative problems confront most large organizations, bureaucracy is not confined to the military and civilian branches of the government but is also found in business, unions, churches, universities, and even in baseball (p. 14).

Bureaucracy is the result of the increasing rationalization of society. The consequences of rationalization have often been deplored, although there is no conclusive proof that such things as alienation actually occur because of it (Blau, 1956). Nearly sixty years ago, Blau wrote that learning to understand bureaucracies is more important than it ever had been, and that the study of bureaucratic organization makes a particular contribution to the advancement of sociological knowledge.

Blau's study of bureaucracy began with *The Dynamics of Bureaucracy* (1955), in which he presented systematic investigations of the bureaucratic structure and function, utilizing the case study method. Blau (and Scott) used the comparative approach in *Formal Organizations* (1962) to explore the role of modern humans in the organizational society. He stated, "Our ability to organize thousands and even millions of men in order to accomplish large-scale tasks—be they economic, political, or military—is one of our greatest strengths" (p. ix). In *The American Occupational Structure* (1967), co-authored with Otis Dudley Duncan, Blau provides a systematic analysis of the American occupational structure. "By analyzing the patterns of these occupational movements, the conditions that affect them, and some of their consequences, we attempt to explain part of the dynamics of the stratification system in the United States" (Blau and Duncan, 1967:1). In *The Organization of Academic Work* (1973), Blau used quantitative empirical data on 115 American universities and colleges to present a systematic study of the relationship between bureaucracy and scholarship, particularly the influences of the administrative structure on academic work. Blau examined how the administrative structure establishes itself in order to organize the many students and faculty members in a university or college. In *On the Nature of Organizations* (1974), Blau presented an overview of his work on organizations and organizational power over twenty years.

Throughout his analysis of organizations, Blau examined the role of organizational substructures, and he found that the system still depends on costs and rewards. If the organization does not make a profit, or a large enough profit, it fails. When it can no longer provide rewards, it has failed. Thus, the principles of exchange theory apply even at the organizational macro level.

KAREN COOK (1946–)

Among the most notable contributions that Karen Cook has made to social thought is her attempt to bridge the micro–macro gap inherent with all social theories. Following in the tradition of Peter Blau and Richard Emerson, Cook has articulated her own version of social exchange theory.

A Brief Biographical Sketch

Karen Schweers Cook was born on July 25, 1946, in Austin, Texas, where she was raised. Karen and her twin brother, Ken, attended college together as undergraduates at Stanford University. She received her bachelor's degree in sociology with distinction and honors in 1968. She remained at Stanford and earned her master's degree in 1970. Cook then served as acting instructor in the Sociology Honors Program and research associate for the Laboratory of Social Research at Stanford. Cook received her Ph.D. with distinction in sociology from Stanford in 1973. After teaching at Washington for two decades, Cook became a Professor of Sociology at Stanford in 1998.

In the area of publishing, Cook generally co-edits and co-authors—instead of producing singled-authored works—a number of books and articles. Cook has published extensively in the area of social exchange theory, social justice, power and trust in social relationships, and social psychology. Among her most recent co-edited books are *Trust and Distrust in Organizations: Emerging Perspectives* (2004), *eTrust: Forming Relationships in the Online World* (2009), and *Whom Can We Trust? How Groups, Networks, and Institutions Make Trust Possible* (2009).

Influences on Cook

Cook is primarily an exchange theorist who is attempting to establish empirical links between specific behaviors and traditional exchange theory. As an exchange theorist, Cook has been influenced by many of the traditional sociologists associated with the field, especially George Homans, Peter Blau, and Richard Emerson.

Among Homans' concepts, Cook was interested in his idea of distributive justice. In an article titled "Distributive Justice, Equity, and Equality" (1983), Cook and Hegtvedt provided a general review of the research conducted since the mid-1980s on individuals' ideas of equity and distributive justice and their reactions to inequality. Cook and Hegtvedt concluded that micro-level concepts of distributive justice have certain limitations, and they suggested that macro-level concepts should be used to integrate equity and distributive justice theories with the grand socio-logical theories of power, conflict, and collective action. If this integration could be achieved, it would bring notions of justice to the forefront in the analysis of social change.

Cook was employed by Peter Blau. Blau had extended the ideas of Homans, especially agreeing with his analysis of individual behavioral processes. However, Blau and Cook were interested in the general characteristics of social structure, rather than just an analysis of small or informal groups, and established social institutions and organizations. Thus, where Homans' focus is on elementary forms of behavior, Blau and Cook's primary focus was the analysis of complex structures. Blau (1964) hoped to establish "an understanding of social structure on the basis of an analysis of the social processes that govern the relations between individuals and groups" (p. 2).

In 1972, Richard Emerson published two essays on power-dependence relations. So important were these essays that they "marked the beginning of a new stage in the develop-ment of social exchange theory" (Molm and Cook, 1995:215). Power is critical in exchange theory, and Emerson articulated this very fact. Like Blau, Emerson has attempted to create a link between the micro and macro aspects of social theory. Emerson's exchange theory has been expanded by his study of "exchange social structures" (Cook, 1987). The actors in Emerson's macro-level exchange theory can be individuals as well as collectivities (such as groups, societies). Cook (1987) indicated that the idea of exchange network structures is critical to the micro–macro link.

Exchange Theory

Like Emerson, Cook began with the basic, micro-level premises of exchange theory. In general, exchange theory is based on the idea that in any social relationship, people calculate the benefits and costs associated with their interaction. People seek to minimize the costs and maximize the rewards, and when a situation is identified as rewarding, attempts to ensure the continuation of the relationship manifest themselves. Cook has examined the costs and reward structures found in social interactions.

For example, Cook examined the relationship between general exchange and social dilemmas. A social dilemma is "a situation involving a particular type of incentive structure, such that, 1) if all group members cooperate, all gain, whereas, 2) for each individual it is more beneficial not to cooperate" (Yamagishi and Cook, 1993:236). Yamagishi and Cook (1993) explained that "in generalized exchange, the rewards that an actor receives usually are not directly contingent on the resources provided by that actor; therefore, free riding can occur" (p. 235). The center of this problem relates to the fact that, if everyone "free-rides"—that is, takes the benefits while contributing nothing—society will eventually suffer. To illustrate this point, Yamagishi and Cook used the example of the stranded motorist. If the car is disabled, eventually someone will come to the rescue. Those coming to the motorist's aid do not expect any immediate reward from the motorist; however, they expect that someone will help them out similarly in the future (a type of reciprocal expectation). If most, or all, people refuse to stop and help others, the exchange system will eventually collapse and everyone may suffer—including society itself. Blau had also addressed the issue of free riders. He believed that the norm of reciprocity is what keeps everyone from being free riders (takers). However, the irony is that without "takers," there cannot be "givers."

Exchange Networks

Research on social exchange networks began with Emerson's (1972a) work on power dependence and his attempt to go beyond small-group analysis. By incorporating networks into exchange theory, Emerson, Cook, and others have extended exchange theory beyond the dyad and have attempted to integrate network-structural principles and power-dependence theory in order to explain the dynamics of power in exchange networks (Bienenstock and Bonacich, 1993:117). An exchange network consists of the following elements (Cook et al., 1983:277):

1. There is a set of either individual or collective actors.
2. Valued resources are distributed among the actors.
3. There is a set of opportunities for exchange among all actors in the network.
4. Exchange relations, or exchange opportunities, exist among the actors.
5. Exchange relations are connected to one another in a single network structure.

In short, "An exchange network is a specific social structure formed by two or more connected exchange relations between actors" (Cook et al., 1983:277). Once this exchange network has been established, the connection between dyadic (two-person) exchange and macro-level structural phenomena is revealed (Yamagishi, Gilmore, and Cook, 1988). Every exchange relation is embedded in a larger exchange network consisting of two or more such networks.

In their study of exchange networks and social dilemmas, Yamagishi and Cook (1993) distinguished between two different types of generalized exchange structures: group-generalized exchange and network-generalized exchange. Group-generalized exchange occurs when all members of the group pool their resources and then eventually share in the rewards generated by pooling (Yamagishi and Cook, 1993). Structures of this type are subject to collapse because everyone involved receives an equal part of what is being shared, but each person within the group may not have contributed resources to the group (free riders). This situation can be illustrated by the classroom group project assignment. Inevitably, not all members of the group participate at an equal rate, and yet the slackers will receive the same rewards as those who worked harder on the project. In other words, within almost any group, there are free riders who take advantage of those who work hard for the benefit of the collectivity. Able-bodied persons who abuse the welfare system are examples of free riders.

Network-generalized exchange is a structure in which each person provides benefits for one other person in the group, rather than benefiting from the group as a whole. Thus, the rewards that one person receives are directly related to the resources given by another specific person (Yamagishi and Cook, 1993).

The research conducted (several four-person groups with multiple variations in testing) by Yamagishi and Cook (1993) revealed that both structures have the benefit of cooperation and the enticement of reaping the rewards but not contributing resources. However, they differ greatly in structure. "Group-generalized exchange involves no internal group structure, whereas the network-generalized exchange takes place in a network of unidirectional relations" (p. 239). Yamagishi and Cook also found that it is easier not to cooperate in group-generalized exchange structures than in network-generalized exchanges. The reason is that it may be more difficult for the rest of the group to notice when someone is failing to participate. Conversely, it is more difficult for someone to free-ride in network-generalized exchange because the group can create and impose sanctions, making it mandatory to participate.

Trust is an extremely important factor in both exchange structures. Because of its strong effect on cooperation in relationships, trust is a necessary component of a functioning exchange structure. Yamagishi and Cook's results showed that people who are more trusting are more likely to contribute their resources to the group than those who are less trusting of others. Interestingly, Yamagishi and Cook also found that within social groups, exchange structures may actually develop trust among group members. Network-generalized exchange groups promote higher levels of trust among their participants, because everyone is directly responsible for benefiting specific members of the group. In group-generalized networks, it is easier for people to become free riders because they are not directly responsible to any one person. Yamagishi and Cook (1993) stated that network-generalized exchange networks are more likely to survive and flourish than group-generalized exchange networks. However, this survival depends on the other members of the group being aware of the actions of others and imposing sanctions to ensure their cooperation. If these sanctions are not implemented, one noncooperative person in the group can cause a domino effect that leads to the degradation and failure of the system.

Trust and Reciprocity

The concept of *trust* has become a primary focus of Cook and her associates the past few years. In *eTrust: Forming Relationships in the Online World* (2009), Cook and contributing authors examine such topics as trusting online product reviews, establishing trust with strangers on the Internet, and the role of reputation in the formation on trust. Using experimental studies and field research, Cook and associates (2009) examine how trust, or the lack thereof, in anonymous online exchanges can create or diminish cooperation between people. That so much of our lives are spent online, whether social networking or purchasing products, trust in the *eworld* is a fascinating topic for exchange theorists. After all, how can there be proper reciprocal action online without trust?

Before publishing *eTrust*, Kramer and Cook (2004) edited a book on the issue of trust and distrust in organizations. In Chapter 1 of this publication (entitled *Trust and Distrust in Organizations: Emerging Perspectives*), Kramer and Cook (2004) describe how important it is for organizations to establish trust with their customers and yet demonstrate how elusive and fragile trust is. Most of us realize, however, that in some cases, organizations such as power companies do not need to develop trust with customers because of their monopolistic advantage. Thus, many of us may not trust the power company that supplies our gas and electric, but what can we do? On the other hand, organizations such as charities, retail stores, and restaurants need to establish trust with their customers or risk losing them to the competition.

Molm, Schaefer, and Collett (2009) provide a nice summary of the role of trust in reciprocal exchange interactions:

> Contracts and formal agreements govern transactions in market exchanges; trust and reciprocity norms govern reciprocal exchanges in socially embedded relationships. Entrepreneurs prefer embedded reciprocal relationships because of both their economic advantages (e.g., securing loans at lower interest rates and obtaining private information about new products or investment opportunities) and their social benefits (p. 1).

Power and Equity

A key element of social exchange theory is the role of power in any given relationship. In Blau's (1964) examination of his large-scale social structures, within an exchange perspective, analysis centered on the development of legitimate institutional power. He argued that the major determinant of legitimacy is found in the exchange aspect of power, specifically, whether subordinates feel that power is exercised fairly and generously. Legitimacy transforms power into authority because legitimacy makes it right and mandatory to obey. The legitimacy of authority develops through group norms that help to enforce members' adherence to the laws (norms).

Emerson (1972b) defined *power* as "the level of potential *cost* which one actor can induce another to 'accept'" and *dependence* as "the level of potential cost an actor will accept within a relation" (p. 64). These concepts became the cornerstone in the development of Emerson's power-dependence theory. Cook and her colleagues summarized Emerson's power-dependence theory this way: "The power of one party over another in an exchange relation is an inverse function of his or her dependence on the other party" (Yamagishi et al., 1988:837).

Karen Cook has examined the role of power and equity in social relationships in a number of articles. In Cook and Emerson's article "Power, Equity, and Commitment in Exchange Networks" (1978), the issue of power, in both the traditional dyadic setting and the macro setting, is explored. They emphasized the importance of social exchange theory in the discussion of power and equity issues.

Cook co-authored with Karen Hegtvedt an article entitled "Distributive Justice, Equity, and Equality" (1983), where they explored how society conceptualizes justice and equity. The sociological approach to justice is to examine how individuals behave when confronted with the distribution of resources in a social setting. They believe that justice is related to individuals' perceptions of fairness.

In their article "Power and Equity: What Counts in Attributions for Exchange Outcomes?" Hegtvedt, Thompson, and Cook (1993) attempted to combine the theoretical perspectives of social exchange and attribution. They proposed a theoretical model that depicts the influence of two fundamental social factors—structural power and outcome equity—on causal attributions for exchange outcomes. Hegtvedt et al. attempted to show how the social factors of structural power and the equity of exchange outcomes affect individuals' causal attributions about these outcomes. The authors made several assumptions in order to complete their study. One assumption is that individuals have the ability to assess the equity of social exchanges, and another is that a balance of power exists when each actor in a social relationship is equally dependent on the others' resources (Hegtvedt et al., 1993). In addition, the authors defined the parameters of attribution in exchange situations (where an individual draws conclusions about another actor's behavior) as the individual's own self, the other individual in the situation, the situation itself, and the interaction between the individuals.

By conducting extensive research on a number of dyadic groups, Cook and her associates attempted to empirically support a number of hypotheses. They found when individuals believe they have greater power, they are more likely to attribute it to their own actions and are thus less likely to attribute their power to the actions of the other members, the situation, or the interaction between the individuals. However, there were some inconsistencies among the dyadic groups:

> In same-sex dyads, the direct effect between structural power and situation attributions is in the direction predicted for perceived power. In opposite-sex dyads, it appears that attributions to self mediate the relationship between perceived power and situation attributions (Hegtvedt et al., 1993:114).

Other hypotheses tested by the authors relate to the idea that an individual's perceived treatment, fair or unfair (in the tradition of Blau), affects the object of the individual's attribution of exchange outcomes, and that the strength of these attributions affects her or his reaction to the situation. The data supported the hypotheses. Cook and associates also found that the results of their study were consistent with the idea that females are more relationship-oriented and tend to see other females as status equals. While there were several limitations to this study, the authors demonstrated the need and value of future research linking exchange relationships with attribution theory.

Social Psychology

Like any theorist who attempts to bridge the micro–macro gap in social theory, Cook has a strong interest in social psychology. Social psychology is a wonderful attempt to inject micro aspects into sociological theory, while reminding psychologists of the major flaw in their discipline: the nearly complete neglect of the effect of macro structural factors on human behavior. Cook has published a number of articles in this area, among them "Recent Theoretical Advances in Social Psychology: Progress and Promises," co-authored with Judith Howard (1992). Cook and Howard believe that the focus of social psychology should be primarily on the relations between individual actors or collectivities and various social factors or forces. They cited Blau (1964) in his work on exchange and power as an example of a theorist who focuses on the dialectic between micro–macro phenomena.

In 1959, Thibaut and Kelley published *The Social Psychology of Groups*. The majority of the book is devoted to dyadic relationships. The concepts of costs and rewards are central to their analysis. Thibaut and Kelley (1959) argue that if both persons involved in a relationship are able to produce maximum rewards at minimum costs to themselves, the relationship will continue.

Molm and Cook (1995) proposed that Thibaut and Kelley's book offers three important contributions to the development of exchange theory:

1. Their interest in power and dependence would later become critical to Emerson and his followers. Unfortunately, Thibaut and Kelley concentrated primarily on dyads, where structural relationships are clearly different from those in triads and larger groups. As Simmel had discovered, in a dyad, each participant is dependent on the other, and therefore each has a degree of power over the other.
2. Thibaut and Kelley discussed the ideas of comparison level and comparison level for alternatives. Both are important in the evaluation of outcomes of relationships. This will become important for future theorists, such as Emerson, who will develop ideas on social networks.
3. The notion of the *outcome matrix* is a way of visually depicting all the possible events that may occur when two persons interact. This matrix provides the individual with options of courses of actions in order to maximize rewards and minimize costs.

The primary task of social psychology is to find the link between micro and macro issues related to social interaction. Consequently, social-psychological elements are inherent in a theory that attempts to sufficiently address the micro and macro variables.

NETWORK ANALYSIS

Contemporary exchange theorists strive to link the micro dynamics of human behavior with the influence of macro structural and organizational influences. Simmel discussed the "web of group affiliations" throughout his works, but contemporary sociologists generally use the term *network*. As discussed previously in this section, Cook, Emerson, and a number of other social theorists have established a field of study referred to as *exchange networks*. Network analysis involves the discovery of patterns of behavior in order to determine how such ramifications influence the behavior of the people involved in the network (Mitchell, 1974).

Network analysis operates on the fundamental premise that social exchange among actors often occurs within a web of larger networks of social exchanges, and not simply between individuals and small groups. Within this context, network analysis is more concerned with the various sizes and connections of the web of networks than with what is actually being exchanged. The influence of Simmel's formal sociology is clearly in play here. Simmel's formal sociology concerned itself with the social form of interactions rather than the content of the interactions. Simmel argued that people interact with one another based on their *forms* of reality. In fact, he believed that society itself consists of a number of social webs (forms) and networks of patterned interactions.

Cook and associates have published a great deal of work in the area of network analysis. In an article titled "Two Approaches to Social Structure: Exchange Theory and Network Analysis," Cook and Whitmeyer (1992) described social structure as "a configuration of social relations among actors where the relations involve the exchange of valued items" (p. 110). Cook explained that the term *network analysis* refers to the patterns of interactions between many actors. These interactions and patterns can be seen as networks. To better understand the concept of social structure, Cook and Whitmeyer used a historical approach by examining the ideas of three exchange theorists: Homans, Blau, and Emerson. Homans studied individuals in the work environment and examined the employee–employer relationship between actors who come into direct contact with each other. Blau has examined social exchange principles in terms of group formation, cohesion, social integration, opposition, conflict, and dissolution. Emerson has attempted to link social structures with exchange principles. Cook and Whitmeyer (1992) concluded that all three theorists had successfully combined exchange theory and social structural parameters. In their network analysis, Cook and Whitmeyer made note that rewards (of some type) always exist, despite the great variety of social actions taken by individuals in a wide disparity of social groups, organizations, and structures.

CRITICISMS OF SOCIAL EXCHANGE THEORY

As with all theories, there are critics of social exchange theory. However, because this theory has variations ranging from elementary exchanges (Homans' original presentation of the theory) to Blau's middle-range theory to Cook, Emerson and others who have popularize network analysis (the macro version), criticisms of one version of the theory are not always applicable to the others. Homans' version of social exchange theory is rightfully criticized for being too micro-oriented for a sociological theory. It is also criticized for ignoring consciousness and the role of large-scale structures and institutions on behavior. In Homans' defense, it was never his intent to explain such things. He hoped to explain everyday exchanges between social actors.

The rational choice aspect of social exchange theory is criticized because of the realization that people do not always act rationally. Indeed, people act in such a manner as to maximize profits, but there are times when people act irrationally in the pursuit of a desired reward that may not be attainable. For example, individuals blinded by love do not always act rationally. They may continue to pursue a relationship even when the costs far outweigh the rewards. In other words, emotion often supersedes rationality.

George Homans has been labeled a reductionist by several of his critics, who have attempted to show that his deductive schemes tend to be either tautological or ad hoc (Coser, 1977). The criticism of reductionism does bring up the question: Should exchange theory incorporate the ideas of symbolic interactionism in order to address the issue of the symbolic meanings of behaviors?

The introduction of network analysis has eliminated much of the criticism directed toward the micro version of social exchange theory. The combination of traditional social exchange theory and network analysis represents a type of grand theory designed to explain social behavior at all levels of interaction. In contemporary sociology, most social theorists seem to have a problem with the establishment of grand theories. This is unfortunate, for the ultimate goal of sociologists, and all social scientists, should be to establish a social theory that *does* explain human behavior at the micro, meso, and macro levels.

APPLICATION OF SOCIAL EXCHANGE THEORY TO CONTEMPORARY SOCIETY

Social exchange theory has a great deal of relevancy to both laypersons and sociologists. Each of us participates in social interactions with individuals, groups, and organizations. It is, perhaps, Homans' work on micro social exchange theory that seems readily applicable to everyday folks. However, his theories, especially his five propositions to explain all human behavior, have great relevancy to micro sociologists as well. Homans dared critics to find any micro social behavior that he could not explain with these propositions. I do the same thing with my students. No one has found an example yet. (To be fair, his propositions can be applied similarly to that of an astrological forecast.) Consider a couple of examples: The success proposition states that individuals will seek out, and maintain, interactions where the rewards outweigh the costs, so that there is a profit. Nearly all of us participate in behaviors we find rewarding repeatedly. A sports fan, for example, will continue to watch sporting events indefinitely. Most sports fans remain so over the course of a lifetime.

Clearly, watching sports provides rewards because such a behavior comes at the cost of doing other things. Most of us will maintain friendships and romantic relationships for as long as the rewards outweigh the costs. The stimulus proposition illustrates the processes of generalization and discrimination, concepts utilized on a regular basis during social interactions. For example, waitresses will find that good service almost always generates good tips, while poor service generally leads to a much smaller tip (generalization). A consumer who prefers "dark" beer (e.g., Guinness) will not like "light" beers (e.g., Miller Lite) (discrimination). The fact is that demonstrating the relevancy of Homans' five propositions would, in itself, fill an entire book. Furthermore, the challenge is offered again to identify *any* behavior that cannot be explained by these propositions.

Homans, Blau, and Cook have all described the importance of understanding group behavior. They have identified elements that lead to its development and maintenance. Nearly everyone is involved in some type of group behavior. It might be a sports team, a study group, a card game gathering, a street gang, or any number of other options. In the analysis of group dynamics, inevitably there must be some discussion of power and authority. Much of the research conducted on power in the exchange tradition is similar to that in conflict theory. In fact, conflict theory and exchange theory are in agreement that power affects the dynamics of the group structure and corresponding interactions. The study of groups and power relationships will always be relevant to sociological theory.

Analysis of bureaucracy and organizations is at least as important as the examination of groups. Blau's work in this area provides a wealth of information relevant to the study of such structures today. Not only do people interact with others in a variety of group settings, but they also often do so within an organizational environment. Cook's network analysis demonstrates how the core premises of micro exchange theory can be applied at the macro level. Entire societies deal with one another in a manner similar to that of individuals.

Blau and Cook (along with other theorists like Emerson) have attempted to bridge the micro–macro divide. All social theories seem to take one approach or the other to their study of human behavior. Symbolic interactionism, ethnomethodology, and phenomenology are micro theories (or theories of the everyday life), while functionalism and conflict theory tend to be macro. Conflict theory and feminism both possess concepts that are concerned with macro and micro issues, but no theory other than social exchange theory has so actively attempted to construct this bridge. Only when a theory has successfully addressed issues of both micro and macro elements will sociology have a true "grand" theory. This grand theory will demonstrate sociology's relevance to the other academic disciplines; consequently, this grand theory will be responsible for sociology's one day reaching the elite status that it so deserves. Social exchange theory is the theory closest to this ultimate goal.

The general acceptance of network analysis in sociology continues to grow. Sociologists see the value of a macro approach to the study of society that incorporates behavior, structure, and the role of power, to mention a few of the attributes of network analysis. The sociology of work and its analysis of collective action and collective goods have found network analysis beneficial. For the past couple decades, network analysis has contributed to the understanding of the collective action of workers as well as the collective good provided by organizations (Simpson and Willer, 2005). In their article "Structural Embeddedness of Collective Goods," Simpson and Willer (2005) found that "(1) collective goods are latent in some, not all types of exchange structures; (2) when present, the size of the collective good is determined by the type of structure; and (3) these goods are made manifest through collective action" (p. 402). Furthermore, Simpson and Willer (2005) found that "networks that generate *identical* exchange ratios when participants act independently produce *different* collective goods when they act collectively" (p. 402).

Hiro Saito has conducted research on cosmopolitanism using an actor-network theory (ANT). Saito (2011) believes that network analysis "is one of the most theoretically robust concepts distilled from the so-called relational perspective in sociology". ANT (described by Saito as a "science of living together" in cosmopolitan areas) represents a variant of network analysis. Saito (2011) argues that ANT helps elaborate mechanisms that mediate the causal relationship between cosmopolitanization as an environmental change and cosmopolitanism as a subjective orientation. Saito (2011) suggests that future research utilizing ANT would be fruitful in the study of the relationship between cosmopolitanization and nationalism; ANT can help clarify how a "world society" is assembled; and third, ANT has the potential to reorient studies of cosmopolitanism beyond sociology.

Jan Fuhse (2009) suggests that research on social networks depicts the structure of relationships as the decisive variable leading to diverse phenomena like status attainment, intellectual creativity, or collective action. However, she also claims that network analysis usually pays little attention to the expectations, symbols, schemata, and cultural practices embodied in interpersonal structures: the *meaning structure of social networks*. Fuhse offers a theory to address the role of meaning in network analysis as a way of meeting this perceived shortcoming. Fuhse (2009) concludes that the *meaning structure of social networks* consists of interpersonal expectations that are embodied in dyadic relationships, role categories, and cultural blueprints found in the social identities of interacting actors.

Summary

Social exchange theory was founded by George Homans. He argued that self-interest is the universal motive for behavior and that people shape their behaviors in terms of the positive or negative reinforcement provided by their environment (Coser, 1977). Homans believed that humans interact with one another by exchanging rewards and punishments. The individual is viewed as a rational being capable of calculating pleasures (rewards) and pains (costs) and is always motivated to maximize profits. Homans' exchange theory is micro-oriented. He believed that all social behaviors could be explained by five psychological principles.

Peter Blau has attempted to extend exchange theory from its micro roots to the macro level. Clearly influenced by Homans, Blau has attempted to remedy some of the deficiencies he perceived in Homans' conceptualizations and to reconcile them within the structural perspective. Blau felt that there were three basic reasons why one should look beyond micro-level interaction patterns. First, humans rarely pursue one goal, forgetting about all others. Second, humans are inconsistent in their performance. Third, humans never have complete information regarding the alternative behaviors that might be available. Turner (2003) stated that "even Blau himself increasingly believed that the isomorphism between micro-level and macro-level exchange processes was forced" (p. 306).

Contemporary social exchange theorists, such as Richard Emerson and Karen Cook, have successfully introduced a macro version of social exchange theory called *network analysis*. Emerson emphasized the concepts of power and dependence and the alternatives available. Emerson and Cook and a number of associates have conducted a number of laboratory studies of exchange relationships in order to determine what costs people are willing to endure in their pursuit of rewards.

Exchange theory and network analysis combined offer sociology the best attempt to bridge the micro–macro schism that generally exists within the discipline. Current and future social theorists must come to grips with the reality that social exchange theory offers valuable insights into social behavior and structural phenomenon.

Study and **Review** on **MySearchLab**

Discussion Questions

1. Describe George Homans' five basic propositions to explain all human behavior. Can you think of an example of a behavior that these propositions could not explain?

2. How does Homans explain the concepts of "power" and "authority"? How do his definitions differ from other social theorists such as Max Weber?

3. Describe Peter Blau's view of group formation and apply the key concepts to your own life.

4. Explain the value of Karen Cook's contributions to social exchange theory.

5. Explain network analysis. Describe two network systems that exist at your college or university.

MySearchLab® Connections

MysearchLab is designed just for you. Each chapter features a customized study plan to help you learn and review key concepts and terms. Dynamic visual activities, videos, and readings found in the multimedia library will enhance your learning experience.

 Watch on **MySearchLab**

▶ Social Interaction and Social Roles
▶ Social Interaction and Technology

 **View** on **MySearchLab**

▶ Social Interactions and Everyday Experiences

12 Ethnomethodology and Phenomenology

 Listen to the **Chapter Audio** on **MySearchLab**

Chapter Outline

- Defining Ethnomethodology
- Key Aspects of Harold Garfinkel's Ethnomethodology
- Studies by Other Ethnomethodologists
- Criticisms of Ethnomethodology
- Application of Ethnomethodology to Contemporary Society
- Defining Phenomenology
- Edmund Husserl and the Phenomenological Approach
- Alfred Schutz and Phenomenology
- Peter Berger and the Social Construction of Reality
- Criticisms of Phenomenology
- Application of Phenomenology to Contemporary Society
- Summary
- Discussion Questions

Ethnomethodology and phenomenology are micro-"sociological theories of the everyday life." Others include symbolic interactionism, dramaturgical analysis, labeling theory, and existentialism. Sociological theories of the everyday life examine how actors come to perceive the world and act according to these perceptions. The world consists of the numerous and shifting inputs of perception. Since most perception is quickly and effortlessly organized into certain customary patterns, the world appears as a familiar one. That is, of course, until a breach interferes with our taken-for-granted assumption and perceptions of our everyday lives.

Among the topics covered in this chapter are degradation ceremonies (formal shamings such as a military court-martial and informal shamings such as a "drunk shaming") and breaching experiments. This author has conducted original research on drunk shamings conducted by college students and has regularly had his students conduct breaching experiments; a number of them appear on YouTube. This is a fun exercise for students, and professors should encourage such an exercise as a way to apply the relevancy of breaching experiments. We begin our coverage with a brief description of both ethnomethodology and phenomenology, and then we will learn more about these two theories.

DEFINING ETHNOMETHODOLOGY

The term *ethnomethodology* was created by Harold Garfinkel (1917–2011). Garfinkel was interested in the study of everyday people, their social worlds, interactions, and conversations. Ethnomethodology is based on the principle that social reality is negotiated by actors interacting with one another who possess a "taken-for-granted" attitude of the social environment that surrounds them. The term *ethnomethodology,* given its Greek roots, literally means the methods of ordinary people that are used on a daily basis to accomplish their everyday needs. If we break the word *ethnomethodology* down into its individual parts, its meaning becomes clearer. The term *ethno* refers to people; *method* simply means method; and *ology*, as always, refers to "the study of." Put together, ethnomethodology is defined as the study of the methods people use to sustain their "everyday lives." In his *Studies in Ethnomethodology*, Garfinkel (1967) used the term "to refer to the investigation of the rational properties of indexical expressions and other practical actions as contingent ongoing accomplishments of organized artful practices of everyday life" (p. 1). Garfinkel believed that life consists of many ordered things and activities. Most people take comfort in the familiar. Garfinkel (1996) refined his definition of *ethnomethodology* as follows:

> Ethnomethodology's fundamental phenomenon and its standing technical preoccupation in its studies is to find, collect, specify, and make inscrutably observable the local endogenous production and natural accountability of immortal familiar society's most ordinary organizational things in the world, *and to provide for them both and simultaneously as objects and procedurally, as alternate methodologies.* The identity of objects and methodologies is key (p. 6).

The study of ordinary society reveals how individuals work hard to maintain consistency, order, and meaning in their lives (Garfinkel, 2002).

Harold Garfinkel, a long-time sociology professor at UCLA, was an innovative sociologist who turned the study of common sense into a dense and arcane discipline (Weber, 2011). As Jeffrey Beemer (2006) states, "Harold Garfinkel's ongoing studies in ethnomethodology defy what many would consider mainstream sociological research" (p. 83). He conducted ethnomethodology studies throughout his life and until his death in 2011.

KEY ASPECTS OF GARFINKEL'S ETHNOMETHODOLOGY

As a sociological theory of the everyday, ethnomethodology examines the taken-for-granted world in which people interact with one another. In an attempt to understand how people create a taken-for-granted world, Garfinkel believed that it was important to ascertain how people account for their own actions and the actions of others during social interaction.

Accounts

Garfinkel's ethnomethodology seeks to understand the methods people employ to make sense of their world. According to Garfinkel, language is important aspect by which social reality is constructed. People regularly use language in an effort to account for their actions. For example, if someone has been accused of saying something unflattering about the other, he may respond verbally by saying, "That comment I made was taken out of context; I would never bad-mouth you. I have great respect for you." In this manner, the actor is trying to use his account of the situation by constructing a sense of reality. Accounts represent the manner in which people attempt to explain specific situations. The accounts of people reflect how social order is possible. "For Garfinkel the answer merges a Durkheimian concern for large collective representations with an interactionist conception of the rules, norms, and meanings that members of any social order daily take for granted" (Denzin, 1969:926–927).

Garfinkel's ethnomethodological studies regard the subject they are studying as the result of accountability production. Accounts are social creations and constructs built from past interactions. The principal aim of ethnomethodology is to investigate the procedural accounts that individuals bring with them during interaction with others. Behaviors that are present in the everyday world are especially interesting to Garfinkel's ethnomethodological studies. As Garfinkel explained in *Studies in Ethnomethodology* (1967):

> In accounting for the stable features of everyday activities sociologists commonly select familiar settings such as familial households or work places and ask for the variables that contribute to their stable features. Just as commonly, one set of considerations are unexamined: the socially standardized and standardizing, "seen but unnoticed," expected, background features of everyday scenes. The member of the society uses background expectancies as a scheme of interpretation. With their use actual appearances are for him recognizable and intelligible as the appearances-of-familiar-events. Demonstrably he is responsive to this background, while at the same time he is at a loss to tell us specifically of what the experiences consist. When we ask him about them he has little or nothing to say. For these background expectancies to come into view one must either be a stranger to the "life as usual" character of everyday scenes, or become estranged from them. As Alfred Schutz pointed out, a "special motive" is required to make them problematic (pp. 36–37).

In an attempt to explain how a taken-for-granted world is created, Garfinkel suggested that sociologists examine how individuals make accounts of their behaviors. He also believed that actors assume certain characteristics of others and of given social situations. This second point leads to Garfinkel's assertion that people attempt to create a common-sense everyday world.

The Common-Sense World

From the theoretical writings of Alfred Schutz, Garfinkel created a number of "determinants" to define an event as an occurrence in the common-sense world (Rogers, 1983). In brief, some of the determinants that assume the label of common sense include viewing specific events as objective facts; viewing the meanings of events as products of a socially standardized process of naming, reification, and idealization of the user's stream of experience (i.e., as the products of language); applying past determinants of events to similar present and future events; and viewing alterations of descriptions of events as remaining in the control of the participating actors. Interacting members of society are not the only ones to utilize a common-sense approach to interaction. Garfinkel acknowledges that researchers often rely on a taken-for-granted, commonsensical approach to the study of human behavior.

Garfinkel (1967) stated,

> Sociologists distinguish the "product" from the "process" meanings of a common understanding. As "product," a common understanding is thought to consist of a shared agreement on substantive matters; as "process," it consists of various methods whereby something that a person says or does is recognized to accord with a rule. With his concepts of *begreifen* and *verstehen,* each with its distinct character as method and knowledge, Weber provided sociologists an authority for this distinction (pp. 24–25).

Furthermore, Garfinkel (1967) stated,

> Much of "core sociology" consists of "reasonable findings." Many, if not most, situations of sociological inquiry are common sense situations of choice. Nevertheless, textbook and journal discussions of sociological methods rarely give recognition to the fact that sociological inquiries are carried out under common sense auspices *at the points where decisions about the correspondence between observed appearances and intended events are being made* (p. 100).

Nonetheless, Garfinkel remains steadfast in the idea that *scientific* sociology is a fact, and not merely based on common sense. It can be a science if it follows certain policies of scientific procedure.

Breaching Experiments

Garfinkel felt it important to conduct empirical studies of social interaction. One of his favorite research methods was the use of breaching experiments. A *breaching experiment* involves deliberately interrupting the taken-for-granted world of actors as they interact with one another. Garfinkel believed that one must "breach" constitutive expectancies in radical ways, since the natural attitude guarantees that people assimilate "strange" into "familiar" without altering the presuppositions underlying a shared world (Rogers, 1983). Breaching experiments are not formally conducted in laboratories like natural scientists conduct; rather, they are quasi-experimental field studies designed to modify the familiar, known-in-common environment by rendering the background expectancies inoperative. Garfinkel (1967) stated:

> Specifically, this modification would consist of subjecting a person to a breach of the background expectancies of everyday life while (a) making it difficult for the person to interpret his situation as a game, and experiment, a deception, a play, *i.e.,* as something other than the one known according to the attitude of everyday life as a matter of enforceable morality and action, (b) making it necessary that he reconstruct the "natural facts" but giving him insufficient time to manage the reconstruction with respect to required mastery of practical circumstances for which he must call upon his knowledge of the "natural facts," and (c) requiring that he manage the reconstruction of the natural facts by himself and without consensual validation (p. 54).

Individuals have no alternative except to try to normalize the resultant incongruities in their social world. Seeking balance and normality in one's life is viewed as a natural need of humans. Examples of this need are endless but especially occur in cases where an unexpected death occurs and people's "normal" lives are disrupted. Consider, for example, the spring 2010 killing of Yeardley Love, a senior lacrosse player on the University of Virginia's (UVA) women's team. Love's boyfriend, George Huguely, a senior on the men's UVA lacrosse team, was charged with her murder. Understandably, the lives of Love's and Huguely's families were disrupted; so too were the lives of two lacrosse teams, and the college community at UVA. As the 2010 NCAA Tournament selections were about to be announced, women's coach Julie Myers proclaimed, "I think that we're kind of building back to normalcy. I think it'll be a new normal. It won't be anything that we're used to" (Teel, 2010: B-1). This same sentiment—the need to get back to normal—was echoed by a number of players on both the men's and women's lacrosse teams at UVA.

We like to think that we are capable of putting meaning on our world, to the point where it can be taken for granted. It makes us feel better, or "normal." Thus, breaching experiments become an effective means of observation of how humans bring order and stability to their lives. Ethnomethodological studies have been conducted in conversation analysis, walking, face-to-face communication, and interactions in various settings. These studies examine how people construct and reconstruct social reality. The researcher enters a social setting, violates or breaches the rules that govern it, and studies how the interactants deal with the breach.

Many of the breaching experiments that Garfinkel utilized were undertaken by his students in casual settings. One example involves the breaching of the basic rules of the game tic-tac-toe. The rules of tic-tac-toe are very simple: Each of the two participants takes a turn placing a mark within one of the cells. In the breaching experiment, the "operative" places a mark between two cells, thus creating confusion about which cell the mark actually belongs in. The game cannot continue "normally," as the taken-for-granted rules have been violated. Ethnomethodologists would examine the reaction of the participant who was being duped.

In another study, Garfinkel had his students act as if they were boarders in their homes. They were instructed to conduct themselves in a circumspect and polite way. "They were to avoid getting personal, to use formal address, to speak only when spoke to" (Garfinkel, 1967:47). Five of his students refused to participate, and four were "unsuccessful." In the other cases, "reports were filled with accounts of astonishment, bewilderment, shock, anxiety, embarrassment, and anger, and with charges by various family members that the student was mean, inconsiderate, selfish, nasty, or impolite" (Garfinkel, 1967:47). Family members demanded to know why the student was behaving in such a way. (They needed an *account* of the student's behavior.) This attempt to put meaning to the breaching behavior reflects their attempt to readjust the social situation to normality. In addition, many students also reported having difficulty with the assignment because of the drastic way it altered their own taken-for-granted world.

By showing how people can give meaning to an intrinsically meaningless situation, Garfinkel provided insight into the creation and maintenance of reality in everyday life. Jeffrey Beemer (2006) concludes,

> As Garfinkel's breaching experiments show, when an individual's social environment becomes unsettled through certain normative disruptions, an active attempt is made to reorganize the taken-for-granted process in recognizable and coherent ways. The "local working out" of a social order is interactively accomplished through indexical practices (pp. 95–96).

Conversation Analysis

Another form of research promoted and utilized by Garfinkel was conversation analysis. Garfinkel interprets an individual's use of words as a means of clarifying or repairing social problems created by human communication. He believes that a large part of human communication is not what *is* said, but what *is not* said. What people leave out of conversation is often far more important than the actual words spoken. The nonverbal communication between the speaker and the spoken-to is of extreme importance. Furthermore, everyone uses anticipatory knowledge gained from previous interactions during verbal discourse: If we did not utilize past knowledge, each conversation would have to begin with a lengthy history lesson of past interaction. Thus, insinuation and alluding to previous events provide an undertone in effective communication. However, until the undertones of discourse are fully exposed, through verbal language, honest communication cannot exist. Garfinkel believes that communication is made possible by a communal agreement, or the appearance of consensus in the spoken word. Previously acknowledged acceptance of events sets patterns of understanding in communication. These patterns are carried into encounters by each participant and assist in effective interaction. Garfinkel and other ethnomethodologists see language as a tool that is used to interpret and clarify social interactions. Breaching the taken-for-granted rules of conversation provides valuable insight into the behaviors of interactants.

The Degradation Ceremony

One's identity is affected by many factors, including both internal reflection (such as sexual identity) and external projection (e.g., a sports coach who states that a player is a discipline problem). Degradation ceremonies are public attempts to inflict identity alteration. They are acts of embarrassment done purposely rather than accidentally.

> With the exception of planned embarrassment, most embarrassing incidents emerge unpredictably; neither their definers nor their actors anticipate their occurrence. These incidents are haphazardly, rather awkwardly accepted instances of status-forcing. The problematic individual is forced to accept an otherwise unacceptable definition of self. Degradation ceremonies describe planned and anticipated instances of status-forcing in which derelict individuals know in advance that they will lose self-credibility (Lindersmith, Strauss, and Denzin, 1991:256).

Examples of accidental embarrassing moments that cause harm to one's stature are numerous, such as a politician who mistakenly uses an ethnically offensive term while making a speech. If the slur is harmful enough, it may cost the politician an election. Among more mundane embarrassing moments that cost someone a degradation of status are a student's falling asleep in the classroom. This student has lost status with the professor and will not be considered a serious student.

Identity degradation involves destroying the offender's current identity and transforming it into a "lower" social type. In 1956, Garfinkel's article "Conditions of Successful Degradation Ceremonies" was published in the *American Journal of Sociology*. In this famous article, Garfinkel described a degradation ceremony as an attempt to transform "an individual's total identity into an identity lower in the group's scheme of social types" (p. 420). Furthermore, "any communicative work between persons, whereby the public identity of an actor is transformed into something looked on as lower in the local scheme of social types, will be called a 'status degradation ceremony'" (p. 420). Garfinkel described the conditions and parameters that give rise to successful degradation ceremonies. Ultimately, individuals who are being degraded must be placed outside the everyday moral order and defined as a threat to that order (Lindersmith et al., 1991). Additionally, since degradation poses a threat to the status of the subject, the ceremony is generally forcibly imposed. The degradation ceremonies discussed by Garfinkel were restricted to those concerned with the alteration of total identities.

The identities referred to must be "total" identities. That is, these identities must refer to persons as "motivational" types rather than as "behavioral" types, not to what a person may be expected to have done or to do (in Parsons' term to his "performance") but to what the group holds to be the ultimate "grounds" or "reasons" for his performance (Garfinkel, 1956:420).

Garfinkel proposed that all moral societies have degradation ceremonies and only those with total anomie do not. In fact, it is highly unlikely that any society does not feature conditions and organization sufficient for inducing shame. Simply put,

There is no society whose social structure does not provide, in its routine features, the conditions of identity degradation. Just as the structural conditions of shame are universal to all societies by the very fact of their being organized, so the structural conditions of status degradation are universal to all societies (Garfinkel, 1956:420).

Garfinkel argued that only the communicative tactics used for the degradation ceremony vary by society.

Degradation ceremonies used at the societal level fall within the scope of moral indignation. They are designed to bring shame and guilt to the violator of the moral code. Moral indignation is equated with public denunciation. In this regard, the accuser is attempting to rally the entire group into believing that the accused is guilty of some wrongdoing. The actions of the violator (accused) are

cast in moral terms which threaten the existence of the social group, and their accuser must be defined as a person who is morally superior. The accuser will evoke higher moral values which witnesses accept, and he will be defined as a legitimate upholder of those values. If the accuser is successful in his attempts, the accused must accept their new status. Degradation ceremonies force them to yield to the wishes of others. They give up control over their own moral career, finding that their fate now lies in the hands of others (Lindersmith et al., 1991:257).

Moral indignation causes the destruction of status of the person denounced, and through ritualistic ceremonies it generally reinforces group solidarity. However, in some cases, the degradation of status inflicted on the accused by one social group may actually lead to rewards by another group. For example, Rosa Parks was a victim of degradation by many southern whites because she refused to give up her bus seat to a white man, but she became a hero and champion of civil rights to the greater American society.

The successful degradation ceremony results in the recasting of the objective character and status of the condemned (accused) person. The person

becomes in the eyes of his condemners literally a different and *new* person. It is not that the new attributes are added to the old "nucleus." He is not changed, he is reconstituted. The former identity, at best, receives the accent of mere appearance.... The new identity is the "basic reality" (Garfinkel, 1956:421–422).

When someone goes through the degradation process, he is removed from the realm of his everyday character. Through the degradation ceremony, the denouncer is attempting to reinforce the values of the greater society; as such, the denouncer must be recognized as a representation of society and its moral code. In other words, the accuser, or denouncer, cannot be guilty of violation of a moral code him- or herself. If any of these or other conditions stipulated by Garfinkel are absent, the denunciation will fail. Unfortunately, for many falsely accused persons, the denouncer is often successful in denouncing an accused in spite of biases and personal agendas.

STUDIES BY OTHER ETHNOMETHODOLOGISTS

A number of ethnomethodologists other than Harold Garfinkel have continued in his tradition. Garfinkel (1988:106–107) briefly acknowledged the work of several studies by ethnomethodologists:

- medicines among the Kpelle of Liberia (Bellman, 1975);
- proving the schedule of thirty-seven theorems and their proof accounts that make up, as instructions, Godel's proof by mathematicians (Livingston, 1986);
- designing and administering a medical school curriculum in pediatrics, and evaluating the competence with that curriculum of medical students, interns, and residents (Robillard and Pack, 1976–1982);
- teaching English as a second language to preschool children from immigrant families (Meyer, 1985, 1988);
- coordinating work site practices of 911 dispatchers in "working" a call (Zimmerman and Whalen, 1987);
- learning to play improvised jazz piano (Sudnow, 1978);
- talking the convict code in an inmate halfway house (Wieder, 1974); and
- designing a Xerox copier to ensure complaint-free operation by office personnel (Suchman, 1987).

These are a few of studies recognized by Garfinkel. He felt that these studies are examples of good ethnomethodology and its attempt to explain everyday behavior and individuals' pursuit of order. Additional ethnomethodological studies are noted below.

Aaron V. Cicourel

Cicourel (1964) has established his own variation of ethnomethodology called *cognitive sociology*. In his research, Cicourel attempts to uncover the universal "interpretive procedures" that humans use to give meaning to social situations. Through these interpretive procedures, humans can put order to their lives and engage in interaction successfully. For example, Cicourel acknowledges how people use the "et cetera" principle (what is left unsaid to fill in the blanks). The TV show *Seinfeld* popularized the "yada, yada, yada" principle to illustrate the et cetera principle. People use this method of storytelling when they don't want to tell the entire story. The audience is left to fill in the blanks form themselves.

Deirdre Boden

Boden (1990b) attempted to integrate ethnomethodology with the more sociological traditional approach to incorporate the role of social structure into human behavior. Boden (1990a) also attempted to incorporate ideas of symbolic interactionism. Her approach to ethnomethodology lies in conversation analysis, with a specific focus on talk. All forms of talk are relevant: work talk, home talk, and every form of mundane talk. Boden has attempted to redefine conversation analysis with elements of symbolic interactionism with her own brand of sociology that she termed *interactional analysis.*

Harvey Sacks

Sacks utilized Garfinkel's concern with verbal accounts. He believed that researchers should examine entire conversations of people in order to properly describe phenomena and social interactions. Sacks and various collaborators have come to realize that interactants involved in conversation expect each other to take turns ("turn talking"). When conversation occurs face to face, they look for cues from one another to know when it is their "turn" to talk. Interruptions in the normal flow of conversation are often viewed as breaches. Sacks's (1992) research has involved the attempt to discover universal forms of interactions that apply to all conversations.

Donald Zimmerman, Melvin Pollner, and Lawrence Wieder

Donald Zimmerman and Melvin Pollner (1970) argued that sociology fails to pay attention to the most important aspect of human behavior. Conventional sociologists use the everyday social world as a *topic* rather than treating the everyday world in its own right, as a *resource.* Traditional sociologists examine communication looking for evidence of values, norms, and prevailing attitudes; the ethnomethodologist examines communication as evidence of how social life is actually carried on. Furthermore, the sociologist attempts to provide causal explanations of observations in terms of patterns and repetitive actions. The ethnomethodologist is concerned with how "members of society go about the task of *seeing, describing,* and *explaining* order in the world in which they live" (Zimmerman and Wieder, 1970:289). Zimmerman, Wieder, and Pollner have all drawn inspiration from Garfinkel, and they have sought to identify universal procedures that people use to maintain a sense of order or normality.

This sampling of ethnomethodological studies reveals that sociologists beyond Harold Garfinkel find the study of everyday life and the methods people use to bring some sense of order to their lives is a dynamic aspect of sociological theory.

CRITICISMS OF ETHNOMETHODOLOGY

Ethnomethodology falls outside the parameters of mainstream sociology. Ethnomethodologists are generally critical of traditional sociologists because they impose their sense of social reality on interactants rather than use the descriptions of those persons under study. In an attempt to be objective and rational, traditional sociologists use some working interpretation of rationality.

> Commonly, sociological researchers decide a definition of rationality by selecting one or more features from among the properties of scientific activity as it is ideally described and understood. The definition is then used methodologically to aid the researcher in deciding the realistic, pathological, prejudiced, delusional, mythical, magical, ritual, and similar features of everyday conduct, thinking, and beliefs (Garfinkel, 1967:262).

Ethnomethodologists remain steadfast in the idea that the everyday world must be treated as a resource rather than as a topic. The primary goal of ethnomethodologists is to specify general rules and procedures that people utilize to maintain a sense of order, a taken-for-granted reality.

Despite much research, ethnomethodology has failed to produce such "laws" of general behavior. Many contemporary sociologists value the contributions of ethnomethodology but feel that its scope of analysis is far too narrow. Macro-structural factors are almost completely ignored, although Garfinkel's study of degradation ceremonies makes cross-cultural reference to the fact that all societies throughout the world utilize such status-reducing rituals. Nonetheless, critics claim that ethnomethodologists make little distinction between micro and macro structures.

APPLICATION OF ETHNOMETHODOLOGY TO CONTEMPORARY SOCIETY

As with all micro-oriented theories, ethnomethodology has its proponents. Although laypersons know very little, if anything at all, about Harold Garfinkel, they do engage in regular conversations with others. And each of us brings to conversations and daily interactions certain expectations of how conversations and interactions should proceed. Throw a curve at people (a breaching experiment) and it is easy to see how most of us prefer a certain sense of normalcy. Although experiments are generally associated with the natural sciences, breaching experiments are fun activities for regular folks and academics. I regularly have my introductory and social theory students conduct breaching experiments. Many of them are posted on YouTube. Although some students are uncomfortable with such assignments, others really enjoy conducting them. In an attempt to breach the norms of everyday life and to test the reactions of others, my students have done such things as place an "out of order" sign on an elevator and then enter the elevator; two of my students set up a little bedroom in an elevator equipped with a bed, end table with lamp, and a stereo; some students have gone shopping at grocery stores and offered advice on produce or taken items from the carts of other shoppers to test their reactions; some students go to class wearing their pajamas during the cold and snowy upstate New York winter; students have walked backwards around campus, stood facing the back of the elevator; and so on. In one case, a student invited friends over to his apartment for a keg party. He actually purchased nonalcoholic beer but did not tell any of the guests. By the time the keg was nearly finished, most of the guests were acting *as if* they were drunk (which would be the normal order of things if one were actually drinking alcohol). It was not until the next day that the student informed his guests they had been drinking nonalcoholic beer—much to their dismay and anger! Breaching experiments reveal many of the taken-for-granted realities that interactants construct in order to proceed smoothly with their daily life.

Perhaps the greatest contribution of ethnomethodology is conversation analysis. The description and explication of everyday talk reveal the many "rules" participants use and rely on while interacting with others. General rules such as taking turns while talking and watching for nonverbal cues indicate to conversation analysts that participants look for order. Conversation analysts generally use audiotapes and videotapes to collect accurate data on naturally occurring dialogues. Garfinkel first used this approach in his research on jury deliberations. This ethnomethodological approach has influenced the labeling school and social psychology (another branch of sociology). The success of many professions is tied directly to effective conversation analysis. Callers to emergency services (e.g., police, firefighters, 911) benefit if the receiver is trained to properly understand what message is being communicated, especially in creating a relaxed conversational tone in order to clearly identify the emergency and the proper method of response. Effective communication skills help to save the lives of those in need and time for those attempting to aid others. Conversation analysis has also been effective in the medical fields. Properly trained doctors and consultants can reduce unnecessary prescribing, overprescribing, and errors in surgery (e.g., amputating the wrong leg). Conflict mediators, marriage counselors, and even politicians can benefit from learning skills in effective public speaking. All persons benefit from effective communication. In short, conversation analysis can assist nearly everyone positively.

Research in the area of degradation ceremonies remains very relevant. Garfinkel was correct in his assertion that all societies use such techniques to control behavior. It is also true that nearly all social groups and organizations have such disciplinary reviews in place to punish those who stray from the expected norm. Degradation ceremonies alter the identity of the subject, who is given a label that is of lesser status than that previously held. This new label brings with it a new identity that compromises full acceptance within the group or society. Among the many examples is the military court-martial, where the convicted person is stripped of former rank and privileges. The disgrace is often too much to bear. Government workers may also be subjected to degradation ceremonies. Other degradation ceremonies include mental health officials' labeling someone insane and the criminal courts' labeling someone a sex offender. The status of sex offender is especially compromised as those so labeled must register with local officials and inform neighbors whenever they move into a new neighborhood.

In *Shameful Behaviors* (2008), I argue that there is a growing culture of shamelessness in society wherein the norms of traditional society are being replaced with new ones that are centered on a lack of feeling shame and embarrassment for behaviors that in the past would have elicited strong negative reactions from others. I distinguish among formal shamings (e.g., military court-martials, judicial punishments designed to shame the offender, and workplace mobbings), which are accompanied by degradation ceremonies; informal shamings (e.g., conducted by friends, family members, and sports teams), which are accompanied by quasi-degradation ceremonies; and self-shaming (people who put themselves in situations destined to cause self-shame). Perhaps the topic students find most interesting in *Shameful Behaviors* is *drunk shamings*.

Drunk shamings are an example of an informal degradation ceremony designed to shame and embarrass the victim. Drunk shamings are most likely to be perpetrated by high school and younger college-aged persons. A drunk shaming occurs when people become too drunk to defend themselves from a private (among friends) or public shaming (via the Internet, such as YouTube or Facebook). Often, the drunk person will have his or her picture taken and/or have items drawn or placed upon them (in an attempt to degrade, or poke fun at, the drunk person). Drunk shamings generally entail a four-step process:

Step 1:   A person(s) drinks excessively (in the company of a group of other people) to the point where he or she passes out drunk.

Step 2:   Someone from the group of other people needs to take action. That is, he or she needs to start the drunk-shaming process.

Step 3:   Some application of a method(s) of drunk shaming must be conducted.

Step 4:   The drunk shaming is captured for posterity on film or video, which may then be posted online.

Drunk shamings involve an emergent form of embarrassment opportunity. Any person who drinks excessively is a potential victim of a drunk shaming. However, there are a number of rules involved with drunk shamings that are designed to protect some forms of drunkenness. For example, if the drunk person is asleep in his or her own bed, they cannot be shamed; however, a person who falls asleep (passes out) with his or her shoes on is fair game for a drunk shaming. In the ethnomethodological tradition, I conducted original research on the drunk-shaming behaviors of college students at a state university. I also conducted traditional data analysis. Thus, this study had aspects of both qualitative and quantitative forms of methodology. Drunk shamings were also analyzed by one's level of self-esteem (to gain a symbolic interactionist approach). I wanted to find to examine whether a person's level of self-esteem was significant with being either a perpetrator or victim of a drunk shaming. Among other findings, it was discovered that most drunk-shaming participants (both victims and perpetrators) found this quasi-degradation ceremony as a fun activity. A person who was a victim of a drunk shaming would usually laugh off the shame and embarrassment the next day by simply saying, "I was drunk!" The growing culture of shameless dictates a general belief that if a person is drunk, he or she should be absolved of any behavior committed while being drunk and that there was no reason to feel shame or embarrassment.

Ethnomethodology would appear to still have relevancy in the present day, both to laypersons and, more importantly, to sociological social theory. Like ethnomethodology, phenomenology is another sociological theory of the everyday life. Let's examine phenomenology next.

DEFINING PHENOMENOLOGY

Phenomenology studies common sense, conscious experience, and routine daily life. In this regard, phenomenology may be placed in the category of sociologies of everyday life. In the preface of *Introduction to the Sociologies of Everyday Life,* Jack Douglas (1980) argued that the sociologists of everyday life have for many years been rebuilding the foundation for understanding all human life and thus rebuilding the foundation of all theory and method in the social sciences.

The term *phenomenological sociology* refers to the work of a number of sociologists who share certain sympathies regarding phenomenological philosophy. Phenomenological analysis has as its subject matter the world of conscious experience. The world consists of the numerous and shifting inputs of perception. Since most perception is quickly and effortlessly organized into certain customary patterns, the world appears as a familiar one. It is common for the familiarity of the world to become so compelling that the work that goes into achieving this familiarity is overlooked. The major goal of phenomenology is to reverse this process by exploring and analyzing the formative core of consciousness (Douglas, 1980). *Phenomenology* can be defined as a philosophical sociology that begins with the individual and his or her own conscious experience as the focus of study and attempts to avoid prior assumptions, prejudices, and other dogmatic forms of thinking while investigating social behavior. A phenomenologist would like people not to take for granted the social world and, instead, to question its formation and maintenance.

EDMUND HUSSERL AND THE PHENOMENOLOGICAL APPROACH

It was Edmund Husserl (1859–1938) who first developed the phenomenological approach. For him, the term *phenomenology* designates two things: a new kind of descriptive method that made a breakthrough in philosophy at the turn of the nineteenth century and a science that is intended to supply the basic instrument for a rigorously scientific philosophy and, in its consequent application, to make possible a methodological reform of all the sciences (McCormick and Elliston, 1981). The roots of phenomenology are firmly entrenched in the German tradition, some of the most important intellectual debates taking place between the world wars.

Edmund Husserl, philosopher and social thinker who helped form phenomenology. (Interfoto/Alamy)

Husserl's Phenomenology

Husserl's philosophy begins with the assumption that every certainty is questionable. In *Ideem I*, Husserl (1950) described phenomenology as a "doctrine of essences" and a doctrine concerned with what things are, not with whether they are. Husserl was not looking to establish absolute presuppositions on which to build a whole system of knowledge. Consequently, he was not interested in being a system builder. In his introduction to *The Phenomenology of Internal Time-Consciousness*, Calvin Schrag says of Husserl, (1966),

> He abhorred system-building as much as did [Søren] Kierkegaard and [Friedrich] Nietzsche. He was always a beginner, reexamining the foundations of his investigations, resisting all fixed formulations and final conclusions. Philosophy for Husserl was a never-ending pursuit of serious and open-ended questions, which lead to further questions that may require a resetting of the original questions. This at the same time accounts for the fertility of his investigations and for the philosophical freedom which his whole philosophy illustrates (p. 11).

In his introduction to *The Idea of Phenomenology*, George Nakhnikian says of Husserl, (1964),

> Husserl's phenomenology as an outgrowth of his attack on psychologism. Psychologism is a species of the view that philosophy is reducible to a factual science, in this case to psychology. Husserl is just as strongly against 'biologism' and 'anthropologism' as he is against psychologism (p. x).

Psychologism is an attempt to reduce the fundamental laws of logic and mathematics to psychological generalizations about the way people think; it is a type of scientific generalization.

> The significance of Husserl's critique of psychologism is basically understandable only in terms of the final goal of the *Logical Investigations,* and that goal in fact lies beyond the two published volumes. The *Investigations* as we have them consist of epistemological clarifications of principles and essential concepts, in the service of laying the theoretical groundwork of a new discipline, pure logic—what Husserl would later call the "logic of the absolute science" (Sheehan, 1981:143).

In his article "A Reply to a Critic of My Refutation of Logical Psychologism," Husserl (1972) stated that

> logic reflects on the reflected consciousness, and endeavors to raise our knowing processes to a higher power by investigating the laws of our reflected consciousness. Psychology, on the other hand, will try to carry reflection raised to a higher power by logic over into the investigation of unreflected consciousness (p. 13).

> Additionally, phenomenology is not interested in the metaphysical world. Husserl's focus on individual consciousness led his phenomenology to be metaphysically neutral. He believed that only through consciousness could a researcher find the true meaning behind behavior. For Husserl (1965), "Consciousness was the 'absolute' being with which philosophy is concerned—his is not a theory of being, as the metaphysician understands it, but only a theory of philosophical

(scientific) being" (p. 67). As Husserl saw it, personal reflection was not a psychological activity of consciousness, but the ideal act of consciousness, which is inescapably linked to an objective structure. The objective world consists of the *Unwelt* (the environing world) and the *Lebenswelt* (the everyday world).

> The *Unwelt* or *Lebenswelt,* then, is the objective counterpart of pre-philosophical consciousness: it is a world in consciousness that has not been rendered "thematic," which is simply taken for granted—it is the familiar world in which men perforce live.... Phenomenology is what it is because it neither seeks nor accepts evidence other than that offered by consciousness itself (Husserl, 1965:67–68).

In short, phenomenology is not a science of facts, but a science of essential being, an eidetic science (meaning an insubstantial empirical science); it is a science that aims at establishing the "knowledge" of essences (Husserl, 1931).

Husserl distinguished between facts and essences. He described sciences of experience as sciences of "fact." Such "facts" are determined by acts of cognition which underline human experiences. Something is real, and thus a fact, because it possesses a spatiotemporal existence, having a particular duration of its own and a "real" content (Husserl, 1931). An essence is that which an individual discloses as a "what is," an empirical possibility—a possibility which is itself to be understood not as empirical, but as an essential possibility (Husserl, 1931). Husserl noted that whatever belongs to the essence of one individual can also belong to another individual. This reality allows for the formation of categories of essences.

The complex ideas that come under the phenomenology umbrella were generated in an atmosphere of heightened social conflict and anxiety about the future. Husserl's phenomenological approach was to examine the phenomena of consciousness and bracket them in order to test their truth.

The Role of Consciousness

There are many differences between phenomenology and sociology. Phenomenologists rely on a reflexive experience as it takes form in consciousness. Their research proceeds on the certain ground of intentional consciousness. Through the techniques of reduction and the capacity for imaginative variation, the phenomenologist is able to find the rudimentary structures and processes of experience. Sociologists, on the other hand, often rely on taking the perspective of the other and imposing a sense of order on the environment so that they may collect data. Phenomenologists are much more concerned with the way individuals construct in their own consciousness the meanings of things. They see the social world as ultimately made up of many more individual constructions than do other sociologists.

> Phenomenological sociology is characterized as a subjective or creative sociology because it seeks to understand the world from the point of view of the acting subject and not from the perspective of the scientific observer. Initially then, the relevant world of study for the sociologist is the world that is inhabited by ordinary people and defined as their common-sense reality (Farganis, 2000:311).

People interact with one another on the basis of a socially created world, where meanings come about through constant negotiation in their everyday lives. Generally, they come to see the world as a natural order, rather than as the socially created one that it is. Phenomenologists question the legitimacy of an "objective" world and therefore prefer to examine the subjective natural of social reality. Edmund Husserl and Alfred Schutz, in particular, concentrate on the reciprocity of perceptions. Their analysis is a result of reflection, attention, and awareness.

Time Consciousness

Husserl (1977) explained,

> The totality of one's consciousness at any given time is a unity within which every element is bound up with every other element. However, in the *manner* of the unification of these elements, as well as in the degree of its fixity and in its immediacy or mediacy, significant differences are to be found (p. 297).

Husserl believed strongly in the link between time and consciousness. The events and content of the past do, in fact, influence one's present consciousness; they are simultaneously linked. Husserl (1931) stated,

> All the essential characteristics of experience and consciousness which we have reached are for us necessary steps towards the attainment of the end which is unceasingly drawing us on, the discovery, namely, of the essence of that *"pure" consciousness* which is to fix the limits of the phenomenological field. Our inquiries were eidetic; but the individual instances of the essences we have referred to as experience, stream of experience, "consciousness" in all its senses, belonged as real events to the natural world (pp. 125–126).

This intentional unity, which we are conscious of, is a continuous flow of perceptual patterns which pass off onto one another.

> These patterns themselves have always their *definite descriptive nature* (*Bestand*), which is *essentially* correlated with that unity. To every phase of perception there necessarily belongs, for instance, a definite content in the way of perspective variations of colour, shape, and so forth. They are counted among the *"sensory data,"* data of a particular region with determinate divisions, which within every such division gather together into concrete unities of experience *sui generis* (*sensory "fields"*) (Husserl, 1931:131–132).

ALFRED SCHUTZ AND PHENOMENOLOGY

Alfred Schutz (1899–1959) was responsible for developing phenomenology as a sociological science. Schutz studied law and social science under Hans Kelsen (philosopher of law) and Ludwig von Mises (economist) at the University of Vienna. His *Phenomenology of the Social World* (1967; Orig. 1932) combined Weber's sociology with Husserl's phenomenological method. Schutz worked with Husserl briefly at Freiburg.

The Phenomenology of the Social World

Schutz spent many years working on *The Phenomenology of the Social World* (1967), and his study is centered on an intensive concern with Weber's subjective approach to the study of human behavior. Schutz (1967) concluded that "only a philosophically founded theory of method can exorcise the pseudo-problems which today hinder research in the social sciences, and especially in sociology" (p. xxxi). Schutz believed that only the works of Henri Bergson and especially Husserl's transcendental phenomenology have a sufficiently deep foundation in the proper methodological approach. When studying the social world, Schutz (1967) argued that we must accept "the existence of the social world as it is always accepted in the attitude of the natural standpoint, whether in everyday life or in the sociological observation" (p. 97). We must accept our own existence and the existence of others. When observing his or her own lived experiences, the individual must perform a reflective act of attention. When observing others, it is not necessary to live their experiences, but rather simply to "look" at (observe) their experiences. Schutz (1967) explained:

> This means that, whereas I can observe my own lived experiences only after they are over and done with, I can observe yours as they actually take place. This in turn implies that you and I are in a specific sense "simultaneous," that we "coexist," that our respective streams of consciousness intersect.... In trying to understand this sychronism we can hardly ignore the fact that when you and I are in the natural attitude we perceive ourselves and each other as psychological unities.... I see, then, my own stream of consciousness and yours in a single intentional act which embraces them both (pp. 102–103).

Thus, one's stream of consciousness is in simultaneous relation to others' streams of consciousness (e.g., as in the expression "growing old together"). An individual's acts are influenced by other people's acts. However, the simultaneity of two streams of consciousness does not mean that the same experiences are shared. For example, a couple may attend a concert; one enjoys it very much, while the other finds the experience unenjoyable. Therefore, even when sharing an experience with someone, one may not share the same stream of consciousness.

In Chapter 4, "The Structure of the Social World," in *The Phenomenology of the Social World* (1967), Schutz explained that once the existence of individuals and the social world is assumed, we have already entered the realm of intersubjectivity.

> The world is now experienced by the individual as shared by his fellow creatures, in short, as a *social* world.... This social world is by no means homogenous but exhibits a multiform structure. Each of its spheres or regions is both a way of perceiving and a way of understanding the subjective experiences of others (p. 139).

In his study of the multiform structure of society, Schutz (1967) attempted to answer three primary questions:

1. How is such an inner differentiation possible?
2. What grounds are there for supposing that the social world has both unity and inner differentiation?
3. Which of these differentiations may usefully serve as a basis for an analysis of understanding the other self?

Schutz (1967) stated that in a certain sense one becomes a social scientist in everyday life whenever one reflects upon his or her fellow humans and their behavior instead of merely experiencing them. The starting point of social science, then, is this *everyday life*. Schutz quickly pointed out that there is a difference between the naive person studying human behavior and the social researcher, who studies behavior scientifically.

Interdifferentiation is evident to all. We are aware of others and can reflect upon their different characteristics; we are consciously aware of this reality. This awareness extends beyond the spatial (the physical space our bodies take within the natural environment); it is a conscious awareness that the world is both united, through streams of consciousness, and divided, based on individual experience and interpretation of events. We not only attend to our own stream of consciousness but can also attend to others, and therefore, we become aware of what is going on in the minds of others. Understanding others is possible because we share the same world and many of the subjective meanings attached to experiences. In this manner, someone else's subjective experiences are "accessible" to me because we share the same world. However, what one interprets as the other's stream of consciousness may not be accurate, because of misinter-pretation, as illustrated by the expression, "I don't know what you mean by that" (just as many students may wonder, "What does the author mean by this?"). Assessing someone else's stream of consciousness is affected by what Schutz called *degrees of interpretability*. Through observa-tion, it is generally clear whether certain people are engaged in social relationships (e.g., a couple walking hand and hand or store employees talking to one another are sure to know one another). However, certain presumptions are often not true; we may misinterpret the interactions among the people we are observing.

So how do we come to understand social action objectively? Schutz altered Weber's defini-tion of *social action*: "Action is social insofar as, by virtue of the subjective meaning attached to it by the acting individual (or individuals), it takes account of the behavior of others, and is thereby oriented in its course"—to "intentional conscious experiences directed toward the other self" (Schutz, 1967:144). Schutz (1967) expanded on this idea:

> Conscious experiences intentionally related to another self which emerge in the form of spontaneous activity we shall speak of as *social behavior*. If such experiences have the character of being previously projected, we shall speak of them as *social action*. Social behavior so defined will embrace all specific Ego-Acts (*Ich-Akte*) which are intention-ally directed upon a Thou as upon another self having consciousness and duration. Here we include experiences such as feelings of sympathy and antipathy, erotic attitudes, and feeling-activities of all kinds (p. 144).

Individuals have many choices in social action. Action represents options of conduct. Action may be covert (the intention of the act is kept private) or it may be overt (the intention of the act is made obvious). In short, "Action may take place—purposely or not—by commission or omission" (Schutz, 1962:67). Acts of omission occur when the individual decides not to act in a given situation (e.g., choosing not to help up off the floor someone who has just fallen).

When two people become reciprocally oriented, we have what Weber called a *social rela-tionship*. In this regard, the behavior (social action) of a plurality of actors is oriented toward each other. Once people are in a social relationship, there are two ways in which a person can become aware of whether her or his intentional acts of consciousness, directed toward another person, are reciprocated. She or he can either live in the mutually related conscious experience (accepting at face value that the relationship is mutual), or she or he can "step out" of the social relationship for a period of time to contemplate whether she or he is the object of attention of the other person (Schutz, 1967). A significant other, in any given social relationship, can be described as a person within reach of direct experience and with whom one shares a community of space and a community of time. In other words, a person who spends a great deal of time and space with someone has a social relationship with that person.

Persons who are in reach of each other's direct experience are involved in "face-to-face" situations.

The face-to-face situation presupposes, then, an actual simultaneity with each other of two separate streams of consciousness.... Spatial and temporal immediacy is essential to the face-to-face situation. All acts of other-orientation and of affecting-the-other, and therefore all orientations and relationships within the face-to-face situation, derive their own specific flavor and style from this immediacy (Schutz, 1967:163).

Face-to-face relationships grow into "we-relationships," where the streams of consciousness are so intertwined that it becomes common for one person to think of the other as a "natural" extension of expression. Schutz also made a distinction between reciprocal and one-sided relationships. In the reciprocal relationship, each partner is benefiting by the experience. As a one-sided relationship would imply, one person is enjoying far more benefits than the other. Friendships are examples of reciprocal relationships, especially in light of the question of why anyone would maintain a friendship that was one-sided. (Work relationships are generally one-sided.) Schutz (1967) described friendship as a series of face-to-face relationships, where behavior is oriented to the "expected and, external obstacles aside, the friends can always get together again and again."

Schutz (1967) concluded that social action is a lived experience; that is guided by a plan or project arising from the subject's spontaneous activity; and that it is distinguished from all other lived experiences by a peculiar act of intention.

Stock of Knowledge

Individuals draw upon their stock of knowledge while interacting with one another in the social environment. The stock of knowledge that people possess is determined by their life experiences and education. Many life experiences and a diverse awareness of events will dramatically increase one's stock of knowledge. With different stocks of knowledge come different behaviors. As Atkinson (2010) explains,

> Importantly, for Schutz the different levels of the stock of knowledge and the attitudes that frame it combine, in conjunction with the characteristics or demands of the situational context in the lifeworld (and sometimes pronounced physiological prompts, e.g., hunger), to give rise to a variety of forms of action, from consciously deliberated projects and long-term plans through habitual or routinized modes of conduct (p. 14).

Schutz and Luckmann (1973) categorized a number of types of stocks of knowledge, some of which seem to overlap. *Routine knowledge* refers to the ability to differentiate between common situations (routine) and unique ones. *Useful knowledge* refers to the awareness of everyday events and being able to accomplish acts that represent a "means to an end." These types of knowledge allow the individual to solve problems. *Knowledge of recipes* is a standardized means of dealing with specific situations that possess a "self-evident" quality or implication. Schutz used as examples a hunter reading tracks, a sailor or mountain climber orienting herself or himself to changes in the weather, and an interpreter who "automatically" translates phrases. *Habitual knowledge* presents "definitive" solutions to problems, which are organized in the flow of lived experiences, and require little attention (e.g., being able to dress and talk on the phone at the same time, or whistling a song while thinking about a mathematical problem). Schutz stated that a certain amount of habitual knowledge belongs to everyone's stock of knowledge. "The 'content' of this knowledge is indeed variable, but not in the same sense that the partial contents of the stock of knowledge are variable from one society to the next and within a society" (Schutz and

Luckmann, 1973:109). Everyone has a certain degree of knowledge; experience is what dictates differences between the stock of knowledge of individuals.

Common Sense

Stocks of knowledge, especially the habitual, come to be so taken for granted that the individual may come to view certain situations as being dictated by rules of common sense. Labeling situations and events as being dictated by common sense presents many potential dangers (for both the researcher and the interactants). Schutz (1962) stated that

> Even the thing perceived in everyday life is more than a simple sense presentation. It is a thought object, a construct of a highly complicated nature.... In other words, the so-called concrete facts of common-sense perception are not as concrete as it seems. They already involve abstractions of a highly complicated nature, and we have to take account of this situation lest we commit the fallacy of misplaced concreteness (pp. 3–4).

All of our knowledge of the world, including common sense and science, involves constructs (e.g., generalizations, formalizations, idealizations). This does not mean that we are incapable of understanding the reality of the world; it just means that we merely grasp only certain aspects of it.

> Common-sense constructs are formed from a "Here" within the world which determines the presupposed reciprocity of perspectives. They take a stock of socially derived and socially approved knowledge for granted. The social distribution of knowledge determines the particular structure of the typifying construct, for instance, the assumed degree of anonymity of personal roles, the standardization of course-of-action patterns, and the supposed constancy of motives (Schutz, 1962:38).

These taken-for-granted and common-sense patterns are relevant only to those with shared life experiences. Thus, the behaviors of one person may seem to violate the common sense of another person, but the person who has no awareness context of the expected and "proper" course of action has not violated common sense. Add to this the reality that many people regularly violate so-called common sense.

The Structure of the Life-World

The Structure of the Life-World (1973) represents the final focus of twenty-seven years of Schutz's labor, encompassing his work between 1932 and his death in 1959. It represents his attempt to achieve a comprehensive grasp of the nature of social reality, and "it presents an integration of his theory of relevance within his analysis of social structures" (quote from Zaner and Engelhardt, translators of *The Structure of the Life-World*, 1973:xxvii).

It is the everyday-life world that remains the cornerstone of interest to phenomenologists. Schutz and Luckmann (1973) stated that

> The everyday life-world is the region of reality in which man can engage himself and which he can change while he operates in it by means of his animate organism.... Only in this realm can one be understood by his fellow-men, and only in it can he work together with them. Only in the world of everyday life can a common, communicative, surrounding world be constituted. The world of everyday life is consequently man's fundamental and paramount reality (p. 3).

Thus, the life world is found in the everyday world. The everyday reality of the life world includes both natural elements found in the environment and the social elements created by culture.

Schutz argued that Husserl's concept of the life world was unacceptable and unworthy of the phenomenological method. It failed because it cannot solve the problem of intersubjectivity.

> Schutz asserted a mundane constitution of intersubjectivity as the foundation of the life-world; he solved the difficult problem of life-worldly transcendences in terms of his rethinking of the concept of the symbol, be deriving "the structure of the life-world from the lived experience of transcendence" (Grafholf, 1989:215).

Schutz believed that the life world is intersubjective and presents itself as a subjective meaning context. That is, it appears meaningful in one's consciousness. In the life world, individuals come to find others who are "like me." Action is therefore embedded for them in meaning contexts and is subjectively motivated and articulated purposefully according to their particular interests and according to what is feasible for them (Schutz and Luckmann, 1973:15). The everyday-life world is the primary reality for individuals because it encompasses most of their daily activities.

Alfred Schutz was a major influence in the development of phenomenological sociology in the English-speaking world and has received recognition as one of the foremost philosophers of social science. Among the more significant contemporary phenomenologists is Peter Berger.

PETER BERGER AND THE SOCIAL CONSTRUCTION OF REALITY

Peter Berger (1929–) is a renowned sociologist and social critic, theologian, and novelist. In his work, Berger attempts to understand reality in modern society. Among his many publications, Berger's most significant contribution to sociology is *The Social Construction of Reality* (1966), which he co-authored with Thomas Luckmann.

The Social Construction of Reality

The Social Construction of Reality (Berger and Luckmann, 1966) was intended as a systematic, theoretical treatise in the sociology of knowledge. Berger and Luckmann argued that reality is socially constructed and that the sociology of knowledge must analyze the processes in which this occurs.

> The key terms in these contentions are "reality" and "knowledge," terms that are not only current in everyday speech, but that have behind them a long history of philosophical inquiry.... for our purposes, [we] define "reality" as a quality appertaining to phenomena that we recognize as having a being independent of our own volition (we cannot "wish them away"), and to define "knowledge" as the certainty that phenomena are real and that they possess specific characteristics (p. 1).

It is difficult to argue with the premise that sociology has a strong interest in regard to "reality" and "knowledge" if for no other reason than their social relativity. Sociology involves the scientific study of society. To study society scientifically (or philosophically), it must consist of a "social reality," and the means about which we examine society is representative in our knowledge of it. However, social reality is greatly influenced by culture, and therefore, one person's (such as a Tibetan monk's) sense of reality may be drastically different from another's (such as an American businessman's). It is the contention of Berger and Luckmann (1980) that

> The sociology of knowledge must concern itself with whatever passes for "knowledge" in a society, regardless of the ultimate validity or invalidity (by whatever criteria) of such "knowledge." And insofar as all human "knowledge" is developed, transmitted and main-tained in social situations, the sociology of knowledge must seek to understand the pro-cesses by which this is done In such a way that a taken-for-granted "reality" congeals for the man in the street. In other words, we contend that *the sociology of knowledge is con-cerned with the analysis of the social construction of reality* (p. 3).

The term *sociology of knowledge* (*Wissenssoziologie*) was coined by German philosopher Max Scheler in the 1920s. This is an important note when one is considering the genesis and development of this new discipline. It is from Marx's *Economic and Philosophical Manuscripts of 1844* that the sociology of knowledge derived its root proposition; that human consciousness is determined by his social being.

> The sociology of knowledge inherited from Marx not only the sharpest formulation of its central problem but also some of its key concepts, among which should be mentioned particularly the concepts of "ideology" (ideas serving as weapons for social interests) and "false consciousness" (thought that is alienated from the real social being of the thinker). The sociology of knowledge has been particularly fascinated by Marx's twin concepts of "substructure/superstructure" (Berger and Luckmann, 1966:5).

According to Berger and Luckmann, other significant social thinkers linked to the origins of the sociology of knowledge include Durkheim, Weber, Pareto, Mannheim, and Parsons.

The foundation of reality is found in everyday life, more precisely, the knowledge that guides conduct in everyday life. Berger and Luckmann (1966) explained that everyday life pres-ents itself as a reality that is subjectively meaningful to actors. The everyday life of individuals is designed to make the world coherent from their perspective. Berger and Luckmann believed that sociologists should examine the everyday life as presented by the actors themselves.

Within the framework of the subjectively established everyday life, the continued con-struction of social reality becomes contingent on a number of processes. One such process is externalization, wherein actors create their own social worlds as they interact with others. From this standpoint, the social construction of reality is accomplished by individuals as a result of their past behaviors and can be continually modified and recreated with current activities. On the other hand, the process of objectivation influences the individual to view the everyday life-world as an ordered reality with phenomena prearranged in patterns that seem to be indepen-dent of the actor. It is this level of consciousness that causes the actor to see the world in a taken-for-granted fashion. The common objectivations of everyday life are maintained primarily by language. The reason for immigrants' reluctance to change their language is not only that it implies giving up their past heritage but that it also results in dramatic changes in their everyday-life world—their very construction of social reality. The same reasoning holds for those who are reluctant to embrace policies that encourage a bilingual society: Their life worlds will be altered. A third process, internalization, is a process in which society attempts to link individual mem-bers in a community through the socialization process. When people share the same norms, values, and behavioral expectations, they share a similar social world.

Marriage and the Construction of Reality

Berger had been contemplating ideas on the social construction of reality since the summer of 1962. In an article that he co-authored with Hansfried Kellner (1964), "Marriage and the Construction of Reality," a specific social institution (marriage) is examined in the context of social construction. "The process that interests us here is the one that constructs, maintains and modifies a consistent reality that can be meaningfully experienced by individuals" (Berger and Kellner, 1964:2). The authors indicated that every society has its own specific way of defining and perceiving reality, and this is true of the institution of marriage. Many rules have been constructed over the years that apply to marriage (e.g., the incest taboo, age restrictions, gender parameters) in any given culture. Society's rules impact the everyday experience and conduct of individuals. The monogamous character of marriage has a profound influence on Americans.

Society's expectations of proper social relationships illustrate the merging point between individual desires and socially acceptable behaviors. Two people who decide to marry realize that each partner's actions must be projected in conjunction with those of the other. Lifestyle changes are implied when one gets married; in other words, the old social reality is abandoned, or at best reconstructed, and a new social reality is constructed. Each partner has new modes of meaningful experience of the world in general, of other people, and of himself or herself. In short, with marriage comes a reconstruction of the everyday-life world. These changes come voluntarily and internally, as few people are literally "forced" to get married.

In *The War over the Family* (1983), co-authored by Brigitte Berger and Peter Berger, the social construction aspect of marriage is expanded to include the changing role of the family in contemporary society. The ideas in this book also demonstrate that changes in the everyday-life world can be caused by external forces, over which actors have little control. The Bergers presented three basic contemporary views of the family: the leftist and feminist critique calling for radical change; the new and largely reactionary "profamily" movement; and the value-free analysis of social scientists. They traced the historical development of the family, giving special notice to the effects of modernization and its pressures. According to the Bergers (1983),

> There is the view that the family and its values are in a steep decline. The decline is variously interpreted in terms of its causes—broad social trends or specific ideological movements or changes in religion and morality—but most of those holding this view agree that the alleged decline of the family is harmful both to the individual and to society (p. 85).

Thus, social forces (e.g., an economic down spiral) which are external to the actor may dictate a change in her or his everyday-life world.

Peter Berger has made significant contributions to the field of sociology in general, and to phenomenology specifically. His and Luckmann's book *The Social Construction of Reality* (1966) remains a classic for all social thinkers.

CRITICISMS OF PHENOMENOLOGY

The criticisms of phenomenology are similar to those of any sociology of the everyday life. Specifically, the critics of phenomenology are generally those who prefer a more scientific or grounded approach to social theory. The concepts used by phenomenologists are very vague and subject to interpretation. This abstract nature clouds the contribution of phenomenology to sociology. But even those who prefer alternatives to scientific social theory question whether the conclusions reached by phenomenologists can be supported by concrete evidence. Scientifically driven social theorists need to acknowledge this diverse approach to the study of human behavior.

Concepts such as *common sense* and *stocks of knowledge* are often problematic. We already know that items treated as "common sense" for some people may not be common sense to others. Thus, the notion of treating things as common sense can become problematic, especially when used as a variable when conducting sociological theory and research. But one's stock of knowledge can be compromised as well and therefore just as problematic. Consider, for example, a person who has acquired knowledge from an unreliable source and then acts as though this information is correct. When this occurs, one's stock of knowledge is compromised and so too is his or her behavior. Shirleene Robinson (2011) discusses the phenomena of the "Outback Steakhouse" restaurant chain being treated as a true representation of Australia for Americans. (There are over 1,200 of these restaurants throughout the United States and across the world. The Australian-themed restaurant was created by four American businessmen who had never been to Australia.) As Robinson (2011) comments,

> The *Outback Steakhouse* is not an authentic Australian restaurant chain by any means.... While there may be some dubious Australiana decorations on the walls and "Australian" images are used in commercials, customers are presented with a nonthreatening construction of Australia that links very closely to the American idea of the "wild west" (p. 559).

People who buy into the concept of *Outback Steakhouses* have added false information to their stocks of knowledge and potentially lose credibility when interacting with people who do know Australian culture. In a related story, it should be noted that Fosters is not "Australian for beer," as the American Fosters beer commercials lead Americans to believe. In fact, as I can attest, if you go to Australia and ask for a Fosters, you will be given looks of bewilderment by younger Australians and comments such as, "You must be an American" by older Australians. Why? Because Fosters beer is not sold in Australia! Someone, like myself, who had added the idea of Fosters as *the* Australian beer to his stock of knowledge was, in reality, working with a false sense of knowledge.

APPLICATION OF PHENOMENOLOGY TO CONTEMPORARY SOCIETY

The relevancy of phenomenology is, in many respects, similar to the relevance of most micro-oriented approaches. However, the very point of studies of the everyday life *is* their relevancy. It provides us with great insights into the everyday, taken-for-granted approach that people utilize in their life worlds. Each of us brings to every social interaction a stock of knowledge. No two persons' stocks of knowledge are the same. As a result, we are constantly reconstructing our sense of social reality as we interact with people who are different from ourselves. Reading the cues of others is a common occurrence in everyday life. Past experiences allow people to bracket possible courses of action in the everyday-life world. An increased stock of knowledge increases the probability of properly interpreting the situation. For example, if your store manager or supervisor, at your first job, does not perform his or her job well, you may become skeptical of your supervisor in your next job. This is because we draw upon previous knowledge and experience. The same concept is true with dating. If the significant other in your first "real" relationship cheated on you, you are likely to be reluctant to trust your next partner. The examples become nearly endless within this scenario.

One's stock of knowledge includes the items found within the realm of common sense. People generally act on what they consider obvious, or what is often referred to as common sense. The problem with "common-sense" attitudes and outlooks on life is highlighted by the reality that people violate common sense regularly. Going through life with a common-sense approach is sure to include many misunderstandings and misinterpretations in the taken-for-granted world. The violation of common sense is so regular and so profound in the life world that I plan on writing an entire book on this subject.

Phenomenologists acknowledge the role of social structure. In *The Social Construction of Social Reality* (1966), Berger and Luckmann acknowledged that social reality is constructed by the everyday interactions of individuals, and also by social institutions. These social institutions are greatly influenced by culture. Thus, perception is influenced by culture and social expectations. The relevancy of Berger's work on the social construction of marriage is applicable to anyone who is married, or in a serious relationship, or about to get married. The rules do change when one gets married because they have to. For example, is it certainly not acceptable to have intimate relations with people other than your partner, and it is expected that couples who share a home also share in the responsibilities of maintaining the home (e.g., cleaning, maintenance, shopping, and cooking).

Just as social researchers continue to use the ethnomethodological approach, so too do a number of researchers utilize the phenomenological approach. One such example involves a study conducted by Shaw and Hector (2010) involving listening to military members' accounts of war when they return from Iraq and/or Afghanistan. The long-lasting wars in the Middle East have many consequences, including an ever-increasing number of veterans returning home with "problems" because of their experiences as military members. As Shaw and Hector (2010) explain, "Talking to military members about their experiences in Iraq and/or Afghanistan via phenomenological interviews may be beneficial for both [researchers] and military members" (p. 128). Many people benefit from telling their stories in a more informal, open-ended style of questioning than they do by answering some sort of list of questions via an exit interview format.

Summary

Ethnomethodology and phenomenology are theories of the everyday life. Their place in sociology is often overshadowed by the traditional sociological theories already discussed and the newer, more popular theories, yet to be discussed (e.g., feminism, critical theory, or postmodern theories). Ethnomethodology is a theoretical perspective that seeks to understand human behavior by examining the methods that people employ to make sense of the world. Created by Harold Garfinkel, ethnomethodology is the study of the everyday practices of people and their attempts to deal with day-to-day life. Clues are provided by individuals through their verbal accounts of social action. People attempt to maintain a sense

of normality and prefer to live in a common-sense world built by a stream of past experiences and interpretations of events.

Phenomenology is a micro-oriented sociological theory which has as its subject matter the conscious experience of individuals. People's view of the world is shaped by varying perceptions that influence their consciousness. Framing our perceptions of the world allows us to envision some sort of social structure, or social order. Most perceptions are quickly organized into customary patterns, which reinforce previous outlooks on things. Phenomenologists attempt to break down these preconceived notions of social reality in order to explore and analyze the formative core of individual consciousness. Phenomenologists attempt to break down the taken-for-granted world of the actors and instead question its formation and maintenance.

Ethnomethodology and phenomenology are theories of the sociology of everyday life, which involve studies of face-to-face interactions by observation. They examine routine life, conscious experience, and common sense. Among the basic premises of these two theories is that people interact with one another on the basis of a socially created, reified world, where meanings come about through constant negotiation in everyday life. Although these theories are rather marginal in the grand scheme of sociological theory, they remain relevant to theorists who attempt to uncover the daily interactions of people.

 Study and **Review** on **MySearchLab**

Discussion Questions

1. Describe what is meant by a degradation ceremony and provide at least three examples from contemporary society.
2. What are breaching experiments? Create, or conduct, your own breaching experiment and write a review of it.
3. What value do the theories of everyday life offer sociology? How do they compare to the traditional theories we have already discussed?
4. Examine your own stock of knowledge. Although this will be difficult to ascertain, is it possible that any of this knowledge is falsely created because of misinformation? How do you handle conflicting information from professors who say one thing in one classroom and then hear another professor say the opposite in a different classroom?
5. Which sociological theory—ethnomethodology or phenomenology—seems more relevant to sociology? Which one seems more relevant to your life? Why?

MySearchLab® Connections

MysearchLab is designed just for you. Each chapter features a customized study plan to help you learn and review key concepts and terms. Dynamic visual activities, videos, and readings found in the multimedia library will enhance your learning experience.

 View on **MySearchLab**

▶ The Social Transformation of Society

 Read on **MySearchLab**

▶ Goffman, Erving. The Presentation of Self in Everyday Life.

CHAPTER

13 Feminist Theory

 Listen to the **Chapter Audio** on **MySearchLab**

Chapter Outline

- Defining Feminism
- Feminist Theory: The First and Second Waves
- Variations in Feminist Theory
- Dorothy E. Smith
- Sandra Harding
- Patricia Hill Collins
- Carol Gilligan
- Joan Jacobs Brumberg
- Barbara Risman
- Application of Feminist Theory and the Third Wave of Feminism
- Criticisms of Feminist Theory
- Summary
- Discussion Questions

Throughout most of history, women have struggled to attain gender equity. The patriarchal design of most societies left women in a secondary power role to men. From the early days of humanity, women, because of their biological make-up, have given birth to children and were the primary caretakers of these children. As a result, men were relegated to the role of hunters in order to secure food for their families. But these biological roles became indoctrinated as gender roles over the millennium, leading many to believe that women should stay at home and take care of the domestic needs of the family while men took on the role of being breadwinners in the workplace. A mindset developed among most cultures that men were meant to perform certain duties and women others. In Western societies, where citizens had the right to vote, such a right was restricted to men until the nineteenth century. It has been a long-time struggle for women in their attempt to gain equality with men. Although many women have voiced a demand for equality throughout the past centuries, it was not until the "first wave" of feminism in the mid-1800s did they gain any significant measure of impending equality. It was the "second wave" of feminism, which started in the 1960s, that really brought about significant changes in the role of women in society. With many battles of equality won, contemporary feminism, or the "third wave," has taken on new challenges in the fight for equality. In this chapter, feminist thought is examined, beginning with a definition of feminism and a brief look at the "first wave" of feminism, continuing with a review of most of the many variations of feminism, along with a review of a few leading feminist theorists, and ending with a look at contemporary feminism. The second and third waves of feminism will also be articulated.

DEFINING FEMINISM THEORY

Feminist theory is an outgrowth of the general movement to empower women worldwide; it is an extension of the idea of feminism. Feminist theory is a broad-based theoretical perspective that attempts to demonstrate the importance of women, to reveal the historical reality that women have been subordinate to men (beginning with the biological division of labor), and to bring about gender equity. Feminism is a women-centered approach to the study of human behavior. It serves as an advocate for oppressed women. Through analysis of gender roles and gender appropriateness, feminist theory demonstrates how women have historically been subjected to a double standard in both their treatment and the evaluation of their worth. With these ideas in mind, feminism can be defined as "a recognition and critique of male supremacy combined with efforts to change it" (Hartmann, 1998:41). Chris Beasley (1999) describes feminism as a doctrine that suggests women are systematically disadvantaged in modern society and that advocates equal opportunities for men and women. Although these two descriptions of feminism are nearly similar, they foreshadow differences in feminist perspectives. That is, some variations of feminism seek equality and others seek to reverse the power differentials between the sexes.

Feminist theory attempts to demonstrate the importance of women and to reveal gender differences that were created socially and not inherent to any sexual classification system. It is this reality that reveals that feminism is more than a theory. And that is why we will use this definition of *feminism*: a social theory and a social movement designed to empower women in an attempt to reach gender equity—especially with regard to sharing scarce resources (e.g., power, prestige, and status). Because gender social differences are the result of cultural norms, values, beliefs, and expectations associated with a sexual category, feminists indicate that such social arrangements can be altered.

In order to accomplish these goals, women activists realized that they needed to change laws, community attitudes, and negative perceptions of women; make changes in existing social institutions (e.g., the family, work, politics, education); and create new social institutions that support women's rights. Women have fought for reproductive rights and protection from domestic violence inflicted upon them by their husbands and boyfriends.

FEMINIST THEORY: THE FIRST AND SECOND WAVES

In Chapter 6, we learned that the abolitionist movement of the 1830s, combined with first Women's Rights Convention, held in Seneca Falls, NY, in 1848, spearheaded the start of the American feminist movement. We can think of this era as the beginning of the "first wave" of feminism.

The First Wave of Feminism

A group of women led by Elizabeth Cady Stanton and Quaker preacher Lucretia Mott spearheaded the first Women's Rights Convention to shed light on the many social institutions that were designed to keep women subordinate to men. The existing sociopolitical structure worked against women. More than 300 people attended the first convention of women's rights in the Wesleyan Methodist Chapel. The convention was gathered to discuss the social, civil, and religious conditions of women. It also led to the Declaration of Sentiments. Elizabeth Cady Stanton wrote the first draft of the Declaration of Sentiments out of a strong desire to fight social injustice. The Declaration of Sentiments was modeled on the Declaration of Independence. Paragraph 2 states,

> We hold these truths to be self-evident; that all men and women are created equal; that they are endowed by their Creator with certain inalienable rights; that among these are life, liberty, and the pursuit of happiness; that to secure these rights governments are instituted, deriving their just powers from the consent of the governed (United States Constitution Online, 2011).

The Declaration of Sentiments also addressed concrete issues that concerned the early feminists. Stating that men have

> framed the laws of divorce, as to what shall be the proper causes of divorce; in case of separation, to whom the guardianship of the children shall be given, as to be wholly regardless of the happiness of women—the law, in all cases, going upon the false supposition of the supremacy of man, and giving all power into his hands....He has monopolized nearly all the profitable employments, and from those she is permitted to follow, she receives but a scanty remuneration....He has denied her the facilities for obtaining a thorough education—all colleges being closed against her (United States Constitution Online, 2011).

The early feminist movement had a strong commitment to gaining rights for women in education. These early feminists argued that women should have the right to attend college and receive a diploma (and not a "testimonial," where such options existed for women at colleges). These feminists also advocated for married women's property reform because women were not allowed to own anything when they married (West and Zimmerman, 2002). They also pushed for changes in inheritance laws that, at the time of the convention, gave full authority to the husband on any decisions on investment of property or money inherited by the wife (Marilley, 1996). This convention also marked the beginning of a seventy-two-year battle to gain women the right to vote in the United States. In 1920, the United States became the seventeenth country in the world to give women the right to vote. New Zealand was the first country to do so, in 1893.

Meanwhile, in early-twentieth-century Germany, feminist thought was being led by such social thinkers as Marianne Weber and grew out of a reaction to the oppressive social system. Germany had been unified in 1871 under the authoritarian and militaristic regime of the monarchy of Prussia led by Otto von Bismarck. The feminist movement in Germany was an active attempt to reach economic and political equality between men and women. Around 1905, another German feminist group emerged whose primary concern was sexual autonomy, which led to what is known as the *erotic movement*. Helene Stocker became the leader of the erotic movement in 1906, and under her leadership, the issues of sexual politics and matrimonial law became the focus. These feminists fought for the right of women to engage in sexual relations regardless of marital and legal considerations (Mommsen and Osterhammel, 1987:486).

Max Weber criticized these women, believing that they were promoting rights of "free love" and "illegitimate" children. He viewed the erotic movement as unethical and hedonistic. Weber's wife, Marianne Weber, agreed and wrote in her own book, *Ehefrau und Mutter in der Rechtsentwicklung* (1907), that the focus of the women's movement should be the equality of women and not sexual and moral emancipation. Marianne Weber believed that marriage should be a lasting relationship between man and woman, with mutual obligations. From this standpoint, Weber made two critical points. First, women should be treated equally in the social institution of marriage, along with all the other social institutions. And second, she made it clear that marriage was strictly a union between a man and a woman, which alienated many other feminists (especially lesbian feminists).

The Second Wave of Feminism

The second wave of feminism began in the 1960s and was influential in the passage of a number of pieces of landmark legislation, including the Equal Pay Act of 1963, the Civil Rights Act of 1964, and Title IX of the Education Amendments of 1972. The 1960s was witness to many changes in the social systems of societies throughout the world. In the United States, there were social movements of all kinds, including Vietnam War protests, a movement promoting "free love" and recreational drug use, civil rights movements, and a women's rights movement. The issues addressed by previous feminists gained ground-level support from many members of society, men included. The "free love" attitude of the 1960s helped women to slowly escape the clutches of the sexual double standard—where young men who had sex with multiple partners were merely sowing wild oats and women who had sex with many partners were labeled "whores" and "sluts." Divorce became so easy to obtain that it is now commonplace. The idea that women were to be happy housewives basking in the glory of their husbands' triumphs was no longer acceptable to many women. The doors to higher-level employment were being knocked down, and women were finding fulfillment outside the home.

A commitment to core feminist beliefs continued during this period. Examining the race–class–gender linkage originated with African American feminists in the 1960s. Concepts such as the *feminization of poverty* arose because of this research. Women are far more likely than men to be poor. Furthermore, poor women are more likely to be single women, women of color, and elderly women living alone. Thus, mainstream white feminists were often negligent of the reality that women of color living in poverty might be more concerned about their economic status than about the disadvantages associated with gender (Lindsey and Beach, 2003). Contemporary feminism is consumed with the idea that women should have equal rights and is reaching this end through legal reform and legislating antidiscriminatory policies. The women's movement does not end with legal reform. It seeks a radical transformation of basic social institutions. Sociological feminist thought was at the forefront of the academic pursuit of equality between the sexes. During the 1974–1983 period, more than 700 gender-related articles appeared in sociology journals alone (Turner, 2003).

Feminism is now one of the largest subject areas in sociological discourse; clearly, its impact on the course of humanity is immense. The two waves of feminism have helped women gain equality, or near equality, in nearly all fields and social institutions. Furthermore, the impact of the "Second Wave" of feminism helped to establish a diversity in feminist thought as well.

VARIATIONS IN FEMINIST THEORY

There is so much theorizing being conducted in feminism that it takes many diverse forms.

> The feminist movement is not completely unified in part because it *is* inclusive, and that very inclusiveness makes it difficult for agreement on some issues. As a result, the movement has several different branches that are divided according to general philosophical differences (Lindsey and Beach, 2003:266).

This inclusiveness leads to an idea that all women are the same. And as Linda Alcoff (1988) points out, this leads to a significant problem for feminist theorists—the very concept of *woman*: "The concept of woman is the central concept for feminist theory and yet it is a concept that is impossible to formulate precisely for feminists.... In attempting to speak for women, feminism often seems to presuppose that it knows what women truly are, but such as assumption is fool-hardy..." (p. 405). The variations in feminist theory are discussed briefly in the following pages.

Liberal Feminism

Liberal (sometimes called *egalitarian*) feminism is the most mainstream perspective. It is based on the idea that all people are created equal and should not be denied equality of opportunity because of their gender. Men who support gender equality are most likely to take the liberal approach to feminism. Liberal feminism is best exemplified by the National Organization for Women (NOW), formed in 1966. It works within the established socioeconomic and political systems to advocate for social changes on behalf of women (Anderson, 1997).

In the mid-1970s, liberal feminism was dismissed as a bourgeois white women's movement. But the gains inspired by liberal feminism have made significant changes in women's lives. On issues ranging from equity in employment to reproductive rights, liberal reforms have resulted in increased opportunities for women and increased public consciousness of women's rights. Working within existing social institutions has most likely contributed to its broad-based support (Anderson, 1997). Believing that all humans have equal rights and should have equal opportunities to secure self-actualization, liberal feminists focus their efforts on social change through the construction of legislation and the regulation of employment practices. They feel that obstacles to equality lie in the traditional laws and behaviors that deny the same rights to women that men enjoy.

The primary obstacle to equality is sexism. Liberal feminists believe that sexist attitudes about appropriate gender role expectations for men and women continue to lead to discrimination and prejudice against women. When women are encouraged to play the role of housewife, it makes them dependent on a male. When men have access to the economic institutions and women do not, females are in a disadvantageous position, a position that leads to an imbalance of power between the sexes. Liberal feminists argue that inequality, then, stems from the denial of equal rights. It is further hampered by women who are reluctant to exercise their rights. Liberal feminism strives for equality and civil rights for all individuals. Equality can best be accomplished through programs that prohibit discrimination and education programs that teach children that society's roles are not gender-specific (e.g., males are doctors, while females are nurses). Education programs can be effective because gender roles are learned and not innate. Consequently, by stressing egalitarian gender roles, the once-dominating patriarchal structure of gender roles found in society's social system will diminish.

Liberal feminism is based on the premise that individuals are autonomous beings, that all individuals are equal, and that women are independent of men. In stressing that women should be treated equally to men, liberal feminism fails to answer "equal to *which* men?" Not all men are treated equally. Class and race also play a role in how people are treated. Thus, liberal feminism is criticized for failing to explain institutionalized social classes and racial oppression (Anderson, 1997). Additionally, liberal feminists have been criticized by nonliberal feminists on a number of grounds, particularly their tendency to overemphasize the importance of individual freedom over the common good and their tendency to valorize a gender-neutral humanism over a gender-specific feminism. Liberal feminists also have a tendency to overestimate the number of women who want to be like men, who want to abandon roles such as "wife" and "mother" for roles such as "citizen" and "worker" (Tong, 1989). As a result, liberal feminism leaves much unanswered. It does not explain the emergence of gender inequality, nor can it account for the effects of class and race. The liberal approach believes that social change can occur through gradual reform and legislation via the existing social institutions. Many other feminists disagree with this approach.

Cultural Feminism

From the liberal feminist perspective, like most other variations of feminist theory, there is a presumption of sameness between men and women; that is to say, "Women are much the same as men [and] women can do what men do" (Beasley, 1999:52). Critics of feminist theory would point out that women and men are not, biologically speaking, the same as each other. This is where cultural feminism steps into theoretical discourse. Cultural feminists argue the biological point that men and women *are* essentially different and add that such differences should be embraced because in many ways the female is more evolved than the male. Cultural feminists would also argue that qualities such as women's love, nurturing abilities, nonviolence, and emotional intelligence should be celebrated. That women are different, and superior to men, leads cultural feminists to endorse such concepts as "sisterhood," or unity and solidarity, and shared identity among females.

Critics of cultural feminist turn the core construct of the theory against proponents of cultural feminism. For the irony of cultural feminism is that males have been using essentially this same argument—that men and women are different—against women to justify why men are best suited for some roles in society and women for others. But the roots of cultural feminism go back to the first wave of feminism, as many early feminists also extolled the value of "the female character" and "feminine personality."

Marxist Feminism

At its most fundamental level, feminism is very similar to the thoughts of Karl Marx and conflict theory. Marx and Engels had shown, starting with the family, how the division of labor was related to gender role expectations (Delaney, 2004). The female, because of her ability to give birth, was generally left to be the homemaker and primary caregiver to children. The male was left to provide for the family, initially as a hunter, and then as the "breadwinner." Marx utilized a theoretical perspective which is often called *historical materialism*. It has as a central thesis that materialism and material conditions caused by capitalism shape people's lives, their behaviors, and their beliefs. Where Marx stated that the means of production were controlled by the bourgeoisie, feminists substitute men. The workers, or proletariat, who are the ones being exploited by the existing social system are the women, according to the feminist perspective. Marx stressed that through productive work, humans can reach their full potential. If women are discriminated against in the economic and political sectors, they will never be able to reach their full human potential.

Marxist feminists stress that only a revolutionary restructuring of property relations can change a social system where women are more likely to be exploited than men. They note that working-class women are hired and paid a cheaper wage than their male counterparts. They produce the necessary work to sustain the capitalistic system, and yet, they do not benefit in the same manner as men (Farganis, 2000). Marx believed that systems of production that distort human potential must be transformed by changing social relations and through revolution (Anderson, 1997).

Karl Marx's theories maintained a focus on how economic systems give rise to social classes; therefore, sexism is a secondary concern yet something that could be eliminated through a restructuring of society. Marx believed that social classes emerge as society produces a surplus. The accumulation of a surplus can be appropriated by one group and places this group in an exploitive position over the workers. Women, because they were left out of the productive system, were always exploited. Consequently, the social system needs to be changed to the point where women have equal access to the control of the means of production. Entering the paid labor force was the first step in equality. Advancing to management positions was the second step. The ultimate goal of Marxist feminists is for women to own the means of production.

Marxist feminists acknowledge class differences, noting that bourgeois women do not experience the same kind of oppression that proletariat women do (Tong, 1989). However, Marxist feminists believe that bourgeois women are also exploited.

> Bourgeois women are not propertied but are kept by propertied men as possessions to perform services that perpetuate the class interests of the bourgeoisie. They produce the heirs to property and provide the emotional support, the nurturing family, and the sexual gratification for the men of property (Farganis, 2000:370).

Thus, Marxist feminism invites all women, whether proletariat or bourgeois, to understand that women's oppression is the product of the political, social, and economic structures associated with capitalism (Tong, 1989).

Radical Feminism

Radical feminism views patriarchy as a sexual system of power in which the male possesses superior power and economic privilege. Sexism is the ultimate tool, used by men, to keep women oppressed. It emphasizes that male power and privilege form the basis of social relations. As Tong (1989) explained, radical feminists generally agree on the following:

1. That women were, historically, the first oppressed group.
2. That women's oppression is the most widespread (it exists in all societies).
3. That women's oppression is the deepest (it cannot be removed as potentially social classes can be removed from society).
4. That it causes the most suffering (e.g., false consciousness).
5. That women's oppression provides a conceptual model for understanding all other forms of oppression.

Radical feminists view patriarchy as having emerged from men's attempt to control females' sexuality. Through patriarchal gender socialization, men attempt to control the bodies of women through the creation of norms of acceptable sexual behavior (MacKinnon, 1982). In MacKinnon's radical feminist perspective, sexuality is the primary sphere of men's power. Men exercise their sexual power over women in many violent forms, including rape, incest, sexual harassment, and battery. Violence against women is not always physical. It can be hidden in more subtle ways, such as encouraging a certain style of dress, beauty standards, motherhood for women, and unpaid housework (Rich, 1976; Wolf, 1991). Radical feminists attack the idea of "love" because they view it as an institution that "promotes vulnerability, dependence, possessiveness, susceptibility to pain and prevents full development of women's human potential" (Donovan, 2000:157). It should come as no surprise then that heterosexuality is also viewed negatively. Heterosexuality is viewed as an institution through which men's power is expressed and is consequently viewed as a tool in institutionalizing male dominance (MacKinnon, 1982). Radical feminists promote lesbianism instead of heterosexuality. They feel that lesbianism encourages women to become strong and independent women. Because lesbianism goes against the male ideal of heterosexuality, from the radical view, radical feminists believe that lesbians suffer from double-jeopardy oppression. Lesbians are exploited not only for being gay, but also because they are women. Radical feminists feel that it is unfair that when women devote their time and energy to maintain a heterosexual relationship, it is viewed as "normal," but when women devote their time and build relations with women, it is seen as sinful (Donovan, 2000).

Radical feminists speak out against all existing social structures because they are believed to be created by men. For example, organized religion generally teaches that God is a "He," and that He is so remote and aloof that He dwells in a place, Heaven, that is beyond earth, reminding us that ultimate power over also implies absolute separation from (Tong, 1989). Interestingly, the radical feminists have had an impact in the area of labeling God as a "He" or "Him" as the 2011 translation of the New International Bible, or NIV, while not completely avoiding the terms "He" and "Him," does avoid using such pronouns as the default reference (*The Citizen*, 2011). The NIV Bible is used by many of the largest Protestant faiths.

MacKinnon (1983) argued that the law views and treats women the same way as men do, and that the state is coercive and ensures men's control over women's sexuality. Although the state professes to be objective, in practice women are "raped" by the state just as they are raped by men (MacKinnon, 1983:643). The implication here is that the state is "male" and acts like a male on behalf of the needs of males. Thus, even though many feminists have demanded state intervention in areas such as sexual abuse, discrimination, and family policy, radical feminism suggests that women cannot entrust their liberation to the state.

Thus, radical feminists have proposed several ways to free women from the cage of femininity. These proposals have ranged from working toward an androgynous culture, in which male and female differences are minimized, to replacing male culture with female culture. To escape from the sexual domination of men, women can resort to celibacy, autoeroticism, or lesbianism. Radical feminists believe that refusing to reproduce is the most effective way for women to escape the snares of patriarchy (Tong, 1989).

Socialist Feminism

Linda Lindsey (1990) suggests that radical feminism deals primarily with ideas, attitudes, or psychological patterns and cultural values rather than with the economics of male domination and that the "sexed body" is often the only concretely "material" elements in its analysis. It is socialist feminism that addresses economic materialism. Whereas radical feminism sees the oppression of women as the result of men's control of female sexuality and the patriarchal institutions that structure sex and gender systems, socialist feminism views women's oppression as stemming from their work in the family and the economy. Socialist feminists believe that the inferior position of women in the social system is the result of class-based capitalism (similar to Marxist feminism). Unpaid housework is used as the primary example of the unequal treatment of men and women.

Socialist feminists argue that women's oppression cannot be reduced to capitalism alone, although capitalism remains a significant factor. The creation of socialist feminism stemmed largely from feminists' dissatisfaction with classical Marxist perspectives on women and the family. Socialist feminists (like Alison Jaggar, Iris Young, and Nancy Fraser) seek to draw components of the radical, Marxist, and psychoanalytic insights under one conceptual umbrella. This feminist perspective attempts to adapt socialist principles to both the workplace and the home in order to increase gender equity (Lindsey and Beach, 2003). Socialist feminism believes that gender relations may be as important as economic class relations in determining women's status. Eradicating social class inequality will not necessarily eliminate sexism (Anderson, 1997). Social change will occur through increased consciousness and knowledge of how society's social structures are designed and operate to oppress women.

The link between the workplace and the home can be illustrated by the concepts of *private sphere* and *public sphere*. Men have typically been associated with the public sphere (the workplace) and women with the private sphere (the home). The private sphere has traditionally been an "invisible" economic factor in terms of production. The goal of feminists is to make the activities of women in the private sphere more visible. Socialist feminists criticize traditional theory because it assumes that the only place where history can be made is in the public sphere. This renders the private sphere (and women) inferior to the public sphere (and men). Women's relegation to the private sphere excludes them from public life and from equal access to sociopolitical and economic resources. Therefore, in order to improve the status and value of women, socialist feminists argue for two things:

1. an increased emphasis on the private sphere and the role of women in the household; and
2. equal opportunities for women in the public sphere.

Socialist feminists argue that change in women's social status will occur only through a transformation of the economic system, along with a change in the way household work is evaluated. It shares with Marxist feminism the position that oppression of women is an economic fact, but it is supplemented by demands for ideological transformation in how women are treated in the private sphere. The economic element presents another concern for socialist feminists—violence. Based on her research findings, Carrie Yodanis (2004) concludes that the more unequal women are when compared to men economically, the more likely men are to be violent toward women.

The continued movement of American society toward socialistic principles scares a great number of people. Not surprisingly, the idea of a socialistic feminist perspective leads to criticisms from many traditional socioeconomic fronts but especially those who promote capitalism and a class system (Beasley, 1999).

Postmodern Feminism

Postmodern feminists attempt to criticize the dominant order, particularly its patriarchal aspects, and to valorize the feminine woman (Tong, 1989). As the name of this perspective implies, postmodern feminism utilizes postmodern theory and its assumption that we no longer live under conditions of modernity, but of postmodernity. The postmodern world is a global economic world highlighted by technology that controls and promotes consumerism. Postmodernists believe that concepts and outlooks used to examine the world in the past no longer apply to the analysis of the world today. Thus, basic forms of knowledge are in question. Postmodernists question definitions from the past that attempt to establish what can be referred to as knowledge in a postmodern world. "Postmodern theorists take the position that all theory is socially constructed and reject the claim of modernists that only rational, abstract thought and scientific methodology can lead to valid knowledge" (Baber and Murray, 2001:23).

Kristine Baber and Colleen Murray (2001) explain that a

> postmodern approach stresses the importance of historical context, variations among people and the expectation of change over time. Postmodernism provides a sophisticated and persuasive critique of essentialism—rejecting the reductionist and naive dualism that result in dichotomous, either-or thinking and embracing ambivalence, paradox, and heterogeneity (pp. 23–24).

Baber and Murray (2001) used a postmodern feminist approach to teaching human sexuality courses. They argued that "such an approach encourages a careful consideration of taken-for-granted information; helps students understand their experiences, even if they are contradictory or incoherent; and is committed to providing information that will be personally and professionally useful to students" (p. 23). Baber and Murray concluded that teaching human sexuality courses from a postmodern feminist perspective offers great opportunities and also considerable challenges. When information is provided as subjective experience, rather than through empirical means, students question its legitimacy.

Dorothy Smith, English-born feminist and women's rights advocate. (Dorothy E. Smith)

Paula Moya (2001) cautioned feminists who believe that postmodern feminist thought is the most productive theoretical framework for feminist discourse. Just as most social thinkers have been hesitant to jump on the postmodern bandwagon, many feminists (such as Barbara Christian, Linda Singer, and Maria Lugones) have acknowledged postmodernism's theoretical limitations. When studying Chicanas and other women of color, feminists are drawn to postmodernism's focus on subjectivity and identity construction. On the other hand, some Chicana feminists demonstrate an ambivalent relationship to postmodernist theory even though they accept many of its presuppositions and claims (Moya, 2001:443).

Attention now shifts to the contributions to contemporary feminist theory of specific feminist social thinkers.

DOROTHY E. SMITH (1926–)

Dorothy E. Smith was born in 1926 in northern England. She earned her B.A. degree in sociology from the London School of Economics in 1955. Smith met her husband while attending college in London. They moved to Berkeley, California, where Smith earned her Ph.D. in sociology from the University of California at Berkeley in 1963. Erving Goffman supervised her Ph.D. studies. By the time she earned her doctorate, she had children and her husband had left her. She found work in the academic world as a lecturer in sociology at Berkeley (Smith, 1979). Smith's personal experiences led her to realize that she occupied two distinct realms of personal identity: in academia, as a member of the public sphere, and in the private sphere as a mother of two small children (Smith, 1987). After teaching at Berkeley (1964–1966), Smith moved back to England, where she taught at the University of Essex from 1966 to 1968; she then taught at the University of British Columbia (1968–1976) and then the Ontario Institute for Studies in Education in Toronto, where she is currently a professor emeritus. Smith's feminist thinking and sociological approach were deeply influenced by her years at Berkeley, where nearly all the professors were males, and, of course, by her experiences as a single mother.

Construction of Knowledge and Bifurcation

Smith's ideas are linked by her concept of *bifurcation.* Bifurcation is a

> conceptual distinction between the world as we experience it and the world as we come to know it through the conceptual frameworks that science invents. In formulating the problem in these terms, Smith is adopting the phenomenological perspective articulated by Alfred Schutz in his distinction between the scientific and the commonsense ways of knowing the world (Farganis, 2000:371).

Smith attempts to expose the gender-biased assumptions within the social sciences. She believes that the male-power-based gender construction of roles has legitimized gender inequality in society. Smith proposes a sociology that utilizes a woman's standpoint and a woman's *construction of knowledge.* Smith believes that mainstream sociological theory has not accessed women's experiences. However, in *The Conceptual Practices of Power: A Feminist Sociology of Knowledge* (1990), Smith questioned whether a feminist sociology can describe the realities of women in terms of the sociological discipline merely by extending the field of interest to include the work on gender roles, the women's movement, women in the labor force, sexuality, and so on. Smith does not believe that it is enough to supplement established sociology by addressing gender issues, because the established objective knowledge in sociology is biased on a male perspective. It is the challenge of feminism to create a new objective knowledge from a female perspective based on female experiences. Smith, then, is attempting to develop a sociology *for,* rather than *about,* women (unfortunately, this creates a new set of biases). Smith (1990) did not propose a radical transformation of the sociological discipline, nor did she promote eliminating all of its methodological procedures. She did suggest that sociology needs a reorganization. Smith especially emphasized the subjective nature of methodology, assuming that the only way researchers can understand subjects under study is from within the subjects themselves. Understanding of this type leads to a bifurcated consciousness. A bifurcated consciousness is an actual representation of the self in the world in which we participate during our daily work life.

Mothering and Schooling

In 1993, Smith described the standard North American family as that of a legally married couple sharing a household. The adult male is in paid employment, his earnings providing the primary economic basis of the family and household. The adult female may also earn an income, but her primary responsibility is the care of the family and the household. Smith (1993) conducted research on schooling and families. During her research, she came to realize that the mothering discourse is actively fed by psychologists and specialists in child development, women's magazines, television programs, and other popular media. An important aspect of the mothering discourse is "managing" women's relation to their children's schooling. As housewives and mothers, many of the women in Smith's study were caught up in the role that society expected of them. Consequently, when interviewing these women, Smith reflected this perspective. She warns researchers not to be caught in the methodological traps that feminists oppose.

In 2004, Smith, with co-author Alison Griffith, would reexamine the role of women and what they do for their children in relation to schooling. Griffith and Smith (2004) provide analysis based on class lines and examine the ways in which women's economic positions further affect their schooling experiences. The authors predict that mothering work with regards to schooling will only intensify as resources are withdrawn from schools. Interestingly, just a few years earlier in her "Schooling for Inequality," Smith (2000) argued that "the topic of schooling as an institution productive of inequalities—of gender, as well as race and class—has never been, as I believe it should be, a major issue for feminism" (p. 1147). Smith certainly views mothering, education, and schooling of children as important concepts for feminists now.

SANDRA HARDING (1935–)

Sandra Harding received her Ph.D. from New York University in 1973. She is a leading feminist and philosopher who taught for two decades at the University of Delaware before joining UCLA in 1996 as a professor of education and women's studies and serving as director of the Center for the Study of Women. Harding is the author or editor of twelve books, including *The Science Question in Feminism* (1986), *Is Science Multicultural? Postcolonialisms, Feminisms and Epistemologies* (1998), and *Science and Social Inequality* (2006).

Feminist Theory

In her article "The Instability of the Analytical Categories of Feminist Theory," Harding (1986) criticized all sociological theories. She believes that theories such as functionalism, critical theory, and hermeneutics somehow fail to apply to women and gender relations. She claims that sociological theories of the past and present are gender-biased (although she fails to offer any support for this claim). Harding also criticizes feminist theory from the perspective of the social experience of Western, bourgeois, heterosexual, white women because it is not applicable to other women. Harding (1986) stated:

> The patriarchal theories we try to extend and reinterpret were created to explain not men's experience but only the experience of those men who are Western, bourgeois, white, and heterosexual. Feminist theorists also come from these categories—not through conspiracy but through the historically common pattern that it is people in these categories who have had the time and resources to theorize, and who—among women—can be heard at all. In trying to develop theories that provide the one, true (feminist) story of human experience, feminism risks replicating in theory and public policy the tendency in the patriarchal theories to police thought by assuming that only the problems of *some* women are human problems and that solutions for them are the only reasonable ones (pp. 646–647).

Harding clearly does not believe in the idea of a universal theory that applies to all humans and their behaviors. She promotes the idea that specific theories should be designed for specific categories of people. Furthermore, Harding (1986) seems to question the validity of theory itself:

> Theorizing itself is suspiciously patriarchal, for it assumes separations between the knower and the known, subject and object, and the possibility of some powerful transcendental, Archimedean standpoint from which nature and social life fall into what we think is their proper perspective (p. 647).

Again, Harding provides no proof to support her contention that theorizing is conducted from a male-centered perspective.

If a social scientist cannot separate the subject from the object and cannot stand outside the realm of study, how is *any* theory or knowledge possible? Harding answers this question in two ways. Harding (1986) stated:

> On the one hand, we can use the liberal powers of reason and the will, shaped by the insights gained through engaging in continuing political struggles, to piece what we see before our eyes in contemporary social life and history into a clear and coherent conceptual form, borrowing from one androcentric discourse here, another one there, patching in between in innovative and often illuminating ways, and revising our theoretical frameworks week by week as we continue to detect yet further androcentrisms in the concepts and categories we are using....On the other hand, we can learn how to embrace the instability of the analytical categories; to find in the instability itself the desired theoretical reflection of certain aspects of the political reality in which we live and think; to use these instabilities as a resource for our thinking and practices. No "normal" science; for us! (p. 648).

Thus, Harding does believe that theory is possible, so long as "normal" science is not used. The implication that males cannot do this and have failed to do this in the past is difficult to comprehend or accept.

Harding promotes the use of "good science" instead of science that has been created by a masculine bias—"science as usual." Harding argues that science created without women researchers is biased and that subject areas chosen without input from women are also biased. The very idea of empirical research is biased. Harding (1986) stated that since

> the very concepts of nature, of dispassionate, value-free, objective inquiry, and of transcendental knowledge are androcentric, white, bourgeois, and Western, then no amount of more rigorous adherence to scientific method will eliminate such bias, for the methods themselves reproduce the perspectives generated by these hierarchies and thus distort our understandings (p. 653).

Not surprisingly, Harding ignores empirical data (e.g., the poor, war veterans, and the homeless) and believes that all males and all whites benefit from their ascribed status. "Objectively, no individual men can succeed in renouncing sexist privilege any more than individual whites can succeed in renouncing racist privilege—the benefits of gender and race accrue regardless of the wishes of the individuals who bear them" (Harding, 1986:658).

In short, Harding believes that social theory must be created by women and must include issues that are central to women.

Sociology of Knowledge

The feminist viewpoint regarding the sociology of knowledge rests primarily on the idea that knowledge was created from the standpoint of men, which implies that it is biased. During the second wave of the women's movement (beginning in the 1960s), feminist research attempted to add to social discourse the perspectives of women in their social activities. The core premise of this approach is the realization that researchers cannot understand women and their lives by adding more studies of men to existing bodies of knowledge. Instead, research should be conducted on women and their social lives (Harding and Hintikka, 1983). Furthermore, Harding and Hintikka (1983) argued that sexist distortions and perversions in epistemology, metaphysics, methodology, and the philosophy of science must be rooted out if an accurate sociology of knowledge is to exist.

In her article "Women as Creators of Knowledge," Harding (1989) acknowledged that some women are making important advances within the social structures of the sciences, and that feminist critiques of the sciences have opened the doors to new research. She described the long battle women have had in their attempts to gain access to the opportunities in sciences that have been available to many men. Harding emphasized that the term *history* should be replaced by *herstory,* which would focus on the achievements of great women (e.g., Maria Mitchell, Dorothy Wrinch, and Rosalind Franklin) who have been otherwise ignored or trivialized, and of less famous women who have also made contributions to science and technology. Harding's description of the lack of women in most academic scientific departments of the past does not apply today, and that is a sure sign of the growing power of women in such areas as the sociology of knowledge.

> In conclusion, I, for one, feel lucky to be living at this exciting, if problematic, moment in the history of women and the history of science....A science that is to be "for humanity" will have to be for women as well as for men; it will have to be a science directed by feminists—males as well as females....It will have to be directed by a global feminism, not by a movement that seeks merely to add women to the group of men in the West who are overadvantaged. The scientific environment and the environment for women today conjoin to create auspicious projects for women as creators of knowledge (Harding, 1989b:706–707).

Neutrality, Objectivity, and Social Inequality in Science

Feminists routinely criticize science as being male-dominated, biased, and lacking in objectivity. "The ideal of objectivity as neutrality is widely regarded to have failed not only in history and the social sciences, but also in philosophy and related fields, such as jurisprudence" (Harding, 1992: 569-570). Harding believes that the sciences are confronted with the demise of objectivism and the threat of relativism. To support her contention, Harding notes that objectivity is difficult in most spheres of life. In academia, issues related to funding requests, sabbaticals, hiring, promotion, and tenure are all subject to the whims and wishes of those with their own agendas. Thus, in these matters, as well as in science, subjectivity continues to interfere with those attempting to conduct "good science." Neutrality is a requirement of objectivity. Those with a bias, or agenda, are not neutral and therefore are not objective.

In *Science and Social Inequality*, Harding (2006) continues her attack on traditional forms of theory and research. Among the chapter titles in this publication are "Thinking About Race and Science" (Harding questions whether or not "science is racist"), "The Political Unconscious of Western Science," and "Are Truth Claims in Science Dysfunctional?" Harding argues that science contributes to worsening of existing gaps between the wealthiest and poorest nations (and people) around the world. She suggests that the hierarchical social formations in modern Western sciences promote antidemocratic principles and practices, particularly in terms of their service to militarism, alienation of labor, Western expansionism, and environmental destruction.

PATRICIA HILL COLLINS (1948–)

Patricia Hill Collins was born in Philadelphia in 1948. She earned her B.A. from Brandeis in 1969, her M.A. from Harvard in 1970, and her Ph.D. from Brandeis in 1984. She is currently teaching at the University of Cincinnati, serving as an associate professor of sociology and African American studies. Her general sociological concerns mirror her experiences as an African American woman who broke many barriers and who often felt marginalized. Her 1990 book, *Black Feminist Thought: Knowledge, Consciousness, and the Politics of Empowerment,* represents her attempt to explain her personal and professional experiences as an African American female. These experiences are expressed in her concept of the *outsider within* (Collins, 1986). The outsider within is similar to Simmel's idea of the *stranger,* where one is a part of the group but feels distanced from the group (in Collins' case because of her race and gender). Collins (1990) recalled how she was often "the first," or "one of the few," or the "only" African American and/or woman in certain schools, communities, and work settings (p. xi).

Black Feminism

Collins agrees with Harding that white male interests have pervaded traditional scholarship. She discards the use of empirical data and statistical analysis in favor of a reliance on the documentation of voices of black women from all social settings. Collins (1989a) described positivism as "Eurocentric masculinist." Collins utilizes her "outsider within" approach to sociological theory throughout her presentations on Black feminism. In her article "Learning from the Outsider Within: The Sociological Significance of Black Feminist Thought" (1986), Collins described how many black women have been privy to some of the most intimate secrets of powerful white families while they have served as domestic servants. "These women have seen white elites, both actual and aspiring, from perspectives largely obscured from their Black spouses and from these groups themselves" (Collins, 1986:514). Their role as servants places them "inside" the house and family structure, but the dual reality that these black women experienced made them realize that they could never join their white families. This "outsider within" status provides Afro-American women with a special standpoint on self, family, and society.

"Black feminist thought consists of ideas produced by Black women that clarify a standpoint of and for Black women.... While Black feminist thought may be recorded by others, it is produced by Black women" (Collins, 1986:516). According to Collins (1986), there are three key themes in black feminist thought:

1. **The meaning of self-definition and self-valuation:** Black feminist thought insists on a black self-definition framework when one is studying the social reality of African American women. Self-valuation involves taking this self-image one step further, to the point where black women learn to value themselves and empower themselves within the societal structure.
2. **The interlocking nature of oppression:** For Collins, gender, race, and class are variables that are interconnected. In *Black Feminist Thought* (1990), Collins argued that society has attempted to teach black women that racism, sexism, and poverty are inevitable aspects

of everyday life for them. Such images are designed to keep black women oppressed. Awareness of this interlocking nature will help make black women more powerful and united in their fight against oppression and discrimination. Patricia Hill Collins further reiterated her position on the interlocking nature of the variables of race, gender, and class in her article "A Comparison of Two Works on Black Family Life" (1989a) when she stated, "The analysis presented in this essay suggests that removing any one piece of the triad of race, gender, or class from the analysis seriously jeopardizes a full understanding of the experiences of any group of people" (p. 884).

3. **The importance of African American women's culture:** A third key element of Black feminist thought involves efforts to empower black women by highlighting the importance of black women's culture. In other words, highlight the importance of the black female experience. Collins (1986) believes that an examination of family life is important in the black women's culture, especially the relationship between black women and their biological children.

When considering these three key themes in black feminist thought, Collins (1986) wrote that the sociological significance lies in two areas: the sociological niche studies of black women's culture and the accumulation of sociological knowledge in general.

Collins' importance placed on using the black women's experiences of everyday life in relation to oppression is furthered examined in her 1989 article "The Social Construction of Black Feminist Thought" (1989b):

Black women's everyday acts of resistance challenge two prevailing approaches to studying the consciousness of oppressed groups. One approach claims that subordinate groups identify with the powerful and have no valid independent interpretation of their own oppression. The second approach assumes that the oppressed are less human than their rulers and, therefore, are less capable of articulating their own standpoint. Both approaches... suggest that oppressed groups lack motivation for political activism because of their flawed consciousness of their own subordination. Yet African American women have been neither passive victims of nor willing accomplices to their own domination (pp. 746–747).

Collins' description of the oppressed certainly is nothing new to sociological thought, as this same argument has been used to describe many other groups that were not willing participants in their oppression by more powerful groups (such as the English over the Irish for centuries), but it does remind us that black women were obviously not willing participants in the discriminatory practices and behaviors to which they have been subjected. The political and economic status of black women directly affects their self-definition and self-valuation.

In her 1996 article "What's in a Name? Womanism, Black Feminism, and Beyond," Collins stated that African American women are a part of a new history, and the recurring theme of giving women a voice resurfaces.

Black women appear to have a voice, and with this new-found voice comes a new series of concerns. For example, we must be attentive to the seductive absorption of black women's voices in classrooms of higher education where black women's texts are still much more welcomed than black women ourselves.... At this point, whether African American women can fashion a singular "voice" about the black *woman's* position remains less an issue than how black women's voices collectively construct, affirm, and maintain a dynamic black *women's* self-defined standpoint (Collins, 1996:9).

Collins believes that such solidarity is essential to ensuring group unity while still recognizing the tremendous heterogeneity that operates among black women. "Current debates about whether black women's standpoint should be named 'womanism' or 'black feminism' reflect this basic challenge of accommodating diversity among black women" (Collins, 1996:9–10).

CAROL GILLIGAN (1936–)

Carol Gilligan is a distinguished psychologist and feminist social thinker with a commitment to providing a forum for female voices. Her most noted theory is the stage theory of moral development for women. Gilligan's works are influenced primarily by Sigmund Freud, Jean Piaget, and Lawrence Kohlberg.

Gilligan received an A.B. (with highest honors in English literature) from Swarthmore College in 1958, an A.M. (with distinction in clinical psychology) from Radcliffe College in 1961, and her Ph.D. from Harvard University in 1964. Her commitment to giving a voice to women began during her graduate studies when she spoke with people in Cleveland at their kitchen tables about voter registration and the need to have a voice in democratic society. She was also involved in the antiwar movement during the 1960s, protesting the University of Chicago's use of grades to determine who would be drafted to serve in Vietnam (Gilligan, 1998). Lower grades increased the likelihood of being drafted. Gilligan began her teaching career as a lecturer at the University of Chicago (1965–1966); moved to Harvard as a lecturer (1967–1969), as an assistant professor from 1971 to 1979, and as an associate professor from 1979 to 1986; and was then promoted to full professor at the Harvard Graduate School of Education. She has published over seventy articles and seven books, *In a Different Voice* (1982) being her most notable.

Gilligan's Stages of Moral Development

Gilligan's stages of moral development for women emphasizes the development of self, rather than changes in cognitive development as one passes from one stage to the next. She also refuses to assign ages to the stages as Piaget and Kohlberg had. There are three stages to Gilligan's (1982) moral development theory:

1. **Orientation to individual survival (preconventional morality):** The primary goal is individual survival (selfishness). A transition occurs when one changes from a selfish focus to a responsibility to others. This is an egocentric level of development where a woman has no feeling of *should* (as in, "I should be more tolerant of others"). Gilligan points out that prospective motherhood often brings about a change in self-concept. Nature has made it difficult for a pregnant woman to feel detached from her fetus, the father, or other mothers. An internal dialogue sparks moral responsibility (Griffin, 1991).

2. **Goodness as self-sacrifice (conventional morality):** Women define their sense of self-worth by their ability to care for others. They search for solutions in which no one gets hurt. Self-sacrifice is goodness, and goodness is measured by caring for others. The woman must seek a balance between helping others and feeling manipulated. A successful transition to the final stage of moral development occurs through a shift from goodness to the truth that she is a person, too.

3. **Responsibility for consequences of choice (postconventional morality):** The essence of a moral decision is the exercise of choice and the willingness to take responsibility for that choice. The principle of nonviolence is critical at this stage. Unlike conventional goodness, the concept of truth requires that a woman extend nonviolence and care to herself as well as to others. She must seek to eliminate tension between herself and others.

The moral development of women can be summed up as a transition from caring only for oneself (Stage 1) to seeing the virtue in caring for others (Stage 2) to the final realization that a woman must seek moral equality between caring for herself and caring for others (Stage 3).

Giving Voice to Women

In her 1982 book *In a Different Voice*, Gilligan pointed out how the developmental theories of Freud and Piaget treat women like men and were built on observations of men's lives. She believes that a different voice needs to be heard in regard to developmental theory and women's lives.

> The failure of women to fit existing models of human growth may point to a problem in the representation, a limitation in the conception of the human condition, an omission of certain truths about life. The different voice I describe is characterized not by gender but theme. Its association with women is an empirical observation, and it is primarily through women's voices that I trace its development (Gilligan, 1982:2).

In a Different Voice represents Gilligan's attempt to show the contrasts between male and female voices and to highlight a distinction between two modes of thought. She points to the interplay of these voices within each sex and suggests that their convergence marks times of crisis and change.

> Clearly, these differences arise in a social context where factors of social status and power combine with reproductive biology to shape the experience of males and females and the relations between the sexes. My interest lies in the interaction of experience and thought, in different voices and the dialogues to which they give rise, in the way we listen to ourselves and to others, in the stories we tell about our lives (Gilligan, 1982:2).

Furthermore, Gilligan (1982) argued that

> women's place in a man's life cycle is to protect this recognition while the developmental litany intones the celebration of separation, autonomy, individuation, and natural rights.... Only when life-cycle theorists divide their attention and begin to live with women as they have lived with men will their vision encompass the experience of both sexes and their theories become correspondingly more fertile (p. 23).

Between Voice and Silence (1995) represents the further attempts of Gilligan, and her colleagues, Jill McLean Taylor and Amy M. Sullivan, to give a forum to the voices of females, especially adolescent girls. The authors reported that when adolescent girls remain silent or censor themselves to maintain relationships, they often become depressed and develop eating disorders or other psychological problems. In contrast, when adolescent girls are outspoken, it is often difficult for others to stay in relationships with them, and they may be excluded or labeled as troublemakers. The research centered on twenty-six girls who were designated "at risk" of high school dropout and early motherhood and covered what they were feeling and thinking about themselves, their relationships, their lives, their futures, their experiences in school, and their decisions concerning sexuality. Taylor, Gilligan, and Sullivan (1995) found that it was the women (especially those who shared the same experiences) in these girls' lives who were most likely to listen, to care, to be interested in knowing about them.

JOAN JACOBS BRUMBERG (1944–)

Joan Jacobs Brumberg is an award-winning author of such publications as *Body Project* (1997a), *Fasting Girls* (1988), and numerous articles on the American woman's experience. She was born and raised in Ithaca, New York, where she would continue to live and work as a professor at Cornell University. Brumberg teaches in the areas of history, human development, and women's studies. Her research and publications have received praise from the Guggenheim Foundation, the National Endowment for the Humanities, and the Rockefeller Foundation. She credits much of her writing direction to her husband, David Brumberg, who helps her with her historical judgments.

Female Bodies and Self-Image

In contemporary Western society, there is an obsession with the female body. In *The Body Project*, Brumberg (1997a) described in great detail how girls' bodies change (they mature much earlier) and why the experience of physical changes affects girls' emotional state and self-image more now than ever before. The mass media, as an agent of culture, has reinforced an ideal image that girls are to strive for and attain, therefore placing more emphasis on "good looks" than on "good works." Parents themselves are responsible for this cultural ideal and often do great disservice to their daughters when they focus too much on physical appearance and attractiveness. In *The Body Project*, Brumberg provided intimate excerpts from girls' diaries between the 1830s and the 1990s. This information reveals how girls' attitudes toward their bodies and sexuality have changed and suggests that although young women today enjoy greater freedom and more opportunities than their counterparts of the past, they are under more cultural pressure to look good. According to Brumberg (1997), the process of sexual maturation is more difficult for girls today than a century ago because girls mature sexually earlier today than ever before. Brumberg also suggests that society provides fewer social protections for girls today, an idea that certainly can be challenged. That girls mature faster today and have more free time (from work obligations as they would have had a century ago), they have become more body-conscious. Girls are also exposed to peer and media pressure to look a certain way, a perspective that centers on body image. "A century ago, American women were lacing themselves into corsets and teaching their adolescent daughters to do the same; today's teens shop for thong bikinis on their own, and their middle-class mothers are likely to be uninvolved until the credit card bill arrives in the mail" (Brumberg, 1997a: xviii).

Brumberg suggested that adolescent girls have always felt angst about their bodies, but the historical moment defines how they react to their changing bodies. The historical moment is a specific environment at a specific point in time. Whether it is the style of the 1920s' flapper or the hourglass figure of the 1950s, women have placed great emphasis on their body image as a means of defining themselves. Brumberg believes that nineteenth-century girls were not as concerned about their physical appearance because of society's emphasis on spiritual rather than physical matters. Many issues related to the changes in the female body were not considered polite public discourse. "In fact, girls who were preoccupied with their looks were likely to be accused of vanity or self-indulgence.... Character was built on attention to self-control, service to others, and belief in God—not on attention to one's own, highly individualistic body project" (Brumberg, 1997a:xx).

Society's Influence on Women's Image

Women found in their body image a sense of self-definition and a way to announce who they are to the world. "Today, many young girls worry about the contours of their bodies—especially shape, size, and muscle tone—because they believe that the body is the ultimate expression of the self"

(Brumberg, 1997a:97). Contemporary adolescent girls learn from their mothers, as well as from the larger culture, that modern femininity requires some degree of exhibitionism. Since the 1920s, it has been fashionable to display certain body parts, such as arms and legs. This freedom to display the body is accompanied by a demand for beauty, and dietary regimens (which involve money and self-discipline) must be met if the young woman is to successfully "pull off the look." As Brumberg (1997a) explained, "What American women did not realize at the time was that their stunning new freedom actually implied the need for greater internal control of the body, an imperative that would intensify and become even more powerful by the end of the twentieth century" (p. 98).

Fashion and the film industry are two huge influences on societal expectations that women display their bodies sexually. The sexual revolution liberated women from the Victorian restraints of modesty but also demanded a commitment to diet and beauty. The 1920s represented the first era when teenage girls made systematic efforts to lower their weight by food restriction and exercise. This dieting craze was referred to as *slimming* and was motivated by new cultural ideals of female beauty. The dominant fashions of the 1920s revealed the shift from the voluptuous Victorian hourglass body shape to an interest in a body shape highlighted by exposed slender legs and a relatively flat chest. After World War II, voluptuous movie stars such as Marilyn Monroe and Jane Russell served as the model for the ideal American woman. The focus became fixated on the size of a woman's breasts, a fascination that continues today, as adolescent boys and men tend to prefer big-breasted women. This cultural reality has led many women to have their breasts enlarged through surgery. In her article "Silicone Valley" (1997b), Brumberg drew attention to the recent phenomenon of plastic surgery. Women not only are changing their breasts; they are changing their noses and having cellulite sucked from their bodies. The pursuit of self-perfection through surgery is now easier than ever before because of greater affluence, decreasing costs, and more board-certified physicians, which make plastic surgery an "acceptable" alternative toward attaining the perfect body. Brumberg (1997b) stated that it is one thing for adult women to have surgery, but it is entirely different for adolescent girls to have plastic surgery as it is potentially damaging to young girls both mentally and physically (p. 2).

Breasts provide visual significance and validation for many women. This is nothing new, as "throughout history, different body parts have been eroticized in art, literature, photography, and film. In some eras, the ankle or upper arm was the ultimate statement of female sexuality" (Brumberg, 1997a:108). The preoccupation with female breasts led to the development of brassieres (bras), a French word for an infant's undergarment or harness. In the United States, the first bras were introduced during the "flapper" era of the 1920s and were designed to flatten the chest in order to conform to the ideal slim, boyish figure that was in vogue. When society placed an emphasis on larger busts, the bra was designed to maximize size and make the breasts conform to an ideal round shape. Today, women are faced not only with wearing a bra, but with wearing a fashionable, sexy bra. Western cultures are characterized by industrial marketers who have cashed in on this preoccupation with fashion and bras. Victoria's Secret and Fredericks of Hollywood specialize in exotic and sexy lingerie. These companies and their advertisers reinforce the image of what a desirable female in contemporary American society should look like.

BARBARA RISMAN (1956–)

Barbara J. Risman was born in 1956 in Lynn, Massachusetts. She was raised in an extended family environment that included grandparents, aunts, uncles, and cousins, often living in the same house. Her grandparents were Jewish immigrants from Russia who spoke only Yiddish. Risman characterizes her family as very traditional. Her father worked for the Army Corps of Engineers, and her mother was a homemaker and nurse. Risman's own family reflects a typical contemporary family, as she and her husband are divorced and have one daughter, Leah. Leah KaneRisman has a last name that is a combination of both her parents'. Risman indicates that people constantly misspell Leah's last name and that this is a sign that the world is not geared to nontraditional names.

Risman attended college at Northwestern University during the height of the feminist movement. She earned her B.A. in sociology in 1976 and her Ph.D. in 1986 from the University of Washington. Risman eventually became a professor of sociology at North Carolina State University and then held the administrative position of Director of Graduate Studies at NCSU. Risman has involved herself in many academic projects, including co-editing the journal *Contemporary Society* and being author and co-editor of many journal articles and author of *Gender Vertigo: American Families in Transition* (1998), her most famous book.

Risman has conducted a great deal of her own research in the area of single parenthood. She believes that men are capable of being single parents and that parent–child attachment, household organization, and child development can all occur successfully in both single-mother and single-father homes (Risman, 1988). The research she collected over the years culminated in *Gender Vertigo* (1998). Risman has attempted to uncover the processes that influence people to act in certain ways regarding gender, and she admits that this has always been her intellectual preoccupation. Basing her conclusions on her own graduate studies and the research of others, Risman (1998) theorized that gender is merely a social structure. She is a supporter and member of the Alternatives to Marriage Project (AMP), an organization that encourages diversity in family structure. The AMP believes that marriage is just one form of family structure and that other healthy alternatives exist (e.g., the single-parent family, same-sex partners). The AMP gives a voice to those raising a family nontraditionally and plays an active role in creating policies and legislation designed to provide same-sex health benefits, family and medical leave, survivor's benefits, and so on.

Doing Gender

Many feminist theorists believe that an individual is labeled at birth as a member of a sex category, either male or female, and from that point on is held to acting accordingly. The individual succumbs to society's expectations, often through the use of, or the threat of, sanctions and therefore "does gender." Individuals who deviate from these expectations are unable to have normal interactions with other members of society. Feminists believe that such expectations reflect a patriarchal society that devalues what is defined as female or feminine and claims that biological differences between males and females exist to justify male dominance (Risman, 1998). Thus, gender is not something that one has or something that one is; rather, it is something that one *does*.

The doing-gender perspective was later extended by West and Fenstermaker (1995) to "doing difference," claiming that what we actually create through interaction is inequality. Risman (1998) believes that just as one uses race to guide interactional encounters despite its lack of biologically based differences, one also uses gender to determine where one stands in daily interactions. Perceived differences between two people play a large role in determining behavior, hence the change from doing gender to doing difference. Risman believes that there is a great difference in how people are treated simply because of their gender categorization.

> Gender polarization is the assumption that not only are women and men different, but that this difference is super-imposed on so many aspects of the social world that a cultural connection is thereby forged between sex and virtually every other aspect of human experience, including modes of dress and social roles and even ways of expressing emotion and experiencing sexual desire (Risman, 1998:2–3).

Since the mid-1990s, Risman has tried to understand why men and women behave so differently, particularly in their intimate relationships. She feels that the doing-gender perspective is helpful, yet incomplete, and that the extension from doing gender to doing difference is an important direction of focus in gender research.

Gender Vertigo

Gender vertigo is a term coined by Robert Connell (1996) in the final chapter of his book *Masculinities*. Risman asked, and was granted permission, by Connell to use this term for the title of her book. Risman suggests that the best solution to society's gender inequalities is going beyond gender, ignoring gendered rules, and "pushing the envelope until we get dizzy" (Risman, 1998:11). Risman (1998) explains:

> Gender vertigo can only help us to destabilize deeply held but incorrect beliefs about the natural differences between women and men. I believe that we will have to be dizzy for a time if we are to hope to deconstruct gender and construct a society based on equality. I argue that as long as behavioral expectations, material advantages, and cultural ideology divide human beings into types based on their ascribed sex (i.e., the shape of their genitals), male privilege will continue (p. 11).

Risman admits that it will be difficult to change people's perceptions of gender and gender role expectations but insists that it must be done in order for equality to occur.

Risman chose the term *gender vertigo* because it is indicative of the profound effect the elimination of gender would have on every person's psyche. Doing gender determines how one walks, talks, dresses, eats, and socializes and nearly all other aspects of everyday life. Gender often plays a significant role in the definition of the self. Freeing individuals from gender restraints will be difficult and marked by feelings of vertigo and disorientation. For these reasons, Risman suggested that society first attack the features of gender structure that immediately uphold differentiation. Family roles requiring women to be financially dependent on men, an economic structure that allows male workers to escape family responsibility, and interpersonal sexism are among the issues that Risman finds the most important. In *Gender Vertigo* (1998), Risman concluded that in order "to move fully toward justice for women and men, we must dare a moment of gender vertigo. My hope is that when the spinning ends we will be in a post-gendered society that is one step closer to a just world" (p. 162).

This concludes our brief look at a few of the key ideas of a select number of contemporary feminists. The great proliferation of feminist thought dictated our limited discussion here. Next, we will examine some of the criticisms of feminist theory and then look at its relevancy to contemporary society.

CRITICISMS OF FEMINIST THEORY

There are many criticisms of feminist theory. The first is the contradictory nature of theory wherein they attack other theories as being gender-biased when, in fact, feminist theory is unapologetically biased to represent the needs of women only. Giving a voice to women is important, but one must question any theory that purposely ignores the perspective of one half of the population: men. For example, Carol Gilligan has articulated a unique developmental theory, in which, instead of concentrating on cognitive development, she examined moral development.

This is a fascinating idea. And yet, her moral development theory is applied to women only. There is no reason why this theory should ignore men. The sociological fight against injustice should not be limited to female injustice; it should include all those who are harmed by a social system designed to disadvantage one person over another.

Second, although a commitment to empirical research is not a must in designs of social theory, relying on such techniques as oral testimony and the analysis of such content as diaries risks a lack of objectivity and bias. When an individual is asked for his or her story, it is always biased from his or her perspective. It is also highly questionable that anyone will find the "truth" in diary entries, as only one side of the story is given voice. Diary entries do provide valuable insights into personal interpretations of events—assuming that the truth is told in a diary. And it is rather common for people not to write the inclusive factual accounts of events in their diaries, or journals. Feminist scholar Jesse Bernard, in her 1972 bestseller *The Future of Marriage,* was among the first to propose the idea that men benefit emotionally from marriage while women suffer. This idea fueled the belief that the social institution of marriage has oppressed women. This theory has persisted among feminists (and is viewed as common knowledge) despite scientists' subsequent findings that Bernard's studies were flawed, and more recent research contradicts her results. Research involving over 10,000 people conducted by David De Vaus, a sociologist at La Trobe University in Melbourne, revealed that emotional problems (e.g., depression and other mental disorders) are equally common among husbands and wives (Ross, 2002). Empirical verification of theory will almost always make it more valid and believable. Nonetheless, feminists and a number of contemporary sociologists value the methodological approach of feminist theory and find great merit in nontraditional forms of research (e.g., from diaries).

Third, most feminist theorists claim that all sociological theories are gender-biased but fail to provide any proof of this claim. It is true that Carol Gilligan provided evidence that Freud's psychological developmental theory is male-biased, but this is hardly a new observation, as relatively few academics take any of Freud's theories seriously today. But just how is a macro-structural theory such as functionalism biased in favor of males? It is an odd accusation. Functionalism is generally criticized for ignoring individuals because of its focus on social structures. It is not designed to deal with such issues as differences between males and females. The five basic propositions that are the cornerstone of Homans' exchange theory apply to women and men. For example, if in the past a behavior was rewarded, that behavior is likely to be repeated in the future; this statement is clearly gender-neutral. The challenge to feminist sociological theory is to support its claim that these two, or any other, sociological theories are biased. Furthermore, how can the sciences of mathematics and biology be gender-biased (Harding claims that past science is "bad science")? Is the law of gravity gender-biased? Are basic mathematical formulas gender-biased? Clearly, they are not. That theorists from the classical era continually used the male perspective in their writings, however, is legitimate complaint from feminists.

Fourth, gender is just one variable in human interaction. Many feminists believe that interactions are based solely on gender distinction. Other feminists realize that it is not that simple. Sandra Harding has noted that gender, class, and race are interlocking variables and cannot be separated. Barbara Risman attempted to deemphasize the importance of gender as a variable in an attempt to eliminate a gender stratification system. As conflict theory has clearly demonstrated, it is power and power differentials that help determine interactions among people, as well as individual interactions in the greater social system. "Power corrupts" is not a gender distinction. Women in power positions can be as vindictive, ruthless, and unfair as men. People in legitimate authority positions have power over others; their sex has little bearing on this reality.

A fifth criticism of feminist theory comes from within feminist sociological theory itself. The fact that there is such a great variety of sociological feminist theories (e.g., liberal, cultural, Marxist, radical, socialist, and postmodern) represents a clear lack of consensus among feminists as to the best means to go about fighting sexism, discrimination, and oppression. If, and when, feminist theory can provide a united front, they will have developed a legitimate sociological theory. When they can provide a clear answer to questions such as "How are women to be paid for housework?" and "How are single moms and single dads to be paid for housework?" they will advance a legitimate sociological theory.

APPLICATION OF FEMINIST THEORY AND THE THIRD WAVE OF FEMINISM

The many criticisms of feminist theory do not detract from its relevancy to contemporary society. Feminist theory is applicable to both laypersons and academics. It is possible for any woman to be a victim of sexism. *Sexism,* which is defined as behavior, conditions, or attitudes that foster stereotypes of social roles based on one's sex and leads to discrimination against a member(s) of one sex due to preferential treatment by a member(s) of the other sex, is more likely to victimize women than men. There are two primary forms of sexism, ideological and institutional. *Ideological sexism* is the belief that one sex is inferior to another and stresses gender appropriateness based on gender roles. *Institutional sexism,* on the other hand, refers to systematic practices and patterns within social institutions that lead to inequality between men and women. Sexual harassment is a byproduct of sexist attitudes, and women are more likely to be a victim than men.

Among the social institutions that foster stereotypes on how women should act and behave is the media. As Brumberg points out, the media sends messages to women on how they are supposed to look, dress, and act. Women are bombarded with images in magazines, television, music videos, and films that suggestively inform, or instruct, women on how to be conscious of their body image and what they need to do to improve themselves—via such physical means as breast augmentation. Most women in magazines and on television are very feminine, are thin, wear the latest trends in clothing style, and engage in acts that society labels as "female roles." Young girls are indoctrinated into a system that seems to dictate how they are supposed to look in order to gain respect and obtain attention. Women of all ages, but especially younger ones, have gone to extremes in order to meet society's ideal image of the idealized female by dieting and getting cosmetic surgery. As Dull and West (2002) explain, women tend to get cosmetic surgery more often than men and then women are far more concerned with their appearance than men are because men expect to be accepted for their flaws while women are taught to correct theirs. Feminist theory has promoted the idea that women should be strong and confident and a woman's image should not be determined by physical looks or ideals established by men. As a result, many contemporary women feel empowered by this ideology. Single mothers now have the opportunity to work as well as raise a child. Women no longer have to live in an unfulfilling marriage because of financial dependency on a husband. Women who are abused either sexually, verbally, or physically do not need to feel afraid to leave their abusers or feel intimidated to report domestic violence to law enforcement officials. Because of strong female role models, such as Hillary Clinton (Secretary of State) and Kathryn Bigelow (film director), young girls have powerful, strong women to admire.

The women's rights convention held in Seneca Falls in 1848 marks the first wave of feminism. At that time women did not attend college. By the end of the second wave of feminism, women outnumbered men attending college. Ironically, the gender "crisis" in higher education is now aimed at males, and efforts to improve their participation rates in college are a top concern among educators. Although complete gender equity has not been accomplished in all spheres of social life, women, arguably, have more overall autonomy and power than ever before. And for that reason, feminist theory is very relevant to many nonacademic women.

The Third Wave of Feminist Theory

The accomplishments achieved by the first two waves of feminism and feminist theory have benefited women around the world. But it is the academic world where feminist theory is most relevant. The growth of women's studies programs (which far outnumber men's studies programs) on college campuses continue to assist the feminist agenda. Furthermore, because of the strides made toward gender equity, much of contemporary feminist theory has shifted its focus toward accomplishing other goals. This shift in focus represents the "third wave" in feminism and feminist theory. Third-wave feminists are concerned about civil rights, gay and lesbian issues, homelessness, AIDS activism, environmental concerns, and human rights in general.

Among the third-wave issues being addressed by feminist theory is the analysis of welfare states. Feminist theorists have documented the link between gender and welfare states for a while now. As Orloff (2009) explains,

> Gender has been at the center of transformations of welfare states, families, and capitalist economies. Social politics increasingly features issues related to gender: fertility, immigration, labor supply, the supply of care workers and services, taxes and mothers' employment; gender equality in households, employment, and polity (p. 335).

Orloff (2005) also states that gendered insights, especially in the area of power and politics have radicalized and transformed the comparative study of welfare states.

Lo and Fan (2010) examine the images of women in Taiwan and Hong Kong from the perspective that cultural codes and styles of expression in civil society are gendered. They challenge innate notions of what it means to be masculine or feminine. For example, Lo and Fan (2010) state, "Just as rationality is not inherently masculine (even if historically regarded as the cultural logic of the male/public sphere), caring is by no means a feminine/private culture, despite a history of cultural biases" (p. 189). Care-giving responsibilities, Lo and Fan, argue have helped to shape women's role in society. The authors suggest that a restructuring of gender roles and their connection to domestic responsibility can bring about equity.

Margaret Hunter (2011) examines gender and its connection to consumerism in hip-hop. Utilizing the feminist-preferred form of research, Hunter conducted a qualitative analysis of the forty-one bestselling rap videos of 2007–2008 and noticed a number of very specific themes.

> Hip-hop's focus on conspicuous consumption, buttressed by the success of entrepreneurial rap moguls, has merged with strip club culture to create a new gender relation based on sexual transaction. The "rap lifestyle," marketed to consumers through multiple media outlets, focuses on the consumption of designer clothes, jewelry, cars, and liquor, often sold by the rap moguls' companies (Hunter, 2011:17).

Hunter believes that rap music videos help to advertise the consumption of the "rap lifestyle." The hip-hop gender perspective has also transformed the idea of strip club themes (e.g., stripper poles and sexual transactions) into mainstream acceptance. The popularity of hip-hop across racial and ethnic lines and among males and females assures that the gendered messages being sent to men and women are influencing a large number of people, especially with the younger generation. Notions of strip club theme have become normalized in a number of ways, including the large numbers of women who have stripper poles in their bedrooms and the advent of promoting pole dancing as a legitimate form of workout. Articles on stripper poles in the home have been commonplace for years. In 2007, Adam Tanner wrote, "Once confined to strip clubs, thin medal poles are popping up in kitchens, bedrooms, and exercise studios across the United States with gym fanatics, moms and even grandmothers using them to get fit" (p. 1). Pole dancing has become popular in the home for women who want to entice their partners and to keep in shape. In order to learn the proper techniques of pole dancing and to avoid injury (e.g., how to avoid pulled muscles and injuries as a result of a fall), women take classes. Oprah Winfrey featured pole dancing in the mid-2000s. What third-wave feminists have discovered is a changing in mentality of women and the strip club mentality. Feminists who studied the strip club culture in the past would have concentrated on the idea that women who shed their clothes for men were demeaning themselves and that men who went to strip clubs wanted to exploit women. Today, we see women embracing the idea of pole dancing. The changing mentality of young women and the strip club culture is revealed in the manner of dress preferred by many young women, casual attitude about having sex, or hooking up, and a willingness to send "sexy" photos of themselves to their boyfriends or husbands (referred to as "sexting") via cell phones.

The third wave of feminist theorists have noticed that many young women recognize that their bodies can be tools of power over men and that they have no problem wearing provocative styles of clothing. Interestingly enough, we can see a pattern of awakening sexuality among women with each wave of feminism. The first wave was accompanied by the erotic movement; the second wave was accompanied by women wearing mini-skirts and going braless and a type of "free love" mentality that "the pill" afforded; and the third wave is characterized by the "slut" culture. Now, before anyone gets upset with the normally derogatory usage of the term slut, let's examine the meaning behind the term slut culture. The *slut culture* concept applies to the growing phenomenon of young women embracing the term slut. In such a scenario, the term slut is being used much like younger gay and lesbian social theorists have come to embrace the term queer. In mainstream society, the terms *queer* and *sluts* are generally used in a derogatory manner. But in an attempt to gain control of their own sense of identities, a number of gay people embrace the queer label (sociology conferences are filled with sessions on "Queer Studies"), and many young women are embracing the slut label. The term slut has been embraced by third wavers because of its popularity on search engines. The theorists wanted ultimate exposure for their version of feminist theory and felt it best to use this term. Many traditional feminists, understandably, are upset with the usage of the term. As one Canadian columnist wrote, "Next thing you know, we'll be reclaiming the 'c' word" (Timson, 2011:L3).

There is evidence to support the contention of the third wave of feminist theory that women are embracing a slut culture. First, there are academic publications such as *Bitch* and *BUST* that promote the third-wave feminist perspective (Snyder, 2008). *Bitch's* stated mission is to provide and encourage an engaged, thoughtful feminist response to mainstream media and popular culture (*Bitch Magazine*, 2011). *BUST Magazine* (2011) also provides a feminist perspective and claims in its mission statement to "tell the truth about women's lives and present a female perspective on pop culture" and they also claim that they have been "BUSTing stereotypes about women since 1993."

Beyond publications such as *Bitch* and *BUST*, the idea of a "slut culture" accompanying the third wave of feminist theory is best supported by the growing phenomenon of "slut walks." Slut walks are a viral trend after the initial walk in Toronto. The purpose of "slut walks" (and there are a lot of local slut walks in cities and towns across the United States, Canada, and Europe) is to underscore the point that blaming victims of sexual assault is unacceptable (Seef, 2011). The origin of slut walks can be traced to an incident in Toronto wherein police officer Michael Sanguinetti suggested that women could avoid being raped if they stopped "dressing like sluts" (Timson, 2011:L3). Toronto-area feminists, and like-minded people everywhere, quickly pointed out that just because a woman wears a sexy, or "slutty," outfit, she is not asking for sex, and she certainly is not asking to be raped. The comment by the Toronto cop quickly led to a response among women in Toronto to congregate and protest such beliefs. The demonstration took to the streets, and many of the women dressed in "slutty" outfits. And with that, a movement was formed.

Another area of concern for third-wave feminists is the role of women in the military. As of mid-2012, women were still officially barred from serving directly in ground combat units and can only be "attached" to those units (*USA Today*, 2012; Roberts and Roberts, 2011). The concern here, beyond seeking equality for women soldiers, is the realization that women do not received full credit or recognition for their service and will therefore find it harder to get promoted and rise to positions of authority within the military. Feminists, among others, point out that present-day policy and law have not kept up with the changing times and present reality of war.

Although there are vague references to a fourth wave of feminist theory, such a thought is premature as the third wave of feminism is still being defined and its impact and longevity have yet to be determined. As Snyder (2008) states, "While a third-wave approach to feminism may not be able to generate a unified vision or inspire a mass movement, it does continue the tradition of feminism as critique, as a critical lens that should be turned on all existing discourses, institutions, and cultural practices" (p. 188). Third wavers are not interested in constructing ambitious theoretical analyses nor do they feel the need to justify the grounds they are acting on; they just do it. Third wavers embrace the anarchic imperative of direct action and criticize academic feminism for losing its critical edge (Snyder, 2008).

Summary

Feminism can be defined as a social movement and an ideology in support of the idea that a larger share of scarce resources (e.g., wealth, power, income, and status) should be allocated to women. Feminists believe that women should enjoy the same rights in society as men and that they should share equally in society's opportunities. Feminists hope to show that gender differences are a result of historical manmade conditions and not natural, biological differences.

Feminist sociological theory arose from the feminist movement in general and maintains as its core mantra expanding the role, power, significance, and status of women. Feminist sociological theory represents an attempt to give a voice to women and the female perspective. It demonstrates how gender roles are learned and not determined by biology. Thus, an individual is doing gender because of the cultural determinants of appropriate behavior based solely on what type of genitals the person has. When boys are taught "big boys don't cry," they are being taught to be strong and emotionally distant. When girls are taught to play quietly with their dolls and to "play house," they are being taught to be subservient. Boys and girls, then, are doing differences in gender expectations. These gender expectations extend throughout all the social institutions (such as economics, politics, military, and family) and are reinforced by the agents of socialization (e.g., the media, the church, the workplace). Dorothy Smith's concept of bifurcation—seeing the world through a preconceived framework—reflects this idea.

Feminist sociological theory is generally critical of the traditional scientific sociological approach that stresses a commitment to neutrality, objectivity, and empirical research. Feminist standpoint theory has become a staple of feminist theory where the development of a sociological method from the "standpoint of women" is the norm (Hekman, 1997; Smith, 1997). Feminists encourage the collection of subjective data, such as life histories, and the content analysis of such materials as diaries and photographs. They strongly encourage a focus on female issues and giving voice to female concerns.

There are three main waves of feminist theory. The first began with the Women's Rights Convention held in Seneca Falls, NY, in 1848 coupled with the abolitionist movement. The second wave of feminism began in the 1960s. These feminists fought for equality for men and women, especially in the workplace and at home. The third wave of feminism, which began, arguably, in the 1990s and continues today, has expanded its scope of feminist thought to include concerns about civil rights, gay and lesbian issues, homelessness, AIDS activism, environmental concerns, and human rights in general.

 Study and **Review** on **MySearchLab**

Discussion Questions

1. Describe each of the three waves of feminist theory articulated in this chapter. Which wave do you think brought about the most significant changes for women?
2. Of the major variations of feminist theory, which theory best reflects your gendered view of the world? Explain.
3. Compare and contrast the ideas of Sandra Harding and Patricia Hill Collins. What are the strengths and weaknesses of their feminist views?
4. What does it mean to give "voice" to women? Provide at least examples from the text.
5. Explain what is meant by the "slut culture." What do you think of the concept of "slut walks"? Would you participate in such a demonstration?

MySearchLab® Connections

MysearchLab is designed just for you. Each chapter features a customized study plan to help you learn and review key concepts and terms. Dynamic visual activities, videos, and readings found in the multimedia library will enhance your learning experience.

 View on **MySearchLab**

▶ Carol Gilligan: Socialization and Girls' Self Esteem

 Watch on **MySearchLab**

▶ Arlene Skolnick: Working Women

CHAPTER

14 Critical Theory

 Listen to the **Chapter Audio** on **MySearchLab**

Chapter Outline

- Defining Critical Theory
- The Roots of Critical Theory
- Herbert Marcuse
- Jürgen Habermas
- Douglas Kellner
- Criticisms of Critical Theory
- Application of Critical Theory to Contemporary Society
- Summary
- Discussion Questions

As you learned in your introductory sociology course, the roots of sociology are firmly entrenched in the social reform of society. The early sociologists shared a sense of concern about the social order of society, especially with the advent of industrialization, and its impact on everyday people. And, as described in Chapter 1, we have learned that social thinkers, in general, have criticized the existing social structure—because it harms the powerless of society—since (at least) the time of Machiavelli and his publication of *The Prince*. The point of these reminders is to reinforce the idea that sociologists have long been known as critics of society. That there is a theoretical perspective that emphasizes criticism, consequently, should not be surprising.

Critical thinking as a school of thought emerged from the work of neo-Marxist German theorists collectively referred to as the Frankfurt School. Critical theory started in 1923 with the founding of the Institute for Social Research at the Frankfurt School in Germany. Funded by private money, the institute enjoyed considerable autonomy and developed with minimal external pressure from the more formal University of Frankfurt (Held, 1980). German ex-patriot Hermann Weil, who lived in Argentina, was persuaded by his son Felix, who obtained a doctorate in political science from Frankfurt, to establish the endowment for an independent research institute to study Marxism and anti-Semitism (Adams and Sydie, 2001).

357

Academic critical thinking is much different than simply criticizing aspects of society, as has become commonplace in contemporary society. Currently, people rely on the Internet for social networking, communication, news, information, and more. And seemingly at every site and at every posting there is a "comments" section that enables viewers to post their own opinions about particular news items. Increasingly, people seemed enamored with the idea of making hateful comments about the most mundane topics (e.g., a celebrity who has put on weight, a politician who makes a comment on society, or an athlete who gets into trouble off the field). In fact, it has become so common for people to post negative comments that the term "hater" is used as an expression to identify a person who posts a contrary, generally very negative comment. But comments from "haters" generally lack any academic integrity or factual evidence to support an opposing viewpoint. In this chapter, we will see that it is possible to criticize society and ways of doing things without being hateful.

DEFINING CRITICAL THEORY

There is no clear-cut definition of critical theory.

> Even a casual glance at general portrayals [(Jay, 1973; Held, 1980)] or at collections of essays on the topic [(Arato and Gebhardt, 1978)] reveals a stunning range of methods, theories, and substantive analyses. Critical theory is immune to brief summary, and even basic familiarity requires effort that few nonspecialists are willing to expend (Antonio, 1983:326).

The term *critical theory* is itself an unfortunate one for it is confused with literary criticism, and a number of other approaches to social theory could be considered "critical" in some sense. Marxist theory is a critical approach to the study of society, feminist theory is a criticism of a male-dominated society, and even positivist researchers make a claim to criticizing the existing understanding of social reality. Thus, to claim to be critical of social conceptions is nothing new or unique. Regardless, a number of social thinkers are drawn to the critical perspective because of a growing dissatisfaction with dominant views of understanding reality.

As Bronner and Kellner (1989) explain, critical theory is a multidisciplinary approach to the study of society that combines such perspectives as sociology, political economy, cultural theory, philosophy, anthropology, and history. Critical theory is able to incorporate such diverse disciplines because it addresses a broader interest—the emancipation from all forms of oppression and commitment to promoting freedom, happiness, and a rational ordering of society. In this regard, critical theory is always subject to change. And yet, it remains fundamentally inspired by the dialectical tradition of Hegel and Marx.

Held (1980) argued that there are six Marxian tenets associated with critical theory:

1. Western societies are dominated by capitalistic principles of production, consumption, and the maximization of profits.
2. The commodity value of products is determined by the market, and labor is not rewarded as equally as ownership.
3. Capitalism fuels the fetishism and reification.
4. Capitalism is alienating because it is not harmonious with the social world.
5. The free market is nearly an illusion because of the dominance of oligarchies and monopolistic mass production of standardized goods.
6. In order for capitalistic societies to survive, they must have an ever-expanding market for consumption. This reality may lead to imperialist expansion and war.

From the critical perspective, it is essential that the capitalistic system be replaced with a system that favors workers and equality.

Contemporary critical theorizing involves a critical assessment of capitalism, disparages the optimism of the Enlightenment, and views the use of science for constructing a better society as naive, illusional, or even harmful. Most critical theorists see "objective" science as an extension of capitalism. "Postmodern" society is also viewed in a negative light (Turner, 2003). The disdain that critical theorists have for science comes from their assumption that dominant political and social interests shape the development of science and technology and from their belief that science and technology are not fully neutral with respect to human values because they inevitably mediate social relations. In other words, science and technology possess ideological implications (Morrow, 1994:63).

In addition to criticizing positivism and modern/postmodern society, Ritzer (2011) argues that contemporary critical theory is also critical of Marxist theory, the field of sociology, and modern culture. The criticism of Marxist theory centers primarily on its economic deterministic flair. Critical theorists believe economics is a cause of societal imbalance but argue that many aspects of social life lead to societal imbalance. The criticisms of contemporary sociology are linked to the critical school's perception of sociology as a positivistic discipline with a primary focus on macro social structures while ignoring (or paying less attention to) the social interactions of individuals. The criticism of culture is directed at the ever-growing power and influence of the media and its ability to create a "culture industry"—the rationalized, bureaucratized structures (e.g., television networks) that control modern society (Kellner and Lewis, 2007; Ritzer, 2011).

THE ROOTS OF CRITICAL THEORY

Critical theory has its roots tied directly to the creation of the Institute for Social Research in Frankfurt and a number of social thinkers who promoted the idealism of Karl Marx.

The Institute for Social Research

The Institute for Social Research was the first Marxist-oriented research school in Europe. Its members attempted to revise both Marx's critique of capitalism and the idea that revolution was the best way to change the social and political structures that had evolved since Marx's death (Bronner and Kellner, 1989). As a result, these social thinkers developed a "critical theory" of society. These German scholars initially used the term *kritische Theorie* to designate a specific approach to interpreting Marxist theory,

> but the term has taken on new meanings in the interim and can be neither exclusively identified with the Marxist tradition from which it has become increasingly distinct nor reserved exclusively to the Frankfurt School, given extensive new variation outside the original German context (Morrow, 1994:6–7).

The institute, under Carl Grunberg's leadership (1923–1929), was the starting point of the Austro-Marxist tradition. Marxism was made the inspiration and theoretical basis of the institute's program (Held, 1980). Under the directorship of Grunberg, the institute was characterized by a rather orthodox scientific Marxism, but this approach was abandoned when

Max Horkheimer assumed control in 1930. Horkheimer and his inner circle of scholars adopted a more philosophical, less dogmatic Marxism that was open to diverse intellectual currents (Jay, 1973). The most active years of the institute (1930–1944) coincided with the prominence of Nazism and fascism. The dilemma of the first generation of critical theorists was

> to reconcile Marx's emancipatory dream with the stark reality of modern society as conceptualized by Max Weber.... There seemed little reason to be optimistic about developing a theoretically informed program for freeing people from unnecessary domination. The defeat of the left-wing working-class movements, the rise of fascism in the aftermath of World War I, and the degeneration of the Russian Revolution into Stalinism had, by the 1930s, made it clear that Marx's analysis needed drastic revision (Turner, 2003:201).

Max Horkheimer, Theodor Adorno, and others who tried to study the power of the masses were put under restraints by Hitler's ascent to power. Anti-Semitism was increasingly evident during the 1930s in Germany, and the Jewish members of the institute were forced into exile. Ironically, the institute relocated to Columbia University (in 1934) in New York City, the center of the capitalist world (Adams and Sydie, 2001).

The term *critical theory* was coined in 1937 after the majority of the institute's members had already emigrated to the United States following Hitler's rise to power. The concept of "critical theory" was initially a type of code used by its adherents to hide their radical commitments to Marxism—an ideology not well received in the United States. But the term stuck and was soon used to encompass and define the emerging general social theories associated with Max Horkheimer, Herbert Marcuse, T. W. Adorno, Leo Lowenthal, and Frederick Pollock, along with Jürgen Habermas and others who would later join the critical school tradition (Bronner and Kellner, 1989).

Max Horkheimer, Friedrich Pollock, and Theodor Adorno represented the institute during the years of exile and its initial reconstitution in New York. In the 1940s, the three theorists went to Los Angeles and remained there until their return to Frankfurt in 1950. Other institute exiles found positions elsewhere (Adams and Sydie, 2001). By 1953, the institute had been reestablished in Germany. In the atmosphere of postwar reconstruction and the cold war, many key intellectuals from Germany's past were subject to attack in the press and in academia because of their continual support of Marxist doctrines (Held, 1980). Most members of the Frankfurt School believed that the individual is enmeshed in a world where capital is highly concentrated and where the economy and the polity are increasingly interlocked.

A number of specific theorists are associated with the formation of critical theory. Steven Smith believed that Hegel was a central figure, while other reviewers of critical theory generally agree that Gyorgy (Georg) Lukacs, Max Horkheimer, and Theodor Adorno are the most important scholars who directly influenced the intellectual development of critical theory and subsequent work by Herbert Marcuse and Jürgen Habermas.

G. W. F. Hegel (1770–1831)

Steven Smith (1987) stated, "Hegel is often regarded as a central figure in the development of the school of modern Critical Theory. Yet while his contribution to this school is often acknowledged, his own practice of critique is seldom given the attention it deserves" (p. 99). Hegel never described himself or his work as critical, but in his *The Phenomenology of Mind* (1931), he revealed a conception of critical theorizing that would have at least two important influences on the development of critical theory:

First, whereas Kant meant by *critique* an inquiry into the nature and limits of rationality as such, for Hegel it took the form of an internal or immanent examination of the various sources of deception, illusion, and distortion that the mind undergoes in its journey to Absolute Knowledge. Such an activity is critical, or in Hegel's term "negative," precisely because it entails a conception of liberation from those historical sources of domination and coercion. Like Marx, Nietzsche, and, later, Freud, Hegel sought to free human agents not only from the coercive illusions that inhibit their capacities for free thought and action, but from the forms of social life within which those coercive illusions thrive and find expression. Philosophical critique necessarily spills over into social theory. Second, underlying the Hegelian conception of critique is the belief that human history expresses an immanent telos the aim of which is the liberation of both the individual and the species from a system of constraints that are at least partially imposed by the minds of the agents to whom the theory is addressed. Hegel's argument depends upon the assumption that human agents are driven by a powerful common interest in freedom that persists through the interplay of their passions and actions (Smith, 1987:99–100).

Questioning what is deemed "absolute knowledge" and realizing that human history is the result of a struggle between interest groups fall within both the Marxist tradition and the critical paradigm.

Antonio (1983) explained that

critical theory is based on the meta-assumptions that derive from Hegel's dialectics, modified by Marx's materialist critique. Hegel's philosophy, which stresses immanent principles of contradiction, change, and movement, constitutes an alternative to the formal and static nature of Kantianism.... For Hegel, the nature of being is characterized by the subject continuously creating, negating, and recreating itself and its object world. Through *labor,* the subject not only makes history, but also produces a movement in history away from "self-estrangement" toward "freedom" (pp. 343–344).

Georg (György) Lukacs (1885–1971)

Lukacs was a part of the early Frankfurt School. In his 1923 publication *History and Class Consciousness* (1923), Lukacs argued that subjectivity is "annihilated" by "commodity production." The capitalistic system creates a "phantom objectivity" that undermines class consciousness.

In his view, emancipatory change does not automatically follow material evolution. Material conditions make revolution possible, but its realization depends upon the "free-action of the proletariat itself." Lukacs' analyses of alienation, commodity fetishism, subjectivity, consciousness, and spontaneous action constitute the theoretical bridge to critical theory; but on the way over, the Frankfurt school discarded other key elements of his approach (Antonio, 1983:328).

Lukacs had come to emphasize the importance Marx placed on the fetishism of commodities, a condition caused when the worker assumes that the commodity produced has an objective quality of its own, rather than realizing the commodity is a result of the worker's labor. "Lukacs' interpretation of Marxism as a dialectical critique of reification placed the problem of ideology to the forefront of attention" (Bailey, 1994:14). According to Jonathan Turner (2003), Lukacs blended Marx's ideas of fetishism of commodities with Weber's belief that rationality is penetrating more spheres of modern life. Combining Weber's and Marx's ideas, Lukacs came to believe that as traditional societies change,

> There is less reliance on moral standards and processes of communication to achieve societal integration; instead, there is more use of money, markets, and rational calculations. As a result, relations are coordinated by exchange values and by people's perceptions of one another as "things" (Turner, 2003:202).

Lukacs' *History and Class Consciousness* (1923), and Karl Korsch's *Marxism and Philosophy* (1971) were written as

> Contributions to the widespread European debates about the "crisis of Marxism" in the early twenties. In the aftermath of World War I, the European socialist movements entered a period of ferment and critical reflection. The experiences of the preceding decade, which had included the capitulation of the German Social Democratic Party to the war effort, the Bolshevik success in Russia and failed revolutionary attempts in Germany, Austria, Hungary and Italy, all seemed to demand a thorough rethinking of the prevailing forms of theory and practice. Lukacs and Korsch had been active participants in the Communist parties of Hungary and Germany respectively, and both were concerned to draw the essential lessons from those experiences (Bailey, 1994:7–8).

Both Lukacs and Korsch were singled out for official denunciation at the Fifth World Congress of the Third International, held in Moscow in 1924, because they questioned prevailing communist sentiments within the party. Lukacs had challenged the philosophical and political assumptions of orthodox dialectical materialism held by party members (Hardt, 1986). By the late 1920s, Soviet Marxism had been transformed into dialectical materialism (Marxism-Leninism), which increasingly contained ideological elements contradictory to Marx's original historical materialism (Antonio, 1983:330). In short, "both Lukacs and Korsch fell victim to the 'Bolshevization' of the European Communist parties in the aftermath of the Russian Revolution" (Bailey, 1994:9). However, "the influence of *History and Class Consciousness* was nonetheless evident in many essays published during the 1930s by Horkheimer, Marcuse, and Adorno in the Institute's journal, the *Zeitschrift für Sozialforschung*" (Bailey, 1994:22).

Max Horkheimer (1895–1973)

Horkheimer attended the universities of Munich, Freiburg, and then Frankfurt, where he earned his doctorate in 1922 with a thesis on Kant. He became a lecturer in 1925 at the Institute for Social Research, and in 1929, he was appointed to the new chair of social philosophy at the institute. A year later, he became director of the institute (Adams and Sydie, 2001). Under Horkheimer, the institute was oriented to developing social theory on an interdisciplinary basis. He wanted theory to benefit from both the reflective capacity of philosophy and the rigorous procedures of the individual sciences. From his inaugural address onward, he stressed the necessity of forging a new unity between philosophy and science, science and criticism, fact and value. For Horkheimer, society was a totality which is continuously restructuring itself. As a result, the idea of a social absolute—a complete or perfect state of social phenomena—is criticized. All factors in the total societal process are held to be in "the process of movement," including the relation of "parts to whole" (Held, 1980:181).

In the 1930s, Max Horkheimer found himself in an intellectual milieu that was marked by a sharp swing away from previously dominant forms of neo-Kantianism and toward pronounced forms of antirationalism. Horkheimer, in his 1934 discussion of "The Rationalism Debate in Contemporary Philosophy," endorsed the idea that there is no absolute truth of reality but warned against extreme antirationalism represented by *Lebensphilosophie* and existentialism (Hoy and McCarthy, 1995). in the direction of sociohistorical inquiry (Hoy and McCarthy, 1995:9).

Horkheimer was also concerned about the increasingly influential sociology of knowledge being developed at the time by Karl Mannheim.

> The appearance of Karl Mannheim's *Ideology and Utopia* in 1929 presented an important challenge to the Marxian theory of ideology.... By linking the ideological distortion of thought to social position, Marxism had raised doubts about the very possibility of its opponents ever attaining an adequate knowledge of social reality (Bailey, 1994:1).

Horkheimer and other members of the Frankfurt School believed that Mannheim's extension of the concept of ideology to encompass all forms of social thought had deprived it of all critical content, by severing it from any definite relation to a concrete historical conception of truth. In short, "Horkheimer judged Mannheim's sociology of knowledge to be practically, no less than theoretically, wrong-headed" (Hoy and McCarthy, 1995:11). Consequently, the Frankfurt School paid close attention to Mannheim's work and subjected it to close scrutiny in order to distinguish it from its own critical theory of society (Bailey, 1994:1–2). Horkheimer's 1937 essay "Traditional and Critical Theory" constitutes the institute's basic manifesto of its theoretical stand and at the same time distinguishes itself from the ideas of Mannheim. In this essay, Horkheimer emphasized a dialectical reinterpretation of Marx's critique of political economy as providing the basic analytical framework for the development of critical theory. During the early 1940s, however, the Frankfurt School's critical theory of society would begin to undergo important changes in orientation (Bailey, 1994:29).

Horkheimer maintained a commitment to the idea that there are no general criteria for critical theory as a whole, for such criteria always depend on a repetition of events and thus on a self-reproducing totality. Critical theory depends on particular historical conditions. Horkheimer maintained that there is a hiatus between concept and object, and between word and thing. These concepts are interdependent but irreducible aspects of the total societal process. Thus, critical theory aims to assess "the breach between ideas and reality." The method of procedure is immanent criticism (Held, 1980:183).

Theodor Wiesengrund-Adorno (1903–1969)

Theodor Adorno was born in Frankfurt. His father was a successful Jewish merchant, and his mother had had a successful singing career prior to her marriage. The name Adorno was from her side of the family (Adams and Sydie, 2001). Martin Jay (1973) explained that some of the members of the institute felt that there were too many Jewish-sounding names on the roster, so Adorno dropped the Wiesengrund part of his name while he was in the United States. Adorno

Theodor Adorno, German critical theorist in the "Frankfurt School" tradition. (A1690 Manfred Rehm Deutsch Presse Agentur/Newscom)

earned his doctorate at the University of Frankfurt in 1924 after completing his thesis on Husserl's phenomenology. He became associated with the institute in 1931 and a full member in 1938.

Adorno attempted to establish a "critical social consciousness" especially in terms of how a philosophy expresses the structure of society. Adorno believed that art expresses social contradictions and antinomies in a mediated form, and so, too, philosophy embodies similar objective structures. Just as forms and pieces of art involve critical perspectives, so could particular philosophies. Adorno's goal was to show how the history of mind—which he conceived of as the attempt of the subject to gain distance from the object—continually reveals the "superiority of objectivity." Adorno argued that objects exist for us through conceptuality (Held, 1980).

> Adorno's complex, aphoristic, and fragmented style is consistent with his view that the language within which we must think and work is not a transparent mirror of reality. What the plain speech of easy and efficacious everyday communication reproduces is the illusion of social harmony and intelligibility. Adorno's highly self-conscious constructions are designed to disrupt the disguised interest in smooth social functioning presupposed by most verbal interchange (Hoy and McCarthy, 1995:132).

In *Negative Dialectics* (1973), Adorno insisted that the dialectic approach is not a middle point between absolutism and relativism. He was also against the idea that critical theory should merely criticize one point of view in favor of another. "This response will not work if the principle and its negation are the only alternatives, and if a double negation formally entails the affirmative" (Hoy and McCarthy, 1995:132). Furthermore, attacking someone else's position as relative does not prove that one's own position is any less relative. As Turner (2003) explains,

> The goal of negative dialectics was to sustain a constant critique of ideas, conceptions, and conditions. This critique could not only by itself change anything, for it operates only on the plane of ideas and concepts. But it can keep ideological dogmatisms from obscuring conditions that might eventually allow emancipatory action (p. 203).

Adorno and Horkheimer shared many ideas and collaborated on a number of works. Adorno was more philosophical but also more research-oriented than Horkheimer. But Adorno was also pessimistic about the chances of critical theory's making great changes in society. Even so, his essays were designed to expose patterns of recognized and unrecognized domination of individuals by social and psychological forces (Turner, 2003).

HERBERT MARCUSE (1898–1979)

Herbert Marcuse was born in Berlin to a prosperous Jewish family. After serving in the German army in World War I, Marcuse became associated with the Social Democratic Party and the revolutionary Soldiers Council in Berlin. In 1919, he left the Social Democratic Party in protest over what he perceived as the betrayal of the proletariat (Jay, 1973). Marcuse then went on to study philosophy at the universities of Berlin and Freiburg. He earned his doctorate in 1923 with a thesis in literature. After spending six years as a bookseller and publisher in Berlin, Marcuse returned to Freiburg in 1929 to study with the philosophers Edmund Husserl and Martin Heidegger, whose right-wing views clashed with his own Marxist views. Despite contradictory philosophical views, Marcuse became a member of the Institute for Social Research in 1933 on Husserl's recommendation (Adams and Sydie, 2001). Furthermore, Marcuse maintained throughout his life that Heidegger was the greatest teacher and thinker whom he had ever encountered (Kellner, 2003).

When the Nazis came into power, and upon Heidegger's advice, Marcuse fled Germany to Geneva, Paris, and finally New York City. Marcuse became a colleague of Horkheimer at the Institute for Social Research—which had emigrated from Germany to New York, at Columbia University—from 1934 to 1940. In December 1942, Marcuse joined the Office of War Information as a senior analyst in the Bureau of Intelligence. In March 1943, he joined the Office of Secret Services (OSS) and identified Nazi and anti-Nazi people and groups and helped to draw up a plan for the "denazifaction" of Germany. After the OSS dissolved in 1951, Marcuse taught at Columbia (1952–1953) and Harvard (1954–1955) and then became a professor of political science at Brandeis (1958–1965). While at Columbia and Harvard, Marcuse began research which led him to the writing of *Soviet Marxism*. In 1967, be began teaching at the University of California at San Diego. Marcuse gained world status during the 1960s as a philosopher, social theorist, and political activist. Through his writings, travels, and media exposure, he became known as the father of the New Left (Kellner, 1984). He tirelessly propagated his critiques of contemporary society and demands for radical social change and attracted a group of devoted followers. "Critiques and commentaries on Herbert Marcuse abound and they abound because his works got hooked up with the global student-youth revolt as have those of no other contemporary Western theorist" (Breines, 1970:1).

Among Marcuse's more significant publications in social theory and political sociology are *Reason and Revolution* (1941), *Eros and Civilization* (1955), *Soviet Marxism* (1958), *One-Dimensional Man* (1964), *A Critique of Pure Tolerance* (1965), *Negations: Essays in Critical Theory* (1968a), *An Essay on Liberation* (1969), *Counterrevolution and Revolt* (1972), *Studies in Critical Philosophy* (1973), and *The Aesthetic Dimension* (1978).

Marcuse shared Adorno's concern about the critique and transcendence of reification and fetishism. In a vein similar to that of Horkheimer, he stressed the unconcluded nature of the dialectic, a potential in humans that is yet to be realized, the centrality of human practice in the constitution and assessment of knowledge, and the importance of interdisciplinary approaches to the comprehension of the social totality. However, despite these overlaps, there are also major differences in their positions (Held, 1980). Marcuse's writings engage more fully than those of Horkheimer and Adorno with the interests of classical Marxism. Politics plays a key, if not central, role in his life and work. His career represents a constant attempt to examine, defend, and reconstruct the Marxist enterprise. He was preoccupied by the fate of revolution, the potentiality for socialism, and the defense of utopian objectives. The goals of his critical approach to society are the emancipation of consciousness, the nurturing of a decentralized political movement, and the reconciliation of humanity and nature (Held, 1980).

Critical Theory

Marcuse did not define explicitly his crucial and critical concepts, nor did he really define *critical theory* itself. Instead, he used abstractions to describe critical theory. For example, critical theory is a process of "bringing to consciousness potentialities that have emerged within the maturing historical situation" (Marcuse, 1968a:158). Critical theory is a theory which was "confronted with the presence of social forces…in the established society which move…toward more rational and freer institutions" (Marcuse, 1964:254). And it is a theory guided by "political practice" (Marcuse, 1969:5). Marcuse believed that "one key task of philosophy is to criticize other philosophy, not only—even if most importantly—in the interests of truth but also because, whether philosophers will it so or not, philosophical ideas are influential in social, moral, and political life" (MacIntyre, 1970a:1).

Marcuse's critical theory was influenced by Hegel and Marx.

> For Marcuse, a critical turning point in the history of philosophy is Hegel's transvaluation of the concept "reason." He sees Hegel as the thinker who projected reason from the subjective sphere in which he found it to its proper role as "a critical tribunal" in and of the world (Bleich, 1977:5–6).

Marcuse placed great value on reason. "In summarizing Hegel's objection to Kant, Marcuse argues that if 'things-in-themselves' are beyond the capacity of reason, reason will remain a mere subjective principle without relevance to the objective structure of reality" (Bleich, 1977:9). Furthermore, Marcuse (1989) described:

> Reason represents the highest potentiality of man and of existence; the two belong together. For when reason is accorded the status of substance, this means that at its highest level, as authentic reality, the world no longer stands opposed to the rational thought of men as mere material objectivity (*Gegenstandlichkeit*). Rather, it is now comprehended by thought and defined as concept (*Begriff*) (p. 58).

Marcuse's study of Hegel contributed to Hegel's renaissance, which was taking place in Europe during the 1930s.

Like all first-generation critical theorists, Marcuse was influenced by the ideas of Karl Marx. Marcuse himself insisted that the primary inspiration and source of critical theory comes from Marx. Interestingly, Marcuse published the first major review (in 1933) of Marx's recently discovered and published *Economic and Philosophical Manuscripts of 1844*. His review of Marx's work revealed Marcuse to be an astute student of Germany philosophy (Kellner, 2003).

> Even in works where Marx is never mentioned, such as *Eros and Civilization,* or in those where traditional Marxism is radically questioned, such as *One-Dimensional Man,* Marcuse is using Marxian concepts and methods to expand Marxian theory, to overcome its limitations and to question aspects that he believes should be revised or rejected. On the whole, Marcuse's version of Marxism consists of a series of revisions and renewals of Marxian theory that provides a theoretical project seeking to comprehend and transform contemporary society (Kellner, 1984:5).

Marcuse praised Marxist materialism because

> Marxist materialism both envisaged a contrast between what man happens to be at the moment and what man could become, and also distinguished between how things really are in a capitalist society and the false consciousness that men in such a society possess, it restored the concept of essence to a central place (MacIntyre, 1970a:8).

Combining the thoughts of Hegel and Marx, Marcuse concluded that history is the arena in which humans seek the freedom to manifest universal rationality (Bleich, 1977). Lipshires (1974) noted that following Marx, Marcuse argues that the material and ideal coexist with neither having priority over the other. While "there exists an objective world of nature transcendentally beyond consciousness" (as Hegel would agree), that world cannot be assigned an onto-logical character as an infrastructure that determines in any way either human nature or human history (p. 3).

Marx was a critic of society and proposed courses of action to change it. However, Marcuse felt that Marxism had neither absorbed the most advanced currents of contemporary thought nor kept pace with changes in contemporary society (Kellner, 1984). Marcuse's critical theory had roots in Marxism, but his reconstruction of it led to the uniqueness of Marcuse's thinking. In short, "For Marcuse, Marxism is a method of analysis and instrument of critique and social transformation and is not a dogma or system of absolute knowledge" (Kellner, 1984:9).

Technological Rationality

In *One-Dimensional Man* (1964), Marcuse extended Weber's idea of rationalization by employ-ing the concept of *technological rationality*. Weber had pointed out that Western society had come to be dominated by science and the "iron cage" of bureaucracy.

> The rationalization process not only manifested itself in the rational behavior of individu-als in bureaucratic settings, but also referred to their method of thinking. Instrumental rationality, a calculating and *means*-oriented mode of thought, had gradually come to replace substantive rationality, or thought dealing with morality, with the validity of the *ends* of action (Farganis, 2000:384).

Marcuse argued that modern industrial society was dominated by a technological rationality, with the working middle class as its vocal supporter and defender.

Among the many shortcomings of Marx's theory was his failure to foresee the develop-ment of a sizeable middle class. The workers of industrial societies enjoy benefits that were never realized at any other time in history. Technology created affluence, and this freedom from mate-rial want led to a relatively happy and materialistically satisfied middle class. When workers are satisfied, their reasons for dissent and protest are eliminated and they become passive members of the dominating system. Marcuse was concerned that the cost of material satisfaction was offset by the loss of individual freedoms and liberties.

> The forms of consumption in an affluent society have, according to Marcuse, a twofold effect. They satisfy material needs which might otherwise lead to protest; and they fos-ter identification with the established order....Moreover the conditions of work in an advanced industrial society tend to render the worker passive. The rhythm of production in a semi-automated factory, the nature of skilled work, the increase in the proportion of white-collar workers all destroy any consciousness of being in opposition to the work system (MacIntyre, 1970b:64–65).

Thus, Marcuse was making two claims. First, the workers of industrial society are suffering from false consciousness. Second, the workers should not be happy with material satisfaction but should be striving for some unidentified (by Marcuse) nonmaterial satisfaction. Marcuse ignored the fact that the history of human kind *is* the pursuit of material success.

As witnessed in the United States in the 2000s (especially since September 2001), Marcuse's prediction of material satisfaction being offset by the loss of individual freedoms and liberties is a reality. People are willingly giving away their individual freedoms in the belief they will garner greater security and protection from the threat of terrorism. Give the people some "toys" (material goods) to play with and they will blindly go along with governmental demands for the right to intrude in the lives of citizens.

Marcuse insisted that modern industrial society produces a "surplus repression" by imposing socially unnecessary labor, unnecessary restrictions on sexuality, and a social system organized around profit and exploitation. Marcuse argued for an end of such "repression" and promoted the creation of a new society. Marcuse believed that industrial society creates false needs, which integrate individuals into the existing system of production and consumption (Kellner, 2003). Technology, mass media, popular culture, and leisure systems are all guilty of being modes of thought that reify the existing social structures.

JÜRGEN HABERMAS (1929–)

Jürgen Habermas was born in Gummersbach, Germany, near Düsseldorf, on June 18, 1929. He grew up during the Nazi regime and World War II, two influences that would have a profound effect on his thinking and future writings. His lifelong work is dedicated to making sure that fascism never reemerges.

Habermas studied philosophy at Göttingen, Zurich, and Bonn, where he earned his doctorate in 1954. He then worked as Adorno's assistant at the Institute for Social Research in Frankfurt (1956–1959). In 1961, he received his second doctorate at Mainz and began teaching at the University of Heidelberg during the same year. In 1964, he became a professor of philosophy at Frankfurt, where he assumed Horkheimer's chair in philosophy and sociology. Habermas then joined the Max Planck Institute for the Study of the Conditions of Life in the Scientific-Technical World, in Starnberg, near Munich, in 1971. In 1982, he returned to the University of Frankfurt as the chair of sociology and philosophy and remained until his retirement in 1993. Since retirement, Habermas has continued to contribute to public discussion through interviews, presentations, and publications. Among Habermas's significant publications are *Communication and the Evolution of Society* (1962), *Knowledge and Human Interests* (1968), *The Theory of Communicative Action* (1981, 1984, 1987), and *The Philosophical Discourse of Modernity* (1987b).

Habermas is perhaps the most well-known and prolific of the second generation of critical theorists. He was influenced by the works of Marx, Weber, and the early members of the Frankfurt School. Habermas's writings are steeped in the German tradition (Held, 1980). In particular, Habermas developed

> Marxist ideas of consciousness, critical theory's critique of instrumental reason, and Weber's critique of rationalization. He attempts to rescue rationality from Weber's pessimistic tendency to couple it with formal rationalization. He also transforms Marxist theory by adding increased emphasis on communication and interaction; this new emphasis, based on twentieth century phenomenology, interactionist theory, and modern theories of communication and cognitive development, clarifies the process by which subjective consciousness can be transformed. Habermas also expands Marxist notions of crisis from economic crisis to crises in political, cultural, and intra-personal spheres—crises of legitimation, rationality, and motivation (Garner, 2000:371).

Habermas seeks a society with the self-emancipation of people from domination. The issue of morality goes hand in hand with this transformation. "In his discussion of the sociocognitive and moral dimensions of the generalized other, Habermas not only underlines the importance of this distinction but also stresses the need to focus on the moral dimension per se" (Strydom, 2001:177). His critical theory is an attempt to further the self-understanding of social groups capable of transforming society.

Critical Theory

In his article "The Tasks of a Critical Theory" (1989), Habermas stated that the work of the Institute for Social Research was basically dominated by six themes until the early 1940s, when the circle of collaborators that had gathered in New York began to break up. These themes were

1. **The forms of integration in postliberal societies:** Whether in a democracy or totalitarian regimes.
2. **Family socialization and ego development:** For example, the structural change of the bourgeois nuclear family and the weakening of the authoritarian position of the father.
3. **Mass media and mass culture:** The development of a culture industry for the manipulative control of consciousness.
4. **The social psychology behind cessation of protest:** Political consciousness of workers and employees.
5. **The theory of art:** The arts as the preferred object of an ideology, whether utopian or critical.
6. **The critique of positivism and science:** science as a tool of the bourgeoisie.

This spectrum of themes reflected Horkheimer's conception of an interdisciplinary social science (Habermas, 1989:292). But this foundation was unable to support an empirical research program, something championed by Habermas.

Utilizing his theory of communicative action, Habermas promoted an analysis that begins reconstructively (or unhistorically) and describes structures of action and structures of mutual understanding that are found in the intuitive knowledge of competent members of modern societies. Nevertheless, Habermas's critical theory was inspired classical Greek and German philosophy, which stressed the inseparability of truth and virtue, of facts and values, and of theory and practice (Held, 1980). The imperative of critical theorists is to reformulate society from its course of history. Habermas maintained that twentieth-century history was primarily shaped by capitalism and Soviet socialism. Agreeing with Horkheimer, Habermas believed that knowledge is historically rooted and interest-bound. The first stage in the redevelopment of society is to provide objectivity in knowledge. Habermas wanted a society where people are free to assemble and communicate openly (politically). In a detailed, historical analysis, Habermas traced the emergence of "public opinion" to the eighteenth century. Forums for public discussion developed rapidly in Europe to mediate the growing division between the state and civil society, a division which developed from the expansion of market economies (Held, 1980).

Communication and the understanding of language are the keys to understanding and comprehending knowledge. "Habermas argued that linguistic communities are predicated upon an understanding that communication should be based upon a free flow of information undistorted by coercion" (Antonio, 1983:335). Habermas described the ideal speech situation as one that is uncoerced, free for all people, and in which all people are treated equally.

Communication Theory

Habermas found the Marxist philosophy of history fragile, especially in regard to its ability to support empirical research. As Horkheimer and Adorno had scaled down Marx's analysis of history in *Dialectic of Enlightenment* (1944), Habermas also retooled Marxian theory.

> Like his critical theory predecessors, Habermas is concerned with reformulating Marxian theory in the light of twentieth-century social changes, and most especially in light of the expansion of state power into all spheres of social life. Habermas expands Marx's conception of humanity by adding language (communication) to work (labor) as a distinct feature of species-being (Adams and Sydie, 2001:413).

Antonio (1983) argued that Habermas's ideas about communication and language are linked to his ideas of social evolution.

> His analysis of the role of language in social evolution rejected views that assign knowledge, values, and ideology a pure epiphenomenal status. Thus, Habermas abandoned the base/superstructure relation and its strict concept of material determinism. He suggested that evolutionary, structural differentiation (rationalization) of productive forces interacts with, establishes limits for, and creates possibilities for the development of communicative action, but does not strictly determine this action (p. 336).

Habermas was especially concerned about Marx's historical-materialist analysis because its assumptions regarding the dialectical relation between productive forces and productive relations were grounded on pseudonormative propositions provided by so-called objective historic accounts. Habermas (1989) argued, instead, that history is written from the point of view of bourgeois idealism. Critical theory questions the validity of historic accounts of events.

To "escape" the philosophical historical materialism of Marxist thought, Habermas proposed that theory cannot be tied to concrete ideals of human life; instead, it must orient itself to the range of learning processes that are opened at any given time. A theory must refrain from critically evaluating and normatively ordering totalities, forms of life and cultures, and life contexts and epochs *as a whole.* Such a theory must feature communicative action (Habermas, 1989:296–297).

The Freudian influence is reflected in the following passage from Habermas's *The Theory of Communicative Action,* Volume 2 (1987):

> The theory of communicative action provides a framework within which the structural model of ego, id, and superego can be recast. Instead of an instinct theory that represents the relation of ego to inner nature in terms of a philosophy of consciousness—on the model of relations between subject and object—we have a theory of socialization that connects Freud with Mead, gives structures of intersubjectivity their due, and replaces hypotheses about instinctual vicissitudes with assumptions about identity formation. This approach can (i) appropriate more recent developments in psychoanalytic research, particularly the theory of object relations and ego psychology, (ii) take up the theory of defense mechanisms in such a way that the interconnections between intra-psychic communicative barriers and communication disturbances at the interpersonal level become comprehensible, and (iii) use the assumptions about mechanisms of conscious and unconscious mastery to establish connection between orthogenesis and pathogenesis (pp. 388–389).

With regard to the media and their role in culture, Habermas (1987a) stated:

> With the shift from writing to images and sounds, the electronic media—first film and radio, later television—present themselves as an apparatus that completely permeates and dominates the language of everyday communication. On the one hand, it transforms the authentic content of modern culture into the sterilized and ideologically effective stereotypes of a mass culture that merely replicates what exists; on the other hand, it uses up a culture cleansed of all subversive and transcending elements for an encompassing system of social controls, which is spread over individuals, in part reinforcing their weakened internal behavioral controls, in part replacing them. The mode of functioning of the culture industry is said to be a mirror image of the psychic apparatus, which, as long as the internalization of paternal authority was still functioning, had subjected instinctual nature to the control of the superego in the way that technology had subjected outer nature to its domination (pp. 389–390).

Habermas argued that an individual's life worlds are influenced by constant interaction with others and with society's social structures:

> The structures of the lifeworld lay down the forms of the intersubjectivity of possible understanding. It is to them that participants in communication owe their extramundane positions vis-à-vis the innerworldly items about which they can come to an understanding. The lifeworld is, so to speak, the transcendental site where the speaker and hearer meet, where they can reciprocally raise claims that their utterances fit the world (objective, social, or subjective) and where they can criticize and confirm those validity claims, settle their disagreements, and arrive at agreements (Habermas, 1987a:126).

Habermas's communication theory involves communicative action, via language, and provides meaning to actors and shapes their life worlds. Habermas's (1987a) communication theory can be summarized as follows:

> Under the functional aspect of *mutual understanding,* communicative action serves to transmit and renew cultural knowledge; under the aspect of *coordinating action,* it serves social integration and the establishment of solidarity; finally, under the aspect of *socialization,* communicative action serves the formation of personal identities. The symbolic structures of the lifeworld are reproduced by way of the continuation of valid knowledge, stabilization of group solidarity, and socialization of responsible actors. The process of reproduction connects up new situations with the existing conditions of the lifeworld; it does this in the *semantic* dimension of meanings or contents (of the cultural tradition), as well as in the dimensions of *social space* (of socially integrated groups), and *historical time* (of successive generations). Corresponding to these processes of *cultural reproduction, social integration,* and *socialization* are the structural components of the lifeworld: culture, society, person (pp. 137–138).

Habermas is perhaps best known for his communication theory. He tried

> to salvage the rational kernel of modern philosophy through his linguistic turn, he thinks that French philosophers like Derrida and Foucault abandon this kernel.... Whereas Habermas takes the linguistic turn to restore and legitimate reason and philosophy, he sees the French poststructuralists' version of the linguistic turn as threatening the preeminence of both reason and philosophy (Hoy and McCarthy, 1995:153).

Habermas (1991) made it clear, however, that he "never had the false ambition of wishing to develop something like a normative political theory from the principle of discourse" (p. 264).

Modernity and Scientism

Habermas was critical of the use of the term *modernity*. Through his research of the use of the term, he discovered that scholars throughout the centuries had used the concept of *modernity*. In Christian lore, the term "new world" was used to describe modern society as the still-to-come age of the world of the future, which was to dawn only on the last day (Judgment Day) of humanity. The secular world eventually used the term *modernity* to apply to chronological eras. In this regard, modernity was identified with an era that had already begun (Habermas, 1987b:5).

Habermas (1997) traced the usage of the word *modern* to the late fifth century, when it was first used to distinguish the present Christian era from the pagan and Roman past. The use of the term modernity brings with it a bias that the current era is more advanced than past eras. Thus, the expression *modern age* is applied whenever a new consciousness is developed. Habermas also underscores the relative meaningless of such a term as *modernity*. After all, those of us alive today live in a modern era (when compared to the past), but centuries, and perhaps mere decades, from now, people would not label the early 2000s as the modern era. Nonetheless, Habermas (1987) believed that the modern world is distinguished from the old by the fact that it opens itself to the future; the epochal new beginning is rendered constant with each moment that gives birth to the new. Modernity, then, is characteristic of a historical consciousness, with the present enjoying a prominent position as contemporary history.

Habermas was also critical of *scientism*—identifying knowledge with science—because of its relation to positivism, since positivism provides scientism's most sophisticated defense. Although positivism began as a critique of certain ideologies (such as religious dogma and speculative metaphysics), it became a central element of technocratic consciousness and a key aspect of modern ideology. Since Habermas believed that (critical) theory should be a critique of knowledge, he opposed positivism because it attempted to objectify knowledge. He believed that knowledge must discard the "illusion" of objectivity—a world viewed as a universe of facts and laws. For Habermas, the goal of the critical sciences is to facilitate the process of methodical self-reflection and to dissolve barriers to the self-conscious development of life (Held, 1980). Habermas prefers a subject-centered philosophy, rather a rational, scientific, objective science (Rasmussen, 1990).

DOUGLAS KELLNER (1943–)

Douglas Kellner was born in 1943 and received his Ph.D. in philosophy from Columbia University in 1973. Kellner can be thought of as a "third-generation" critical theorist in the tradition of the Frankfurt School. (The first generation consists of such theorists as Horkheimer, Adorno and Marcuse; and the second generation is identified with Habermas.) Kellner is especially known for his systematic and critical review of television in the United States. He believes that the media— and in particular, television—have long served the interests of the powerful. Among his most recent publications are *Camera Politica: The Politics and Ideology of Contemporary Hollywood Film* (co-authored with Michael Ryan) (1988) and *Media Spectacle and the Crisis of Democracy* (2005); he is co-editor of *Media and Cultural Studies: KeyWorks* (2005), *Guys and Guns Amok: Domestic Terrorism and School Shootings from Oklahoma City Bombings to the Virginia Tech Massacre* (2008), and *Media/Cultural Studies* (2009); and he is co-author of *Cinema Wars: Hollywood Film and Politics in the Bush–Cheney Era*.

Critical Theory

In his book *Karl Korsch: Revolutionary Theory* (1977), Kellner reviewed the work of Karl Korsch. Kellner (1977) described Korsch as

> being increasingly recognized as one the most interesting, neglected, and relevant political theorists of the century.... Korsch was also an early opponent of nazism and developed a theory of fascism and counterrevolution on a world-wide scale to explain the defeats of the working-class movement and their failure to follow the Marxian scenario.... Further, Korsch was one of the first Western theorists to call attention to developments in the so-called Third World, which he perceived might be a locale for the sort of social revolution that had failed to materialize in Europe and America (p. 3).

The relevance of this book to Kellner's critical theory lies in the fact that while Kellner reviewed Korsch's concern about such issues as the crisis of Marxism, he remained committed to the core ideas of Marxist thought. In his review of Jean Baudrillard (*Jean Baudrillard: From Marxism to Postmodernism and Beyond*, 1989b), Kellner specifically defended Marx's concepts of *use values* and *commodities*. Kellner (1989b) believed that most individuals and societies *do* prioritize needs and the use values of commodities in everyday consumer practices and social policies. Kellner does, however, question whether or not individuals and societies have a clear idea as to what they actually need or what is useful. Kellner also remains committed to Marxist analysis and critical scrutiny of human behavior, especially in regard to commodities and consumption.

Kellner believes that we live in an era still dominated by capitalism, and as a result, we are still in the "modern" era and not a postmodern era as some theorists would argue (see Chapter 15). As a result, Kellner argues that Marxist terms and concepts such as reification and alienation are still relevant in the analysis of technocapitalism. Kellner (1989a:178) described *technocapitalism* as a capitalist society structured so that technical and scientific knowledge, automation, computers, and advanced technology play such a significant role in the process of production that they parallel the role of human labor power in early capitalism. Technocapitalism is a variation of capitalism, but it is, nonetheless, capitalism. Kellner's examination of the media—and in particular, television— reveals his technoapproach to the understanding of human behavior, society, and culture.

In their co-edited *Media and Cultural Studies: KeyWorks* (2005), Durham and Kellner examine culture via a collection of articles on culture, media, and communication. Utilizing the Frankfurt tradition, this collection of articles offers a critical assessment of contemporary culture by some of the leading critical theorists of the past and present eras.

Media and Culture

Kellner's ideas on the effect of the media on culture are influenced by the work of Baudrillard. As Kellner (1989b) stated,

> During the 1980s Jean Baudrillard has been promoted in certain circles as the most advanced theorist of the media and society in the so-called postmodern era. His theory of a new, postmodern society rests on a key assumption that the media, simulations and what he calls "cyberblitz" constitute a new realm of experience and a new stage of history and type of society. To a large extent Baudrillard's work consists in rethinking radical social theory and politics in the light of developments in the consumer, media, information and technological society (p. 60).

But Kellner (1989b) criticized Baudrillard for ignoring the important terrain of cultural politics, for not addressing alternative media practices, for believing that all media are mere producers of noise and are devoid of meaning, and for believing that the media are merely an example of one-way communication.

Kellner's views of the effect of media on culture are presented in his *Television and the Crisis of Democracy* (1990). In Chapter 1 of his book, Kellner provides statistics (which are outdated now but still illustrate his point) that demonstrate how prevalent television is in contemporary society: "In excess of 750 million TV sets in more than 160 countries are watched by 2.5 billion people per day" (p. 1). Nearly every home in the United States has a television set that is turned on for more than seven hours per day. Furthermore, Kellner stated that watching television is the most popular leisure activity of Americans. Frey and Delaney (1996) found that watching television was the most popular leisure activity among prison inmates as well.

In short, television has a tremendous impact on culture, and consequently, many people have analyzed the effects of television on viewers.

> Television thus has many critics, commentators, and celebrants—but few theorists. The critiques themselves have largely been determined by the political views of the critics. Conservatives, for example, claim that television is a liberal medium that subverts traditional values. Liberals and radicals, by contrast, often criticize television for its domination by business imperatives and conservative values (Kellner, 1990:3).

Postmodern theorists have conceptualized contemporary capitalist society in terms of the proliferation and dissemination of images, citing the media as the primary culprit in creating "hyperreal" images that replace reality. In contrast to the postmodern theory of the media, and to Horkheimer and Adorno's 1972 study of the media *(Dialectic of Enlightenment),* Kellner (1990) presented a multidimensional approach:

> My aim, by contrast, is to develop a critical theory that analyzes television in terms of its institutional nexus within contemporary U.S. society. Moreover, rather than seeing contemporary U.S. society as a monolithic structure absolutely controlled by corporate capitalism (as the Frankfurt School sometimes did), I shall present it as a contested terrain traversed by conflictual mass medium in which competing economic, political, social, and cultural forces intersect....I contend that U.S. society is highly conflictual and torn by antagonisms and struggles, and that television is caught up in these conflicts, even when it attempts to deny or cover them over, or simply to "report" them (pp. 14–15).

Kellner criticized the early critical school because of its narrow view of the media and mass culture as mere instruments of capitalist ideology. Kellner does not see television as a tool of oppression used by corporate entities to subvert the members of society.

However, Kellner is concerned that television is a threat to democracy. The term *democracy* is problematic in its own right, but Kellner (1990) stated,

> In its broadest signification, democracy refers to economic, political, and cultural forms of self-management. In an "economic democracy," workers would control the work place, just as citizens would control their polity through elections, referenda, parliaments, and other political processes. "Cultural democracy" would provide everyone access to education, information, and culture, enabling people to fully develop their individual potentials and to become many-sided and more creative (p. 15).

From this standpoint, the United States has a political democracy (citizens have the right to vote), but certainly not an economic democracy (workers do not control the workplace) or a cultural democracy (there is unequal access to education and information). Kellner argued that the United States does not have a fully democratic polity.

Kellner realizes what many first-generation critical theorists failed to notice: the importance of conflicts within the ruling class and challenges to liberal and conservative positions by radical movements and discourses.

> Given the ubiquity and power of television, it is a highly desired prize for ruling groups. Unlike most critical theorists, however, I attempt to specify both the ways in which television serves the interests of dominant economic and political forces, and the ways in which it serves to reproduce conflicts that traverse contemporary capitalist societies. Accordingly, I shall attempt to present a more comprehensive and multidimensional theoretical analysis than the standard Marxist and neo-Marxist accounts, which tend to conceptualize the media and the state simply as instruments of capital (Kellner, 1990:15).

Kellner also argued that television contributes to social integration and implies that democratized media could be the basis for a revitalized public sphere (Antonio, 1983:340). Through his examination of television in the 1980s, Kellner concluded that television has worked increasingly to further conservative hegemony. In so doing, television has helped produce a crisis in democracy. To his credit, Kellner goes beyond mere criticism of television and offers alternative models to the existing structure of commercial broadcasting—ones that may enhance political knowledge and participation.

Many of these "alternative" approaches to broadcasting have been realized, especially with the Federal Communication Commission's (FCC) implementation of deregulation in 1984. Among the alternative television systems promoted by Kellner (1990) is public-access television, which he described as "one of the few real forms of alternative television, and it provides the best prospect for using the broadcast media to serve the interests of popular democracy" (p. 207). The advent of cable television in the 1970s and satellite TV in the 1980s was directly responsible for the increase in public access programs, channels for government, and educational programming.

Kellner's recent publications continue to examine political discourse and the role of the media in culture from a critical perspective. In *Media Spectacle and the Crisis of Democracy* (2005), Kellner highlights the changing role of the media after the momentous political events that followed 9/11 (the September 11, 2001, terrorist attacks on U.S. soil) and warns that Americans' core freedoms are becoming jeopardized. Kellner demonstrates how corporate media ownership linked with a right-wing political agenda to disadvantage the Democrats while benefiting Republicans. Kellner describes how a number of "media spectacles" have come to dominate news coverage while distracting Americans from the substance of real public issues.

In *Guys and Guns Amok* (2008), Kellner examines recent shootings and reflects upon their cultural meaning and interpretation by the media—often resulting in the creation of media spectacles. Kellner also explores the continued fascination among Americans, especially males, with guns and how males equate a gun fetish with masculinity. Kellner proposes that individual acts of gun violence are connected to the militarism of American society as a whole. The socialization process of males, especially via the media, encourages the use of weapons and violence as a means of solving problems and exerting power over others. Consistent with his previous works, Kellner highlights the pervasive power of the media over popular culture and cultural norms.

Cinema Wars (2009) is another recent publication of Kellner's that examines the impact of the media on culture. In this publication, Kellner examines a number of films and connects his analysis of them to major political issues, events, and developments of the contemporary era. Once again, Kellner describes the importance of the September 2001 terrorist attacks on the United States and the political decision-making of the Bush–Cheney Administration. Ross Lynchehaun (2011) describes ways in which Kellner connects the film industry with the Bush-era politics. First, Kellner provides an overview of the "horrors" or apocalyptic visions of the Bush Administration based on the idea that the world is in a state of ecological crisis. Second, the terrorist attacks of 9/11 are typically presented in American film in a manner consistent with the Bush Administration's political agenda of what "really" happened that day. Third, according to Lynchehaun (2011), the rise of documentary-style films, such as those by Michael Moore, is the result of the documentary-style presentation of the terrorist attacks. Fourth, the fictional accounts of many Hollywood films have mirrored the fictional accounts of the terrorist attacks presented by the Bush Administration.

In yet another publication on the role of the media in culture, Hammer and Kellner (2009) provide an inclusive anthology on critical examinations of the media and its impact on culture designed for teachers and students who want to learn how to interpret our common culture and the everyday life. *Media/Cultural Studies* (2009) is divided into four sections, with chapters covering key theories, concepts, and methodologies of critical cultural and media studies. *Media/Cultural Studies* also presents practical advice to teachers on how to teach critical analysis of the media and culture to students.

CRITICISMS OF CRITICAL THEORY

As with any social theory, there are criticisms of critical theory—something that certainly does not surprise critical theorists, as they encourage the dissemination of knowledge and culture-based information. Consequently, there are a number of criticisms of critical theory.

The first criticism of critical theory is that it reproduces idealist (utopian) positions. For example, Habermas's concepts of ideal speech (uncoerced, free for all), undistorted communication (communication is seldom free from bias, whether purposeful or not), and political autonomy (self-rule) are philosophical ideals not grounded in everyday reality. The second criticism is related to the first: Critical theory shows undue concern about philosophical and theoretical problems. In this regard, critical theorists are accused of failing to support their ideas with facts, data, and research. The critical approach has a general disdain for positivistic methods. As Antonio (1983) explained,

> Though critical theory should neither embrace positivist methods uncritically nor fuse with sociology, it should be open to those techniques that can be harmonized with dialectical method as well as be useful for collecting and analyzing data necessary for the empirical moment of immanent critique (p. 348).

It is important for critical theorists to at least provide adequate empirical grounding for their theories (e.g., as Kellner has consistently provided in his analysis of television broadcasting).

The third criticism of critical theory is its preoccupation with negativity. This should be treated as a given, really. Since the purpose of this theoretical approach is to criticize, it will always be viewed as "negative." Some people value the role of critics (e.g., movie critics, sports critics, and food critics) because of their "valued" and "knowledgeable" opinions. However, critics must have some legitimate credential to claim such a role. On the other hand, most members of society do not like to be criticized (even "constructively"), especially if a viable alternative is not provided. For example, if a parent criticizes a child's school science project without providing help toward the desired goal, of what benefit is the criticism? Eliminating this negative slant remains critical theory's biggest challenge.

The fourth criticism of critical theory is the claim that it developed from a purely academic setting and thus was isolated from working-class politics (add to this the fact that Marx's conception of the working class as a revolutionary force is untrue) and became increasingly embroiled in abstract issues and "second-order" discourse. This criticism is reflected in the lack of empirical research conducted by critical theorists. Contemporary critical theorists are increasingly meeting this concern.

The fifth criticism leveled against critical theory is that it is ahistorical. Critical theorists have examined a variety of events without paying much attention to their historical and comparative contexts. Given its Marxist roots, this criticism is especially severe as Marx was well versed in the historic method. The ahistorical nature of critical theory is especially true of the first generation of this school of thought.

> The first generation of critical theorists (most of whom were trained in philosophy, not sociology), though they stressed the importance of history, did not go far enough in incorporating concrete historical and empirical work into their analyses. Their philosophical training and overly broad definition of positivism caused some of their theoretical work to rely upon less than adequate empirical/historical grounding (Antonio, 1983:348).

Breaking further away from the Marxist tradition is the criticism that critical theory does not pay enough attention to economics and the role of economic power in decision-making. Once again, however, Kellner has addressed this criticism by linking political decision-making (e.g. the Bush Administration) to cultural norms and values that are upheld and reinforced by most forms of media.

Criticisms such as these have led many sociologists to consider critical theory, at best, a marginal field. Tom Bottomore (1984:76), a traditional Marxist, declared the Frankfurt School "dead." Harvey Greisman (1986:273) labeled critical theory "the paradigm that failed." Despite these criticisms, critical theory is relevant and has been applied to such areas as postmodernity, popular culture (e.g., music), education, and crime and delinquency. Ruane and Todd (1988) believe

> The application of critical theory to the practical world has been a goal of critical theorists since the foundation of the Frankfurt School. The early critical theorists stressed the practical relevance of their project but their most influential work was highly theoretical and remote from concrete issues and problems (p. 533).

Before we declare critical theory "dead," let's examine its application to contemporary society.

APPLICATION OF CRITICAL THEORY TO CONTEMPORARY SOCIETY

As with our review of the application of specific schools of thought to contemporary society in previous chapters, we will examine the usefulness of critical theory to laypersons and professionals. If critical theory is negative in design and lacking in supporting data as critics claim, that would qualify many laypersons as critical theorists, although in reality, they might more accurately be viewed as complainers and not social critics. By some stretch of social reality, most of us are social critics. It is common for people in all walks of life to offer opinions, including criticisms, solicited or unsolicited, on nearly every subject imaginable, including restaurant food and service; preferred soda, alcohol, and coffee tastes; desired sexual partners and the attractiveness of others; television, movies, and video games; athletes and sports; Medicaid and Medicare; the federal deficit; health care; cyber-bullying; politics and politicians; art and artists; and so on. The examples of topics each of us is willing to comment on are nearly limitless. In many cases, however, much of the criticisms expressed by individuals is based on little, or no, experience and empirical knowledge. And that is why it could be said that critical theory, but not critical analysis, is applicable to laypersons.

Shifting our attention to the application of critical theory to contemporary sociology (and related disciplines), we may discover that this theoretical perspective is not "dead," as some critics may claim. Critical theory might be a relatively marginal theory in sociology, but there are many theorists conducting sociological research within its framework.

Applying a theoretical perspective to issues of concern in popular culture is one sure way to guarantee its relevance. Many critical theorists have examined the role of the media and other forms of communication. As we have already learned, Kellner and associates have examined many forms of the media. Music is also important to nearly all cultures. "Music like poetry is a *form* of critical theory in that it stimulates and solicits resignation or rebellion" (Agger, 1976:19). Whether it is classical, heavy metal, rock, rap, or country, music *does* something for people. For example, "Rock music and drugs are sources of prepolitical ecstasy which in their ecstatic moments free the person from the space-time of serial bourgeois life" (Agger, 1976:29). The study of music is relevant because music itself is relevant to people's lives. Certain songs remind individuals of past events, and these songs allow the individual to transcend the present place and time.

> Critical theory must surpass *itself* in remaining within the dialectic of the real and the possible. New science recovers grounds for positive rebellion in the carnal body, the body politic. "Critical theory" is not a school but rather the way we choose to oppose inhumanity in different songs of joy (Agger, 1976:32).

Another type of popular culture is public opinion. Perrin and Jarkko (2005) translated Adorno's (1964) "Opinion Research and Publicness" (*Meinungsforschung und Offenlichkeit*) and applied his public opinion thesis to Glynn et al.'s (1999) textbook, *Public Opinion,* and Bryan's (2004) *Real Democracy. Public Opinion*'s front cover consists of a Norman Rockwell painting, *Town Meeting*—a painting of an apparent working-class man standing at a rail in some sort of public forum. Perrin and Jarkko (2005) concur with Bourdieu (1979) and others who find this cover to be an odd choice because public opinion conjures images of an aggregation of opinions held by citizens who make up the public, and not of an individual's opinion. The cover of *Real Democracy* consists of another Rockwell painting, Freedom of Speech. This book cover is deemed "naïve" by Perrin and Jarkko. Perrin and Jarkko (2005) argue that "public opinion is not produced, manipulated, silenced, or channeled; it predates public discourse and, when things are working properly, finds transparent representation in that discourse" (p. 117). Adorno (1964) had criticized the notion that public opinion is simply the aggregate of private opinions and that is why Perrin and Jarkko are critical of the book cover choices of these two texts, as they do not accurately reflect the nature of public opinion. Perrin and Karkko (2005) also warn that "opinion research, without social-critical intentions, spontaneously turns into social criticism" (p. 122).

Thus, there must be some sort of substance (social-critical) to public opinion to make it a worthwhile endeavor for critical theorists.

Critical theory is relevant to the field of education. *Critical Theories in Education* by Popkewitz and Fendler (1999) is a book about the changing discourses of critical educational theory that examines claims to "truth" about knowledge that are imposed on students from the dominant class's point of view. In the preface, the editors wrote,

> Critical theory addresses the relations among schooling, education, culture, society, economy, and governance. The critical project in education proceeds from the assumption that pedagogical practices are related to social practices, and that it is the task of the critical intellectual to identify and address injustices in these practices....In education, critical theory has been an important impulse for a wide range of educational practices. In short, critical theory is concerned with the workings of power in and through pedagogical discourses (Popkewitz and Fendler, 1999:xiii).

A critical assessment of the educational system remains an important and relevant topic in contemporary society.

Critical theory has also been applied to issues related to crime and delinquency.

> In general terms, critical theorists have clarified theoretical and methodological boundaries which have on occasion been blurred by criminologists, and their unified model of empirical and interpretive analysis can help make sense of recent developments in criminological theory. In addition, critical theory draws its orientation from a broad range of disciplines, including linguistics, psychology, sociology, philosophy, and Marxism (Groves and Sampson, 1986:538).

The critical approach to the study of crime and delinquency challenges the status quo, examines power (class) differentials, and investigates the creation of law.

Scott and Thorpe (2006) examine the work of psychiatrist R. D. Laing and his interpretation of schizophrenia from a critical perspective.

> The critical dimension of Laing's work can be seen clearly by comparing his approach with Jürgen Habermas's project of critical theory. Anti-psychiatry can be seen as an example *par excellence* of the type of new social movement emerging in the 1960s, which Habermas saw as constructing a new politics, aimed at defending the lifeworld against the encroachment of scientific-instrumental-economistic rationality or "system" (p. 343).

Laing's work, on the other hand, can be "understood as a critical theory of the psychiatric colonization of the lifeworld" (Scott and Thorpe, 2006:343). Laing's work on schizophrenia can "be seen as a critical theory with problems of power and domination as its key preoccupation" (Scott and Thorpe, 2006:350).

By criticizing and drawing upon a variety of seemingly quite different schools of thought, critical theorists break out of the protected positions often given to established members of a theoretical tradition. With their focus on a critique of all existing social theories, the critical school risks alienating all established approaches (Held, 1980). Nonetheless, the critical approach to examining society is fully entrenched in sociology dating back to its birth and the rise of industrialization. It is perhaps in "the blood" of sociologists to criticize the perceived injustices of society.

If this is true, then critical theory surely has its place in sociology. There will be social thinkers criticizing the injustices of the world until they cease to exist. In other words, there will always be a need for constructive criticism and a place for those who offer alternative approaches in the fight against injustice.

Summary

There is neither a single definition of critical theory nor a single approach to its examination of society. Critical theory is generally about the role of power in social relations. It is also concerned with action and political involvement. It separates itself from conflict theory by avoiding the idea of economic determinism, and it disagrees with the positivistic style of functionalist theory and its attempt to explain social life by discovering universal "social laws."

Critical theory has existed since the formation of the Institute for Social Research at Frankfurt University in 1923. The institute conducted independent studies of Marxism and anti-Semitism. Critical theory can be divided into three eras: the first generation of Frankfurt philosophers who maintained a commitment to Marxist ideology; the second generation, beginning with Jürgen Habermas, among others, who reconstructed Marxist ideology; and the contemporary, or third, generation of critical theorists, such as Douglas Kellner (and Ben Agger), who have used a more multidimensional approach to their study of modern culture (especially the media). In light of the rise of Nazism, fascism, and socialism, the first generation of critical theorists had a difficult time defending Marxist idealism and a single-focused (the economic realm) approach to explaining behavior. Axel van den Berg (1980) went as far as stating, "Perhaps the first generation of Frankfurt philosophers can be accused of a certain cowardice for not directly facing up to the seamier sides of Soviet reality until after World War II" (p. 450).

The second generation of critical thinkers made amends for the short-sightedness of the original Frankfurt scholars. However, "after the dissolution of the Frankfurt School, the meaning of critical theory was more elusive than ever" (Antonio, 1983:337). Habermas has maintained the belief that Western society promotes a distorted conception of rationality and continues its destructive impulse to dominate. Contemporary critical theorists have increasingly turned their attention to the media and other forms of entertainment in their examination of modern culture.

In summary,

> Critical theory cannot be characterized by a particular set of methodological techniques and theoretical propositions; however, it is still a coherent approach to the social world that is separate from other types of sociology and Marxism. This fact is obscured by the great diversity of studies in critical theory and by the loose application of this term by some sociologists (Antonio, 1983:343).

Critical theory is comfortable with its commitment to a critique of society by attempting to uncover distorting forms of consciousness, or ways of thinking. "To be sure, the results of rational dialogue and critique cannot add up to absolute knowledge; but in the current intellectual and political context, it seems important to stress that they are not entirely trivial either" (Bailey, 1994:121).

Study and **Review** on **MySearchLab**

Discussion Questions

1. What is the value of critical theory for sociology? How do you view its effectiveness in addressing issues of sociological concern?
2. Explain the origins of the critical perspective and the major influences on its formation.
3. Compare and contrast the critical theories of Marcuse and Habermas. Which approach is most relevant today? Why?

4. Douglas Kellner has examined the role of the media and its influence on society. How do your beliefs compare to his? For example, how would you critique the role of the media in contemporary society?
5. Summarize the criticisms of critical theory. Do you think these criticisms are fair, too harsh, or not critical enough?

MySearchLab® Connections

MysearchLab is designed just for you. Each chapter features a customized study plan to help you learn and review key concepts and terms. Dynamic visual activities, videos, and readings found in the multimedia library will enhance your learning experience.

 Read on **MySearchLab**

▶ Husserl, Edmund. Phenomenology.
▶ Marx, Karl, Friedrich Engels. Economic and Philosophic Manuscripts of 1844.

Listen to the Chapter Audio on MySearchLab

The development of alternative sociological theories to the mainstream theories of functionalism, conflict, symbolic interactionism, and social exchange continues with postmodernism. Postmodern theory attempts to reflect Western societies' transition from "modernity" to "postmodernity." Postmodern theorists have attempted to develop new concepts and new ways of analyzing society in light of this transitionary period. As Allan and Turner (2000) explained, sociology emerged as a discipline to explain the dramatic transformations associated with industrialization, which was at that time referred to as modernity. Western societies have a new interpretation of what constitutes modernity now that we have reached postindustrialization. The changes in some societies seem so different from the changes dating back to the birth of sociology that some theorists and laypersons use the term *postmodernity* to describe contemporary society.

As society embarks on the "postmodern era," Marxism and critical theory also seem to be at a crossroads. Will they continue to find supporters, or will they be overwhelmed by postmodernists? Critical theorist Ben Agger (1992) addressed this issue:

It is commonly said that civilization has entered an era (sometimes called postmodernity) in which political contention can be put behind. . . . In this context, the crisis of Marxism requires a serious reappraisal of traditional left "certainties" such as the inevitability of capitalism's demise. Both *perestroika* and postmodernism seem to call into question venerable Marxist speculation about the direction of history. Everywhere old-guard leftists fall by the wayside, overtaken by all manner of political factions who have little use for the Marxist catechism. Some of these factions claim to be neoconservative, others post-Marxist. In any case, to be a Marxist today is to be unfashionable (p. 3).

Agger (1992, 1996) argues that the left has developed its own right wing, composed of both orthodox Marxist and postmodern theorists. Critical, or left, postmodernists like Fredric Jameson (to be discussed later in this chapter) use postmodernism as a way to defend the significance of Marx's world historical eschatology against other postmodernists, like Baudrillard, who celebrate postmodernity's break with modernity (Agger, 1996). Promoting a more enduring, flexible critical theory, Agger encourages interrogating traditional Marxist ideas by means of postmodern thought.

According to Agger, (1996), *postmodernity* is a utopian category—something to be achieved. In this regard, postmodernism is viewed as an extension of Marxism.

Postmodernism, conceived within the eschatological or "critical" framework of Marxist critical theory, does not betray Marxism but extends Marxism into the late 20th century, formulating postmodernity as the latter-day version of Marx's socialism. In particular, postmodern critical theory is the first narrative to pose a possible utopian future not as a determinate outcome of nature-like social laws but rather as one conceivable discursive accomplishment among many (p. 37).

Agger (1996) views postmodernism as Marxist because Marx foresaw the need to fulfill the "project of modernity," as Habermas termed it. Agger (1996) states:

Postmodernity, then, is not to be located off the Marxist map, a time after when leftist eschatological aims no longer apply. Instead, postmodernity is a contemporary formulation of utopia that can only be reached through modernity. It has much the same status as Marx's notion of how socialism would end prehistory. Only with postmodernity will modernity achieve its telos—dialogical democracy. In appearing to claim postmodernism "for" Marxism I am not making a one-sided appropriation. Marxism is transformed by its engagement with postmodernism and feminism, perhaps beyond recognizability. I contend that it is also revivified now that discursive politics and personal politics matter like never before (p. 45).

In this chapter, we will learn more about the transition from modernity to postmodernity and rise of postmodern theory. We begin with a definition of postmodernism theory.

DEFINING POSTMODERNISM THEORY

Although most classically trained sociologists consider sociology a science, there has always been an active debate about whether the scientific model is an appropriate one for studying society. The earliest sociologists (beginning with Claude-Henri Saint-Simon and Auguste Comte), in an attempt to gain some credibility for the field of sociology, borrowed the methodologies utilized by the natural sciences in the hope that they too could establish "laws" just as the natural scientists had. Traditionally, most classical social theorists embraced the concept that science could help change society for the better. Postmodernists strongly disagree with this outlook. "The most important component of postmodernism is its rejection of this scientific canon, of the idea that there can be a single coherent rationality or that reality has a unitary nature that can be definitively observed or understood" (Wallace and Wolf, 1999:406). Postmodernists go so far as to proclaim traditional sociological theory dead and say that postmodernism will revitalize social theory. Steven Seidman (1991) encouraged a renunciation of scientism and its "absurd" claim to speak the truth. There are some postmodernists who

> concede that the physical world might operate by laws, [but] the very process of discovering these laws creates culture that, in turn, is subject to interests, politics, and forms of domination. For example, law-like knowledge in subatomic physics has reflected political interests in war-making or the laws of genetics can be seen to serve the interests of biotechnology firms.... From a postmodernist's view, "truth" in science, especially social science, is not a correspondence between theoretical statements and the actual social universe, but a cultural production like any other sign system (Turner, 2003:228–229).

Defining postmodernism is difficult. Many postmodernist theorists disagree with one another about what are the parameters of postmodernism. Norman Denzin (1991), for example, has provided numerous definitions for the term *postmodernism*, one of which claims that the term is "undefinable." Postmodernists are often consumed with jargon that is lacking in clarity and inconsistently applied, thus making clear-cut determinations of the theory and its concepts vague and open to interpretation (Kivisto, 1998). Another problem associated with defining postmodernism is the vast diversity among scholars who claim to be postmodernists. Carol Nicholson (1989) agrees that the controversy among scholars on how to define and interpret postmodern theory is tied to its diversity and complexity and states, "Given the complexity and diversity of the postmodern movement, it would be foolish to try and capture its significance in a precise definition" (p. 197).

However, there are others who contend in order to discuss a topic, such as postmodernism, parameters must be established. Riley (2002) states that the most celebrated definition is that of Lyotard (1979),

> who talks of the postmodern condition as the collapse of grand narratives, that is, of uniform and orthodox worldviews that can encompass everything and claim widespread adherence based on this purported epistemological inclusivity and certainty. Pluralism is an obvious outcome of this situation, something Lyotard regards as salutary, but others have contended that a certain anxiety equally arises with the death of these comforting grand narratives (p. 244).

Allan and Turner (2000:365) define social postmodernism as "a critical form of theorizing that is concerned with the unique problems that are associated with culture and subjectivity in late capitalist societies" (p. 365).

FROM MODERNISM TO POSTMODERNISM

Many disciplines use the terms *modernism* and *postmodernism*; this is potentially problematic as they are vague, ambivalent concepts that are arbitrarily applied to social phenomena. Stephen Feldman (2000) applied the terms to his study of the legal profession and identified the construct of time to distinguish between such concepts: "To travel from premodernism through modernism and into post-modernism might take several centuries and even millennia" (p. 3). Postmodernism is especially prevalent in the world of art, where its vagueness as a category onto itself is awkward. Francis Berry (2006), for example, distinguishes postmodern art from modern art by claiming that postmodern art abandons political advocacy for a singular ideology whereas modernist avant-garde art was an agent of social change that helped to shape many of the political movements of the twentieth century (e.g., Italian fascism art). Obviously, art is much more than a political forum, so Berry's explanation of the difference between modern and postmodern art does not hold true for all artists, or fans of art.

For the past few decades, the term *postmodernism* has also found its way into sociological discourse. As described in Chapter 14, scholars have been using the term *modernism* for centuries (dating back at least to the fifth century C.E.), usually in connection with technological advancements or new levels of consciousness. Habermas (1997) traced the use of the word *modern* to the late fifth century, when Christians used the term to distinguish the present from the pagan and Roman past. Bill Martin (1992) used a Hegelian explanation of modernity in terms of eras of time:

> With Western humanity's emergence into modernity, the conditions, in totality, are finally set for the "completion" of history. Hegel's philosophy of history is most of all recognition of these conditions in his own day: the passage of humanity through the four cultural and spiritual levels of development (called by Hegel the "Oriental," "Greek," "Roman," and "Christian" Worlds), the emergence of the modern nation state and the instantiation of Christian Universality in modern individuality (p. 34).

Thus, each era considers itself modern. This implies that all of history leads to any given era. "Hegel does not say that history has reached its point of completion with the achievement of the Christian World; rather the stage is set for this completion" (Martin, 1992:34).

When scholars think beyond the present (modernity), they allow for both a future (postmodernity) and, consequently, postmodern thought. According to Alexander Riley (2002),

> The history of postmodern thought...begins in the French Third Republic, roughly during the second half of the life of the Republic, from about 1900 to the outbreak of World War II in 1939. In the aftermath of the fall of the second Bonaparte Empire and of the Paris Commune's rise and demise, the late nineteenth century saw the emergence of a great number of political and cultural debates that would touch on the entire French society (p. 245).

The social force that would change French society was secularism. C. Wright Mills (1959:166) simply stated that the modern age was being succeeded by a postmodern period. John Deely (1994), agreeing with the simplicity of the term *postmodernism,* argued that there is "a nearly indisputable consensus that the word 'post' can only exist in opposition, continuity, or complementarity with the universe which it presupposes, that is, the world of modernity" (p. xi). Kellner (1989a) explained that when society breaks from current modes of thinking, it has emerged into a postmodern era. To accomplish this, social thinkers must question the taken-for-granted world, the rules of society, and the claims to authority found in society. The use of such methodological techniques as deconstruction, reversal, and inversion assist the postmodern thinker. Kellner (1983) believed that the postmodern attitude is reflected in expressionist art because it can be viewed as a critical source of knowledge.

As for American sociological theory, postmodernism followed the dominance of functionalism in the 1950s and the prevalence of neo-Marxist and conflict theory in the 1960s and 1970s. Many social theorists point to Thomas Kuhn's book *The Structure of Scientific Revolutions* (1962) as a significant indicator that a reliance on science and scientific analysis was not a criterion shared by sociologists. Michael Friedman (1993) argued that Kuhn's book had forever changed the perception of the philosophical importance of the history of science:

> Reacting against what he perceived as the naively empiricist, formalist, and ahistorical conception of science articulated by the logical positivists, Kuhn presented an alternative conception of science in flux, of science driven not so much by the continuous accumulation of uncontroversial observable facts as by profoundly discontinuous conceptual revolutions in which the very foundations of old frameworks of scientific thought are replaced by radically new ones. When such a revolution occurs, we do not simply replace old "false" beliefs with new "true" beliefs; rather, we fundamentally change the system of concepts (p. 37).

Kuhn described these revolutions in thought as *paradigm shifts*. Kuhn had argued that the history of science is not gradual and cumulative but punctuated by a series of more-or-less radical "paradigm shifts." Summarizing Kuhn's ideas of paradigm shifts in simplistic terms, Conant and Haugeland (2000), in their editors' introduction to *The Road since Structure*, wrote "Shifts happen" (p. 1).

Kuhn questioned scientific claims to objectivity, absolute truth, and rationality.

> Kuhn's critique called into question many of the central elements of the traditional picture—the concept of absolute truth, the observation/theory distinction, the determinacy of rational choice, and the normative function of philosophy of science—and it provided an alternative model of scientific change that dispensed with these notions altogether. Kuhn's radical views have been the focus of much debate not only by philosophers, historians, and sociologists of science but also by large numbers of practicing scientists (Horwich, 1993:1).

Postmodernists continue in the tradition of Kuhn by challenging claims to objectivity and the neutrality of "facts."

According to Dmitri Shalin (1993), "Postmodernism has been around for decades now, but it was not until the 1980s that social scientists started paying this intellectual current serious attention" (p. 303). Many sociologists in the 1980s and 1990s believed that there was a

> decisive shift in the nature of society, from "modernity" to "postmodernity"; that, as a result, the distorted nature of many of the concepts and ideas used by modern theorists (including scientists and social scientists) is increasingly apparent; and that a postmodernist vocabulary and discourse should henceforth be adopted instead (Wallace and Wolf, 1999:402).

Charles Lemert (1997) in particular argued that there has been a major shift in the nature of society, and that the description *modern* is no longer characteristic of the present day.

Shalin (1993) believes that the primary reason that postmodernism has received a "half-hearted" reception by social scientists is that postmodernists do not look favorably at the scientific model, especially such ideals as objective reporting and valid generalizations. Symbolic interactionists were among the first in the social science community to join with the concerns of postmodernism (Faberman, 1991; Denzin, 1991; Fontana and Preston, 1990; Shalin, 1991), perhaps because of symbolic interactionism's relatively marginal status in sociology, along with their "maverick" status. "The postmodernist critique of formal logic, positivism, and scientism also strikes a responsive chord with interactionist sociologists, as is the emphasis on the marginal, local, everyday, heterogeneous, and indeterminate" (Shalin, 1993:303).

To a large degree, postmodern thought has been the product of nonsociologists, such as Jean-François Lyotard, Jacques Derrida, and Fredric Jameson. Recently, a number of sociologists have incorporated the ideas of postmodernism into sociological discourse.

> In social theory, postmodernism rejects grand narratives on the nature of the universe, doubts the advantages of technology, reduces science to a language game, criticizes the exigencies of the market and the hyperreality of advertising, and offers no vision of theory beyond many voices in continual play (Allan and Turner, 2000:364).

In general, postmodern thinkers attack the idea of objectivity in social research, an autonomous rational mind, and grand narratives (grand theorizing). In addition,

> postmodernism emphasizes the role of unconsciousness, reinterpreting knowledge as socially constructed and historically situated instead of a timeless representation of the world by separate individuals. In the absence of criteria for distinguishing discourse that accurately represents reality from other uses of language, the traditional distinctions between logic and rhetoric, literal language and metaphor, argument and narrative break down (Nicholson, 1989:198).

Wallace and Wolf (1999) stated that two famous names in postmodernism are Jacques Derrida and Michel Foucault, both of whom are French. This in itself is noteworthy, in that the French intellectual tradition is in conflict with the Anglo-Saxon approach of North American, Australian, and British social scientists.

There are a number of significant postmodern theorists who deserve to be mentioned. In the pages that follow, discussion will center on the key thoughts, concepts, and contributions of David Riesman, Jean-François Lyotard, Michel Foucault, Jean Baudrillard, Jacques Derrida, and Fredric Jameson.

DAVID RIESMAN (1909–2002)

David Riesman was born in Philadelphia in 1909 and was the son of a professor at the University of Pennsylvania Medical School. Riesman graduated from Harvard College in 1931 and earned a degree from Harvard Law School in 1934. He served as a clerk for U.S. Supreme Court Justice Louis Brandeis and later taught at the University of Buffalo Law School. In 1949, he joined the social science faculty of the University of Chicago. "*The Lonely Crowd* was published in 1950, and became a best seller, as well as winning the admiration of

David Riesman, postmodern theorist who incorporated the impact of technology on society and individuals. (Jane Reed/Harvard Staff Photographer)

his academic peers. He co-authored the book with Nathan Glazer, professor emeritus of education and social structure, and Reuel Denney, but, according to Glazer, Riesman was the real author of the work" (American Sociological Association, 2002:1). Riesman's other publications include *Faces in the Crowd* (1952, in collaboration with Nathan Glazer), *Thorstein Veblen: A Critical Interpretation* (1953), *Individualism Reconsidered* (1955), *Constraint and Variety in American Education* (1956), *The Academic Revolution* (1968, with Christopher Jencks), *On Higher Education* (1980), and many others. Riesman taught at Chicago until 1958 and then moved to Harvard University, where he taught for over thirty years. Riesman attained much recognition throughout his academic life.

The Lonely Crowd

The Lonely Crowd (1950/2001) can be viewed as a modern to postmodern discourse in that Riesman discussed dramatic social changes that were reshaping American society. According to Todd Gitlin, who wrote the foreword in the 2001 publication of *The Lonely Crowd*, this book represents a study of the changing American character:

> As America was moving from a society governed by the imperative of production to a society governed by the imperative of consumption, the character of its upper middle classes was shifting from "inner-directed" people, who as children internalized goals that were essentially "implanted" by elders, to "other-directed" people, "sensitized to the expectations and preferences of others." In Riesman's wonderful metaphor, the shift was from life guided by an internal gyroscope to life guided by radar. The new American no longer cared much about adult authority but rather was hyperalert to peer groups and gripped by mass media.... *The Lonely Crowd* went on to become, according to a 1997 study by Herbert J. Gans, the best-selling book by a sociologist in American history, with 1.4 million copies sold, largely in paperback editions. For years, the book made "inner-direction" and "other-direction" household terms, canapés for cocktail party chat (p. xii).

Wilfred McClay (2009) claims that *The Lonely Crowd* was initially an attempt to study political apathy in the time following World War II, but as the postwar lifestyle changed dramatically, the publication was pushed to discuss many more issues in society. McClay (2009) adds that *The Lonely Crowd* focused on the dramatic increase in corporatizing, bureaucratizing, and suburbanizing, and an increase in white-collar America that was emerging, creating a society filled with "anxious, over socialized, and glad handling personality mongerers, salesman, trimmers, empty suits, and artful dodgers" (p. 22).

In the preface to *Faces in the Crowd* (1952), Riesman spelled out his intent for *The Lonely Crowd* as a

> wholly tentative effort to lay out a scheme for the understanding of character, politics, and society in America. The book moved on the most general levels (as in its discussion of the possible relations between growth of population and change in character type) and also on the most concrete (as in its use of particular American movies and comic strips as illustrations of some of its theses) (p. v).

The postmodern approach is illustrated by Riesman's attention to the change in America's social character from the nineteenth century to the mid-twentieth century. Riesman defined social character as that part of "character" which is shared by significant social groups and is the product of the experiences of these groups.

> The link between character and society ... is to be found in the way in which society ensures some degree of conformity from the individuals who make it up. In each society, such a mode of ensuring conformity is built into the child, and then either encouraged or frustrated in later adult experience (Riesman, et al., 1950/2001:5–6).

In other words, the agents of socialization (beginning with the family and extending to the media, employers, religion, and so on) attempt to make individuals conform to the expectations of specific social groups and of society in general. Riesman used the term *mode of conformity* interchangeably with the term *social character,* although noting that conformity is just one aspect of social character. "However, while societies and individuals may live well enough— if rather boringly—without creativity, it is not likely that they can live without some mode of conformity—even be it one of rebellion" (Riesman et al., 1950/2001:6).

Riesman analyzed the anxieties of American life that were associated with the fast-changing post–World War II culture. In other words, society was changing, from a modern one to a postmodern one, and with this change, Americans expressed a great number of concerns. In *The Lonely Crowd,* along with his other works, Riesman attempts to provide middle-class Americans with a brunt look at their major cultural preoccupations; especially consumerism and mass consumption (Patterson, 2002). Riesman used a number of significant terms in *The Lonely Crowd.* Among them are *tradition-direction, inner-direction, outer-direction, the oversteered child, bohemia,* and *self-consciousness.*

In *tradition-directed* societies, social change is at a minimum. Conformity is ensured by incorporating a near-automatic obedience to tradition. Individuals learn

> To understand and appreciate patterns which have endured for centuries, and are modified but slightly as the generations succeed each other. The important relationships of life may be controlled by careful and rigid etiquette, learned by the young during the years of intensive socialization that end with initiation into full adult membership. Moreover, the culture, in addition to its economic tasks, or as part of them, provides ritual, routine, and religion to occupy and to orient everyone (Riesman et al., 1950/2001:11).

Little effort is spent on alternative ways of thinking: As a result, technology seldom finds a welcome in tradition-based societies.

The concept of *inner-direction* is intended to cover a very wide range of social types. Riesman et al. (1950/2001) stated:

> In western history the society that emerged with the Renaissance and Reformation and that is only now vanishing serves to illustrate the type of society in which inner-direction is the principle mode of securing conformity. Such a society is characterized by increased personal mobility, by a rapid accumulation of capital (teamed with devastating techno-logical shifts), and by an almost constant *expansion:* intensive expansion in the production of goods and people, and extensive expansion in exploration, colonization, and imperial-ism. The greater choices this society gives—and the greater initiatives it demands in order to cope with its novel problems—are handled by character types who can manage to live socially without strict and self-evident tradition-direction. These are the inner-directed types (p. 14).

Riesman is clearly utilizing the modern–postmodern analysis approach by describing such issues as technology and economic production affecting the very character of individuals, which, in turn, led to a dramatic change in society. "The problem facing the societies in the stage of transitional growth is that of reaching a point at which resources become plentiful enough or are utilized effectively enough to permit a rapid accumulation of capital" (Riesman et al., 1950/2001:17). To secure rapid development, countries are often dependent on the resources of other countries.

Riesman (1950/2001) applied the term *other-direction* especially to upper-middle-class persons in large cities:

> The type of character I shall describe as other-directed seems to be emerging in very recent years in the upper middle class of our larger cities: more prominently in New York than in Boston, in Los Angeles than in Spokane, in Cincinnati than in Chillicothe. Yet in some respects this type is strikingly similar to the American, who Tocqueville and other curious and astonished visitors from Europe, even before the Revolution, thought to be a new kind of man (p. 19).

The other-directed person is shallow, freer with money, friendlier, and more demanding of approval. The other-directed person gains his or her sense of self from the reactions of oth-ers. "Of course, it matters very much who these 'others' are: whether they are the individual's immediate circle or a 'higher' circle or the anonymous voices of the mass media; whether the individual fears the hostility of chance acquaintances or only of whose who 'count'" (Riesman et al., 1950/2001:20). In other words, the other-directed person cares more about the feelings and reactions of significant others than those of strangers or ancestors. Riesman (1950/2001) acknowledged that people of all eras cared about how others felt about them, but "it is only the modern other-directed types who make this their chief source of direction and chief area of sensitivity" (p. 21).

Individuals who attempt to meet the standards of significant others risk being "over-steered." This is especially true of children. There is a danger for children who are born to and raised by exemplary persons to be *oversteered,* that is, to find themselves set on a course they cannot realistically follow. Although some children can handle the pressure of being born into famous families (e.g., the son or daughter of a politician or a professional athlete), the result for many is a dreadful insecurity about whether they can live up to these exalted models (Riesman et al., 1950/2001:95).

An aspect of any "modern" society is the fact that some individuals do not wish to conform or blend into the mode dictated by "other-directed" forces. Such people attempt to find autonomy or harmony. Riesman believed that *Bohemia* was such a "place." "Among the groups dependent on inner-direction the deviant individual can escape geographically or spiritually, to Bohemia; and still remain an individual. Today, whole groups are matter-of-factly Bohemian; but individuals who compose them are not necessarily free" (Riesman et al., 1950/2001:258). On the contrary, they are often zealously tuned in to the signals of a group that finds the meaning of life in a strict adherence to alternative codes of acceptable behavior.

Riesman (1950/2001) believed that *self-consciousness* constitutes the insignia of the autonomous in an era dependent on other-direction:

> For, as the inner-directed man is more self-conscious than his tradition-directed predecessor and as the other-directed man is more self-conscious still, the autonomous man growing up under conditions that encourage self-consciousness can disentangle himself from the adjusted others only by a further move toward even greater self-consciousness. His autonomy depends not upon the ease with which he may deny or disguise his emotions but, on the contrary, upon the success of his effort to recognize and respect his own feelings, his own potentialities, his own limitations. This is not a quantitative matter, but in part an awareness of the problem of self-consciousness itself, an achievement of a higher order of abstraction (p. 259).

Riesman had a very profound idea regarding self-consciousness. Achieving self-consciousness is undoubtedly difficult, and even those who attain it often fail to mold it into the structure of an autonomous life and succumb to anomie. "Yet perhaps the anomie of such processes is preferable to the less self-conscious, though socially supported, anxiety of the adjusted who refuse to distort or reinterpret their culture and end by distorting themselves" (Riesman et al., 1950/2001: 259–260).

In *Faces in the Crowd* (1952), Riesman and Glazer continued with the same sorts of issues presented in *The Lonely Crowd,* but with a greater emphasis on individuals. Research came as a result of interviews conducted with a number of people in the continental United States. *Faces in the Crowd* contains the stories of individuals who are grouped roughly in terms of the character types they illustrate (e.g., forty interviews were conducted with residents of East Harlem). Riesman and Glazer (1952) concluded that most individuals attempt to be both a part of society and alone from it.

> Indeed the moving about between being in the crowd and being in the wilderness, between society and solitude contains much of the American experience and the American tension. We did not invent the elevator so that we could jam together, but the invention helped spur our "need" to do so, to build cities which would loom like mirages over the all too open spaces.... By moving in a crowd, we seek to deny the accidental and chancy nature of our national life. But we also, the more autonomous of us for whom accident is more liberating than frightening, win the courage to single out the faces in the crowd that please us and stimulate us. By moving about both in crowds and in the wilderness, we assure ourselves that we still have room "inside" and "outside" us (pp. 740–741).

Thus, someone may be just as alone and lonely in Los Angeles as in rural Montana. On the other hand, one may find peace and self-consciousness as easily in Los Angeles as in rural Montana.

Social Research, Theory, and Narratives

In his article "Some Observations on Social Science Research" (1951), Riesman stated,

> Every work of social science today establishes itself on a scale whose two ends are "theory" and "data": that is, the great theoretical structures by which we attempt to understand our age at one end, and the relatively minuscule experiments and data which we collect as practicing social scientists at the other (p. 259).

Sociologists generally accept the scientific method and empiricism as the "standard" for conducting sound research. It is what makes them "scientists." And sociologists who embrace the scientific method would not agree with Riesman's contention that the discipline has conducted minuscule amounts of data via its diverse research studies. There are, however, some people who claim to be sociologists and argue against the use of the scientific method—among them, the postmodernists. Patterson (2002) is one such theorist who disagrees with empirical social research in sociology:

> Anxious to achieve the status of economics and other "soft sciences," the gatekeepers of sociology have insisted on a style of research and thinking that focuses on the testing of hypotheses based on data generated by measurements presumed to be valid (p. 15).

Although Patterson underestimated the American public's desire for scientific validity in social matters, he corrected indicated that that Riesman utilized statistical analysis. For example, in *Faces in the Crowd* (1952), Riesman and Glazer collected data from 180 interviews. "Interviews are simply one of a number of ways of understanding human character in a society that trains people in many analogous kinds of social conversation and encounter" (Riesman and Glazer, 1952:31). They found that working with interviews preserves the "freshness of first impression," while the data allowed them to quantify their results. The importance of interviewing reflects Riesman's postmodern commitment to social research because it avoids the narrative, grand-theorizing approach of traditional sociology.

JEAN-FRANÇOIS LYOTARD (1924–1998)

Jean-François Lyotard was born in Versailles, France, in 1924. He was one of the world's foremost philosophers and a noted postmodernist. His interdisciplinary discourse covers a wide variety of topics, including the postmodern conditions, modernist and postmodernist art, knowledge and communication, language, metanarratives, and legitimization. Lyotard taught at many universities, including the University of California at Irvine for several years. At the time of his death in 1998, Lyotard was professor emeritus of the University of Paris VIII and professor at Emory University in Atlanta.

Legitimation, Language, and Narratives

Lyotard's (1999) definition and usage of *postmodernism* are linked to the three concepts of *legitimation, language,* and *narratives*:

Simplifying to the extreme, I define *postmodern* as incredulity toward metanarratives. This incredulity is undoubtedly a product of progress in the sciences: but that progress in turn presupposes it. To the obsolescence of the metanarrative apparatus of legitimation corresponds, most notably, the crisis of metaphysical philosophy and of the university institution which in the past relied on it. The narrative function is losing its functors, its great hero, its great dangers, its great voyages, its great goal. It is being dispersed in clouds of narrative language elements—narrative, but also denotative, prescriptive, descriptive, and so on (p. xxiv).

Lyotard firmly believed that the grand narratives of knowledge had lost their credibility in the postmodern society and that proponents of positivism had lost their claims of legitimacy. Lyotard used the term *metanarratives* to mark the progressive emancipation of reason and to draw attention to the postmodern break from tradition dominated by positivistic grand narratives.

According to Lyotard (1999:19–23), narration is a quintessential form of customary knowledge in at least five ways:

1. Popular stories recount the successes and failures of the hero's undertakings. These successes bestow legitimacy upon the hero (which may be an individual or a social institution). Thus, the narratives allow the society in which they are told, on the one hand, to define its criteria of competence and, on the other hand, to evaluate according to those criteria what is performed or can be performed within it.
2. The narrative form, unlike the developed forms of the discourse of knowledge, lends itself to a great variety of language games.
3. The pragmatic rules that constitute the social bond are transmitted through these narratives.
4. Rhythm, time, and metrical beat are emphasized because they make narratives easy to remember.
5. A culture that gives precedence to the narrative form doubtless has no more of a need for special procedures to authorize its narratives than to remember its past. It is even harder to imagine a society handing over the authority for its narratives to some opposing narrator.

Narratives are an integral aspect of culture and directly affect the language of any given society. Lyotard utilized a methodology he called *language games*.

In *The Postmodern Condition* Lyotard uses the method of language game analysis to contrast the pragmatics of narrative and scientific knowledge. He defines modernism as the attempt to legitimate science by appeal to "metanarratives," or philosophical accounts of the progress of history in which the hero of knowledge struggles toward a great goal such as freedom, universal peace, or the creation of wealth (Nicholson, 1989:198).

In describing language games, Lyotard used Wittgenstein's study of language, where he focused on the effects of different modes of discourse or what he called the various categories of utterances. Lyotard (1999) wrote that

each of various categories of utterance can be defined in terms of rules specifying their properties and the uses to which they can be put—in exactly the same way as the game of chess is defined by a set of rules determining the properties of each of the pieces, in other words, the proper way to move them (p. 10).

Lyotard (1999) continued to articulate on language games by making three observations:

> The first is that their rules do not carry within themselves their own legitimation, but are the object of a contract, explicit or not, between players (which is not to say that the players invent the rules). The second is that if there are no rules, there is no game, that even an infinitesimal modification of one rule alters the nature of the game, that a "move" or utterance that does not satisfy the rules does not belong to the game they define. The third remark is suggested by what has just been said: every utterance should be thought of as a "move" in a game (p. 10).

Language can be used for the sheer pleasure of "making a move" in the game of life, and it can be used as a weapon, for if knowledge is power, communicating in a tactical and purposeful manner may allow individuals (or societies) to gain an advantage over others.

Language exemplified the first efforts of legitimacy. Rulers of past societies utilized language constructs when they formed governments and regimes (*forma regiminis*). Kant referred to this as the legitimation of the normative instance. Rigid designators define the world. Each human who is born into the world comes to a place that has been previously labeled, or constructed. Furthermore, these labels or constructions have been legitimized by past events, and by those in power (Lyotard, 1993:45). Lyotard explained in his 1992 article "Mainnise" that it is up to all infants to emancipate themselves, to become owners of themselves. Language is a tool of emancipation. Language is also a requirement for a society to exist. Therefore, to understand social relations, what is necessary is not only a theory of communication, but also a theory of language games.

Postmodernism and Knowledge

In *The Postmodern Condition: A Report on Knowledge* (1999), Lyotard drew attention to the shift in thinking among many social scientists, namely, away from a reliance on and belief in universals (positivism). In this book, Lyotard wrote about the condition of knowledge as a postmodern one and believed that this condition can be used to describe the condition of knowledge in most highly developed societies. In the introduction to *The Postmodern Condition*, Lyotard (1999) wrote,

> The object of this study is the condition of knowledge in the most highly developed societies. I have decided to use the word *postmodern* to describe that condition. The word is in current use on the American continent among sociologists and critics; it designates the state of our culture following the transformations which, since the end of the nineteenth century, have altered the game rules for science, literature, and the arts (p. xxiii).

Lyotard described positivist science as a "fable" with a methodology that produces legitimization with respect to the rules of its own game.

Lyotard (1999) made it clear that there is a distinction between knowledge and science:

> Knowledge [*savoir*] in general cannot be reduced to science, not even to learning [*connaissance*]. Learning is the set of statements which, to the exclusion of all other statements, denote or describe objects and may be declared true or false. Science is a subset of learning. It is also composed of denotative statements, but imposes two supplementary conditions on their acceptability: the objects to which they refer must be available for repeated access, in other words, they must be accessible in explicit conditions of observation; and it must be possible to decide whether or not a given statement pertains to the language judged relevant by the experts (p. 18).

Knowledge includes notions of "knowing" how to do things, such as knowing how to listen, how to live, how to enjoy life. Science is a type of knowledge.

With the above position in mind, Lyotard proposed a postmodern approach to the study of society and the advancement of knowledge, one that does not involve positivism.

> Science does not expand by means of the positivism of efficiency. The opposite is true: working on a proof means searching for and "inventing" counter examples, in other words, the unintelligible; supporting an argument means looking for a "paradox" and legitimating it with new rules in the games of reasoning (Lyotard, 1999:54).

Lyotard believed that with every new theory, hypothesis, statement, or observation, the question of legitimacy remains. He explained that legitimation

> is the process by which a "legislator" dealing with scientific discourse is authorized to prescribe the stated conditions determining whether a statement is to be included in that discourse for consideration by the scientific community.... For it appears in its most complete form, that of reversion, revealing that knowledge and power are simply two sides of the same question: who decides what knowledge is, and who knows what needs to be decided? (1999:8)

In short, Lyotard wanted to eliminate the reliance on positivism (a methodology linked to the modern era) and abolish the monopoly that such orthodoxies have enjoyed over claims to "truth" and "knowledge production."

MICHEL FOUCAULT (1926–1984)

Foucault led an interesting life that was cut short when he died of AIDS in 1984 at fifty-seven. He was born on October 15, 1926, in Poitiers, France, and was named after his father, Paul-Michel Foucault. In 1940 he enrolled at the Jesuit secondary school Collège St. Stanislas. In 1946, he was admitted to École Normale Supérieure, where he received the *licence de philosophie* (1948), the *licence de psychologie* (1949), and the *agrégation de philosophie* (1952). After teaching at the University of Uppsala in Sweden (1955–1958) and the University of Clermont-Ferrand (1960), Foucault received his doctorate degree in 1961. He then taught at various colleges around the world and first visited the United States in 1970. Foucault continued to travel and teach at a variety of places globally.

Foucault's works are in areas familiar to sociologists: prisons, asylums, medicine, and changing sexual attitudes and practices. Among his more significant publications are *Mental Illness and Psychology, Discipline and Punish, Madness and Civilization,* and *The Birth of the Clinic.* His book trilogy devoted to sex—*The History of Sexuality* (1976), *The Care of the Self* (1984), and *The Use of Pleasure* (1984)—revealed his lifelong obsession with sex. His personal lifestyle included homosexuality and sadomasochism, an attraction to impersonal sex characteristic of gay bathhouses, and a deep attraction to San Francisco's flourishing gay community. Foucault also experimented with the drug LSD in the spring of 1975 and spoke highly of its positive effect in expanding his mind and redirecting his focus on the "truth"—a reference to his homosexuality (Miller, 1993).

Foucault's Theories

There is some debate as to whether Foucault was a postmodernist, a functionalist, or something else. Lemert and Gillan (1982) asked the questions that many social thinkers ponder when examining Foucault's works. Was he a Marxist? A structuralist? A semiotician? Foucault uses Marx's terms of "class," "political economy," "commodity," "capital," "labor power," and "struggle," but he also demonstrated a structuralist interest in the universal forms of culture. Then again, he renounces his own use of structuralism (Lemert and Gillian, 1982). Lemert and Gillian also suggest that Foucault displays a "semiotician's hand" in his studies of general grammar in *The Order of Things* (1966a) and of the relation between signs and symptoms in *Birth of the Clinic* (1975).

Strictly speaking, Foucault was not a structuralist, although he thought that structuralism was the most advanced position in the human sciences. "Foucault was primarily an historian of psychiatry who saw the connections between his specialty and other institutional spheres" (Collins, 1990:462). Additionally, "Foucault never posited a universal theory of discourse, but rather sought to describe the historical forms taken by discursive practices" (Dreyfus and Rabinow, 1982:vii). Ritzer (2011) describes Foucault as somewhere between a structuralist and a poststructuralist with an element of phenomenological influence who also adopted Nietzsche's interest in the relationship between power and knowledge from a sociological perspective.

Foucault's work is difficult to understand because of his wide range of historical reference and his use of new concepts, but perhaps most of all because his theories do not fit very well into any of the established disciplines. His early works (*Madness and Civilization,*1965; *Birth of the Clinic,*1975) center on the analysis of historically situated systems of institutions and discursive practices.

> The discursive practices are distinguished from the speech acts of everyday life. Foucault is interested only in what we will call *serious* speech acts; what experts say when they are speaking as experts. And he furthermore restricts his analyses to the serious speech acts in those "dubious" disciplines which have come to be called the human sciences (Dreyfus and Rabinow, 1982:xx).

Methodology

Foucault, a postmodernist, presented a further paradox in his use of methodology. One of the central tenets of postmodernism is to criticize empiricism; however, as Mirchandani (2005) states, "Foucault's work was certainly catalyzed by empirical conditions" because he was frustrated by the abstractness of the philosophy he studied. Foucault also embraced value neutrality, a strong tenet of positivism, and seemed to downplay the method of hermeneutics. In *The Archaeology of Knowledge*, Foucault (1969) insisted that human sciences (social sciences) can be treated as autonomous systems of discourse. In methodological approaches to the study of human societies, the researcher must remain neutral as to the truth and meaning of the discursive system studied. He proposed to treat all human sciences as a "discourse-object." Dreyfus and Rabinow (1982) stated,

> Foucault is not interested in recovering man's unnoticed everyday self-interpretation. He would agree with Nietzsche and the hermeneutics of suspicion that such an interpretation is surely deluded about what is really going on. But Foucault does not believe that a hidden deep truth is the cause of the misinterpretation embodied in our everyday self-understanding (p. xix).

This statement strongly suggests that Foucault did not value the hermeneutic approach, because he did not attempt to uncover any hidden meanings behind written words.

Sexuality

In *The History of Sexuality* (1978), "Foucault challenges the hermeneutic belief in deep meaning by tracing the emergence of sexual confession and relating it to practices of social domination" (Dreyfus and Rabinow, 1982:xxi). Foucault was concerned about such social systems as psychotherapy and medicine. He questioned their power position and their corresponding ability to dictate to others what is "normal" and how one "should" feel.

> Foucault saw these changes in the treatment of the mad and the criminal as a central feature of the modern discursive formation, characterized by the dominance of the sciences—biology, psychology, sociology—and by the translation of these disciplines' claims into fields of practice such as medicine, psychotherapy, and social work. All of these fields constitute disciplines of power; that is, they are focused on the imposition of order, regulation of behavior, and social control (Garner, 2000:433).

Technologies of all kind are designed to control the free-thinking behavior of individuals (e.g., surveillance cameras in many walks of life). Individuals are taught self-control. In short, the modern world attempts to suppress impulses of all kinds, especially sexual, violent, and unruly ones (Garner, 2000). As Collins (1990b) explained, "In Foucault's effort to theorize, he hit on a more modern sociological theme, the relationship between micro processes and the macro structure of power. Again, bravo; but frankly, it is an amateur's performance" (p. 462).

Power

From the tradition of Nietzsche, Foucault believed that power and knowledge were intertwined. Social institutions that are in power positions generally have the knowledge to manipulate others in an effort to maintain the status quo (especially in regard to norms, values, and expectations). Foucault (1983) argued that one's very identity and sense of self are shaped by one's position in the power structure. Foucault (1983) stated that power "applies itself to immediate everyday life which categorizes the individual, marks him by his own individuality, attaches himself to his identity, imposes a law of truth on him which we must recognize and which others have to recognize in him" (p. 212). Markula (2003) noted that in his later years, Foucault "concentrated on the relationship of the self to power and truth: how the human being turns him- or herself into a subject through the technologies of the self" (p. 94). Throughout his life, Foucault sought to understand the role of the individual in society, the changing nature of the self as power relations change, and the "effects of power relations and the possibilities of their transformation" (Markula, 2003:97). No doubt, some of his own questions about his sense of self, his sexuality, and his corresponding position in society reveal themselves in his work.

Wallace and Wolf (1999) argued that since the death of Foucault there have been no major sociological theorists who can be categorized as active and unequivocally postmodern. "At the same time there *are* important continuities between postmodernism and some of the major concerns and emphases in contemporary sociology and in social science as a whole" (Wallace and Wolf, 1999:409). David Harvey, for example, writing at the end of the 1980s, described a number of contemporary concerns of society that fit the postmodern mode.

Postmodernism has come of age in the midst of this climate of voodoo economics, of political image construction and deployment, and of new social class formation. That there is some connection between this postmodernist burst and the image-making of Ronald Reagan, the attempt to deconstruct traditional institutions of working-class power (the trade unions and the political parties of the left), the making of the social effects of the economic politics of privilege, ought to be evident enough (Harvey, 1989:336).

JEAN BAUDRILLARD (1929–2007)

Jean Baudrillard was born in 1929 in the northern French town of Reims. Jean's parents were civil servants, and his grandparents were peasant farmers. He was the first member of his family to attend university. He taught German in a lycée before completing his doctoral thesis in sociology under the guidance of Henri Lefebvre. Baudrillard became an assistant professor in September 1966 at Nanterre University of Paris. Identifying with student protests at Nanterre in 1968, Baudrillard began publishing a number of theoretical articles bashing capitalist affluence and the growth of technology. Over the years, Baudrillard became a notorious French sociologist (Baudrillard, 2003).

Baudrillard was a postmodern theorist and social philosopher and the author of such publications as *System of Objects, Consumer Society, Critique of the Political Economy of the Sign, The Mirror Production, Symbolic Exchange and Death, On Seduction, America, On the Beach,* and *Cool Memories.*

Baudrillard's work was quite diversified and ever-changing. In the 1960s, he was both a modernist and a Marxist. He was especially critical of the consumer society. He was also influenced by the fields of linguistics and semiotics. By the 1980s, Baudrillard could be considered both a postmodernist and a critic of Marxism. Douglas Kellner (1989b) wrote in the introduction to *Jean Baudrillard* that Baudrillard

> is now sliding toward center stage of the cultural scene in some circles. In a number of "postmodern" journals and grouplets, Baudrillard is being proclaimed as a fundamental challenge to our orthodoxies and the conventional wisdom in Marxism, psychoanalysis, philosophy, semiology, political economy, anthropology, sociology and other disciplines (p. 1).

Christopher Norris (1990) added,

> Baudrillard is undoubtedly the one who has gone furthest toward renouncing enlightenment reason and all its works, from the Kantian-liberal agenda to Marxism, Frankfurt Critical Theory, the structuralist "sciences of man," and even—on his view—the residual theoreticist delusions of a thinker like Foucault (p. 164).

Postmodernism

Baudrillard was a part of the French tradition challenging traditional sociological thought. In the 1960s and 1970s, his ideas included Marxist criticism of capitalism in studies of consumption, fashion, media, sexuality, and the consumer society.

From this perspective, Baudrillard's early work can be interpreted as a response to neo-capitalism, which, in the 1960s, came with a vengeance to France, with contradictory consequences. The Monnet Plan of the 1940s had inaugurated state planning, and by the 1960s modernization, technological development and the growth of both monopoly firms and a technocratic state sector were evident (Kellner, 1989b:2).

France was also experiencing new architecture and many new expressions of the consumer society such as drugstores, advertising, and mass media—especially television. The France of the 1960s was dramatically different from the France of the 1950s. Social theorists attempted to explain this societal transformation. "These socioeconomic developments stirred a remarkable series of attempts to reconstruct radical social theories to account for the changes in social conditions and everyday life, and spawned many new critical discourses" (Kellner, 1989:3). Baudrillard refers to France as a "consumer society."

The critique of society is a postmodernist creed, where ideas of truth, validity, or claims to being "right" are challenged. Baudrillard (1981, 1983) argued that the empirical object is a myth. He believes that there was a time when signs stood for something real; now they refer to little more than themselves. Thus, signs are created for their own sake; they have become self-referential. Distinctions between what is real and what is fabricated are the cornerstone of the postmodern world.

In a world where signs no longer have a "natural" meaning and are instead manufactured, they take on symbolic meaning. In this regard, Baudrillard's postmodernist thinking is familiar to symbolic interactionists. For example, in the medieval world, symbols had an unbroken bond with reality—an individual's identity was brutally and unequivocally stamped by the rigid estate system. Everyone *was* exactly as he or she appeared to be (Shalin, 1993). Today, this is not necessarily true. Instead, the postmodern world is characterized by simulation. According to Baudrillard (1983), we live in the "age of simulation." Simulations dominate society and have produced a new kind of social order. Simulations lead to the creation of simulacra—the reproductions of objects or events. Baudrillard viewed "simulacra" as reproductions of objects or events. During industrialization, when infinite reproducibility appeared in the world, industrial simulacra dominated. Mass production replaced the "natural" form of production that existed in feudal-medieval times.

Dramatic changes in society cause a ripple effect throughout the social system. The technological world of capitalism requires a technical language (signs, simulacra) to describe the new systems of objects and their relations. Baudrillard's postmodernist perspective led him to believe that the new technical world of objects causes changes in values, modes of behavior, and relations to objects and to other people. The modern individual is portrayed as a "cybernetician" who is induced to order objects in accordance with the imperatives of the technical world (Baudrillard, 1968). The new morality ushered in by technical advancements affects all the structures of society, and life in its totality. (This is similar to structural functionalist thought: A dramatic change in one part of the system causes dramatic changes in the remaining parts.)

In short, the system of objects leads people to adapt to a new, modern world which represents a transition from a traditional, material organization of the environment to a more rationalized and cultural one. Baudrillard provides a multidimensional analysis of this new world, and attempts to elucidate the ways in which objects and individuals are "liberated" from traditional systems and usages, yet constrained by the technical imperatives of the new environment (Kellner, 1983:10–11).

According to Baudrillard (1981), we live in a world that is not "real." (Note: He influenced the novel *The Matrix*.) Instead, we live in a *hyperreal* world where signs have acquired a life of their own and serve no other purpose than symbolic exchange. Symbolic exchange involves the continuous cycle of taking and returning, giving and receiving, a cycle of gifts and countergifts (Baudrillard, 1973/1975:83). Furthermore, individuals caught up in this exchange are convinced that the objects they consume have intrinsic use value. However, this use value is really a "sign exchange value" that the technical system maintains only because consumers choose to give it meaning (a classical Marxist perspective). Shalin (1993) argued that Baudrillard took his cue from Thorstein Veblen (e.g., Veblen's study of the leisure class) and supplemented it with his own original insights into the age of mass media, mass production, and mass consumption.

In sum, Baudrillard (1983) argued that society in the postmodern era is dominated by simulacra and simulation and falls into the domain of a hyperreal sociality, where "referential reason disappears."

To further illustrate his postmodern analysis of simulacra and hyperreality, Baudrillard used the events of the first Gulf War, of 1991, and September 11 (9/11), 2001. Baudrillard had predicted that the first Gulf War would never take place. During the war, he said it was not really taking place. At the conclusion of the war, he announced that it had not taken place. Instead, Baudrillard insisted that the war was conducted as a media spectacle rehearsed as a wargame or simulation. The viewing public saw this simulation as a news event with the real violence as, essentially, an electronic narrative—by simulation (Baudrillard, 1995; Poole, 2007). Baudrillard characterized the 1990s as a media presentation of doom and gloom depicting an impending "end of history" as we know it. This doom and gloom was further fueled by threats of terrorism. In his 2001 article, "The Spirit of Terrorism," Baudrillard (2001/2003) claimed the attacks on the United States on 9/11 were the "ultimate event, the mother of all events" (Baudrillard and Turner, 2003; Poole, 2007). Baudrillard further shocked mainstream society by claiming in his 2005 article, *War Porn*, that the photographs from Abu Ghraib enacted scenes of fetishistic pornography, concluding, "It is really America that has electrocuted itself" (Baudrillard, 2005; Poole 2007).

The Mass Media and Entertainment

Baudrillard (1983) believed that the mass media are so dominant and powerful that they have created a culture characterized by hyperreality. That is, the media no longer mirror reality: They have become more real than reality itself. Entertainment media present images that are both not real and, yet, more real than real (Baudrillard, 1983). As Delaney and Wilcox (2002) explained:

> Contemporary society can be characterized as a *mass-mediated culture,* that is, a culture in which the mass media play a role in both shaping and creating cultural perceptions. The media do not simply mirror society, they help to shape it. With a nearly endless array of events occurring constantly around the world, the media require some way to selectively manage a number of items. This is accomplished by the "categorization of news," selecting events to cover that "fit" the given format. Categorization limits the number of stories deemed worthy of coverage, and also helps to shape how the coverage is presented. Consequently, if the media decide not to cover an event, it is not *news*—at least not public news (pp. 202–203).

Ryan and Wentworth (1999) argued that another important element of the media's presentation of events is their "over-simplification of complex issues." In this regard, events are streamlined by the media and are limited by time and space. The categorization and oversimplification of events by the media are packaged in such a way as to appeal to the largest audience of consumers.

Best and Kellner (1991) used as an example of Baudrillard's hyperreality a television show where the actor Robert Young played the role of Dr. Welby. Young received thousands of letters asking for medical advice because the audience could not separate the "real" Robert Young from the "unreal" Dr. Welby. Young later capitalized on this misinterpretation of his television role by appearing in commercials saying that he was not a doctor, but that if he were, he would recommend this product. Tabloid news shows, infomercials, and so-called reality TV shows can be viewed as hyperreal as well because of the distortions of reality they represent.

According to Baudrillard, the mass media are not the only social institution responsible for hyperreality. He believed that hyperreality extends to all aspects of postmodern culture and comes in the form of entertainment as well. Baudrillard (1983) was critical of Disneyland and remarked, "Disneyland is presented as imaginary in order to make us believe that the rest is real, when in fact all of Los Angeles, and the America surrounding it, are no longer real, but of the order of the hyperreal and of simulation" (p. 25). (Imagine how Baudrillard must have reacted to Euro Disney in Paris.) Such generalized statements certainly leave Baudrillard open to criticism (Kivisto, 1998:143). Citizens of the United States, in general, and of Los Angeles, specifically, may live in a hyperreal world as described by Baudrillard, but their world *is* real, as demonstrated by the daily events and chores that each person must accomplish in order to live. Kivisto (1998) took exception to Baudrillard's rather unflattering portrait of the role of individuals in postmodern society, stating that we appear to have reduced to roles of mall rats in quest of objects of desire and excitement, couch potatoes playing with television remotes (and today with video game consoles), and voyeurs peering into the private lives of the rich and famous. Despite the protests of Kivisto and others, one could certainly argue in favor of Baudrillard's claim that we are voyeurs. For evidence of this, one merely as to acknowledge the predominance of so-called reality TV, and the preoccupation that many people have with photographing and video-recording nearly all aspects of life via cell phones and other modern, or postmodern, devices. We are, as Baudrillard claims, in an era in which new technologies (e.g., the media, cybernetic models, and computers) have replaced industrial production and political economy as the organizing principle of society. The important issue is: What will we, as a society, do about it? Will we find a way to survive with an emphasis on industry? The next "modern" or "postmodern" era will reveal the answers.

JACQUES DERRIDA (1930–2004)

Jacques Derrida was born in El-Biar, Algeria, in 1930. Derrida was a French philosopher and essayist, rather than a sociologist. His works utilize a deconstructivist approach (Martin, 1992). Deconstruction is a strategy of analysis that has been applied to such areas as literature, linguistics, philosophy, law, and architecture. Derrida's deconstructive approach is illustrated in his three 1967 books: *Speech and Phenomena, Of Grammatology,* and *Writing and Difference.* Additional publications include *Glas* (1974) and *The Post Card* (1980). Derrida's publications are focused on the deconstructive analysis of language. The concept of *discourse* is derived from his works. In using the term *discourse,* Derrida sought to uncover the meanings of words and their understanding by those who communicate with one another. Words and concepts are used to mediate reality, according to Derrida. Derrida took his first teaching job at a lycée in Le Mans. He then taught at the Sorbonne for four years, before moving to the position he was to occupy until 1984 at the École Normale (Attridge and Baldwin, 2004).

Logocentrism

Derrida was critical of grand narratives and viewed their construction as the product of what he referred to as *logocentrism*. Logocentrisms are modes of thinking that apply truth claims to universal propositions. Thus, our knowledge of the social world is grounded in a belief that we can make sense of our ever-changing and highly complex societies by clinging to old models of thinking. "The postmodernist stance articulated by Derrida (1976, 1978) calls for a repudiation of logocentrism, which entails taking what postmodernists refer to as an antifoundational stance" (Kivisto, 1998:130–140). Postmodernists would like us to repudiate the entire traditional Western way of looking at the world.

The Hermeneutical Method

Social thinkers that do not employ the methods of science (empiricism, data collection, and data analysis) must find alternative ones. Max Weber (1864–1920) promoted the use of *verstehen* as a method of study. *Verstehen* is the German word for "to understand." Weber's sociological approach was primarily interpretive and based on *verstehen*. He believed that sociologists should look at the actions of individuals and examine the meanings attached to behaviors. Weber's use of the term *verstehen* was common among German historians of his day and was derived from a field of study known as *hermeneutics* (Pressler and Dasilua, 1996). "The German tradition of *hermeneutics* was a special approach to the understanding and interpretation of published writings. The goal was not limited to merely understanding the basic structure of the text, but the thinking of the author as well" (Delaney, 2004:137).

In response to Foucault's *The History of Madness in the Classical Age* (1961), Derrida wrote an article, "To Do Justice to Freud: The History of Madness in the Age of Psychoanalysis" (1997). Derrida (1997:60) wanted to study the "role of psychoanalysis in the Foucauldian" tradition of a history of madness. Derrida utilized the hermeneutical method in his analysis of Foucault. Derrida (1997) stated that the hermeneutical method is

> valid for the historian of philosophy as well as for the psychoanalyst, namely, the necessity of first ascertaining a surface or manifest meaning, and, thus, of speaking the language of the patient to whom one is listening; the necessity of gaining a good understanding, in a quasi-scholastic way, philologically and grammatically, by taking into account the dominant and stable conventions, of what Descartes *meant* on the already so difficult surface of his text, such as it is interpretable according to classical norms of reading; the necessity of gaining this understanding *before* submitting the first reading to a symptomatic and historical interpretation regulated by other axioms or protocols, *before and in order to* destabilize, wherever this is possible and if it is necessary, the authority of canonical interpretations (p. 61).

This quote of Derrida's reflects his commitment to the hermeneutical approach, but it also reveals how difficult his translated works are to read.

Fredric Jameson (1934–)

Fredric Jameson was born on April 14, 1934, in Cleveland, Ohio. He received his M.A. from Yale University in 1956 and his Ph.D. from Yale in 1959. He taught at Harvard University from 1959 to 1967; at the University of California at San Diego from 1967 to 1976; at Yale from 1976 to 1983; at the UC at Santa Cruz from 1983 to 1985; and at Duke starting in 1986. Jameson then served as Distinguished Professor of Comparative Literature at Duke University, where he directed the Graduate Program in Literature and the Center for Cultural Theory. Among his publications are *Marxism and Form* (1971), *The Political Unconscious* (1981a), and "Postmodernism, or, After the Cultural Logic of Late Capitalism" (1984).

Jameson is considered to be one of the foremost contemporary Marxist literary critics writing in English. He studied Marxist theory in the 1960s when he was influenced by the New Left and the antiwar movement. His *Marxism and Form* (1971) introduced a tradition of dialectical neo-Marxist theory to the English-speaking world (Kellner, 2011). Jameson's dialectic approach involves an attempt to synthesize competing positions and methods of Marxism into a more comprehensive theory (see *The Prison-House of Language*, 1972).

Postmodernism

Jameson equates postmodernism with late capitalism. He believes that distinct phases of the mode of production have distinct "cultural dominants," or forms of culture.

> Jameson gives relatively little attention to classes as coherent purposive social actors. Rather, the cultural dominant is a pattern of representation that appears across different media and art forms. It is an indirect reflection of the underlying mode of production and social conditions, not the product of a class-conscious dominant class (Garner, 2000:536).

Late capitalism is characterized by commodity production, "high tech" or electronic technology, multinationalism and globalization, and media penetration into our unconscious, as well as into our consciousness. Late capitalism represents the shift from modern society to postmodern society. According to Jameson (1981b), in late capitalism, culture is dominated by consumerism and mass media. Never, at any other point in history, has society been so saturated with signs and messages (e.g., advertising, information, and communication technologies). The impact of consumerism and the mass media is felt in all spheres of life, including socialization, education, and leisure.

Unlike many postmodern theorists, Jameson does not reject Marxian theory. Jameson used Marxist analyses of six continental writers in his 1971 publication *Marxism and Form*. Jameson (2000) believes that with late capitalism, aesthetic production has become integrated into commodity production. Aesthetic production has spilled over into architecture as well, with many new buildings described as postmodern. According to Jameson, styles such as those produced by Frank Lloyd Wright illustrate this point, while Las Vegas epitomizes aesthetic populism.

An interesting concept of Jameson's is *hyperspace,* an area where modern conceptions of space are useless in helping us to orient ourselves. Jameson (1984) used as an example the Los Angeles Hotel Bonaventure, with its lobby design that leaves visitors unable to get their bearings. The lobby contains rooms surrounded by four absolutely symmetrical towers, which contain the rooms. Visitors to Las Vegas' gambling rooms complain of the same thing: Where is the exit? It is very easy to lose one's bearings in the casinos of Las Vegas. Jameson uses the concept of *hyperspace* to illustrate the point that people develop cognitive maps in order to maneuver in the complexity of society. The use of maps reinforces the reality that people define the world spatially rather than temporally. Interestingly, Jameson (1989) admitted that cognitive mapping is in reality nothing but a code word for "class consciousness."

It is highly questionable whether the concepts of *hyperspace* and *cognitive mapping* are unique to the postmodern era. Throughout history, cultures have designed unique architecture that may have left visitors confused. The pyramids come to mind immediately, and a number of castles have been designed symmetrically. The University of Moscow has an awesomely huge administrative and dorm building designed in a mirror fashion. As a visitor to that wonderful campus, this author was left confused more than once about whether he was facing the front or the back of the building. As a final note, this building is more than 150 years old—clearly not a product of postmodernism.

Modernism and Capitalistic Imperialism

History has shown that imperialism and colonization have existed for thousands of years and therefore are clearly not to be blamed on modernism or postmodernism. Jameson (1990), however, attempted to show a relationship between modernism and imperialism in his article "Modernism and Imperialism" (1990), in which he wrote,

> If it is the link between imperialism and modernism that is in question here (and between imperialism and Western modernism at that), then clearly imperialism must here mean the imperialist dynamic of capitalism proper, and not the wars of conquest of the various ancient empires (p. 46).

Thus, Jameson had to admit that imperialism is not a modern construct; however, he relabeled imperialism to fit his argument against capitalism. Jameson believed that most people think of Marx when they think of imperialism, but even Marx's theories of imperialism are subject to a historical qualification.

Jameson (1990) focused on imperialism not as the relationship between metropolis and colony, but as the rivalry of the various imperial and metropolitan nation-states:

> For it is in our time, since World War II, that the problem of imperialism is as it were restructured: in the age of neocolonialism, of decolonization accompanied by the emergence of multinational capitalism and the great transnational corporations, it is less the rivalry of the metropolitan powers among each other that strikes the eye (our occasional problems with Japan, for example, do not project that impending World War-type conflict that nagged at the awareness of the *belle époque*); rather, contemporary theorists, from Paul Baran on to the present day, have been concerned with the internal dynamics of the relationship between First and Third World countries, and in particular the way in which this relationship—which is now very precisely what the word "imperialism" means for us—is one of necessary subordination or dependency, and that of an economic type, rather than a primarily military one (pp. 47–48).

Jameson's belief that imperialism is significantly different from in the past is flawed. Imperialism has always been about expanding markets and spreading culture (including religion). The danger of late-capitalistic imperialism is expanding military modes of destruction. Since the third millennium began, the threat of worldwide war has been ever-present. The terrorist attacks on New York City on September 11, 2001, were a wake-up call to all citizens of the world.

The Political Unconscious

Jameson wrote in *The Political Unconscious* (1981a) that our understanding of the world is influenced by the concepts and categories that we inherit from our culture's interpretive tradition. With this in mind, Jameson (1981a) wondered, "How can readers of the present understand literature of the past when it was written in such a culturally different context?" (p. 281). The answer, according to Jameson, lies in Marxism and Marx's perspective that history is a single collective narrative that links past and present:

> The most influential lesson of Marx—the one which ranges him alongside Freud and Nietzsche as one of the great negative diagnosticians of contemporary culture and social life—has, of course, rightly been taken to be the lesson of false consciousness, of class bias and ideological programming, the lesson of the structural limits of the values and attitudes of particular social classes, or in other words of the constitutive relationship between praxis of such groups and what they conceptualize as value or desire and project in the form of culture (Jameson, 1981:281–282).

Determining what is "false" and what is "objective" fact continues to dominate modern thought. When it is applied to the political arena, the distinction becomes increasingly cloudy.

Jameson (1981a:296) maintained a commitment to the Marxist approach of understanding literature by promoting a general theoretical framework in which a Marxist negative hermeneutic and a Marxist positive hermeneutic method are used. "It is only at this price—that of the simultaneous recognition of the ideological and Utopian functions of the artistic text—that a Marxist cultural study can hope to play its part in political praxis, which remains, of course, what Marxism is all about" (Jameson, 1981a:299).

CRITICISMS OF POSTMODERN THEORY

There are those who wonder whether modern and postmodern theories are actually theories at all. Sociological theory has traditionally consisted of grand narratives and "schools of thoughts." Consequently, rejecting grand theorizing is similar to rejecting sociological theory. Sociological analysis is the examination of large social events: societies, organizations, cultures, and so on. Successful sociological analysis is, for the most part, dependent on a broad and macro approach. With this reality in mind, it is easy to understand why a large number of criticisms are levied against postmodern social thought.

The first criticism directed toward postmodern theories is aimed at their refusal to employ empirical studies with statistical analysis. It is difficult to examine whether their observations and theories are accurate, because "there are no systematic tests of these assertions" (Turner, 2003:246). In this regard, postmodern theories present the same potential problems as critical theories; they question existing sociological interpretations of events but offer little concrete evidence that their perspective is any better. Sociological theory must be, at the very least, falsifiable; otherwise, we are no better than philosophy. It may be that postmodern theorists are indeed onto some new revelation and insight regarding society and social interaction. However, if it remains unsubstantiated with "proof" (evidence of some sort), its validity is questionable. The obvious suggestion is not to be afraid to try empirical testing of theories that lead to grand narratives. Insights regarding social life are the goal of sociological theory. Free and unconstrained by the rules of science and the dispassionate rhetoric of the modern scientist, postmodernists have allowed themselves to create broad generalizations without qualification (Ritzer, 2011).

Since every society has considered itself "modern," the term is too vague to apply to a theoretical approach. Within a short period of time (50–100 years) from now, future generations will look back at this era and laugh at claims of modernity, just as we do to past generations. The term postmodernism, therefore, becomes equally problematic.

It is possible to question whether or not postmodernism is a theory at all; it may more accurately be viewed as an ideological belief system. Furthermore, postmodern discourse is itself vague and abstract, so it is difficult to connect to the social world (Calhoun, 1993).

Postmodernists work with the vague assumption that society indeed made a decisive shift in the 1980s and 1990s. By some definitions this may be true. Western societies have evolved into what is referred to as the *service economy,* and yet industrialization is as prevalent as ever before. Industry has slowly left the dominant societies and has shifted into Third World nations, but it remains the fuel that runs the global market. Kivisto (1998) concurred with this idea:

> By claiming that we have moved from production to consumption, this version of postmodernism shows evidence of a serious blind spot. It is obvious that goods continue to be produced, although in a global economy this might mean that they are being produced in poor countries, where workers (too frequently including children) are paid abysmal wages and are forced to work exploitatively long hours in unsafe and unsanitary factories (p. 145).

The point remains, then, for postmodernists to show proof that such a dramatic change in society has occurred that it warrants the label *postmodernism.*

Ritzer (2011) offers a number of other criticisms of postmodern theory. Postmodern critics of sociological theory reveal the questionable validity with which they work, for they generally lack a normative basis with which to make their judgments. Given their rejection of an interest in the subject and subjectivity, postmodernists often lack a theory of agency. Postmodern social theorists are best at critiquing society, but they lack any vision of what society ought to be. Postmodern social theory is very pessimistic. Postmodern social theorists argue about what they consider major social issues, while ignoring what many consider the key problems of our time.

Despite these and other criticisms of postmodern theory, the postmodern approach encourages sociologists to reexamine long-held, traditional beliefs about human behavior and society. And this reality is something that objective-minded sociologists should embrace.

APPLICATION OF POSTMODERN THEORY TO CONTEMPORARY SOCIETY

Many of the ideas brought forth by the postmodern theorists discussed in this chapter are relevant to contemporary sociologists and nonacademics. A variety of nonacademic persons utilize a postmodern approach to business (as in a "thinking-outside-the-box" philosophy), architecture (e.g., the construction of "green" buildings), means of communications (e.g., social networking), and entertainment (e.g., art, film, music, and video gaming). However, everyday conversations about postmodernism and its implications among people are not as common as references to conflict, functionality, critical analysis, cost–benefits awards, gender differences, and so on that make up the foundation of other sociological theories.

In academic circles, postmodern thought was common among scholars in the 1990s and early 2000s. Whether or not the postmodern movement is alive or dead is a matter of opinion; and it may simply be too soon to make such declarations of a theoretical perspective that is still young in development. One thing is certain: Postmodern theory remains in discourse and its applicability to contemporary society can be articulated in a number of ways. For example, David Riesman expressed a premise that is common among postmodernists, namely, that society has become increasingly oriented toward spending and consumerism. Our consumption of consumerism has affected our very character. Evidence of this orientation is bountiful. Citizens of Western societies are treated as a collection of consumers eager to purchase products, even if their purchases mean going into debt. We are encouraged to purchase items that we cannot afford by using credit cards and taking out loans.

The federal government and many state governments utilize this very principle by operating on a deficit budget principle. It is noteworthy to point out that in my 2005 *Contemporary Social Theory* text (a text written in 2004), I spoke of a federal budget deficit that exceeded $100 billion as an example of federal spending gone astray. As this book was written between 2012–2013 (with an August 2013 estimated publication release), the U.S. national debt was nearly $17 *trillion*! [Note: On May 4, 2013, according to the U.S. National Debt Clock, the national debt was over $16.8 trillion (U.S. National Debt Clock, 2013).] On August 2, 2011, the federal government risked its first ever shutdown because it could not pay its bills. Elected lawmakers from both major parties were divided on the best strategy to avoid a federal government shutdown and decided that *increasing* the deficit limit by another $2.4 trillion (to carry the government through the end of 2012) was the best strategy. The plan also called for cuts to spending that would decrease the overall federal deficit by a mere (approximately) $2 trillion over a ten-year period. The negative backlash as a result of lawmakers' decision led to Standard & Poor's (S&P) lowering the United States' AAA credit rating one notch to AA-plus. It was the first time the U.S. had its credit rating reduced since it was granted AAA status in 1917 (Standard & Poor's, 2011). Is this the postmodern way of running a government? If so, no wonder there are still traditionalists who theorize that spending should never exceed income.

Riesman also described the changing nature of colleges and universities and especially the modern trend toward designing specialized courses and majors to meet the needs of postmodern students. It is also common now for students to take courses online. Does this represent a postmodern approach to higher education? Some professors worry about the potential harm in changing the traditional format, which consists of students and professors together in the classroom (what is now referred to as "brick and mortar" classes). Would professors become obsolete? After all, if courses can be taught online and on television, the rerun of taped broadcasts could phase professors out of jobs. Lyotard sounded an alarm to educators when he predicted the "death of the professor." "His proposal to replace professors with computers poses more problems than the obvious one in massive unemployment for those of us in the teaching profession" (Nicholson, 1989:199). A truly postmodern thought has occurred to me. Why would professors be phased out when really what can be eliminated is the institution itself? Professors could become accredited, teach from their home computers online, and collect tuition payments directly from students (the plan is a little more complicated than presented here, but this would be the general idea and illustrates "thinking outside the box"). Administrators would become obsolete under this plan as well. Without institutional costs, student tuition would be greatly reduced. After all, any college or university *needs* only students and professors. When something like this happens, we will have reached a postmodern form of education.

Michel Foucault used his theories on domination, power, and sense of self to describe the different ways through which humans define their experiences. A number of sport sociologists have applied these ideas to the study of sport (Barker-Ruchti and Tinning, 2010). Chapman (1997) showed how female rowers "made weight" by embracing a process (losing weight) that enabled them to fulfill feminine ideals, and Johns and Johns (1998, 2000) pointed out the negative experiences of "making weight" in gymnasts. Barker-Ruchti and Tinning (2010) conducted their own study on female gymnasts using Foucault's theories and concluded that "the degree of discipline and submissiveness required by gymnasts is key in preventing these athletes from reflecting upon themselves as individuals" in a positive manner (p. 246).

Jean Baudrillard's ideas on symbolic exchange are especially noteworthy and offer an expansion on the prevalence of consumerism. Gift-giving has indeed become a part of a continuous-feedback loop of giving and receiving. When one receives a gift from another, there is a social expectation that the "receiver" will return the gesture to the "giver." Although it is true that there cannot be "givers" without "takers," it is a social faux pas to take and take without ever giving something in return. There are also a growing number of occasions where giving gifts (among close friends and relatives) is the expected norm: birthdays, weddings, anniversaries, Valentine's Day, job promotions, book publications, graduations, house warmings, religious holidays, and so on. This expectation of gift exchange often leads to frustration and the realization that one is seemingly always purchasing a gift for someone for some reason. Receiving a "last-minute" holiday card from someone whom you did not send a card to results in a last-minute purchase and mailing of a card on your part. Giving gifts is not unique to the modern world, but the excess emphasis on materialism and consumerism is a characteristic of modern society.

In his book *The Self after Postmodernity* (1997), Calvin Schrag challenged the bleak deconstructionist and postmodernist views of the human self as something ceaselessly changing. Schrag described the self as a being open to understanding through its discourse, its actions, its being with other selves, and its experience of transcendence. When examining the self, the theorist needs to realize that the self is exposed to a wide diversity of external stimuli but can only be truly understood through introspection. Schrag's (1997) postmodern perspective on the self is exemplified in this quote:

> Human bodies exist in space, are open to inspection by external observers, and are subject to the laws of mechanics that govern the movements of physical objects. Human minds, in contrast, are not in space, are known through introspection rather than by observation, and are exempt from models of mechanistic explanation. Human bodies are public, and the events that they exhibit are external; the career of mind is private, and the events that compose its workings are internal. It is thus that the official doctrine delivers a dualism—a dualism of body versus mind, the public versus the private, the external versus the internal, and the mechanistic versus the vitalistic (p. 11).

Schrag attempted to avoid what he called the modernists' overdetermination of unity and identity and the postmodernists' self-enervating pluralism. "The portrait of the self has been...designed to bring the legacy of modernity into confrontation with the sensibilities and deconstructive strategies of postmodernity" (Schrag, 1997:148).

Interestingly, Schrag also addressed the issue of gift-giving but came to a different conclusion than Baudrillard. Schrag (1997) stated that "a gift, to be genuinely a gift, is given without any expectation of return. There can be no expectation of a 'countergift,' for such would place the giving within the context of a contractual rather than a gift-giving relation" (p. 139). Schrag acknowledged that there is a phenomenon of gift-giving and gift-receiving that is a part of the economy of production and consumption, distribution, and exchange.

Postmodern theory has new frontiers. Jagtenberg and McKie (1997), for example, envision a postmodern society marked by social movements that will help the ecology. They predict "the greening of social movements" and the utilization of "green maps":

Green maps and new paradigms have their origins in this changing world, but they have not come from the reflexive, relativizing social theory of postmodernism or from the reflection of sociologists on globalization, new communications technology, and risk society. The green ideas we are exploring here have come mainly from the cultures of social movements (pp. 90–91).

According to these authors, there is a growing "culture of the environment," one that has been ushered into existence because of a paradigm shift away from a patriarchal, European, human-centered focus. Only time will tell whether a significant enough change occurs in society to bring about a "greening of culture."

Mirchandani (2005) believes that postmodern epistemology can be extended to embrace empiricism. Empirical postmodernism, grounded in empirical research Mirchandani (2005) proposes, would help to support the epistemology of postmodernism. Without empiricism, postmodernism research is "sketchy and generalized," Mirchandani argues (2005), adding that "by embracing empirical study, postmodernists would generate supporting evidence for their often vague terms. It could also help postmodernists reshape current postmodern thought that does not stand up to empirical verification. Mirchandani (2005) also believes that empirical postmodernism would be useful in the examination of the future, which would supplement its current ability to examine the past.

Summary

Postmodern theories are promoted as alternatives to the more traditional sociological theories. The terms *modern* and *postmodern* are themselves problematic, in that they are vague and have been applied to a wide variety of phenomena over a period of many centuries. The concepts of *modernism* and *postmodernism* are usually used in connection with technological advancements and new modes of thinking (such as preindustrial, industrial, and postindustrial). Not surprisingly, every era (since at least the fifth century) has considered itself "modern." When social thinkers and policymakers think beyond the current era, they may be thought of as postmodernists. Thus, in order to think as a postmodernist, a social theorist must break from the taken-for-granted world, the given rules, and the claims to authority found in a society. The popular image in American society currently is "thinking outside the box." In other words, social thinkers must break from current modes of thinking *and* doing. The doing aspect refers to the methodological techniques used

by social thinkers. Postmodern theorists have a general disdain for positivism and the scientific methods of data collection and analysis. They reject the grand theorizing and narratives that are common in the more traditional sociological theories. With their French origins, postmodern theories became relatively popular in the 1980s following the heyday of functionalism in the 1950s and conflict theory in the 1960s and 1970s.

Keith Kerr's 2009 *Postmodern Cowboy* promotes the idea of sociologists, postmodernists in particular, as cowboys attempting to tame the "Wild West." Kerr argues that there are plenty of new frontiers (the Wild West) that need to be explained from a new perspective, or way of thinking. This frontier perspective is postmodernism. In the Foreword to *Postmodern Cowboy*, Stjepan Mestrovic, a student of David Riesman's, states that Riesman advised him to go into sociology because the field remains "like the Wild West, and you can still make new discoveries." In contrast, Riesman described psychology and other neighboring disciplines as "too civilized" because they offered only "paved highways" of constricted and forced thought into specific directions of study. Kerr (2009) concludes that sociologists should never completely abandon the work that has come before each of us but states, "It is often said that the destiny of each new generation of sociologists to take the sociological knowledge that came before them and make it their own—making it relevant for the new world in which it must resonate" (p. 129).

Postmodernism, then, may indeed represent the future of sociological theory, but postmodernists should be careful not to abandon all the work conducted by the brilliant sociologists who preceded them.

 ## Study and Review on MySearchLab

Discussion Questions

1. What do the terms *modernity* and *postmodernity* mean to you? Is your conception of these terms similar or different as what has been presented here? Explain.
2. Describe the premise of David Riesman's *The Lonely Crowd* and demonstrate its relevancy to contemporary society.
3. What is the connection between Marxism and postmodernism? Provide specific examples from the ideas of multiple postmodern theorists.
4. Using a postmodern perspective, describe the future of the institution of education in the United States.
5. Is postmodernism a valid sociological theory? Why or why not?

MySearchLab® Connections

MysearchLab is designed just for you. Each chapter features a customized study plan to help you learn and review key concepts and terms. Dynamic visual activities, videos, and readings found in the multimedia library will enhance your learning experience.

 ## Read on MySearchLab

▶ Derrida, Jacques. Of Grammatology: The Written Being/The Being Written.

Consistent and Significant Themes in Sociological Theory

Part III, "Consistent and Significant Themes in Sociological Theory," is applicable to the study of both classical and contemporary social theory. The lone chapter, Chapter 16, provides an overview of the primary themes of sociological significance that have revealed themselves over the past five centuries. These themes include a general belief in progress and cultural evolution, technological growth, scarce resources, threats associated with overpopulation, capitalism and globalization, the importance of language and development of a universal language, the dominant role of religion in society, and social injustice and the imbalance of power. Past and present sociological social thinkers have concerned themselves with some or all of these eight social themes. Undoubtedly, future social thinkers will also address these social themes; after all, any social trend that has existed for five centuries is likely to extend itself into the future.

16 Five Centuries of Social Theory

 Listen to the **Chapter Audio** on **MySearchLab**

Chapter Outline

- Major Themes in Sociological Thought
- Parting Thoughts
- Discussion Questions

Among the primary purposes of *Classical and Contemporary Social Theory: Investigation and Application* was to provide the reader with an extensive, but clearly presented, review of key concepts and contributions from a select number of brilliant classical social thinkers and contemporary "schools of thought" over a 500-year period (beginning with Machiavelli's *The Prince*) and to demonstrate the relevancy of this material to contemporary society. The ability to link social thought with "real," everyday events is critical if the social sciences hope to maintain any sense of legitimacy in the academic and secular worlds. As George Homans noted, sociologists and other social scientists have made empirical discoveries and behavioral psychologists have established general propositions, but he insisted that the key *now* is to apply such propositions to all forms of human behavior, thus demonstrating their relevancy. As seen in Chapter 11, Homans outlined five distinct propositions that he felt explained all human behaviors. And whether or not one agrees with Homans' premise that all behavior can be reduced to psychological principles, the point is that he attempted to demonstrate the relevancy of his theory. Many of the great classical theorists were involved in the practical implications of their theories, especially Marx, Durkheim, Simmel, and Weber. While ignoring grand theorizing in favor of analysis of slices of social reality, contemporary social theorists, ranging from functionalists to postmodernists, continue in the tradition of demonstrating the relevancy of their theories. Thus, one may, or may not, agree with the postmodernist view of society and the need to deconstruct and reconstruct our means of analyzing society, but, as open-minded persons, we need to acknowledge the postmodern application of theoretical constructs. In short, we learn of a variety of theoretical perspectives in order to enlighten ourselves in our own attempt to explain human behavior and social society.

When we open ourselves to multiple theoretical perspectives, we not only help to eliminate bias; we stimulate objectivity. And among the primary purposes of sociological theory is to objectively examine society and human behavior. Along with other goals, sociological theorists look to discover social arrangements and patterns of social behavior, signs of inequality and injustice, and are generally critical of any societal arrangement that disadvantages any segment of humanity. If they are activists, sociological theorists will promote the idea that something needs to be done to correct social injustice; in some cases, they will serve as leaders of such social movements.

MAJOR THEMES IN SOCIOLOGICAL THOUGHT

When one examines a scope of 500 years of social theory, as we have done in this text, a number of themes of sociological significance reveal themselves. That is to say, there are a number of specific themes of social significance that have interested social theorists throughout the past five centuries. Students and sociologists alike might identify any number of general trends that have consumed the concerns of social theorists. I have identified eight: a general belief in progress and cultural evolution; technological growth; scarce resources; threats associated with overpopulation; capitalism and globalization; the development of a universal language; the dominant role of religion in society; and social injustice and the imbalance of power. Not only have past and present sociological social thinkers concerned themselves with these eight themes, but it is likely that future social thinkers will also have to contend with them. After all, any theme that has existed for 500 years is likely to extend itself into the future.

Let's take a brief look at each of these persistent general themes in sociological thought for the past five centuries.

Belief in Progress and Cultural Evolution

Social theorists, especially those grounded in the scientific tradition, tend to share in a belief that society is continuously progressing and culture is generally evolving. Progressive thinking and scientific reason are essential elements in cultural evolution. Since at least the time of the Greeks, enlightened thinkers have faced the challenges presented by those who possess an allegiance to religious faith, tradition, and/or other forms of dogmatic thinking. The Age of Enlightenment was a period in history when social thinkers were convinced that society was emerging from centuries of darkness and ignorance into an age of scientific reason and progress. These thinkers held a firm belief in the power of human reason and the ability of people to act rationally. They believed that humanity itself could be progressively altered.

Saint-Simon, Comte, Spencer, Marx, Durkheim, Weber, Cooley, and Mead are among the classical theorists who proposed a variation of a theory that suggested society has evolved over time and that cultural evolution would continue to flourish in the future. Social theorists who promote progress and cultural evolution may warn that humanity is capable of going through periods of stagnation but promote the idea that further knowledge will bring about progress.

Contemporary theorists, as a whole, generally accept the idea and value of continued societal progress and cultural evolution. The social thinkers who do not perceive that society is progressing "properly" generally have ideas on how to reach a more desired variation of society. Feminists, for example, would equate a progressive society as one where power is shared equally among men and women. Social theorists, like most academics, equate a belief in progress as fairly logical and point out that any alternative belief is not only pessimistic; it is detrimental in efforts to improve society.

Technological Growth

Continued evolutionary growth and progress in human society are dependent upon technological growth. Since the time of the Industrial Revolution, the human species has witnessed and enjoyed tremendous societal improvements due to the benefits of technological growth. Examples of these benefits are nearly endless but include such areas as a significant increase in life expectancy and overall quality of life due to improvements in the medical profession and a wide variety of the material goods that make everyday tasks simple (e.g., in transportation, automobiles, subways, and airplanes; in food production, farm equipment, such as tractors, combines, and hay balers; in forms of communication, satellites, cellular telephones, and the Internet) and other everyday products of technological development that we take for granted (such as indoor plumbing and electricity).

In the past 500 years, human society has clearly profited from the development of technology. Undoubtedly, technology will continue to benefit humanity (and ideally the other species and the environment). It is a necessary criterion of progress and cultural evolution.

Limited Scarce Resources

Nearly all classical theorists and contemporary theoretical perspectives warn that technological growth and "progress" may be linked to a number of costs, especially due to the limited scarce social and natural resources available to sustain growth. The examination of limited social resources has led sociological theorists to discuss such important issues as social stratification and conflict. Clearly, neither are all people within a given society born equal, nor do they enjoy an equal quality of life. The unequal distribution of significant social resources leads to social stratification. The stratification system of a society reveals the dichotomy in the possession of scarce social resources. Those in a position of power and authority do not want to, nor should they be expected to, voluntarily redistribute their resources to others without receiving some sort of compensation (something else of value in return). Those in a position of authority make every attempt to maintain and legitimize their power. Those without power seek to exercise some control over their lives and may even challenge the existing social authority. Those in power are always smaller in number but much more organized than the masses. (The role of power in society is so important that it is discussed later under a separate theme heading.) The stratification system can create tension between the haves and have-nots, and this tension can transform itself into conflict. Marx and conflict theorists go so far as to claim that conflict is inevitable in society because of social class distinctions.

As for natural resources, it is important to acknowledge that the earth has a limited capacity to support life. This "carrying capacity," as Catton (1980) described it, is the maximum feasible load, just short of the level that would end the environment's ability to support life. The limits of the natural world, consequently, make scarce natural resources, at the very least, just as important to humans as social resources. It should be pointed out that a concern over the limited number of natural resources is a rather recent development. But many social thinkers today realize the importance of protecting the natural environment to the point where it can sustain all living creatures on earth. The demands placed on our planet are huge. Humanity is still primarily dependent on the conversion of fossil fuels (e.g., for heating oil and gasoline) to meet its energy needs. The consumption of fossil fuels has grown rapidly since the time of industrialization and economic development. Among the potential undesirable side effects of a dependence on fossil fuels are pollution (e.g., smog and acid rain), ravaged topsoil, and changes in the global economy. The third millennium will undoubtedly witness a number of tragic events related to the seriousness of a limited number of scarce natural resources. Water will prove to be the most precious of these resources. Maintaining the rainforest, protecting ample agricultural topsoil suitable for growing food, and developing new methods to secure the energy needs of an ever-expanding population are among the critical issues related to the scarcity of natural resources. Scientists must continue to explore and develop such energy alternatives as nuclear, solar, and wind energy sources and must build more efficient homes, office buildings, automobiles, and so on.

Overpopulation

As hinted at above, the scarce natural and social resources will be further drained by the expanding population. Many classical and contemporary social theorists have expressed concern, sometimes alarming levels of concern, for the number of people on the planet. They worry that overpopulation can cause many harmful effects, even to the point where humanity and the planet itself are threatened. The first "alarmist" to express grave concerns about overpopulation was Thomas Malthus. In *An Essay on the Principle of Population*, Malthus (1798) presented a pessimistic view of human society. He believed that the world's population was growing too quickly in proportion to the amount of food available. Malthus feared that the lack of natural resources would lead to such social problems as crime, poverty, and greed. Herbert Spencer felt that overpopulation and the search for scarce resources would inevitably lead to the *survival of the fittest*. People, and whole societies, would be in conflict with one another over the scarcity of desired resources. These conflicts would lead to political and territorial conflicts.

Although the threats of overpopulation are staring at us face to face, demographic analysis is among the most underused determining factors for the evolution of economy and society (Cooper and Layard, 2002). By 2050, the world's population is likely to range from 8 to 12 billion, up from 3 billion in 1960. The U.S. Census Bureau (2011), for example, predicts that the world population will be over 9.3 billion in 2050. In 2012, anyone forty years old or older has been alive long enough to have seen the earth's population double. Rapid population growth is especially evident in the developing nations of the world. Accompanying this rapid growth is the shift of large numbers of people from rural areas to urban areas. On the positive side, the improvement in the status of women (e.g., in the cash economy) in the twentieth century and especially in the last third of it is a direct result of the spread of social civil rights among the growing masses (Cohen, 2002).

Sociological concerns regarding overpopulation extend way beyond Malthus and Spencer. From Marx to modern-day, sociologists have expressed trepidation because of overpopulation. Hoffmann (2004) notes that the sociological community, especially recently, has conducted research to determine the effects of human-controlled activities over other species that coexist in our shared environments. Hoffmann examined neo-Malthusian models of human pressures on the environment, especially human demand for land.

> The needs of a rapidly growing population are assumed to outpace the supply of natural resources such as timber and water and increase the demand for land.... Deforestation is a prime example of what happens as populations increase and more land must be co-opted to house a greater number of people, produce subsistence crops, provided for energy needs (e.g., mining, power plants), build transportation conduits, or develop other infrastructure components.... This has an obvious impact on animal species [as well] (Hoffmann, 2004:81–82).

The five horrorists, the new and more deadly "destroyers of life." (Jarrad Lokes)

Clark Abt (2002) argues that the ever-expanding numbers of people may increase as much as seven-fold to eightfold by 2025. The world's increased need for electricity alone underscores the reality that over-population will undoubtedly lead to conflict over the scarcity of natural energy.

As first presented in *Contemporary Social Theory: Investigation and Application* (2005), I used a neo-Malthusian model that established a theoretical construct of the "Five Horrorists"—an updated version of the "Four Horsemen." The latest version of this model appears in *Environmental Sustainability*, co-written by Tim Madigan (2011). The *five horrorists* represent an advanced evolutionary interpretation and development of the four horsemen concept. Breaking completely from the religious roots and de-emphasizing the natural component of the four horsemen, the five horrorists emphasize the social forces that will lead to the destruction of humanity and the environment if left unchecked by global political powers. Along with an updated version of Malthus's four horsemen—war, famine, pestilence, and disease—is the introduction of a new, and equally deadly partner—the *enviromare*. Enviromares are environmental-related threats, or nightmares, to humanity and the environment and, if left unchecked, will spell the doom of human and planetary existence as we know it. In short, the five horrorists are the new and more deadly "destroyers of life." The five horrorists come about as the result of overpopulation and the threat posed by humans to the sustainability of the environment. Although there is a clear pessimistic feel to the impact of the five horrorists, there is still a chance that humans can save themselves and the planet from the harmful effects of overpopulation (Delaney, 2004; Delaney and Madigan, 2011).

Capitalism, the Worldwide Community, and Globalization

The roots of Western sociology, arguably, reside with the rise of industrialization and subsequent creation of capitalism. Under capitalism, wealth is concentrated in the hands of private individuals and is used to create more wealth. Governments may own property and provide services, but the private sector dominates the economy. As an ideology, capitalism implies that all individuals have the opportunity to be successful through hard work, effort, and determination. Inevitably, this system will create poorer citizens among those who do not, or cannot, flourish even when presented with nearly limitless opportunities to do so. In an effort to provide for such persons, capitalist countries in the West have developed welfare programs with varying degrees of benefits. It is the capitalistic system and its effects on people, particularly social arrangements, that many sociologists have examined for the past centuries. Most of the schools of thought in sociological theory, especially conflict theory, feminism, critical theory, and postmodern theories, attack the tenets of capitalism. Other social thinkers point out that inequality exists in all societies regardless of their socioeconomic systems. However, the vast majority of sociological thought is generated in Western societies, and these societies are most directly influenced by capitalism.

Capitalism is fueled by growth via consumerism and spending. When one marketplace becomes saturated, a new one must be developed. Large corporations have expanded their markets throughout the world. These multinational corporations, or "multinationals," are economic enterprises that have headquarters in one country and conduct business in one or more other countries (Barnet, 1980). Multinationals are not a new phenomenon, as commerce among nations is at least as old as the Phoenicians, whose trading ships sailed from what is now Lebanon to foreign lands more than 3,000 years ago. From then on, trading routes crisscrossed the globe, as silk, gold, spices, and tools were bartered or sold. Trading firms like the Hudson's Bay Company and the Dutch East India Company were chartered by major colonial powers and granted monopolies over the right to trade with native populations.

The trading among nations and business practices of multinationals have led to a world-wide community interconnected by the economic order. There are a number of globalizing developments that have contributed to a worldwide community: the emergence of the global communications industry; the previously mentioned growth of the multinationals; the influence of global financial markets; global warming; and international action in support of human rights. Developments like these have brought the idea of a global society to the forefront. Of special note, the world today is more closely tied into a single economy than ever before in human history. The process of linking nations of the world together is referred to as *globalization*.

> Globalization appears to be the buzzword of the 1990s, the primary attractor of books, articles, and heated debated, just as postmodernism was the most fashionable and debated topic of the 1980s. A wide and diverse range of social theorists are arguing that today's world is organized by accelerating globalization, which is strengthening the dominance of a world capitalist economic system, supplanting the primacy of the nation-state with trans-national corporations and organizations, and eroding local cultures and traditions through a global culture (Kellner, 2002:285).

Globalization can be defined as "a social process in which the constraints of geography on social and cultural arrangements recede and in which people become increasingly aware that they are receding" (Waters, 1995:3). Globalization represents the evolution of heterogeneous cultures into a homogeneous culture that transcends all topographical boundaries placed on maps. Discussion on matters related to globalization have become commonplace since the mid-1990s.

The global economy has expanded to incorporate all or almost all areas of the world into a single, integrated economic system. This has led to greater profits for the multinationals and their stockholders but has left the less-developed nations in a state of uneasiness and even hostile resentment. According to Kellner (2002), many contemporary social theorists argue

> that today's world is organized by accelerating globalization, which is strengthening the dominance of a world capitalist economic system, supplanting the primacy of the nation-state with transnational corporations and organizations, and eroding local cultures and traditions through a global culture. Marxists, world-systems theorists, functionalists, Weberian, and other contemporary theorists are converging on the position that globalization is a distinguishing trend of the present moment (p. 265).

As the late 2000s revealed, the global economy, with its interlinking networks and emerging markets, is vulnerable to a domino-style economic crisis. A major breakdown anywhere in the system can cause problems throughout the network. Such a breakdown will have tremendous sociological impact on cultures across the globe. Clearly, sociologists will be discussing the impact of capitalism, the world community, and globalization in the future.

The Importance of Language and Developing a Universal Language

When early humans began to interact with people from different societies, finding an effective means of communication was often a challenge. Each culture develops its own language to represent their particular values and norms. Language is a quick, efficient, and flexible means of communication. Language not only makes communicating easier but also actually makes conceivable some ideas that would otherwise be inconceivable. Philosophy, science, and literature would not exist without language. The value of language far exceeds the obvious benefit of making communication between individuals easier.

Sociologists have long examined the role of language in society. Auguste Comte believed that it is language that keeps the members of a society bound to one another. Language itself is a social institution because it allows people to interact with one another. From this standpoint, Comte believed that language not only promotes unity among people, but also connects them with preceding generations and the culture of their ancestors. Thus, language creates an ancestral community. Comte viewed language as one of the most critical ingredients in the human community. In fact, many of the theorists discussed throughout this text the importance of language and communication.

As a result of the world community and globalization, many diverse people come into contact with one another. If such people do not share the same language, communication becomes more difficult. Although many sociologists are concerned that the powerful nations, and especially the multinational corporations, most of which have English as a primary or secondary language, have too much influence on native cultures (and thus language), the development of a *universal language* does not have to be a negative theme. We have already witnessed an increased efficiency in the development of global communications. Because of this, it is just a matter of time before advancements in technology and future communications will allow all the diverse people of the world to keep their own languages. Thus, the universal language concept proposed here would be assisted by communication devices that will allow others to "hear" or "read" foreign languages in their own language. This technology is already in use. Telephone companies have already marketed telephones that translate language (e.g., the iTranslate app available on certain cell phones), there are computer translation programs, and the use of such advancements as holograms will become routine midway through the twenty-first century. Additionally, it seems inevitable that someday very soon, the public will have access to and the option of inserting a chip (a type of hearing aid) into their ears allowing them to understand all people. As mentioned in Chapter 3, social network sites such as Facebook are capable of translating posts instantly (although sometimes we are reminded that not all words translate from one language to another). This author has Facebook friends in Russia, and while my posts are in English and all posts on their pages are in Russian, it is possible for us to read each other's pages.

All of these advancements in communication could have a huge effect on universal understanding.

The Role of Religion

Social thinkers have pondered the validity of a god or a higher power for multiple millennia. Philosophers generally debate the existence of a god, while sociologists tend to focus on the role of religion in human society. Religion has played an important role in nearly all societies throughout time. The earliest forms of religion were polytheistic. Religious answers to life's mysteries were often very irrational and seldom based on fact or technological knowledge. As society evolved, a new force emerged: science. The once unexplainable natural phenomena were now being answered coherently through science. During the nineteenth century, many intellectuals believed that religion would eventually be replaced by science. Religion, they believed, was irrational, and science therefore was better equipped to answer the questions that plagued humankind. Most of the classical social theorists were exposed to a religious indoctrination and came to reject its tenets. Contemporary social thinkers are less likely to embrace religion (compared to the general population) but generally restrict their discussion of religion to its role in society.

Social thinkers, and especially sociologists, have been interested in the role of religion in society for centuries. A few conclusions can be drawn. First, religion has a number of functional aspects; primarily, it provides meaning and identity to billions of people. It can be a beacon of light directing people toward a path of cooperativeness and understanding. Unfortunately, as history has demonstrated, the dysfunctional aspects of religion may outnumber the positive ones. Fanatical attachment to a belief system that lacks grounding in empirical reality continues to foster intolerance and hatred toward others, which inevitably leads to conflict and war. Attempts to foster peace in the Middle East, for example, will never be met as long as religion remains the guiding force of bigotry and hatred toward those who are different simply because of different interpretations of a god(s). In 2012, for example, violence erupted in the form of an attack on the U.S. Embassy in Cairo, then quickly spread to Libya, where a September 11th attack on the U.S. Consulate in Benghazi left the U.S. ambassador and three other Americans dead in the midst of a mob frenzy protesting the release of an anti-Islam video which portrays the prophet as a fraud, womanizer, and child molester. The film was made in the United States but with no connection to the U.S. government. Adding fuel to the fire of two radical defenses of respective religions was the September 19, 2012, issue of the *Charlie Hebdo*, a French weekly satirical publication that included a crude, lewd caricature of Islam's Prophet Muhammad (*Chicago Sun Times*, 2012). Islamic faith forbids imagery of Muhammad. While the vast majority of Christians and Muslims are against religious-based violence, extremists on either side can cause tension, violence, and even war.

From a sociological perspective, religion is a belief system consumed with ritualistic behavior based on traditions handed down from the past. Science, on the other hand, relies on rational thought, with theory supported by empirical data. The scientific approach to understanding life is often contradictory to the religious interpretation of life. Because of advancements in technology, science is ever expanding its level of knowledge and its ability to explain things that previously were left to religious explanations. This helps to explain that despite the advancements in science and rational thought, or perhaps because of, religion generally claims responsibility for whatever science cannot explain. For example, if a medical doctor gives a grave opinion about a patient's potential recovery and then suddenly the patient regains her health, religious proponents will claim it was a "miracle" or "God's will." The medical doctor may have simply underestimated her ability to heal or misdiagnosed the patient's ability to recover. In some cases, we will never know for sure. Scientists will admit to their limits of knowledge and ability to explain all events but explain that it's just a matter of time before they can provide a rational explanation. Religious persons also remain steadfast in their belief that a higher, spiritual power exists.

The power and influence of religion over people across the world will not disappear anytime soon. As a result, sociologists will continue to study this social institution and its role in society indefinitely.

Social Injustice and the Imbalance of Power

Perhaps the topic that concerns the greatest number of sociologists, past or present, is social injustice and the imbalance of power. Sociology is all about the examination of social systems and the design of society and its impact on humans. It comes as no surprise, then, that sociologists for centuries have well documented social inequality in its many forms. At the root of all social injustice is power imbalance. This inequality of decision-making capabilities afforded to those in a position of power over those without has led to conflict, prejudice, discrimination, and general social inequality. This is why power is one of the most precious of all scarce social resources. The imbalance of power exists at the individual, group, and societal levels. Those with power use the available resources to maintain their advantageous position. They may even resort to force (the capacity to persuade or convince, to produce with unnatural or unwilling effort) and coercion (compulsions, enforcement) as a means to influence the behavior of others. This type of abuse often leads to illegitimate forms of authority and power.

Social injustice and an unequal distribution of power will most certainly exist throughout the third millennium; it would be naive to think otherwise. This does not imply that social activism should be discouraged; in fact, those who feel strongly about acts of injustice should attempt to make necessary changes. Among the biggest challenges for sociologists in general and social justice activists in particular is the inequality found between social classes and between racial/ethnic groups.

Wealth and income not only lie at the core of socioeconomic stratification but are also important sources of power. After all, having wealth and high income is almost synonymous with having power. Any attempt to eradicate the imbalance of power caused by the disparity of wealth and income involves a major overhaul in the social system of entire societies. While some sociologists promote this very idea, others support the social system but seek ways to stimulate assistance to the less fortunate by the government and wealthy. Sociologists who study the effects of globalization on world populations point out how the imbalance of power contributes to global stratification. Once again, the solutions promoted by sociologists range from a more equitable distribution of wealth to providing greater assistance to the world's poor.

Racial and ethnic social inequality is a given in human society. In many instances across the globe, people are treated unequally simply because of their race or ethnicity. Racial and ethnic social injustice is manifested in a variety of forms, but the power that one racial or ethnic category of people has over the other(s) is its accessibility to scarce resources and the control over its distribution. Thus, the power race or ethnicity is not always the majority (in terms of total numbers) in any given society, although that is generally the case. Among the negative byproducts of the imbalance of power between categories of people are racism, prejudice, and discrimination—topics that have long concerned sociologists.

Racism involves any attitude, belief, behavior, or social arrangement that has the intent, or the ultimate effect, of favoring one racial category of people over another. Racism involves denying equal access to goods and services among all racial groups of society. A racist perspective denies the idea of equality among all people and promotes an ideology that one racial category is superior to another (Doob, 1999). Prejudice and discrimination are other forms of social injustice. *Prejudice* refers to negative beliefs about a group of people, while *discrimination* is actual behavior that treats people unequally on the basis of an ascribed status. A *stereotype* is a common type of prejudice and involves an exaggerated belief concerning a group of people. Thus, prejudice is a belief, but someone who acts upon it has discriminated. For example, one might think that a certain group of people is lazy (prejudice) and then purposely not hire a member of that group for a job (discrimination).

As social injustice and an imbalance in power seem to be fixtures of human societies, these topics will remain at the forefront of sociological theoretical discourse.

PARTING THOUGHTS

What does the future hold for sociological thought? The idea of grand theorists, such as those described in this text (Marx, Durkheim, Simmel, Weber, and Mead), proposing theoretical perspectives that attempt to explain huge segments of sociological concerns has long been replaced by an overabundance of sociologists promoting their own specialized banners and flag-waving concerns linked together by some general umbrella of a "school of thought." A number of niche theories exist today but none worthy of a "school of thought" categorization. And yet, it has already been three decades since the concept of "postmodernism" theory. For today's college students, there doesn't seem to be anything so postmodernist about a theory created before most of them were born. Perhaps it is time for some sociological "giant" to formulate a grand theory, emerge, and present it to us all. Then again, perhaps it is not. It seems, however, that the time has come for some significant new theory worthy of the umbrella categorization of "school of thought" to emerge. Are there any takers?

 Study and **Review** on **MySearchLab**

Discussion Questions

1. Now that you have read the entire text, identify at least five sociological themes of interest among social thinkers that have existed the past 500 years. How does your list compare and contrast to that of the author?

2. Of all the sociological themes identified by the author, which ones concern you the most? Explain why.

3. What do you think should be done to fight social injustice? What do you think should be done to help alleviate the imbalance of power in society? Or, do you think that social injustice and the imbalance of power in society are inevitable? Explain.

4. What would be the foundation of your own grand sociological theory? That is, what elements should be included? Would your theory be a micro or macro approach? What social issues would your theory address?

5. What has sociological theory done right? Where has it failed? Explain.

MySearchLab® Connections

MysearchLab is designed just for you. Each chapter features a customized study plan to help you learn and review key concepts and terms. Dynamic visual activities, videos, and readings found in the multimedia library will enhance your learning experience.

 Watch on **MySearchLab**

▶ John Macionis: Is There a Global Population Crisis?

 View on **MySearchLab**

▶ Population Growth in Global Perspective

BIBLIOGRAPHY

24/7 Wall St. 2012. "The 10 Poorest Countries in the World." Available: http://247wallst.com/2012/09/14/the-10-poorest-countries-in-the-world/2/

Aboulafia, Mitchell. 1986. *The Mediating Self: Mead, Sartre, and Self-Determination*. New Haven: Yale University Press.

Abrahamson, Mark. 1978. *Functionalism*. Englewood Cliffs, NJ: Prentice-Hall.

Abt, Clark. 2002. "The Future of Energy from the Perspective of the Social Sciences," 77–122 in *What the Future Holds*, edited by Richard Cooper and Richard Layard. Cambridge, MA: MIT Press.

Acevedo, Gabriel. 2005. "Turning Anomie on its Head: Fatalism as Durkheim's Concealed and Multidimensional Alienation Theory." *Sociological Theory*, 23(1): 75–85.

Acton, H. B. 1967. *What Marx Really Said*. New York: Schocken.

Adams, Bert, and R. A. Sydie. 2001. *Sociological Theory*. Thousand Oaks, CA: Pine Forge Press.

Addams, Jane. 1906. *The Modern City and the Municipal Franchise for Women*. New York: National American Woman Suffrage Associates.

Addams, Jane. 1910. *Twenty Years at Hull-House*. New York: Macmillian.

Addams, Jane. 1916. *The Long Road of Women's Memory*. New York: Macmillian.

Addams, Jane. 1922. *Peace and Bread in the Time of War*. New York: Macmillian.

Addams, Jane. 1930. *The Second Twenty Years at Hull-House*. New York: Macmillan.

Adler, Patricia, and Peter Adler. 2000. "The Gloried Self," pp. 185–197 in *Social Theory*, edited by Roberta Garner. Orchard Park, NY: Broadview.

Adorno, Theodor. 1972 [1964]. "Meinungsforschung and Offenlichkeit," pp. 532–37 in *Sociologische Schriften*. Frankfurt: Sukrkamp.

Adorno, Theodor. 1973. *Negative Dialectics*. New York: Seabury.

Agger, Ben. 1976. "On Happiness and the Damaged Life," pp. 12–33 in *On Critical Theory*, edited by John O'Neill. New York: Seabury.

Agger, Ben. 1992. *The Discourse of Domination: From the Frankfurt School to Postmodernism*. Evanston, IL: Northwestern University Press.

Agger, Ben. 1996. "Postponing the Postmodern." *Cultural Studies*. Vol. 1:37–46.

Alcoff, Linda. 1988. "Cultural Feminism Versus Post-Structuralism: The Identity Crisis in Feminist Theory." *Signs*, 13(3): 405–436.

Alexander, Elizabeth. 1995. "We Must Be About Our Father's Business" *Signs*. Winter: 336–356.

Alexander, Jeffrey C. 1985. *Neofunctionalism and After*. Beverly Hills, CA: Sage.

Alexander, Jeffrey C. 1987. *Twenty Lectures: Sociological Theory Since World War II*. New York: Columbia University Press.

Alexander, Jeffrey C. 1998. *Neofunctionalism and After*. Malden, MA: Blackwell.

Alfonso III, Fernando. 2011. "Questioning Authority." *The Post-Standard*, May 12: A-3.

Allan, Kenneth and Jonathan H. Turner. 2000. "A Formalization of Postmodern Theory." *Sociological Perspectives*, Vol. 43, No.3:363–385.

American Sociological Association. 2002. "David Riesman." *Footnotes*, 30 (5):1.

American Sociological Association. 2011. "Arlie Hochschild Award Statement." Available: http://www.asanet.org/about/awards/bernard/hochschild.cfm.

Anderson, Margaret L. 1997. *Thinking About Women: Sociological Perspectives on Sex and Gender*. Boston: Allyn and Bacon.

Anderson, Ralph E., Irl Carter, and with Gary R. Lowe. 1999. *Human Behavior in the Social Environment: A Social Systems Approach*, 5th edition. New York: Aldine de Gruyter.

Andreski, Stanislav. 1971. *Herbert Spencer: Structure, Function and Evolution*. London: Michael Joseph.

Antonio, Robert J. 1983. "The Origin, Development, and Contemporary Status of Critical Theory." *Sociological Quarterly*, 24 (Summer):325–351.

Arato, Andrew and Eike Gebhardt, eds. 1982 [1978]. *The Essential Frankfurt School Reader*. New York: Continuum.

Armstrong, Dave. 2012. "Martin Luther's Devotion to Mary." *Catholic Culture*. Available: http://www.catholicculture.org/culture/library/view.cfm?id=788

Aron, Raymond. 1970. *Main Currents in Sociological Thought*. Garden City, NY: Doubleday.

Aschcraft, Richard. 1987. *Locke's Two Treatises of Government*. London: Allen & Unwin.

Ashley, David, and David Orenstein. 1985. *Sociological Theory*. Boston: Allyn & Bacon.

Atkinson, Will. 2010. "Phenomenological Additions to the Bourdieusian Toolbox: Two Problems for Bourdieu, Two Solutions from Schutz." *Sociological Theory*, 28(1): 1–19.

Attridge, Derek and Thomas Baldwin. 2004. "Jacques Derrida." Guardian.co.uk, October 11. Available: http://www.guardian.co.uk/news/2004/oct/11/guardianobituaries.france.

Ayers, Michael. 1999. *Locke*. New York: Routledge.

Baber, Kristine and Colleen I. Murray. 2001. "A Post Modern Feminist Approach to Teaching Human Sexuality." *Family Relations*, 50 (1):23–31.

Bacon, Margaret. 1999. *Valiant Friend: The Life of Lucretia Mott*. Philadelphia: Friends General Conference.

Baggerman, Arianne and Rudolf M. Dekker. 2004. "The Enlightenment," *Encyclopedia of Children in History and Society*, Vol. 1: 321–324.

Bailey, Leon. 1994. *Critical Theory and the Sociology of Knowledge*. New York: Peter Lang.

Baldwin, John. 1986. *George Herbert Mead: A Unifying Theory for Sociology*. Beverly Hills: Sage Publishing.

Barker-Ruchti, Natalie and Richard Tinning. 2010. "Foucault in Leotards: Corporeal Discipline in Women's Artistic Gymnastics." *Sociology of Sport Journal*, 27: 229–250.

Barnet, R. 1980. *The Lean Years*. New York: Simon & Schuster.

Baron, Robert, and Donn Byrne. 1997. *Social Psychology*, 8th edition. Boston: Allyn & Bacon.

Baudrillard, Jean. 1968. *Le Systeme des Objets*. Paris: Denoel-Gonthier.

Baudrillard, Jean. 1970. *The Consumer Society*. London: Sage.

Baudrillard, Jean. 1975 [1973]. *The Mirror of Production*. St. Louis: Telos Press.

Baudrillard, Jean. 1981. *For a Critique of the Political Economy of the Sign*. St. Louis: Telos.

Baudrillard, Jean. 1983. *Simulations*. New York: Semiotext(e).

Baudrillard, Jean. 1995. *The Gulf War Did Not Take Place*. Bloomington, IN: The Indiana University Press.

Baudrillard, Jean. 2003. "Jean Baudrillard Biography." Available: www.egs.edu/faculty/baudrillard.html.

Baudrillard, Jean. 2005. "War Porn." *International Journal of Baudrillard Studies*, 2(1) (January). Available: http://www.ubishops.ca/baudrillardstudies/vol2_1/taylor.htm.

Baudrillard, Jean and Chris Turner. 2003. *The Spirit of Terrorism and Other Essays*. New York: Verso.

BBC News. 1999. "Marx the Millennium's 'Greatest Thinker.'" October 1. Available: http://news.bbc.co.uk/2/hi/461545.stm.

BBC News. 2006. "Judge's Own Da Vinci Code Cracked." April 28. Available: http://news.bbc.co.uk/2/hi/entertainment/4953948.stm.

Beasley, Chris. 1999. *What is Feminism?: An Introduction to Feminist Theory*. Thousand Oaks, CA: Sage.

Beemer, Jeffrey K. 2006. "Breaching the Theoretical Divide: Reassessing the Ordinary and Everyday in Habermas and Garfinkel." *Sociological Theory*, 24(1): 81–104.

Bellah, Robert N. 1973. *Emile Durkheim on Morality and Society*. Chicago: The University of Chicago Press.

Bellman, Beryl. 1975. *Village of Curers and Assassins: On the Production of Fala Kpelle Cosmological Categories*. The Hague: Mouton.

Bendix, Reinhard. 1960. *Max Weber: An Intellectual Portrait*. Garden City, New York: Doubleday.

Berger, Brigitte and Peter Berger. 1983. *The War Over the Family*. Garden City, NY: Anchor.

Berger, Peter and Hansfried Kellner. 1964. "Marriage and the Construction of Reality." *Diogenes*, 46:1–24.

Berger, Peter and Thomas Luckmann. 1966. *The Social Construction of Reality*. Garden City, NY: Anchor.

Berger, Peter and Thomas Luckmann. 1980. *The Social Construction of Reality*. New York: Irvington.

Berlin, Isiah. 1971. *Karl Marx: His Life and Environment*, 3rd ed. New York: Oxford University Press.

Bernard, Jessie. 1972. *The Future of Marriage*. New York: World Pub.

Berry, Francis. 2006. "Difference Between Modern Art and Postmodern Art." Available: http://postmodern-art.com/index.html.

Best, Steven and Douglas Kellner. 1991. *Postmodern Theory: Critical Interrogations*. New York: Guilford.

Bienenstock, Elisa Jayne and Philip Bonacich. 1993. "Game-Theory Models for Exchange Networks: Experimental Results." *Sociological Perspectives*. 36 (2):117–135.

Birnbaum, Pierre, and Jane Marie Todd. 1995. "French Jewish Sociologists Between Reason and Faith: The Impact of the Dreyfus Affair." *Jewish Social Studies*. 2:1–35.

Bitch Magazine. 2011. "About Us: Who We Are." Available: http://search.aol.com/aol/search?s_it=topsearchbox. search&v_t=comsearch50ct5&q=Bitch+Magazine.

Blau, Peter. 1955. *The Dynamics of Bureaucracy*. Chicago: University of Chicago Press.

Blau, Peter. 1956. *Bureaucracy in Modern Society*. New York: Random House.

Blau, Peter. 1964. *Exchange and Power in Social Life*. New York: Wiley.

Blau, Peter. 1973. *The Organization of Academic Work*. New York: Wiley.

Blau, Peter. 1974. *On the Nature of Organizations*. New York: Wiley.

Blau, Peter. 1994. *Structural Contexts of Opportunities*. Chicago: University of Chicago Press.

Blau, Peter and Otis Dudley Duncan. 1967. *The American Occupational Structure*. New York: Wiley.

Blau, Peter and Robert Merton, editors. 1981. *Continuities in Structural Inquiry*. Beverly Hills, CA: Sage.

Blau, Peter and Joseph E. Schwartz. 1997. *Crosscutting Social Circles: Testing a Macrostructural Theory of Intergroup Relations*. New Brunswick, NJ: Transaction Pubs.

Blau, Peter and W. Richard Scott. 1962. *Formal Organizations*. Scranton, PA: Chandler.

Bleich, Harold. 1977. *The Philosophy of Herbert Marcuse*. Washington, DC: University Press of America.

Blum, Christopher Olaf. 2006. "On Being Conservative: Lessons from Louis de Bonald." *The Intercollegiate Review* (Spring): 23–31.

Blumer, Herbert. 1940. "The Problem of the Concept in Social Psychology." *American Journal of Sociology*. 45 (5):707–719.

Blumer, Herbert. 1954. "What is Wrong with Social Theory?" *American Sociological Review*. 19 (1):3–10.

Blumer, Herbert, *Symbolic Interactionism: Perspective & Method*, 1st Ed., © 1969. Reprinted and electronically reproduced by permission of Pearson Education, Inc., Upper Saddle River, New Jersey.

Blumer, Herbert. 1980. "Mead and Blumer: The Convergent Methodological Perspectives of Social Behaviorism and Symbolic Interaction." *American Sociological Review*. 45 (3):409–419.

Blumer, Herbert. 1990. *Industrialization as an Agent of Social Change*, edited with an introduction by David R. Maines and Thomas J. Morrlowe. New York: Aldine de Gruyter.

Blute, Marion. 2002. Review of *Theories of Distinction: Redescribing the Descriptions of Modernity* in the *Canadian Journal of Sociology Online* (Nov-Dec). Available: http://www.cjsonline.ca/pdf/luhmann.pdf.

Boden, Deirdre. 1990A. "People are Talking: Conversation Analysis and Symbolic Interaction," pp. 244–273 in *Symbolic Interactionism and Cultural Studies*, edited by H.S. Becker and M. McCall. Chicago: University of Chicago Press.

Boden, Deirdre. 1990B. "The World as it Happens: Ethnomethodology and Conversation Analysis," pp. 185–213 in *Frontiers of Social Theory: The New Syntheses*, edited by George Ritzer. New York: Columbia University Press.

Bottomore, Tom. 1984. *The Frankfurt School*. Chichester, England: Ellis Horwood.

Bourdieu, P. 1979. "Public Opinion Does Not Exist," pp. 124–30 in *Communication and Class Struggle: Capitalism and Imperialism*, Vol. 1. New York: International Mass Media Research Center.

Boyd, Melba Joyce. 1994. "Canon Configuration for Ida B. Wells-Barnett." *The Black Scholar*, Vol 24, No.1:8–13.

Brazill, William. 1970. *The Young Hegelians*. Yale University Press.

Brecht, Martin. 1985. *Martin Luther: This Road to Reformation, 1483–1521*, translated by James L. Schaaf. Philadelphia: Fortress.

Breckman, Warren. 1999. *Marx, the Young Hegelians and the Origins of Radical Social Theory*. Cambridge: University Press.

Breen, Tom. 2011. "Army Group says there ARE Atheists in Foxholes." Baxterbulletin.com. Available: http://www.baxterbulletin.com/article/20110416/NEWS01/104160304.

Breines, Paul. 1970. "From Guru to Spectre: Marcuse and the Implosion of the Movement," pp. 1–21 in *Critical Interruptions*, edited by Paul Breines. New York: Herder and Herder.

Brewster, Mary. 2002. "Theories, Research and Practice Implication," pp. 23–48 in *Handbook of Domestic Violence Intervention Strategies: Policies, Programs, and*

Legal Remedies, edited by Albert R. Roberts. New York: Oxford University Press.

Bronner, Stephen Eric, and Douglas Kellner, editors. 1989. *Critical Theory and Society*. New York: Routledge.

Broome, J. H. 1963. *Rousseau: A Study of His Thought*. Alva, Scotland: Edward Arnold Publishers.

Brooks, David. 2012. "When the Good Do Bad." New York Times, March 19. Available: http://www.nytimes.com/2012/03/20/opinion/brooks-when-the-good-do-bad.html.

Broschart, Richards Kay. 1991. "Ida B. Wells Barnett," pp. 433–448 in *Women in Sociology: A Bio-Bibliographical Sourcebook*, edited by Mary Jo Deegan. New York: Greenwood Press.

Brown, Victoria Bissell. 2004. *The Education of Jane Addams*. Philadelphia: University of Pennsylvania Press.

Brumberg, Joan Jacobs. 1988. *Fasting Girls: The Emergence of Anorexia Nervosa as a Modern Disease*. Cambridge, MA: Harvard University Press.

Brumberg, Joan Jacobs. 1997a. *The Body Project: An Intimate History of American Girls*. New York: Random House.

Brumberg, Joan Jacobs. 1997b. "Silicone Valley." *The Nation*. December 29.

Bryan, F. M. 2004. *Real Democracy: The New England Town Meeting and How it Works*. Chicago: University of Chicago Press.

BUST Magazine. 2011. "About BUST." Available: http://www.bust.com/info/about-bust.html.

Buxton, William. 1985. *Talcott Parsons and the Capitalist Nation-State: Political Sociology as a Strategic Vocation*. Toronto: University of Toronto Press.

Calhoun, Craig. 1993. "Habitus, Field, and Capital: The Question of Historical Specificity," pp.61–88 in *Bourdieu: Critical Perspectives*, edited by Craig Calhoun, E. LiPuma and M. Postone. Chicago: University of Chicago Press.

Calhoun, Craig. 2003. "Robert K. Merton Remembered." *ASA Footnotes* (March). Available: http://www.asanet.org/footnotes/mar03/indextwo.html.

Camic, Charles. 1991. *Talcott Parsons: The Early Essays*. Chicago: University of Chicago Press.

Caplan, Jason R., Lucy A. Epstein, Davin K. Quinn, Jonathan R. Stevens and Theodore A. Stern. 2007. "Neuropsychiatric Effects of Prescription Drug Abuse." *Journal of Neuropsychology Review*, 17: 363–380.

Carlebach, Julius. 1978. *Karl Marx and the Radical Critique of Judaism*. Boston: Routledge & Kegan Paul.

Carneiro, Robert, editor. 1967. *The Evolution of Society: Selections From Herbert Spencer's Principles of Sociology*. Chicago: University of Chicago Press.

Carr, E. H. 1934. *Karl Marx, A Study in Fanaticism*. London: Dent.

Catton, W.R. 1980. *Overshoot: The Ecological Basis of Revolutionary Change*. Urbana: University of Illinois Press.

Centers for Disease Control (CDC). 2009. "Press Release." November 12. Available: http://www.cdc.gov/media/pressrel/2009/r091112.htm.

Centers for Disease Control (CDC). 2010. "Suicide: Facts at a Glance." Summer 2010. Available: http://www.cde.gov/violenceprevention/pdf/Suicide_DataSheet-a.pdf.

Centers for Disease Control (CDC). 2011. "Quick Facts About Suicide." Available: http://www.spanusa.org/index.cfm?fuseaction=home.viewPage&page_id=0D213AD4-C50A-1085-4DD96CE0EEED52A0.

Centers for Disease Control (CDC). 2012a. "Suicide and Self-Inflicted Injury." Available: http://www.cdc.gov/nchs/fastats/suicide.htm.

Centers for Disease Control (CDC). 2012b. "Suicide Rates Among Persons Ages 10 Years and Older, by Race/Ethnicity and Sex, United States, 2005–2009." Available: http://www.cdc.gov/violenceprevention/suicide/statistics/rates02.html

Center on Budget and Policy Priorities. 2010. "Critics Still Wrong on What's Driving Deficits in Coming Years: Economic Downturn, Financial Rescues, and Bush-era Policies Drive the Numbers." June 28. Available: http://www.cbpp.org/cms/index.cfm?fa=view&id=3036.

Cetina, Karin Knorr. 2009. "The Synthetic Situation: Interactionism for a Global World." *Symbolic Interactionism*, 32 (1): 61–87.

Chapman, G. E. 1997. "Making Weight: Lightweight Rowing, Technologies of Power, and Technologies of the Self." *Sociology of Sport Journal*, 14: 205–223.

Charon, Joel M. 1989. *Symbolic Interactionism*, 3rd ed. Englewood, Cliffs, NJ: Prentice Hall.

Chesterton, G. K. 1995 [1908]. Orthodoxy. San Francisco: Ignatius Press.

Chriss, James J. 1993. "Durkheim's Cult of the Individual as Civil Religion: Its Appropriation by Erving Goffman." *Sociological Spectrum*. 13:251–275.

Cicourel, Aaron V. 1964. *Method and Measurement in Sociology*. New York: Free Press.

Cockerham, William. 1995. *The Global Society*. New York: McGraw-Hill.

Cohen, Joel. 2002. "The Future of Population," pp. 29–75 in *What the Future Holds*, edited by Richard Cooper and Richard Layard. Cambridge, MA: MIT Press.

Collins, Patricia Hill. 1986. "Learning From the Outsider Within: The Sociological Significance of Black Feminist Thought." *Social Problems*. 33 (6):514–532.

Collins, Patricia Hill. 1989a. "A Comparison of Two Works on Black Life." *Signs*, 14 (4):875–884.

Collins, Patricia Hill. 1989b "The Social Construction of Black Feminist Thought." *Signs*. 14 (4):745–773.

Collins, Patricia Hill. 1990. *Black Feminist Thought*. Cambridge, MA: Unwin Hyman.

Collins, Patricia Hill. 1996. "What's in a Name? Womanism, Black Feminism, and Beyond." *Black Scholar*. 26 (1):9–17.

Collins, Randall. 1971A. "A Conflict Theory of Sexual Stratification." *Social Problems*. 19:3–12.

Collins, Randall. 1971b. "Functional and Conflict Theories of Educational Stratification." *American Sociological Review*. 36:1002–1019.

Collins, Randall. 1974. *Conflict Sociology: Toward an Explanatory Science*. New York: Academic Press.

Collins, Randall. 1975a. "The Basics of Conflict Sociology," pp. 56–61 in *Conflict Sociology*. New York: Academic Press.

Collins, Randall. 1975b. *Conflict Sociology*. New York: Academic Press.

Collins, Randall. 1979. *The Credential Society*. New York: Academic Press.

Collins, Randall. 1981. "On the Micro Foundations of Macro Sociology." *American Journal of Sociology*. 86:984–1014.

Collins, Randall. 1986. *Weberian Sociological Theory*. Cambridge: University Press.

Collins, Randall. 1990. "Market Dynamics as the Engine of Historical Change." *Sociological Theory*. 8 (2): 111–135.

Collins, Randall. 1990b. "Reply: Cumulation and Anticumulation in Sociology." *American Sociological Review*, 55 (3):462–463.

Collins, Randall. 1993. "Maturation of the State-Centered Theory of Revolution and Ideology." *Sociological Theory*. 11 (1):117–128.

Collins, Randall. 1997. "An Asian Route to Capitalism: Religious Economy and the Origins of Self-transforming Growth in Japan." *American Sociological Review*. 62 (6):843–865.

Collins, Randall. 1999. *Macro-History: Essays in Sociology of the Long Run*. Stanford, CA: University Press.

Collins, Randall. 2000. "The Sociology of Philosophies: A Precis." *Philosophy of the Social Sciences*. 30(2):157–201.

Collins, Randall. 2000. 2009. *Conflict Sociology" A Sociological Classic Updated*. Boulder, CO: Paradigm.

Collins, Randall and Michael Makowsky. 2010. *The Discovery of Society*, 8th edition. Boston: McGraw-Hill.

Conant, James and John Haugeland (Eds.). 2000. *The Road Since Structure*. Chicago: The University of Chicago Press.

Connell, Robert W. 1995. *Masculinities*. Cambridge, UK: Polity Press.

Cook, Karen. 1987. "Emerson's Contribution to Social Exchange Theory," pp. 209–222 in *Social Exchange Theory*, edited by Karen Cook. Beverly Hills, CA: Sage.

Cook, Karen and Richard Emerson. 1978. "Power, Equity and Commitment in Exchange Networks." *American Sociological Review*. 43 (October): 721–739.

Cook, Karen and Karen Hegtvedt. 1983. "Distributive Justice, Equity and Equality." *Annual Review of Sociology*. 9:217–241.

Cook, Karen, Richard Emerson, Mary Gilmore, Toshio Yamagishi. 1983. "The Distribution of Power in Exchange Networks: Theory and Experimental Results." *American Journal of Sociology*. 89:275–305.

Cook, Karen and Mary Gilmore. 1984. "Power, Dependence, and Coalitions." *Advances in Group Processes*. 1:27–58.

Cook, Karen and J.M. Whitmeyer. 1992. "Two Approaches to Social Structure: Exchange theory and Network Analysis." *Annual Review of Sociology*. 18:109–127.

Cook, Karen and Judith Howard. 1992. "Recent Theoretical Advances in Social Psychology: Progress and Promises." *Social Psychology Quarterly*. 55(2):87–93.

Cook, Karen, Chris Snijders, Vincent Buskens, and Coye Cheshire (eds). 2009. *eTrust: Forming Relationships in the Online World*. New York: Russell Sage Foundation.

Cooley, Charles. 1902. *Human nature and the Social Order*. New York: Scribners.

Cooley, Charles. 1909. *Social Organization*. New York: Scribners.

Cooley, Charles. 1964. *Human Nature and the Social Order*, introduction by Philip Rieff, Foreword by Herbert Mead. New York: Schocken.

Cooper, Derick. 1991. "On the Concept of Alienation." *International Journal of Contemporary Sociology*. 28:7–26.

Cooper, Richard and Richard Layard, editors. 2002. *What the Future Holds*. Cambridge, MA: MIT Press.

Cope, Kevin L. 1999. *John Locke Revisited*. New York: Twayne.

Coser, Lewis. 1956. *The Functions of Social Conflict*. New York: Free Press.

Coser, Lewis. 1964. "The Political Functions of Eunuchism." *American Sociological Review*. 29 (6):880–885.

Coser, Lewis. 1965a. *Georg Simmel*. Englewood Cliffs, NJ: Prentice Hall.

Coser, Lewis. 1965b. *Men of Ideas: A Sociologist's View*. New York: Free Press.

Coser, Lewis. 1967. *Continuities in the Study of Social Conflict*. New York: Free Press.

Coser, Lewis. 1972a. "The Alien as a Servant of Power: Court Jews and Christian Renegades." *American Sociological Review*. 37 (5):574–581.

Coser, Lewis. 1972b. "Marxist Thought in the First Quarter of the 20th Century." *American Journal of Sociology*. 78 (1): 173–201.

Coser, Lewis. 1974. *Greedy Institutions: Patterns of Undivided Commitment*. New York: Free Press.

Coser, Lewis. 1975. "Presidential Address: Two Methods in Search of a Substance." *American Sociological Review*. 40 (6): 691–700.

Coser, Lewis. 1976. "Sociological Theory From the Chicago Dominance to 1965." *Annual Review of Sociology*. (2):145–160.

Coser, Lewis. 1977. *Masters of Sociological Thought*, 2nd ed. New York: Harcourt, Brace & Jovanovich.

Coser, Lewis. 1982. "Remembering Gouldner: Battler, Conquistador, and Free Intelligence." *Theory and Society*. 11 (6): 885–888.

Coser, Lewis. 1988. "Primitive Classification Revisited." *Sociological Theory*. 6, (1):85–90.

Coser, Lewis. 1993. "A Sociologist's Atypical Life." *Annual Review of Sociology*. Vol. 19:1–15.

Cranston, Maurice. 1983. *Jean-Jacques: The Early Life and Work of Jean-Jacques Rousseau, 1712–1754*. Suffolk, Great Britain: Chaucer Press.

Crisis Intervention Center. 2011. "What is Sexting?" Available: http://www.crisisinterventioncenter.org/index.php?option=com_content&view=article&id=147:what-is-sexting&catid=39:teens&Itemid=79.

Crocker, Lester G. 1968. *Jean-Jacques Rousseau: The Quest, 1712–1758*, Vol.1. New York: Macmillan.

Cullen, Daniel E. 1993. *Freedom in Rousseau's Political Philosophy*. DeKalb, IL: Northern Illinois University Press.

Curra, John. 2003. *The Human Experience*. Boston: Allyn and Bacon.

Cuzzort, R. P. 1969. *Humanity and Modern Sociological Thought*. New York: Holt, Rinehart and Winston.

Cuzzort, R.P. and Edith W. King. 1995, 5th ed. *Twentieth-Century Social Thought*. Fort Worth: Harcourt Brace.

Dahrendorf, Ralf. 1959. *Class and Class Conflict in Industrial Society*. Stanford, CA: University Press.

Dant, Tim. 1996. "Fetishism and the Social Value of Objects." *Sociological Review*. 44:495–516.

Davis, Allen F. 1973. *American Heroine: The Life and Legend of Jane Addams*. New York: Oxford Press.

Davis, Kingsley. 1959. "The Myth of Functional Analysis as a Special Method in Sociology and Anthropology." *American Sociological Review*. 24:757–772.

Deegan, Mary Jo. 1989. *American Ritual Dramas*. New York: Greenwood Press.

Deely, John. 1994. *New Beginnings; Early Modern Philosophy and Postmodern Thought*. Buffalo: University of Toronto Press.

De La Fuente, Eduardo. 2008. "The Art of Social Forms and the Social Forms of Art: The Sociology-Aesthetics Nexus in Georg Simmel's Thought." *Sociological Theory*, 26(4): 344–362.

Delaney, Tim. 2001. *Community, Sport and Leisure*, 2nd edition. Auburn, NY: Legend Books.

Delaney, Tim. 2004. *Classical Social Theory: Investigation and Application*. Upper Saddle River, NJ: Prentice Hall.

Delaney, Tim. 2006. *Seinology: The Sociology of Seinfeld*. Amherst, NY: Prometheus.

Delaney, Tim. 2008. *Shameful Behaviors*. Lanham, MD: University Press of America.

Delaney, Tim. 2012. *Connecting Sociology to Our Lives: An Introduction to Socioilogy*. Boulder, CO: Paradigm.

Delaney, Tim. 2012b. "Georg Simmel's *Flirting* and *Secrecy* and Its Application to the Facebook Relationship Status—"It's Complicated." Journalism and Mass Communication Journal, 2(5): 530–540.

Delaney, Tim and Tim Madigan. 2011. *Environmental Sustainability*. Available online at: http://www.lulu.com/product/file-download/environmental-sustainability/16054869?productTrackingContext=search_results/search_shelf/center/1.

Delaney, Tim and Allene Wilcox. 2002. "Sports and the Role of the Media," pp. 199–215 in *Values, Society and Evolution*, edited by Harry Birx and Tim Delaney. Auburn, NY: Legend Books.

della Cava, Marco R. 2005. "Art Museum: Modern or McArchitecture?" *USA Today*, October 7: 9D.

Denzin, Norman K. 1969. "Symbolic Interaction and Ethnomethodology: A Proposed Synthesis." *American Sociological Review*, 34 (6):922–934.

Denzin, Norman K. 1991. *Images of Postmodernism: Social Theory and Contemporary Cinema*. London: Sage.

Derrida, Jacques. 1976. *Of Grammatology*. Baltimore, MD: Johns Hopkins University Press.

Derrida, Jacques. 1978. *Writing and Difference*. Chicago: University of Chicago Press.

Derrida, Jacques. 1997. "To Do Justice to Freud: The History of Madness in the Age of Psychoanalysis," pp. 57–104 in *Foucault and His Interlocutors*, edited by Arnold I. Davidson. Chicago: The University of Chicago Press.

Deutsch, Morton and Robert M. Krauss. 1965. *Theories in Social Psychology*. New York: Basic Books.

Diliberto, Gioia. 1999. *A Useful Woman*. New York: Scribner.

Domhoff, G. William. 2006. *Who Rules America?: Power and Politics and Social Change*, 5th edition. Boston: McGraw Hill.

Doob, Christopher Bates. 1999. *Racism: An American Cauldron*. New York: Longman.

Douglas, Jack. 1980. *Introduction to the Sociologies of Everyday Life*. Boston: Allyn and Bacon.

Dreyfus, Hubert L. and Paul Rabinow. 1982. *Michel Foucault*. Chicago: University Press.

Dronberger, Ilse. 1971. *The Political Thought of Max Weber: In Quest of Statesmanship*. New York: Meredith Corporation.

Dull, Diana and Candace West. 2002. "Accounting for Cosmetic Surgery: The Accomplishment of Gender," pp. 119–140 in *Doing Gender, Doing Difference: Inequality, Power, and Institutional Change*, edited by Sarah Fenstermaker and Candance West. New York: Routledge.

Dunn, Robert G. 1997. "Self, Identity and Difference: Mead and Poststructuralists." *Sociological Quarterly*, 38: 687–705.

Durham, Meenakshi Gigi and Douglas Kellner (Eds.). 2005. *Media and Cultural Studies: KeyWorks*. New York: Wiley-Blackwell.

Durkheim, Emile. 1928. *Socialism*. New York: Collier Books.

Durkheim, Emile. 1938. [1895]. *The Rules of Sociological Method*. New York: Free Press.

Durkheim, Emile. 1957. *Professional Ethics and Civil Morals*. London: Routledge & Kegan Paul.

Durkheim, Emile. 1965 [1912]. *The Elementary Forms of Religious Life*. New York: Free Press.

Durkheim, Emile. 1973 [1914]. "The Dualism of Human Nature and its Social Condition," pp. 149–163 in *Émile Durkheim: On Morality and Society*, edited by K. Bellah. Chicago: University of Chicago Press.

Durkheim, Emile. 1973 [1925]. *Moral Education: A Study in the Theory and Application of the Sociology of Education*. New York: Free Press.

Durkheim, Emile. 1984. *The Division of Labor in Society*, translated by W. D. Halls. New York; Free Press.

Dwyer, Devin and Huma Khan. 2011. "'I Don't Hide': Wisconsin Gov. Defends Comments on Prank Phone Call." *ABC News*, February 23. Available: http://abcnews.go.com/Politics/gov-scott-walker-pranked-reporter-posing-david-koch/story?id=12980381.

Edwards, Paul. 1997. *The Encyclopedia of Philosophy*. New York: Macmillan.

Eliaeson, Sven. 2002. *Max Weber's Methodologies: Interpretation and Critique*. Malden, MA: Polity.

Ellul, Jacques. 1964. *The Technological Society*. New York: Vintage.

Elshtain, Jean Bethke. 2002. *Jane Addams and the Dream of American Democracy: A Life*. New York: Basic Books.

Emerson, Richard. 1972a. "Exchange Theory, Part I: A Psychological Basis for Social Basis for Social Exchange," pp. 38–57 in *Sociological Theories in Progress*, Vol. 2, edited by J. Berger, M. Zelditch, and B. Anderson. Boston: Houghton Mifflin.

Emerson, Richard. 1972b. "Exchange Theory, Part II: Exchange Relations and Networks," pp. 58–87 in *Sociological Theories in Progress*, edited by J. Berger, M. Zelditch, and B. Anderson. Boston: Houghton Mifflin.

Engels, Frederick. 1869. "Karl Marx," translated by Joan and Trevor Walmsley in *Die Zukunft* (185): August 11.

Engels, Frederick. 1883. "On the Death of Karl Marx." *Der Sozialdemokrat*. No. 13.

Engerman, Stanley L. and Kenneth L. Sokoloff. 2006. "The Persistence of Poverty In the Americas: The Role of Institutions," pp. 43–78 in *Poverty Traps*, edited by

Samuel Bowles, Steven N. Durlauf, and Karla Hoff. Princeton University Press: Princeton, N.J.

Entertainment Weekly. 2011. "The White Stripes Announce That They Have 'Officially Ended.'" February 2. Available: http://music-mix.ew.com/2011/02/02/the-white-stripes/

Etzkorn, Peter. 1968. *Georg Simmel*. New York: Teachers College Press.

Ewin, R. E. 1991. *Virtues and Rights: The Moral Philosophy of Thomas Hobbes*. Boulder, CO: Westview Press.

Faberman, Harvey A. 1991. "Symbolic Interaction and Postmodernism: Close Encounter of a Dubious Kind." *Symbolic Interaction*, 14:471–488.

Farganis, James. 2000. *Readings in Social Theory: The Classic Tradition to Post-Modernism*, 3rd ed. Boston: McGraw Hill.

Farganis, James. 2011. *Readings in Social Theory: The Classic Tradition to Post-Modernism*, 6th edition. Boston: McGraw-Hill.

Faris, Robert. 1967. *Chicago Sociology 1920–1932*. San Francisco: Chandler.

Farrington, Karen. 2000. *The History of Torture & Execution*. New York: Lyons Press.

Fay, Brian. 1975. *Social Theory and Political Practice*. Boston: Unwin Hyman.

Fay, Brian. 1987. *Critical Social Science: Liberation & Its Limits*. Ithaca, NY: Cornell University Press.

Feldman, Stephen M. 2000. *American Legal Thought From Premodern to Postmodern: An Intellectual Voyage*. New York: Oxford Press.

Fine, Gary Alan. 1993. "The Sad Demise, Mysterious Disappearances, and Glorious Triumph of Symbolic Interactionism." *Annual Review of Sociology*. 19:61–87.

Fish, Jonathan S. 2005. "Talcott Parsons and the Sociology of Emotion." *Sociological Perspectives*, 48 (1): 135–152.

Fontana, Andrea, and James Frey. 1983. "The Place Kicker in Professional Football: Simmel's Stranger Revisited." *Qualitative Sociology*. 6(1) Winter: 308–321.

Fontana, Andrea and Frederick Preston. 1990. "Postmodern Neon Architecture: From Signs to Icons." *Studies in Symbolic Interaction*, 11:3–24.

Foucault, Michel. 1965. *Madness and Civilization: A History of Insanity in the Age of Reason*. New York: Vintage.

Foucault, Michel. 1966a. *The Order of Things: An Archaeology of the Human Sciences*. New York: Vintage.

Foucault, Michel. 1969. *The Archaeology of Knowledge and the Discourse on Language*. New York: Harper Collophon.

Foucault, Michel. 1975. *The Birth of the Clinic: An Archaeology of Medical Perception*. New York: Vintage.

Foucault, Michel. 1978. *The History of Sexuality*. New York: Pantheon Books.

Foucault, Michel. 1983. "Afterword: The Subject and Power," pp. 208–226 in *Michel Foucault: Beyond Structuralism and Hermeneutics*, edited by H.L. Dreyfus and P. Rabinow. Chicago: The University of Chicago Press.

Foucault, Michel. 1985. *The Use of Pleasure: The History of Sexuality*. Vol. 2. New York: Pantheon.

Fournier, Marcel. 2007. *Emile Durkheim*. Paris: Fayard.

Freund, Julien. 1968. *The Sociology of Max Weber*. New York; Random House.

Frey, James H. and Tim Delaney. 1996. "The Role of Leisure Participation in Prison: A Report From Consumers." *Journal of Offender Rehabilitation*, 23(1/2):79–89.

Friedman, Michael. 1993. "Remarks on the History of Science and the History of Philosophy," pp. 37–54 in *World Changes*, edited by Paul Horwich. Cambridge, MA: The MIT Press.

Frisby, David. 1981. *Sociological Impressionism: A Reassessment of George Simmel's Social Theory*. London: Heinemann.

Frisby, David. 1984. *Georg Simmel*. Chichester, England: Ellis Horwood.

Frisby, David. 2002. *Georg Simmel* (revised edition). New York: Routledge.

Fuchs, Stephan. 2001. "Networks and Systems," pp. 129–139 in *Talcott Parsons Today*, edited by A. Javier Trevino, foreword by Neil J. Smelser. New York: Rowman & Littlefield.

Fuhse, Jan A. 2009. "The Meaning Structure of Social Networks." *Sociological Theory*, 27(1): 51–73.

Garfinkel, Harold. 1956. "Conditions of Successful Degradation Ceremonies." *American Journal of Sociology*. 61 (March):420–424.

Garfinkel, *Studies In Ethnomethodology*, 1st Ed., © 1967. Reprinted and electronically reproduced by permission of Pearson Education, Inc., Upper Saddle River, New Jersey.

Garfinkel, Harold. 1996. "Ethnomethodology's Program." *Social Psychology Quarterly*. 59 (1):5–21.

Garfinkel, Harold. 2002. *Ethnomethodology's Program: Working out Durkheim's Aphorism*, edited and introduced by Anne Warfield Rawls. New York: Rowman & Littlefield.

Gaona, Elena. 2003. "Tattoos Portray Life in Los Angeles Gangs," pp. 114–124 in *Body Piercing and Tattoos*, edited by J.D. Lloyd. New Haven, CT: Greenhaven/Thomson.

Garcelon, Marc. 2010. "The Missing Key: Institutions, Networks, and the Project of Neoclassical Sociology." *Sociological Theory*, 28(3): 326–353.

Garner, Roberta (editor). 2000. *Social Theory*. Orchard Park, NY: Broadview.

Gartner, Lloyd. P. 2001. *History of the Jews in Modern Times*. New York: Oxford University Press.

Gay, Peter. 1969. *The Enlightenment: An Interpretation*. New York: Norton & Company.

Geertz, C. 1973. "The Growth of Culture and the Evolution of Mind." *The Interpretation of Culture*. New York: Basic.

Gerth, Hans, and C. Wright Mills. 1946. *From Max Weber: Essays in Sociology*. New York: Oxford University Press.

Giddens, Anthony. 1971. *Capitalism and Modern Social Theory*. Cambridge: University Press.

Giddens, Anthony. 1976. *New Rules of Sociological Method*. London: Hutchinson

Giddens, Anthony. 1977. *Studies in Social and Political Theory*. London: Hutchinson.

Giddens, Anthony. 1979. *Central Problems in Social Theory: Action, Structure and Contradiction in Social Analysis*. Berkeley: University of California Press.

Giddens, Anthony. 1984. *The Constitution of Society: Outline of the Theory of Structuration*. Cambridge: University Press.

Giddens, Anthony. 1987. *Sociology: A Brief But Critical Introduction*, 2nd edition. New York: Harcourt, Brace & Jovanovich.

Giddens, Anthony. 1990. *The Consequence of Modernity*. Stanford, CA: Stanford University Press.

Giddens, Anthony. 1991. *Modernity and Self-identity: Self and Society in the Late Modern Age*. Cambridge: Polity Press.

Giddens, Anthony. 1992. *The Transformation of Intimacy*. Stanford, CA: Stanford University Press.

Giddens, Anthony. 1994. *Beyond Left and Right*. Cambridge: Polity Press.

Giddens, Anthony. 2000a. *Runaway World*. New York: Routledge.

Giddens, Anthony. 2000b. *The Third Way and its Critics*. Malden, MA: Polity Press.

Giddens, Anthony. 2007. *Over to You, Mr. Brown*. Malden, MA: Polity Press.

Giddens, Anthony. 2009. *Politics of Climate Change*. Malden, MA: Polity Press.

Giddens, Anthony. 2010. *The Third Wave: The Renewal of Social Democracy*. Malden, MA: Polity Press.

Giddens, Anthony. 2011. "Facebook: Home Page". Available: http://www.facebook.com/pages/Anthony-Giddens/54819020784.

Giddens, Anthony and Patrick Diamond (Eds.). 2005. *The New Egalitarian*. Malden MA: Polity Press.

Gildin, Hilail. 1983. *Rousseau's Social Contract: The Design of the Argument*. Chicago: University of Chicago Press.

Gilligan, Carol. 1982. *In a Different Voice*. Cambridge, MA: Harvard University Press.

Gilligan, Carol. 1998. "Remembering Larry." *Journal of Moral Education*. (2)125–140.

Gilman, Charlotte Perkins. 1887. "The Right to Earn Money." *Woman's Journal*. 18 (January 8):12.

Gilligan, Carol. 1892/1973. *The Yellow Wall-Paper*. New York: Feminist Press.

Gilligan, Carol. 1898. *Women and Economics*. Boston: Small and Maynard.

Gilligan, Carol. 1935. *The Living of Charlotte Perkins Gilman*. New York: D. Appleton-Century Company.

Gilligan, Carol. 1998. *The Abridged Diaries of Charlotte Perkins Gilman*, edited by Denise D. Knight. Charlottesville, VA: University of Virginia Press.

Gilligan, Carol. 2002. *The Dress of Women*, edited with an introduction by Michael R. Hill and Mary Jo. Deegan. Westport, CT: Greenwood Press.

Glaser, Barney G. and Anselm L. Strauss. 1965. *Awareness of Dying*. Chicago: Aldine.

Glynn, C. J., S. Herbst, G.J. O'Keefe, and R.Y. Shapiro. 1999. *Public Opinion*. Boulder: Westview.

Goffman, Erving. 1952. "On Cooling the Mark Out." *Psychiatry: Journal of Interpersonal Relations*, 15(4): 451–463.

Goffman, Erving. 1953. "Communication Conduct in an Island Community." Ph.D. dissertation, University of Chicago.

Goffman, Erving. 1956. "Embarrassment and Social Organization." *American Journal of Sociology*, 62 (3): 264–271.

Goffman, Erving. 1959. *Presentation of Self in Everyday Life*. Garden City, NY: Anchor.

Goffman, Erving. 1961a. *Asylums*. Garden City, NY: Doubleday Anchor Books.

Goffman, Erving. 1961b. *Encounters: Two Studies in the Sociology of Interaction*. Indianapolis: Bobbs-Merrill.

Goffman, Erving. 1963. *Stigma*. Englewood Cliffs, NJ: Prentice Hall.

Goffman, Erving. 1967. *Interaction Ritual*. Garden City, NY: Anchor.

Goffman, Erving. 1983a. "Felicity's Condition." *American Journal of Sociology*. 89 (1):1–53.

Goffman, Erving. 1983b. "The Interaction Order: American Sociological Association, 1982 Presidential Address." *American Sociological Review*. 48 (1):1–17.

Goldberg, Chad Alan. 2008. "Introduction to Emile Durkheim's 'Anti-Semitism and Social Crisis.'" *Sociological Theory*, 26(4): 299–321.

Goldberg, Chad Alan. 2011. "The Jews, the Revolution, and the Old Regime in French Anti-Semitism and Durkheim's Sociology." *Sociological Theory*, 29(4): 248–271.

Goldin-Meadow, Susan. 2003. *Hearing Gesture: How Our Hands Help Us Think*. Cambridge, MA: Harvard University Press.

Goodwin, Albert. 1970. *The French Revolution*. London: Hutchinson.

Gordon, Bill. 2007. "Original Sin." 4Truth.net: *A Reasoned Approach to Christianity*. Available: http://www.4truth. net/fourtruthpb.aspx?pageid=8589951952

Gospel-driven Disciples. 2011. "McChurches." Available: http://gospeldrivendisciples.blogspot.com/2011/03/mcchurches.html.

Grafholf, Richard, editor. 1978. *The Theory of Social Action*. Bloomington; Indiana University Press.

Grafholf, Richard. 1989. *Philosophers in Exile*. Bloomington, IN: Indiana University Press.

Gray, John. 2003. "The Beast Stirs." *New Statesman*, April 21. Available: http://www.newstatesman.com/200304210037.

Green, Adam Isaiah. 2007. "Queer Theory and Sociology: Locating the Subject and the Self in Sexuality Studies." *Sociological Theory*, 25(1): 26–45.

Green, Martin. 1974. *The Von Richtofen Sisters*. New York: Basic.

Greenhouse, Steven. 2011. "Mural of Maine's Workers Becomes Political Target." *The New York Times*, March 23.

Available: http://www.nytimes.com/2011/03/24/us/24lepage.html?_=1.

Greisman, Harvey C. 1986. "The Paradigm that Failed," pp.273–291 in *Structures of Knowing*, edited by R.C. Monk. Lanhan, MD: University Press of America.

Griffin, Em. 1991. "A Different Voice of Carol Gilligan." *A First Look at Communication Theory*. Boston: McGraw Hill.

Griffith, Alison L. and Dorothy E. Smith. 2005. *Mothering for Schooling*. New York: Psychology Press.

Griffith, Elisabeth. 1984. *In Her Own Right*. New York: Oxford University Press.

Groves, W. Byron and Robert J. Sampson. 1986. "Critical Theory and Criminology." *Social Problems*. 33(61): 538–575.

Guardian.co.uk. 2011. "Anthony Giddens Profile." Available: http://www.guardian.co.uk/global/2007/jun/04/anthonygiddens

Gurko, Miriam. 1974. *The Ladies of Seneca Falls*. New York: Schocken Books.

Habermas, Jurgen. 1970. *Toward A Rational Society: Student Protests, Science, and Politics*. Boston: Beacon.

Habermas, Jurgen. 1973. "What Does a Crisis Mean Today: Legitimation Problems in Late Capitalism." *Social Research*. 40 (4): 39–64.

Habermas, Jurgen. 1984. *The Theory of Communicative Action*, Volume One. Boston: Beacon.

Habermas, Jurgen. 1987a. *The Theory of Communicating Action*, Volume Two. Boston: Beacon Press.

Habermas, Jurgen. 1987b. *The Philosophical Discourse of Modernity*, translated by Frederick Lawrence. Cambridge, MA: The MIT Press.

Habermas, Jurgen. 1989. "The Tasks of a Critical Theory of Society," pp. 292–312 in *Critical Theory and Society*, edited by Stephen Eric Bronner and Douglas Kellner. New York: Routledge.

Habermas, Jurgen. 1991. "A Reply," pp.214–264 in *Communicative Action*, edited by Alex Honneth and Hans Joas. Cambridge, MA: The MIT Press.

Habermas, Jurgen 1997. "Modernity," Habermas & Unfinished Project of Modernity, ed. d'Entreves & Benhabib. Cambridge, MA: MIT Press.

Habermas, Jurgen. 1998. "Remarks on Legitimation Through Human Rights." *The Modern Schoolman*. 75:87–100.

Hadden, Richard W. 1997. *Sociological Theory*. Orchard Park, NY: Broadview.

Hall, Richard. 1987. *Organizations: Structures, Processes, and Outcomes*, 4th edition. Englewood Cliffs, NJ: Prentice-Hall.

Hammer, Rhonda and Douglas Kellner. 2009. *Media/Cultural Studies*. New York: Peter Lang.

Hampson, Norman. 1963. *The Social History of the French Revolution*. Toronto: University of Toronto Press.

Harcourt, Bernard. 2001. *Illusion of Order: The False Promise of Broken Windows Policing*. Harvard: University Press.

Harding, Sandra. 1986. "The Instability of the Analytical Categories of Feminist Theory." *Signs*, 11 (4):645–664.

Harding, Sandra. 1989. "Women as Creators of Knowledge." *American Behavioral Scientist*, 32 (6): 700–707.

Harding, Sandra. 1992. "After the Neutrality Ideal; Science, Politics, and Strong Objectivity." *Social Research*, 59 (Fall): 567–87.

Harding, Sandra. *Science and Social Inequality: Feminist and Postcolonial Issues*. Urbana, IL: University of Illinois Press.

Harding, Sandra and Merrill B. Hintikka, editors. 1983. *Discovering Reality*. Boston: D. Reidel.

Hardt, Hanno. 1986. "Critical Theory in Historic Perspective." *Journal of Communication*. 36:144–154.

Harrison, Ross. 2003. *Hobbes, Locke, and Confusion's Masterpiece: An Examination of Seventeenth-Century Political Philosophy*. New York: Cambridge University Press.

Hartmann, Susan. 1998. "Feminism and Women's Movements," pp.41–45 in *Reading Women's Lives*, edited by Mary Margaret Fonow. Needhan Heights, MA: Simon & Schuster.

Harvey, David. 1989. *The Condition of Postmodernity*. Cambridge, MA: Blackwell.

Hechter, Michael. 1987. "Rational Choice Foundations of Social Order," in *Theory Building in Sociology*, edited by Jonathan Turner. Newbury Park, CA: Sage.

Hegel, Georg Wilhelm Friedrich. 1931. *The Phenomenology of Mind*. New York: Macmillan.

Hegtvedt, Karen, Elaine Thompson and Karen S. Cook. 1993. "Power and Equity: What Counts in Attributions for Exchange Outcome?" *Social Psychology Quarterly*. 56:100–119.

Heilbroner, Robert L. 1970. *Between Capitalism and Socialism*. New York: Random House.

Held, David. 1980. *Introduction to Critical Theory*. Berkeley: University of California Press.

Helle, Horst J. 2009. "Introduction to the Translation," pp. 1–18 in *Sociology* by Georg Simmel, translated and edited by Anthony J. Blasi, Anton K. Jacobs, and Mathew Kanjirathinkal. Boston: Brill.

Heller, Agnes. 1976. *The Theory of Need in Marx*. New York: St. Martin's Press.

Hilgart, Art. 1997. "Sanctioned Sociopathy." *Humanist*. 57(1):3.

Hill, Michael R. 1991. "Harriet Martineau," pp. 289–297 in *Women in Sociology: A Bio-Bibliographical Sourcebook*, edited by Mary Jo Deegan. New York: Greenwood Press.

Hobbes, Thomas. 1994. *Leviathan*, edited, with an Introduction by Edwin Curry. Indianapolis: Hackett.

Hochschild, Arlie Russell. 1973. *The Unexpected Community*. Berkeley: University of California Press.

Hochschild, Arlie Russell. 1979. "Emotion Work, Feeling Rules, and Social Structure." *American Journal of Sociology*. 85:551–573.

Hochschild, Arlie Russell. 1983. *The Managed Heart: Commercialization of Human Feeling*. Berkeley: University of California Press.

Hochschild, Arlie Russell. 1994. "Inside the Clock Work of Male Careers," pp. 125–139, in *Gender and the Academic Experience*, edited by Kathryn P. Meadow Orlans and Ruth A. Wallace. Lincoln: University of Nebraska Press.

Hochschild, Arlie Russell. 2003a. *Global Woman: Nannies, Maids and Sex Workers in the New Economy*, edited by Barbara Ehrenreich and Arlie Hochschild. New York: Metropolitan Press.

Hochschild, Arlie Russell. 2003b. *The Commercialization of Intimate Life: Notes From Home and Work*. Los Angeles: University of California Press.

Hoecker-Drysdale, Susan. 1992. *Harriet Martineau: The First Woman Sociologist*. Oxford, England: Berg Publishers.

Hoffmann, John P. 2004. "Social and Environmental Influences on Endangered Species: A Cross-National Study." *Sociological Perspectives*, 47(1): 79–107.

Homans, George. 1941. *English Villagers of the Thirteenth Century*. Cambridge, MA: Harvard University Press.

Homans, George. 1950. *The Human Group*. New York: Harcourt & Brace.

Homans, George. 1951. "The Western Electric Researches," pp. 201–241 in *Human Factors in Management*, edited by S.D. Hoslett. New York: Harper.

Homans, George. 1958. "Social Behavior as Exchange." *American Journal of Sociology*. 63:597–606.

Homans, George. 1961. *Social Behavior: Its Elementary Forms*. New York: Harcourt, Brace and World.

Homans, George. 1962. *Sentiments and Activities*. New York: Free Press.

Homans, George. 1967. *The Nature of Social Science*. New York: Harcourt, Brace and World.

Homans, George. 1984. *Coming to My Senses: The Autobiography of a Sociologist*. New Brunswick, NJ: Transaction Books.

Homans, George and Charles Curtis. 1934. *An Introduction to Pareto and His Sociology*. New York: Knopf.

Hook, Sydney. 1962. *From Hegel to Marx*. Ann Arbor, MI: University Press.

Horkheimer, Max. 1947. *The Eclipse of Reason*. New York: Oxford University Press.

Horkheimer, Max. 1974. *Critique of Industrial Reason*. New York: Seabury Press.

Horkheimer, Max. 1982. *Critical Theory: Selected Essays*. New York: Continuum. .

Horkheimer, Max and Theodor W. Adorno. 1944. *Dialectic of Enlightenment*. New York: Continuum.

Horkheimer, Max and Theodor W. Adorno. 1972. *Dialectic of Enlightenment*. New York: Herder and Herder.

Horowitz, Irving L. 1983. *C. Wright Mills: An American Utopian*. New York: Free Press.

Horwich, Paul, editor. 1993. *World Changes: Thomas Kuhn and the Nature of Science*. Cambridge, MA: MIT Press.

Hoy, David Couzens and Thomas McCarthy. 1995. *Critical Theory*. Oxford: Blackwell.

Hudson, Kenneth and Andrea Coukos. 2005. "The Dark Side of the Protestant Ethic: A Comparative Analysis of Welfare Reform." *Sociological Theory*, 23(1): 1–24.

Hughes, John A., Peter J. Martin, and W.W. Sharrock. 1995. *Understanding Classical Sociology: Marx, Weber, Durkheim*. Thousand Oaks, CA: Sage.

Hunter, Margaret. 2011. "Shake it Baby, Shake it: Consumption and the New Gender Relations in Hip-Hop." *Sociological Perspectives*, 54(1): 15–36.

Husserl, Edmund. 1931. *Ideas*. New York: Macmillan.

Husserl, Edmund. 1950. *Ideem I*. The Hague: Martinus Nijholf.

Husserl, Edmund. 1964. *The Idea of Phenomenology*, translated by William P. Alston and George Nakhnikian, and introduction by George Nakhnikian. The Hague: Martinus Nijhoff.

Husserl, Edmund. 1965. *Phenomenology and the Crisis of Philosophy*, translated with an introduction by Quentin Lauer. New York: Harper & Row.

Husserl, Edmund. 1966. *The Phenomenology of Internal Time-Consciousness*, edited by Martin Heidegger, introduction by Calvin O. Schrag. Bloomington, IN: Indiana University Press.

Husserl, Edmund. 1972. "A Reply to a Critic of My Refutation on Logical Psychologism." *Personalist*, 53:5–13.

Husserl, Edmund. 1977. "Psychological Studies in the Elements of Logic." *Personalist*, 58:297–320.

Husserl, Edmund. 1998. "The Phenomenology of Monadic Individuality and the Phenomenology of the General Possibilities and Compossibilities of Lived-Experiences: Static and Genetic Phenomenology." *Continental Philosophy Review*, 31:143–152.

Hutchinson, Louise Daniel. 1981. *Anna J. Cooper: A Voice from the South*. Washington, DC: Smithsonian Institution Press.

Jagtenberg, Tom and David McKie. 1997. *Eco-Impacts and the Greening of Postmodernity*. Thousand Oaks, CA: Sage.

James, William. 1948 [1890]. *Principles of Psychology*. Cleveland: World Publishing.

Jameson, Fredric. 1971. *Marxism and Form*. Princeton: Princeton University Press.

Jameson, Fredric. 1972. *The Prison-House of Language: A Critical Account of Structuralism and Russian Formalism*. Princeton, NJ: University of Princeton Press.

Jameson, Fredric. 1981a. *The Political Unconscious*. Ithaca, NY: Cornell University Press.

Jameson, Fredric. 1981b. "Reification and Utopia in Mass Culture." *Social Text*. 1:139.

Jameson, Fredric. 1984. "Postmodernism on the Cultural Logic of Late Capitalism." *New Left Review*. 146:53–92.

Jameson, Fredric. 1989. "Afterward—Marxism and Postmodernism," pp. 369–387 in *Postmodernism, Jameson, Critique*, edited by Douglas Kellner. Washington, DC: Maisonneuve Press.

Jameson, Fredric. 1990. "Modernism and Imperialism," pp. 43–66 in *Nationalism, Colonialism, and Literature*, edited by Terry Eagleton, Fredric Jameson and Edward W. Said. Minneapolis: University of Minnesota Press.

Jameson, Fredric. 2000. "Postmodernism on the Cultural Logic of Late Capitalism," pp. 539–557 in *Social Theory*, edited by Roberta Garner. Orchard Park, New York: Broadview.

Jay, Martin. 1973. *The Dialectical Imagination: A History of the Frankfurt School and the Institute of Social Research 1923–1950*. Boston: Little & Brown.

Jefferson, Gail. 1979. "A Technique for Inviting Laughter and Its Subsequent Acceptance Declination," pp. 79–96 in *Everyday Language; Studies in Ethnomethodology*, edited by G. Psathas. New York: Irvington.

Jefferson, Gail. 1984. "On the Organization of Laughter in Talk About Troubles," pp. 346–369 in *Structures of Social Action*. Cambridge: Cambridge University Press.

Jimerson, Jason B. 1999. "'Who Has Next?': The Symbolic, Rational, and Methodical Use of Norms in Pickup Basketball." *Social Psychology Quarterly*, 62(2): 136–156.

Joas, Hans. 1985. *George Herbert Mead: A Contemporary Re-Examination of his Thought*. Cambridge: MIT Press.

Johns, D. P. 1998. "Fasting and Feasting: Paradoxes of the Sport Ethic." *Sociology of Sport Journal*, 15: 41–63.

Johns, D.P. and J.S. Johns. 2000. "Surveillance, Subjectivism and Technologies of Power." *International Review for the Sociology of Sport*, 35(2): 219–234.

Johnson, Benton. 1975. *Functionalism in Modern Sociology: Understanding Talcott Parsons*. Morristown, NJ: General Learning Press.

Johnson, Laurie M. 1993. *Thucydides, Hobbes, and the Interpretation of Realism*. DeKalb, IL: Northern Illinois University Press.

Jones, S.G. Stedman. 1995. "Charles Renouvier and Emile Durkheim." *Sociological Perspectives*, 38(1): 27–40.

Kalberg, Stephen. 1980. "Max Weber's Types of Rationality: Cornerstones for the Analysis of Rationalization Processes in History." *American Journal of Sociology*, 85:1145–1179.

Kallen, Horace. 1953. *The Philosophy of William James: Selected From His Chief Works*. New York: Modern Library.

Kallen, Horace. 1956. *The Social Dynamics of George H. Mead*. Washington, DC: Public Affairs Press.

Kasler, Dirk. 1988. *Max Weber: An Introduction to His Life and Work*. Chicago: University of Chicago Press.

Kaufman, Michael. 2003. "Robert K. Merton, Versatile Sociologist and Father of the Focus Group, Dies at 92." *New York Times*. February 24.

Kellner, Douglas. 1977. *Karl Korsch: Revolutionary Theory*. Austin: University of Texas Press.

Kellner, Douglas. 1983. "Expressionism and Rebellion," pp. 3–39 in *Passion and Rebellion*, edited by Stephen Eric Bronner and Douglas Kellner. New York: Universe Books.

Kellner, Douglas. 1984. *Herbert Marcuse and the Crisis of Marxism*. Berkeley: University of California Press.

Kellner, Douglas. 1989a. *Critical Theory, Marxism, and Modernity*. Baltimore: John Hopkins University Press.

Kellner, Douglas. 1989b. *Jean Baudrillard: From Marxism to Post Modernism and Beyond*. Stanford, CA: Stanford University Press.

Kellner 1990: 14-15; 15. Kellner, Douglas. 1990. Television and the Crisis of Democracy. Boulder, CO: Westview.

Kellner, Douglas. 2002. "Theorizing Globalization." *Sociological Theory*, 20 (3):285–305.

Kellner, Douglas. 2003. "Herbert Marcuse." Available: www.uta.edu/huma/illuminations/kellner.

Kellner, Douglas. 2005. *Media Spectacle and the Crisis of Democracy: Terrorism, War, and Election Battles*. Boulder, CO: Paradigm.

Kellner, Douglas. 2008. *Guys and Guns Amok: Domestic Terrorism and School Shootings from the Oklahoma City Bombings to the Virginia Tech Massacre*. Boulder, CO: Paradigm.

Kellner, Douglas. 2009. *Cinema Wars: Hollywood Film and Politics in the Bush-Cheney Era*. New York: Wiley-Blackwell.

Kellner, Douglas. 2011. "Fredric Jameson." Available: http://gseis.ucla.edu/faculty/kellner/papers/JamesonJH.htm

Kellner, Douglas and Tyson Lewis. 2007. "Cultural Critique," pp. 896–898 in *The Blackwell Encyclopedia of Sociology*, edited by George Ritzer. Oxford: Blackwell.

Kelton Research and Support. 2008. "News & Information." Available: http://sev.prnewswire.com/computer-electronics.

Kemper, Theodore D. and Randall Collins. 1990. "Dimensions of Microreintation." *American Journal of Sociology*. 96 (1):32–68.

Kenny, Robert Wade. 2010. "Beyond the Elementary Forms of Moral Life: Reflexivity and Rationality in Durkheim's Moral Theory." *Sociological Theory*, 28(2): 215–244.

Kerr, Keith. 2009. *Postmodern Cowboy*, foreword by Stjepan Mestrovic. Boulder, CO: Paradigm.

Kuhn, Thomas. 1962, *The Structure of Scientific Revolutions.* Chicago: University of Chicago Press.

Kivisto, Peter. 1998. *Key Ideas in Sociology.* Thousand Oaks, CA: Pine Forge Press.

Knight, Denise. 1997. *Charlotte Perkins Gilman.* New York: Twayne.

Knoke, David. 1990. *Political Networks.* Cambridge: University Press.

Kornblum, William. 1994. *Sociology,* 3rd edition. Fort Worth, TX: Harcourt Brace.

Korsch, Karl. 1971. *Marxism and Philosophy.* New York: Monthly Review Press.

Kramer, Roderick and Karen Cook (Eds.). 2004. *Trust and Distrust in Organizations: Emerging Perspectives.* New York: Russell Sage Foundation.

Krantz, Matt and Barbara Hansen. 2011. "CEO Pay Soars While Workers' Pay Stalls." *USA Today,* April 4. Available: http://www.usatoday.com/money/companies/management/2011-03-31-ceo-pay-2010.htm#

La Capra, Dominick. 1972. *Emile Durkheim: Sociologist and Philosopher.* Ithaca, NY: Cornell University Press.

Lachmann, L.M. 1971. *The Legacy of Max Weber.* Berkley: Glendessary Press.

Lawrence, P. A. 1976. *George Simmel: Sociologist and European.* New York: Barnes & Noble.

Lawson, David M. 2003. "Incidence, Explanations, and Treatment of Partner Violence." *Journal of Counseling & Development,* 81(1), Winter: 19–32.

Lemert, Charles. 1997. *Postmodernism is Not What You Think.* Malden, MA: Blackwell.

Lemert, Charles C. and Garth Gillan. 1982. *Michel Foucault: Social Theory and Transgression.* New York: Columbia University Press.

Lengermann, Patricia Madoo, and Jill Niebrugge-Brantley. 1998. *The Women Founders.* Boston: McGraw Hill.

Lengermann, Patricia Madoo, and Jill Niebrugge-Brantley. 2000. "Early Women Sociologists and Classical Sociological Theory: 1830–1930," pp. 289–321, in *Classical Sociological Theory,* written by George Ritzer. Boston: McGraw Hill.

Lenin, Vladimir. 1896. "Biographical Article on Friedrich Engels," in *Collected Works.* Moscow: Progress.

Levin, William C. 1991. *Sociological Ideas,* 3rd ed. Belmont, CA: Wadsworth.

Levine, Daniel. 1971. *Jane Addams and the Liberal Tradition.* Madison, WI: State Historical Society of Wisconsin.

Levine, Donald. 1971. *Georg Simmel.* Chicago: University of Chicago Press.

Lichtheim, George. 1970. *A Short History of Socialism.* New York: Prager.

Lindersmith, Alfred R., Anselm L. Strauss, and Norman K. Denzin. 1991. *Social Psychology,* 7th edition. Englewood Cliffs, NJ: Prentice Hall.

Lindsey, Linda. 1990. *Gender Roles: A Sociological Perspective.* Englewood Cliffs, NJ: Prentice Hall.

Lindsey, Linda L. and Stephen Beach. 2003. *Essentials of Sociology.* Upper Saddle River, NJ: Prentice Hall.

Lindsey, Linda L. and Stephen Beach. 2004. *Sociology.* Upper Saddle River, NJ: Prentice Hall.

Lipshires, Sidney. 1974. *Herbert Marcuse: From Marx to Freud and Beyond.* Cambridge, MA: Schenkman.

Livingston, Eric. 1986. *The Ethnomethodological Foundations of Mathematics.* London: Routledge and Kegan Paul.

Lo, Ming-Cheng M. and Yun Fan. 2010. "Hybrid Cultural Codes in Nonwestern Civil Society: Images of Women in Taiwan and Hong Kong." *Sociological Theory,* 28(2): 167–192.

Locke, John. 1967 [1690]. *Two Treatises of Government: A Critical Edition,* introduction by Peter Laslett. London: Cambridge.

Locke, John. 1975 [1690]. *Essay Concerning Human Understanding,* edited with an Introduction by Peter H. Nidditch. New York: Oxford University Press.

Locke, John. 1991 [1689]. *Letter Concerning Toleration,* translated by William Popple. London: Routledge.

Lopreato, Joseph. 1967. "Class Conflict and Images of Society." *The Journal of Conflict Resolution.* 11 (3):281–293.

Lowith, Karl. 1982. *Max Weber and Karl Marx,* edited with an Introduction by Tom Bottomore and William Outhwaite; translated by Hans Fantel. London: George Allen & Unwin.

Lukacs, Georg. 1923. *History and Class Consciousness.* Berlin: Malik Verlag.

Lukes, Steven. 1972. *Emile Durkheim: His Life and Work.* New York: Harper & Row.

Lukes, Steven. 2008. "Zero Confidence." *New Humanist,* November/December: 10–11.

Luhmann, Niklas. 1983. "Insistence on Systems Theory: Perspectives From Germany—An Essay." *Social Forces.* 61 (June):987–996.

Luhmann, Niklas. 1984. "The Self-Description of Society: Crisis Fashion and Sociological Theory." *International Journal of Comparative Sociology*, 25 (Jan/Apr):59–72.

Lynchehaun, Ross. 2011. "Cinema Wars: Hollywood Film and Politics in the Bush-Cheney Era." *Screen*, 52(1): 128–131.

Lyotard, Jean-Francois. 1979. *The Postmodern Condition: A Report on Knowledge*. Minneapolis: University of Minnesota Press.

Lyotard, Jean-Francois. 1992. "Mainmise." *Philosophy Today*, (Winter):419–427.

Lyotard, Jean-Francois. 1993. *The Postmodern Explained*. Minneapolis: University of Minnesota Press.

Lyotard, Jean-Francois. 1999 [1984]. *The Postmodern Condition: A Report on Knowledge*. Minneapolis: University of Minnesota Press.

Machiavelli, Niccolo Machiavelli. 2006 [1532]. *The Prince*, translated by W.K. Marriott. The Project Gutenberg EBook. Available: http://www.gutenberg.org/files/1232/1232-h/1232-h.htm.

Mackinnon, Catherine A. 1982. "Feminism, Marxism, Method and the State: An Agenda for Theory." *Signs*, 7:515–544.

MacIntyre, Alasdair. 1970a. *Herbert Marcuse*. New York: Viking.

MacIntyre, Alasdair. 1970b. *Marcuse*. Bungay, Suffolk, Great Britain: Fontana.

Macrae, Donald. 1974. *Max Weber*. New York: Viking.

Malinowski, Bronislaw. 1926. *Crime and Custom in Savage Society*. London: Routledge and Kegan Paul.

Mallard, Gregoire. 2011. "*The Gift* Revisited: Marcel Mauss on War, Debt, and the Politics of Reparation." Sociological Theory, 29(4): 225–247.

Malthus, Thomas. 1798. *An Essay on the Principle of Population*. London. (Available: http://www.esp.org/books/malthus/population/malthus.pdf)

Mannheim, Karl. 1936. *Ideology and Utopia*. New York: Harvest Books.

Manning, Philip. 1992. *Erving Goffman and Modern Sociology*. Sanford, CA: Stanford University Press.

Maps of World. 2008. "Top Ten Poorest Countries." Available: http://www.mapsofworld.com/world-top-ten/world-top-tenj-poorest-countries-map.html.

Marcuse, Herbert. 1960. "Activity of Dialectic." *Diogenes*. 31:80–88.

Marcuse, Herbert. 1964. *One-Dimensional Man*. Boston: Beacon Press.

Marcuse, Herbert. 1966. *Eros and Civilization*. Boston: Beacon Press.

Marcuse, Herbert. 1968a. *Negations*. Boston: Beacon Press.

Marcuse, Herbert. 1968b. "Re-examination of the Concept of Revolution." *Diogenes*. 64:17–26.

Marcuse, Herbert. 1969. *Essay of Liberation*. Boston: Beacon Press.

Marcuse, Herbert. 1972. *Studies in Critical Philosophy*. Boston: Beacon Press.

Marcuse, Herbert. 1989. "Philosophy and Critical Theory," pp. 58–74 in *Critical Theory and Society*, edited with an Introduction by Stephen Eric Bronner and Douglas Kellner. New York: Routledge.

Mariani, John. 2011. "Protesters Decry Business Breaks." *The Post-Standard*. April 19: A–8.

Marilley, Suzanne M. 1996. *Woman Suffrage and the Origins of Liberal Feminism in the United States, 1820–1920*. Cambridge, MA: Harvard University Press.

Markula, Pirkko. 2003. "The Technologies of the Self: Sport, Feminism, and Foucault." *Sociology of Sport Journal*, 20 (2):87–107.

Martin, Bill. 1992. *Matrix and Line*. Albany: State University of New York Press.

Martindale, Don. 1981. *The Nature and Types of Sociological Theory*. Boston: Houghton Mifflin Harcourt.

Martindale, Don. 1988. *The Nature and Types of Sociological Theory*. Prospect Heights, IL: Waveland Press.

Martineau, Harriet. 1822 "Female Writers on Practical Divinity." *Monthly Repository*, 17:593–96.

Martineau, Harriet. 1832–34. *Illustrations of Political Economy*. 9 vols. London: Charles Fox.

Martineau, Harriet. 1836–37. *Society in America*, 2 vols. New York: Saunders and Otley.

Martineau, Harriet. 1838. *How to Observe Morals and Manners*. London: Charles Knight and Company.

Martineau, Harriet. 1841a. *The Hour and the Man: An Historical Romance*, 3 vols. London: Cassell.

Martineau, Harriet. 1841b. *The Playfellow*, 4 vols. London: Charles Knight and Company.

Martineau, Harriet. 1844. *Life in the Sick-Room: Essays by an Invalid*. London: Edward Moxon.

Martineau, Harriet. 1845. *Letters on Mesmerism*. London: Edward Moxon.

Martineau, Harriet. 1848. *Eastern Life: Past and Present*, 3 vols. London: Edward Moxon.

Martineau, Harriet. 1852. *Letters From Ireland*. London: John Chapman.

Martineau, Harriet. 1853. *The Positive Philosophy of Auguste Comte, Freely Translated and Condensed by Harriet Martineau*. London: John Chapman.

Martineau, Harriet. 1859. "Female Industry." *Edinburgh Review*. 109:293–336.

Martineau, Harriet. 1877. *Harriet Martineau's Autobiography, with Memorials by Maria Westin Chapman*, 3 vols. London: Elder.

Martineau, Harriet, and Henry George Atkinson. 1851. *Letters on the Laws of Man's Nature and Development*. London: John Chapman.

Marx, Eleanor. 1897. "Biographical Comments on Karl Marx." *Neue Zeit*, Vol.1.

Marx, Karl. 1852. *The 18th Brumaire of Louis Bonaparte*. Online version available: http://www.marxists.org/archive/marx/works/1852/18th-brumaire/.

Marx, Karl. 1964 [1844]. *The Economic & Philosophic Manuscripts of 1844*, edited by Dirk Strunk. New York: International Publishers.

Marx, Karl, and Friedrich Engels. 1978. "Manifesto of the Communist Party," pp. 469–500 in *The Marx and Engels Reader*, edited by Robert Tucker. New York: Norton.

Marx, Karl, and Friedrich Engels. 1980. *Collected Works*. New York: International Publishers.

Mauss, Marcel. 2005 [1924]. *The Gift*. Abingdon, Oxon: Routledge.

Mazlish, Bruce. 1993. *A New Science: The Breakdown of Connections and the Birth of Sociology*. University Park, PA: Pennsylvania State University Press.

McClay, Wilfred M. 2009. "David Riesman and the *Lonely Crowd*." *Society*, 46 (Spring): 21–28.

McCormick, Peter and Frederick A. Elliston, editors. 1981. *Husserl: Shorter Works*. Notre Dame, IN: Notre Dame University Press.

McLellan, David. 1969. *The Young Hegelians and Karl Marx*. New York: Macmillan.

McLellan, David. 1987. *Marxism and Religion*. New York: Harper and Row.

McLellan, David. 1990. *Karl Marx: Selected Writings*. Oxford: Oxford Press.

McPhail, Clark and Cynthia Rexroat. 1979. "Mead vs. Blumer: The Divergent Methodological Perspectives of Social Behaviorism and Symbolic Interaction." *American Sociological Review*. 44 (3):449–467.

Mead, George Herbert. 1936. *Movements of Thought in the Nineteenth Century*. Chicago: University of Chicago Press.

Mead, George Herbert. 1938. *The Philosophy of the Act*. Chicago: University of Chicago Press.

Mead, George Herbert. 1959. *The Philosophy of the Present*. LaSalle, IL: Open Court.

Mead, George Herbert. 1962 [1934]. *Mind, Self & Society: From the Standpoint of a Social Behaviorist*, edited and with introduction by Charles W. Morris. Chicago: University of Chicago Press.

Mead, George Herbert. 1964. *Selected Writings*, edited by Andrew Reck. Indianapolis, IN: Bobbs-Merrill.

Mead, George Herbert. 1964. *On Social Psychology*, edited by Anselm Strauss. Chicago: University Press.

Mead, George Herbert. 1982. *The Individual and the Social Self: Unpublished Work of George Herbert Mead*. Chicago: University of Chicago Press.

Merton, Robert K. 1938. "Social Structure and Anomie." *American Sociological Review*. 3:672–682.

Merton, Robert K. 1968 [1949]. *Social Theory and Social Structure*. New York: Free Press.

Merton, Robert K. 1957a. "Priorities in Scientific Discovery: A Chapter in the Sociology of Science." *American Sociological Review*. 22 (6):635–659.

Merton, Robert K. 1957b. "The Role Set: Problems in Sociological Theory." *British Journal of Sociology*. 2:106–120.

Merton, Robert K. 1957c. "Social Structure and Anomie." *American Sociological Review*. 22 (6):672–682.

Merton, Robert K. 1959. "Social Conformity Deviation and Opportunity—Structure." *American Sociological Review*. 24: 177–189.

Merton, Robert K. 1987. "The Focused Interview and Focus Groups: Continuities and Discontinuities." *Public Opinion Quarterly*. 51 (4):550–565.

Merton, Robert K. 1996 [1994]. "A Life of Learning," pp. 339–359 in *Robert K. Merton: On Social Structure and Science*, edited by Piotr Sztompka. Chicago: University Press.

Merton, Robert K. 1995. "The Thomas Theorem and the Matthew Effect." *Social Forces*, 74 (2): 379–424.

Merton, Robert K. 1997. "On the Evolving Synthesis of Differential Association and Anomie Theory: A Perspective from the Sociology of Science." *Criminology*, 35 (3):517–523.

Merton, Robert K., Alisa P. Gray, Barbara Hockey, and Hanan C. Selvin, editors. 1952. *Reader in Bureaucracy.* New York: Free Press.

Mestrovic, Stjepan G. 1988. *Emile Durkheim and the Reformation of Sociology.* Totowa, NJ: Rowman and Littlefield.

Meyer, Lois. 1985. *Making a Scene: Probing the Structure of Language in Sibling Interaction.* Unpublished manuscript. University of California, Berkeley.

Meyer, Lois. 1988. "It was No Trouble: Achieving Communicative Competence in a Second Language," pp. 195–221 in *Developing Communicative Competence in a Second Language,* edited by Robin Scarcella, Elain Anderson and Stephen Krashin. New York: Newbury House.

Michelmore, Bill. 2000. "Cataracts Big Suicide Lure." *Buffalo News.* May 1:A1.

Miller, David. 1973. *George Herbert Mead; Self, Language, and the World.* Austin: University of Texas Press.

Miller, James. 1993. *The Passion of Michel Foucault.* New York: Anchor.

Miller, S.M. 1963. *Max Weber.* New York: Crowell.

Mills, C. Wright. 1948. *The New Men of Power.* New York: Harcourt, Brace and Jovanovich.

Mills, C. Wright. 1956. *The Power Elite.* New York: Oxford University Press.

Mills, C. Wright. 1958. *The Causes of World War Three.* New York: Simon & Schuster.

Mills, C. Wright. 1959. *The Sociological Imagination.* New York: Oxford University Press.

Mills, C. Wright. 1958b. "The Structure of Power in American Society." *British Journal of Sociology,* 9(1): 29–41.

Mills, C. Wright. 1962. *The Marxists.* New York: Dell.

Mills, C. Wright. 2002. "The Promise," pp. 1–7 in Mapping the Social Landscape, edited by Susan J. Ferguson. Boston: McGraw Hill.

Mirchandani, Rekha. 2005. "Postmodernism and Sociology: From the Epistemological to the Empirical." *Sociological Theory,* 23(1): 86–115.

Mitchell, J. Clyde. 1974. "Social Networks." *Annual Review of Anthropology,* 3: 279–99.

Molm, Linda and Karen Cook. 1995. "Social Exchange and Exchange Networks," pp. 209–235 in *Sociological Perspectives in Social Psychology,* edited by K.S. Cook, G.A. Fine, and J. House. Boston: Allyn and Bacon.

Molm, Linda, David R. Schaefer and Jessica L. Collett. 2009. "Fragile and Resilient Trust: Risk and Uncertainty in Negotiated and Reciprocal Exchange." *Sociological Theory,* 27(1): 1–32.

Mommsen, Wolfgang, and Jurgen Osterhammel, editors. 1987. *Max Weber and His Contemporaries.* Boston: Allen & Unwin.

Morrow, Raymond A. with David D. Brown. 1994. *Critical Theory and Methodology.* Thousand Oaks, CA: Sage.

Moses, Sarah. 2011. "Superintendents Resist Pay Cap." *The Post-Standard,* March 15:A-1, A-6.

Moya, Paula M.L. 2001. "Chicana Feminism and Post Modernist Theory." *Signs,* 26 (2): 441–483.

Muggeridge, Kitty, and Ruth Adam. 1968. *Beatrice Webb.* New York: Knopf.

Mukerji, Chandra. 2010. "The Territorial State as a Figured World of Power: Strategies, Logistics and Impersonal Rule." *Sociological Theory,* 28 (4): 402–424.

National Coalition on Health Care. 2009. "Health Insurance Costs." Available: http://www.nchc.org/facts/cost.shtml.

National Health Care Anti-Fraud Association. 2009. "What is Health Care Fraud?" Available: http://www.nhcaa.org/eweb/DynamicPage.aspx?webcode=anti_fraud_resource_centr&wpscode=ConsumerAndActionInfo.

Nemedi, Denes. 1995. "Collective Consciousness, Morphology, and Collective Representations: Durkheim's Sociology of Knowledge, 1894–1900." *Sociological Perspectives,* 38(1): 41–56.

Nicholson, Carol. 1989. "Postmodernism, Feminism, and Education: The Need for Solidarity." *Educational Theory,* 39 (3):197–205.

Nisbet, Robert. 1974. *The Sociology of Emile Durkheim.* New York: Oxford University Press.

Nord, Deborah Epstein. 1985. *The Apprenticeship of Beatrice Webb.* Amherst, MA: The University of Massachusetts Press.

Norris, Christopher. 1990. *What's Wrong with Postmodernism.* Baltimore: Johns Hopkins University Press.

Ollman, Bertell. 1976. *Alienation,* 2nd edition. Cambridge MA: University Press.

On Campus. 2011(March/April). "Defending Public Services." 30(4): 8–10.

Orloff, Ann Shola. 2005. "Social Provision and Regulation: Theories of States, Social Policies and Modernity," pp. 190–224 in *Remaking Modernity: Politics, History, and Sociology,* edited by J. Adams, E.S. Clemens, and A.S. Orloff. Durham, NC: Duke University Press.

Orloff, Ann Shola. 2009. "Gendering the Comparative Analysis of Welfare States: An Unfinished Agenda." *Sociological Theory*, 27(3): 317–343.

Palmer, Joy A., editor. 2001. *Fifty Modern Thinkers on Education: From Piaget to the Present*. London: Rutledge.

Pampel, Fred. 2000. *Sociological Lines and Ideas*. New York: Worth Publishers.

Paretskaya, Anna. 2010. "The Soviet Communist Party and the Other Spirit of Capitalism." *Sociological Theory*, 28(4): 377–401.

Parsons, Talcott. 1942. "Some Sociological Aspects of the fascist Movements." *Social Forces*, 21:138–147.

Parsons, Talcott. 1949 [1937]. *The Structure of Social Action*. Glencoe, IL: Dorsey Press.

Parsons, Talcott. 1951. *The Social System*. Glencoe, IL: Free Press.

Parsons, Talcott. 1954. *Essays in Sociological Thought*. Glencoe, IL: Free Press.

Parsons, Talcott. 1956a. "A Sociological Approach to the Theory of Organizations I." *Administrative Science Quarterly*. June: 63–85.

Parsons, Talcott. 1956b. "A Sociological Approach to the Theory of Organizations II." *Administrative Science Quarterly*. Sept: 225–239.

Parsons, Talcott. 1965 [1960]. *Structure and Process in Modern Societies*. New York: Free Press.

Parsons, Talcott. 1964. *Social Structure and Personality*. New York: Free Press.

Parsons, Talcott. 1966. *Societies*. Englewood Cliffs, NJ: Prentice Hall.

Parsons, Talcott. 1969. *Politics and Social Structure*. New York: Free Press.

Parsons, Talcott. 1971. *The System of Modern Sociology*. Englewood Cliffs, NJ: Prentice Hall.

Parsons, Talcott and Robert Bales. 1955. *Family, Socialization and Interaction*. Glencoe, IL: Free Press.

Parsons, Talcott, Robert F. Bales and Edward A. Shils. 1953. *Working Papers in the Theory of Action*. Glencoe, IL: The Free Press.

Parsons, Talcott and Gerald Platt. 1973. *The American University*. Cambridge, Mass: Harvard University Press.

Parsons, Talcott and Neil Smelser. 1956. *Economy and Society*. New York: Free Press.

Patterson, Orlando. 2002. "The Last Sociologist." *New York Times*, May 19:15.

Peel, J.D.Y. 1971. *Herbert Spencer: The Evolution of a Sociologist*. New York: Basic.

Perrin, Andrew. 2003. "Lewis Coser Remembered." *ASA Footnotes* (Sept/Oct). Available: http://www.asanet.org/footnotes/septoct03/indexthree.html.

Perrin, Andrew and Lars Jarkko. 2005. "Opinion Research and Publicness." *Sociological Theory*, 23(1) (March): 116–123.

Perrow, Charles. 1986. *Complex Organizations*, 3rd edition. New York: Random House.

Pfuetz, Paul. 1954. *Self, Society and Existence; Human Nature and Dialogue in the Thoughts of George Herbert Mead and Martin Buber*. New York: Harper Torch Books.

Pichanick, Valerie Kossew. 1980. *Harriett Martineau: The Women and Her Work, 1802–76*. Ann Arbor, MI: The University of Michigan Press.

Pickering, Mary. 1993. *Auguste Comte: An Intellectual Biography*, Vol.1. Cambridge: Cambridge University Press.

Pickering, Mary. 2000. "Auguste Comte," pp. 25–52 in *The Blackwell Companion to Major Social Theories*, edited by George Ritzer. Malden, MA: Blackwell.

Platt, Jennifer. 1995. "The United States Reception of Durkheim's *The Rules of Sociological Method*." 38(1): 77–105.

Poggi, Gianfranco. 2006. *Weber: A Short Introduction*. Malden, MA: Polity Press.

Poole, Steven. 2007. "Jean Baudrillard: Philosopher and Sociologist who Blurred the Boundaries between Reality and Simulation." Guardian.co.uk, March 7. Available: http://www.guardian.co.uk/news/2007/mar/07/guardianobituaries.france.

Popkewitz, Thomas and Lynn Fendler, editors. 1999. *Critical Theories in Education*. New York: Routledge.

Porter, Theodore M. 1995. "Statistical and Social Facts From Quetelet to Durkheim." 38(1): 15–26.

Pressler, Charles and Fabio Dasilua. 1996. *Sociology and Interpretation: From Weber to Habermas*. Albany: State University of New York Press.

Radice, Lisanne. 1984. *Beatrice and Sidney Webb: Fabian Socialists*. New York: St. Martin's Press.

Raison, Timothy, editor. 1969. *The Founding Fathers of Social Science*. Baltimore, MD: Penguin.

Rammstedt, Otthein. 1991. "On Simmel's Aesthetics: Argumentation in the Journal *Jugend*, 1897–1906." *Theory, Culture, and Society.* 8:125–144.

Rasmussen, David M. 1990. *Reading Habermas.* Cambridge, MA: Blackwell.

Reck, Andrew. 1964. *Selective Writings; George Herbert Mead.* Chicago: University of Chicago Press.

Riesman, David. 1951. "Some Observation of Social Science Research." *Antioch Review*, S51(11):259–278.

Riesman, David with Nathan Glazer and Reuel Denney. 2001 [1950]. *The Lonely Crowd*, foreword by Todd Gitlin. New Haven, CT: Yale University Press.

Riesman, David, with Nathan Glazer. 1952. *Faces in the Crowd.* New Haven, CT: Yale University Press.

Reynolds, Larry. 1990. *Interactionism; Exposition and Critique*, 2nd ed. Dix Hills, NY: General Hall.

Rich, Adrienne. 1976. *Of Women Born: Motherhood as Experience and Institution.* Cambridge, MA: Harvard University Press.

Riley, Alexander Tristan. 2002. "Durkheim Contra Bergson? The Hidden Roots of Postmodern Theory and the Postmodern Return of the Sacred." *Sociological Perspectives*, 45(3):243–265.

Risman, Barbara. 1986. "Can Men 'Mother'?: Life as a Single Father." *Family Relations*, 35:95–102.

Risman, Barbara. 1988. "Just the Two of Us: Parent-Child Relationships in Single-Parent Homes." *Journal of Marriage and the Family*, 50:1049–1062.

Risman, Barbara. 1998. *Gender Vertigo: American Families in Transition.* New Haven, CT: Yale University Press.

Ritzer, George. 2000. *Sociological Theory*, 5th edition. Boston: McGraw Hill.

Ritzer, George. 2000b. *Classical Social Theory*, 3rd edition. Boston: McGraw Hill.

Ritzer, George. 2000c. *The McDonaldization of Society*, New Century Edition. Thousand Oaks, CA: Pine Forge Press.

Ritzer, George. 2010. *Contemporary Sociological Theory and Its Classical Roots: The Basics*, 3rd edition. Boston: McGraw Hill.

Ritzer, George. 2011. *Sociological Theory*, 8th edition. Boston: McGraw Hill.

Roberts, Cokie and Steven V. Roberts. 2011. "Women are Still Waiting for Equality." Syndicated column (as it appeared in *The Citizen* newspaper, Auburn, NY), December 30: A1.

Robillard, Albert B. and Christopher Pack. 1976–1982. Research and didactic videotapes, occasional papers, in-house memoranda, tape and video recorded rounds and medical and clinic conferences, and lectures. Department of Human Development, Michigan State University.

Robinson, Laura. 2010. "The Cyberself: The Self-ing Project Goes Online, Symbolic Interaction in the Digital Age." *New Media & Society*, 9(1): 93–110.

Robinson, Shirleene. 2011. "Inventing Australia for Americans: The Rise of the *Outback Steakhouse* Restaurant Chain in the USA." *The Journal of Popular Culture*, 44(3): 545–562.

Roche de Coppens, Peter. 1976. *Ideal Man in Classical Theory: The Views of Comte, Durkheim, Pareto, and Weber.* London: Pennsylvania State University Press.

Rogers, Mary F. 1983. *Sociology, Ethnomethodology, and Experience.* New York: Cambridge University Press.

Rogow, Arnold A. 1986. *Thomas Hobbes: Radical in the Service of Reaction.* New York: Norton.

Rose, Peter. 1981. *They and We*, 3rd ed. New York: Random House.

Ross, Emma. 2002. "Husbands, Too, May Be Suffering, Study Suggests." *Buffalo News.* October 5:A2.

Ruane, Joseph and Jennifer Todd. 1988. "The Application of Critical Theory." *Political Studies*, 36:533–538.

Rubel, Maximilien and Margaret Manale. 1975. *Marx Without Myth: A Chronological Study of His Life and Work.* New York: Harper & Row.

Rude, George. 1988. *The French Revolution.* New York: Weidenfeld & Nicholson.

Ruelas, Richard. 2011. "Tucson Shooting Victim Honored by Angel Statue." *USA Today*, April 2. Available: http://www.usatoday.com/news/nation/2011-04-01-tucson-victim-honored_N.htm#.

Ryan, John and William Wentworth. 1999. *Media and Society.* Boston: Allyn and Bacon.

Sabine, George. 1965. *A History of Political Theory.* New York: Holt, Rinehart & Winston.

Sacks, Harvey. 1992. *Lectures on Conversation.* New York: Blackwell.

Saito, Hiro. 2011. "An Actor-Network Theory of Cosmopolitanism." *Sociological Theory*, 29(2): 124–149.

Scharff, Robert. 1995. *Comte After Positivism.* New York: Cambridge.

Scheffler, Israel. 1974. *Four Pragmatists: A Critical Introduction to Pierce, James, Mead, and Dewey.* New York: Humanities Press.

Schegloff, Emmanuel. 1979. "Identification and Recognition in Telephone Conversation Openings, pp. 23–78 in *Language: Studies in Ethnomethodology*, edited by G. Psathas. New York: Irvington.

Schellenberg, James. 1978. *Masters of Social Psychology.* New York: Oxford University Press.

Schiller, Friedrich. 1967. *On the Aesthetic Education of Man in a Series of Letters*, edited by Wilkinson and Willoughby. New York: Oxford Press.

Schluchter, Wolfgang. 1981. *The Rise of Western Rationalism: Max Weber's Developmental History.* Berkley: University of California Press.

Schmaus, Warren. 1995. "Explanation and Essence in *The Rules of Sociological Method* and *The Division of Labor in Society*." *Sociological Perspectives*, 38(1): 57–75.

Schmidt, Emerson P., editor. 1937. *Man and Society: A Substantive Introduction to the Social Sciences.* New York: Prentice Hall.

Schmitt, Richard. 1987. *Introduction to Marx and Engels: A Critical Reconstruction.* Boulder, CO: Westview.

Schrag, Calvin O. 1997. *The Self After Postmodernity.* New Haven CT: Yale University Press.

Schutz, Alfred. 1962 [1932]. *Collected Papers.* The Hague: Marinus Nijhoff.

Schutz, Alfred. 1967. *The Phenomenology of the Social World*, introduction by George Walsh. Evanston, IL: Northwestern University Press.

Schutz, Alfred and Thomas Luckmann. 1973. *The Structures of the Life-World*, translated by Richard M. Zaner and H. Tristram Engelhardt, Jr. Evanston, IL: Northwestern University Press.

Scimecca, Joseph. A. 1997. *The Sociological Theory of C. Wright Mills.* Port Washington, NY: Kennikat.

Scott, Susie and Charles Thorpe. 2006. "The Sociological Imagination of R. D. Laing." *Sociological Theory*, 24(4) (Dec.): 331–352.

Seef, Amanda. 2011. "Students to Hold Walk to Raise Awareness of Sexual Assault." WebsterPost.com. May 5. Available: http://www.websterpost.com/latestnews/x527528915/Students-to-hold-walk-to-raise-awareness-of-sexual-assault.

Seidman, Steven. 1983. *Liberalism and the Origins of European Social Theory.* Los Angeles: University Press.

Seidman, Steven. 1991 [1983]. *Liberalism and the Origins of European Social Theory.* Los Angeles: Norton.

Seinfeld. 1995. "The Label Maker." Episode # 98, first air date January 19.

Shalin, Dmitri 1986. "Pragmatism and Social Interactionism." *American Sociological Review.* 51:9–29.

Shalin, Dmitri. 1991. "The Pragmatic Origins of Symbolic Interactionism and the Crisis of Classical Science." *Studies in Symbolic Interaction*, 12:223–251.

Shalin, Dmitri. 1992. "Critical Theory and the Pragmatist Challenge." *American Journal of Sociology*, Vol. 98 (2) (Sept):237–79.

Shalin, Dmitri. 1993. "Modernity, Postmodernity, and Pragmatist Inquiry: An Introduction." *Symbolic Interaction*, 16 (4): 303–332.

Shalin, Dmitri. 2000. "George Herbert Mead," pp. 302–344 in *The Blackwell Companion to Major Social Theorists*, edited by George Ritzer. Malden, MA: Blackwell Publishers.

Sheehan, Thomas. 1981. "Husserl's Critique of Psychologism," pp.143–145 in *Husserl: Shorter Works*, edited by Peter McCormick and Fredrick A. Elliston. South Bend, IN: University of Notre Dame Press.

Shibutani, T. and K. Kwan. 1965. *Ethnic Stratification: A Comparative Approach.* New York: Macmillan.

Simmel, Georg. 1890. "Über soziale differenzierung." *Staats—und Sozialwissenschaftliche Sprachwissenschaft.* XX:6–46.

Simmel, Georg. 1893. "Moral Deficiencies as Determining Intellectual Functions." *International Journal of Ethics.* 111:490–507.

Simmel, Georg. 1895. "The Problem of Sociology." *Annals of the American Academy of Political and Social Science.* VI:412–23.

Simmel, Georg. 1896. "Friedrich Nietzsche: Eine Moral Philsophische Silhovette." *Seitschrift fur Philosphie und Philosophische Kritk.* CVII:202–05.

Simmel, Georg. 1896–97. "Superiority and Subordination as Subject-matter for Sociology." *American Journal of Sociology*, 167–89.

Simmel, Georg. 1897–99. "The Persistence of the Social Group." *American Journal of Sociology*, 662–98.

Simmel, Georg. 1900. *Philosophie des Geldes.* Leipzig: Duncker und Humblot.

Simmel, Georg. 1950 [1906]. "The Secret and the Secret Society," pp. 307–376 in *The Sociology of Georg Simmel*, edited and translated by K. Wolff. New York: Free Press.

Simmel, Georg. 1955 [1908]. *Conflict and the Web of Group Affiliates*. New York: Free Press.

Simmel, Georg. 1959 [1908]. "The Problem of Sociology," pp. 310–336 in *Essays in Sociology, Philosophy and Aesthetics*, edited by K. Wolff. New York: Harper Torch Books.

Simmel, Georg. 1964. "The Web of Group Affiliations," translated by Reinhard Bendix, edited by Kurt H. Wolff, Reinhard Bendix, *Simmel: Translation of Chapters from "Soziologie."* New York: The Free Press.

Simmel, Georg. 1965. *Makers of Modern Social Science*, edited by Lewis Coser. Englewood Cliffs, NJ: Prentice Hall.

Simmel, Georg. 1971 [1903]. "The Metropolis and Mental Life," pp. 324–339 in *George Simmel*, edited by D. Levine. Chicago: University of Chicago Press.

Simmel, Georg. 1971 [1904]. "Fashion," pp. 294–323 in *George Simmel*, edited by D. Levine. Chicago: University of Chicago Press.

Simmel, Georg. 1971 [1908]. "The Poor," pp. 150–178 in *Georg Simmel*, edited by D. Levine. Chicago: Chicago Press.

Simmel, Georg. 1971 [1908]. "The Stranger," pp. 143–199 in *Georg Simmel*, edited by D. Levine. Chicago: Chicago Press.

Simmel, Georg. 1978 [1907]. *The Philosophy of Money*, edited and translated by Tom Bottomore and David Frisby. London: Routledge.

Simmel, Georg. 2009. *Sociology: Inquiries into the Construction of Social Forms, Volume I*, translated by Anthony J. Blasi, Anton K. Jacobs and Mathew Kanjirathinkal, with an introduction by Horst J. Helle. Boston: Brill.

Simpson, George. 1969. *Auguste Comte: Sire of Sociology*. New York: Crowell.

Simpson, George. 1963. *Emile Durkheim*. New York: Crowell.

Simpson, Brent and David Willer. 2005. "The Structural Embeddedness of Collective Goods: Connection and Coalitions in Exchange Networks." *Sociological Theory*, 23(4): 386–407.

Singular Investor. 2012. "Top Ten Most Expensive Women's Handbags." Available: http://singularinvestor.hubpages.com/hub/Top-Ten-Most-Expensive-Womens-Handbags.

Skvoretz, John David Willer and Thomas J. Fararo. 1993. "Toward Models of Power Development in Exchange Networks." *Sociological Perspectives*. 36 (2):95–115.

Smelser, Neil J. 1966. *Social Structure and Mobility in Economic Development*. Chicago: Aldine.

Smelser, Neil J. 1998. "The Rational and the Ambivalent in Social Sciences." *American Sociological Review*. 63 (1):6.

Smith, Dorothy. 1979. "A Sociology for Women," in *The Prism of Sex: Essays in the Sociology of Knowledge*, edited by J.A. Sherman and E.T. Beck. Madison: University of Wisconsin Press.

Smith, Dorothy. 1987. *The Everyday World as Problematic: A Feminist Sociology*. Boston: Northeastern University Press.

Smith, Dorothy. 1990. *The Conceptual Practices of Power: A Feminist Sociology of Knowledge*. Boston, Northeastern University Press.

Smith, Dorothy. 1993. "The Standard North American Family." *Journal of Family Issue*. 14 (5):50–65.

Smith, Dorothy. 2000. "Schooling for Inequality." *Signs*, 25 (4): 1147–1151.

Smith, Preserved. 1962 [1934]. *A History of Modern Culture*. New York: Collier.

Smith, Steven B. 1987. "Hegel's Idea of a Critical theory." *Political Theory*, 15 (1):99–126.

Snyder, R. Claire. 2008. "What is Third-Wave Feminism?: A New Directions Essay." *Signs: Journal of Women in Culture and Society*, 34(1): 175–196.

So, Alvin, 1990. "Class Theory or Class Analysis? A Re-examination of Marx's Unfinished Chapter of Class." *Critical Sociology*. 17:35–55.

Spencer, Herbert. 1851. *Social Statics*. London: Chapman.

Spencer, Herbert. 1860. *The Social Organism*. London: Greenwood.

Spencer, Herbert. 1898. *Principles of Sociology*. New York: Appleton.

Spencer, Herbert. 1904. *An Autobiography*. New York: Appleton.

Spykman, Nicholas. 1965. *The Social Theory of Georg Simmel*. New York: Atherton.

Suchman, Lucy. 1987. *Plans and Situated Actions: The Problem of Human-Machine Communication*. New York: Cambridge University Press.

Sundow, David. 1978. *Ways of the Hand*. Cambridge, MA: Harvard University Press.

Stammer, Otto, editor. 1971. *Max Weber and Sociology Today*. New York: Harper & Row.

Standard & Poor's. 2011. "'AAA/A-1+' Rating on United States of America Affirmed; Outlook Revised to Negative." Available: http://www.standardandpoors.com/ratings/articles/en/us/?assetID=1245302886884.

Standley, Arline Reilein. 1981. *Auguste Comte*. Boston: Twayne.

Stayer, James M. 2000. *Martin Luther, German Saviour: German Evangelical Theological Factions and the Interpretation of Luther, 1917–1933*. Montreal: McGill-Queen's University Press.

Sterling, Dorothy. 1979. *Black Foremothers: Three Lives*. Old Westbury, NY: The Feminist Press.

Stone, Gregory P. 1962. "Appearance and the Self," pp.86–118 in *Human Behavior and Social Processes*, edited by Arnold Rose. Boston: Houghton Mifflin.

Stone, Gregory P. and Harvey A. Farberman. 1970. *Social Psychology Through Symbolic Interaction*. Waltham, MA: Ginn-Blaisdell.

Strathern, Paul. 2001. *Marx in 90 Minutes*. Chicago: Ivan R. Dee Publishing.

Strauss, Anselm. 1956. *The Social Psychology of George Herbert Mead*. Chicago: University Press.

Strauss, Anselm. 1964. *George Herbert Mead on Social Psychology: Selected Papers*. Chicago: University of Chicago Press.

Strenski, Ivan. 1997. *Durkheim and the Jews of France*. Chicago: University of Chicago Press.

Strydom, Piet. 2001. "The Problem of Triple Contingency in Habermas." *Sociological Theory*. 19 (2):165–186.

Stryker, Sheldon. 1987. "The Vitalization of Symbolic Interactionism." *Social Psychology Quarterly*. 50 (1):83–94.

SUNY. 2012. "SUNY Chancellor Nancy L. Zimpher: 'Systemness' To Drive Success in 2012." January 9. Available: http://www.suny.edu/sunynews/News.cfm?filname=2012-01-09-FINAL-SOU-RELEASE.htm.

Symonds, Michael and Jason Pudsey. 2006. "The Forms of Brotherly Love in Max Weber's Sociology of Religion." *Sociological Theory*, 24(2): 133–149.

Tanner, Adam. 2007. "Stripper Poles Pop Up in Homes as Exercise Tool." Reuters.com. Available: http://www.reuters.com/article/2007/08/23/us-poledancing-idUSN1624103720070823.

Tavory, Iddo. 2011. "The Question of Moral Action: A Formalist Position." *Sociological Theory*, 29(4):272–293.

Taylor, Jill McLean, Carol Gilligan and Amy M. Sullivan. 1995. *Between Voice and Silence*. Cambridge, MA: Harvard University Press.

Teel, David. 2010. "Virginia LAX Teams Seek Normalcy in Tournament." *The Post-Standard*, May 12: B-1.

Thayer, H. S. 1968. *Meaning and Action: A Critical History of Pragmatism*. New York: Bobbs-Merrill.

The Declaration of Independence. 1776. Available: http://www.ushistory.org/Declaration/document/index.htm.

The Citizen. 2011. "Legality of Assisted Suicide Varies Around the World." June 4: A9.

The Economist. 2009. "Big Mac Index." January 22. Available: http://www.economist.com/node/12991434.

The Economist. 2011. "Big Mac Index." May 31. Available: http://www.economist.com/markets/bigmac/about.cfm.

Theopedia Encyclopedia of Biblical Christianity. 2012. "Original Sin." Available: http://www.theopedia.com/Original_sin

The Post-Standard. 2004. "Still a Mystery." June 17: A-2.

The Post-Standard. 2011. "WTC Steel to Help Honor Shooting Victim." March 24: A-11.

The Southern Business Journal. 2011. "Need a McJob? McDonald's Hosting National Hiring Day April 19." Available: http://thesouthern.com/business/local/article_ffc9967a-62ef-11e0-8f15-001cc4c002e0.html.

Thibaut, John and Harold Kelley. 1959. *The Social Psychology of Groups*. New York: Wiley.

Thio, Alex. 2010. *Deviant Behavior*, 10th edition. Boston: Allyn & Bacon.

Thomas, Cal. 2011. "America's New Gilded Age," as it appeared in *The Post Standard*, April 6: A-14.

Thompson, Kenneth. 1975. *Auguste Comte: The Foundation of Sociology*. New York: Wiley & Sons.

Thompson, Kenneth. 1982. *Emile Durkheim*. London: Tavistock.

Thompson, Mildred I. 1990. *Ida B. Wells-Barnett: An Exploratory Study of an American Black Woman, 1893–1930*. Brooklyn, NY: Carlson.

Thomson, Garret. 1993. *Descartes to Kant*. Prospect Heights, IL: Waveland Press.

Time.com. 2011A. "Bouaziz: The Man Who Set Himself and Tunisia on Fire." January 21. Available: http://www.time.com/time/world/article/0,8599,2043557,00.html.

Timson, Judith. 2011. "Why Slut Walk Raises Hackles—and Hopes." *The Globe and Mail*, May 13: L3.

Tole, Lise Ann. 1993. "Durkheim on Religion and Moral Community in Modernity." *Sociological Inquiry*. 63:1–29.

Tong, Rosemarie. 1989. *Feminist Thought*. Boulder, CO: Westview Press.

Trevino, A. Javier. 2008. *The Sociology of Law: Classical and Contemporary Perspectives*. New Brunswick, NJ: Transaction.

Tucker, Robert, editor. 1978. *The Marx-Engels Reader*, 2nd edition. New York: Norton.

Turner, Bryan. 1990. *Theories of Modernity and Post-Modernity*. London: Sage.

Turner, Jonathan. 1973. "From Utopia to Where?: A Strategy for Reformulating the Dahrendorf Conflict Model." *Social Forces*. 52 (2) :236–244.

Turner, Jonathan H. 1974. The Structure of Sociological Theory. Homewood, IL: Dorsey Press.

Turner, Jonathan. 2003. *The Structure of Sociological Theory*, 7th edition. Belmont, CA: Wadsworth.

Turner, Stephen P. 1993. "The End of Functionalism." *Philosophy of the Social Science*. 23:228–242.

Turner, Stephen P. 1995. "Durkheim's *The Rules of Sociological Method*: Is It a Classic?" *Sociological Perspectives*, 38(1): 1–13.

United Press International. 2011. "Subway Passes McDonald's in Total Outlets." March 7. Available: http://www.upi.com/Business_News/2011/03/07/Subway-passes-McDonalds-in-total-outlets/UPI-33891299550287/

United States Census Bureau. 2011. "International Programs." Available: http://www.census.gov/population/international/data/idb/worldpopgraph.php.

United States Census Bureau. 2012. "About Poverty: Highlights." Available: http://www.census.gov/hhes/www/poverty/about/overview/

United States Constitution Online. 2011. "Declaration of Sentiments." Available: http://www.usconstitution.net/sentiments.html.

USA Today. 2012. "Military to Ease Rules on Women in Combat." January 9. Available: http://www.usatoday.com/news/washington/story/2012-02-08/war-women-pentagon/53017764/1

van den Berb, Axel. 1980. "Critical Theory; Is There Still Hope?" *American Journal of Sociology*. 86 (3):449–478.

Vital, David. 1999. *A People Apart: The Jews in Europe, 1789–1939*. New York: Oxford University Press.

Von Scheve, Christian. 2012. "The Social Calibration of Emotion Expression: An Affective Basis of Micro-social Order." *Sociological Theory*, 30(1): 1–14.

Wallace, David. 1967. "Reflection on the Education of George Herbert Mead." *American Journal of Sociology*. Vol. 72(4):396–408.

Wallace, Ruth A.; Wolf, Alison, *Contemporary Sociological Theory: Expanding The Classical Tradition*, 5th Ed., © 1999. Reprinted and electronically reproduced by permission of Pearson Education, Inc., Upper Saddle River, New Jersey.

Wallechinsky, David. 2007. "Is America Still No. 1?" *Parade*. January 14: 4–6.

Waters, Malcolm. 1995. *Globalization*. London: Routledge.

Weingartner, Rudolph. 1962. *Experience and Culture: The Philosophy of Georg Simmel*. Middletown, CT: Wesleyan University Press.

Webb, Beatrice Potter. 1891/1904. *The Co-operative Movement in Great Britain*. London: Swan, Sonnenschein and Company.

Webb, Beatrice Potter. 1926. *My Apprenticeship*. London: Longmans Green.

Webb, Beatrice Potter. 1982. *The Diary of Beatrice Webb*, Vol. 1, edited by Norman and Jeanne MacKenzie. Cambridge, MA: Harvard University Press.

Webb, Beatrice Potter. 1983. *The Diary of Beatrice Webb*, Vol. 2 Edited by Norman and Jeanne Mackenzie. Cambridge, MA: Harvard University Press.

Webb, Robert K. 1960. *Harriet Martineau: A Radical Victorian*. New York: Columbia University Press.

Weber, Bruce. 2011. "Harold Garfinkel, a Common-Sense Sociologist, Dies at 93." *The New York Times*, May 3. Available: http://search.aol.com/aol/search?s_it=topsearchbox.search&v_t=comsearch50ct5&q=Harold+Garfinkel.

Weber, Marianne. 1975 [1926]. *Max Weber: A Biography*, translated and edited by Harry Zohn. New York: Wiley & Sons.

Weber, Marianne. 1988. *Max Weber: A Biography*. New Brunswick, NJ: Transaction Books.

Weber, Marianne. 2003. "Authority and Autonomy in Marriage," translation with introduction and commentary by Craig R. Bermingham. *Sociological Theory*, 21 (2): 65–102.

Weber, Max 1946. *From Max Weber: Essays in Sociology*, translated and edited by H. Gerth and C. Wright Mills. New York: Oxford University Press.

Weber, Max. 1947. *The Theory of Social and Economic Organization*, translated by A. M. Parsons and T. Parsons. New York: Free Press.

Weber, Max. 1949 [1903–1917]. *The Methodology of the Social Sciences*, Edward Shils and Henry Rinch, editors. New York: Free Press.

Weber, Max. 1958 [1904–1905]. *The Protestant Ethic and the Spirit of Capitalism*. New York: Scribners.

Weber, Max. 1958 [1915]. "Religious Rejections of the World and Their Directions," pp. 323–359 in *From Max Weber: Essays in Sociology*, edited by H. Gerth and C. W. Mills. New York: Oxford University Press.

Weber, Max. 1958 [1916–1917]. *The Religion of India: The Sociology of Hinduism and Buddhism*. Glencoe, IL: Free Press.

Weber, Max. 1958 [1921]. *The Rational and Social Foundations of Music*. Carbondale: Southern Illinois University Press.

Weber, Max. 1963 [1921]. *The Sociology of Religion*. Boston: Beacon Press.

Weber, Max. 1964 [1916]. *The Religion of China: Confucianism and Taoism*. New York: Macmillan.

Weber, Max. 1964. *Basic Concepts in Sociology*. New York: Citadel Press.

Weber, Max. 1968 [1921]. *Economy and Society*, 3 vols. Totowa, NJ: Bedminstor Press.

Weber, Max. 1976 [1896–1906]. *The Agrarian Sociology of Ancient Civilizations*. London: NLB.

Weber, Max. 1976 [1903–1906]. *Roscher and Knies; The Logical Problems of Historical Economics*. New York: Free Press.

Weber, Max. 1978a. *Economy and Society*, edited by Guenter Roth and Claus Wittich. Berkley: University of California Press.

Weber, Max. 1978b. *Selections in Translation*, edited by W. Runciman, translated by Matthews. New York: Oxford University Press.

Weber, Max. 1985 [1906]. " 'Churches' and 'Sects' in North America: An Ecclesiastical Social-Political Sketch." *Sociological Theory*. 3:7–13.

Wells-Barnett, Ida. 1895. *A Red Record*. Chicago: Donohue and Henneberry.

Wells-Barnett, Ida. 1900/1969. "Mob Rule in New Orleans," reprinted in *On Lynchings*. New York: Arno Press.

Wells-Barnett, Ida. 1970. *Crusade for Justice: The Autobiography of Ida B. Wells*, edited by Alfreda M. Duston. Chicago: University of Chicago Press.

West, Candance and Sarah Fenstermaker. 1995. "Doing Gender." *Gender and Society*, 9:8–37.

West, Candace and Don H. Zimmerman. 2002. "Doing Gender," pp. 3–24 in *Doing Gender, Doing Difference: Inequality, Power, and Institutional Change*, edited by Sarah Fenstermaker and Candace West. New York: Routledge.

Westley, Frances. 1983. *The Complex Forms of Religious Life: A Durkheimian View of New Religious Movements*. Chico, CA: Scholars Press.

Whitmeyer, Joseph M. 2001. "Measuring Power in Exchange Networks." *Sociological Perspectives*. 44 (2):141–162.

Wieder, D. Lawrence. 1974. *Language and Social Reality*. The Hague: Mouton.

Willis, James J., Stephen D. Mastrofski, and David Weisburd. 2004. "COMPSTAT and Bureaucracy: A Case Study of Challenges and Opportunities for Change." *Justice Quarterly*, 21(3): 463–497.

Wolf, Naomi. 1991. *The Beauty Myth; How Images are Used Against Women*. New York: William Morrow.

Wolff, Kurt. 1950. *The Sociology of Georg Simmel*. New York: Free Press.

World Bank. 2012. "World Bank Updates Poverty Estimates for the Developing World." Available: http://econ.worldbank. org/WBSITE/EXTERNAL/EXTDEC/EXTRESEARCH/0,, contentMDK:21882162~pagePK:64165401~piPK:64165026 ~theSitePK:469382,00.html

Women's Rights National Historical Park. 2011. "Women's Rights." Pamphlets available at the Seneca Falls location of Women's Rights National Historical Park.

Wrenn, Eddie. 2012. "The Biggest Phobia in the World? 'Nomophobia'—the Fear of Being Without Your Mobile—Affects 66 per cent of Us." The Daily Mail, May 8. Available: http://www.dailymail. co.uk/sciencetech/article-2141169/The-biggest-phobia-world-Nomophobia--fear-mobile--affects-66-cent -us.html.

Yamagishi, Toshio and Karen Cook. 1993. "Generalized Exchange and Social Dilemma." *Social Psychology Quarterly*. 56(4):235–248.

Yamagishi, Toshio, Mary Gilmore, and Karen Cook. 1988. "Network Connections and the Distribution of Power in Exchange Networks." *American Journal of Sociology*. 93:833–851.

Yates, Gayle Graham (Ed). 1985. *Harriet Martineau on Women*. New Brunswick, NJ: Rutgers University Press.

Yodanis, Carrie L. 2004. "Gender Inequality, Violence Against Women, and Fear: A Cross-National Test of the Feminist Theory of Violence Against Women." *Journal of Interpersonal Violence*, 19(6): 655–675.

Yuille, Judith. 1991. *Karl Marx: From Trier to Highgate.* London: Highgate Cemetery.

Zeccola, Dorothy. 1996. "Ida B. Wells Barnett," pp. 338–442 in *Women in Communication: A Biographical Sourcebook*, edited by Nancy Signorielli, foreword by Alan M. Rubin. Westport, CT: Greenwood Press.

Zeitlin, Irving. 1968. *Ideology and the Development of Sociological Thought.* Englewood Cliffs, NJ: Prentice Hall.

Zeitlin, *Ideology And The Development Of Sociological Theory*, 2nd Ed., © 1981. Reprinted and electronically reproduced by permission of Pearson Education, Inc., Upper Saddle River, New Jersey.

Zimmerman, Don and Melvin Pollner. 1970. "The Everyday Life," pp. 80–103 in *Understanding Everyday Life*, edited by Jack Douglas. Chicago: Aldine.

Zimmerman, Don and Jack Whalen. 1987. "Multi-party Management of Single Telephone Calls: The Verbal and Gestural Organization of Work in an Emergency Dispatch Center." Presented at the Surrey Conference on Video, University of Surrey, Guildford, England.

INDEX